Man against Nature

Man against *Nature*

Tales of Adventure and Exploration

Collected and Edited by CHARLES NEIDER

harper & brothers - publishers - new york

Library of Congress catalog card number: 54-8974

To my dear friend

ALEXANDER KLEIN

Contents

ADVENTURE—THE UNENDING CHALLENGE   xi
by Maurice Herzog

INTRODUCTION   xv
by Charles Neider

EARTHQUAKE AT SAN FRANCISCO   1
by Frank W. Aitken *and* Edward Hilton

THE STRANGE DEATH OF LOUIS SLOTIN   8
by Stewart Alsop *and* Ralph E. Lapp

VOYAGE TO THE SOUTH POLE   19
by Roald Amundsen

THE JUST VENGEANCE OF HEAVEN   35
Anonymous

FORTY-FIVE SECONDS INSIDE A TORNADO   48
by Ira J. Baden, as told to Robert H. Parham

DESCENT INTO PERPETUAL NIGHT   61
by William Beebe

THE PLAGUE   78
by Giovanni Boccaccio

HEAD HUNTERS OF NEW GUINEA   83
by Sidney Spencer Broomfield

ALONE   88
by Richard E. Byrd

LOST IN THE SAHARA   95
by Donald R. G. Cameron

THE GREAT LISBON EARTHQUAKE   114
by Samuel Chase

THE CHAMPAWAT MAN-EATER 128
  by Jim Corbett

THE SILENT WORLD 150
  by J. Y. Cousteau, *with* Frédéric Dumas

INDIANS! 158
  by George A. Custer

ROUNDING THE HORN 167
  by Richard Henry Dana

BATTLE WITH A WHALE 196
  by William M. Davies

ON THE BOTTOM 203
  by Edward Ellsberg

LOST IN THE CANADIAN WILDERNESS 214
  by John Grant

THE GREAT CHICAGO FIRE 222
  by Samuel S. Greeley

BAILING OUT AT SUPERSONIC SPEED 229
  by Arthur Ray Hawkins, as told to Wesley Price

DEATH IN THE AFTERNOON 239
  by Ernest Hemingway

BRIDGING THE HELLESPONT 247
  by Herodotus

KON-TIKI 252
  by Thor Heyerdahl

TO THE SUMMIT OF EVEREST 264
  by Sir Edmund Hillary

MAN AGAINST BRONCO 274
  by Emerson Hough

THE TIDAL WAVE 285
  by Louis V. Housel

HUNTING THE AFRICAN BUFFALO 294
  by J. A. Hunter

CONTENTS

MASAI SPEARMEN   309
by J. A. Hunter

WE JUMP INTO FIRE   317
by Starr Jenkins

ROCKET SHOOT AT WHITE SANDS   328
by Jonathan Norton Leonard

NEW YORK TO PARIS   338
by Charles A. Lindbergh

ATTEMPTS ON THE EIGERWAND   344
by C. F. Meade

THE BUFFALO CHASE   354
by Francis Parkman

THE NORTH POLE CONQUERED   360
by Robert E. Peary

THE ERUPTION OF VESUVIUS   369
by Pliny the Younger

ON THE EDGE OF THE PRIMEVAL FOREST   375
by Albert Schweitzer

THE LAST MARCH   389
by Robert Falcon Scott

THE OPEN BOAT   402
by Sir Ernest Shackleton

CRATERS OF FIRE   423
by Haroun Tazieff

THE JOHNSTOWN FLOOD   437
by Peter J. Toner

TEN THOUSAND MILES IN THE SADDLE   443
by A. F. Tschiffely

BUZZING DEATH   452
by Tursa

ANNAPURNA   455
by James Ramsey Ullman

A WATERSPOUT IN THE PACIFIC   466
   by James J. Wait

SUCCESS AT KITTY HAWK   475
   by Orville Wright

SOURCES AND ACKNOWLEDGMENTS   481

Adventure----The Unending Challenge

by MAURICE HERZOG

We live in an era of exploration—the British scaling earth's "Third Pole," Everest; the Germans topping Nanga-Parbat; the Americans' gallant, tragic try for K-2; other expeditions, Japanese, Indian, Swiss, Norwegian, pursuing their goals on the roof of the world. Men have sounded great depths as well—Professor Piccard, Jacques-Yves Cousteau and others plumbing the eerie ocean bottoms, and the speleologists, the cave-plungers, groping farther and farther down into underground darkness. Why is all this going on? What makes men behave this way?

The answer is, the spirit of adventure—a yearning for the unknown, for risks, that moves Western men who live in modern "comfort," the heaven and hell of our days.

My own awakening to the magical spirit of adventure came in my university days. In Paris, I was a student, dividing my time between law and speculation in the pure sciences. Then, one February, I had the chance to go to the Alps. I came to a village peacefully hibernating among snow-covered mountains. I started at sunrise and climbed the lower mountain slopes until I came to a small forest. Far from any inhabited place, I had only myself to count on. The solitude suddenly made me feel extremely vulnerable. I had the sensation that my life was in danger. I was venturing alone up immense snow slopes. Avalanches were a constant threat.

I was part of nature, like an animal among other animals—white hares, marmots, chamois, jackdaws, foxes. I felt my muscles acting as muscles naturally should. I was steeped in brilliant sunshine, although I fought against the piercing cold. Finally, worn and hungry, I reached the crest. I had striven against nature like a primitive man to gain that goal, and suddenly I experienced a vast exultancy.

I believe that what I felt that day closely resembles what we call happiness. I also believe that if I felt such happiness in such rigorous circumstances it is because the planned, organized, predigested happiness that the modern world offers is not complete. It leaves certain sides of man's nature unsatisfied.

After all, man is only an animal with a big brain. He makes such a fuss about the brain that he forgets arms, legs, pectoral muscles, as if he were ashamed of them. A human being is constructed to defend his life—and not merely by trickery, malice or cunning. If we are here today it is because our ancestors learned how to fight against the elements and against other animals. If they could win those fights it was not only because they were crafty but also because they knew how to run, jump, strike, swim and climb; because they had a powerful physical mechanism, great vigor, incredible resistance and a skill and suppleness not combined in any other animal in creation.

Nowadays "comfort" means that the whole marvelous, miraculous organization of man's muscles may eventually become useless to him. Now he is still able to recapture the great primeval satisfaction of his forebears. He can be totally exhilarated. And this, indeed, is a sign that he is on the right road, that he is, at last, completely at one with himself.

All this has not gone unnoticed among the races which have managed to acquire the peak of worldly comfort. As life has grown progressively easier over the centuries, with adventure disappearing from the face of the earth, man's physical organism has protested. Society's solution is sport. It is notable that sports have developed most brilliantly in advanced societies. Sport has no meaning when daily life provides its parallel.

For the ultimate stage of our comfort-keyed civilization man will doubtless sustain himself by consuming a variety of little pills. But, just as swallowing nourishment through pills will never entirely supplant gourmandizing and the pleasures of the table, so sport will never abolish a thirst for natural activity without training manuals or tricks. And the solution is not a super-sport. The solution is adventure—adventure in which a man's total energies, all his physical and mental resources, are involved. In adventure, muscles, nerves, instincts, reflexes, even brains —in a word, the entire man—are taxed to the full.

Please understand me: everything that involves danger is not necessarily adventure. Often it is mere prowess, a gratuitous, barren exploit. Valid adventure, so far as I am concerned, is not pursued at all costs, or artificially created. A great French philosopher, Alain, recently dead, put it this way: "He who seeks adventure is condemned never to find it."

When a mountaineer decides to climb he foresees everything possible to foresee, organizes the smallest details of his ascent precisely so as to avoid "adventure." Those who do not proceed thus are mental cases who need a psychoanalyst and generally won't live long. Most mountaineers are anxious not to die. We are truly afraid of dangers and try from the start to be forewarned and to avoid them. Despite the general impression, we do not start off seeking adventure.

Often enough during a climb, however, circumstances arise that put us in a difficult spot. Sometimes it is a rock or ice fall that we must avoid, sometimes a blizzard that threatens to overwhelm us; or it may be a track that leads us astray and cannot be retraced, a misplotting of our course bringing us to unscalable barriers, an injured comrade who must be carried back, the fall of darkness paralyzing an advance, a slip into a crevasse, fog in a wide snowfield confusing us into going in circles—a thousand such incidents, often several of them at once in a single day.

Face to face with these life-and-death crises, a man's real character appears. He is brave or cowardly, skillful or clumsy, patient or impulsive. Death stalks him and he must utilize all his forces to survive. All his qualities as a man are involved, and they must be complete. The slightest faltering, the slightest weakness, can be fatal.

No mountaineer exults in a ticklish situation. But when, thanks to energy and skill, he overcomes a critical obstacle or conquers an unforeseen emergency, he reacts with a kind of pride that seems to me legitimate. He has managed, unaided, to dominate hostile nature and he feels a great self-satisfaction—just as his ancestors must have felt when they had warded off the attack of a ferocious beast or slain a creature larger than themselves.

The true joy of living, simple as it may seem, is harder to manufacture than a jet engine. It must be in one's self—and then one must win it. The true value of life is never apparent until one has risked losing it. A man who has triumphed over mortal danger is born again. It is a birth without indebtedness to anything on earth. It endows one with a serenity and independence which are truly unutterable.

Mountain climbers, polar explorers, pioneers in unknown, hostile regions, in the caves of the earth and the sea's depths, are all linked by the same vision. All of them stake their native, human gifts against the unknown. Their reward is to enrich mankind's heritage, and the sense of this is their common bond.

When all the mountains in the world have been scaled, when the poles hold no more secrets, when the last acre of the last continent has been traversed, when, in short, everything on our planet is known and catalogued, the way will still be open for discovery. The world will never be conquered so long as the zest for conquest, for adventure, is in men's hearts.

Introduction

Recently I had a curious experience. I was at the periscope of a submarine which dived and surfaced repeatedly. What was so curious was not the action of the periscope itself, which interested me with its bulk and hydraulic power, but what it revealed to me. For it revealed to me not only the sunlit ocean and the whitecaps, the distant shore, our bow and stern rising and disappearing, but also something of myself.

There I was, inside the control room, peering—and what I saw startled me. Not that I saw anything outwardly unexpected. What startled me was the fact that I could see ourselves disappear—I was under water and yet I wasn't, we were all submerged so that nothing of us was visible, and yet I could see the air frothing where we had just been, and I could see the sunlight and the whitecaps and the angry green of the cold ocean.

All of us are more or less split psychologically. This was nothing new to me. What startled me was that I should be sensing this lesson vividly from the inside of a submarine, where I had expected to forget all "inner" psychology. Perhaps I had failed to imagine adequately the psychological possibilities of a life of submersion and crowdedness; or perhaps, being entirely fresh to the experience, I was tempted to find aspects of it long forgotten by veterans of it. I kept the matter to myself and glued my gaze to the instrument, fascinated each time I saw us rise or disappear. I remember wondering what Robert Louis Stevenson would have thought if he were viewing the action with me, he who created the dual personality of Dr. Jekyll and Mr. Hyde; or what Dostoyevsky would have thought, the writer who specialized in the submerged personality. Part of me was trapped beneath the water; part was as free as a bird, looking down at the trapped part. I tried to imagine how a doctor feels who operates on himself, or how it feels to be insane, to be two people at once. It was a startling lesson that I am not likely ever to forget.

The crew about me were men against nature, wresting from the ocean a privilege she accorded only to fish and the sounding whale. It was made possible by machines, of course; and sometimes as I moved about the sub and saw the incredible array of dials and knobs and felt the great power of the boat I wondered if it weren't also a matter of men against machine. It seemed fabulous that mere men could be trained to subdue such a complex monster. Then I thought of Hillary and Tenzing reaching the top of Mt. Everest in their oxygen masks and their clothes which a highly industrialized nation had made possible; and I thought of the men at White Sands, New Mexico, experimenting with rockets, and those in the same state releasing atomic power; and I realized afresh how much of the conquest of nature is preceded by the conquest of the machine, and how sometimes it seems that the machine is threatening to become the master.

When we docked at the submarine base these thoughts were still with me, and they led back naturally to another curious experience I had not long ago, on Mt. Etna in Sicily. I was in the lava zone. Some of the lava patches were hundreds of yards wide, and often they were of great height, standing like hills. These cold ribbons stretched for miles, flinty, barren, with great sharp edges. I imagined the molten stuff streaming out of the mountain's fissures, burying chunks of forest, setting fields afire, then slowly cooling, the gases erupting, the most porous stuff on top, and down beneath, the solid lava rock.

I had been standing awe-struck before all this, when quite suddenly the experience became intolerable. For the first time in my life I was in an entirely inorganic world, without life or souvenir of life: a moon-world, barren, pitted, inhospitable to man. I felt like a traveler to the moon who had been deprived of his space suit and oxygen mask. It was a new experience of the awesome loneliness of man in the inorganic universe, and I felt a close kinship with every form of life I could imagine, however lowly or primitive. Like the experience at the periscope, it was largely a psychological one: a revelation of mind brought about by a strange environment. Again it was man against nature, this time without benefit of machine, only now it was a nature which was unearthly because it emanated from inside the earth rather than from its surface, from a place where no life could be sustained and where the inorganic realm reigned without dispute.

What I have been suggesting is that adventure, large or small, is exciting not only to our physical selves but to our imaginative side as well: that a true adventure is also a psychological affair and a spiritual matter. Seen from this point of view, many of the hazardous experiences in this book can, I think, be more fully understood.

What impelled Byrd to brave the Antarctic winter alone was not only the advisability of making accurate weather observations but also the opportunity to experience utter and sustained solitude and in that solitude to take stock of himself, his life, his future, and his relations with the community of men. Such motivations tend to ennoble the adventures which are outwardly one's chief pursuit.

One of the most fascinating aspects of Corbett's hunting of man-eating tigers is that the man becomes the beast, with a cunning, instinct, and a sense of survival approximating the tiger's; while at the same time the tiger, in its seeming intelligence, reasoning and ability to outguess the man at times, even to the point of hunting down the hunter, begins to take on the contours of a human being. This, of course, is not mere fantasy: there is the beast in all of us, and there is no sure borderline between the animal and his human counterpart.

Aside from the feat itself, the most remarkable thing, it seems to me, about Beebe's descent into the ocean is that it is a descent into the experience of great darkness, broken only by the remarkable flashes of phosphorescent fish, like the flashes of image and thought deep in our night world of dreams, hate, love and desire for womb-shelter. It is beautiful and awful at the same time. That the experience of great darkness is a wonderful thing in itself, awe-inspiring and frightening, can be attested to by all those persons who have experienced the unimaginable darkness of great caverns.

But these are only random thoughts and tentative suggestions. I leave it to the reader to enjoy and to understand according to his own lights and his own fashion the book of man and the book of nature which the accounts here gathered together so nobly constitute.

Needless to say, I derived great pleasure from editing this collection, and I am grateful to Harper & Brothers for asking me to take on the assignment. What I had previously read in the field had led me to believe there were great things in it, and I was not disappointed. Perhaps the reader will forgive me for thinking that this book is unique in several respects: as regards quality, variety, and the depth of its exploration of theme. As far as I am aware, nothing quite like it exists in any language. There have been collections of discoveries and explorations; others of adventures; but none so closely united by a common great theme; none so intent on including narrative of eyewitness authenticity and vividness as well as of excellence in style.

I have tried to place the reader at the summit or the depth of the event, so that he may experience for himself as much as can be done by reading, and so that he may judge for himself the meaning of the particular occasion. If I have succeeded I will have brought before him a rich experience, in time and space, of man's indomitable curiosity and courage, his will to conquer his environment, his ingenuity in surviving, and his willingness to die if necessary as part of the "game." No greater theme exists than is inherent in the present volume.

Some accounts, such as Corbett's, I have included because they are fabulous in themselves, without regard to historic occasion. Others mark great steps in man's exploration of his planet: such as those by Peary, Amundsen, Wright, Lindbergh and Hillary. But above and beyond every other consideration I have selected the accounts for the depth and freshness of their probing of our theme. I am happy to say that despite the exigencies which encompass the editing of every volume, no narrative pressed to be included here which was in the end discarded for one reason or another. The results are as much what I desired as it is possible for them to be.

CHARLES NEIDER

Cumberland, Indiana
April 18, 1954

Man against Nature

Earthquake at San Francisco

by FRANK W. AITKEN
and EDWARD HILTON

The California earthquake of 1952, which caused damage at Bakersfield, had greater force than that of 1906, but because the latter afflicted the city of San Francisco it has become known as the most terrible earthquake in United States experience. Had the 1952 quake centered in a great urban community the devastation would have been ghastly. Some of the more dramatic details of the San Francisco quake are given below. Following it came a great fire, which almost destroyed the central business and residential sections. An area of four square miles was leveled, 28,000 buildings were brought down, hundreds of lives lost, and about half a billion dollars in property consumed. For weeks afterwards thousands of the city's residents slept in the parks and streets. Meanwhile direct aid was rushed to the city, and indirect aid amounting to about $10,000,000 was given by the entire world.

APRIL, 1906, FOUND SAN FRANCISCO LIVING ITS LIFE intensely, pulsating with the vigor of achievement and hope, full of the "joy of living." The year had been one of unexampled prosperity; trade had never been so brisk, business never so good before. Again and again the real estate sales, the building operations, the volume of business, had surpassed all records. Population was increasing with wonderful rapidity. Never had the city's future seemed so bright, its destiny so certain, as in those early days of April.

San Francisco had probably never been more carefree in all its laughing years than on the night of April 17. Easter Sunday had just

passed and a new season of jollity had begun. Society was awhirl with
a merry dance of pleasure. Festivities were everywhere. Theaters and
other places of amusement were thronged. The Metropolitan Grand
Opera Company had just started upon a long engagement at the Grand
Opera House. That night Caruso, in Carmen, was at his best. The house
was filled to the foyer, and the great audience left the theater still thrilled
by his magic tones.

Toward midnight the cafés and restaurants began to fill. Parties
dropped in for those quiet little suppers that were a part of the city's
fame. The rattle of dishes and clink of glasses, a merry laugh or a happy
chuckle, a snatch of a stage joke or a bit of repartee—this for an hour
or two; then all was still.

The city slept. A lone policeman on his rounds, the clanging bell of
some owl car anxious to be off the street, the tread of a man hurrying
home, the uncertain antics of some befuddled fellow—scarcely more
than this anywhere. The city slept, unconscious of the manner of its
awakening.

Slowly dawn crept over the hills; some sleepy folk were getting their
wares out for the early buyers. A sudden rumbling hurried closer and
closer. The houses of the sleeping city shook as if seized with a sudden
ague. At first came a sharp but gentle swaying motion that grew less and
less; then a heavy jolting sidewise—then another, heaviest of all. Finally
a grinding round of everything, irregularly tumultuous, spasmodic, jerky.
It was as if some Titans, laying hold of the edge of the world, were
trying to wrest it from each other by sudden wrenchings.

Plaster showered from the walls; nails creaked in their sockets and
pulled and tried to free themselves. Crockery and glassware smashed
upon the floor. Doors flew open—swung round—jerked off their hinges.
Furniture toppled. Pianos rattled their keys in untimed janglings. Chimneys snapped and fell. Houses groaned and twisted and reeled on their
foundations. Outside, streets were seized with writhings. Hillsides slid.
The city shook itself like a dog coming out of the water.

People ran from their houses and crowded into the streets. In hotels
and other places where many lived under one roof the commotion nearly
reached a panic. They crowded and jostled one another in their flight
down the stairs and, reaching the street, ran about in varicolored night
garments, overawed by the unaccustomed experience. Some women
screamed, some wild-eyed men wept in the frenzy of their fear. And as
they ran and wept and screamed, the temblor ceased. Abruptly it was

gone—mysteriously, without warning. Some said it had lasted two minutes—five—an eternity. In reality it was over in forty-eight seconds. Throughout the city was heard the grating and grinding and rattling of houses and the crash of falling chimneys. In the neighborhood of the City Hall the noise was appalling. The heavy iron columns filled with concrete, with their massive cornices, on the west and south sides; the greater portion of the dome; and much of the roof of the south and west wings of that great monument of graft and incompetence fell with a crash into the street. Across Market Street the roof of the Majestic Theater fell in. Other buildings downtown collapsed. As the crashing of falling walls and subterraneous rumblings died away there came the cry of dying horses, the appeals for help of men and women pinned beneath the debris, and the laughter of a few hysterical ones; while here and there explosions of gas escaping from broken mains occurred with loud reports.

The first wild moment passed and an intense quiet pervaded the people of the city. Cowed and tongue-tied by this manifestation of the supernatural, they huddled, half-dressed, in the streets, and looked at the swaying roof-lines silhouetted against the half-lit sky. Then some, from courage or shame, went inside to dress; others had the hardihood to return to bed for one more nap. In the streets a few low words were spoken—the hushed words of a great fear; but in the main the people waited objectless in the streets, wondering if it was all over.

Then the drollery of the situation broke in upon them. It occurred to them that their sudden unclothed flight was undignified, even ludicrous. Some began to smile, shamefacedly; others crept under cover. The suspense was over; straightway all began to talk and gossip. The earthquake was a general introduction; everybody knew everybody else. They laughed together at chimneys sprawled in the street and houses tilted out of plumb. Tales of the freaks of the temblor began to circulate—of chimneys that were cracked across but not thrown down, of bronze that broke and china that survived. Soon everybody knew that Jones' house had moved on its foundation and that Smith's marble steps had cracked and that Brown's chimney was split across but still stood and that Black had run frightened into the street and then dressed on the front porch.

Throughout the greater part of the city—north of Market Street and out in the Western Addition and over in the Mission—there was never a thought that the earthquake would be found any different in its results from any other. It was a heavier shock than usual—that was all.

It became a holiday—a carnival. Leaving their bric-a-brac where it lay, people went to see the sights, to laugh at their neighbors' experiences, and to congratulate each other that it was no worse. They set out to go downtown. Crowds collected on Market Street to see if any damage had been done to the big buildings. They sauntered along easily and laughed at the strange appearance of rooms exposed by the falling of the front walls, and at the terror the occupants must have felt. They smiled knowingly and murmured "Graft" as they saw the City Hall walls lying in the street. An occasional businessman hurried along, anxious to protect his records. But for the most part the procession was one of curious sightseers.

The smoke of many fires rose before them, and they wended their way to vantage places, with never a thought that the fire department would be unequal to its task. Never before had it failed to handle every fire that occurred; always it had protected them and their wooden city from the greedy flames.

They were in the best of humor. When the soldiers took possession of Market Street, the people took to more circuitous routes without complaint. They had not waited for breakfast at home, and soon discovered that they could get none downtown. They walked far before they discovered that the cars were not running. It was a long way home. Yet they were happy, for they were viewing a spectacle that was worth while.

It was all a play—a fantastic comedy. This, north of Market Street.

South of Market the play was a tragedy. There the decrepit ramshackles, remnants of another generation, flimsy with age, tottering on their foundations, had fallen into masses of splintered wood. Cheap lodginghouses and hotels had gone down burying their guests in the ruins. Quickly, on the wings of terror, spread the news—that many buildings were down and many people injured and dying; that fires had started all about.

Hereabout dwelt one-sixth of the city's population. Here the roll of the dead was longest, here the fires sprung up the quickest, and spread, uncontrolled, with greatest fury, leaping across the little by-ways and racing pell-mell from street to street.

It was an agony of fear. People saved a little, whatever came handiest —needful or useless—and waited for the moment when they must give up their little remaining hope and flee. Some there were, not strong enough to wait, who gathered up their pitiful bundles in panic and hurried out into the suburbs. Many struggled bravely to rescue the injured from the oncoming flames.

In addition to the innumerable tumbledown structures which the earthquake brought to the ground as scarce more than kindling—in many of which people were pinioned and burned to death—a number of hotels and lodginghouses collapsed, and buried in their ruins many who could not be extricated before the fire reached them. Such were the Cosmopolitan, the Brunswick, the Denver.

Wild rumors of cruelty and greed and murder among the injured afterward got about; stories of men who begged to be killed, and others who cursed their mothers, of parents who left their wounded children unaided, while they, unheeding, made their selfish way to safety; stories, too, of fiends who cut rings from the fingers of the dead, and of swift punishment by quick-shooting soldiers. But followed out to the end most of these stories have been proved mere rumors, the weird hallucinations of overstrained minds. To the eternal credit of mankind it is known that here uncountable deeds of kindness were done; and that many who died beyond the reach of help closed their eyes without complaint—stoics to the end.

The people who had gone about sightseeing after the earthquake found much to interest and amaze them. Although the big buildings downtown seemed entirely uninjured, there were startling instances of the earthquake's power in various parts of the city. Imposing brick and stone buildings had collapsed, streets and car tracks had been twisted out of shape in a few neighborhoods that seemed to have been especially hardhit by the shock.

At the City Hall hundreds of tons of brickwork had crashed to earth; in a moment the once imposing building had been stripped of all its pretense and its seeming strength. Half the building was in ruins. The great bronze dome, three hundred and thirty-five feet in height, rose airily out of the huge piles of brick that had been its walls and columns, its frame seeming strangely slight in the absence of the brickwork which had surrounded it and lay in monumental ruin below. A group of massive columns, with their gigantic cornice, crashing into an apartment house across Larkin Street, brought down its whole front wall.

The Majestic Theater building, a short distance away from the City Hall, was also demolished. Half the roof fell in; at both front and rear the walls fell away for half their height.

The Hall of Justice, on Kearny Street opposite Portsmouth Square, lost much of the brickwork of its tower. Out in the Park one end of the refreshment house at the children's playground—a picturesque lodge, of brick covered with sandstone—completely collapsed.

At the Girls' High School, which cost over $90,000 to build, great quantities of the walls fell, and all around the building cracks zigzagged up and down the bulging brickwork.

In the same neighborhood as the Girls' High School stood St. Dominic's Church—a massive structure of brick covered with cement. One of its lofty spires was completely stripped of its covering. From the companion spire all the brickwork of the tower proper fell away, leaving only the rounded, domelike top, like a giant toadstool balanced high on its fragile stem. The walls of the church spread; the roof fell in; great cracks split the structure clear to the foundations.

A few other large buildings met the same fate—the Beth Israel Synagogue, the Scottish Rite Temple, and the Knight Templar Asylum, all within a few blocks of St. Dominic's. In each case, the story was the same: much of the walls fell away; the roof dropped; the wreck was complete.

A storage warehouse of four stories nearby presented a unique spectacle. On all sides the wall of its upper story had fallen, leaving exposed to view the varied collection of household goods stored within, so that the roof seemed to rest on nothing but the close-packed goods beneath. Further downtown, in the district of hotels and apartment houses, other brick structures lost one or more stories from their façades in the same way.

Apart from the large brick buildings so damaged, and the numerous wooden shanties detroyed, the most striking manifestations of the power of the shock were to be found in its effect on the earth itself here and there in various parts of the city.

On Valencia Street, near Nineteenth, about a mile southwest of the City Hall, stood the Valencia Street Hotel, a four-story wooden structure. The earthquake spilled it out into the street. From the windows of its upper story the guests stepped out onto the car track; but in the rooms below some twenty persons were crushed to death. The street in front of the hotel was twisted far to one side, and had dropped several feet below its level; the cable tracks, heavy concrete conduits on steel yokes, were bent sharply aside and broken, as if made of clay. On Howard Street, two blocks away (just beyond the fire line), a row of houses leaned drunkenly on each other for support. Through here ran Willow Creek years ago; and even yet, perhaps some of the waters find their outlet beneath the loose soil which has been placed on the old bed. It was on this filled soil that the Valencia Street Hotel stood, as well as the leaning houses on Howard Street. When the earthquake shook things up the whole fill settled a little more compactly and slid a few feet along the course of the creek. Sidewalks and pavements and car tracks were twisted; houses reeled from their foundations; water pipes (one of them forty-four inches in diameter) were torn apart. Brick foundations at the edge of the fill cracked across and sagged; the side walls of the Youths' Directory, a four-story brick building, resting on ground which moved unequally, split from its base clear to its cornice.

Fully as interesting as the row of houses on Howard Street were those on Van Ness Avenue, near Vallejo Street, far to the north. Here the whole side of the gently sloping hill had been brought up to the grade by being filled with sand, and here some of the most interesting results of the earthquake were shown. On Van Ness, just above Vallejo, the street lengthened out. The cement squares of the pavement, separating, tilted slightly on the shifting sand beneath and, twisting about with the shock, arranged themselves fantastically *en échelon*. The bituminous pavement, on its concrete base, split from curb to curb in several places and, sliding down the hill, produced alarming fissures in some places and in another a ridge of jammed-up ends of bitumen, a foot in height. Houses and fences and backyards on the hillside moved down the hill; strange curves appeared in the retaining walls along Vallejo Street. But while the effect of the earthquake here was startling, the amount of actual displacement was small, four feet, with a drop of about two feet in Vallejo Street. On Union Street, near Pierce, however, the car track was shoved some six feet to the side and dropped almost as much. The sidewalk, indeed, dropped several feet. The street there, however, was merely a fill on a side hill; when the earthquake came, it slid down into an adjoining truck garden.

Lower Market Street and the other streets on made land near the waterfront sank noticeably, though without such picturesque results. Some old buildings tilted and twisted and leaned queerly and lost much of their brickwork, and in some cases roof trusses unseated themselves.

These were some of the things seen by the crowds who wandered about the streets after the temblor. No one, individually, saw very much of the damage, for soon the people looked at the sky. Smoke was curling heavenward in many places—lazily, with all the assumption of a fiend sure of its power.

The Strange Death of Louis Slotin

by STEWART ALSOP
and RALPH E. LAPP

*One of the most deadly products of an atomic explosion is radia-
tion, as everyone knows. But radiation is not restricted to explosions.
The following story was long withheld by the United States Government.
It is a brilliant example of man's duel with energies which he himself
has learned to release and which he is now striving to control.*

D R. LOUIS SLOTIN, A YOUNG AND BRILLIANT ATOMIC
scientist, began to die at precisely twenty minutes past
three o'clock, on the afternoon of May 21, 1946. The story of how he
began to die, and of what happened afterward—which can only now be
fully told—is in some ways a rather horrible story. Yet, if only because
it helps strip the mystery from the most terrifying effect of atomic
weapons—the invisible killer, nuclear radiation—Louis Slotin's story
is worth telling all the same.

The place where Louis Slotin began to die was a laboratory in a
canyon near Los Alamos, the war-built town in New Mexico where the
world's first atomic bomb was made. A few minutes after he began to
die, Doctor Slotin, with the precision of a trained scientist, drew a careful chart of this laboratory, showing the exact location of its occupants
at the time. From this chart, and from the accounts of those who were
present and survived, it is possible accurately to reconstruct the scene.

Visualize, then, a large, oblong, white-painted room, unfurnished except for a metal desk near the center, and a table against one wall, bearing the complicated equipment of the atom-bomb-maker's trade. The

spring sunshine floods obliquely through the single large window. There are eight people in the room. Their silence is broken only by the staccato clicking of a Geiger counter, as all attention is focused on a short figure standing over the metal desk.

This is Louis Slotin, thirty-four years old, five feet six inches in height, slender, wiry, his face heavily bronzed by the New Mexico sun, his black hair already graying a little at the temples. He is wearing an open sports shirt, a rather gaudy Mexican belt and khaki trousers tucked into cowboy boots. Through thick, horn-rimmed spectacles—which betray the scientist and the intellectual, despite the cowboy boots—he is peering intently at certain objects on the desk.

These are two hollow, silvery-gray half globes of metal, which Slotin is deliberately manipulating closer to each other, using an ordinary screw driver as a lever. These hunks of metal are the guts of an atomic bomb.

Standing behind Slotin is a fellow scientist—Scientist X, we shall call him—a quiet-mannered, pleasant-faced man, also thirty-four years old. Scientist X has his hand resting casually on Slotin's shoulder, and he is leaning forward with intense interest—he has never seen this experiment before.

The six other people in the room are laboratory assistants, technicians and others gathered more or less by chance to watch the experiment. Two are standing in front of the desk, at a distance of about six feet. The four others are grouped behind the desk, at a distance of eight feet or more. The scene is a casual one. Like Slotin, the others are dressed informally, in open shirts or sweaters. Slotin himself appears confident, almost gay. He loves this experiment—"tickling the dragon's tail," he calls it—and he has already performed it at least forty times. Even so, there is a certain tension in the room. Those present are aware that manipulating the guts of an atomic bomb is no child's play.

Slotin has his ear cocked to the click of the Geiger counter, and he also glances frequently at an instrument called a "neutron monitor," which is recording on a roll of paper, in a thin, wavy line of red ink, the radiation emitted by the lumps of metal. As Slotin slowly moves the lumps, the red line staggers upward and the Geiger counter clicks erratically, always a little faster, like a deranged clock.

Suddenly the Geiger counter begins to click insanely, and then stops dead. All in a moment, the people in the room sense rather than see a strange blue glow, stronger than the spring sunlight. Instantly, Slotin throws himself forward, thrusting the half globes of deadly metal apart with his naked hands. Then he stands up, his face a chalky white beneath the tan.

In a concerted, instinctive, almost somnambulistic movement, the eight people file quickly from the room, without speaking. Some of them are aware of a dry, prickly, sour sensation on their tongues—a sign of excessive radiation. Some of them are no doubt also aware of a little flicker of fear in their hearts. Yet aside from the sour taste, they feel nothing else at all—not even Louis Slotin, who has already begun to die.

To understand what happened, and why, and what it means, it is necessary to know something about Louis Slotin, and the reason he tickled the dragon's tail. The bare facts of Slotin's thirty-four years can be quickly recited.

He was born, Louis Alexander Slotin, in 1912, of prosperous Jewish parents in Winnipeg, Canada. At the tender age of fifteen, he entered Winnipeg's University of Manitoba, and received his master-of-science degree at the equally tender age of twenty-one. He studied physics for four years at the University of London, and got his Ph.D. in 1936.

In 1937 he was in Chicago, apparently on his way home to Winnipeg, when he ran into Prof. William D. Harkins, pioneer atomic chemist of the University of Chicago. Harkins remarked that he badly needed an assistant for cyclotron work, but he had no money to pay an assistant. Slotin immediately went to work for nothing a week—a salary for which he worked for almost two years.

His work at Chicago University led him directly into the Manhattan District, the supersecret wartime atomic project. He worked for a time in Chicago, then at Indiana University, and later at Oak Ridge. In late 1943, Slotin came to Los Alamos, when the job of actually putting the atomic bomb together was started, and there he began to tickle the dragon's tail.

So much for the bare facts. The bare facts, of course, do not answer the question: What kind of man was Louis Alexander Slotin?

"No man," John Donne wrote, "is an island unto himself." Yet Louis Slotin was more nearly an island unto himself than most men. He was extraordinarily reserved. "Louis was a sweet kind of guy," one of his former colleagues has remarked, "but no one ever got to know him really well."

Even so, certain well-marked characteristics of the man emerge through the mists of time. In the first place, Slotin was a brave man—but brave in an odd sort of way. "Slotin had a positive hankering for danger," another of those who knew him says. "He seemed to be suffering from some sort of inner tension, and he was always very quiet. But he was downright gay when he was doing something dangerous."

This hankering for danger led Slotin to pester the Manhattan District authorities to allow him to accompany the first atomic bombs to their Japanese targets, as a scientific observer. When the authorities refused, Slotin was deeply depressed for weeks. And the same strange hankering no doubt also led Slotin to become the Manhattan District's chief practitioner of the art of tickling the dragon's tail.

This experiment, it must be understood, was not a kind of scientific Russian roulette which Slotin and the other young physicists at Los Alamos thought up to relieve their boredom. It was a vitally important experiment, absolutely essential to the bomb-making process—and, indeed, it is still essential today.

Fissionable material—uranium 235 and plutonium—is queer stuff. Below a certain size and weight, a lump of this very heavy, greasy-gray metal is no more dangerous than a lump of lead. But it has one special characteristic which may one day destroy civilization as we know it. For if a certain amount of this metal is brought together all in one place, a chain reaction starts within the mass of metal. It is the chain reaction, of course, which lends to the atomic bomb the power to blast and sear a whole city. The amount of the metal required for the chain reaction to start is called a "critical mass"—a "crit," to use the physicists' shorthand.

But how much is a crit? There were and are ways of calculating theoretically the amount of fissionable material required to form a critical mass. But such calculations can never be wholly precise. Moreover, in order to achieve "optimum efficiency"—for which read killing power— in an atomic bomb, the size of the crit had to be determined—and still must—under various conditions.

Even today, for reasons of security, it is necessary to be a little imprecise about the experiment which Louis Slotin performed that May day in 1946—and which his successors are still performing under very different conditions. But it can be said, accurately though unscientifically, that the idea was to shove together lumps of fissionable material in such quantities, and in such a geometric relationship to each other, that the whole amount *just* went critical. In other words, a chain reaction was permitted to begin—thus establishing the crit—but it was stopped before the material became dangerously overcritical. The problem, of course, was to know when to stop.

No one at Los Alamos had any illusions about the danger involved.

There was, to be sure, no danger that Los Alamos might be blown off the face of the map if something went wrong. In order to generate true explosive power, the critical mass must somehow be held together by an outside force—this is called "maintaining assembly." Otherwise the power of the chain reaction automatically "disassembles the crit." In the meantime, however, if a true chain reaction is permitted really to get under way, the critical mass of fissionable material becomes briefly but intensely radioactive. It sends out precisely the same lethal radioactive rays as an atomic bomb does when it explodes over a city.

Slotin particularly had good reason to be aware of this danger. Before the day when Slotin tickled the dragon's tail for the last time, at least three people at Los Alamos had fallen victim to the invisible killer. One of these was Slotin's friend and laboratory assistant, Harry Daglian. Slotin spent many hours at his assistant's bedside, during the month that it took Daglian to die.

Particularly after Daglian died, those in authority at Los Alamos worried about the radiation danger. One Nobel Prize winner told Slotin, "I predict you won't last a year if you keep on doing that experiment." But Slotin happily carried on.

"Sure, it's dangerous," Slotin remarked to one colleague, "but it has to be that way." One suspects that Slotin, perhaps unconsciously, wanted it to be that way.

Ironically, on May 21, 1946, Slotin was performing his beloved experiment for what he knew to be the last time. For more than two years he had performed the experiment again and again in different ways and under various conditions. He was particularly proud of the fact that he had been chosen to test the criticality of the world's first atomic bomb—he cherished the receipt for this bomb which he got when he returned it to be exploded at Alamogordo, after having tickled its tail. Now he had been ordered to Bikini, to participate in the bomb tests there. He was eager to be off—when final orders came to perform the experiment just once more, for the benefit of Scientist X. So Slotin tickled the dragon's tail just once more—and the dragon lashed back to destroy him.

What went wrong? Part of the answer may no doubt be found in Slotin's hankering for danger—such a man may always be tempted to go too far. But part of the answer is also certainly found in the fact that Slotin, at the age of thirty-four, was already an old-fashioned scientist.

Slotin received his whole training as a physicist in the '30's, before the time when national survival depended on the special skills of his kind. It was quite typical of those days that a brilliantly qualified physicist like

matter of manipu-
the rest of the as-
hed," one of those
was closed." The
tion combines the
al use of an ordi-
. In a word, the

ned, and his re-
and pulled the
ass." If he had
table, he might
that he would

that I and per-
I do not know
have objected

ssary to under-
gamma rays
one sufficiently
A grim pecu-
fore this kill-
ls do not die
all the time
injury is the
d reproduce
cells fail to

for all of us
ar radiation
dose." The
n a person
to know is
and for a
ath rate.
ause there
he human
nt, it was

'30's physicists led a hand-
pment, their experiments and
nificent Government, but on
w great universities.

rform their experiments with
ry screw driver. This cavalier
ced period of the Manhattan
n pride in their own casual ap-
ces locked up in matter. After
ple spring-actuated safety device
ionable material apart as soon as
y radioactive.

ad, he said proudly, "a feeling for
ed, such devices would cause acci-
xperimenter would come to rely on
own judgment.

tomic Energy Commission recently
t between present and past. These
icated "critical assembly machines"
sy" and the other "Godiva" because
e only "barely" critical. There is an-
control panel used to work these ma-
rge Orwell's "1984"—complete with
reens and a blond lady in an aseptic
according to the AEC release, "control-
t a distance of a quarter of a mile.

ly is manipulating the guts of an atomic
doing that day in May when the nuclear
case, the deadly stuff was right under his
knobs, no television screens, no remote-
iger counter, his neutron monitor, his skill
driver.

what happened that day in May or about
rd of the neutron monitor which Slotin used
ed-ink line mounts gradually across the paper,
iation emitted by the lumps of metal at each
y 3:20 P.M., the line simply disappears. At
tion became so intense that the instrument was

d, no one, not even Slotin himself, was entirely

sure. The experiment was almost finished—it was a
lating one last piece of metal an eighth of an inch from
sembly. "When the point of criticality was almost reac
present writes, "the piece somehow slipped and the gap
"somehow" is still unexplained. But the best explana
overconfidence of an over-brave man with Slotin's casu
nary screw driver to lever the deadly hunks of metal
screw driver slipped.

At any rate, Slotin knew instantly what had happe
action was instantaneous. When he lunged forward
chunks of metal apart, he "disassembled the critical n
not done so, if he had instantly ducked away from the
conceivably have saved himself. It is far more probabl
have condemned others in the room to death.

"It is unquestionably true," Scientist X has written, "
haps others of those present owe our lives to his action.
whether this is heroism or not. I suspect that Louis woul
to such a term."

To understand the meaning of Slotin's action, it is nece
stand something of the nature of the invisible killer. Th
emitted by a chain reaction penetrate into the body of any
exposed, and kill individual cells deep within the body.
liarity of radiation injury is that there is a latent period b
ing of the cells becomes apparent. This is because the ce
until the periodic cell division—a process which is going o
in everyone's body—takes place. Thus in a sense, radiation
opposite of cancer. Cancer kills when the cells divide ar
themselves too rapidly. Nuclear radiation kills when the
divide and do not reproduce themselves at all.

But, even more than in the case of cancer, it is important
who live in the age of nuclear war to understand that nucle
need not be fatal. Everything depends on the size of the "
"dose" is measured in r's, or roentgens, of radiation. Whe
receives a radiation injury, the first thing the doctors want
whether he has received "LD/50." This is medical shorth
"median lethal dose," which causes a 50 per cent average d

LD/50 has never been precisely determined, simply bec
have not been many human guinea pigs on whom to test t
body's resistance to radiation injury. At the time of the accide

thought that LD/50 was in the neighborhood of 400 roentgens. The best estimates now place LD/50 at 525 roentgens, plus or minus 75.

The number of roentgens of radiation a person receives depends principally on the power of the radiation source and the time of exposure. When Slotin lunged forward to disperse the critical assembly and break the chain reaction, he sharply reduced the danger to the other people in the room, by reducing both the power of the radiation and the time of exposure of the others. He also, of course, exposed himself to actual physical contact with the lumps of fissionable material at the very moment the chain reaction was taking place.

Within an hour of the accident, all the eight people in the laboratory were taken to the Los Alamos hospital—a temporary, wartime, shack-like, wooden structure—and placed under close observation. Other than Scientist X, the man who had been closest to Slotin was an unmarried fifty-four-year-old technician, who was standing about six feet in front of the metal desk. He was kept in the hospital for two weeks, and he showed certain symptoms of radiation injury, including measurable radio-sodium and radio-phosphorus in his urine. But he felt quite well—and six weeks later this man, who was something of an athlete, was happily hiking six miles in one day without ill effect.

Others who were standing somewhat farther away had even less reason to complain, although everyone in the room had taken a dose of radiation. So much nonsense has been spread abroad about the silent nuclear killer that many people have come to feel that it is absolutely lethal at almost any range. Actually, the athletic technician took a dose of about 100 roentgens, according to later calculations—the same dose he would have taken if he had been wholly exposed to the radiation effect of a modern, 100-kiloton atomic bomb exploding at a distance of 6500 feet.

Despite the technician's rapid and complete recovery, a dose of 100 roentgens is no laughing matter. If Slotin had not reacted so quickly, if the technician had been exposed only a little longer, the technician would certainly have suffered as Scientist X suffered—and he might well have died.

Scientist X, remember, was standing with his hand on Louis Slotin's shoulder, watching intently the experiment which he himself would have to perform later, when the accident happened. According to later calculations, he took a dose of about 180 roentgens. This is still well under LD/50, but it is nevertheless in the danger area. It is the same dose he would have taken if he had been about 6000 feet from a modern atomic bomb, only a few hundred feet less than the athletic technician. Where nuclear radiation is concerned, short distances can make an enormous difference.

A courageous and unexcitable man by nature, Scientist X was calm and made no complaints when he was admitted to the hospital. Shortly after being admitted, he vomited once. The feeling of nausea passed away in about ten hours, leaving Scientist X feeling weak and tired, with little appetite, but otherwise well enough. He continued thus for about five days. On the fifth day the delayed effect of the gamma rays on his cell tissue began to make itself felt. His temperature climbed close to 103 degrees, and two blood transfusions were required. For some time he felt terribly drowsy and highly irritable, but his temperature fell gradually, and after the fifteenth day he was well enough to be sent home to rest.

But the gamma rays were not yet through with him. He had lost ten pounds, and for some weeks he tired very easily, and spent upward of sixteen hours in bed each day. On the seventeenth day after the accident an unpleasant experience, which Scientist X had known enough to expect, began. On that day the skin on his left temple and on the left side of his head—which had been most exposed—began to feel sensitive. In the two following days this sensitive feeling increased to the point of acute pain. On the twentieth day Scientist X was combing his hair, and found large tufts coming out in the comb.

Thereafter, his hair came out easily by the handful. He lost almost all the hair on the left side of his head, and his beard also stopped growing over most of his left cheek. He also became temporarily sterile, according to the AEC report on the case—a normal and expected symptom of radiation damage. But the point to emphasize is that such symptoms were wholly temporary.

The only permanent aftereffect which Scientist X has suffered is a moderate radiation cataract in the left eye, which reduces his vision from 20/20 to 20/40. The fact that he has suffered no other ill effect is underscored by his brilliant subsequent contributions to our atomic-energy program, notably in the development of that most terrible of weapons, the hydrogen bomb.

In short, a man can survive even a vicious attack by the silent radiation killer on his living cell tissue. But Scientist X unquestionably had a close brush with death. Of Louis Slotin, to whom, as he says, he owes his life, Scientist X has written:

"I can perhaps tell you as much about his personality and character as I could in very many words if I merely quote to you his first statement to me when we were alone together in a hospital room. He said, 'I'm sorry

I got you into this. I am afraid I have less than a fifty-fifty chance of living. I hope you have better than that.' My own estimate of our chances coincided pretty well with his. I felt I had a pretty good chance. I only hoped he had."

For some days there seemed reason for hope. Slotin vomited twice before he got to the hospital, and in the first twelve hours thereafter he continued to vomit repeatedly. But he, too, like Scientist X, recovered from his initial nausea, and his only other immediate general symptoms were a slight temperature and feeling of tiredness.

His hands, of course, had taken a terrible dose, since he had used them to shove the metal apart and break the chain reaction. Within three hours Slotin's left hand became very red, swollen and bluish under the nails. Twenty-eight hours after the accident this hand began to blister painfully, and the symptoms spread to his right hand and both arms. From this time on, both arms were packed in ice, to reduce the swelling and the pain. His lower abdomen also became red and tender, and this spread gradually and became more intense.

Yet aside from these local symptoms, Slotin's general condition seemed greatly to improve after the first twenty-four hours. What had happened quickly became known throughout the Manhattan District, and everything possible was done to help him. No fewer than ten doctors were called in to consult on his case. Maj. Gen. Leslie Groves wrote to him: "I have nothing but admiration for your heroic actions. . . . Your quick reactions and disregard for the danger to yourself undoubtedly prevented a much more serious accident."

Groves' letter cheered Slotin, and he was cheered more when Groves ordered a special Army plane to bring his mother and father from Winnipeg to his bedside. When they arrived, they found their son normal, composed and even downright cheerful, despite the pain in his arms. When friends and colleagues came to visit him, he would introduce them to his parents, and then ask, half jokingly, the crucial question: "Well, what's the dose?"

For five days no one knew. But on the fifth day the answer became tragically obvious—the dose was more than LD/50. That morning Slotin had a new complaint—his tongue was sore opposite a tooth which had a gold inlay. The doctors found a small whitish ulceration on his tongue, and immediately suspected the cause. The gold in his tooth was heavily radioactive. The inlay was capped with gold foil and the pain eased. But this was a bad sign.

There was a worse sign on the same day, when Anna May Dickey, then a nurse in the Los Alamos hospital, took Slotin's blood count. When she looked at the results, she began to weep. She knew the meaning of the sudden, precipitous fall in the leucocyte, or whiteblood-cell, count. The silent killer was at work on Louis Slotin's blood, and the lifesaving white blood cells were failing to reproduce themselves.

On this same day Slotin's pulse rate rose very rapidly. Thereafter he could eat nothing, and visibly lost weight. On the seventh day his mind began to fail, and he had long periods of mental confusion, in which he could not recognize his parents or colleagues. Gradually, he sank into a coma. Early in the morning of the ninth day, May 30, 1946, Louis Slotin quietly died.

That is about the end of Louis Slotin's story. His parents flew back to Winnipeg with his corpse, and scientists and others from all over the United States and Canada attended his funeral. His parents offered a last sacrifice to the cause of science, when they permitted an autopsy to be performed on his body, although this was against the tenets of their religion. It was later estimated, according to the Atomic Energy Commission's recently declassified report on his case, that Slotin had taken about 880 roentgens of nuclear radiation. This was as though he had been fully exposed to the explosion of a modern atomic bomb at a distance of 4800 feet. Nothing could have saved him.

Louis Slotin was not a great or famous man, and he has been in his grave now for almost eight years. Yet his story has seemed worth telling, and not only because nuclear radiation, which kills without being seen or felt, is more terrifying than need be, just because it is so mysterious. It has seemed worth telling also because it is a story of human bravery and sacrifice, qualities which may yet save a civilization threatened with destruction by the very weapons Louis Slotin helped to make.

Voyage to the South Pole

by ROALD AMUNDSEN

The Norwegian explorer, Roald Amundsen (1872-1928), was the first to reach the South Pole, on December 14, 1911, beating Captain Robert Falcon Scott's party by less than a month. His expedition of 1910-12 was originally intended as a North Polar expedition, but Amundsen, by a dramatic surprise, changed his plans and sailed secretly from Madeira to Ross Sea without calling at any port. Amundsen relied entirely on dogs, and his journey to the Pole was comparatively fast and easy, in contrast to that of the ill-fated Scott, who depended on motor sledges and ponies. In 1928, when General Nobile's airship, Italia, was wrecked on its return from the North Pole, Amundsen went to search for him. Leaving Bergen, Norway, for Spitsbergen, the Norwegian archipelago in the Arctic Ocean, on June 17, 1928, he was never heard of again.

I N LAT. 87° S.—ACCORDING TO DEAD RECKONING—WE SAW the last of the land to the northeast. The atmosphere was then apparently as clear as could be, and we felt certain that our view covered all the land there was to be seen from that spot. We were deceived again on this occasion, as will be seen later. Our distance that day (December 4) was close upon twenty-five miles; height above the sea, 10,100 feet.

The weather did not continue fine for long. Next day (December 5) there was a gale from the north, and once more the whole plain was a mass of drifting snow. In addition to this there was thick falling snow, which blinded us and made things worse, but a feeling of security had come over us and helped us to advance rapidly and without hesitation, although we could see nothing. That day we encountered new surface conditions—big, hard snow waves (*sastrugi*). These were anything but

19

pleasant to work among, especially when one could not see them. It was of no use for us "forerunners" to think of going in advance under these circumstances, as it was impossible to keep on one's feet. Three or four paces was often the most we managed to do before falling down. The *sastrugi* were very high, and often abrupt; if one came on them unexpectedly, one required to be more than an acrobat to keep on one's feet. The plan we found to work best in these conditions was to let Hanssen's dogs go first; this was an unpleasant job for Hanssen, and for his dogs too, but it succeeded, and succeeded well. An upset here and there was, of course, unavoidable, but with a little patience the sledge was always righted again. The drivers had as much as they could do to support their sledges among the *sastrugi,* but while supporting the sledges, they had at the same time a support for themselves. It was worse for us who had no sledges, but by keeping in the wake of them we could see where the irregularities lay, and thus get over them. Hanssen deserves a special word of praise for his driving on this surface in such weather. It is a difficult matter to drive Eskimo dogs forward when they cannot see; but Hanssen managed it well, both getting the dogs on and steering his course by compass. One would not think it possible to keep an approximately right course when the uneven ground gives such violent shocks that the needle flies several times round the compass, and is no sooner still again than it recommences the same dance; but when at last we got an observation, it turned out that Hanssen had steered to a hair, for the observations and dead reckoning agreed to a mile. In spite of all hindrances, and of being able to see nothing, the sledge meters showed nearly twenty-five miles. The hypsometer showed 11,070 feet above the sea; we had therefore reached a greater altitude than the Butcher's.

December 6 brought the same weather: thick snow, sky and plain all one, nothing to be seen. Nevertheless we made splendid progress. The *sastrugi* gradually became leveled out, until the surface was perfectly smooth; it was a relief to have even ground to go upon once more. These irregularities that one was constantly falling over were a nuisance; if we had met with them in our usual surroundings it would not have mattered so much; but up here on the high ground, where we had to stand and gasp for breath every time we rolled over, it was certainly not pleasant.

That day we passed 88° S., and camped in 88° 9′ S. A great surprise awaited us in the tent that evening. I expected to find, as on the previous evening, that the boiling point had fallen somewhat; in other words, that it would show a continued rise of the ground, but to our astonishment this was not so. The water boiled at exactly the same temperature as on the preceding day. I tried it several times, to convince myself that there was nothing wrong, each time with the same result. There was great rejoicing among us all when I was able to announce that we had arrived on the top of the plateau.

December 7 began like the 6th, with absolutely thick weather, but, as they say, you never know what the day is like before sunset. Possibly I might have chosen a better expression than this last—one more in agreement with the natural conditions—but I will let it stand. Though for several weeks now the sun had not set, my readers will not be so critical as to reproach me with inaccuracy. With a light wind from the northeast, we now went southward at a good speed over the perfectly level plain, with excellent going. The uphill work had taken it out of our dogs, though not to any serious extent. They had turned greedy—there is no denying that—and the half kilo of pemmican they got each day was not enough to fill their stomachs. Early and late they were looking for something—no matter what—to devour. To begin with they contented themselves with such loose objects as ski bindings, whips, boots, and the like; but as we came to know their proclivities, we took such care of everything that they found no extra meals lying about. But that was not the end of the matter. They then went for the fixed lashings of the sledges, and—if we had allowed it—would very quickly have resolved the various sledges into their component parts. But we found a way of stopping that: every evening, on halting, the sledges were buried in the snow, so as to hide all the lashings. That was successful; curiously enough, they never tried to force the "snow rampart."

I may mention as a curious thing that these ravenous animals, that devoured everything they came across, even to the ebonite points of our ski sticks, never made any attempt to break into the provision cases. They lay there and went about among the sledges with their noses just on a level with the split cases, seeing and scenting the pemmican, without once making a sign of taking any. But if one raised a lid, they were not long in showing themselves. Then they all came in a great hurry and flocked about the sledges in the hope of getting a little extra bit. I am at a loss to explain this behavior; that bashfulness was not at the root of it, I am tolerably certain.

During the forenoon the thick, gray curtain of cloud began to grow thinner on the horizon, and for the first time for three days we could see a few miles about us. The feeling was something like that one has on waking from a good nap, rubbing one's eyes and looking around. We had become so accustomed to the gray twilight that this positively dazzled us. Meanwhile, the upper layer of air seemed obstinately to remain the same and to be doing its best to prevent the sun from showing itself. We badly wanted to get a meridian altitude, so that we could determine our latitude. Since 86° 47′ S. we had had no observation, and it was not easy to say when we should get one. Hitherto, the weather conditions on the high ground had not been particularly favorable. Although the prospects were not very promising, we halted at 11 A.M. and made ready to catch the sun if it should be kind enough to look out. Hassel and Wisting used one sextant and artificial horizon, Hanssen and I the other set.

I don't know that I have ever stood and absolutely pulled at the sun to get it out as I did that time. If we got an observation here which agreed with our reckoning, then it would be possible, if the worst came to the worst, to go to the Pole on dead reckoning; but if we got none now, it was a question whether our claim to the Pole would be admitted on the dead reckoning we should be able to produce. Whether my pulling helped or not, it is certain that the sun appeared. It was not very brilliant to begin with, but, practiced as we now were in availing ourselves of even the poorest chances, it was good enough. Down it came, was checked by all, and the altitude written down. The curtain of cloud was rent more and more, and before we had finished our work—that is to say, caught the sun at its highest, and convinced ourselves that it was descending again—it was shining in all its glory. We had put away our instruments and were sitting on the sledges, engaged in the calculations. I can safely say that we were excited. What would the result be, after marching blindly for so long and over such impossible ground, as we had been doing? We added and subtracted, and at last there was the result. We looked at each other in sheer incredulity: the result was as astonishing as the most consummate conjuring trick—88° 16′ S., precisely to a minute the same as our reckoning, 88° 16′ S. If we were forced to go to the Pole on dead reckoning, then surely the most exacting would admit our right to do so. We put away our observation books, ate one or two biscuits, and went at it again.

We had a great piece of work before us that day: nothing less than carrying our flag farther south than the foot of man had trod. We had our silk flag ready; it was made fast to two ski sticks and laid on Hanssen's sledge. I had given him orders that as soon as we had covered the distance to 88° 23′ S., which was Shackleton's farthest south, the flag was to be hoisted on his sledge. It was my turn as forerunner, and I pushed on. There was no longer any difficulty in holding one's course; I had the grandest cloud formations to steer by, and everything now went like a machine. First came the forerunner for the time being, then Hanssen, then Wisting, and finally Bjaaland. The forerunner who was not on duty went where he liked; as a rule he accompanied one or other of the sledges. I had long ago fallen into a reverie—far removed from the scene in which I was moving; what I thought about I do not remember now, but I was so preoccupied that I had entirely forgotten my surroundings. Then suddenly I was roused from my dreaming by a jubilant shout, followed by ringing cheers. I turned round quickly to discover the reason of this unwonted occurrence, and stood speechless and overcome.

I find it impossible to express the feelings that possessed me at this moment. All the sledges had stopped, and from the foremost of them the Norwegian flag was flying. It shook itself out, waved and flapped so that the silk rustled; it looked wonderfully well in the pure, clear air and the shining white surroundings. 88° 23′ was past; we were farther south than any human being had been. No other moment of the whole trip affected me like this. The tears forced their way to my eyes; by no effort of will could I keep them back. It was the flag yonder that conquered me and my will. Luckily I was some way in advance of the others, so that I had time to pull myself together and master my feelings before reaching my comrades. We all shook hands, with mutual congratulations; we had won our way far by holding together, and we would go farther yet— to the end.

We did not pass that spot without according our highest tribute of admiration to the man who—together with his gallant companions— had planted his country's flag so infinitely nearer to the goal than any of his precursors. Sir Ernest Shackleton's name will always be written in the annals of Antarctic exploration in letters of fire. Pluck and grit can work wonders, and I know of no better example of this than what that man has accomplished.

The cameras of course had to come out, and we got an excellent photograph of the scene which none of us will ever forget. We went on a couple of miles more, to 88° 25′, and then camped. The weather had improved, and kept on improving all the time. It was now almost perfectly calm, radiantly clear, and, under the circumstances, quite summerlike: −0.4° F. Inside the tent it was quite sultry. This was more than we had expected.

After much consideration and discussion we had come to the conclusion that we ought to lay down a depot—the last one—at this spot. The advantages of lightening our sledges were so great that we should have to risk it. Nor would there be any great risk attached to it, after all, since we should adopt a system of marks that would lead even a blind man back to the place. We had determined to mark it not only at right angles to our course—that is, from east to west—but by snow beacons at every two geographical miles to the south.

We stayed here on the following day to arrange this depot. Hanssen's dogs were real marvels, all of them; nothing seemed to have any effect on them. They had grown rather thinner, of course, but they were still as strong as ever. It was therefore decided not to lighten Hanssen's sledge, but only the two others; both Wisting's and Bjaaland's teams had suffered, especially the latter's. The reduction in weight that was effected was considerable—nearly 110 pounds on each of the two sledges; there was thus about 220 pounds in the depot. The snow here was ill-adapted for building, but we put up quite a respectable monument all the same. It was dogs' pemmican and biscuits that were left behind; we carried with us on the sledges provisions for about a month. If, therefore, contrary to expectation, we should be so unlucky as to miss this depot, we should nevertheless be fairly sure of reaching our depot in 86° 21′ before supplies ran short. The cross-marking of the depot was done with sixty splinters of black packing case on each side, with 100 paces between each. Every other one had a shred of black cloth on the top. The splinters on the east side were all marked, so that on seeing them we should know instantly that we were to the east of the depot. Those on the west had no marks.

The warmth of the past few days seemed to have matured our frost sores, and we presented an awful appearance. It was Wisting, Hanssen, and I who had suffered the worst damage in the last southeast blizzard; the left side of our faces was one mass of sore, bathed in matter and serum. We looked like the worst type of tramps and ruffians, and would probably not have been recognized by our nearest relations. These sores were a great trouble to us during the latter part of the journey. The slightest gust of wind produced a sensation as if one's face were being cut backward and forward with a blunt knife. They lasted a long time, too; I can remember Hanssen removing the last scab when we were coming into Hobart—three months later. We were very lucky in the weather during this depot work; the sun came out all at once, and we had an excellent opportunity of taking some good azimuth observations, the last of any use that we got on the journey.

December 9 arrived with the same fine weather and sunshine. True, we felt our frost sores rather sharply that day, with −18.4° F. and a little breeze dead against us, but that could not be helped. We at once began to put up beacons—a work which was continued with great regularity right up to the Pole. These beacons were not so big as those we had built down on the Barrier; we could see that they would be quite large enough with a height of about 3 feet, as it was very easy to see the slightest irregularity on this perfectly flat surface. While thus engaged we had an opportunity of becoming thoroughly acquainted with the nature of the snow. Often—very often indeed—on this part of the plateau, to the south of 88° 25′, we had difficulty in getting snow good enough—that is, solid enough for cutting blocks. The snow up here seemed to have fallen very quietly, in light breezes or calms. We could thrust the tent pole, which was 6 feet long, right down without meeting resistance, which showed that there was no hard layer of snow. The surface was also perfectly level; there was not a sign of *sastrugi* in any direction.

Every step we now took in advance brought us rapidly nearer the goal; we could feel fairly certain of reaching it on the afternoon of the 14th. It was very natural that our conversation should be chiefly concerned with the time of arrival. None of us would admit that he was nervous, but I am inclined to think that we all had a little touch of that malady. What should we see when we got there? A vast, endless plain, that no eye had yet seen and no foot yet trodden; or—— No, it was an impossibility; with the speed at which we had traveled, we must reach the goal first, there could be no doubt about that. And yet—and yet—— Wherever there is the smallest loophole, doubt creeps in and gnaws and gnaws and never leaves a poor wretch in peace. "What on earth is Uroa scenting?" It was Bjaaland who made this remark, on one of these last days, when I was going by the side of his sledge and talking to him. "And the strange thing is that he's scenting to the south. It can never be——" Myliuns, Ring, and Suggen showed the same interest in the southerly direction; it was quite extraordinary to see how they raised their heads, with every sign of curiosity, put their noses in the air, and sniffed due south. One would really have thought there was something remarkable to be found there.

From 88° 25′ S. the barometer and hypsometer indicated slowly but surely that the plateau was beginning to descend toward the other side.

This was a pleasant surprise to us; we had thus not only found the very summit of the plateau, but also the slope down on the far side. This would have a very important bearing for obtaining an idea of the construction of the whole plateau. On December 9 observations and dead reckoning agreed within a mile. The same result again on the 10th: observation 2 kilometers behind reckoning. The weather and going remained about the same as on the preceding days: light southeasterly breeze, temperature −18.4° F. The snow surface was loose, but ski and sledges glided over it well. On the 11th, the same weather conditions. Temperature −13° F. Observation and reckoning again agreed exactly. Our latitude was 89° 15′ S. On the 12th we reached 89° 30′, reckoning 1 kilometer behind observation. Going and surface as good as ever. Weather splendid—calm with sunshine. The noon observation on the 13th gave 89° 37′ S. Reckoning 89° 38.5′ S. We halted in the afternoon, after going eight geographical miles, and camped in 89° 45′, according to reckoning.

The weather during the forenoon had been just as fine as before; in the afternoon we had some snow showers from the southeast. It was like the eve of some great festival that night in the tent. One could feel that a great event was at hand. Our flag was taken out again and lashed to the same two ski sticks as before. Then it was rolled up and laid aside, to be ready when the time came. I was awake several times during the night, and had the same feeling that I can remember as a little boy on the night before Christmas Eve—an intense expectation of what was going to happen. Otherwise I think we slept just as well that night as any other.

On the morning of December 14 the weather was of the finest, just as if it had been made for arriving at the Pole. I am not quite sure, but I believe we dispatched our breakfast rather more quickly than usual and were out of the tent sooner, though I must admit that we always accomplished this with all reasonable haste. We went in the usual order —the forerunner, Hanssen, Wisting, Bjaaland, and the reserve forerunner. By noon we had reached 89° 53′ by dead reckoning, and made ready to take the rest in one stage. At 10 A.M. a light breeze had sprung up from the southeast, and it had clouded over, so that we got no noon altitude; but the clouds were not thick, and from time to time we had a glimpse of the sun through them. The going on that day was rather different from what it had been; sometimes the ski went over it well, but at others it was pretty bad. We advanced that day in the same mechanical way as before; not much was said, but eyes were used all the more. Hanssen's neck grew twice as long as before in his endeavor to see a few inches farther. I had asked him before we started to spy out ahead for all he was worth, and he did so with a vengeance. But, however keenly he stared, he could not descry anything but the endless flat plain ahead of us. The dogs had dropped their scenting, and appeared to have lost their interest in the regions about the earth's axis.

At three in the afternoon a simultaneous "Halt" rang out from the drivers. They had carefully examined their sledge meters, and they all showed the full distance—our Pole by reckoning. The goal was reached, the journey ended. I cannot say—though I know it would sound much more effective—that the object of my life was attained. That would be romancing rather too barefacedly. I had better be honest and admit straight out that I have never known any man to be placed in such a diametrically opposite position to the goal of his desires as I was at that moment. The regions around the North Pole—well, yes, the North Pole itself—had attracted me from childhood, and here I was at the South Pole. Can anything more topsy-turvy be imagined?

We reckoned now that we were at the Pole. Of course, every one of us knew that we were not standing on the absolute spot; it would be an impossibility with the time and the instruments at our disposal to ascertain that exact spot. But we were so near it that the few miles which possibly separated us from it could not be of the slightest importance. It was our intention to make a circle round this camp, with a radius of twelve and a half miles, and to be satisfied with that. After we had halted we collected and congratulated each other. We had good grounds for mutual respect in what had been achieved, and I think that was just the feeling that was expressed in the firm and powerful grasps of the fist that were exchanged. After this we proceeded to the greatest and most solemn act of the whole journey—the planting of our flag. Pride and affection shone in the five pairs of eyes that gazed upon the flag, as it unfurled itself with a sharp crack, and waved over the Pole. I had determined that the act of planting it—the historic event—should be equally divided among us all. It was not for one man to do this; it was for *all* who had staked their lives in the struggle, and held together through thick and thin. This was the only way in which I could show my gratitude to my comrades in this desolate spot. I could see that they understood and accepted it in the spirit in which it was offered. Five weatherbeaten, frostbitten fists they were that grasped the pole, raised the waving flag in the air, and planted it as the first at the geographical South Pole. "Thus we plant thee, beloved flag, at the South Pole, and give to the plain on which it lies the name of King Haakon VII's Plateau." That moment will certainly be remembered by all of us who stood there.

One gets out of the way of protracted ceremonies in those regions—the shorter they are the better. Everyday life began again at once. When we had got the tent up, Hanssen set about slaughtering Helge, and it was hard for him to have to part from his best friend. Helge had been an uncommonly useful and good-natured dog; without making any fuss he had pulled from morning to night, and had been a shining example to the team. But during the last week he had quite fallen away, and on our arrival at the Pole there was only a shadow of the old Helge left. He was only a drag on the others, and did absolutely no work. One blow on the skull, and Helge had ceased to live. "What is death to one is food to another," is a saying that can scarcely find a better application than these dog meals. Helge was portioned out on the spot, and within a couple of hours there was nothing left of him but his teeth and the tuft at the end of his tail. This was the second of our eighteen dogs that we had lost. The Major, one of Wisting's fine dogs, left us in 88° 25′ S., and never returned. He was fearfully worn out, and must have gone away to die. We now had sixteen dogs left, and these we intended to divide into two equal teams, leaving Bjaaland's sledge behind.

Of course, there was a festivity in the tent that evening—not that champagne corks were popping and wine flowing—no, we contented ourselves with a little piece of seal meat each, and it tasted well and did us good. There was no other sign of festival indoors. Outside we heard the flag flapping in the breeze. Conversation was lively in the tent that evening, and we talked of many things. Perhaps, too, our thoughts sent messages home of what we had done.

Everything we had with us had now to be marked with the words "South Pole" and the date, to serve afterward as souvenirs. Wisting proved to be a firstclass engraver, and many were the articles he had to mark. Tobacco—in the form of smoke—had hitherto never made its appearance in the tent. From time to time I had seen one or two of the others take a quid, but now these things were to be altered. I had brought with me an old briar pipe, which bore inscriptions from many places in the Arctic regions, and now I wanted it marked "South Pole." When I produced my pipe and was about to mark it, I received an unexpected gift: Wisting offered me tobacco for the rest of the journey. He had some cakes of plug in his kit bag, which he would prefer to see me smoke. Can anyone grasp what such an offer meant at such a spot, made to a man who, to tell the truth, is very fond of a smoke after meals? There are not many who can understand it fully. I accepted the offer, jumping with joy, and on the way home I had a pipe of fresh, fine-cut plug every evening. Ah! that Wisting, he spoiled me entirely. Not only did he give me tobacco, but every evening—and I must confess I yielded to the temptation after a while, and had a morning smoke as well—he undertook the disagreeable work of cutting the plug and filling my pipe in all kinds of weather.

But we did not let our talk make us forget other things. As we had got no noon altitude, we should have to try and take one at midnight. The weather had brightened again, and it looked as if midnight would be a good time for the observation. We therefore crept into our bags to get a little nap in the intervening hours. In good time—soon after 11 P.M.—we were out again, and ready to catch the sun; the weather was of the best, and the opportunity excellent. We four navigators all had a share in it, as usual, and stood watching the course of the sun. This was a labor of patience, as the difference of altitude was now very slight. The result at which we finally arrived was of great interest, as it clearly shows how unreliable and valueless a single observation like this is in these regions. At 12.30 A.M. we put our instruments away, well satisfied with our work, and quite convinced that it was the midnight altitude that we had observed. The calculations which were carried out immediately afterward gave us 89° 56′ S. We were all well pleased with this result.

The arrangement now was that we should encircle this camp with a radius of about twelve and a half miles. By encircling I do not, of course, mean that we should go round in a circle with this radius; that would have taken us days, and was not to be thought of. The encircling was accomplished in this way: Three men went out in three different directions, two at right angles to the course we had been steering, and one in continuation of that course. To carry out this work I had chosen Wisting, Hassel, and Bjaaland. Having concluded our observations, we put the kettle on to give ourselves a drop of chocolate; the pleasure of standing out there in rather light attire had not exactly put warmth into our bodies. As we were engaged in swallowing the scalding drink, Bjaaland suddenly observed: "I'd like to tackle this encircling straight away. We shall have lots of time to sleep when we get back." Hassel and Wisting were quite of the same opinion, and it was agreed that they should start the work immediately. Here we have yet another example of the good spirit that prevailed in our little community. We had only lately come in from our day's work—a march of about eighteen and a half miles—and now they were asking to be allowed to go on another twenty-five miles. It seemed as if these fellows could never be tired. We therefore turned this meal into a little breakfast—that is to say, each man ate what he wanted of his bread ration, and then they began to get ready for the work. First, three small bags of light windproof stuff were made, and in each of these was placed a paper, giving the position of our camp. In addition, each of them carried a large square flag of the same dark brown material, which could be easily seen at a distance. As flagpoles we elected to use our spare sledge runners, which were both long—12 feet—and strong, and which we were going to take off here in any case, to lighten the sledges as much as possible for the return journey.

Thus equipped, and with thirty biscuits as an extra ration, the three men started off in the directions laid down. Their march was by no means free from danger, and does great honor to those who undertook it, not merely without raising the smallest objection, but with the greatest keenness. Let us consider for a moment the risk they ran. Our tent on the boundless plain, without marks of any kind, may very well be compared with a needle in a haystack. From this the three men were to steer out for a distance of twelve and a half miles. Compasses would have been good things to take on such a walk, but our sledge compasses were too heavy and unsuitable for carrying. They therefore had to go without. They had the sun to go by, certainly, when they started, but who could say how long it would last? The weather was then fine enough, but it was impossible to guarantee that no sudden change would take place. If by bad luck the sun should be hidden, then their own tracks might help them. But to trust to tracks in these regions is a dangerous thing. Before you know where you are the whole plain may be one mass of driving snow, obliterating all tracks as soon as they are made. With the rapid changes of weather we had so often experienced, such a thing was not impossible. That these three risked their lives that morning, when they left the tent at 2.30, there can be no doubt at all, and they all three knew it very well. But if anyone thinks that on this account they took a solemn farewell of us who stayed behind, he is much mistaken. Not a bit; they all vanished in their different directions amid laughter and chaff.

The first thing we did—Hanssen and I—was to set about arranging a lot of trifling matters; there was something to be done here, something there, and above all we had to be ready for the series of observations we were to carry out together, so as to get as accurate a determination of our position as possible. The first observation told us at once how necessary this was. For it turned out that this, instead of giving us a greater altitude than the midnight observation, gave us a smaller one, and it was then clear that we had gone out of the meridian we thought we were following. Now the first thing to be done was to get our north and south line and latitude determined, so that we could find our position once more. Luckily for us, the weather looked as if it would hold. We measured the sun's altitude at every hour from 6 A.M. to 7 P.M., and from these observations found, with some degree of certainty, our latitude and the direction of the meridian.

By nine in the morning we began to expect the return of our comrades; according to our calculation they should then have covered the distance —twenty-five miles. It was not till ten o'clock that Hanssen made out the first black dot on the horizon, and not long after the second and third appeared. We both gave a sigh of relief as they came on; almost simultaneously the three arrived at the tent. We told them the result of our observations up to that time; it looked as if our camp was in about 89° 54' 30" S., and that with our encircling we had therefore included the actual Pole. With this result we might very well have been content, but as the weather was so good and gave the impression that it would continue so, and our store of provisions proved on examination to be very ample, we decided to go on for the remaining ten kilometers (five and a half geographical miles), and get our position determined as near to the Pole as possible. Meanwhile the three wanderers turned in—not so much because they were tired, as because it was the right thing to do— and Hanssen and I continued the series of observations.

In the afternoon we again went very carefully through our provision supply before discussing the future. The result was that we had food enough for ourselves and the dogs for eighteen days. The surviving sixteen dogs were divided into two teams of eight each, and the contents of Bjaaland's sledge were shared between Hanssen's and Wisting's. The abandoned sledge was set upright in the snow, and proved to be a splendid mark. The sledge meter was screwed to the sledge, and we left it there; our other two were quite sufficient for the return journey; they had all shown themselves very accurate. A couple of empty provision cases were also left behind. I wrote in pencil on a piece of case the information that our tent—"Polheim"—would be found five and a half geographical miles northwest quarter west by compass from the sledge. Having put all these things in order the same day, we turned in, very well satisfied.

Early next morning, December 16, we were on our feet again. Bjaaland, who had now left the company of the drivers and been received with jubilation into that of the forerunners, was immediately entrusted with the honorable task of leading the expedition forward to the Pole itself. I assigned this duty, which we all regarded as a distinction, to him as a mark of gratitude to the gallant Telemarkers for their pre-eminent work in the advancement of ski sport. The leader that day had to keep as straight as a line, and if possible to follow the direction of our meridian. A little way after Bjaaland came Hassel, then Hanssen, then Wisting, and I followed a good way behind. I could thus check the direction of the march very accurately, and see that no great deviation was made. Bjaaland on this occasion showed himself a matchless forerunner; he went perfectly straight the whole time. Not once did he incline to one side or the other, and when we arrived at the end of the distance, we could still clearly see the sledge we had set up and take its bearing. This showed it to be absolutely in the right direction.

It was 11 A.M. when we reached our destination. While some of us were putting up the tent, others began to get everything ready for the coming observations. A solid snow pedestal was put up, on which the artificial horizon was to be placed, and a smaller one to rest the sextant on when it was not in use. At 11:30 A.M. the first observation was taken. We divided ourselves into two parties—Hanssen and I in one, Hassel and Wisting in the other. While one party slept, the other took the observations, and the watches were of six hours each. The weather was altogether grand, though the sky was not perfectly bright the whole time. A very light, fine, vaporous curtain would spread across the sky from time to time, and then quickly disappear again. This film of cloud was not thick enough to hide the sun, which we could see the whole time, but the atmosphere seemed to be disturbed. The effect of this was that the sun appeared not to change its altitude for several hours, until it suddenly made a jump.

Observations were now taken every hour through the whole twenty-four. It was very strange to turn in at 6 P.M., and then on turning out again at midnight to find the sun apparently still at the same altitude, and then once more at 6 A.M. to see it still no higher. The altitude had changed, of course, but so slightly that it was imperceptible with the naked eye. To us it appeared as though the sun made the circuit of the heavens at exactly the same altitude. The times of day that I have given here are calculated according to the meridian of Framheim; we continued to reckon our time from this. The observations soon told us that we were not on the absolute Pole, but as close to it as we could hope to get with our instruments.

On December 17 at noon we had completed our observations, and it

is certain that we had done all that could be done. In order if possible
to come a few inches nearer to the actual Pole, Hanssen and Bjaaland
went out four geographical miles (seven kilometers) in the direction
of the newly found meridian.

Bjaaland astonished me at dinner that day. Speeches had not hitherto
been a feature of this journey, but now Bjaaland evidently thought the
time had come, and surprised us all with a really fine oration. My amazement reached its culmination when, at the conclusion of his speech, he
produced a cigar case full of cigars and offered it round. A cigar at the
Pole! What do you say to that? But it did not end there. When the cigars
had gone round, there were still four left. I was quite touched when
he handed the case and cigars to me with the words: "Keep this to re-
mind you of the Pole." I have taken good care of the case, and shall
preserve it as one of the many happy signs of my comrades' devotion on
this journey. The cigars I shared out afterward, on Christmas Eve, and
they gave us a visible mark of that occasion.

When this festival dinner at the Pole was ended, we began our preparations for departure. First we set up the little tent we had brought with
us in case we should be compelled to divide into two parties. It had been
made by our able sailmaker, Rönne, and was of very thin windproof
gabardine. Its drab color made it easily visible against the white surface.
Another pole was lashed to the tent pole, making its total height about
13 feet. On the top of this a little Norwegian flag was lashed fast, and
underneath it a pennant, on which "Fram" was painted. The tent was
well secured with guy ropes on all sides. Inside the tent, in a little bag,
I left a letter, addressed to H.M. the King, giving information of what
he had accomplished. The way home was a long one, and so many
things might happen to make it impossible for us to give an account of
our expedition. Besides this letter, I wrote a short epistle to Captain
Scott, who, I assumed, would be the first to find the tent. Other things we
left there were a sextant with a glass horizon, a hypsometer case, three
reindeerskin foot bags, some kamiks and mitts.

When everything had been laid inside, we went into the tent, one by
one, to write our names on a tablet we had fastened to the tent pole. On
this occasion we received the congratulations of our companions on the
successful result, for the following messages were written on a couple
of strips of leather, sewed to the tent: "Good luck," and "Welcome to
90°." These good wishes, which we suddenly discovered, put us in very
good spirits. They were signed by Beck and Rönne. They had good faith
in us. When we had finished this we came out, and the tent door was

securely laced together, so that there was no danger of the wind getting a hold on that side.

And so good-by to Polheim. It was a solemn moment when we bared our heads and bade farewell to our home and our flag. And then the traveling tent was taken down and the sledges packed. Now the homeward journey was to begin—homeward, step by step, mile after mile, until the whole distance was accomplished. We drove at once into our old tracks and followed them. Many were the times we turned to send a last look to Polheim. The vaporous, white air set in again, and it was not long before the last of Polheim, our little flag, disappeared from view.

TRANSLATED BY A. G. CHATER

The Just Vengeance of Heaven

Anonymous

The following eighteenth-century narrative was contained in a journal discovered on the island of Ascension by Captain Mawson of the ship Compton *as the captain was homeward bound to England from India. In the words of the title page of an old edition, the journal offers "a full and exact relation of the author's being set on shore there by order of the commodore and captains of the Dutch fleet, for a most enormous crime he had been guilty of, and the extreme and unparalleled hardships, sufferings and misery he endured from the time of his being left there to that of his death. All wrote with his own hand and found lying near the skeleton."*

B Y ORDER OF THE COMMODORE AND CAPTAINS OF THE DUTCH fleet I was set on shore the 5th of May, 1725, upon the Island of Ascension, which struck me with great dread and uneasiness, having no hopes remaining but that the Almighty God would be my protector. They put on shore with me a cask of water, a hatchet, two buckets, an old frying pan, a fowling piece, teakettle, tarpaulin, onions, pease, calivances,* rice, etc. I pitched my tent on the beach and put some of my clothes on the sand near a rock, that I might the better know where to find them again.

On Sunday, the 6th, I went to the top of a hill to see whether I could discover any living creatures that were good for food, or any greens whereby I might satisfy my raging hunger; but to my great sorrow and confusion found nothing. I began then seriously to reflect upon my misspent life and the justice of the Almighty, who had thought fit to punish me in so exemplary a manner for the foul crimes I had committed; and

* Chick-peas.

sincerely wished that some unforeseen accident would put a period to those days which my malpractices had rendered miserable.

In the evening I returned to my tent with much difficulty, not being acquainted with the way, walking very melancholy along the sand, praying to God to further my escape from this desolate island. When I was arrived at my tent I fortified it with stones and covered it with a tarpaulin to screen me from the weather. About four or five o'clock I killed three birds, called boobies, which I skinned, salted and put in the sun to dry, and were the first birds I killed upon the island.

On the 7th in the morning I went to my water cask, which was full half a league from my tent, and broached it, by which I lost a great quantity of water; but afterwards turning the cask upon its head, with much difficulty I saved the rest. I then made a white flag out of one of my old shirts, which I placed on the top of a hill very near the sea, making my fowling piece as part of the standard, having nothing proper, it being rendered entirely useless for want of powder and shot; and employed myself for the remaining part of the evening in carrying stones to make my tent the stronger.

On the 8th early in the morning I took down my flag in order to place it on a hill the other side of the island. In my way thither I found a turtle, which I killed with the butt end of my piece, and returned back to my tent to rest my limbs, still flattering myself that some ship or other would speedily come to my deliverance. At night I removed my tent to the other side of the rock, being apprehensive of the destruction threatened by the moldering stones that were impending and unwilling to be accessory to my own death, trusting that the Omnipotent would still permit me to see better days. There was not a more commodious place on the whole island where I could have pitched my tent, which was no small satisfaction to one who labored under such deplorable circumstances. And what illustrated more the beauty of divine Providence, I still enjoyed my health. In the evening I killed more birds.

On the 9th in the morning I went to search for the turtle I had killed the day before, carrying my ax with me and split it down the back, it being so large that I could not turn it whole: cut some of the flesh from off the forefin which I carried to my tent, salted and dried in the sun; and having a second time screened my tent with a tarpaulin, I began to build my bulwark of stones about it.

On the 10th in the morning I took four or five onions and a few pease and carried them to the south part of the island to find a proper place for them, looking carefully all the way on the sand in order to discover a rivulet of water or the footsteps of some beast, by whose track I might in time find out the place where they drank. I also diligently sought after some herbage, and after a tedious walk over barren sands, hills and rock, almost inaccessible, I discovered a little purslane, part of which I eat for my refreshment. And being both weary and thirsty and having no water to drink, put the remainder into a sack which I had with me. In returning to my tent I found some other greens, but not knowing what they were did not dare to eat of them.

On the 11th in the morning I went into the country again and found some roots which had a taste not unlike that of potatoes, but was apprehensive they were not wholesome. I endeavored to make other necessary discoveries but to no purpose, which made me very disconsolate. Being almost choked with thirst, I returned to my tent, which was situated on the side of a hill, near which was another hill of a larger size, and adjacent to that a sandy bay. Upon the largest hill in the evening I boiled some rice, being much disordered in mind and body.

On the 12th in the morning I boiled some rice again and, having eat a small quantity, offered my prayers to God for a speedy deliverance. I then went toward the shore in hopes of seeing some friendly vessel approaching but found none; then walking on the beach till I was weary, seeing nothing but empty shells, returned to my tent. It was my usual custom to walk out every day in hopes of a distant view of ships upon the ocean, forced by stress of weather to make toward this desolate island to repair their damages. Afterward I read till I was tired and employed the remainder of the day in mending my clothes and the chief part of the night in meditations and dismal reflections on my unhappy state.

On the 13th in the afternoon I put the onions, together with some pease and calivances, into the ground near my tent, to try if they would grow. The 13th early in the morning went in search of some sea fowls but found none. In my return back I found a turtle, with whose eggs and flesh I made an excellent dinner, boiling them with some rice, and buried the remainder that could not be immediately used, for fear the stench would offend me, the turtles being of so large a size that it is impossible for one man to eat a whole one whilst sweet. I also found some nests of turtle eggs, which I boiled, melting some of the fat of the turtle to mingle with them, burning the remainder of it in the night in a saucepan, not having a lamp. On the 14th after prayers I took my walk as usual, but finding nothing new returned to my tent, mended my clothes and continued writing this my journal. On the 15th, before I took my walk, I eat some rice and then followed my usual employment, viz. the catching of those birds called boobies. I afterwards amused myself with reading and then endeavored to ease my tortured mind by a calm repose. On the 16th and 17th I caught several of the before-mentioned birds, one of which I kept alive for the space of eight days, and then it died. On the 18th two more. On the 19th and 20th nothing worth note.

On the 22nd I went to the other side of the island to try to make some discovery, but to no purpose. In the afternoon made a line and fished from a rock near four hours but had no success. Judge then what anxiety of mind, what midnight horrors I must undergo, whilst the night is an emblem of my crimes and each clear day renews my punishment. At my return my tent was filled with smoke, and remembering my tinder box was left upon the quilt, I hastened to the seaside for a bucket of salt water and soon quenched the flames. I immediately returned God thanks that all my wearing apparel was not consumed, having lost nothing but a banian, a shirt, the corner of the quilt and my Bible singed; and intreating the Almighty to give me patience to bear with these my present afflictions.

The 23rd I spent the whole day in admiring the infinite goodness of Almighty God, who had so miraculously preserved the small remainder of my worldly treasure; and sometime tortured myself with the melancholy reflection of the inexpressible punishment my crimes deserved, well knowing the wages of sin was inevitable death and that my crime was of the blackest dye; nor could I possibly form an idea in my mind of a punishment that could make the least atonement for so great an offence.

On the 24th I walked to my flag and returned again to my tent, having caught one bird only, which I broiled on the embers and eat. On the 25th after breakfast I went to catch sea fowls, then returned to my tent and dried them. On the 26th I repeated my usual endeavors in order to descry some ships sailing on the ocean, but to my great disappointment found my hopes frustrated; neither could I find any fowls or eggs that day. On the 27th met with the same ill success. On the 28th I ascended a hill so high that had my foot slipped I had inevitably been lost, but found nothing remarkable nor any food wherewith to satisfy my craving appetite. On the 29th and 30th I met the same disappointment. On the 31st I secured the provisions I had before salted and laid in the sun to dry. From the 1st to the 4th of June it would be useless to relate how often I strained my eyes, misled with distant objects, which the earnest desire of my delivery made me believe to be some ships approaching. The roaring torrent of the ocean, intermixed with the sun's bright rays, presented to my view a yellow gloom, not much unlike the moon when part obscured. The streaks of the element and every cloud seemed to me as a propitious sail. But reflect how dreadful was the shock when from my tired eyes the object flew and left behind sad scenes of black despair. When I was put on shore the captain told me it was the time for ships to pass that way, which made me more diligent in my search. From the 5th to the 7th I never failed to take my usual walks, although in vain.

On the 8th my water grew so scanty that I had but two quarts left, and so thick that I was obliged to strain it through my handkerchief. I then, too late, began to dig in the middle of the island, and after digging six or seven foot deep could find no moisture. I then returned to my tent and endeavored to make a new well, but found it impracticable. After having gone a fathom deep my grief was inexpressible to find no water to relieve me from this desolate island, where there is nothing left that can long subsist a human creature. On the 9th, finding no manner of food, I spent my time in meditating on my future state, and to appease the wrath of Him I had so highly offended. On the 10th I boiled some rice in the little water I had remaining, having little hopes of any relief but perishing. I recommended my soul to the Supreme Governor of all things. But recollecting that I had formerly heard there was a well of water on this island, whilst I was able to walk I traveled over hills and rocks to the other side, being determined to leave no place unsearched.

After four tedious hours' search I began to grow thirsty, and the intolerable heat of the sun made my life a burden to me, but was resolved to proceed, though very faint, and almost dead with heat and excessive fatigue. But God of his gracious goodness led me to a hollow place in a rock, from whence issued forth a stream of fresh water.

It is impossible for me to express my great joy and satisfaction at so agreeable a sight. I drank to that excess as to almost hurt myself, then sat down by the current for some time and drank again. After which refreshment I returned to my tent, having no vessel to carry any water away with me. On the 11th in the morning, after returning my sincere and humble thanks to the Maker of all things, I took my teakettle, together with some rice and wood, to the place where the spring was, and there boiled my rice and eat it. On the 12th I boiled some rice for my breakfast and afterward with much trouble carried two buckets of water to my tent. My shoes being worn out, the rocks cut my feet in a terrible manner, insomuch that I was often in danger of falling and breaking my buckets, without which I could not possibly live. On the 13th I went out to look for food but found none, but chanced to meet with some small weeds like birch, which I brought to my tent and boiled some rice for my dinner. After which I walked to the seashore to look out as usual, but my flattened hopes created in me a deep melancholy.

On the 14th and 15th I took my teakettle and some rice to the place above mentioned and after having refreshed myself returned to my tent, mended my clothes and spent the remainder of the day in reading. On the 16th I took my walk on the beach as usual and with as little success as ever, then returned to my tent to repose myself, where in the solemn gloom and dead of night I was surprised by an uncommon noise that surrounded me, of bitter cursing and swearing mixed with the most blasphemous and libidinous expressions I ever heard. My hair stood on end with horror and cold sweat trickled down my pallid cheeks. Trembling I lay, fearful to speak, least some vile fiend more wicked than the rest should make a prey of me, food fit for devils after my revolt from the just laws of Heaven. For no man living but would have thought the Devil had forsook his dark abode and come attended by infernal spirits to keep his hell on earth, being very certain there was not a human creature on the island except myself, having never observed the footsteps of a man since my being there.

Their discourse and their actions was such that nothing but devils could be guilty of, and one more busy than the rest kept such a continual whisking of his tail about my face that I expected nothing less than to be instantly torn to pieces by them. Among the rest I imagined to have heard the voice of a friend of mine, with whom in this lifetime I was very conversant. Sometimes I imagined myself to be agitated by an evil spirit, which made me apply to the Almighty for succor and forgiveness of my sin. I believe it was near three o'clock in the morning before this hellish tumult ceased; and then, being quite weary and spent, I fell asleep. About seven I arose and returned God thanks for my safe deliverance, but still heard bitter shrieks near my tent, yet could see nothing. Then, taking my prayerbook, read those prayers proper for a person in my condition; at the same time heard a voice saying, "Bugger, Bugger." I cannot afford paper sufficient to set down every particular of this unhappy day.

On the 17th I fetched two buckets of water but dreaded the ensuing night and interceded that God would not suffer me to be haunted any more with evil spirits. I believe my petition was heard, not being troubled with them that night. The day following, an apparition came to me in the likeness of a man that I perfectly knew. He conversed with me and touched so sensibly in exposing the diabolical life of Nature, for which I was then a sufferer and fiercely repented of, that I wished the shock would have ended my miserable life.

On the 18th, after my devotions, I went to look out as usual and took my hatchet with me; but, finding myself disappointed, made all possible haste to the other part of the island, where to my great satisfaction I found a tree, which I believe Providence had thrown on shore in some measure to alleviate my present misery. I divided it with my hatchet, the whole being more than I was capable of carrying at once. I took part of it on my shoulder, and having carried it halfway to my tent, laid it down and rested myself thereon. Alas! how wretched is that man whose bestial pleasures have rendered him odious to the rest of his fellow-creatures and turned him loose on a barren island, Nebuchadnezzar-like, to herd and graze with beasts, till, loathsome to himself and spurned by man, he prays to end his wretched days! His guilty conscience checks him, his crimes flare him full in the face, and his misspent life calls aloud for vengeance from on high. Such was the case of me, unhappy wretch, which proves the justice of All-gracious Heaven; and whilst I was resting my wearied limbs and seriously reflecting with myself the apparition again appeared to me, which gave me horror inexpressible.

His name I am unwilling to mention, not knowing what the consequence may be. He haunted me so long that he began to be familiar with me. After I had rested some time I carried my burden to the tent and returned to fetch the other part. On the 19th I went in the morning to see my colors, where for some time I fed my longing eyes with the ocean in hopes to see some ship approaching, but being denied so agreeable a prospect, when night came on I laid me down to rest and found no interruption by those evil voices which had before disturbed me, nor heard anything of them the next day, which made me hope the damned had reassumed their dismal caves. But when night came on, to my great surprise the restless apparitions grew more enraged and doubled their fury, tumbling me up and down so in my tent that in the morning my flesh appeared like an Egyptian mummy. The person I had formerly been acquainted with spoke several times to me, nor could I think he meant any harm, for when he was living we were as friendly as brothers. He was a soldier in Batavia. The saucepan was thrown down, the light put out and all my things left in a strange disorder. I then began to hope that if just Heaven did not think fit to end my perfect torments these punishments would serve as an atonement for my heinous crimes, in making use of man to satisfy my hellish and ungovernable lust, despising woman, which his hand had made a far more worthy object. My death begins to draw near, my strength decays and life is now become an insupportable burden.

On the 21st I lifted up my voice to Heaven, imploring mercy, then went abroad to search for daily food, but found the hand of Providence withdrawn. Insuperable grief and care oppressed my anxious soul. My senses were overwhelmed in depth of thought and every moment threatened my destruction. What pangs, alas! do wretched mortals feel who headstrong tread the giddy maze of life and leave the beauteous paths of righteousness, pleased to increase the number of the damned.

On the 22nd I took my buckets to fetch more water to my tent, which I could not accomplish till the day was far spent, being forced to travel in great misery barefooted over the rocks. The 23rd I spent my time in prayer, viewed with eager eyes the raging main, and from the 24th to the 27th incessantly continued my prayers. On the 28th in the morning I went to see whether my flag was standing, and after having humbled myself before God and desired his mercy and forgiveness I returned to my tent, took my bedding and some other necessaries and went to the middle of the island, where I fixed a new habitation in the cavity of a rock, it being much nearer the rivulet of water before mentioned. But, to my great astonishment, when I went to get some there was not one drop. I fetched a few eggs and boiled them in my teakettle with some of the water I had left, then went to the south side of the island, where there is a large hill of sand and rocks, upon which I found more purslane, which I gathered and put into my sack, together with some eggs. I fried both and eat them with a good appetite but was obliged to return lest I should be belated and not be able to find my new abode. Before I arrived at the rock I was almost dead for want of drink and my skin blistered in a terrible manner with the scorching heat of the sun, so that it was ready to peel from my flesh.

On the 29th I went to the top of the hill to look out for shipping. Afterward, walking on the seashore, I perceived a piece of wood sinking in the sand. At first I took it for a tree but, coming nearer, I found it to be a cross. I embraced it in my arms and prayed fervently to God to deliver me. I believe there had been a man buried there belonging to some ship. In my return to my cave my feet were miserably cut with the sharp stones, that I had liked to have perished in coming down the hill. When I had got to my tent I rested and then went out again and in my walk found a piece of glass bottle with which I descended into a deep pit and found some water of brackish taste, so that my search proved of no effect. As I was returning to my cave in a disconsolate manner, bemoaning my wretched fate, I found some scattered wood, which I made up into a bundle and carried with me. I was no sooner come to my cavern but I heard a dreadful noise, resembling many coppersmiths at work. I went again to get some greens and eggs, with which I eat and drank the last of the water I had left.

On the 30th I went in search of water but could find none, and now all hopes were lost, a ghastly skeleton appeared to me with his hand uplifted, pointed to his throat and seemed to tell me I should die with drought.

July the 1st. The water being dried up in every place where I was used to get it, I was ready to perish with thirst, therefore offered up my prayers to God to deliver and preserve me as he did Moses and the children of Israel, by causing the water to gush out of the rock; esteeming their sufferings not to equal mine, seeing that I was not only bereft of food and raiment but banished from all human society and left to be devoured by the birds of prey, who infest this desolate island. Whilst I was rambling up and down in quest, ascending the top of a hill, I espied a great number of goats a-grazing at a distance, which I chased with all the speed I was able, but to my sorrow found they were too swift for me. I still followed them at a distance, in hopes of finding the place where they watered, when, after a long pursuit, I came to a pit five or six fathom deep, which I descended, but found no water. I believe by the goats frequenting it there is sometimes water, chiefly occasioned by the fall of rain. It is a miracle to me how the goats keep themselves alive in a dry season, since water is so scarce throughout the whole island. I should long before this have perished had it not been for a gallon of water that I had before preserved, with a full resolution not to make use of it unless compelled by dire necessity.

I afterward went to the strand but could discover nothing that would be of any service to me. I then proceeded farther up the island and, having ascended a lofty hill, espied a greater number of goats, with their kids accompanying them, which I pursued with the like ill success. As there are so many on the island it is surprising I had not discovered them sooner, but believe they give their young ones suck in the holes of the rocks, till the sun has drawn the moisture thence, then sally out abroad in search of more. Here I found about two gallons of water more in a rock.

July the 4th I moved my things from my cave and went to the other side of the island to settle my abode, being sure there was no water on this side. I prayed to God to send a plenteous rain but, waiting from the 5th to the 8th, found my prayers ineffectual.

On the 9th, as I was walking pensively on the sand, half dead with thirst, I heard a dismal noise of cursing and swearing in my own language, during which time a cloud of birds obscured the light of the sun. On the 10th I ascended another steep hill but found nothing but a piece of wood, which I took with me to prop my new habitation. From the 11th to the 18th nothing remarkable happened. On the 19th I went out in search of water but found none. I found some birds' eggs and brought them home to eat, using my water very sparingly, which lasted me only the next day. From the 21st to the 31st tongue can't express nor thought devise the wretched torments I endured.

From the 1st to the 3rd of August I walked out with my bucket and found a little water which the goats had left in the hollow of a rock, which I carried to my tent. On the 4th I went to the sands and found a broken oar and three or four small pieces of wood, which was very acceptable. Proceeding a little further, I espied something which appeared to me at a distance like a house and, calling to mind that I had heard the Portuguese formerly inhabited this island, made all the haste possible thither, and to my great surprise found it to be a white hollow rock, in the cavity of which were some nails and broken glass bottles. These were but of little service to me; therefore I took my wood and went home.

On the 5th I went abroad again to seek for food but returned overwhelmed with grief and want. On the 6th I went to the beach and observed three or four of the calivances which I had before set were coming up, but upon a strict inquiry found the vermin had devoured all the rest, which damped my former joy. There has not been half an hour's rain for the space of three months, neither is there one drop of water to be found on the whole island except what I have preserved in my cask, and if God of his great goodness does not speedily refresh the earth with a plentiful rain I must inevitably perish.

From the 8th to the 10th could find no water, therefore endeavored to prepare myself for that great and terrible change which I was sufficiently convinced was near at hand, begging for salvation through the merits of my blessed Lord and Savior Jesus Christ, who shall change our vile bodies and make them like unto his.

On the 11th I went to my tent on the strand, where I again heard a terrible noise, but could not tell from whence it proceeded. I was resolved to go up the hill to endeavor to inform myself, but saw nothing there but a cloud of birds (of which mention has been made before) and am therefore fully persuaded the noise was made by them.

From the 12th to the 17th I could get no water, though I lost no time in search after it. I had not now above six gallons left in my cask, which made me boil nothing and drink but little. On the 18th and 19th the same; but, being near sunset, and I a great distance from my tent on the other side of the island, I lost my way; therefore was compelled to lie all night between two rocks; where I was disturbed with so great a number of rats that I was afraid of being devoured by them, heartily wishing myself on the strand again.

On the 20th I prayed incessantly to Almighty God to send rain, then took my spade and dug two fathoms, but found no moisture. I viewed the motions of the heaven, in hopes to see some friendly cloud o'er-charged with water, that might disgorge itself upon the barren rocks and grant relief to me in this distress, but my hopes were vain; then wildly wandered over the sterile hills and begged the rocks and sands might cover me, deeming the goats that browsed about the island far happier than that man whose boundless lust had been the occasion of his suffering.

On the 21st I went rambling about the island with my scoop in hand but found no refreshment. The small quantity of water I had left being almost exhausted, I was forced to make water in my scoop and drank my urine, thinking it wholesomer than salt water. I was so extremely thirsty that my lips stuck together.

On the 22nd I took a walk (after having offered up my sacrifice of prayer) on the strand, where I found a turtle, which I killed, and drank near a gallon of the blood instead of water, and took some of the fat and eggs and fried them together and eat them. But the blood did not agree with me, neither did it quench my raging thirst, so that I was forced to drink a large quantity of my urine.

On the 23rd, having no hopes of finding any more water, I took some of the turtle blood, which I had killed the day before, after letting it settle all night, which I mixed with my own urine and boiled some tea in it, and thought it far preferable to raw blood. About four in the afternoon I returned to my tent, having nothing to drink but turtle blood, but presently was taken so violently with the flux, occasioned by the drinking it, that I could hardly stand. This was rather a satisfaction to me than a shock, hoping the sooner to end my miserable days, desiring nothing more. I with great difficulty got to my tent.

From the 24th to the 27th I had no thought of anything but death, continuing very ill, but prayed earnestly that God would put an end to my misery. The fowl's eggs no way relieving my thirst, I was therefore forced to boil me some more tea in my urine and settled blood, there being plenty of the turtles on the island. On the 28th at three in the morning I went out and killed one turtle with my hatchet and put the blood in my bucket. There was a great quantity of water in the bladder which I drank, it being much better than the blood, but it did not continue long upon my stomach. I then cut off some of the flesh and carried it to my tent. And, being very dry, I boiled some more tea in the turtle blood, but my stomach, being weak, required greater nourishment; and the blood, being bitter, proved a strong emetic and I could no longer retain it. On the 29th I could not sleep, occasioned by a drought and dizziness in my head, which afflicted me to that degree that I thought I should have run mad. I once more went to search for water but found none.

On the 30th I prayed to be dissolved and be with Christ, for most part of the day thinking my sufferings exceeded that of Job, I being debarred the pleasure of human conversation, sick and had no clothing; my actions unjustifiable, my torments inexpressible and my destruction unavoidable. I tried to compose myself after I had prayed to the Almighty for rain or that I might die before morning. In the afternoon I endeavored to get out of my tent but could not walk, I was so weak; therefore dressed some turtle eggs. I had some turtle flesh in my tent but it was not sweet, but was in such agony for want of water that tongue can't express. I caught three boobies and drank the blood of them.

On the 31st as I was crawling on the sand, for I could not walk three steps, I espied a turtle and, being so weak that I could not carry my buckets, I cut off his head with my hatchet, then laid myself on my side and sucked the blood as it ran out; afterwards put my arm into the body and plucked his bladder out, which I crawled away with to my tent, and put the water into a teakettle; then returned back and cut it up, in order to get the eggs, in doing of which the helve of my hatchet broke. This was still an addition to my misfortunes; but I got out some of the eggs, carried them to my tent and fried them, then boiled me some tea in my own urine, which was very nauseous to me but revived me very much.

September the 1st I killed another turtle; but having broke my hatchet I crushed it to pieces and raking among the entrails broke the gall, which made the blood very bitter; but was forced to drink it or should instantly have died. My thoughts were bent upon another world, and the ardent desire to meet approaching death both cherished and tortured my departing soul. Drank a quart of salt water and expecting nothing but an immediate dissolution, I prostrate, begging to taste the bitter cup; till, oppressed and harassed out with care, obtained some interrupted slumbers. On the 3rd I awoke and, finding myself something better, employed my time in fitting a helve to my hatchet and eat some of the turtle which I had killed the night before.

From the 5th to the 8th I lived upon turtle blood and eggs, from the 8th to the 14th I lingered on with no other food to subsist me.

I am become a moving skeleton, my strength is entirely decayed, I cannot write much longer. I sincerely repent of the sins I committed and pray, henceforth, no man may ever merit the misery which I have undergone. For the sake of which, leaving this narrative behind me to deter mankind from following such diabolical inventions, I now resign my soul to him that gave it, hoping for mercy in . . .

Forty-five Seconds Inside a Tornado

by IRA J. BADEN
as told to ROBERT H. PARHAM

In May, 1953, a tornado struck the city of Waco, Texas, cutting a path of tremendous destruction. A close-up of this whirling demon, which could strip a man of all his clothes without harming him while exploding houses as though they were made of cards, is given in the accompanying eyewitness report. Usually such power is exercised in the countryside—earthquakes, falling meteors, great fires—and we are only remotely aware of them. But occasionally they encroach upon our city lives, at which time they become a common experience of the disaster which nature is always ready to bring to bear upon us.

WHAT IS IT LIKE TO VIEW A TORNADO FROM THE INSIDE OUT? What is it like to cling to a thin steel railing and watch nature's ultimate fury bear down on you with the roar of a hundred express trains, its blasting force leveling all in its path? What is it like to feel that you cannot survive this horror which engulfs you, and yet live to tell the tale?

All of this was my experience on Waco's dark Monday when, at 4:45 o'clock in the afternoon, a twister dipped from the sky into that 104-year-old city of 90,000 persons and in its wake left 114 dead, more than 500 injured, and two square miles of the business district a mass of twisted rubble—a $50,000,000 loss.

From the sidewalk where I clung desperately to my steel rail to avoid being sucked into the vortex, I saw the tornado's incredible forty-five-second thrust through the business heart of the city. I saw the fronts and the walls of buildings explode outward and roofs collapse into their own basements. I saw roofs pop up like corks from champagne bottles and burst apart, while their supporting walls remained intact. I saw automobiles—some unoccupied, others bearing passengers—crushed like bugs and buried out of sight under great mounds of brick, timber, steel and glass. I saw one car, an old model, leap upward and disappear into the air as if by magic.

I saw blocks of stone and timbers blown horizontally through the atmosphere at unbelievable speed, and razor-sharp chunks of steel and glass flew toward me as though shot from rifles—only to change their course at the instant before impact and leave me unharmed.

Others may have witnessed what I saw. But, so far as I know, nobody else who saw as much of the storm as I, lived to tell of it.

I am no weather expert. I don't know much about how a tornado is supposed to act. But, experts report, they twist counterclockwise, and their movement, both as to the direction they travel and their upward and downward motion, is highly erratic. Visually speaking, they are said to descend in the form of a dark, funnel-shaped cloud—some tilted, others vertical—and to taper from a relatively large top to a relatively narrow base.

I saw no such funnel—although doubtless there was one—and I heard no one else say that he saw it. This might be attributable to the fact that such a cloud could have been no darker than was the general cloud layer which gave it birth, thus the element of contrast was missing. Moreover, the storm moved in from a direction outside my line of vision.

I did not at first recognize the storm as a twister. The wind which preceded it seemed to blow in straight, and it was not until I saw and felt the curling action of the force which followed that I knew it to be tornadic.

Such storms in the Midwest and Southwest are not uncommon. They occur so frequently, in fact, that the United States Weather Bureau has a warning system to announce to threatened areas the existence of climatic conditions conducive to the spawning of twisters. Generally, tornadoes spend their destructive force on the open countryside or rip through the outskirts of small towns or cities. Never before had one struck at the business heart of a city the size of Waco, Texas, though tornadoes twice have ravaged the residential areas of St. Louis.

Waco, moreover, had been considered immune to the tornado scourge. From the time that Indians roamed over the Texas plains the legend grew that this spot, in a low valley sheathed by rolling hills, was one place where the "dancing devil" could not dance. Thus little heed was paid on that Monday, May 11, 1953, when the Weather Bureau warned of a tornado possibility.

At noon, Roy Miller, our company's mechanical engineer, and I stopped for lunch at Hillsboro. We were en route from Dallas to Waco to complete the job we had started ten days earlier. Our job with the Nichols Engineering Company is to install the operating mechanism for automatic doors. At Waco we were installing four sets of them on the old, twenty-one-story Amicable Life Building.

When we left Hillsboro the sky was heavily overcast. We had not listened to the automobile radio, so knew nothing of the tornado warnings being broadcast. The wind, out of the southwest, was against us and it was difficult to make time. We had promised to be in Waco at two o'clock in the afternoon and were running late.

As we neared Waco, I had the curious sensation of traveling in sudden bursts of speed. The speedometer would steady at seventy-five miles per hour for a mile or so; then suddenly spin upward. Once it hit ninety-five; another time 100.

I said to Roy, "We're hitting air pockets. This thing keeps trying to run away from us."

"Must be coming into a low-pressure area," Roy said.

"If those clouds start churning," I said, "let's turn around and get out of here."

"I'm with you," Roy replied—but we continued on into town.

We arrived at the Amicable Building at 2:15 P.M., forgot the weather and went to work.

Two of the heavy automatic doors for the Amicable installation had to be trimmed before they could be hung on their pivots. I worked on them in the basement until about four o'clock. It was time for the building employees to change shifts. The locker rooms were in the basement, and several passing workers stood around and watched me operate the power saw. Louis Overton, the building manager, came down. He called for the attention of the men.

"There's a storm warning out," he said, "and it looks like it might hit here. I want you to go upstairs to all washrooms and all offices where no one is working and close the windows. Two of you go to the roof and close the vents and the elevator power room."

"Sounds like you're expecting something, Mr. Overton," I remarked.

"Yeah," he said, "it doesn't look good."

Ten minutes later I went upstairs. It was raining lightly. I went to the doorway and started marking out on the tile floor the position for the door pivots. Roy Miller and Mr. Overton walked out the door to go across the street.

"Don't get wet," I called to them.

At 4:35 I finished laying out the pivot positions. I went next door to the drugstore, in the same building, and ordered a cup of coffee. Outside, it was dead calm and growing dark. The air was uncomfortably warm, damp and sticky. With my cup in my hand, I walked out the door for a look at the sky. It was like looking into nightfall, and I held my watch to my ear to make sure it was running. Despite the stillness at ground level, the clouds moved fast across the gloomy sky.

Roy and Mr. Overton hurried back across the street, glancing upward.

"Looks bad," Roy said, as he joined me at the drugstore entrance. Mr. Overton went into the Amicable lobby. I went back to the drugstore, left the coffee cup on a counter, then returned to the doorway. Now the wind began to blow in gusts. My ears popped from pressure, and I felt lightheaded.

The automatic doors are not supposed to yield to wind. But Roy and I noticed that one of the doors was slightly ajar—pushed outward. Roy said, "We've got to put stronger springs on these, Ira."

My reaction was different. I recalled that in situations of intensely low pressure the windows and doors of buildings usually burst outward, the greater pressure on the inside thrusting out to fill the vacuum created by the lower pressure of the outside air. We opened and braced the doors to equalize the pressure.

Again I walked outside. The wind was even stronger; I grew conscious of an ominous roar. It was raining again, but horizontally—the huge raindrops, driven by the wind, seemed not to hit the street.

The distant roar became almost deafening, and above it I suddenly heard the sound of shattering glass. I was at the outward end of the guide rail—the steel rail anchored into the sidewalk to divide traffic coming in and going out of the automatic doors. I locked my arm around the rail, crouched and turned to look up the street. At that instant a steel mailbox flew by within inches of my head. A jeep parked in front jerked forward several feet and jammed against the curb.

It's hard to judge the speed of wind. But I felt sure that by now it reached upwards of 100 miles per hour, and it seemed to move straight down Austin Street from northwest to southeast. The Amicable Building is at the corner of Austin and 5th streets. Directly across stood the six-story Dennis Furniture Company Building, with five stories above ground and one below, and back of it on 5th street was the four-story Tom Padgitt Building. At the other end of the block from the Dennis Building, and on the same side of Austin, was the Roosevelt Hotel. Between these two larger structures lay a series of one- and two-story buildings—the Joy Theater, Chris's Café, a tailor shop, a men's store, a cafeteria, a jewelry store and another clothing store.

All of a sudden the flying debris and the wind-driven rain tripled or quadrupled their speed, blasting like rockets. I was conscious of trying to move back into the building, but I could not. The enormous pressure, plus the hypnotic terror of witnessing this unbelievable scene, kept me glued to the rail.

Bricks, individually and in cemented clusters, were ripping past. Plate glass in large pieces and small whizzed by with the peculiar whine that only flying glass or a ricocheting bullet can make. The air burst from my lungs and I could not seem to refill them. How my spectacles remained bridged to my nose I cannot guess. But they protected my eyes from the screaming wind and permitted me to see.

Up Austin Street, some three blocks northward, a force more powerful than anything I had yet seen suddenly ripped the buildings clean of their façades. One structure exploded and collapsed. In a second's time its debris had rocketed in a swift curving sweep into the fronts of the buildings across the street from me.

Time could be measured only in instants and fractions thereof. Everything seemed to happen at once. In the flash of a camera bulb the front of the Joy Theater, directly opposite me, erupted into the street and its arched roof pancaked downward atop the seats. Simultaneously, plate glass in all the store fronts along that side of the block blasted outward, as though clawed out by some giant mailed hand. Meanwhile high-voltage electric wires, whipped from their moorings, writhed like the hair of an injured Medusa the length of Austin Street. Torn by glass and flying steel, the wires lay bare in a hundred places. Each sharp lash against the wet pavement brought a pistol crack and a shower of sparks which lighted the scene in a brilliant fireworks display.

The tornado's business end appeared to describe the action of a great, single-tipped auger, slightly tilted, the whirling tip gashing one spot and missing another as it moved along. It seemed to miss entirely the Roosevelt Hotel, but reached beyond to flatten the smaller Joy Theater. On the next turn it reached backward to rip off the second floor of the two-story building lying immediately adjacent to the hotel. Then it dumped its burden of debris atop the lower-lying buildings to the south. These smaller buildings, which included Chris's Café, caved in, their fronts spouting outward into the street.

In another split instant the storm's tip caught the Dennis Building. This old edifice was not of modern steel-and-stone construction. It was capable of carrying a heavy weight load—but not of withstanding a violent, twisting wind.

The Dennis Building became the focal point of the storm's tragedy. The wind struck, and in less time than it would take to snap your fingers, the structure wrenched off at the second floor. The top four floors whirled upward, exploded and, as though snatched downward by some magnetic force, crashed at an angle back upon their own base.

A great part of the debris cascaded atop the adjoining Joy Theater and onto the roof of the Torrance Recreation Hall, toward the rear. Other tons of wood, brick and mortar poured down into 5th Street alongside the building. The Tom Padgitt Building to the rear must have collapsed at the same time. I did not see it go. But when I looked, it no longer was there.

Only now did I realize for certain that the storm was a tornado. The fact that flying debris had seemed to bear straight at me, but curved away before reaching me; the fact that every wind-borne object had seemed to rip in a swirling motion into the buildings across the street—neither fact had impressed itself on me as being indicative of a twister. Nor had I realized that for at least a part of the time I had been within the cone of that twister. Not until I saw the motion of the tall building across the street—wrenching, rising and tearing apart—did I realize the true nature of the storm.

After demolishing the Dennis Building, the storm seemed to change its course. It zoomed over the small tavern across 5th Street, then dipped again onto Franklin Street. Now it hopscotched its way across the city toward the southwest. I saw no more of its fury, but next day learned more of its destructive force. As it moved away, the great moaning roar dwindled with the same rapidity with which it had intensified to its climax. My ears continued to pop. There was sharp pain again as the pressure returned toward normal.

I eased my grip on the guide rail and looked around. The plate glass was gone from the drugstore show window to my right, and small fragments of it surrounded my feet. The window contained a jewelry display. I called to the store's porter, who stood in the doorway and whose name was Alphonse, "Better collect these things and put them away." He found a box, while I pushed the wrist watches, rings and costume jewelry into a small pile in one corner of the window. They would have proved tempting to anyone with looting instincts.

The blowing rain continued. It had been impossible to gauge the heaviness of the downpour during the seconds of the storm because of the flying debris with which it mixed. The water ran curb to curb. And there had been hail. You could see it now, great ice balls glistening among the rubble in the streets. The rubble piles, many covering crushed automobiles, stood out like small volcanic islands rising above the sea.

By now all the able-bodied who had had the good fortune to find refuge in buildings like the Amicable and the Roosevelt Hotel poured out into the streets to begin rescue efforts. Roy Miller, who had been somewhere behind me in the drugstore entrance, came to my side. He must have been as confused as I—and as was the girl counter waitress. He wore a new gray hat and a dark blue sports jacket. He removed the jacket and handed it to the girl. He took off the hat and jammed it on my head—down over my ears, his head being larger. "Here, look after these," he said, and he started across the street to begin digging at the rubble.

I placed the hat inside on a counter, then went to join Roy. The girl took the jacket to the rear of the store, neatly folded it, and crammed it into the refrigerator. The jacket was not discovered until some hours later, when, during a respite, Roy returned to the drugstore and ordered a ham sandwich.

As the storm approached, we had seen several people scurry into Chris's Café for refuge. It was that time of day, too, when many employees of businesses along the block gathered at the restaurant for coffee. From our position during the storm it looked as though, except for the Dennis Building, Chris's was the spot hit hardest. So that was where our rescue efforts began.

The café's roof was smashed in, but tilted crazily upward. Ton upon ton of debris was piled on top. The rubble had not quite settled when we reached it, and it made our work precarious. The odor of gas escaping from broken mains was strong and growing stronger. We called warnings to one another not to smoke.

We heard a woman's moan from beneath the rubble, and the call of a man for help. We dug frantically toward the sounds. Within minutes we brought out the man, scratched and bruised, but otherwise uninjured.

Extricating the woman proved more difficult. By now a fire-department crew had arrived to direct rescue efforts. The firemen organized a chain system, passing chunks of debris from hand to hand into the street.

Within a short time they brought out the woman, still alive, but badly injured.

No further signs of life came from Chris's, but here and there in the rubble could be seen the arms and legs of victims protruding from crushed and lifeless bodies. Roy Miller and some others located the bodies of Vic and Angelo Sermas, two of the three brothers who owned the café.

It seemed senseless at this early hour to expend our efforts in the removal of the dead while others might still be brought out alive. Roy and I left the tomb that was Chris's to search elsewhere for signs of the trapped, but still living. The Joy Theater was our next stop. The marquee, which advertised a double feature including, ironically, a picture called *The Lucky Texan*, was intact, but supporting tons of debris. Most of those persons who had been inside were, indeed, lucky Texans, because the arched roof of the structure protected them from being crushed.

By now hundreds were engaged in the rescue work. Police threw up a rope barricade around the worst-devastated area to keep back sight-seers and expedite the work. Shortly after five o'clock it was estimated that more than 10,000 persons surged around the roped-off section seeking a better view. Police had a busy time restraining the crowd and comforting those among them who feared for the lives of relatives. Screams of anguish mingled with audible prayers around the waiting circle.

I climbed atop the theater's debris and through a small opening along-side the Dennis Building. I could hear voices calling for help from what seemed like the rear end of the latter place. From a pile of rubbish at the edge of the narrow passageway, the twisted, shoeless feet of a man protruded grotesquely. I felt the ankle and found no pulse.

The passage was blocked beyond. So I returned to the street, went around the corner and found a littered path to the rear. I told others of the voices I'd heard, and several joined me. We listened, heard a voice and began to dig. We took out two men alive, both badly injured. As we dug for these two injured, a heavily built, overalled man of about forty-five emerged from the wreckage of the Torrance Recreation Hall, which opened onto the alley. He had clawed his own way out of entombment. I stopped to ask him about others who might have been trapped with him.

"It's a miracle—a miracle," he stammered incoherently. "Everybody dead in there but me—a miracle."

We learned later that others were rescued alive from the pool hall.

But it did yield a great toll of dead. Most of the victims were teen-age boys who had come after school to while away a rainy afternoon shooting pool.

From the direction of Franklin Street came calls for help. There I found several persons digging at a mountainous pile of brick and mortar in the street. Underneath was an automobile, crushed to the level of its wheels. Someone said there were two persons inside. We dug straight down through the center until we reached the top of the car. A man appeared with a cutting torch, which he used to remove the car top. First taken out was a man, horribly crushed. I did not wait to see the other body.

By the time I got back to Austin Street, the military had taken over. The effect was the same as martial law, although martial law was not actually declared. A sound truck was stationed in front of the Amicable Building, and headquarters were established in the building's First National Bank offices. Instructions from the sound truck rose above the clatter of the equipment used by the digging crews.

"We have the Army in here now," the loud-speakers announced. "We have plenty of help. Will all civilians not needed in the area please go home. We want to save as many lives as we can. Too many people create a hazard. Please go home."

It was now approximately 5:30, only forty-five minutes since the storm had struck. The military held the area under tight control, and rapidly restored a semblance of order. The rescue crews of Army and Air Force men dug at the debris expertly. MP's and National Guardsmen patrolled against possible looting and to keep the streets clear of non-workers.

By dark, scores of trucks of all descriptions—bulldozers, cranes and other huge pieces of earth-moving equipment—were clawing away at the rubble, loading and hauling it to the city dump. Relief items, ranging from bandages and blankets to money and blood, began to pour in from across the nation. Stricken Waco had begun to feel the gentle hand of neighborliness.

Thus far, I have only told about the storm's slash across the face of the city, and a little about the rescue efforts which followed. The brief forty-five seconds of the tornado's onslaught were so full of sound and fury that to try to tell it all in sequence would be impossible.

At the time the plate-glass windows of the bank in the Amicable Building exploded on my right and the glass in the drugstore show window blasted outward past me, I was in perhaps my own greatest danger. But so hypnotized was I by the storm's force that I took no notice. Nor did I feel a personal danger when the violent wind clutched at me, swept away my feet and almost dislodged me from my rail.

Most of my fear, strangely, was for others. At the instant of the storm's peak a man ran from the Amicable lobby and started across the street. Roy Miller and I both called to him to come back. He shouted that his wife was in the Dennis Building and he had to go to her. As he stepped from the curb the wind engulfed him. He simply disappeared.

In the same instant the wind ripped off the roof and the second-floor front and side walls of the building adjacent to the Roosevelt Hotel. The scene was much like a cross-section drawing. Here was an office, the desk, chairs and filing cases in place. A man stood near the desk with his hat on, an incredulous look on his face. He walked to the edge of the open floor and peered over the side. Then he turned and ran to the back wall, opened the door into what a moment before had been a hallway, and stepped out into space. I did not see him again.

When the high-voltage wires snapped and started their fiery dance on the pavement of Austin Street, a man in a new black sedan pulled up in the center of the street abreast of the Amicable Building. He stopped his car and set his brakes against the twister. The car hopped and sidled a few paces forward, then came to an abrupt stop as one of the crackling wires whipped across the hood and held taut against the radiator grille. As the wind's peak passed, the man jumped from the car door and headed for the radiator.

Roy Miller and I both screamed, "Don't touch that wire! It's hot!"

He picked it up before he heard us and tried to pull it loose from the bumper guard. "What's that?" he called back, turning to look as he tugged at the wire.

"Forget it!" shouted Roy.

The man could not budge the tightened wire. So he got back into his car and backed a foot or two. Then he got out again, pulled the wire loose, laid it gently on the street, got back in and pulled away. As the rear wheel of the car passed over the wire there was a report like a pistol shot, and it burned in two in a volcano of sparks.

How many automobiles were destroyed in the twister only a final count by the insurance companies can say. At least half a dozen rolled down Austin Street, not on their wheels but sideways—top, side, wheels, side, top—as an oblong stone might roll downstream in a swift-moving current. Several were stopped in their rolling motion by the downpour of debris from shattered buildings, which crushed them the way your foot might squash a beetle.

Oddly enough, every car parked along the east side of Austin Street was either demolished or badly damaged, while a few parked along the west, or my side, suffered no more than scratches. Roy Miller's car was picked up from the curb and deposited in the center of the street. A split second later tons of rubble filled the spot next the curb where the car had been—the car thus escaped damage.

It was strange about the rolling cars. Once stopped, they gathered flying debris the way the camel thorn of the Sahara gathers grains of blowing sand, piling it higher until a dune is formed. So grew the brick dunes in Austin Street. Many persons were entombed in the buried cars. Some lived; others were crushed to death.

Freakish incidents are recorded in the annals of all tornadoes. Tales abound of wheat straws being blown through heavy oak posts; of heavy objects being picked up from one spot and deposited in another, miles away and undamaged. In the Waco blow a light car of uncertain vintage was parked across the street. The wind picked it up, bounced it once on its tires, then sucked it out of sight. I heard later that such a car had been blown completely through a closed freight car sitting on a siding near the railway freight terminal.

Immediately following the storm, many dazed individuals wandered about aimlessly. Some had been stripped of strategic articles of clothing. One man, uninjured, had had every shred torn from his body except his shoes and socks. He walked along the street, apparently unaware of his nudity, until he encountered a reporter. The newsman inquired his name and asked if he could be of help.

"Help?" he said, emerging from his trance as he looked downward. "My God, yes! Get me a barrel—quick! And forget you asked my name!"

On Austin Street between 3rd and 4th I encountered a pretty red-haired woman. Her skirt was gone and she was bare of foot, but she wore a fine fur stole and a perky hat—one she might have bought for Easter. I asked if I could help her.

She stared at me blankly and sobbed, "Where did it go? Where can I find it?"

"What did you lose?" I asked, surmising it must have been the articles of missing clothing—or perhaps her purse, since she carried none. She repeated her questions.

"They probably went that way, lady," I said, pointing in the direction the twister had traveled.

"Thank you," she said, and plodded away into the glass-strewn rubble.

How she managed it barefooted, I don't know. I had trouble navigating with my shoes on.

By seven o'clock I was dead tired and soaked with rain and perspiration. I walked to the Roosevelt, hoping to get a room for a brief rest. Instead of taking guests, however, the hotel was busy evacuating them. There were no lights, and the threat of explosion from escaping gas had increased throughout the demolished area. Another warning of the possibility of a second tornado had been issued. Fearful persons jammed the lobby in silent wait for the next blow.

The Roosevelt switchboard had one telephone circuit in operation. The operator called the Raleigh Hotel up the street and reserved rooms for Roy Miller and me, although I did not know Roy's whereabouts at the time. Next time I saw him he said he had driven to Hillsboro, about thirty-five miles away, to telephone his wife and reassure her of his safety. He was fuming.

"I drive seventy miles to call my wife," he said; "I says, 'Honey, I'm all right. I'm safe. You don't need to worry any longer.' And what do I get? She says, 'Who's worried? You always have been all right. Why do you have to call me long distance to tell me so? Roy Miller,' she says, 'what have you been up to?' " Mrs. Miller had not heard of the storm.

I learned later that Roy's wife had called my wife to relay the glad tidings. When told that I was all right, Mrs. Baden said, simply, "I'm glad somebody thinks so." I don't know whether I should credit that to her not having heard of the tornado or to a somewhat more obvious fact: sometimes wives can be difficult.

Roy and I worked until well after midnight. We supplied tools, such as hacksaws, where needed, to the laboring rescue crews. During a part of the time I relieved Mr. Overton on guard duty at the Amicable Building. He admonished me to let no one enter, explaining that many of the upstairs offices were wide open to looting.

In the next half hour I turned away a hundred or more persons each seeking entry to find a usable telephone. None, I feel certain, was a potential looter. Most were simply thoughtful individuals wanting to telephone anxious relatives and let them know they were safe. There was little evidence of looting. One man, a small fellow, passed along the street wearing a new topcoat many sizes too large. I noticed the price tag still attached. These may have been looters, but it is more charitable to think that they were among those stripped of clothing by the storm.

Another man, I heard later, showed up at the city dump to salvage a few pieces of furniture. He was arrested, lectured sternly by the police and released.

When the rescue workers changed shifts, Roy and I went to the Raleigh and to bed. I didn't get much sleep. The horror of the past hours kept revolving through my mind. Roy called me at 6:00 A.M. We went back to the Amicable Building. Mr. Overton was still there, red-eyed and weary. "I think we'll just leave those doors off for a while," he said. "Why don't you two go on back to Dallas and get some rest?" We agreed that would be smart.

We went out for a daylight look at the damage that had been done. It was indescribable. The sweating rescue crews toiled monotonously at their forbidding task. Here and there, lifeless victims were brought out and hauled to the morgue. But hope still survived. At 6:45 we witnessed the most dramatic rescue of the tornado's aftermath. Miss Lillie Matkin, telephone operator for the Dennis Furniture Company, was hoisted, still alive, from deep within the rubble of the company's building. Hers, undoubtedly, was one of the voices I had heard at 5:30 the previous afternoon, when I entered that passageway alongside the Joy Theater. The rescue teams began at that time to dig for her—I, for a while, among them—and had toiled in shifts throughout the night until their efforts were rewarded. Miss Matkin suffered only shock from her fourteen-hour ordeal.

At ten o'clock we left Waco to return to our jobs in Dallas. As we drove out of town the rains came again. This time it was the seven-inch downpour that followed up the storm. We felt for Waco's rescue workers, and for those among the ruins who still might be alive.

Descent Into Perpetual Night

by WILLIAM BEEBE

*The great American naturalist, William Beebe, has been con-
nected for many years with the New York Zoological Society. In August,
1934, together with Otis Barton, he made the then world's deepest dive,
of half a mile, in the Bathysphere off Bermuda. Although this dive has
been surpassed by thousands of feet by Professor Piccard and others, it
is unlikely that Beebe's account of his adventure will be outdone by any
other diver. Beebe was fortunate in being able to see in the depths. Reports from Professor Piccard indicate that there is almost nothing to be
distinguished in the great depths, the blackness being extremely intense.*

A T 9:41 IN THE MORNING* WE SPLASHED BENEATH THE
surface, and often as I have experienced it, the sudden shift
from a golden yellow world to a green one was unexpected. After the
foam and bubbles passed from the glass, we were bathed in green; our
faces, the tanks, the trays, even the blackened walls were tinged. Yet
seen from the deck, we apparently descended into sheer, deep ultra-
marine. The only hint of this change of color vouchsafed those above
was the increasing turquoise of the bathysphere as it approached the
vanishing point, about 100 feet.

We were dropped several fathoms and dangled there awhile, until all
the apparatus on deck was readapted to the vertical cable close to the
ship's side. I made the most of my last glimpse of the upper world. By
peering up I could see the watery ceiling crinkling, and slowly lifting
and settling, while here and there, pinned to this ceiling, were tufts of
sargassum weed. I could see small dots moving just below the weed,

* April 11th.

and for the first time I tried, and successfully, to focus low power binoculars through the water. I had no trouble in recognizing a small ocean turbot and a flyingfish, trailing its half-spread wings as it swam. The bathysphere then revolved slightly and the hull of the *Ready* came into view. It was even more like a coral reef than it had appeared four years ago, great streamers of plant and animal life floating out from it. There is something wholly unreal and at the same time rather amusing about an upward view of the slow-rolling bottom of an unanchored boat, whose deck, a few minutes before, had seemed so solid and staunch.

The sun was blazing over the ocean, the surface was unusually quiet; conditions were perfect for whatever the eyes could carry to the brain. A question came over the phone, an answer went, and down we slipped through the water. As I have said, the first plunge erases, to the eye, all the comforting, warm rays of the spectrum. The red and the orange are as if they had never been, and soon the yellow is swallowed up in the green. We cherish all these on the surface of the earth and when they are winnowed out at 100 feet or more, although they are only one-sixth of the visible spectrum, yet, in our mind, all the rest belongs to chill and night and death. Even modern war bears this out; no more are red blood and scarlet flames its symbols, but the terrible grayness of gas, the ghastly blue of Very lights.

The green faded imperceptibly as we went down, and at 200 feet it was impossible to say whether the water was greenish-blue or bluish-green. At this depth I made my eyes focus in mid-water and saw small creatures clearly, copepods and others of the innumerable swarms which haunt the upper layers.

At 320 feet a lovely colony of siphonophores drifted past. At this level they appeared like spun glass. Others which I saw at far greater and blacker depths were illumined, but whether by their own or by reflected light I cannot say. These are colonial creatures like submerged Portuguese men-o'-war, and similar to those beautiful beings, and are composed of a colony of individuals, which perform separate functions, such as flotation, swimming, stinging, feeding, and breeding, all joined by the common bond of a food canal. Here in their own haunts they swept slowly along like an inverted spray of lilies-of-the-valley, alive and in constant motion. In our nets we find only the half-broken swimming bells, like cracked, crystal chalices, with all the wonderful loops and tendrils and animal flowers completely lost or contracted into a mass of tangled threads. Twenty feet lower a pilot fish looked in upon me— the companion of sharks and turtles, which we usually think of as a surface fish, but with only our pitiful, two-dimensional, human observation for proof.

When scores of bathyspheres are in use we shall know much more about the vertical distribution of fish than we do now. For example, my next visitors were good-sized yellow-tails and two blue-banded jacks which examined me closely at 400 and 490 feet respectively. Here were so-called surface fish happy at 80 fathoms. Several silvery squid balanced for a moment, then shot past, and at 500 feet a pair of lanternfish with no lights showing looked at the bathysphere unafraid.

At 600 feet the color appeared to be a dark, luminous blue, and this contradiction of terms shows the difficulty of description. As in former dives, it seemed bright, but was so lacking in actual power that it was useless for reading and writing.

There are certain nodes of emotion in a descent such as this, the first of which is the initial flash. This came at 670 feet, and it seemed to close a door upon the upper world. Green, the world-wide color of plants, had long since disappeared from our new cosmos, just as the last plants of the sea themselves had been left behind far overhead.

At 700 feet the light beam from our bulb was still rather dim; the sun had not given up and was doing his best to assert his power. At 800 feet we passed through a swarm of small beings, copepods, sagitta or arrow worms and every now and then a worm which was not a worm but a fish, one of the innumerable round-mouths or *Cyclothones*. Eighty feet farther and a school of about 30 lantern fish passed, wheeled and returned; I could guess *Myctophum laternatum*, but I cannot be certain. The beam of light drove them away.

At 1000 feet we took stock of our surroundings. The stuffing box and the door were dry, the noise of the blower did not interfere with the telephone conversation, the humidity was so well taken care of that I did not need a handkerchief over nose and mouth when talking close to the glass. The steel was becoming very cold. I tried to name the water; blackish-blue, dark gray-blue. It is strange that as the blue goes, it is not replaced by violet—the end of the visible spectrum. That has apparently already been absorbed. The last hint of blue tapers into a nameless gray, and this finally into black, but from the present level down, the eye falters, and the mind refuses any articulate color distinction. The sun is defeated and color has gone forever, until a human at last penetrates and flashes a yellow electric ray into what has been jet black for two billion years.

I kept the light on for a while and at 1050 feet through a school of little flying snails there suddenly passed a "large dark body, over four feet long" (so I telephoned it). I shut off the light, but looked into empty gray space without a trace of lumination—the fish had dissolved. Later, with the light on again, ten feet lower, a pilotfish appeared, showing how easily his kind can adapt itself to a shift of more than 30 atmospheres and from 15 pounds an inch at the surface to 480 at this level.

Lights now brightened and increased, and at 1100 feet I saw more fish and other organisms than my prebathysphere experience had led me to hope to see on the entire dive. With the light on, several chunky little hatchet-fish approached and passed through; then a silver-eyed larval fish two inches long; a jelly; suddenly a vision to which I can give no name, although I saw others subsequently. It was a network of luminosity, delicate, with large meshes, all aglow and in motion, waving slowly as it drifted. Next a dim, very deeply built fish appeared and vanished; then a four-inch larval eel swimming obliquely upward; and so on. This ceaseless telephoning left me breathless and I was glad of a hundred feet of only blue-blackness and active sparks.

At 1200 feet an explosion occurred, not at the window but a few feet away, so baffling that I decided to watch intently for repetitions. The large fish came again, and a loose, open school of pteropods and small shrimps bobbed about. The snails were shield-shaped as I well knew from having handled thousands in the deep-sea nets. Their empty shells form most of the sea bottom hereabouts.

Suddenly in the distance a strong glow shot forth, covering a space of perhaps eight inches. Not even the wildest guess would help with such an occurrence. Then the law of compensation sent, close to the window, a clean-cut, three-inch, black anglerfish with a pale, lemon-colored light on a slender tentacle. All else my eye missed, so I can never give it a name.

One great source of trouble in this bathysphere work is the lag of mind behind instantaneous observation. For example, at 1300 feet a medium-sized, wide-mouthed angler came in sight, then vanished, and I was automatically describing an eight-inch larval eel looking like a transparent willow leaf, when my mind shot back to the angler and demanded how I had seen it. I had recorded no individual lights on body or tentacle, and now I realized that the teeth had glowed dully, the two rows of fangs were luminous. It is most baffling to gaze into outer darkness, suddenly see a vision, record the bare facts—the generality of the thing itself—and then, in the face of complete distraction by another spark or organism, to have to hark back and recall what special characters escaped the mind but were momentarily etched upon the retina. On this point I had thoroughly coached Miss Hollister at the other end of the telephone, so I constantly received a fire of questions, which served to focus my attention and flick my memory. Again and again when such a question came, I willfully shut my eyes or turned them into the bathysphere to avoid whatever bewilderment might come while I was searching my memory for details of what had barely faded from my eye. At a few stops on the descent, as I have said, I permitted myself a minute or two of emotional debauch, of reciting to myself the where and the what of locality, surroundings, time of day, pressure, temperature, and so on. But all the rest of the time I allowed myself no rest from direct observation and reporting. The unproductive Oh's! and Ah's! of my first few dives were all too vivid in my mind.

Just above 1400 feet two black eels, about eighteen inches in length, went through the beam—distinctly *Serrivomer*. At 1400 feet my recent studies came to mind, and told me that I saw a male golden-tailed seadragon with a big cheek light (*Idiacanthus*), but before it vanished I saw it was black, and considerably larger even than the giant female of the species. So it was wholly unknown.

At 1500 I swung for two and a half minutes, and here occurred the second memorable moment in these dives—opportunity for the deliberate, accurate record of a fish wholly new to science, seen by one or both of us, the proof of whose existence, other than our word, must await the luck of capture in nets far more effective than those we now use in our oceanographic work. First, a quartet of slender, elongate fish passed through the electric light literally like arrows, about twenty inches long, whether eels or not I shall never know; then a jelly, so close that it almost brushed the glass. Finally, without my seeing how it got there, a large fish swung suspended, half in, half out of the beam. It was poised with only a slow waving of fins. I saw it was something wholly unknown, and I did two things at once; I reached behind for Mr. Barton, to drag him away from his camera preparations to the windows, to see and corroborate, and I disregarded Miss Hollister's insistent questions in my ears. I had to grunt or say something in reply to her, for I had already exceeded the five seconds which was our danger duration of silence throughout all the dives. But all this time I sat absorbing the fish from head to tail through the wordless, short-circuiting of sight, later to be materialized into spoken and written words, and finally into a painting dictated by what I had seen through the clear quartz.

The strange fish was at least two feet in length, wholly without lights or luminosity, with a small eye and good-sized mouth. Later, when it shifted a little backwards I saw a long, rather wide, but evidently filamentous pectoral fin. The two most unusual things were first, the color, which, in the light, was an unpleasant pale, olive drab, the hue of water-soaked flesh, an unhealthy buff. It was a color worthy of these black depths, like the sickly sprouts of plants in a cellar. Another strange thing was its almost tailless condition, the caudal fin being reduced to a tiny knob or button, while the vertical fins, taking its place, rose high above and stretched far beneath the body, these fins also being colorless. I missed its pelvic fins and its teeth, if it had any, while such things as nostrils and rays counts were, of course, out of the question.

There is a small family of deep-sea fish known as *Cetomimidæ*, and somewhere in or close to this the strange apparition belongs. Only three species are known, and only twenty-four individuals have so far been captured, sixteen of which have been in our own deep nets drawn through these very waters. I have called the fish we saw the Pallid Sailfin, and am naming it *Bathyembryx istiophasma*, which is a Grecian way of saying that it comes from deep in the abyss and swims with ghostly sails.

Although I had already seen many deep-sea forms on this dive, yet here was one larger than any we had ever taken in nets. The Sailfin was alive, quiet, watching our strange machine, apparently oblivious that the hinder half of its body was bathed in a strange luminosity. Preëminently, however, it typified the justification of the money, time, trouble, and worry devoted to bringing the bathysphere to its present efficiency. Amid nameless sparks, unexplained luminous explosions, abortive glimpses of strange organisms, there came, now and then, adequate opportunity to add a definite new fish or other creature to our knowledge of the life of the deep sea. At the possible risk of cumbering taxonomy with a *nomen nudum,* I have chosen to give definite names to a very few of these clearly seen fish, the physical type of which must, for a time, be represented by a drawing, made under my direction, with only the characters of which I am certain. With no visible increase of fin vibration, my Pallid Sailfin moved into outer darkness, and when I had finished telephoning the last details I ordered a further descent. This entire volume would not contain the detailed recital of even a fraction of all the impressive sights and forms I saw, and nothing at these depths can be spoken of without superlatives.

At 1630 feet a light grew to twice its diameter before our eyes, until it was fully the diameter of a penny, appearing to emanate from some creature which bore irregular patches of dull luminosity on its body. The outline was too indistinct to tell whether it was with or without a backbone.

At 1900 feet, to my surprise, there was still the faintest hint of dead gray light, 200 feet deeper than usual, attesting the almost complete calm of the surface and the extreme brilliancy of the day far overhead. At 2000 feet the world was forever black. And this I count as the third great moment of descent, when the sun, source of all light and heat on the earth, has been left behind. It is only a psychological mile-post, but it is a very real one. We had no realization of the outside pressure but the blackness itself seemed to close in on us.

At 2000 feet I made careful count and found that there were never less than ten or more lights—pale yellow and pale bluish—in sight at any one time. Fifty feet below I saw another pyrotechnic network, this time, at a conservative estimate, covering an extent of two by three feet. I could trace mesh after mesh in the darkness, but could not even hazard a guess at the cause. It must be some invertebrate form of life, but so delicate and evanescent that its abyssal form is quite lost if ever we take it in our nets. Another hundred feet and Mr. Barton saw two lights blinking on and off, obviously under control of the fish.

At this level and again on the way up, I saw at the very end of our beam some large form swimming. On earlier dives I had observed this and had hesitated even to mention it, for it savored too much of imagination backed by imperfect observation. But here it was again. The surface did not seem black, and what outline came momentarily to view was wholly problematic. But that it was some very large creature or creatures of which we had glimpses five separate times on dives separated by years, we are certain. Whether fish or squid or other organism we cannot say.

At 2300 some exclamation of mine was interrupted by a request from above to listen to the tug's whistles saluting our new record, and my response was, "Thanks ever so much, but take this: two very large leptocephali have just passed through the light, close together, vibrating swiftly along; note—why should larval eels go in pairs?" And with this the inhabitants of our dimly remembered upper world gave up their kindly efforts to honor us. On down we went through a rich, light-filled 2400, and to rest at 2500 feet, for a long half hour.

A pair of large, coppery-sided scimitar-mouths (*Gonostoma*

elongatum) swam past; *Sternoptyx,* the skeletonfish, appeared in a group of four; a fish as flat as a moonfish entered the beam, and banking steeply, fled in haste. One flying snail, from among the countless billions of his fellows, flapped back and forth across my glass. Three times, at different levels, creatures had struck against the glass and, utterly meaningless as it sounds, exploded there, so abruptly that we instinctively jerked back our heads.

We tried out the full power of the 1500-watt light, heating the bathysphere and window considerably, but not too dangerosuly. At 11:17 o'clock I turned the light on suddenly, and saw a strange quartet of fish to which I have not been able to fit genus or family. Shape, size, color, and one fin I saw clearly, but Abyssal Rainbow Gars is as far as I dare go, and they may be anything but gars. About four inches over all, they were slender and stiff with long, sharply pointed jaws. They were balanced in the center of the electric ray when it was first turned on, and the unheard-of glare affected them not at all. There they stood, for they were almost upright, and I could see only a slight fanning with a dorsal fin. Keeping equal distances apart, and maintaining their upright pose, they swam slowly into the uttermost dark. The amazing thing about them was their unexpected pattern and color. The jaws and head were brilliant scarlet, which, back of the gills, changed abruptly into a light but strong blue and this merged insensibly into clear yellow on the posterior body and tail. Unless in the light of some other fish, or in my electric path, their colors could never have been visible, and were assuredly useless by-products.

I alternated with Mr. Barton's camera at the window and there were hardly any seconds without lights or definite organisms coming into view. In one period of this duration, chosen at random, I counted 46 lights, ten of which were of unusual size, most of them pale yellow, but a few bluish. The sight I enjoyed most was a momentary glimpse of what I am certain was the same, or another, Pallid Sailfin. In all this vast extent in three dimensions, of black water, the chance of confirming at a wholly different depth a new observation made my satisfaction complete.

The change in the electric beam itself from 1000 feet downward was interesting. At the upper layers it was weak but decidedly yellow, with a turquoise cap at the farther end of the oblique luminous shaft. As we descended, the yellow changed to a luminous gray, and the turquoise crept down, until, at this extreme depth, it reached to the very window. Along each side of the sharply marked beam extended a broad border of rich, velvety, dark blue, and abruptly outside of this came the black pit itself. At two well-separated depths, I focused very carefully on the rain of small creatures passing and repassing through the farthest extreme end of the light. In both cases the focus was the same and I brought the glass to the surface without changing it. On deck, walking back from the bow until it was in perfect focus with the glass, I found that the visible end of the beam of electric light was 45 feet distant from the bathysphere window, five feet farther than I had been estimating.

The several nodes of high lights of which I have written occur on every descent, but there is in addition a compounding of sensations. At first we are quick to see every light, facile in sending up notes, but when we have used up most of our adjectives it is difficult to ring changes on sparks, lights, and darkness. More and more complete severance with the upper world follows, and a plunging into new strangenesses, unpredictable sights continually opening up, until our vocabularies are pauperized, and our minds drugged.

Over two hours had passed since we left the deck and I knew that the nerves both of my staff and myself were getting ragged with constant tenseness and strain. My eyes were weary with the flashing of eternal lights, each of which had to be watched so carefully, and my mind was surfeited with visions of the continual succession of fish and other organisms, and alternately encouraged and depressed by the successful or abortive attempts at identification. So I asked for our ascent.

One minute later, at 2470 feet, all my temporarily relaxed attention was aroused and focused on another splendid piece of luck. A tie rope had to be cut and in this brief interval of suspension, extended by my hurried order, a new anglerfish came out of all the ocean and hesitated long enough close to my window for me to make out its dominant characters. I am calling it the Three-starred Anglerfish, *Bathyceratias trilynchnus.* It was close in many respects to the well-known genera *Ceratias* and *Cryptosparas,* but the flattened angle of the mouth and the short, even teeth were quite different. It was six inches long, typically oval in outline, black, and with small eye. The fin rays were usual except that it had three tall tentacles or illicia, each tipped with a strong, pale yellow light organ. The light was clearly reflected on the upper side of the fish. In front of the dorsal fin were two pear-shaped organs exactly like those of the common *Cryptosparas.* The paired fins escaped me. No pioneer, peering at a Martian landscape, could ever have a greater thrill than did I at such an opportunity.

Once more I rearranged my aching limbs, stretched and twisted to make my muscles cease complaining, and watched the small fry slip downward through the beam, as the winch drew us steadily upward. Everything of interest was still relayed through the phone, but I was slumped down, relaxed. Suddenly I leaned forward, banging my head against the steel but not losing a second of observation. A small school of luminous fish had just passed, when, fortunately at a moment of suspension, came a new and gorgeous creature. I yelled for continuance of the stop, which was at 1900 feet, and began to absorb what I saw; a fish almost round, with long, moderately high, continuous, vertical fins; a big eye, medium mouth, and small pectoral fins. The skin was decidedly brownish. We swung around a few degrees to port, bringing the fish into the dark blue penumbra of the beam, and then I saw its real beauty. Along the sides of the body were five unbelievably beautiful lines of light, one equatorial, with two curved ones above and two below. Each line was composed of a series of large, pale yellow lights, and every one of these was surrounded by a semicircle of very small, but intensely purple photophores.

The fish turned slowly and, head on, showed a narrow profile. If it were at the surface and without lights I should, without question, have called it a butterflyfish (*Chætodon*) or a surgeonfish (*Acanthurus*). But this glowing creature was assuredly neither, unless a distant relation, adapted for life at three hundred fathoms. My name for it is *Bathysidus pentagrammus,* the Five-lined Constellationfish. In my memory it will live throughout the rest of my life as one of the loveliest things I have ever seen.

Soon after I returned to the surface I reviewed my telephoned notes, especially of the several new fish of which I had given such excellent sights. I added all the details that came to mind. Then, with my artist Mrs. Bostelmann, I went into an artistic huddle, made scrawling attempts myself, and then carefully corrected her trained drawing. Little by little my brain fish materialized, its proportions, size, color, lights, fins interdigitated with those of my memory, and we have a splendid finished painting, which represents the vision in front of my window at 11:52 in the morning of August eleventh, 1900 feet below the surface of the Atlantic Ocean.

In the never-ceasing excitement of abounding life I had completely forgotten the idea of a half-mile record and when on deck, in exactly another hour, we were reminded that an additional 130 feet would have done the trick, I had no regrets. A man-made unit of measure is of far less importance than my Three-starred Angler which otherwise we should surely have missed.

As for this particular dive, we started up from the lowest depth, 2510 feet, with 650 pounds of oxygen left in the tank and reached the surface just as the last hiss of gas escaped from the valve, and the recording ball settled to rest. Unfortunately for any sensational news value, we had a second valve and full tank ready to use. We had been sealed up for more than three hours and when we stepped out the air was as fresh as that on deck, the pressure was exceedingly slight and while we were both glad of the relaxing of constant tenseness, and our legs and feet were sound asleep, our mechanical apparatus had worked without a hitch, and was ready for a new dive. In fact in the afternoon we made an hour's contour dive near shore, and mapped about a mile of Bermuda's slopes some ten fathoms under water. But that is another story.

Late in the afternoon as we reached the entrance of St. Georges harbor, the mighty *Queen* of the Furness Line passed close to us, outward bound. She saw the 2510 chalked on the bow of the *Ready* and roared a salute of congratulations.

Sunday we devoted to translating and augmenting our notes with added remembered details, and getting everything ready for the next dive. Believing that the best kind of rest is a change of activity, on Monday, August thirteenth, we took the *Skink,* our launch, and went ten miles out from shore to North Rock, the last forlorn hope of old Bermuda. Diving in the helmet in seven fathoms at the edge of a magnificent reef, I had the amazing luck of seeing all the so-called dangerous fish of Bermuda, sharks, barracudas, and green moray eels, within a space of twenty square feet.

The following day we went to sea in the *Gladisfen* and drew deep-sea nets across the very place I had dived in the bathysphere so few hours before. As always we were delighted with the sight and touch of beings from the icy depths, and at the same time amazed at the meagerness of the haul compared with what I knew of the abundance of life through which the nets had passed. However each net was filled with glorious creatures, many of which were unknown. Best of all, instant transference into iced salt water revived many of them.

Here again John Tee-Van was in charge of the deck machinery with Bass and Ramsey as aides. I was winchman except at the actual incoming of the nets, when Miss Crane and I watched and took notes of the movements and colors of the living and just dead catch. A pair of ten-inch scimitar-mouths, such as I had seen on the last dive at a depth of four hundred and sixteen fathoms, were alive, and for the first time we had a black swallower, *Chiasmodon niger,* swimming full speed about his jar. Unlike most of his kind, his stomach was empty and not distended with one of his unbelievably enormous meals. Another treasure was a living, gay-colored, semi-transparent, telescope-eyed *Dolichopteryx,* the Long-finned Ghostfish, probably a new species. It was the sixteenth of the whole genus to be taken by man, and the first ever to be seen alive.

Day after day my weather held good and Wednesday, August fifteenth, was no exception. At 6:45 in early morning we were arranging to leave St. Georges anchorage, the barge *Ready* with the bathysphere and ourselves, and the tug *Gladisfen* towing. Three hours later Mr. Barton and I were dropped overboard far out at sea. As well as we could determine from sights on the lighthouses we submerged at the identical spot into which we had splashed four days before.

The same spot, but far from the same visible life. Surprises came at every few feet and again the mass of life was totally unexpected, the sum total of creatures seen unbelievable. At 1000 feet I distinctly saw a shrimp outlined and distinguished several of its pale greenish lights. Although I delayed very little at the hundred foot stops, when the rope guys were attached, yet I dictated page after page of observations. I used the light as little as possible and carefully shielded my eyes, so that very soon they became dark adapted. I was watching for two or three things which I wanted to solve. Large Melanostomiatid dragon-fish with their glowing port-hole lights showed themselves now and then, by which I mean on three separate occasions; and more than elsewhere, in our electric light, we had frequent glimpses of small opalescent copepods, appropriately called *Sapphirina,* which renewed for us all the spectrum of the sunlight.

I have spoken of the three outstanding moments in the mind of a bathysphere diver, the first flash of animal light, the level of eternal darkness, and the discovery and description of a new species of fish. There is a fourth, lacking definite level or anticipation, a roving moment which might very possibly occur near the surface or at the greatest depth, or even as one lies awake, days after the dive, thinking over and reliving it. It is, to my mind, the most important of all, far more so than the discovery of new species. It is the explanation of some mysterious occurrence, of the display of some inexplicable habit which has taken place before our eyes, but which, like a sublimated trick of some master fakir, evades understanding.

This came to me on this last deep dive at 1680 feet, and it explained much that had been a complete puzzle. I saw some creature, several inches long, dart toward the window, turn sideways and—explode. This time my eyes were focused and my mind ready, and at the flash, which was so strong that it illumined my face and the inner sill of the window, I saw the great red shrimp and the outpouring fluid of flame. This was a real Fourth Moment, for many "dim gray fish" as I had reported them, now resolved into distant clouds of light, and all the previous "explosions" against the glass became intelligible. At the next occurrence the shrimp showed plainly before and during the phenomenon, illustrating the value in observation of knowing what to look for. The fact that a number of the deep-sea shrimps had this power of defense is well known, and I have had an aquarium aglow with the emanation. It is the abyssal complement of the sepia smoke screen of a squid at the surface.

Before this dive was completed, I had made a still greater refinement in discernment, perceiving that there were two very distinct types of defense clouds emitted, one which instantly diffused into a glowing mist or cloud, and the other which exploded in a burst of individual sparks, for all the world like a diminutive roman candle. Both occurred at the window or near it a number of times, but it was the latter which was the more startling.

Another advance in bathyspheric educational technique was unconscious and was only accidentally brought to conscious realization. On a succeeding dive I went down fifteen hundred feet and took Mr. Tee-Van and he wondered at my ability to identify organisms which to him, on this first descent into the dark zone, were only individual lights. As we compared notes I realized that I had learned instinctively to ignore the light as soon as possible and look to left or right of it. Exactly as the spiral nebula in Andromeda can be seen most clearly by looking a little to one side, so the sudden flashing out of a light is less blinding when viewed indirectly, and simultaneously its author may more than likely come into focus. Before we returned to the surface Tee-Van had followed this method and we saw eye to eye in subsequent identifications.

At 1800 I saw a small fish with illumined teeth, lighted from below, with distinct black interspaces; and ten feet below this my favorite seadragons, *Lamprotoxus,* appeared, they of the shining green bow. Only sixteen of these fish have ever been taken, seven of which came up in our own nets. The record size is about eight inches, while here before me were four individuals all more than twice that length, and very probably representing a new species. The green side line glowed but the long chin tentacle was quite invisible, certainly giving out no light. At 2100 feet two large fish, quite three feet over all, lighted up and then became one with the darkness about them, a tantalizing glimpse which made me, more than ever, long for bigger and better nets.

At 2450 a very large, dim, but not indistinct outline came into view for a fraction of a second, and at 2500 a delicately illumined ctenophore jelly throbbed past. Without warning, the large fish returned and this time I saw its complete, shadow-like contour as it passed through the farthest end of the beam. Twenty feet is the least possible estimate I can give to its full length, and it was deep in proportion. The whole fish was monochrome, and I could not see even an eye or a fin. For the majority of the "size-conscious" human race this MARINE MONSTER would, I suppose, be the supreme sight of the expedition. In shape it was a deep oval, it swam without evident effort, and it did not return. That is all I can contribute, and while its unusual size so excited me that for several hundred feet I kept keenly on the lookout for hints of the same or other large fish, I soon forgot it in the (very literal) light of smaller, but more distinct and interesting organisms.

What this great creature was I cannot say. A first, and most reasonable guess would be a small whale or blackfish. We know that whales have a special chemical adjustment of the blood which makes it possible for them to dive a mile or more, and come up without getting the "bends." So this paltry depth of 2450 feet would be nothing for any similarly equipped cetacean. Or, less likely, it may have been a whale shark, which is known to reach a length of forty feet. Whatever it was, it appeared and vanished so unexpectedly and showed so dimly that it was quite unidentifiable except as a large, living creature.

Alexander the Great still holds the record for size of a deep-sea fish, when, in the Ethiopic version of Pseudo-Callisthenes, we are told that he looked out of his glass cage, and was shown by an angel of the Lord a monster which, swimming rapidly, took three days and three nights to pass before him! Nevertheless, my creature is a good beginning. Seriously, it shows what still remains for the pioneer explorer of the depths of the sea.

Anyone who, from an airplane high above the earth, has tried to spot another plane somewhere near, in full view, will appreciate the even greater difficulty of focusing in this three-dimensional, stygian blackness, upon some creature, suddenly appearing six inches from our faces, or forty-five feet away. Again and again before the eye can re-focus, the flash and its owner have vanished.

Mr. Barton saw no trace of the large creature I have mentioned, al-though I called out to him and got him at the window immediately. Soon after, when we were both looking out, he saw the first living *Stylophthalmus* ever seen by man, which completely escaped me, al-though it must have been within a foot of the windows. This is one of the most remarkable of deep-sea fish, with the eyes on the ends of long, periscope stalks, almost one-third as long as the entire body. My miss-ing the fish was all the more disappointing because I had recently been thoroughly studying these strange beings, and in fact had abolished their entire family, after proving that they were the larvæ of the golden-tailed serpent-dragons, *Idiacanthus*.

The next fish of unusual size was seen at 2900 feet. It was less than three feet long, rather slender, with many small luminous spots on the body, and a relatively large, pale green, crescent-shaped light under the eye. Near it were five lanternfish, unlike all others I had seen. They swam so slowly that I made certain before they disappeared that they were of the genus *Lampadena*.

At 11:12 A.M. we came to rest gently at 3000 feet, and I knew that this was my ultimate floor; the cable on the winch was very near its end. A few days ago the water had appeared blacker at 2500 feet than could be imagined, yet now to this same imagination it seemed to show as blacker than black. It seemed as if all future nights in the upper world must be considered only relative degrees of twilight. I could never again use the word BLACK with any conviction.

I looked out and watched an occasional passing light and for the first time I realized how completely lacking was the so-called phospho-rescence with which we are familiar at the surface. There, wherever an ordinary fish passes, it becomes luminous by reflection from the lights of the myriads of the minute animals and plants floating in the water. Here each light is an individual thing, often under direct control of the owner. A gigantic fish could tear past the window, and if unillumined might never be seen.

My eyes became so dark adapted at these depths that there was no possibility of error; the jet blackness of the water was broken only by sparks and flashes and steadily glowing lamps of appreciable diameter, varied in color and of infinite variety as regards size and juxtaposition. But they were never dimmed or seen beyond or through any lesser mist or milky-way of organisms. The occasional, evanescent, defense clouds of shrimps hence stand out all the more strongly as unusual phenomena, and are quite apart from the present theme. If the surface light is emitted chiefly by *Noctiluca* and single-celled plants, the explanation of its abyssal absence is easy, for all surface forms of these groups have died out hundreds of feet overhead.

A second thing which occurred to me as I sat coiled in the bathysphere, *more* than half a mile down, was the failure of our powerful beam of light to attract organisms of any kind. Some fled at its appearance, others seemed wholly unconcerned, but not a single copepod or worm or fish gathered along its length or collected against the starboard window from which it poured. We sometimes kept the lesser beam on for three minutes at a time, so there was abundance of time for the plankton, which abounded in all parts of the path of light, to feel and react to its influence. The reason for this demands far more study than I have been able to give it. One factor is doubtless not only lack of the rhythm of day and night, but the eternal absence of all except animal light.

Even in this extremity of blackness I sensed the purity of the water, its freedom from sediment and roiling; six miles from shore and a full mile from the-bottom insured this. So there was no diffusion of light, no trails, no refraction. When sparks or larger lights moved they were as distinct as when they were motionless. But reflection was noticeable, as upon the eye or skin from a sub-ocular or a lateral photophore, or upon my face when a shrimp exploded close in front.

Now and then I felt a slight vibration and an apparent slacking off of the cable. Word came that a cross swell had arisen, and when the full weight of bathysphere and cable came upon the winch, Captain Sylvester let out a few inches to ease the strain. There were only about a dozen turns of cable left upon the reel, and a full half of the drum showed its naked, wooden core. We were swinging at 3028 feet, and, Would we come up? We would.

Whatever I thought about the relative value of intensive observation as compared with record-breaking, I had to admit that this ultimate depth which we had attained showed a decided increase in the number of large fish—more than a dozen from three to twenty feet having been seen—and a corresponding greater number of lights, though not in actual size of their diameters.

Now and then, when lights were thickest, and the watery space before me seemed teeming with life, my eyes peered into the distance beyond them, and I thought of the lightless creatures forever invisible to me, those with eyes which depended for guidance through life upon the glow from the lamps of other organisms, and strangest of all the inhabitants of the deeper parts of the ocean, those blind from birth to death, whose sole assistants, to food, to mates and from enemies, were cunning sense organs in the skin, or long, tendril-like rays of their fins.

Before we began to ascend, I had to stop making notes of my own, so numb were my fingers from the cold steel of the window sill, and to change from my cushion to the metal floor, was like shifting to a cake of ice. Of the blackness of the outside water I have already written too much. As to pressure, there seemed no reason why we should not be outside in a diving helmet as well as in. I thought of a gondola 60,000 feet up in the stratosphere with a pressure of one pound to the square inch. And then through the telephone we learned that at this moment we were under a pressure of 1360 pounds to each square inch, or well over half a ton. Each window held back over nineteen tons of water, while a total of 7016 tons were piled up in all directions upon the bathysphere itself. Yes, we had heard clearly, we were ready to be pulled up at once!

At 2929 feet I heard a metallic twang through the phone, asked what it was, and got some noncommittal answer. I found out later that one of the guy ropes used in spooling the incoming cable on the drum had suddenly given way with a terrific report—a ghastly shock to everyone on deck until they realized it was a rope and not the cable. Truly we in the bathysphere had the best of it at all times.

Whenever I sink below the last rays of light, similes pour in upon me. Throughout all this account I have consciously rejected the scores of "as ifs" which sprang to mind. The stranger the situation the more does it seem imperative to use comparisons. The eternal one, the one most worthy and which will not pass from mind, the only other place comparable to these marvelous nether regions, must surely be naked space itself, out far beyond atmosphere, between the stars, where sunlight has no grip upon the dust and rubbish of planetary air, where the blackness of space, the shining planets, comets, suns, and stars must really be closely akin to the world of life as it appears to the eyes of an awed human being, in the open ocean, one half mile down.

The Plague

by GIOVANNI BOCCACCIO

*The pestilence of which Boccaccio writes in "The First Day"
of his* Decameron *was the Black Death of 1348, a general epidemic of
which bubonic plague was probably a prominent part. The Black Death
claimed three out of five persons in the city of Florence, Italy, where
Boccaccio resided, and, because of the exodus of citizens, caused grass
to grow in the streets.*

IN THE YEAR OF OUR LORD 1348, THERE HAPPENED AT FLOR-
ence, the finest city in all Italy, a most terrible plague; which
whether owing to the influence of the planets, or that it was sent from God
as a just punishment for our sins, had broken out some years before in
the Levant; and after passing from place to place, and making incredible
havoc all the way, had now reached the West; where, spite of all the
means that art and human foresight could suggest, as keeping the city
clear from filth, and excluding all suspected persons; notwithstanding
frequent consultations what else was to be done; nor omitting prayers
to God in frequent processions: in the spring of the foregoing year, it
began to show itself in a sad and wonderful manner; and, different from
what it had been in the East, where bleeding from the nose is the fatal
prognostic, here, there appeared certain tumors in the groins, or under
the armpits, some as big as a small apple, others as an egg; and afterwards purple spots in most parts of the body: in some cases large and
but few in number, in others less and more numerous, both sorts the
usual messengers of death.

To the cure of this malady, neither medical knowledge, nor the power
of drugs was of any effect; whether because the disease was in its own
nature mortal, or that the physicians (the number of whom, taking

78

quacks and women pretenders into the account, was grown very great) could form no just idea of the cause, nor consequently ground a true method of cure; which ever was the reason, few or none escaped; but they generally died the third day from the first appearance of the symptoms, without a fever or other bad circumstance attending. And the disease by being communicated from the sick to the well, seemed daily to get ahead, and to rage the more as fire will do, by laying on fresh combustibles. Nor was it given by conversing with only, or coming near the sick, but even by touching their clothes, or anything that they had before touched.

It is wonderful, what I am going to mention; which had I not seen it with my own eyes, and were there not many witnesses to attest it besides myself, I should never venture to relate, however credibly I might have been informed about it; such I say, was the quality of the pestilential matter, as to pass not only from man to man, but what is more strange, and has been often known, that anything belonging to the infected, if touched by any other creature, would certainly infect, and even kill that creature in a short space of time; and one instance of this kind I took particular notice of; namely, that the rags of a poor man just dead, being thrown into the street, and two hogs coming by at the same time, and rooting amongst them, and shaking them about in their mouths, in less than an hour turned around, and died on the spot.

These accidents, and others of the like sort, occasioned various fears and devices amongst those people that survived, all tending to the same uncharitable and cruel end; which was, to avoid the sick, and everything that had been near them; expecting by that means to save themselves. And some holding it best to live temperately, and to avoid excesses of all kinds, made parties, and shut themselves up from the rest of the world; eating and drinking moderately of the best, and diverting themselves with music, and such other entertainments as they might have within doors; never listening to anything from without, to make them uneasy.

Others maintained free living to be a better preservative, and would baulk no passion or appetite they wished to gratify, drinking and reveling incessantly from tavern to tavern, or in private houses, which were frequently found deserted by the owners, and therefore common to every one; yet avoiding, with all this irregularity, to come near the infected. And such, at that time was the public distress, that the laws, human or divine, were not regarded; for the officers, to put them in force, being either dead, sick, or in want of persons to assist them; every one did just as he pleased.

A third sort of people chose a method between these two; not confining themselves to rules of diet like the former, and yet avoiding the intemperance of the latter; but eating and drinking what their appetites required, they walked everywhere with odors and nosegays to smell to; as holding it best to corroborate the brain: for they supposed the whole atmosphere to be tainted with the stink of dead bodies, arising partly from the distemper itself, and partly from the fermenting of the medicines within them. Others, of a more cruel disposition, as perhaps the more safe to themselves, declared, that the only remedy was to avoid it: persuaded, therefore of this, and taking care for themselves only, men and women in great numbers left the city, their houses, relations, and effects, and fled into the country: as if the wrath of God had been restrained to visit those only within the walls of the city; or else concluding, that none ought to stay in a place thus doomed to destruction.

Divided as they were, neither did all die nor all escape; but falling sick indifferently, as well those of one as of another opinion; they who first set the example by forsaking others, now languished themselves, without mercy. I pass over the little regard that citizens and relations showed to each other; for their terror was such, that a brother even fled from his brother, a wife from her husband, and what is more uncommon a parent from its own child. On which account numbers that fell sick could have no help but what the charity of friends, who were very few, or the avarice of servants supplied; and even these were scarce, and at extravagant wages, and so little used to the business, that they were only fit to reach what was called for, and observe when they died; and this desire of getting money often cost them their lives.

From this desertion of friends, and scarcity of servants, an unheard of custom prevailed; no lady, however young or handsome, would disdain being attended by a manservant, whether young or old it mattered not; and to expose herself naked to him, the necessity of the distemper requiring it, as though it was to a woman; which might make those who recovered, less modest for the time to come. And many lost their lives, who might have escaped, had they been looked after at all. So that, between the scarcity of servants, and violence of the distemper, such numbers were continually dying, as made it terrible to hear as well as to behold. Whence, from mere necessity, many customs were introduced, different from what had been before known in the city.

It had been usual, as it now is for the women who were friends and neighbors to the deceased, to meet together at his house, and to lament with his relations; at the same time the men would get together at the door, with a number of clergy, according to the person's circumstances; and the corpse was carried by people of his own rank, with the solemnity of tapers and singing, to that church where the person had desired to be buried; which custom was now laid aside, and, so far from having a crowd of women to lament over them, that great numbers passed out of the world without a single person: and few had the tears of their friends at their departure; but those friends would laugh, and make themselves merry; for even the women had learned to postpone every other concern to that of their own lives. Nor was a corpse attended by more than ten, or a dozen, nor those citizens of credit, but fellows hired for the purpose; who would put themselves under the bier, and carry it with all possible haste to the nearest church; and the corpse was interred, without any great ceremony, where they could find room.

With regard to the lower sort, and many of a middling rank, the scene was still more affecting; for they, staying at home either through poverty, or hopes of succor in distress, fell sick daily by thousands, and, having nobody to attend them, generally died: some breathed their last in the streets, and others shut up in their own houses, when the stench that came from them, made the first discovery of their deaths to the neighborhood. And, indeed, every place was filled with the dead.

A method now was taken, as well out of regard to the living, as pity for the dead, for the neighbors, assisted by what porters they could meet with, to clear all the houses, and lay the bodies at the doors; and every morning great numbers might be seen brought out in this manner; from whence they were carried away on biers, or tables, two or three at a time; and sometimes it has happened, that a wife and her husband, two or three brothers, and a father and son, have been laid on together: it has been observed also, whilst two or three priests have walked before a corpse with their crucifix, that two or three sets of porters have fallen in with them; and where they knew but of one, they have buried six, eight, or more: nor was there any to follow, and shed a few tears over them; for things were come to that pass, that men's lives were no more regarded than the lives of so many beasts. Hence it plainly appeared, that what the wisest in the ordinary course of things, and by a common train of calamities, could never be taught, namely, to bear them patiently; this, by the excess of those calamities, was now grown a familiar lesson to the most simple and unthinking.

The consecrated ground no longer containing the numbers which were continually brought thither, especially as they were desirous of laying every one in the parts allotted to their families; they were forced to dig trenches, and to put them in by hundreds, piling them up in rows, as goods are stowed in a ship, and throwing in a little earth till they were filled to the top.

Not to rake any farther into the particulars of our misery, I shall observe, that it fared no better with the adjacent country; for to omit the different castles about us, which presented the same view in miniaure with the city, you might see the poor distressed laborers, with their families, without either the plague or physicians, or help of servants, languishing on the highways, in the fields, and in their own houses, and dying rather like cattle than human creatures; and growing dissolute in their manners like the citizens, and careless of everything, as supposing every day to be their last, their thoughts were not so much employed how to improve, as to make use of their substance for their present support: whence it happened that the flocks, herds, etc., and the dogs themselves, ever faithful to their masters, being driven from their own homes, would wander, no regard being had to them, among the forsaken harvest; and many times, after they had filled themselves in the day, would return of their own accord like rational creatures at night.

What can I say more, if I return to the city? unless that such was the cruelty of Heaven, and perhaps of men, that between March and July following, it is supposed, and made pretty certain, that upwards of a hundred thousand souls perished in the city alone; whereas, before that calamity, it was not supposed to have contained so many inhabitants. What magnificent dwellings, what noble palaces were then depopulated to the last person! what families extinct! what riches and vast possessions left, and no known heir to inherit! what numbers of both sexes in the prime and vigor of youth, whom in the morning neither Galen, Hippocrates, nor Asclepius himself, but would have declared in perfect health; after dining heartily with their friends here, have supped with their departed friends in the other world!

Head Hunters of New Guinea

by SIDNEY SPENCER BROOMFIELD

Broomfield's life was an incredible one—he was a prime example of the nineteenth-century adventurer: ivory hunter, prospector, pioneer, pearl fisher and—doctor of medicine. One suspects that it was incredible even to himself. Perhaps the essence of his genius, apart from its versatility, was his ability to survive. From this perspective one can better appreciate the amazing story I have selected from his book, Kachalola, *published in 1930 when Broomfield was 83.*

Under the heading of "nature" it seemed to me worth while to include primitive man. This by no means is meant to imply that there is an absence of primitive man in the so-called civilized species.

IT WAS FULLY FIFTY MILES UP THAT WE FOUND THE FIRST village, and only found it when we captured a small dugout with three natives in it. These natives were very short of stature, the tallest only measured five feet three. They were filthy, ugly little devils. The boy Hayes had loaned me could talk to them, and through him I found out about the village. I tied these three natives up and they acted as guides. They said there was a great sickness at their village, that a number of them had died. I took twenty of my men, leaving Ali in charge of the fleet. Had we not have captured these natives we would never have found their village. They took us along several paths; one path would peter out and they would cross the bush and pick up another path. This happened three times before we reached the village.

I sent one of the guides forward to let his chief know we were friendly, and that I would do anything I could for the sick natives. Hayes' boy explained this to the guide. We came to the village, and I found that

83

the natives were suffering from dysentery. It was a queer place. All the huts were built on piles, and the natives had to climb a ladder to reach them. The huts were scattered, and the village covered quite a few acres of the bush. They were built in two stories, with a platform underneath the hut, and a ladder leading from the hut to the platform. They were a filthy lot, and more than two-thirds of them suffering from dysentery, and unable to get about. In all there were about three hundred and eighty men and youths, the remainder women and children. The women were even shorter than the men; the tallest did not stand more than four feet ten inches, or five feet in height. They were dressed in kilts made from the bark of the sago palm.

I sent back to the boats, ordering Ali to look out a high place and make a camp, and send my medicine chest, tent and kit along. I made up my mind to stay with this crowd until I had beaten the dysentery. This turned out a good move on my part. I only lost nine cases, women and children, and in three weeks had all the rest on their feet.

These people used stone axes and knives, and seemed to take great care of their stone implements. I found out after that making a good axe or knife took weeks and sometimes months of time and work.

Their food consisted of sago, yams and breadfruit. Also fish and birds when they could shoot or trap them. They used bows and arrows, the arrows tipped with bone; also spears. Some of the spears had flint blades, but most of them had bone blades.

There was a devil-devil house, and a platform. The platform I heard later was called the Sing Sing Platform. They had an idol in the devil-devil house, made of reeds, about four feet high. This was covered with clay, and there was a human skull with a clay mask, very much like the face of a boar, covering it, with boar tusks and crocodile teeth. The eyes were made of mother of pearl, and the edges of the frame were fringed with plumes of cassowary and birds of paradise. There were a few human skulls and crocodile skulls in the devil-devil house, and seven or eight drums, some long and some short. I saw lots of these houses later, and always set fire to them. I hated the looks of the wretched things.

After I became friendly with this crowd, I learned of several other villages and sent presents to the chiefs, asking them to visit me at my camp. I had shifted from the village to my camp as soon as I had the dysentery well in hand.

Three of the chiefs came in to my camp, and I managed to get altogether sixty carriers from these people. I started from these villages with fourteen dugouts and two whaleboats to go further up the Sepik.

The first day after leaving the Pygmies, we had to scrap a party of head-hunters on the river. They did not get near enough to do any harm. We opened with our rifles, and I did not think the report of a rifle could terrify people as these people were scared. They simply left their dug-outs, swam to the bank of the river, and disappeared into the dense bush. It was hopeless to try and follow them.

I saw numbers of crocs on the sandbanks, yet I did not notice any of the natives dragged under when they jumped out of their dugouts and swam for the bank.

I went up the river about one hundred and eighty or two hundred miles, then hid the dugouts and boats in a small river running into the Sepik, and started with the carriers to try and cross the island to the other coast.

Two days from the river I sent four of my men out to try and shoot meat for the carriers. One returned with a spear wound in his arm, and reported that the other three had been wounded and captured by a large party of natives. The boy loaned me by Hayes questioned the carriers and discovered that there was a large tribe of cannibals living in this part of the island. Leaving Ali and fourteen of my men to guard the camp, I went forward with forty carriers and thirty-two of my own men, to look for the people who had captured my men. It was a nasty job; we had a lot of cutting to do through the bush and undergrowth, and had to camp in the thick bush that night. I did not enjoy that trip. Snakes, scorpions and centipedes were very plentiful, and mosquitoes swarmed. I killed two snakes and several scorpions in my tent. I was giving quinine to my own people and taking heavy doses myself. I expected to see some of my Indians go down with fever, but up to the present time none had suffered. The heat was terrific during the day, and the work of cutting a path in some places very hard.

The following morning we came on a path leading up a ridge and fol-lowed it for about two miles, when we heard natives beating drums and kicking up an awful row. I took three men and went forward. I saw the village through the bush, which was more open on this ridge, and also saw that there was a dance in progress.

Returning to my men, I sent one half under Da Silva to attack the vil-lage from the other side. After giving Da Silva time to get round to his position, I rushed the village from my side, firing as we charged. These people put up a good fight and several of my carriers went down and some of my Indians stopped arrows. I had one or two narrow shaves, two arrows lodged in my shirt and one knocked off my hat. I heard Da Silva shooting on the other side of the village, and saw some of the natives who were resisting us clear out. We had some close up fighting after that, and then it was a hut to hut fight. The natives seemed to lose their heads and cleared into their huts. The fight was won after about one and a half hours from the time I gave the signal to rush the village.

We captured fifty-eight full grown men, forty youths and nearly one hundred and sixty women and children. I gave orders to the carriers under Da Silva to search the huts and try to find our men, and with the aid of Hayes' boy I started to question our prisoners.

One of the prisoners said he was the chief's son. His father was killed. This lad denied any knowledge of our men. They had not been on the warpath for many moons. After a lot of talk, he said there was another village between here and the river, and it must have been them that had been on the warpath, and captured my men. While we were talking, Da Silva came back; his men were dragging a filthy-looking native. Da Silva looked quite ill. He had discovered this old devil in the devil-devil house, and he also discovered the heads of our men there. Some of the carriers brought further proof. They had found two hands and a foot of the missing men.

We tied up all the men and youths and put the women and children into some of the huts. I was very angry at the fate of my chaps, and determined to put a stop to this kind of thing if I was able to.

I had a talk with Da Silva and told him I was going to make an example of the witch-doctor, for so his prisoner turned out to be. I would make these people kai-kai the brute. I told Hayes' boy to tell my carriers what I had determined on doing.

Those little devils were delighted. Many of their people had been kai-kai by this same tribe. I called up the man, who said he was son of the chief, and told him to tell his people that I was going to give them a feast, so soon as they had cleaned up the village, and planted the dead. There were no wounded amongst the cannibals; my carriers had seen to that. Amongst ourselves there had been twenty-three casualties, nine killed outright and fourteen wounded, only two very badly. I attended to the wounded and had my tent put up in the middle of the kraal, and then ordered the neck chains to be removed from six of the prisoners, and made them tie up the witch-doctor. The women were ordered to get their pots and fires ready. I ordered the son of the chief to kill and cook their witch doctor. This he refused to do. I asked through Hayes' boy, did they not kill and eat three of my people? This they denied; they had eaten them but my boys had been killed in battle.

"Right oh," said I, "Da Silva, hang this man," and Da Silva with the assistance of some of the carriers hanged him. I then ordered another man to carry on, and he refused. I ordered him to be hanged, but when he felt himself being pulled up to the limb of the tree, he offered to carry out my orders, and he did so. I then ordered the men to cut off the body, and hand the meat over to the women to be cooked. This was also done. When the meal was ready, I told the men who had been released from neck chains to carry the pots to their friends. They refused to eat. I was determined to give them a dose of their own medicine, and ordered one of the men to start eating. He refused. I ordered him to be hanged, and he followed the chief's son. I had to hang a third prisoner before I could get the others to obey my orders. But they did eat this filthy witch doctor, and if I was not mistaken some of them seemed to enjoy doing it after they got started.

Then I ordered them through Hayes' man to send forward by the drums news as to what had been done here, and to add that a white man was traveling through this part of the country, and intended to repeat what was done here, in every case. That he wanted to be friends with the natives, pay them when they helped him, and trade peaceably with them. But if the natives attacked him and his people, he would in every case make the natives who killed and ate his people not only kill and eat their own chief and witch doctor, but kill and eat their own wives and children, capture all he could, and make slaves of the people he captured. This was the gist of the message I ordered them to beat out on their drums. Of course the eating of wives and children was only bluff. But there was no bluff about the other part of the message, as a good many of the witch doctors and chiefs found out later.

People may think I took drastic measures with these natives. Let those who do try and put themselves in my place, amongst a nation of cannibals, with no hopes of outside help, being continually attacked night and day. I did not interfere with the women and kids. I punished grown men and I had to be severe in the punishment I dealt out.

I took the whole of the grown men from this village, and made them carry and do other work for me. I burned down the devil-devil house and their idols, and also burned the bodies of the three men I had ordered to be hanged. Da Silva planted the heads and remains of our own three people. We got seven very well preserved heads in this devil-devil house. These I kept, and they are now in museums.

Alone

by RICHARD E. BYRD

During the Antarctic winter night of 1934 Admiral Byrd manned alone Bolling Advance Weather Base, situated on the Ross Ice Barrier on a line between Little America and the South Pole. He very nearly died in the task. The record of his heroism is contained in a book of modesty, intelligence and beauty—Byrd's Alone, *from which I have selected this adventure. Byrd, as an explorer, thinker and stylist, is among the finest that the United States has produced.*

MAY WAS A ROUND BOULDER SINKING BEFORE A TIDE. TIME sloughed off the last implication of urgency, and the days moved imperceptibly one into the other. The few world news items which Dyer read to me from time to time seemed almost as meaningless and blurred as they might to a Martian. My world was insulated against the shocks running through distant economies. Advance Base was geared to different laws. On getting up in the morning, it was enough for me to say to myself: Today is the day to change the barograph sheet, or, Today is the day to fill the stove tank. The night was settling down in earnest. By May 17th, one month after the sun had sunk below the horizon, the noon twilight was dwindling to a mere chink in the darkness, lit by a cold reddish glow. Days when the wind brooded in the north or east, the Barrier became a vast stagnant shadow surmounted by swollen masses of clouds, one layer of darkness piled on top of the other. This was the polar night, the morbid countenance of the Ice Age. Nothing moved; nothing was visible. This was the soul of inertness. One could almost hear a distant creaking as if a great weight were settling.

Out of the deepening darkness came the cold. On May 19th, when I took the usual walk, the temperature was 65° below zero. For the first time the canvas boots failed to protect my feet. One heel was nipped, and I was forced to return to the hut and change to reindeer mukluks. That day I felt miserable; my body was racked by shooting pains—exactly as if I had been gassed. Very likely I was; in inspecting the ventilator pipes next morning I discovered that the intake pipe was completely clogged with rime and that the outlet pipe was two-thirds full. Next day—Sunday the 20th—was the coldest yet. The minimum thermometer dropped to 72° below zero; the inside thermograph, which always read a bit lower than the instruments in the shelter, stood at −74°; and the thermograph in the shelter was stopped dead—the ink, though well laced with glycerine, and the lubricant were both frozen. So violently did the air in the fuel tank expand after the stove was lit that oil went shooting all over the place; to insulate the tank against similar temperature spreads I wrapped around it the rubber air cushion which by some lucky error had been included among my gear. In the glow of a flashlight the vapor rising from the stovepipe and the outlet ventilator looked like the discharge from two steam engines. My fingers agonized over the thermograph, and I was hours putting it to rights. The fuel wouldn't flow from the drums; I had to take one inside and heat it near the stove. All day long I kept two primus stoves burning in the tunnel.

Sunday the 20th also brought a radio schedule; I had the devil's own time trying to meet it. The engine balked for an hour; my fingers were so brittle and frostbitten from tinkering with the carburetor that, when I actually made contact with Little America, I could scarcely work the key. "Ask Haines come on," was my first request. While Hutcheson searched the tunnels of Little America for the Senior Meteorologist, I chatted briefly with Charlie Murphy. Little America claimed only −60°. "But we're moving the brass monkeys below," Charlie advised. "Seventy-one below here now," I said. "You can have it," was the closing comment from the north.

Then Bill Haines's merry voice sounded in the earphones. I explained the difficulty with the thermograph. "Same trouble we've had," Bill said. "It's probably due to frozen oil. I'd suggest you bring the instrument inside, and try soaking it in gasoline, to cut whatever oil traces remain. Then rinse it in ether. As for the ink's freezing, you might try adding more glycerine." Bill was in a jovial mood. "Look at me, Admiral," he boomed. "I never have any trouble with the instruments. The trick is in having an ambitious and docile assistant." I really chuckled over that because I knew, from the first expedition, what Grimminger, the Junior

Meteorologist, was going through: Bill, with his back to the fire and blandishment on his tongue, persuading the recruit that duty and the opportunity for self-improvement required him to go up into the blizzard to fix a balky trace; Bill humming to himself in the warmth of a shack while the assistant in an open pit kept a theodolite trained on the sounding balloon soaring into the night, and stuttered into a telephone the different vernier readings from which Bill was calculating the velocities and directions of the upper air currents. That day I rather wished that I, too, had an assistant. He would have taken his turn on the anemometer pole, no mistake. The frost in the iron cleats went through the fur soles of the mukluks, and froze the balls of my feet. My breath made little explosive sounds on the wind; my lungs, already sore, seemed to shrivel when I breathed.

Seldom had the aurora flamed more brilliantly. For hours the night danced to its frenetic excitement. And at times the sound of Barrier quakes was like that of heavy guns. My tongue was swollen and sore from drinking scalding hot tea, and the tip of my nose ached from frostbite. A big wind, I guessed, would come out of this still cold; it behooved me to look to my roof. I carried gallons of water topside, and poured it around the edges of the shack. It froze almost as soon as it hit. The ice was an armor plating over the packed drift.

At midnight, when I clambered topside for an auroral "ob," a wild sense of suffocation came over me the instant I pushed my shoulders through the trapdoor. My lungs gasped, but no air reached them. Bewildered and perhaps a little frightened, I slid down the ladder and lunged into the shack. In the warm air the feeling passed as quickly as it had come. Curious but cautious, I again made my way up the ladder. And again the same thing happened; I lost my breath, but I perceived why. A light air was moving down from eastward; and its bitter touch, when I faced into it, was constricting the breathing passages. So I turned my face away from it, breathing into my glove; and in that attitude finished the "ob." Before going below, I made an interesting experiment. I put a thermometer on the snow, let it lie there awhile, and discovered that the temperature at the surface was actually 5° colder than at the level of the instrument shelter, four feet higher. Reading in the sleeping bag afterwards, I froze one finger, although I shifted the book steadily from one hand to the other, slipping the unoccupied hand into the warmth of the bag.

Out of the cold and out of the east came the wind. It came on gradually, as if the sheer weight of the cold were almost too much to be moved. On the night of the 21st the barometer started down. The night was black as a thunderhead when I made my first trip topside; and a tension in the wind, a bulking of shadows in the night indicated that a new storm center was forming. Next morning, glad of an excuse to stay underground, I worked a long time on the Escape Tunnel by the light of a red candle standing in a snow recess. That day I pushed the emergency exit to a distance of twenty-two feet, the farthest it was ever to go. My stint done, I sat down on a box, thinking how beautiful was the red of the candle, how white the rough-hewn snow. Soon I became aware of an increasing clatter of the anemometer cups. Realizing that the wind was picking up, I went topside to make sure that everything was secured. It is a queer experience to watch a blizzard rise. First there is the wind, rising out of nowhere. Then the Barrier unwrenches itself from quietude; and the surface, which just before had seemed as hard and polished as metal, begins to run like a making sea. Sometimes, if the wind strikes hard, the drift comes across the Barrier like a hurrying white cloud, tossed hundreds of feet in the air. Other times the growth is gradual. You become conscious of a general slithering movement on all sides. The air fills with tiny scraping and sliding and rustling sounds as the first loose crystals stir. In a little while they are moving as solidly as an incoming tide, which creams over the ankles, then surges to the waist, and finally is at the throat. I have walked in drift so thick as not to be able to see a foot ahead of me; yet, when I glanced up, I could see the stars shining through the thin layer just overhead.

Smoking tendrils were creeping up the anemometer pole when I finished my inspection. I hurriedly made the trapdoor fast, as a sailor might batten down a hatch; and knowing that my ship was well secured, I retired to the cabin to ride out the storm. It could not reach me, hidden deep in the Barrier crust; nevertheless the sounds came down. The gale sobbed in the ventilators, shook the stovepipe until I thought it would be jerked out by the roots, pounded the roof with sledge-hammer blows. I could actually feel the suction effect through the pervious snow. A breeze flickered in the room and the tunnels. The candles wavered and went out. My only light was the feeble storm lantern.

Even so, I didn't have any idea how really bad it was until I went aloft for an observation. As I pushed back the trapdoor, the drift met me like a moving wall. It was only a few steps from the ladder to the instrument shelter, but it seemed more like a mile. The air came at me in snowy rushes; I breasted it as I might a heavy surf. No night had ever seemed so dark. The beam from the flashlight was choked in its throat; I could not see my hand before my face.

My windproofs were caked with drift by the time I got below. I had a vague feeling that something had changed while I was gone, but what, I couldn't tell. Presently I noticed that the shack was appreciably colder. Raising the stove lid, I was surprised to find that the fire was out, though the tank was half full. I decided that I must have turned off the valve unconsciously before going aloft; but, when I put a match to the burner, the draught down the pipe blew out the flame. The wind, then, must have killed the fire. I got it going again, and watched it carefully.

The blizzard vaulted to gale force. Above the roar the deep, taut thrumming note of the radio antenna and the anemometer guy wires reminded me of wind in a ship's rigging. The wind direction trace turned scratchy on the sheet; no doubt drift had short-circuited the electric contacts, I decided. Realizing that it was hopeless to attempt to try to keep them clear, I let the instrument be. There were other ways of getting the wind direction. I tied a handkerchief to a bamboo pole and ran it through the outlet ventilator; with a flashlight I could tell which way the cloth was whipped. I did this at hourly intervals, noting any change of direction on the sheet. But by 2 o'clock in the morning I had had enough of this periscope sighting. If I expected to sleep and at the same time maintain the continuity of the records, I had no choice but to clean the contact points.

The wind was blowing hard then. The Barrier shook from the concussions overhead; and the noise was as if the entire physical world were tearing itself to pieces. I could scarcely heave the trapdoor open. The instant it came clear I was plunged into a blinding smother. I came out crawling, clinging to the handle of the door until I made sure of my bearings. Then I let the door fall shut, not wanting the tunnel filled with drift. To see was impossible. Millions of tiny pellets exploded in my eyes, stinging like BB shot. It was even hard to breathe, because snow instantly clogged the mouth and nostrils. I made my way toward the anemometer pole on hands and knees, scared that I might be bowled off my feet if I stood erect; one false step and I should be lost forever.

I found the pole all right; but not until my head collided with a cleat. I managed to climb it, too, though ten million ghosts were tearing at me, ramming their thumbs into my eyes. But the errand was useless. Drift as thick as this would mess up the contact points as quickly as they were cleared; besides, the wind cups were spinning so fast that I stood a good chance of losing a couple of fingers in the process. Coming down the pole, I had a sense of being whirled violently through the air, with no control over my movements. The trapdoor was completely buried when I

found it again, after scraping around for some time with my mittens. I
pulled at the handle, first with one hand, then with both. It did not give.
It's a tight fit, anyway, I mumbled to myself. The drift has probably
wedged the corners. Standing astride the hatch, I braced myself and
heaved with all my strength. I might just as well have tried hoisting the
Barrier.

Panic took me then, I must confess. Reason fled. I clawed at the three-
foot square of timber like a madman. I beat on it with my fists, trying to
shake the snow loose; and, when that did no good, I lay flat on my belly
and pulled until my hands went weak from cold and weariness. Then I
crooked my elbow, put my face down, and said over and over again,
You damn fool, you damn fool. Here for weeks I had been defending
myself against the danger of being penned inside the shack; instead, I
was now locked out; and nothing could be worse, especially since I had
only a wool parka and pants under my windproofs. Just two feet below
was sanctuary—warmth, food, tools, all the means of survival. All these
things were an arm's length away, but I was powerless to reach them.

There is something extravagantly insensate about an Antarctic blizzard at night. Its vindictiveness cannot be measured on an anemometer
sheet. It is more than just wind: it is a solid wall of snow moving at gale
force, pounding like surf.* The whole malevolent rush is concentrated
upon you as upon a personal enemy. In the senseless explosion of sound
you are reduced to a crawling thing on the margin of a disintegrating
world; you can't see, you can't hear, you can hardly move. The lungs
gasp after the air sucked out of them, and the brain is shaken. Nothing in
the world will so quickly isolate a man.

Half-frozen, I stabbed toward one of the ventilators, a few feet away.
My mittens touched something round and cold. Cupping it in my hands,
I pulled myself up. This was the outlet ventilator. Just why, I don't
know—but instinct made me kneel and press my face against the opening. Nothing in the room was visible, but a dim patch of light illuminated
the floor, and warmth rose up to my face. That steadied me.

Still kneeling, I turned my back to the blizzard and considered what
might be done. I thought of breaking in the windows in the roof, but
they lay two feet down in hard crust, and were reinforced with wire
besides. If I only had something to dig with, I could break the crust and
stamp the windows in with my feet. The pipe cupped between my hands
supplied the first inspiration; maybe I could use that to dig with. It, too,

* Because of this blinding, suffocating drift, in the Antarctic winds of only
moderate velocity have the punishing force of full-fledged hurricanes elsewhere.

was wedged tight; I pulled until my arms ached, without budging it; I had lost all track of time, and the despairing thought came to me that I was lost in a task without an end. Then I remembered the shovel. A week before, after leveling drift from the last light blow, I had stabbed a shovel handle up in the crust somewhere to leeward. That shovel would save me. But how to find it in the avalanche of the blizzard?

I lay down and stretched out full length. Still holding the pipe, I thrashed around with my feet, but pummeled only empty air. Then I worked back to the hatch. The hard edges at the opening provided another grip, and again I stretched out and kicked. Again no luck. I dared not let go until I had something else familiar to cling to. My foot came up against the other ventilator pipe. I edged back to that, and from the new anchorage repeated the maneuver. This time my ankle struck something hard. When I felt it and recognized the handle, I wanted to caress it.

Embracing this thrice-blessed tool, I inched back to the trapdoor. The handle of the shovel was just small enough to pass under the little wooden bridge which served as a grip. I got both hands on the shovel and tried to wrench the door up; my strength was not enough, however. So I lay down flat on my belly and worked my shoulders under the shovel. Then I heaved, the door sprang open, and I rolled down the shaft. When I tumbled into the light and warmth of the room, I kept thinking, How wonderful, how perfectly wonderful.

Lost in the Sahara

by DONALD R. G. CAMERON

The following is part of a longer account by an Englishman of a journey carried out across the Central Sahara. The author apologizes in his preface for being unpracticed in "the art of the pen" and for having set down his story in the somewhat unfavorable conditions of barrack and camp life, but he might have spared himself the trouble. In my opinion his is one of the finest books on the desert. Specifically, his description of how it feels to be lost in the desert and dying of thirst is not surpassed anywhere. He made his trip in the middle twenties of this century.

I WOKE ON THE FOLLOWING MORNING TO FIND EVERYTHING, myself included, covered with a thin layer of sand. The wind which had risen during the night had worked itself up to the velocity of half a gale, and sleep had been intermittent only. Every now and then I had been compelled to rise and readjust the waterproof sheet which formed my shelter, for the strength of the wind was too much for its rather crude support, and time and again I had found it lying flat on top of me. It was bitterly cold, and there was a thick sand haze all round. The feeling of relief at not having to rise at the first glimmer of dawn and trudge on through the long day until sunset was too pleasant to describe, and the temptation to lie on between the blankets was great. However, all chances of succumbing to this temptation were destroyed by this vile wind. My little shelter was always carefully erected with its only opening to the leeward side, and that had achieved its object in the open desert through which we had come, where the direction of the wind was constant. But now, in hilly country, the vagaries of this infernal

wind seemed to be directed against me personally, and, in spite of my
having arranged the shelter in a manner which gave the best protection,
it seemed to take a fiendish delight in changing completely round and
blowing a stinging cloud of sand all over me. This, I must confess, was
the only reason why I got up early. My tent, which so far had hardly
justified the trouble of carrying so much extra weight, was now to be
useful, and after a rather long struggle with the canvas bellying out in
the wind, we managed to get it firmly pitched. Inside its shelter it was
possible to get a little peace and to eat a meal that did not include 50
per cent of sand.

Atahair went off to find the water hole, the actual location of which
I was not very much surprised that he was not sure of, considering the
long period which had elapsed since his last and only visit to this place.
I sent Mahomed back to see if he could persuade my camel to move,
hoping that I would soon be able to give it water and food in order to
revive it. In the meantime there was nothing to do but wait for Atahair's
return. A rather disconcerting discovery was that there seemed to be
little more in the way of camel pasture than the few bare trees we had
found the previous night. We had found a few more trees, bearing a
very scanty amount of foliage, in a re-entrant in the northern side of
the bluff, but they were lamentably bare and could provide nothing like
a good feed for the wretched animals.

An hour or two had elapsed since Atahair's departure, when I was
interrupted in the middle of a fit of quiet chuckling to myself at Falstaff's
ignominious adventures amongst the foul linen by the flap of my tent
being thrown open and, bunched outside it, all six natives pressing in at
me. There was obviously something wrong. It is not difficult to sense
trouble when you are in contact with natives. The fact of their appearance in a bunch and the rather vacant looks on their faces that seemed
to say, "Well, what are you going to do about it?" told me that something was amiss, although I was not prepared for the alarming news
which was broken to me by Baragai that Atahair had failed to find the
water hole; for such was their reason for interrupting my engrossment
in Mr. Shakespeare's comedy.

To say that I was surprised is hopelessly inadequate, for Atahair
had appeared so confident of the route that no doubts whatever had
crossed my mind. His admission now, that not only could he not find the
water hole, but that this place was not Katelet and the surroundings
were quite unfamiliar to him, was startling, to say the least of it. There
was no doubt as to the first thing to be done: and that was to collect

together all the remaining water and place it under lock and key. In one respect the cold weather had been a blessing, for since leaving Tadeghat we had not required our full ration of water, but the saving on this had, to a certain extent, been counteracted by the partial drying up of the "salkas"* by the wind. Our total supply when augmented by every drop we could squeeze out of the water bottles amounted to just over one and a half drums full, or six or seven gallons. The only complete drumful was the one we had luckily brought with us from Tadeghat, and, as it proved, it saved our lives. The two drums, containing all that stood between us and an unpleasant death from thirst, I kept locked under my own eye and retained the keys myself. I had a few tins of the smallest size of tinned milk, but that was not much use as a thirst-quencher. Now to decide the question of how the supply was to be rationed. When and where we were to obtain any more Heaven alone knew, and the only thing to do seemed to be to limit the ration to the smallest possible quantity conducive to keeping us alive, and a little less than a mugful each daily was decided upon.

Atahair said that when he had gone off on his own from Taghazi the Tuaregs he had met had mentioned to him the whereabouts of some Ahaggaren Tuaregs grazing their camels in the neighborhood of Katelet, and he suggested that he and Mahomed should go off in search of them. If they were found all would be well. I acceded to his request, and they left in the afternoon, Mahomed riding the strongest of the baggage camels. Mahomed had returned, having failed to move my camel.

The remaining members of the party then set about a search in the surrounding country with the hope of finding an isolated and hidden waterhole, which might possibly have previously escaped notice. The bluff under the side of which we were camped was rectangular in shape, and so regular in its lines that it might almost have been the work of human hands. The flat and sheer sides rose up out of a sloping heap of disintegrated rock which had gradually piled up at the base, and ended at their upper extremities with corrugated edges, which from a distance had the appearance of battlements and tended to give the impression that this rugged outcrop was the relic of some ancient fortress. At its northwestern corner it was joined by a saddle to the main formation of bleak and rocky hills, of which it formed a southern spur. Surrounding us on all sides except the south were other groups of these bare and desolate hills of broken and heaped-up rock. The ground surface between the rocks was sandy and fairly level. The most

* Waterskins (Hausa).

likely places for finding water appeared to be up in the torrent beds with which some of these hills were gashed, and it was up in these that the remainder of the day was spent. Clambering over enormous boulders and flat rocks, searching in the hollows scooped out in the sand at their bases on a happier day when rain had fallen and rushed down the steep slope in a bubbling and sparkling torrent, scratching out the sand in the torrent bed; but always with the same result—not a drop of moisture was to be found anywhere. An exceptionally long period had elapsed all over this region of the Sahara since rain had fallen—and everywhere was dry, dry as sun-bleached bones.

We wandered back to camp that evening one by one, all with the same doleful news, beginning now to feel thirsty and realizing that there is not much satisfaction in only a mugful of water a day. The very knowledge of the fact that there was so little water tended to make you feel more thirsty than you really were, and never in my life have I missed anything so much as those mugs of hot, steaming tea with which I had been accustomed to regale myself on the completion of a day's march.

Atahair and Mahomed returned the following afternoon with the news that they had found nothing, the former having found no clue as to where we were—in fact, he said he was quite lost. My feelings toward him now were far from brotherly, for it was obvious that he must have wandered from the correct route days before and, instead of informing me, had kept it quietly to himself, hoping either to meet Tuaregs who could put him right or by a stroke of good luck to regain the route. When I had commented on what my compass showed to be a tendency to travel more into the west than I calculated we should have done, not a word of his deviation from the right route had he mentioned, but had calmly left me under the delusion that all was well. Had he only confessed his error, how different things would have been. The water would have been more strictly rationed and the supply conserved, and had the worst befallen we could have retraced our steps to Tadeghat.

What were we to do? The camels, although a little rested, were in a terribly weak condition from lack of food, and the quest for pasture had become equally important, as far as they were concerned, as that for water. The chances of their surviving the six long and exhausting marches back over the grim and barren stretch of desert across which we had just come seemed only too slender; and there was the probability that our previous tracks had been completely obliterated by the wind. Besides, after having surmounted the many difficulties that had arisen all along in attempting to prevent my reaching Djanet, the thought of turning back after having come so far was repugnant. My map gave me no assistance, for it had a very small scale, and it was not possible to rely on its accuracy for anything but very large and general features. Plotting out the bearings I had kept since leaving the last waterhole did not help very much on such a small-scale map, because my calculations of the length of the daily marches had necessarily been approximate, as I had no other means of judging them than by the rate the camels moved and the duration of the day's march. The one thing that appeared more or less certain was that we had come too far to the west, and in order to regain our proper route we must turn into the east. There was one danger in this. If the point we had now reached was some distance south of the parallel of latitude on which Katelet lies, and if, as it would be the simplest thing in the world to do, we missed the waterhole or even the track, we might unwittingly go wandering on into the absolutely unknown desert which stretched away to the east for several hundred miles as far as the Djado region. This, however, had to be risked, and it was decided to move off in a N.N.E. direction, following the line of a small valley between the hills, the next morning.

I made Atahair go off again that afternoon in that direction, and see if he could not pick up some landmark that was familiar to him. He returned in the evening, and said that he thought he could recognize a hill in the distance, and he felt sure that he could bring us to water in three days' time. This was a little more cheering, but my faith in him was somewhat shaken by this time, and I did not feel unduly optimistic.

That night, as I lay in my tent pondering over our predicament, I could not escape the feeling that the whole situation was incongruous and foolish; for so it seemed. It was difficult to reconcile myself with the same person who, just over three months before, had been sitting in the security of a mess verandah in Nigeria, where a call of "Boy!" brought you just what you wanted—or, to be strictly accurate, two or three calls of "Boy!" for the Nigerian native is not noted for his alacrity in answering a summons! But a sore feeling in the throat, and a leathery tongue that impelled a longing glance at the mug containing the remaining third of my day's water ration and all that I could have until the evening of the morrow, forcibly reminded me that there was no doubt but that I was one and the same person.

The next morning, the 12th, we packed up and moved off in a N.N.E. direction, following the line of a sandy valley bordered by hills. It had, of course, been impossible to send back either food or water to the two camels that had been left behind, but the precarious position in which the whole party stood had rather reduced thought of them to a place of secondary importance. Nevertheless, it was with the greatest reluctance that I had to leave them to a slow death from thirst and starvation.

After wending our way through the hills for an hour we saw the welcome sight of a patch of dried grass growing under the shelter of a steep-sided gap between hills which would have escaped notice unless you were actually traveling through the gap itself. We stopped here and let the camels feed, and I gave orders for as much of the grass as could be carried to be made into bundles. Atahair, however, interjected with a remark that this was unnecessary, for he now recognized some small features that he knew, and there was plenty of grass ahead. Still I demurred, for it seemed wisest to take every advantage of what we were quite sure of rather than rely on the hypothetical existence of what was in front of us, and, besides, it seemed odd that he had not noticed it during his excursions from camp, for he must have ridden considerably further afield than this. He continued to persist in its existence, and knowing that in this broken type of country it was simple to pass very close to an object without seeing it, I decided to push on without wasting any time, for it appeared that he really had got his bearings at last. For the remainder of the day not a single blade of grass did we see.

The whole of that day we spent in marching over completely barren country, made up for the most part of small semi-sand and rock hills. The faint track of one camel pad pointing in an easterly direction to a range of hills which appeared to run north and south and was discernible in the distance made us swing our course round until we were traveling about due east. Pasture was more likely to be found growing in the shelter of a range such as that, and there might be more likelihood of finding water there. Sunset arrived with not a vestige of vegetation in sight, the only change in the landscape being that the hills had become larger and more scattered. The range was still a long way off. It was an exhausted and low-spirited party that wearily off-loaded the camels that night. Not a scrap of wood with which to kindle a fire for protection from the biting wind; not a mouthful for the camels to eat; and we were reduced again to tearing up the straw saddle pads to give them, which were little better than nothing at all. They just knelt huddled together gazing listlessly at one another, and I wondered how many of them would get through another day such as this. One of the smaller of them had only just struggled in, and had needed urging along most of the way, even though we had disposed of its load.

Despondency was beginning to possess the natives, and all were praying hard and calling on Allah to send water. It required a little effort to maintain a cheerful countenance and to assure them that all would be well in the end, and that I knew we should find water. While I lay trying to make myself eat something Sakari came over from the natives' shelter, which was only a few yards from mine, and asked me if I would give him one of my biscuits. I asked him what he wanted it for, and he said as an offering to Allah, which they were all making, and they would like the "Bature" to give something, too. I gave it to him and watched him put it in a small calabash containing contributions from each of the natives. Then they all stood up in front of it, while Sakari called on Allah to send us water, bowing in unison with him and giving vent to frequent cries of "Allah! Ba mu ruwa."* There was something terribly pathetic about those earnest but simple figures as they stood there shivering in the night wind, and I could not altogether escape a guilty feeling that it was I who was responsible for their being in this position; for but for me they would never have come to this merciless desert.

The march over this dreary desolation was resumed soon after sunrise, still making for the range of hills, which I calculated we should reach that evening. Two or three hours were sufficient for the young camel which had been so weak the previous day. It just sank down on its knees, and nothing that we could do would move it. It, at any rate, need not be left to a lingering death, and I put it out of its misery with my revolver and hurried on. My reason for hurry was that I did not desire to be a spectator of the operation that the natives were now going to perform on it; and that was to open its stomach and extract what fluid remained inside. They caught me up some minutes afterward and showed me two large French water bottles which they had managed to fill. Thirsty as I was, never once during the day did I feel tempted to go to one of those water bottles—rather did the thought of it fill me with sickness. The fluid was not drunk by the natives either, but they used it for cooking their food with that night and the next.

The nearer we got to the range the more open the country became, there being fewer hills and more sand-and-shingle plains. A few rocky stretches had occurred, and here the rock was conspicuous by reason of its bright colors. There were two types: one green, which lay about in large blocks that looked as if they might have been fossilized tree trunks, and the other blue, which was chiefly in a diagonal slate forma-

* "Allah! Give us water."

tion and gave the impression that regularly placed rows of slates had been laid down, but had become rounded off at the edges and partially covered with sand.

By about four o'clock in the afternoon I was beginning to feel desperate—very thirsty and exhausted. Except for a short period of not more than an hour each day, when I rode on top of one of the baggage camels, I had walked the whole distance, and this, combined with the fact that I had eaten practically nothing since we had been on a short water ration, was beginning to have its effect. We were within a few miles of the range, but, scrutinize it through my field glasses as I would, not a sign of vegetation could I see. The prospect of a similar dismal night to the last was before us. But we pushed on.

We had almost reached the range when, on topping the rise at the commencement of a depression in the ground, we espied something white lying ahead. Hurrying forward we discovered, to our great joy, that it was the skeleton of a camel, and lying near it a few pieces of dead wood. Farther on was a small patch of tufted grass which, on reaching it, we found to be in a shallow "agoras"* running parallel to the hills, and on looking along it, we perceived several other similar patches. Our quest for pasture, at any rate, was ended, but the most hopeful discovery was that a faint track could be discerned following the bed of the watercourse.

A more cheerful and hopeful spirit pervaded the party that night. Atahair was bubbling over with optimism, and swore by all he knew that we were on the Katelet-Tighighi track, and that we would reach the latter place by noon the next day. If we did not, he said, I could slay him. Little he realized perhaps the many occasions on which I had felt like doing so. The affair of the patch of grass had been but one of several equally exasperating incidents. On one occasion he had said that he recognized a hill, and that he knew Djanet was only one day's march the other side. This I knew to be ridiculous, for I knew by the map that an expanse of sand dunes lay to the west of the oasis, and we could not get there without crossing it; besides, we were many days away yet. I had no faith in him now whatsoever, but realized that all his wild statements were perhaps just his way of creating a hopeful spirit, and also that if by chance any of them proved correct his prestige as a guide would be partially reinstated. The better outlook and Atahair's prophecy had brought forth a request from Sakari for an extra ration of water, but I had to tell them that I did not share the former's optimism,

* Vegetated watercourse or valley.

and I thought it wiser to keep to the same ration. I did not wish them to become too elated, for, should the next day find us no better off, a contingency for which I was fully prepared, their disappointment would be great. They all seemed to understand, and made no further request. When I was giving out the water I think that I did give them a little extra, however—a full mug instead of a nearly full one.

It was only now that I realized that it was almost impossible for the natives to eat anything at all. Their food consisted of flour and grain chiefly, which must be cooked in order to be eaten, but in order to cook it you need to have water—the one thing we had not got. The small daily allowance was insufficient for drinking purposes, let alone for cooking. From now onwards they used my own stores, but biscuits, chocolate, and a very littly bully beef or tinned salmon did not give them the same satisfaction as their own stodgy food, with which they like to fill themselves. When suffering from thirst it is impossible to eat very much, and the lack of sufficient nourishment was having a very weakening effect on the party.

Following the line of the watercourse in the morning, in places where the surface was not too sandy, tracks were plainly visible, and the increasing amount of vegetation raised our hopes. After two hours' march we came to clearly marked crosstracks where another track cut across the one we were following at right angles. I now began to feel that perhaps Atahair was right. He said that this was the In-Azaoua-Ghat route, and it seemed quite feasible. Still pushing on along the track we had been following, we wound through groups of conical-shaped slag-heap-like hills, finally entering a valley lying in an extensive hilly formation. Here vegetation was thicker, but most of the grass had been chewed up by animals on a previous occasion. Tracks of camels and goats abounded, and this had evidently been a feeding ground for numbers of Tuaregs; but not a sign of life or water could be found.

On we went through the valley for the remainder of the day, and by evening it had narrowed, the vegetation had dwindled to nothing, and we came out on to a small gravel plain. Here we found a patch of grass and pitched camp. Another blank day! Although our failure to find water was not unexpected, the finding of so many traces of Tuaregs had certainly raised our hopes, and inwardly I felt a great disappointment.

A measure that I had resolved to adopt when the situation began to look desperate was that of sending off Atahair on his strong riding camel to ride ahead of us as hard as he could until he did find something, and, if he proved successful in his quest, to bring back water in the skins he would take with him. His camel was still quite strong, and he himself, being a Tuareg and accustomed to long rides and existing on a very little water for a long period, was capable of greater endurance than the remainder. I rather prematurely decided on giving effect to this by reason of a suggestion of the same nature from Sakari that night. His addition to the idea was that he should go with the guide and ride behind him on the riding camel. The natives distrusted the guide, and feared that he might go off without intending to return—a distrust which, to a certain extent, I shared myself. However, I was doubtful whether Sakari's power of endurance would be anything like equal to Atahair's, and told him that we had better risk his going off by himself, as I did not think that he, Sakari, would stand the strain of an exhausting ride on so little water. He insisted that he was quite strong enough, and was so keen that I gave in, and they started off by moonlight that night, taking with them some biscuits and tinned food and the equivalent of two full mugs of water. I impressed on them the importance of making some sort of mark which we could identify at all places where the path was not clear, and in rocky regions where the tracks of their camels could not be seen, so that we should have no difficulty in following them.

We followed on in the morning as fast as our weary, laden camels would allow. It happened to be my birthday, and I could not help hoping that it would bring good luck with it. The most acceptable present that could have been wished for was a large tank of cool, clear water.

Gravel and sand were met with most of the way, where the tracks of the guide's camel were easy to follow; but in the broken rocky stretches in the small regions of hills which sometimes had to be negotiated it was not so easy, although with the aid of the indications left by Sakari we managed to keep to the trail.

We had not traveled for long when it was found that the guide had picked up the tracks of four other camels that looked to be not more than two or three days old. Tracks of goats and donkeys were all visible from time to time. A donkey will not go for more than four days without water, and it was beginning to look as if we really were in sight of safety.

The physical condition of the party was now becoming alarmingly weak. Marching for eight or nine hours a day, mostly on foot, on top of a raging thirst and insufficient nourishment, was having a telling effect, and the limit of the party's endurance was not far distant. Plod, plod along, hour after hour, forcing unwilling feet to keep moving; eager and longing eyes eating up the landscape for some sign of succour, and anxiously topping the crest of every rise, hoping that the view the other side would hold some great and happy surprise. Sometimes I would get ahead of the caravan and, taking advantage of the lead, would lie down to rest, praying the while that they would take a long time to catch me up. One became a little lightheaded, and by noon it seemed that one was living in a trance. The mind seemed to divorce itself from the body, and from somewhere above to look down on the pitiful little group of animals and men that groped its way through this wilderness.

By good fortune, except for odd periods when the wind dropped, it was not hot, and often the sky was cloudy. Had it been really hot we should never have come as far as we had done.

About three o'clock in the afternoon we were approaching an extensive formation of fairly high hills by way of a broad and sandy watercourse when I heard a shout from behind, and on looking round saw that the camels had stopped and Mallam was running toward me. The fact that the latter was running was a sure sign that something unusual was afoot, for in normal circumstances he would have indulged in nothing so undignified. On reaching me I saw that he was clutching a handful of dark earth, and he eagerly told me that he had spotted a dark patch in the bank of the watercourse, and on examining it had found the ground to be damp. I hurried back with him and examined it myself. Sure enough he was correct, and we hastily grabbed our machetes and the one shovel from the backs of the camels and proceeded to dig. For an hour we dug feverishly, but we had to give it up, exhausted and with a terribly increased thirst. Hainja, the camelman, who was experienced in the digging of wells and waterholes, examined the changing color of the earth as we got deeper, and said that the water, if any, was probably very deep down—40 or 50 feet at the least. However, it was decided to camp here for the night and make a further attempt at digging after we had unloaded the camels and rested a while. To move on whilst there was the remotest chance of finding water would have been foolish.

A second attempt lasted little longer than the first, and we abandoned it, having obtained nothing more beneficial than the damp taste of earth sucked through a handkerchief. It seemed maddening that here we were, probably sitting right on top of the one thing that could save us, and yet it was as good as a thousand miles away. All our hopes rested on the guide and Sakari, and eyes were constantly strained for a sign of them returning. They had not returned by the next morning, and we started off again. A few hundred yards from camp we turned off into a broad and very well vegetated valley, where our camels had been pastured during the halt. Here there were countless tracks of camels and goats and donkeys, but not one living soul to be seen. It had obviously been a popular pasture ground for the nomads, but the drying up of pools in the rock had driven them away. Many tracks would lead up to places where pools had been, but always were they found to be dry.

Three hours had passed when we met the other two wearily returning, and by their dejected appearance it was obvious that their quest had been unsuccessful. They had ridden for nearly forty hours with only one halt, but Atahair said that, on coming to the end of the valley which we were following a barren stretch of open desert commenced, and there were no more tracks to follow. I questioned him about the four fairly fresh tracks we had been following but had lost in the mass of footprints near the head of the valley. His reply was not very encouraging, for he said that he thought they were those of robbers from the Fezzan.

Sakari was very "done," and when he dismounted from the camel lay exhausted on the ground. We put him on one of the baggage animals and wearily retraced our steps back to the previous night's camping place. That was a black day, and our last few days' wanderings had drawn a complete blank. But a cheerful face had, as far as it was possible, to be shown, and our thoughts turned to some other direction for a way out of the desperate situation.

We made a third attempt at digging, but that was no more successful than the previous ones. A gang of fit and strong men digging for days would probably not have reached water, should it have existed.

In the afternoon Atahair again went off, accompanied by Mahomed on the strongest baggage camel, to search in the surrounding hills for a possible pool, saying that they would return not later than that night. I had decided that the following day he should go off carrying a S O S note addressed to the Commandant at Djanet, and make off in either one of two directions in which I thought the oasis lay, and to go on until he did find some human beings, however long it took him. There was the possibility that a patrol had been sent from Djanet to meet me, and he might run into it. The question was to decide on which direction, and that I decided to leave until his return and discover his opinion. There appeared to be two possible routes: the first to return to the crosstracks that we had passed on the 14th and there take the easterly branch and follow it up; the second to make off in a N.N.E. direction, following what looked like the faint traces of a track leading toward a mountain range which could be seen in the distance. Either one was pure chance, but something had to be done. The remainder of the caravan, I hoped, would be able to follow in his tracks.

I had studied the map until my eyes were sore trying to reconcile some feature with the surrounding country, but it was useless. The only possible reconciliation I could make was that the mountain range we could see was the same as a rather prominent range marked on the map as Tadent and possessing a permanent waterhole at the northern extremity. On a previous occasion I had cross-examined the guide about this place, but he said he had never heard of it.

Atahair and Mahomed had not returned late that night, but I told Baragai to wake me, should I be asleep, immediately on their return. When I awoke in the morning they were still absent. I was surprised and a little perturbed, for I wanted to get Atahair off as soon as possible. The water ration was down to nearly half a mugful now, and by cutting it down a little more it would last five more days. I made the discovery that the camelmen had commenced opening veins in the camels' necks, and were drinking the blood obtained thereby. I told them that this must stop, for, apart from weakening the camels, I did not want to resort to such a measure until our water supply was completely exhausted. It is apparently a common practice with the Tuareg when he is on a long ride and has no water.

When necessity demands it is strange how one can accustom oneself to doing without that which in normal times would seem indispensable. To refrain from drinking from early morning until nightfall had now become a matter of course, and it was not until camp was pitched that the first drink would be taken. My pipe was a blessing, and I smoked it continuously throughout the day's march. When one was finished and thirst began to take a hold another would be lighted, and so on throughout the march. I had made every experiment I could think of for eking out my miserable mug of water to its fullest benefit, at first by adding a little tinned milk and finally by flavoring it with a few drops of "Alcohol de Menthe," of which I had a very small bottle, obtained in exchange for jam from Campbell at Iferuan. My ration I divided into three parts, one of which I drank after we had made camp, another some time during the evening, after a little food had been eaten, and the other in the morning after a meager breakfast. During many nights this last portion was in grave danger of coming to a sudden and premature end, for on awaking during the night with a throat like the inside of a limekiln it needed a great exercise of will power to resist the longing to grab the mug and gulp down its contents. I had discovered that much more satisfaction was obtained by drinking it out of a spoon. It lasted longer that way, and seemed to be more than if drunk straight off out of the mug.

Sakari, after a long sleep, felt much better, but was still very weak. He had admitted to Baragai that during his ride with the guide the latter had persuaded him to drink urine when they had finished their water. He, the guide, on whom nothing seemed to have much effect, could do this without very serious consequences; not so Sakari, and his condition was no doubt chiefly due to having allowed himself to be persuaded into what he knew was a mad thing to do. After this knowledge had come to light the danger of such foolishness was impressed both on him and on the others, and that under no circumstances were they to resort to this, however great the temptation.

It was an unpleasant situation having Sakari in this condition and not being able to do very much for him. As much extra water as I dared spare, together with a little tinned milk and whisky, was all that could be given to him. A small tot of whisky now preceded the daily issue of water, and the natives much appreciated it for the stimulating effect it gave. They were becoming very low-spirited and beginning to feel that things were hopeless. The one exception was Baragai, whose behavior at this crisis, as it was throughout the journey, was splendid. Suffering as he was himself, he did his utmost to show a cheerful face to adversity, and encouraged the remainder as best he could. I owe a great debt to him for his loyalty during that period.

The day wore on, but still no sign of Atahair and Mahomed, and I was becoming seriously anxious. Welcome as the day's rest had been, I was keen to get the party on the move again, for this enforced inaction and just sitting and waiting was not a thing for which the native temperament was suited.

Another night and day passed without their return. What could have happened to them? What were we to do? To go on waiting or to try and make a move on our own? The fact had gradually forced itself upon me that we had no alternative. Waiting was all that we were physically capable of doing. Looking around the party and seeing their hollow cheeks and eyes and their generally emaciated bodies, the realization came that even if they were capable of performing the heavy task of loading the camels, which was doubtful, anything but the very shortest of marches was a physical impossibility.

So we had to wait, hoping that they had picked up some fresh clue leading to water, but always with the fear lurking at the back of our minds that perhaps they would never return. Short excursions in an easterly direction were made during the day, but all proved abortive. In between whiles one rested, for much exertion left you weakened. My volume of Shakespeare, one of the few books I had with me, was a godsend, for with its help it was possible to become transplanted to an altogether different world.

Still another night went by without their returning, and we entered on the tenth day, January 19th, since it had been discovered that we were lost. A thorough search through the stores was made for anything that might possibly be called drinkable. Even the medicine chest was gone through and most of its contents tasted, but beyond getting a foul taste in my mouth and an increased thirst I did not gain anything from it. "Friar's balsam" is most certainly for external use only! Sakari, although still weaker than the remainder, had bucked up considerably, and suggested that a little Worcester sauce mixed with their food would improve the taste and would not increase their thirst. On trying to open a bottle I was alarmed to discover that I could not pull out the stopper with the strength of my fingers alone, but had to use a knife. I had realized that I had become fairly weak, but not that it was as bad as that.

Later in the morning I sent Hainja down to the camels' feeding place in order to bring one of them back for me to mount and go and reconnoiter. During the last few days the former had shown a somewhat unusual anxiety for the animals' welfare, and whenever I wanted him I was told that "he go for look dem camel." The suspicion that I had formed proved to be correct, for on examining the necks of the camels I discovered that most of them had been punctured. Far from anxiety for their welfare, his numerous visits to the animals had been to quench his thirst. I thought I had noticed a telltale dark stain round his mouth on more than one occasion.

I started off on the camel—or rather with it, for it behaved in a swinish manner and refused to allow me to mount—and made for a hill lying to the N.N.E. with the intention of ascending it and studying the landscape. I left my camel hobbled at the bottom and began to climb the steep rocky side of the hill. The effort of climbing was too exhausting, and I gave it up halfway from the summit and laid myself down to watch from there. The only living things in sight were my camel browsing on some tufts of grass below and a few birds flitting amongst the rocks. After half an hour had gone by I began to find the wind chilly, and descended and started on my way back to camp. I did not go right back, however, but stopped five or six hundred yards short of the camp, and lay basking in the sun behind a rock which sheltered me from the wind. Here I lay for an hour or so, glad to be away from the depressing atmosphere of the camp, and trying to banish the peril of our situation from my mind by daydreams of kinder countries and of all the most refreshing drinks I had tasted in my life, and those I intended having in the future. As I lay sprawled on my back gazing at the blue sky I conjured up a picture of a little English wayside inn, the door leading down below the road level to a spotlessly clean floor sprinkled with sawdust, and on the counter inside a long row of large tankards capped with white froth hiding below it clear and cool depths of beer. I made a vow that on reaching civilization I would walk down a street and have a drink in every place that sold any sort of beverage, be it beer, milk, or lemonade. This was not kept, for when you have plenty you do not appreciate your good fortune but take everything for granted.

I was interrupted in my dreaming by the gentle rustle of something on the sand, and, on looking round, saw that it was the paper cover of the bottle of sauce I had opened in the morning. I do not know, but I suppose it must have been superstition, but the manner in which it had blown straight from the camp to where I was lying made me wonder if anything had happened, and I decided to go back, in case the two absentees should have returned with water. On my closer approach to camp the somnolent figures of the natives did not indicate that there had been any unusual occurrence. Baragai and Mallam awoke and rose when I arrived, and I inquired of the former as to Sakari, and he said that he was all right and still sleeping. I then went to the top of the bank and put an old and torn sheet on two sticks, for it had struck me as I was returning how concealed from view we were, the camp lying right under the bank of the watercourse, which was between four and five feet high, and how easy it would have been for anyone to pass comparatively close on the eastern side but not see us. This done, I went to my little shelter to lie down.

I had hardly settled down when Baragai came over to me, and said in his quaint pidgin English, "Sah, I tink Sakari, him go finish!" I jumped up at this and said, "What do you mean—he go die?" "I tink so, sah!" he answered.

I hurried over to examine him myself. Sure enough, he was dead. Nothing I could do would revive him. Neat whisky was forced between his teeth and every possible means resorted to to bring back some life to him, but all without avail. It came as a great shock and amazement, for I had had no idea that his condition was so precarious. Only the previous morning he had run round the camp to show how much better he felt, and that very morning had been, considering the circumstances, comparatively cheerful. I asked the other two "boys" if they had thought that he was as bad as this, and they both expressed the same surprise. He had been sleeping covered with a blanket, and thinking that he had been still for an unusually long time, they lifted it and found that he was dead. Baragai now told me that he had caught him again drinking urine and had taken it from him. This, on top of the exhausting ride which he had courageously volunteered to undertake, was no doubt the cause of his death. It was a sad blow, for he was a very capable and intelligent type of native, and, considering that he had made a comparatively long visit to England, very little spoiled by his contact with Western civilization. His loss was greatly felt, and emphasized by the fact that we were a small party in a very lonely and desolate place.

We dug his grave up on top of the bank, and there buried him in Mohammedan fashion, lying on his right side facing the east. Mallam, who was very much affected, as Sakari had been his great friend, performed the last rites of the Mohammedan burial service, whilst Baragai and Hainja stood by the grave.

I left them and sat down to look through Sakari's kit, and had not been there many minutes when a cry from Mallam of "Duba, bature; duba, bature; dauke maidubi. Akwoi mutane"* made me run for my field glasses. Approaching down the slope of the watercourse from a southerly direction were some figures, but too distant to recognize with the naked eye. A few seconds' scrutiny through my glasses and I felt like making a tremendous bound in the air for joy. Atahair and Mahomed were returning, and by the presence of an additional man and camel and the prominent bulges on the sides of the camels, which I recognized as filled waterskins, I knew that our ordeal was over. It was a curious fact that water should have arrived at the one moment during that period when our thoughts were not dwelling on the subject, for the recent loss to the party had temporarily expelled it from our minds. More often than not this is the case, and if you are waiting expectantly for the arrival of somebody or something it happens at one of those rare moments when one's thoughts have been diverted in another direction. It was an ironic stroke of Fate that sent the water only a few hours after Sakari had died, although it is doubtful if it would have saved him.

The thought of those bulging skins made me hurry forward to meet the approaching figures, and as I met them Mahomed jumped off his camel without delay, and in no time handed me a calabash of clear, sparkling water. I then had my first proper drink for ten days. I expected to see the calabash empty as if a suction pump were at work on it, but

* "Look, master! Look, master! Get your glasses; there are some men!"

was rather disappointed at the smallness of my swallow, for I could only take one or two inches off the top. It was just as well, because I had only just been impressing on the natives the necessity for being abstemious in their first drink in case of ill-effects after so long an abstinence. They were all very sensible except Hainja, who gulped and gulped away as if he would never stop. The result was that he became violently sick, rather to the secret amusement of the rest of the party, for his behavior during the last few days had been anything but plucky, and he had spent most of his time cowering down underneath a blanket bemoaning his unfortunate fate.

No time was lost in pouring the water from the skins into the drums, where there was no chance of its leaking away. Fires were lighted and water put on to boil in order to make a hot meal for the natives and tea for myself. That first mug of tea was the most exquisite sensation of my life, and closing my eyes, I rolled every drop of it round my tongue. What gave me almost equal pleasure was to watch the poor devils of natives putting some warm slop inside them, and the joyful and thankful expressions on their faces as they did so.

It appeared that Atahair and Mahomed had decided after leaving camp to go back to the crosstracks, and doing this they took the eastern branch. Picking up some fresh camel tracks leading off to the north, they had followed them and found one Asgur Tuareg looking after some camels in the vicinity of a pool known as Taruadi. After a drink and rest they had filled up the skins and returned by the shortest route under the guidance of the nomad. If only we had taken that right-hand turning at the crosstracks! We must have passed within a few miles only of that very pool. It only serves to show the absolute necessity of having a very good guide who knows the actual location of water, for hidden away up amongst the rocks or in a depression in the ground, as the pools or waterholes often are, it is possible to pass within a few hundred yards and be quite ignorant of their existence. Very often, too, there are alternative pools or holes within a few miles of one another, for after a long drought one may dry up quicker than the other, and a first-hand knowledge of both is essential. When I reached Djanet I was told that the commandant, although he had six years' experience of that region, never left the post without a guide.

It had been an unpleasantly critical situation, and the release from the strain of those ten days was as if a tremendous weight had been lying on top of you which had been suddenly lifted. Less than one and a half mugfuls of water each remained, and the party were getting rapidly weaker. The three days' wait had told heavily on the natives, and on several occasions they had asked, "What are you going to do, Master?" and I could only answer, "Wait." They are queer creatures, little more than children, and it was amazing the way they thanked me, who was responsible for ever having brought them to this God-forsaken land, for their deliverance, as if I had personally brought them the water. Baragai seemed to have been more concerned that his master should have had to go without than for his own welfare. That night he opened his heart to me and said: "Sometimes I go tink I no fit to see Nigeria again, but I 'member what you say, dat we go catch water some time and it all be all right for end, and I tink for my heart dat I go see him again."

The undertone of sadness which had pervaded the party at the loss of one of their number gradually wore off, for natives soon forget, and, as Baragai said to Mallam when consoling him, "It is no good for you to worry. Allah says his time has come, and there is no more to say." Soon they were eating, chatting, and laughing away around a large and cheerful fire, with the camp flooded in the brilliant light of a full moon.

The Great Lisbon Earthquake

by SAMUEL CHASE

The following account was written by Chase as a letter to his sister in England. The Lisbon earthquake was probably the most famous of the eighteenth century. It did much to shake up that century's complacency about the sweet reasonableness of nature, and had considerable influence upon the thought of specific philosophers. Chase's account of the quake and consequent fire is extremely graphic and portrays not only his own perilous condition but the emotions and situation of many around him.

ABOUT THREE-QUARTERS AFTER NINE O'CLOCK IN THE MORNing, on Saturday, the 1st of November, 1755, I was alone in my bedchamber, four stories from the ground, opening a bureau, when a shaking or trembling of the earth (which I knew immediately to be an earthquake), gentle at first, but gradually becoming violent, much alarmed me. Turning round to look at the window, the glass seemed to be falling out. Surprised at the continuation of the motion, and calling to mind the miserable fate of Callao, in the Spanish West Indies, I dreaded a like catastrophe; and, remembering that our house was so old and weak that any heavy carriage passing made it shake throughout, I ran directly into the Arada, to see if the neighboring houses were agitated with the same violence. This place was a single room at the top of the house, with windows all round the roof, supported by stone pillars. It was only one story higher than my chamber, but commanded a prospect of some part of the river, and of all the lower part of the city, from the king's palace up to the castle.

I was no sooner up the stairs than the most horrid prospect that imagination can figure appeared before my eyes. The house began to heave to that degree that, to prevent being thrown down, I was obliged to put my arm out of a window and support myself by the wall. Every stone in the wall separating and grinding against each other (as did the walls of the other houses, with variety of different motions), causing the most dreadful jumbling noise ears ever heard. The adjoining wall of Mr. Goddard's room fell first; then followed all the upper part of his house, and of every other as far as I could see toward the Castle. When, turning my eyes quickly to the front of the room (for I thought the whole city was sinking into the earth), I saw the tops of two of the pillars meet, and saw no more. I had resolved to throw myself upon the floor, but suppose I did not; for I immediately felt myself falling, and then, after I know not how long, just as if waking from a dream, with confused ideas, I found my mouth stuffed full of something that with my left hand I strove to get out; and not being able to breathe freely, struggled till my head was quite disengaged from the rubbish. In doing this I came to myself, and, recollecting what had happened, supposed the earthquake to be over; and from what I had so lately seen, expected to find the whole city fallen to the ground, and myself at the top of the ruins. When attempting to look about me, I saw four high walls near fifty feet above me (the place where I lay was about ten feet in length and scarcely two feet wide), without either door or window in any of them. Astonished to the last degree at my situation, I remembered that there was such a place between the houses; and, having seen the upper parts of both fall, concluded that either the inhabitants must be all destroyed, or at least that there was no probability of their looking down there again in time for my preservation; so that, struck with horror at the shocking thought of being starved to death immured in that manner, I remained stupefied, till the still falling tiles and rubbish made me seek for shelter under a small arch in the narrow wall opposite my head as I lay, at the bottom of which there appeared to be a little hole quite through it. Upon approaching the aperture, with difficulty dragging myself out of the rubbish, I found it much larger than I had imagined; and, first getting in my head and arm, by degrees I pulled all my body after, and fell about two feet into a small dark place, arched over at the top, which I supposed to be only a support for the two walls; till, feeling about, I found on one side a narrow passage that led me round a place like an oven, into a little room where stood a Portuguese man covered with dust, who, the moment he saw me coming in that way, started back and, crossing himself all over, cried out, as their custom is when much surprised, "Jesus, Mary, and Joseph! Who are you? Where do you come from?" Of which being informed, he placed me in a chair. This done, clasping his hands together he lifted them and his eyes toward the ceiling, in show of the utmost distress and concern. This made me examine myself, which before I had not leisure to do. My right arm hung down before me motionless like a dead weight, the shoulder being out and the bone broken; my stockings were cut to pieces, and my legs covered with wounds; the right ankle was swelled to a prodigious size, with a fountain of blood spouting upward from it; the knee also was much bruised, and my left side felt as if beaten in, so that I could scarcely breathe; all the left side of my face likewise swelled up—the skin was beat off, and the blood streaming from it; with a great wound above, and a small one below the eye, and several bruises on my back and head. Barely had I perceived myself to be in this mangled condition when another shock, threatening as the first, came on.

The Portuguese flew directly out of the door. The violence of the shock, and the falling of the houses, with the screams of the people, made me again seek shelter below the arch I had entered in at; where waiting till it had abated, I returned back again, and, nobody appearing, went out at the same door I had seen the man do, in hopes to find him again, or meet with some other person; but instead of a room as I expected, it was only a narrow staircase, which with a few steps brought me, to my surprise, into the street, not imagining myself to have been so near it.

The people were all at prayers, covered with dust, and the light appeared as of a dark, cloudy day; when, flattering myself that my legs might still support me to the waterside, I turned and saw the street below (which was very narrow) filled with fallen houses as high as the tops of the remaining ones. I then, in hopes to get into the country, advanced a few steps up the hill, but the same sad prospect appeared above! and in a street to the right I saw no other. I knew not what to do, my strength failed, and I fell prostrate just where the three streets met. I then thought myself so much past all assistance that, though Mr. Branfill, Mr. Goddard, and their people came to the very spot where I lay, I spoke not to any of them, although they stood close by me, till Mr. John Ernest Jorg, a German, and merchant of the city of Hamburg, coming to his door, told them he saw no way for their escaping out of the city; therefore begged they would go up into a garden he had by the top of his house, which was the safest place he knew of. This they complied with, and how long afterward I lay there I know not; but, recovering a little strength, I raised myself up, and set my back against the wall of this gentleman's house, who appearing again at his door, I heard him say, "What miserable wretch is this? He seems by his dress to be a stranger"; and coming down from his door round to the other side of my face, he cried out, "Dear Mr. Chase, what a shocking sight is this! Let me carry you upstairs, and try what we can do for you."

My answer was, "Many thanks, but it is now too late." "Never think so," said he; "I hope the worst is past, and you shall have the very first assistance that can be procured": then calling some of his people, he had me conveyed upstairs, and put me in a chair till he had got me something to drink; and a bed being made ready, he laid me there, desiring me to compose myself as much as possible. But he had not left me long before another shock made me lay my left arm over my eyes, expecting soon to be released from further misery, till all the plaster falling from the walls covered the beds, causing such a dust that I was roused to exert all my strength to open the door just at the bed's head, and get out.

The noise I made soon brought Mr. Jorg out of his garden, when, begging of him to lay me there with the other people, to abide the common chance, he said there was a room on one side of it, and he would order a bed to be made ready immediately. He placed me there accordingly, telling me he had already sent for the English surgeon, Mr. Scrafton; but his house was down, and there was no knowing what had become of him.

Mr. Jorg and Mrs. Goddard came constantly between the shocks (now much less violent and frequent), to offer me their assistance; and during one of the intervals Mr. Jorg and his uncle dressed my leg with some plasters that they happened to have in the house.

Mr. Jorg's uncle would not go into the garden during the shocks, but remained in the house, declaring he had lived a long time, and, if it so pleased Providence, he was as ready to die in that manner as in any other. Mrs. Goddard also acquainted me with the deaths of several already known (whose fate I then thought much happier than my own), and that three fires had broken out in the city, which did not then alarm me much. One of the fires and a large part of the city I could see from the bed as I lay, for it was now again at the top of a high house, some part of which had fallen, and the remainder was much shattered.

About two o'clock, the earth having enjoyed some little respite, the cloud of dust was dissipated, and, the sun appearing, we began to hope the worst was over; as, indeed, it was with regard to earthquakes, but still every succeeding shock, though it did little harm, was attended with the same dread and terror as the foregoing ones. However, this made the people in the garden (consisting of English, Irish, Dutch, and Portuguese) recover spirits enough to think of attempting to get out of the ruinous city; when Mr. Jorg, wholly intent on assisting everybody, desired them only just to stay to eat some fish he had ordered to be got ready, and they would then be the better enabled to bear any future fatigue. To oblige his great care, I ate a little, without any inclination; imagining, from the painful condition I was in, a very few hours more would release me from further suffering; nor did anybody hitherto flatter me with other hopes. This was one reason, as well as knowing that all people were so intent upon their own preservation as not to be at leisure to assist others, that I suffered Mr. Jorg's garden by degrees to grow quite empty—and Mr. Branfill, Mr. Goddard, and their people, after dining and taking leave of me, to go away without asking their assistance, or even desiring them to send any help to me, till finding Mr. Jorg was left with only his old uncle, an old lame lady of his acquaintance, whom he had sent his servants to fetch from her house (where she was left alone, and very probably would have perished had he not thought of her), and two or three of his people; and supposing he intended to quit his house, I begged of him to endeavor to hire some people to carry me out of town. He said he feared it would be impossible—that all his servants but one had left him, and the city was quite deserted; that if it was my request, he would try, but for his own part, he was determined to take the fate of his house, as he thought venturing out of it would be only to encounter greater danger; and in my condition he would advise me to do the same. This assurance quite satisfied me, little imagining how much more distress I had still to support.

All that afternoon I passed in most melancholy reflections, while the flames spread everywhere within my view with inexpressible swiftness, till about five o'clock they seemed approaching close to the window of the room where I lay. Mr. Jorg then came in, and, looking at me without speaking, which hitherto he had always done, retired, shutting the door close after him. Full of suspicions from what he had before said, that there was no assistance to be had, I was struck by the stillness in the adjacent room, and with difficulty raising myself up, listened a considerable time without hearing anything stir, when I concluded that he had found himself obliged to leave his house, and, lacking courage to tell me the horrid fate I must submit to, he had quitted it without speaking at all.

In the utmost agony of body and mind, I determined to ascertain if this were the case; and if so, to endeavor, if possible, to reach the gallery on the east side of the window, and, by throwing myself down the hill, put an end to all my excessive miseries at once.

By the help of two chairs I just got within reach of the door, with the greatest pain, and was then so spent I was obliged to sit down, nor could I have gone a step farther had the room been on fire. Recovering a little strength, I opened the door and found Mr. Jorg, the old lady, and two persons, all silently sitting round the outer room. Surprised to see me got so far, he asked me the reason of it; to which I replied that, as I was fully sensible both of the great distress we were reduced to, and of his inability to assist me, I begged (with tears in my eyes) as the greatest favor, that before he found himself obliged to quit his house, he would either throw me over the gallery, or in any other way dispatch me, and not leave me in agony, lingering a few hours, to die a dreadful death! He desired me not to talk in that manner, and assured me most affectionately he never had intended to leave me, and if no other help came, he would himself carry me upon his back, and we should take our chance together—that the fire had not yet surrounded us, and that there was still a passage free to the Seorio do Paco (a large square before the king's palace), and, as soon as necessity obliged us, he hoped we might all get there very safe; therefore I had much better lie down again, and he would be careful to acquaint me in time. But as I still suspected that only his good nature made him promise this, I desired to stay with them, which he permitted me; going up himself every half-hour to the top of his house, to observe what progress the fire made; till about eleven o'clock, when there came two servants of a German gentleman, who I think was his nephew, at that time also in the house.

Mr. Jorg then declared he thought it time to remove; and with great composure going for his hat and cloak, returned with a cap and quilt for me, telling me perhaps I might find it cold when I was carried out; and then desired the German gentleman and his servants to carry me to the square first, and return again to fetch the lame lady.

They carried me in one of the room chairs, with the quilt over me (which proved afterward of great service), and another person went before with a torch. I heard some poor wretches begging for help as I was carried through a narrow alley down a steep hill, which was the only passage left free from ruins.

To find myself thus, so much beyond all expectation, suddenly relieved from the constant apprehension of falling houses and dangers of the fire (as I thought, at least), when I was in the greatest despair, and had given up all hopes of assistance, raised my spirits to that degree that now, for the first time, notwithstanding the great pain I was in, I began to hope it was possible still to live, till new terrors employed my thoughts. For the people, all full of the notion that it was the day of judgment, and

willing therefore to be employed in good works, had loaded themselves
with crucifixes and saints; and men and women equally the same, during
the intervals between the shocks, were either singing litanies, or cruelly
tormenting the dying with religious ceremonies; and whenever the earth
trembled, all on their knees roaring out *"Misericordia!"* in the most
dismal voice imaginable. The fear, then, that my presence might excite
their fanaticism at such a time, when all government was at an end (and
it was impossible to guess what turn their furious zeal might take against
that worst of criminals, a heretic), made me dread the approach of every
person. Add to this, that the Caista Pedra (or stony quay), adjoining to
this square, had already sunk, and the least rising of the water would
overflow us all. In such reflections there passed about two hours, during
which time Mr. Jorg and his family were come to the square to Mr.
Grave's family. The fire was now almost opposite, and under the shed,
which had at first been quite crowded, there was nobody left but myself;
when I heard a cry of "Beat down the cabaras" (stalls), some of which,
it seems, had taken fire; and, telling all that were under them to get out,
they began immediately to knock down that where I lay. With the greatest
difficulty I got myself out before it tumbled down; and, meeting with Mr.
Jorg and another person, they carried me to Mr. Grave's family, and
laid me on their bundles.

Mrs. Graves I found to be of the common opinion that it was the last
day; and, attempting to persuade her to the contrary, she told me it was
but of little consequence to us, as the fire was just approaching to the
gunpowder shops opposite, and she expected they would blow up every
moment. This new terror stopped my further speaking, and we silently
waited the event, which proved, however, most favorable; for there were
only three explosions, one after the other, making a great report, but not
attended with mischief.

About this time a poor Irish beggarwoman who seemed to be half mad,
putting her trust in some saint with a strange name, went through the fire
in the Rua Nora to Mr. Houston's cellar, and brought from thence a
bottle of wine to Mr. Graves, from whom she would receive no gratuity at
such a time as that. Of this Mrs. Adford gave me some.

On Sunday morning, about five o'clock, the wind changing, it blew
very fresh, and drove the fire with the utmost rapidity down the hill from
the cathedral to one side of the square, which obliged us immediately to
move; and their blacks, carrying me opposite to the customhouse, left me
there till they had conveyed their master's bundles to the other side. But

so quick was the progress of the flames that they presently seized upon the customhouse, bursting out all at once with a violent heat.

I attempted to get away, but was unable; so remained scorching there till Mr. Jorg removed me; and the blacks came and conveyed me again to Mrs. Graves's family, laying me, as before, on their bundles.

We were now very near the palace, the roof of which had already tumbled in, and the fires were so much decreased that there seemed to be but little left to burn, and we apprehended no danger except from the falling of the walls, almost all of which were still standing.

About nine o'clock, the sun shining very bright, some boats came to the shore and carried off a number of persons. A young man, son to our housekeeper, finding me out, told me he was endeavoring to hire a boat to carry his mother (also much hurt, and then in the square) on board ship, and asked me to go with them. To this I hardly answered in the affirmative, supposing all the danger from the fire to be over, and therefore unwilling to leave only my friend, Mr. Jorg, behind me.

We were now again in a crowd of people with their bundles, all endeavoring to procure boats. Among them I saw Mr. George Barclay lying on a mattress, who had (as I learned afterward) one of his feet smashed by a stone; but I saw no more either of him or the housekeeper's son. Mr. Jorg, returning from the waterside, desired us all to remove thither, or else it would be impossible to procure a boat, for the moment they reached the shore they were filled with people. This was directly complied with, and I found the cool air from the water very refreshing; but it did not long continue so; for in a little time it grew excessively hot, and we soon perceived that the fire, which we imagined we had left so far behind us, had crept along through the low buildings by the waterside, and was just breaking out in a penthouse close by us. This obliged our immediate return into the square; soon after which the fire, by means of a large quantity of timber which lay upon the shore, gained the end of the palace next to the water, and there, to our great surprise, blazed out fresh again, though it had seemed before to be almost extinguished; and presently we found ourselves every way surrounded with such a shower of ashes from the timber by the waterside, that, to keep them off, I was forced (notwithstanding the violent heat) to close my quilt quite over my face. About this time two chaise *machos* (or mules), with all their furniture on, were running about loose. The harness of one of them caught fire, and, blazing all over its back, made the mule gallop with the greatest violence backward and forward over the people, the other following; while I, unable to get out of the way, lay listening to the screams of the people to guess the distance they might be from me, till I heard somebody cry out, "You are on fire!" and, feeling my quilt snatched away, saw it thrown on the ground, where the fire being stamped out with their feet, the quilt was returned to me again.

I then told Mrs. Graves if she did not remove we should be on fire again; that it was better to go into the corner of the square (where the entrance to the palace had been), the only place free from bundles, and whither the wind did not blow the flames, and run the risk of the falling of the walls, than to remain there for the certainty of the fire; but Mrs. Graves, whose spirits were quite exhausted, replied that it was impossible to go anywhere to avoid it; that having already removed several times to no purpose, she would stir no farther.

Mr. Jorg, however, told me that, if I desired it, he would carry me there, and accordingly did so with the help of the blacks, and, placing me upon a small bundle of a Portuguese, they returned. Soon after I heard several Portuguese men and women encouraging each other to attempt an escape through the ruins of the palace, and soon, mounting over the rubbish, they disappeared. Just then part of an arch, through which they were supposed to pass, fell in, causing a kind of compassionate cry among the people; but as none of them returned, I concluded they were successful. About an hour after, the fire still gaining ground, I attracted the attention of a Portuguese woman, who began her prayers in a melancholy tone, holding a crucifix over my head, and the people on their knees, forming a circle round us, joined with her.

As this was what I had all along much feared would happen, I waited the event with the utmost horror, and had determined to feign insensibility, when she abruptly stopped, and immediately the dismal roar of *"Misericordia!"* always attendant on the earthquakes (of which there had been several uncounted by me, as the fire had become the more threatening danger), made me expect another shock; but, perceiving no motion, I was surprised, and, venturing to open my quilt, I saw all kneeling down, and that the great square was full of flames; for the people from the adjoining streets had filled it with bundles, which they had left there when the increase of the fire had driven themselves away. These bundles were now all in a blaze, except just in one corner, and under the palace walls, whither Mr. Graves's family had retired; but as the wind blew very fresh and drove the flames in sheets of fire close slanting over our heads, expecting them every minute to seize upon us, I lost all my spirits, and, again abandoning myself to despair, thought it was still impossible, after so many escapes, to avoid the sort of death I most dreaded.

After some time passed in these dreadful apprehensions, the wind suddenly abated, and the fire, burning upward, made no farther progress. This again restored hope to us, and hunger obliged those that had provisions to think of eating, when an Irish Roman Catholic gentlewoman sitting near me asked if my name was not Chase, and said she knew my father many years, and gave me a large piece of watermelon and some bread and water. Mr. Jorg also, soon after, brought me some bread, and, carrying me on his back to Mr. Graves's family, left me there; and presently after, going himself with his uncle and the old lady to the waterside (to which there was now a passage, the penthouses being burned down), and not returning soon, I began to imagine they were gone, till it was confirmed to me, by Mr. Waubbes (who was the gentleman that assisted in bring me to the square) saying that "he was surprised Mr. Jorg had left me at last." But, for my own part, I had more reason to be surprised he had not done it before, and to think myself very happy that, after saving my life so many times, he had not deserted me till the most threatening dangers were almost over. Therefore, far from making any complaints, I only wished him the utmost happiness, excited thereto by the warmest gratitude for my preservation. However, as he had been almost the only person that had showed me any attention, I could not but be very uneasy at my present situation; and, determining to exert myself as much as possible, now I had nobody left to depend upon for assistance, I applied immediately to Mr. Graves to beg a place in the boat he was endeavoring to procure for his family; to which he replied, "that his own family was sufficient to fill any boat he was likely to get; that it was no time for ceremony; therefore he could not pretend to offer any such thing." Surprised at such an answer, especially as the boats on that river are so large, I asked if his black servants were reckoned part of his family, or, if not, whether he would permit me to employ one of them to try to hire a boat for me? To which Mr. Waubbes (to whom one of the blacks, it seemed, belonged) directly answered I was welcome to his servant to go wherever I pleased. Mr. Graves also said I might if I liked it, but that it was impossible to get a boat, even if I was to offer a hundred mocdas for one. Knowing that I could not be in a worse situation, I accepted their offers directly, and desired one of the blacks to go immediately to the waterside, to wait there, and to endeavor to procure me a place in a boat, telling him I would give him a thirty-six-shilling piece to get me conveyed up the river to the Convent of Madre de Dios, and to carry me thence to Mr. Hake's house, just by it, upon his back; to make the best bargain he could, and the remainder to be for himself.

After which, if I remember well, Mr. Graves having removed us more into the square, nearer to the waterside, placed his own family in a great glass coach, which stood at a little distance, leaving only the maidservant with her bundles, upon which I was laid. There came to her then a poor boy, who seemed to have a crust over his face, begging earnestly for some water. There being but little left, he was refused. He laid himself down, and, shrieking in the most dreadful agonies, prevailed with her to give him all that there was. Soon after, seeing the two women who had given me the melon going with a man toward the waterside, I desired Mr. Graves's maid to apply to them, to ask them if they had any room in their boat, but she was answered in the negative. I begged of her also to call to the watermen, who began now to appear. At last one of them came. I offered him half a moidore, which he refused, saying they were sent only for the servants of the palace—however, that he would go and consult with his companions upon it. About three o'clock, as I suppose, we began to hear a dreadful rumbling noise underground. It seemed to proceed from under the ruins of the palace—as if the earth had opened there, and the river was rushing in, forcing great stones along with it. The cause of it I could not tell, but it continued till my departure.

Mr. Houston, a coffeehouse man, with whom I had not the least acquaintance, seeing the miserable condition I lay in, came and offered me any assistance in his power. I asked him directly if he was attempting to quit the square before night; to which he answered he was not, because he wanted to carry away with him some pieces of holland he had saved, and for which he supposed he should hardly be able to procure a conveyance before the next day. I desired him to bring them and sit down by me, which he complied with, to my very great satisfaction; for I almost despaired of receiving any further assistance from Mr. Graves's family; and, as the night was coming on, I knew not what would become of me without some friendly help. Some time afterward, when I had given up all hopes of their return, came the two watermen, and offered to carry me, provided they were paid beforehand.

Mr. Houston said it was too much, which would have been of little consideration to me at such a time, had not the black boy returned also to tell me he had agreed for a place for eighteen shillings, and that I must go directly. With the greatest joy imaginable I desired him to take me on his back; nor do I know why I did not ask Mr. Houston to go with me, or why he did not himself offer it. I took my leave of him and of Mr. Graves's family, who were all just returned from the glass coach, and were in tears, disputing among themselves (the cause I did not then know).

Mr. Jorg's partner, Mr. Brockleman, was with them, who came ashore in a ship's boat on purpose to carry them away; but, as I learned afterward, they would not accept his offer, because his boat was not large enough to carry all of them and their bundles together at once; they therefore chose rather to remain in the square another night than divide.

We were once more put to great distress by the fire; and Mr. Houston, in the confusion endeavoring to save their bundles, lost his own pieces of holland; however, the next day they all got away safe.

But to return to myself; another black boy offered to attend me. I made no objection, and between the two was conveyed into a large boat almost full of people, and there laid upon a board along the middle of it. A priest that came in afterward treading upon my lame leg, the increase of pain almost overcame me; however, the coolness of the water, which was very smooth and pleasant, and the evening fine, soon brought me to myself. Going a little way up the river, just beyond the fire, the boat stopped at the Ribeira, or fish market—a large place—from which there was an open way along the riverside into the country. The people were all put on shore; and, to my great surprise, they were going to put me there likewise. Vexed to the last degree at my disappointment, I exerted all the spirits I had left, and told them that they might see in my condition it was to no purpose to set me on shore there; if they could not comply with their agreement I desired to be carried back to the place whence they had brought me, where the fire had almost spent itself, rather than be placed here to meet with it again.

One of them said he knew nothing of any such agreement, that his partner was wrong to make it, for they belonged to a town on the other side of the river, and could not have time sufficient. I desired them to carry me as far as they could, and they accordingly proceeded forward. I saw Mr. Home going on shore in a ship's boat, but did not speak to him.

When we came to the Horse Guards, at the end of the city, the watermen said the tide was turning, and, muttering together, I heard them call me a heretic and the blacks devils; so that I was glad to be rid of them at any rate, and was but roughly put on shore, where, deeming it unsafe they should know I had more money about me than the thirty-six-shilling piece, I chose rather to send the blacks with one of the boatmen to get the change, and remained myself lying on the ground close to the water, during which a Galician porter came and offered to carry me anywhere I pleased for eighteen shillings; but as the night was coming on I had not confidence sufficient to trust him. Upon their return, which seemed to me a long time at first, the boatman asked me whether I did not think he had run away with my money; then said it was not good, and talked in an odd kind of manner, to which I made no reply. The black boys also showed no inclination to go any farther, saying they could not get back to their masters in the night unless the watermen would wait, as by their agreement at first they had promised to do. This the watermen said they would still comply with, if they made haste back again, upon which they set out, carrying me by turns on their shoulders, often setting me down to rest themselves, for they were so weakly that I expected them every step to tumble. The distance, I think, cannot be above a mile, but it seemed to us then a long way indeed; and it was with great difficulty I prevailed with them to get on as far as Mr. Hake's *juinte*, or country house. The road was pretty full of people going silently along with the most dejected countenances. At one of their resting places the blacks put me upon some stone steps leading up to a nobleman's house, which brought the ladies to the window. Imagining I was coming to them, they told me that part of the large house of retirement for widows had just tumbled down. At last they brought me, almost overcome with the increase of pain, to the first gate of Mr. Hake's garden, which, standing open, we went in, and found the walk leading to the house full of people; but as it was growing dark I could not distinguish them.

I asked, however, immediately, if Mr. Hake were living, and if he were there; neither of which they knew. Proceeding on a little farther, I heard a man speaking English, and, repeating the same question to him, was only answered that he had lost his wife and three fine children; and even at the house, which was standing, they either knew nothing or did not mind me; whence, concluding that the family had quit the place, most likely to go on board ship, I was quite in despair what to do with myself, when Mr. Joseph Hake, who was at some distance, astonished to hear the voice of a person he had been informed the preceding day was either dead or dying, called out in the greatest surprise to tell his father and mother, and came running immediately to me.

Mr. Hake said that he had believed my case to be desperate, and therefore had wished most heartily to hear I was released from suffering. They received me in the most affectionate manner possible, which filled me with so much joy to be taken so much notice of, that I could not help telling Mr. Hake that I sincerely thanked God for lengthening out my days to die under his protection.

They carried me to a tent made of carpets under a vine walk where their beds were placed, and gave me some strong wine and bread and butter, at that time exquisite and refreshing to me; but they feared to give me as much as I would have desired. The two black boys I joyfully dismissed, equally pleased with eighteen shillings each.

On the Tuesday, Mr. Scrafton, the surgeon, came to me with great difficulty from Belem; said he was almost pulled to pieces by the people, and, confirming the former opinion of my case, told me he was very glad to hear I had fallen into such good hands as he esteemed the bonesetter's to be. [The bone-setter was a man who had already examined and treated his wounds.]

Mr. Hake from the first assured me of his assistance and protection; yet when I heard the clamor of the starving people for bread, threatening to break in upon us (so that we were forced to eat our victuals almost by stealth), as also the variety of reports of robberies and murders which were committed all around us, while all government was at an end, and at the same time the English were pressing him for his own safety to go on board ship, I expected every day necessity would force him to compliance, and should that happen I knew not whither to look with hope.

With what gratitude then did my heart overflow (a gratitude which no time can ever efface) to hear him declare, when earnestly entreated to go on board a ship of which he himself was an owner, and where there was a place reserved for him, that he could not leave his family. On being told they would make room for his sons, he said he not only meant his sons, but myself also, whom he could not abandon in so distressful a condition, and therefore it would be in vain to mention it any more to him.

And, indeed, in every respect he most fully complied with his promise to me, carrying me on board the aforementioned ship on Saturday, the 29th of November.

The next day she sailed for England with twenty-four passengers, being the second ship after the earthquake; the *Expedition* packet, Captain William Clies, having sailed about ten days before us with seventeen passengers.

The Champawat Man-Eater

by JIM CORBETT

I know of no hunter whom I would rather read than Corbett; no sportsman either, and I am tempted to say no naturalist. Not the least astonishing thing about this extraordinary British citizen—he recently retired from India to Nairobi, in Africa—is that, despite his fabulously intimate encounters with man-eating tigers and leopards, some of whom hunted him while he thought he was hunting them, he never lost a sportsman's fairness toward them. Great hunter and brilliant writer— his accounts are amazingly observant and detailed—he also deserves to be called a great man, whose essential spirit, despite his modesty, rises out of his books. There is no doubt that in his field he is unsurpassed and a genius.

I WAS SHOOTING WITH EDDIE KNOWLES IN MALANI WHEN I first heard of the tiger which later received official recognition as the "Champawat man-eater."

Eddie, who will long be remembered in this province as a sportsman *par excellence* and the possessor of an inexhaustible fund of shikar yarns, was one of those few, and very fortunate, individuals who possess the best of everything in life. His rifle was without equal in accuracy and striking power, and while one of his brothers was the best gun shot in India, another brother was the best tennis player in the Indian Army. When therefore Eddie informed me that his brother-in-law, the best shikari in the world, had been deputed by Government to shoot the Champawat man-eater, it was safe to assume that a very definite period had been put to the animal's activities.

The tiger, however, for some inexplicable reason, did not die, and was

128

causing Government a great deal of anxiety when I visited Naini Tal four years later. Rewards were offered, special shikaris employed, and parties of Gurkhas sent out from the depot in Almora. Yet in spite of these measures, the toll of human victims continued to mount alarmingly.

The tigress, for such the animal turned out to be, had arrived in Kumaon as a full-fledged man-eater, from Nepal, whence she had been driven out by a body of armed Nepalese after she had killed two hundred human beings, and during the four years she had been operating in Kumaon had added two hundred and thirty-four to this number.

This is how matters stood when shortly after my arrival in Naini Tal I received a visit from Berthoud. Berthoud, who was Deputy Commissioner of Naini Tal at that time, and who after his tragic death now lies buried in an obscure grave in Haldwani, was a man who was loved and respected by all who knew him, and it is not surprising therefore that when he told me of the trouble the man-eater was giving the people of his district, and the anxiety it was causing him, he took my promise with him that I would start for Champawat immediately on receipt of news of the next human kill.

Two conditions I made, however: one that the Government rewards be canceled, and the other, that the special shikaris, and regulars from Almora, be withdrawn. My reasons for making these conditions need no explanation, for I am sure all sportsmen share my aversion to being classed as a reward-hunter and are as anxious as I am to avoid the risk of being accidentally shot. These conditions were agreed to, and a week later Berthoud paid me an early morning visit and informed me that news had been brought in during the night by runners that a woman had been killed by the man-eater at Pali, a village between Dabidhura and Dhunaghat.

In anticipation of a start at short notice, I had engaged six men to carry my camp kit, and leaving after breakfast, we did a march the first day of seventeen miles to Dhari. Breakfasting at Mornaula next morning, we spent the night at Dabidhura, and arrived at Pali the following evening, five days after the woman had been killed.

The people of the village, numbering some fifty men, women, and children, were in a state of abject terror, and though the sun was still up when I arrived I found the entire population inside their homes behind locked doors, and it was not until my men had made a fire in the courtyard and I was sitting down to a cup of tea that a door here and there was cautiously opened, and the frightened inmates emerged.

I was informed that for five days no one had gone beyond their own doorsteps—the insanitary condition of the courtyard testified to the truth of this statement—that food was running short, and that the people would starve if the tiger was not killed or driven away.

That the tiger was still in the vicinity was apparent. For three nights it had been heard calling on the road, distant a hundred yards from the houses, and that very day it had been seen on the cultivated land at the lower end of the village.

The Headman of the village very willingly placed a room at my disposal, but as there were eight of us to share it, and the only door it possessed opened on to the insanitary courtyard, I elected to spend the night in the open.

After a scratch meal which had to do duty for dinner, I saw my men safely shut into the room and myself took up a position on the side of the road, with my back to a tree. The villagers said the tiger was in the habit of perambulating along this road, and as the moon was at the full I thought there was a chance of my getting a shot—provided I saw it first.

I had spent many nights in the jungle looking for game, but this was the first time I had ever spent a night looking for a man-eater. The length of road immediately in front of me was brilliantly lit by the moon, but to right and left the overhanging trees cast dark shadows, and when the night wind agitated the branches and the shadows moved, I saw a dozen tigers advancing on me, and bitterly regretted the impulse that had induced me to place myself at the man-eater's mercy. I lacked the courage to return to the village and admit I was too frightened to carry out my self-imposed task, and with teeth chattering, as much from fear as from cold, I sat out the long night. As the gray dawn was lighting up the snowy range which I was facing, I rested my head on my drawn-up knees, and it was in this position my men an hour later found me—fast asleep; of the tiger I had neither heard nor seen anything.

Back in the village I tried to get the men—who I could see were very surprised I had survived the night—to take me to the places where the people of the village had from time to time been killed, but this they were unwilling to do. From the courtyard they pointed out the direction in which the kills had taken place; the last kill—the one that had brought me to the spot—I was told, had taken place round the shoulder of the hill to the west of the village. The women and girls, some twenty in number, who had been out collecting oak leaves for the cattle when the unfortunate woman had been killed, were eager to give me details of the occurrence. It appeared that the party had set out two hours before midday and, after going half a mile, had climbed into trees to cut leaves. The victim and two other women had selected a tree growing on the edge of a ravine, which I subsequently found was about four feet deep and ten to twelve feet wide. Having cut all the leaves she needed, the woman was climbing down from the tree when the tiger, who had approached unseen, stood up on its hind legs and caught her by the foot. Her hold was torn from the branch she was letting herself down by, and, pulling her into the ravine, the tiger released her foot, and while she was struggling to rise caught her by the throat. After killing her it sprang up the side of the ravine and disappeared with her into some heavy undergrowth.

All this had taken place a few feet from the two women on the tree, and had been witnessed by the entire party. As soon as the tiger and its victim were out of sight, the terror-stricken women and girls ran back to the village. The men had just come in for their midday meal and, when all were assembled and armed with drums, metal cooking-pots—anything in fact that would produce a noise—the rescue party set off, the men leading and the women bringing up the rear.

Arrived at the ravine in which the woman had been killed, the very important question of "what next?" was being debated when the tiger interrupted the proceedings by emitting a loud roar from the bushes thirty yards away. As one man, the party turned and fled helter-skelter back to the village. When breath had been regained, accusations were made against one and another of having been the first to run and cause the stampede. Words ran high until it was suggested that if no one was afraid and all were as brave as they claimed to be, why not go back and rescue the woman without loss of more time? The suggestion was adopted, and three times the party got as far as the ravine. On the third occasion the one man who was armed with a gun fired it off, and brought the tiger roaring out of the bushes; after this the attempted rescue was very wisely abandoned. On my asking the gun man why he had not discharged his piece into the bushes instead of up into the air, he said the tiger was already greatly enraged and that if by any mischance he had hit it, it would undoubtedly have killed him.

For three hours that morning I walked around the village looking for tracks and hoping, and at the same time dreading, to meet the tiger. At one place in a dark heavily-wooded ravine, while I was skirting some bushes, a covey of kaleege pheasants fluttered screaming out of them, and I thought my heart had stopped beating for good.

My men had cleared a spot under a walnut tree for my meals, and after breakfast the Headman of the village asked me to mount guard while the wheat crop was being cut. He said that if the crop was not harvested in my presence, it would not be harvested at all, for the people were too frightened to leave their homes. Half an hour later the entire population of the village, assisted by my men, were hard at work while I stood on guard with a loaded rifle. By evening the crop from five large fields had been gathered, leaving only two small patches close to the houses, which the Headman said he would have no difficulty in dealing with the next day.

The sanitary condition of the village had been much improved, and a second room for my exclusive use placed at my disposal; and that night, with thorn bushes securely wedged in the doorway to admit ventilation and exclude the man-eater, I made up for the sleep I had lost the previous night.

My presence was beginning to put new heart into the people and they were moving about more freely, but I had not yet gained sufficient of their confidence to renew my request of being shown round the jungle, to which I attached some importance. These people knew every foot of the ground for miles round, and could, if they wished, show me where I was most likely to find the tiger, or in any case, where I could see its pug marks. That the man-eater was a tiger was an established fact, but it was not known whether the animal was young or old, a male or a female, and this information, which I believed would help me to get in touch with it, I could only ascertain by examining its pug marks.

After an early tea that morning I announced that I wanted meat for my men and asked the villagers if they could direct me to where I could shoot a ghooral (mountain goat). The village was situated on the top of a long ridge running east and west, and just below the road on which I had spent the night the hill fell steeply away to the north in a series of grassy slopes; on these slopes I was told ghooral were plentiful, and several men volunteered to show me over the ground. I was careful not to show my pleasure at this offer and, selecting three men, I set out, telling the Headman that if I found the ghooral as plentiful as he said they were, I would shoot two for the village in addition to shooting one for my men.

Crossing the road we went down a very steep ridge, keeping a sharp lookout to right and left, but saw nothing. Half a mile down the hill the ravines converged, and from their junction there was a good view of the rocky and grass-covered slope to the right. I had been sitting with my back to a solitary pine which grew at this spot for some minutes, scanning the slope, when a movement high up on the hill caught my eye. When the movement was repeated I saw it was a ghooral flapping its ears; the animal was standing in grass and only its head was visible. The men had not seen the movement, and as the head was now stationary and blended in with its surroundings it was not possible to point it out to them. Giving them a general idea of the animal's position, I made them sit down and watch while I took a shot. I was armed with an old Martini Henry rifle, a weapon that atoned for its vicious kick by being dead accurate—up to any range. The distance was as near two hundred yards as made no matter and, lying down and resting the rifle on a convenient pine root, I took careful aim and fired.

The smoke from the black powder cartridge obscured my view and the men said nothing had happened and that I had probably fired at a rock or a bunch of dead leaves. Retaining my position I reloaded the rifle and presently saw the grass, a little below where I had fired, moving, and the hind quarters of the ghooral appeared. When the whole animal was free of the grass it started to roll over and over, gaining momentum as it came down the steep hill. When it was half-way down it disappeared into heavy grass, and disturbed two ghooral that had been lying up there. Sneezing their alarm call, the two animals dashed out of the grass and went bounding up the hill. The range was shorter now, and, adjusting the leaf sight, I waited until the bigger of the two slowed down, and put a bullet through its back, and as the other one turned and made off diagonally across the hill, I shot it through the shoulder.

On occasions one is privileged to accomplish the seemingly impossible. Lying in an uncomfortable position and shooting up at an angle of sixty degrees at a range of two hundred yards at the small white mark on the ghooral's throat, there did not appear to be one chance in a million of the shot coming off, and yet the heavy lead bullet driven by black powder had not been deflected by a hair's breadth and had gone true to its mark, killing the animal instantaneously. Again, on the steep hillside which was broken up by small ravines and jutting rocks, the dead animal had slipped and rolled straight to the spot where its two companions were lying up; and before it had cleared the patch of grass the two companions in their turn were slipping and rolling down the hill. As the three dead animals landed in the ravine in front of us it was amusing to observe the surprise and delight of the men who never before had seen a rifle in action. All thought of the man-eater was for the time being forgotten as they scrambled down into the ravine to retrieve the bag.

The expedition was a great success in more ways than one; for in addition to providing a ration of meat for everyone, it gained me the confidence of the entire village. Shikar yarns, as everyone knows, never lose anything in repetition, and while the ghooral were being skinned and divided up, the three men who had accompanied me gave full rein to their imagination, and from where I sat in the open, having breakfast, I could hear the exclamations of the assembled crowd when they were told that the ghooral had been shot at a range of over a mile, and the magic bullets used had not only killed the animals—like that—but had also drawn them to the sahib's feet.

After the midday meal the Headman asked me where I wanted to go, and how many men I wished to take with me. From the eager throng of men who pressed round I selected two of my late companions, and with them to guide me set off to visit the scene of the last human tragedy.

The people of our hills are Hindus and cremate their dead, and when one of their number has been carried off by a man-eater it is incumbent on the relatives to recover some portion of the body for cremation even if it be only a few splinters of bone. In the case of this woman the cremation ceremony was yet to be performed, and as we started out, the relatives requested us to bring back any portion of the body we might find.

From early boyhood I have made a hobby of reading and interpreting jungle signs. In the present case I had the account of the eye-witnesses who were present when the woman was killed, but eye-witnesses are not always reliable, whereas jungle signs are a true record of all that has transpired. On arrival at the spot a glance at the ground showed me that the tiger could only have approached the tree one way without being seen, and that was up the ravine. Entering the ravine a hundred yards below the tree, and working up, I found the pug marks of a tiger in some fine earth that had sifted down between two big rocks; these pug marks showed the animal to be a tigress, a little past her prime. Further up the ravine, and some ten yards from the tree, the tigress had lain down behind a rock, presumably to wait for the woman to climb down from the tree. The victim had been the first to cut all the leaves she needed, and as she was letting herself down by a branch some two inches in diameter the tigress had crept forward and, standing up on her hind legs, had caught the woman by the foot and pulled her down into the ravine. The branch showed the desperation with which the unfortunate woman had clung to it, for adhering to the rough oak bark where the branch, and eventually the leaves, had slipped through her grasp were strands of skin which had been torn from the palms of her hands and fingers. Where the tigress had killed the woman there were signs of a struggle and a big patch of dried blood; from here the blood trail, now dry but distinctly visible, led across the ravine and up the opposite bank. Following the blood trail from where it left the ravine we found the place in the bushes where the tigress had eaten her kill.

It is a popular belief that man-eaters do not eat the head, hands, and feet of their human victims. This is incorrect. Man-eaters, if not disturbed, eat everything—including the blood-soaked clothes, as I found on one occasion; however, that is another story, and will be told some other time.

On the present occasion we found the woman's clothes, and a few pieces of bone which we wrapped up in the clean cloth we had brought for the purpose. Pitifully little as these remains were, they would suffice for the cremation ceremony which would ensure the ashes of the high-caste woman reaching Mother Ganges.

After tea I visited the scene of yet another tragedy. Separated from the main village by the public road was a small holding of a few acres. The owner of this holding had built himself a hut on the hillside just above the road. The man's wife and the mother of his two children, a boy and a girl aged four and six respectively, was the younger of two sisters. These two sisters were out cutting grass one day on the hill above the hut when the tigress suddenly appeared and carried off the elder sister. For a hundred yards the younger woman ran after the tigress brandishing her sickle and screaming at the tigress to let her sister go and take her instead. This incredible act of heroism was witnessed by the people in the main village. After carrying the dead woman for a hundred yards the tigress put her down and turned on her pursuer. With a loud roar it sprang at the brave woman who, turning, raced down the hillside, across the road, and into the village, evidently with the intention of telling the people what they, unknown to her, had already witnessed. The woman's incoherent noises were at the time attributed to loss of breath, fear, and excitement, and it was not until the rescue party that had set out with all speed had returned, unsuccessful, that it was found the woman had lost her power of speech. I was told this tale in the village, and when I climbed the path to the two-roomed hut where the woman was engaged in washing clothes, she had then been dumb a twelvemonth.

Except for a strained look in her eyes the dumb woman appeared to be quite normal and, when I stopped to speak to her and tell her I had come to try and shoot the tiger that had killed her sister, she put her hands together and stooping down touched my feet, making me feel a

wretched impostor. True, I had come with the avowed object of shooting the man-eater, but with an animal that had the reputation of never
killing twice in the same locality, never returning to a kill, and whose
domain extended over an area of many hundred square miles, the chance
of my accomplishing my object was about as good as finding a needle
in two haystacks.

Plans in plenty I had made, way back in Naini Tal; one I had already
tried and wild horses would not induce me to try it again, and the others
—now that I was on the ground—were just as unattractive. Further,
there was no one I could ask for advice, for this was the first man-eater
that had ever been known in Kumaon; and yet something would have
to be done. So for the next three days I wandered through the jungles
from sunrise to sunset, visiting all the places for miles round where the
villagers told me there was a chance of my seeing the tigress.

I would like to interrupt my tale here for a few minutes to refute a
rumor current throughout the hills, that on this, and on several subsequent occasions, I assumed the dress of a hill woman and, going into
the jungle, attracted the man-eaters to myself and killed them with
either a sickle or an ax. All I have ever done in the matter of alteration
of dress has been to borrow a sari and with it draped round me cut
grass, or climbed into trees and cut leaves, and in no case has the ruse
proved successful; though on two occasions—to my knowledge—man-
eaters have stalked the tree I was on, taking cover, on one occasion
behind a rock and on the other behind a fallen tree, and giving me no
opportunity of shooting them.

To continue. As the tigress now appeared to have left this locality I
decided, much to the regret of the people of Pali, to move to Champawat,
fifteen miles due east of Pali. Making an early start, I breakfasted at
Dhunaghat, and completed the journey to Champawat by sunset. The
roads in this area were considered very unsafe, and men only moved
from village to village or to the bazaars in large parties. After leaving
Dhunaghat, my party of eight was added to by men from villages adjoining the road, and we arrived at Champawat thirty strong. Some of the
men who joined me had been in a party of twenty men who had visited
Champawat two months earlier, and they told me the following very
pitiful story.

"The road for a few miles on this side of Champawat runs along the
south face of the hill, parallel to and about fifty yards above the valley.
Two months ago a party of twenty of us men were on our way to the
bazaar at Champawat, and as we were going along this length of the

road at about midday, we were startled by hearing the agonized cries of a human being coming from the valley below. Huddled together on the edge of the road we cowered in fright as these cries drew nearer and nearer, and presently into view came a tiger, carrying a naked woman. The woman's hair was trailing on the ground on one side of the tiger, and her feet on the other—the tiger was holding her by the small of the back—and she was beating her chest and calling alternately on God and man to help her. Fifty yards from, and in clear view of us, the tiger passed with its burden, and when the cries had died away in the distance we continued on our way."

"And you twenty men did nothing?"

"No, sahib, we did nothing for we were afraid, and what can men do when they are afraid? And further, even if we had been able to rescue the woman without angering the tiger and bringing misfortune on ourselves, it would have availed the woman nothing, for she was covered with blood and would of a surety have died of her wounds."

I subsequently learned that the victim belonged to a village near Champawat, and that she had been carried off by the tiger while collecting dry sticks. Her companions had run back to the village and raised an alarm, and just as a rescue party was starting the twenty frightened men arrived. As these men knew the direction in which the tiger had gone with its victim, they joined the party, and can best carry on the story.

"We were fifty or sixty strong when we set out to rescue the woman, and several of the party were armed with guns. A furlong from where the sticks collected by the woman were lying, and from where she had been carried off, we found her torn clothes. Thereafter the men started beating their drums and firing off their guns, and in this way we proceeded for more than a mile right up to the head of the valley, where we found the woman, who was little more than a girl, lying dead on a great slab of rock. Beyond licking off all the blood and making her body clean the tiger had not touched her, and, there being no woman in our party, we men averted our faces as we wrapped her body in the loincloths which one and another gave, for she looked as she lay on her back as one who sleeps, and would waken in shame when touched."

With experiences such as these to tell and retell through the long night watches behind fast-shut doors, it is little wonder that the character and outlook on life of people living year after year in a man-eater country should change, and that one coming from the outside should feel that he had stepped right into a world of stark realities and the rule of the tooth and claw, which forced man in the reign of the sabre-toothed tiger to shelter in dark caverns. I was young and inexperienced in those far-off Champawat days, but, even so, the conviction I came to after a brief sojourn in that stricken land, that there is no more terrible thing than to live and have one's being under the shadow of a man-eater, has been strengthened by thirty-two years' subsequent experience.

The Tahsildar of Champawat, to whom I had been given letters of introduction, paid me a visit that night at the Dak Bungalow, where I was putting up, and suggested I should move next day to a bungalow a few miles away, in the vicinity of which many human beings had been killed.

Early next morning, accompanied by the Tahsildar, I set out for the bungalow, and while I was having breakfast on the verandah two men arrived with news that a cow had been killed by a tiger in a village ten miles away. The Tahsildar excused himself to attend to some urgent work at Champawat, and said he would return to the bungalow in the evening and stay the night with me. My guides were good walkers, and as the track went downhill most of the way we covered the ten miles in record time. Arrived at the village I was taken to a cattle shed in which I found a week-old calf, killed and partly eaten by a leopard. Not having the time or the inclination to shoot the leopard I rewarded my guides, and retraced my steps to the bungalow. Here I found the Tahsildar had not returned, and as there was still an hour or more of daylight left I went out with the chowkidar of the bungalow to look at a place where he informed me a tiger was in the habit of drinking; this place I found to be the head of the spring which supplied the garden with irrigation water. In the soft earth round the spring were tiger pug marks several days old, but these tracks were quite different from the pug marks I had seen, and carefully examined, in the ravine in which the woman of Pali village had been killed.

On returning to the bungalow I found the Tahsildar was back, and as we sat on the verandah I told him of my day's experience. Expressing regret at my having had to go so far on a wild-goose chase, he rose, saying that as he had a long way to go he must start at once. This announcement caused me no little surprise, for twice that day he had said he would stay the night with me. It was not the question of his staying the night that concerned me, but the risk he was taking; however, he was deaf to all my arguments and, as he stepped off the veranda into the dark night, with only one man following him carrying a smoky lantern which gave a mere glimmer of light, to do a walk of four miles

in a locality in which men only moved in large parties in daylight, I took
off my hat to a very brave man. Having watched him out of sight I
turned and entered the bungalow. . . .

II

I spent the following morning in going round the very extensive fruit
orchard and tea garden and in having a bath at the spring, and at about
midday the Tahsildar, much to my relief, returned safely from Champawat.

I was standing talking to him while looking down a long sloping hill
with a village surrounded by cultivated land in the distance, when I
saw a man leave the village and start up the hill in our direction. As the
man drew nearer I saw he was alternately running and walking, and
was quite evidently the bearer of important news. Telling the Tahsildar
I would return in a few minutes, I set off at a run down the hill, and
when the man saw me coming he sat down to take breath. As soon as I
was near enough to hear him he called out, "Come quickly, sahib, the
man-eater has just killed a girl." "Sit still," I called back, and turning
ran up to the bungalow. I passed the news on to the Tahsildar while I
was getting a rifle and some cartridges, and asked him to follow me
down to the village.

The man who had come for me was one of those exasperating individuals whose legs and tongue cannot function at the same time.
When he opened his mouth he stopped dead, and when he started to
run his mouth closed; so telling him to shut his mouth and lead the way,
we ran in silence down the hill.

At the village an excited crowd of men, women, and children awaited
us and, as usually happens on these occasions, all started to talk at the
same time. One man was vainly trying to quieten the babel. I led him
aside and asked him to tell me what had happened. Pointing to some
scattered oak trees on a gentle slope a furlong or so from the village, he
said a dozen people were collecting dry sticks under the trees when a
tiger suddenly appeared and caught one of their number, a girl sixteen
or seventeen years of age. The rest of the party had run back to the
village, and as it was known that I was staying at the bungalow a man
had immediately been dispatched to inform me.

The wife of the man I was speaking to had been of the party, and she
now pointed out the tree, on the shoulder of the hill, under which the
girl had been taken. None of the party had looked back to see if the

tiger was carrying away its victim and, if so, in which direction it had gone.

Instructing the crowd not to make a noise, and to remain in the village until I returned, I set off in the direction of the tree. The ground here was quite open and it was difficult to conceive how an animal the size of a tiger could have approached twelve people unseen, and its presence not detected, until attention had been attracted by the choking sound made by the girl.

The spot where the girl had been killed was marked by a pool of blood and near it, and in vivid contrast to the crimson pool, was a broken necklace of brightly colored blue beads which the girl had been wearing. From this spot the track led up and round the shoulder of the hill.

The track of the tigress was clearly visible. On one side of it were great splashes of blood where the girl's head had hung down, and on the other side the trail of her feet. Half a mile up the hill I found the girl's sari, and on the brow of the hill her skirt. Once again the tigress was carrying a naked woman, but mercifully on this occasion her burden was dead.

On the brow of the hill the track led through a thicket of blackthorn, on the thorns of which long strands of the girl's raven-black hair had caught. Beyond this was a bed of nettles through which the tigress had gone, and I was looking for a way round this obstruction when I heard footsteps behind me. Turning round I saw a man armed with a rifle coming toward me. I asked him why he had followed me when I had left instructions at the village that no one was to leave it. He said that Tahsildar had instructed him to accompany me, and that he was afraid to disobey orders. As he appeared determined to carry out his orders, and to argue the point would have meant the loss of valuable time, I told him to remove the heavy pair of boots he was wearing and, when he had hidden them under a bush, I advised him to keep close to me, and to keep a sharp lookout behind.

I was wearing a very thin pair of stockings, shorts, and a pair of rubber-soled shoes, and as there appeared to be no way round the nettles I followed the tigress through them—much to my discomfort.

Beyond the nettles the blood trail turned sharply to the left, and went straight down the very steep hill, which was densely clothed with bracken and ringals.* A hundred yards down, the blood trail led into a narrow and very steep watercourse, down which the tigress had gone with some

*Hill bamboos.

difficulty, as could be seen from the dislodged stones and earth. I followed this watercourse for five or six hundred yards, my companion getting more and more agitated the further we went. A dozen times he caught my arm and whispered—in a voice full of tears—that he could hear the tiger, either on one side or the other, or behind us. Halfway down the hill we came on a great pinnacle of rock some thirty feet high, and as the man had by now had all the man-eater hunting he could stand, I told him to climb the rock and remain on it until I returned. Very gladly he went up, and when he straddled the top and signaled to me that he was all right I continued on down the watercourse, which, after skirting round the rock, went straight down for a hundred yards to where it met a deep ravine coming down from the left. At the junction was a small pool, and as I approached it I saw patches of blood on my side of the water.

The tigress had carried the girl straight down to this spot, and my approach had disturbed her at her meal. Splinters of bone were scattered round the deep pug marks into which discolored water was slowly seeping and at the edge of the pool was an object which had puzzled me as I came down the watercourse, and which I now found was part of a human leg. In all the subsequent years I have hunted man-eaters I have not seen anything as pitiful as that young comely leg—bitten off a little below the knee as clean as though severed by the stroke of an axe—out of which the warm blood was trickling.

While looking at the leg I had forgotten all about the tigress until I suddenly felt that I was in great danger. Hurriedly grounding the butt of the rifle, I put two fingers on the triggers, raising my head as I did so, and saw a little earth, from the fifteen-foot bank in front of me, come rolling down the steep side and plop into the pool. I was new to this game of man-eater hunting or I should not have exposed myself to an attack in the way I had done. My prompt action in pointing the rifle upwards had possibly saved my life, and in stopping her spring, or in turning to get away, the tigress had dislodged the earth from the top of the bank.

The bank was too steep for scrambling, and the only way of getting up was to take it at a run. Going up the watercourse a short distance I sprinted down, took the pool in my stride, and got far enough up the other side to grasp a bush and pull myself on to the bank. A bed of Strobilanthes, the bent stalks of which were slowly regaining their upright position, showed where, and how recently, the tigress had passed, and a little further on under an overhanging rock I found where she had left her kill when she came to have a look at me.

Her tracks now—as she carried away the girl—led into a wilderness of rocks, some acres in extent, where the going was both difficult and dangerous. The cracks and chasms between the rocks were masked with ferns and blackberry vines, and a false step, which might easily have resulted in a broken limb, would have been fatal. Progress under these conditions was of necessity slow, and the tigress was taking advantage of it to continue her meal. A dozen times I found where she had rested, and after each of these rests the blood trail became more distinct.

This was her four hundred and thirty-sixth human kill and she was quite accustomed to being disturbed at her meals by rescue parties, but this, I think, was the first time she had been followed up so persistently and she now began to show her resentment by growling. To appreciate a tiger's growl to the full it is necessary to be situated as I then was—rocks all round with dense vegetation between, and the imperative necessity of testing each footstep to avoid falling headlong into unseen chasms and caves.

I cannot expect you who read this at your fireside to appreciate my feelings at the time. The sound of the growling and the expectation of an attack terrified me at the same time as it gave me hope. If the tigress lost her temper sufficiently to launch an attack, it would not only give me an opportunity of accomplishing the object for which I had come, but it would enable me to get even with her for all the pain and suffering she had caused.

The growling, however, was only a gesture, and, when she found that instead of shooing me off it was bringing me faster on her heels, she abandoned it.

I had now been on her track for over four hours. Though I had repeatedly seen the undergrowth moving I had not seen so much as a hair of her hide, and a glance at the shadows climbing up the opposite hillside warned me it was time to retrace my steps if I was to reach the village before dark.

The late owner of the severed leg was a Hindu, and some portion of her would be needed for the cremation, so as I passed the pool I dug a hole in the bank and buried the leg where it would be safe from the tigress, and could be found when wanted.

My companion on the rock was very relieved to see me. My long absence, and the growling he had heard, had convinced him that the tigress had secured another kill and his difficulty, as he quite frankly admitted, was how he was going to get back to the village alone.

I thought when we were climbing down the watercourse that I knew of no more dangerous proceeding than walking in front of a nervous man carrying a loaded gun, but I changed my opinion when on walking behind him he slipped and fell, and I saw where the muzzle of his gun— a converted .450 without a safety catch—was pointing. Since that day— except when accompanied by Ibbotson—I have made it a hard and fast rule to go alone when hunting man-eaters, for if one's companion is unarmed it is difficult to protect him, and if he is armed, it is even more difficult to protect oneself.

Arrived at the crest of the hill, where the man had hidden his boots, I sat down to have a smoke and think out my plans for the morrow.

The tigress would finish what was left of the kill during the night, and would to a certainty lie up among the rocks next day.

On the ground she was on there was very little hope of my being able to stalk her, and if I disturbed her without getting a shot, she would probably leave the locality and I should lose touch with her. A beat therefore was the only thing to do, provided I could raise sufficient men.

I was sitting on the south edge of a great amphitheater of hills, without a habitation of any kind in sight. A stream entering from the west had fretted its way down, cutting a deep valley right across the amphitheater. To the east the stream had struck solid rock, and turning north had left the amphitheater by a narrow gorge.

The hill in front of me, rising to a height of some two thousand feet, was clothed in short grass with a pine tree dotted here and there, and the hill to the east was too precipitous for anything but a ghooral to negotiate. If I could collect sufficient men to man the entire length of the ridge from the stream to the precipitous hill, and get them to stir up the tigress, her most natural line of retreat would be through the narrow gorge.

Admittedly a very difficult beat, for the steep hillside facing north, on which I had left the tigress, was densely wooded and roughly three-quarters of a mile long and half-a-mile wide; however, if I could get the beaters to carry out instructions, there was a reasonable chance of my getting a shot.

The Tahsildar was waiting for me at the village. I explained the position to him, and asked him to take immediate steps to collect as many men as he could, and to meet me at ten o'clock the following morning at the tree where the girl had been killed. Promising to do his best, he left for Champawat, while I climbed the hill to the bungalow.

I was up at crack of dawn next morning, and after a substantial meal told my men to pack up and wait for me at Champawat, and went down to have another look at the ground I intended beating. I could find nothing wrong with the plans I had made, and an hour before my time I was at the spot where I had asked the Tahsildar to meet me.

That he would have a hard time in collecting the men I had no doubt, for the fear of the man-eater had sunk deep into the countryside and more than mild persuasion would be needed to make the men leave the shelter of their homes. At ten o'clock the Tahsildar and one man turned up, and thereafter the men came in twos, and threes, and tens, until by midday two hundred and ninety-eight had collected.

The Tahsildar had let it be known that he would turn a blind eye towards all unlicensed fire-arms, and further that he would provide ammunition where required; and the weapons that were produced that day would have stocked a museum.

When the men were assembled and had received the ammunition they needed I took them to the brow of the hill where the girl's skirt was lying, and pointing to a pine tree on the opposite hill that had been struck by lightning and stripped of bark, I told them to line themselves up along the ridge and, when they saw me wave a handkerchief from under the pine, those of them who were armed were to fire off their pieces, while the others beat drums, shouted, and rolled down rocks, and that no one was on any account to leave the ridge until I returned and personally collected him. When I was assured that all present had heard and understood my instructions, I set off with the Tahsildar, who said he would be safer with me than with the beaters whose guns would probably burst and cause many casualties.

Making a wide detour I crossed the upper end of the valley, gained the opposite hill, and made my way down to the blasted pine. From here the hill went steeply down and the Tahsildar, who had on a thin pair of patent leather shoes, said it was impossible for him to go any further. While he was removing his inadequate foot-gear to ease his blisters, the men on the ridge, thinking I had forgotten to give the pre-arranged signal, fired off their guns and set up a great shout. I was still a hundred and fifty yards from the gorge, and that I did not break my neck a dozen times in covering this distance was due to my having been brought up on the hills, and being in consequence as sure-footed as a goat.

As I ran down the hill I noticed that there was a patch of green grass near the mouth of the gorge, and as there was no time to look round for a better place, I sat down in the grass, with my back to the hill down which I had just come. The grass was about two feet high and hid half my body, and if I kept perfectly still there was a good chance of my not being seen. Facing me was the hill that was being beaten, and the gorge that I hoped the tigress would make for was behind my left shoulder.

Pandemonium had broken loose on the ridge. Added to the fusillade of guns was the wild beating of drums and the shouting of hundreds of men, and when the din was at its worst I caught sight of the tigress bounding down a grassy slope between two ravines to my right front, and about three hundred yards away. She had only gone a short distance when the Tahsildar from his position under the pine let off both barrels of his shotgun. On hearing the shots the tigress whipped round and went straight back the way she had come, and as she disappeared into thick cover I threw up my rifle and sent a despairing bullet after her.

The men on the ridge, hearing the three shots, not unnaturally concluded that the tigress had been killed. They emptied all their guns and gave a final yell, and I was holding my breath and listening for the screams that would herald the tigress's arrival on the ridge, when she suddenly broke cover to my left front and, taking the stream at a bound, came straight for the gorge. The .500 modified cordite rifle, sighted at sea level, shot high at this altitude, and when the tigress stopped dead I thought the bullet had gone over her back, and that she had pulled up on finding her retreat cut off; as a matter of fact I had hit her all right, but a little far back. Lowering her head, she half turned toward me, giving me a beautiful shot at the point of her shoulder at a range of less than thirty yards. She flinched at this second shot but continued, with her ears laid flat and bared teeth, to stand her ground, while I sat with rifle to shoulder trying to think what it would be best for me to do when she charged, for the rifle was empty and I had no more cartridges. Three cartridges were all that I had brought with me, for I never thought I should get a chance of firing more than two shots, and the third cartridge was for—an emergency.

Fortunately the wounded animal most unaccountably decided against a charge. Very slowly she turned, crossed the stream to her right, climbed over some fallen rocks, and found a narrow ledge that went diagonally up and across the face of the precipitous hill to where there was a great flat projecting rock. Where this rock joined the cliff a small bush had found roothold, and going up to it the tigress started to strip its branches. Throwing caution to the winds I shouted to the Tahsildar to bring me his gun. A long reply was shouted back, the only word of which I caught was "feet." Laying down my rifle I took the hill at a run, grabbed the gun out of the Tahsildar's hands and raced back.

As I approached the stream the tigress left the bush and came out on the projecting rock towards me. When I was within twenty feet of her I raised the gun and found to my horror that there was a gap of about three-eighths of an inch between the barrels and the breech-lock. The gun had not burst when both barrels had been fired, and would probably not burst now, but there was danger of being blinded by a blow back. However, the risk would have to be taken, and, aligning the great blob of a bead that did duty as a sight on the tigress's open mouth, I fired. Maybe I bobbed, or maybe the gun was not capable of throwing the cylindrical bullet accurately for twenty feet; anyway, the missile missed the tigress's mouth and struck her on the right paw, from where I removed it later with my fingernails. Fortunately she was at her last gasp, and the tap on the foot was sufficient to make her lurch forward. She came to rest with her head projecting over the side of the rock.

From the moment the tigress had broken cover in her attempt to get through the gorge I had forgotten the beaters, until I was suddenly reminded of their existence by hearing a shout, from a short distance up the hill, of "There it is on the rock! Pull it down and let us hack it to bits." I could not believe my ears when I heard "hack it to bits," and yet I had heard aright, for others now had caught sight of the tigress and from all over the hillside the shout was being repeated.

The ledge by which the wounded animal had gained the projecting rock was fortunately on the opposite side from the beaters, and was just wide enough to permit my shuffling along it sideways. As I reached the rock and stepped over the tigress—hoping devoutly she was dead, for I had not had time to carry out the usual test of pelting her with stones —the men emerged from the forest and came running across the open, brandishing guns, axes, rusty swords, and spears.

At the rock, which was twelve to fourteen feet in height, their advance was checked, for the outer face had been worn smooth by the stream when in spate and afforded no foothold even for their bare toes. The rage of the crowd on seeing their dread enemy was quite understandable, for there was not a man among them who had not suffered at her hands. One man, who appeared demented and was acting as ringleader, was shouting over and over again as he ran to and fro brandishing a sword. "This is the *shaitan** that killed my wife and my two sons." As happens with crowds, the excitement died down as suddenly as it had flared up, and to the credit of the man who had lost his wife and sons be it said that he was the first to lay down his weapon. He came near to the rock and said, "We were mad, sahib, when we saw our enemy, but the madness

* Devil.

has now passed, and we ask you and Tahsildar sahib to forgive us." Extracting the unspent cartridge, I laid the gun across the tigress and hung down by my hands and was assisted to the ground. When I showed the men how I had gained the rock the dead animal was very gently lowered and carried to an open spot, where all could crowd round and look at her.

When the tigress had stood on the rock looking down at me I had noticed that there was something wrong with her mouth, and on examining her now I found that the upper and lower canine teeth on the right side of her mouth were broken, the upper one in half, and the lower one right down to the bone. This permanent injury to her teeth— the result of a gunshot wound—had prevented her from killing her natural prey, and had been the cause of her becoming a man-eater.

The men begged me not to skin the tigress there, and asked me to let them have her until nightfall to carry through their villages, saying that if their womenfolk and children did not see her with their own eyes, they would not believe that their dread enemy was dead.

Two saplings were now cut and laid one on either side of the tigress, and with pugrees, waistbands, and loincloths she was carefully and very securely lashed to them. When all was ready the saplings were manned and we moved to the foot of the precipitous hill; the men preferred to take the tigress up this hill, on the far side of which their villages lay, to going up the densely wooded hill which they had just beaten. Two human ropes were made by the simple expedient of the man behind taking a firm grip of the waistband, or other portion of clothing, of the man in front of him. When it was considered that the ropes were long and strong enough to stand the strain, they attached themselves to the saplings, and with men on either side to hold the feet of the bearers and give them foothold, the procession moved up the hill, looking for all the world like an army of ants carrying a beetle up the face of a wall. Behind the main army was a second and a smaller one—the Tahsildar being carried up. Had the ropes broken at any stage of that thousand-foot climb, the casualties would have been appalling, but the rope did not break. The men gained the crest of the hill and set off eastwards, singing on their triumphal march, while the Tahsildar and I returned west and made for Champawat.

Our way lay along the ridge and once again I stood among the blackthorn bushes on the thorns of which long tresses of the girl's hair had caught, and for the last time looked down into the amphitheater which had been the scene of our recent exploit.

On the way down the hill the beaters had found the head of the unfortunate girl, and a thin column of smoke rising straight up into the still air from the mouth of the gorge showed where the relations were performing the last rites of the Champawat man-eater's last victim, on the very spot on which the man-eater had been shot.

After dinner, while I was standing in the courtyard of the Tahsil, I saw a long procession of pine torches winding its way down the opposite hillside, and presently the chanting of a hill song by a great concourse of men was borne up on the still night air. An hour later, the tigress was laid down at my feet.

It was difficult to skin the animal with so many people crowding round, and to curtail the job I cut the head and paws from the trunk and left them adhering to the skin, to be dealt with later. A police guard was then mounted over the carcass, and next day, when all the people of the countryside were assembled, the trunk, legs, and tail of the tigress were cut up into small pieces and distributed. These pieces of flesh and bone were required for the lockets which hill children wear round their necks, and the addition of a piece of tiger to the other potent charms is credited with giving the wearer courage, as well as immunity from the attacks of wild animals. The fingers of the girl, which the tigress had swallowed whole, were sent to me in spirits by the Tahsildar, and were buried by me in the Naini Tal lake close to the Nandadevi temples.

While I had been skinning the tigress the Tahsildar and his staff, assisted by the Headmen and graybeards of the surrounding villages and merchants of the Champawat bazaar, had been busy drawing up a program for a great feast and dance for the morrow, at which I was to preside. Round about midnight, when the last of the great throng of men had left with shouts of delight at being able to use roads and village paths that the man-eater had closed for four years, I had a final smoke with the Tahsildar, and telling him that I could not stay any longer and that he would have to take my place at the festivities, my men and I set off on our seventy-five-mile journey, with two days in hand to do it in.

At sunrise I left my men and, with the tigress's skin strapped to the saddle of my horse, rode on ahead to put in a few hours in cleaning the skin at Dabidhura, where I intended spending the night. When passing the hut on the hill at Pali it occurred to me that it would be some little satisfaction to the dumb woman to know that her sister had been avenged, so leaving the horse to browse—he had been bred near the snow-line and could eat anything from oak trees to nettles—I climbed the hill to the hut, and spread out the skin with the head supported on a stone facing the door. The children of the house had been round-eyed spectators of these proceedings and, hearing me talking to them, their mother who was inside cooking, came to the door.

I am not going to hazard any theories about shock, and countershock, for I know nothing of these matters. All I know is that this woman, who was alleged to have been dumb a twelvemonth and who four days previously had made no attempt to answer my questions, was now running backwards and forwards from the hut to the road calling to her husband and the people in the village to come quickly and see what the sahib had brought. This sudden return of speech appeared greatly to mystify the children, who could not take their eyes off their mother's face.

I rested in the village while a dish of tea was being prepared for me and told the people who thronged round how the man-eater had been killed. An hour later I continued my journey and for half a mile along my way I could hear the shouts of good will of the men of Pali. . . .

At a durbar held in Naini Tal a few months later Sir John Hewett, Lieutenant-Governor of the United Provinces, presented the Tahsildar of Champawat with a gun, and the man who accompanied me when I was looking for the girl, with a beautiful hunting-knife, for the help they had given me. Both weapons were suitably engraved and will be handed down as heirlooms in the respective families.

The Silent World

by J. Y. COUSTEAU
with FRÉDÉRIC DUMAS

Cousteau and Dumas have come to be known in some quarters as "the first of the menfish." Cousteau is a French Navy gunnery officer who was awarded the Legion of Honor for his wartime underground activities. Dumas is sometimes referred to as the world's most experienced diver. He is a civilian physiologist with the French Navy's Undersea Research Group. Rachel Carson, author of The Sea Around Us, *has written: "We owe Captain Cousteau an immense debt of gratitude. He has revolutionized the means of human access to the undersea world. . . . But all of us, whether we enter the sea or merely read about it, are indebted to Captain Cousteau for this completely fresh and unhackneyed account of what the diver sees and feels when he descends into the sea."*

OUR WORST EXPERIENCE IN FIVE THOUSAND DIVES DID NOT come in the sea but in an inland water cave, the famous Fountain of Vaucluse near Avignon. The renowned spring is a quiet pool in a crater under a six-hundred-foot limestone cliff above the River Sorgue. A trickle flows from it the year around, until March comes; then the Fountain of Vaucluse erupts in a rage of water which swells the Sorgue to flood. It pumps furiously for five weeks, then subsides. The phenomenon has occurred every year of recorded history.

A retired Army officer, Commandant Brunet, who had settled in the nearby village of Apt, became an addict of the Fountain as had Petrarch six hundred years before. The Commandant suggested that the Undersea Research Group dive into the Fountain and learn the secret of the mechanism. In 1946 the Navy gave us permission to try. We journeyed to Vaucluse on the 24th of August, when the spring was quiescent. There seemed to be no point in entering a violent flood, if its source might be discovered when the Fountain was quiet.

Embarrassed by our pendant gadgetry and requiring the support of our comrades, we waded into the pool. We looked around for the last time. I saw the reassuring silhouette of Fargues and the crowd jutting around the amphitheater. In their forefront was a young *abbé*, who had come no doubt to be of service in certain eventuality.

As we submerged, the water liberated us from weight. We stayed motionless in the pool for a minute to test our ballast and communications system. Under my flexible helmet I had a special mouthpiece which allowed me to articulate under water. Dumas had no speaking facility, but could answer me with nods and gestures.

I turned face down and plunged through the dark door. I rapidly passed the buttress into the shaft, unworried about Dumas's keeping pace on the thirty-foot cord at my waist. He can outswim me any time. Our dive was a trial run: we were the first *cordée* of a series. We intended to waste no time on details of topography but proceed directly to the pig iron and take it on to the elbow of Negri's siphon, from which we would quickly take up a new thread into the secret of the Fountain. In retrospect I can also find that my subconscious mechanism was anxious to conclude the first dive as soon as possible.

I glanced back and saw Didi gliding easily through the door against a faint green haze. The sky was no longer our business. We belonged now to a world where no light had ever struck. I could not see my flashlight beam beneath me in the frightening dark—the water had no suspended motes to reflect light. A disc of light blinked on and off in the darkness, when my flashlight beam hit rock. I went head down with tigerish speed, sinking by my overballast, unmindful of Dumas. Suddenly I was held by the belt and stones rattled past me. Heavier borne than I, Dumas was trying to brake his fall with his feet. His suit was filling with water. Big limestone blocks came loose and rumbled down around me. A stone bounced off my shoulder. I remotely realized I should try to think. I could not think.

Ninety feet down I found the pig iron standing on a ledge. It did not appear in the torch beam as an object from the world above, but as something germane to this place. Dimly I recalled that I must do something about the pig iron. I shoved it down the slope. It roared down with Dumas's stones. During this blurred effort I did not notice that I lost

the lines coiled on my arm. I did not know that I had failed to give
Fargues three tugs on the line to pay out the weight. I had forgotten
Fargues, and everything behind. The tunnel broke into a sharper decline.
I circled my right hand continuously, playing the torch in spirals on the
clean and polished walls. I was traveling at two knots. I was in the Paris
subway. I met nobody. There was nobody in the Metro, not a single rock
bass. No fish at all.

At that time of year our ears are well trained to pressure after a summer's diving. *Why did my ears ache so?* Something was happening. The
light no longer ran around the tunnel walls. The beam spread on a flat
bottom, covered with pebbles. It was earth, not rock, the detritus of the
chasm. I could find no walls. I was on the floor of a vast drowned cave.
I found the pig iron, but no zinc boat, no siphon and no teetering rock.
My head ached. I was drained of initiative.

I returned to our purpose, to learn the geography of the immensity
that had no visible roof or walls, but rolled away down at a forty-five-
degree incline. I could not surface without searching the ceiling for the
hole that led up to the inner cavern of our theory.

I was attached to something, I remembered. The flashlight picked out
a rope which curled off to a strange form floating supine above the pebbles. Dumas hung there in his cumbersome equipment, holding his torch
like a ridiculous glowworm. Only his arms were moving. He was sleepily
trying to tie his *piolet* to the pig-iron line. His black frogman suit was filling with water. He struggled weakly to inflate it with compressed air.
I swam to him and looked at his depth gauge. It read one hundred and
fifty feet. The dial was flooded. We were deeper than that. We were at
least two hundred feet down, four hundred feet away from the surface
at the bottom of a crooked slanting tunnel.

We had rapture of the depths, but not the familiar drunkenness. We
felt heavy and anxious, instead of exuberant. Dumas was stricken worse
than I. This is what I thought: *I shouldn't feel this way in this depth. . . .
I can't go back until I learn where we are. Why don't I feel a current?
The pig-iron line is our only way home. What if we lose it? Where is the
rope I had on my arm?* I was able in that instant to recall that I had lost
the line somewhere above. I took Dumas's hand and closed it around the
guide line. "Stay here," I shouted. "I'll find the shaft." Dumas understood me to mean I had no air and needed the safety aqualung. I sent
the beam of the flashlight around in search of the roof of the cave. I
found no ceiling.

Dumas was passing under heavy narcosis. He thought I was the one in danger. He fumbled to release the emergency lung. As he tugged hopelessly at his belt, he scudded across the drowned shingle and abandoned the guide line to the surface. The rope dissolved in the dark. I was swimming above, mulishly seeking for a wall or a ceiling, when I felt his weight tugging me back like a drifting anchor, restraining my search.

Above us somewhere were seventy fathoms of tunnel and crumbling rock. My weakened brain found the power to conjure up our fate. When our air ran out we would grope along the ceiling and suffocate in dulled agony. I shook off this thought and swam down to the ebbing glow of Dumas's flashlight.

He had lost the better part of his consciousness. When I touched him, he grabbed my wrist with awful strength and hauled me toward him for a final experience of life, an embrace that would take me with him. I twisted out of his hold and backed off. I examined Dumas with the torch. I saw his protruded eyes rolling inside the mask.

The cave was quiet between my gasping breaths. I marshaled all my remaining brain power to consider the situation. Fortunately there was no current to carry Dumas away from the pig iron. If there had been the least current we would have been lost. *The pig iron must be near.* I looked for that rusted metal block, more precious than gold. And suddenly there was the stolid and reassuring pig iron. Its line flew away into the dark, toward the hope of life.

In his stupor, Didi lost control of his jaws and his mouthpiece slipped from his teeth. He swallowed water and took some in his lungs before he somehow got the grip back into his mouth. Now, with the guide line beckoning, I realized that I could not swim to the surface, carrying the inert Dumas, who weighed at least twenty-five pounds in his waterlogged suit. I was in a state of exhaustion from the mysterious effect of the cave. We had not exercised strenuously, yet Dumas was helpless and I was becoming idiotic.

I would climb the rope, dragging Dumas with me. I grasped the pig-iron rope and started up, hand over hand, with Dumas drifting below, along the smooth vertical rock.

My first three hand holds on the line were interpreted correctly by Fargues as the signal to pay out more rope. He did so, with a will. I regarded with utter dismay the phenomena of the rope slackening and made superhuman efforts to climb it. Fargues smartly fed me rope when he felt my traction. It took an eternal minute for me to form the tactic that I should continue to haul down rope, until the end of it came into Fargues's hand. He would never let that go. I hauled rope in dull glee.

Four hundred feet of rope passed through my hands and curled into the cavern. And a knot came into my hands. Fargues was giving us more rope to penetrate the ultimate gallery of Vaucluse. He had efficiently tied on another length to encourage us to pass deeper.

I dropped the rope like an enemy. I would have to climb the tunnel slope like an Alpinist. Foot by foot I climbed the fingerholds of rock, stopping when I lost my respiratory rhythm by exertion and was near to fainting. I drove myself on, and felt that I was making progress. I reached for a good hand hold, standing on the tips of my fins. The crag eluded my fingers and I was dragged down by the weight of Dumas.

The shock turned my mind to the rope again and I received a last-minute remembrance of our signals: six tugs meant pull everything up. I grabbed the line and jerked it, confident that I could count to six. The line was slacked and snagged on obstacles in the four hundred feet to Maurice Fargues. *Fargues, do you not understand my situation?* I was at the end of my strength. Dumas was hanging on me.

Why doesn't Dumas understand how bad he is for me? Dumas, you will die, anyway. Maybe you are already gone. Didi, I hate to do it, but you are dead and you will not let me live. Go away, Didi. I reached for my belt dagger and prepared to cut the cord to Dumas.

Even in my incompetence there was something that held the knife in its holster. *Before I cut you off, Didi, I will try again to reach Fargues.* I took the line and repeated the distress signal, again and again. *Didi, I am doing all a man can do. I am dying too.*

On shore, Fargues stood in perplexed concentration. The first *cordée* had not been down for the full period of the plan, but the strange pattern of our signals disturbed him. His hard but sensitive hand on the rope had felt no clear signals since the episode a few minutes back when suddenly we wanted lots of rope. He had given it to us, eagerly adding another length. *They must have found something tremendous down there,* thought Fargues. He was eager to penetrate the mystery himself on a later dive. Yet he was uneasy about the lifelessness of the rope in the last few minutes. He frowned and fingered the rope like a pulse, and waited.

Up from the lag of rope, four hundred feet across the friction of rocks, and through the surface, a faint vibration tickled Fargues's finger. He reacted by standing and grumbling, half to himself, half to the cave watchers, *"Qu'est-ce que je risque? De me faire engueuler?"* (What do I risk? A bawling out?) With a set face he hauled the pig iron in.

I felt the rope tighten. I jerked my hand off the dagger and hung on.

Dumas's air cylinders rang on the rocks as we were borne swiftly up. A hundred feet above I saw a faint triangle of green light, where hope lay. In less than a minute Fargues pulled us out into the pool and leaped in the water after the senseless Dumas. Tailliez and Pinard waded in after me. I gathered what strength I had left to control my emotions, not to break down. I managed to walk out of the pool. Dumas lay on his stomach and vomited. Our friends stripped off our rubber suits. I warmed myself around a flaming caldron of gasoline. Fargues and the doctor worked over Dumas. In five minutes he was on his feet, standing by the fire. I handed him a bottle of brandy. He took a drink and said, "I'm going down again." I wondered where Simone was.

The Mayor said, "When your air bubbles stopped coming to the surface, your wife ran down the hill. She said she could not stand it." Poor Simone had raced to a café in Vaucluse and ordered the most powerful spirit in the house. A rumor monger raced through the village, yelling that one of the divers was drowned. Simone cried, "Which one? What color was his mask?"

"Red," said the harbinger.

Simone gasped with relief—my mask was blue. Then she thought of Didi of the red mask and her joy collapsed. She returned distractedly up the trail to the Fountain. There stood Didi, a miracle to her.

Dumas's recuperative powers put the color back on him and his mind cleared. He wanted to know why we had been drugged in the cavern. In the afternon another *cordée*, Tailliez and Guy Morandière, prepared to dive, without the junk we had carried. They wore only long underwear and light ballast, which rendered them slightly buoyant. They planned to go to the cavern and reconnoiter for the passage which led to the secret of Vaucluse. Having found it they would immediately return and sketch the layout for the third *cordée*, which would make the final plunge.

From the diving logs of Captain Tailliez and Morandière, I am able to recount their experience, which was almost as appalling as ours. Certainly it took greater courage than ours to enter the Fountain from which we had been luckily saved. In their familiarization period just under the surface of the pool, Morandière felt intense cold. They entered the tunnel abreast, roped together. Second *cordée* tactics were to swim down side by side along the ceiling.

When they encountered humps sticking down from the roof, they were to duck under and return to follow closely the ceiling contour. Each hump they met promised to level off beyond, but never did. They went down and down. Our only depth gauge had been ruined, but the veteran

Tailliez had a sharp physiological sense of depth. At an estimated one hundred and twenty feet he halted the march so they might study their subjective sensations. Tailliez felt the first inviting throbs of rapture of the depths. He knew that to be impossible at a mere twenty fathoms. However, the symptoms were pronounced.

He hooted to Morandière that they should turn back. Morandière maneuvered himself and the rope to facilitate Tailliez's turnabout. As he did so, he heard that Talliez's respiratory rhythm was disorderly, and faced his partner so that Tailliez could see him give six pulls on the pig-iron rope. Unable to exchange words under water, the team had to depend on errant flashlight beams and understanding, to accomplish the turn. Morandière stationed himself below Tailliez to conduct the Captain to the surface. Tailliez construed these activities to mean that Morandière was in trouble. Both men were slipping into the blank rapture that had almost finished the first *cordèe*.

Tailliez carefully climbed the guide line. The rope behind drifted aimlessly in the water and a loop hung around his shoulders. Tailliez felt he had to sever the rope before it entangled him. He whipped out his dagger and cut it away. Morandière, swimming freely below him, was afraid his mate was passing out. The confused second *cordée* ascended to the green hall light of the Fountain. Morandière closed in, took Tailliez's feet and gave him a strong boost through the narrow door. The effort upset Morandière's breathing cycle.

We saw Tailliez emerge in his white underwear, Morandière following through the underwater door. Tailliez broke the surface, found a footing and walked out of the water, erect and wild-eyed. In his right hand he held his dagger, upside down. His fingers were bitten to the bone by the blade and blood flowed down his sodden woolens. He did not feel it.

We resolved to call it a day with a shallow plunge to map the entrance of the Fountain. We made sure that Didi, in his anger against the cave, could not slip down to the drowned cavern that had nearly been our tomb. Fargues lashed a one hundred and fifty foot line to Dumas's waist and took Didi's dagger so he couldn't cut himself loose and go down further.The final reconnaissance of the entrance shaft passed without incident.

It was an emotional day. That evening in Vaucluse the first and second *cordées* made a subjective comparison of cognac narcosis and rapture of the Fountain. None of us could relax, thinking of the enigmatic stupor that had overtaken us. We knew the berserk intoxication of *l'ivresse des grandes profondeurs* at two hundred and twenty feet in the sea, but why did this clear, lifeless limestone water cheat a man's mind in a different way?

Simone, Didi and I drove back to Toulon that night, thinking hard, despite fatigue and headache. Long silences were spaced by occasional suggestions. Didi said, "Narcotic effects aren't the only cause of diving accidents. There are social and subjective fears, the air you breathe . . ." I jumped at the idea. "The air you breathe!" I said. "Let's run a lab test on the air left in the lungs."

The next morning we sampled the cylinders. The analysis showed 1/2000 of carbon monoxide. At a depth of one hundred and sixty feet the effect of carbon monoxide is sixfold. The amount we were breathing may kill a man in twenty minutes. We started our new Diesel-powered free-piston air compressor. We saw the compressor sucking in its own exhaust fumes. We had all been breathing lethal doses of carbon monoxide.

Indians!

by GEORGE A. CUSTER

As almost every American schoolboy knows, General George Armstrong Custer (1839–76) was a handsome, youthful and daring cavalry officer who emerged with a brilliant reputation from the Civil War. He had everything he wanted out of life, or so it seemed. During several leisurely years he wrote My Life on the Plains *(1874), from which the following account is drawn. In 1876 Custer and the 7th Regiment were ordered against the Sioux in Montana and Dakota. Custer arrived at the junction of the Big Horn and Little Big Horn Rivers in Montana Territory on June 24th. On the 25th he advanced in three columns to surround a supposedly small force of hostile Indians and was attacked by the enemy's full force—a disaster caused largely by faulty intelligence. Custer and the center column rode into the midst of the Indians and were slaughtered—265 of them—in what came to be known as Custer's Last Stand.*

THE MARCH FROM CAMP TO BEAVER CREEK WAS MADE WITHout incident. Here the combined forces of Colonel West and Lieutenant Robbins encamped together during the night. Next morning at early dawn Lieutenant Robbins's party, having the train in charge, continued the march toward Fort Wallace, while Colonel West sent out scouting parties up and down the stream to search for Indians.

As yet none of their party were aware of the hostile attitude assumed by the Indians within the past few hours, and Colonel West's instructions contemplated a friendly meeting between his forces and the Indians should the latter be discovered. The march of the train and escort was made to Fort Wallace without interruption. The only incident worthy of remark was an observation of Comstock's, which proved how thoroughly he was familiar with the Indian and his customs.

The escort was moving over a beautifully level plateau. Not a mound or hillock disturbed the evenness of the surface for miles in either direction. To an unpracticed eye there seemed no recess or obstruction in or behind which an enemy might be concealed, but everything appeared open to the view for miles and miles, look in what direction one might. Yet such was not the case. Ravines of greater or less extent, though not perceptible at a glance, might have been discovered if searched for, extending almost to the trail over which the party was moving. These ravines, if followed, would be found to grow deeper and deeper, until, after running their course for an indefinite extent, they would terminate in the valley of some running stream. These were the natural hiding places of Indian war parties, waiting their opportunities to dash upon unsuspecting victims. These ravines serve the same purpose to the Indians of the timberless plains that the ambush did to those Indians of the Eastern States accustomed to fighting in the forests and everglades. Comstock's keen eyes took in all at a glance, and he remarked to Colonel Cook and Lieutenant Robbins, as the three rode together at the head of the column, that "If the Injuns strike us at all, it will be just about the time we are comin' along back over this very spot. Now mind what I tell ye all." We shall see how correct Comstock's prophecy was.

Arriving at the fort, no time was lost in loading up the wagons with fresh supplies, obtaining the mail intended for the command, and preparing to set out on the return to camp the following day. No late news regarding Indian movements was obtained. Fortunately, my letter from Fort McPherson to Mrs. Custer, asking her to come to Fort Wallace, miscarried, and she did not undertake a journey which in all probability would have imperiled her life, if not terminated it in a most tragic manner.

On the following morning Colonel Cook and Lieutenant Robbins began their return march. They had advanced one half the distance which separated them from Colonel West's camp without the slightest occurrence to disturb the monotony of their march, and had reached the point where, on passing before, Comstock had indulged in his prognostication regarding Indians; yet nothing had been seen to excite suspicion or alarm.

Comstock, always on the alert and with eyes as quick as those of an Indian, had been scanning the horizon in all directions. Suddenly he perceived, or thought he perceived, strange figures, resembling human heads, peering over the crest of a hill far away to the right. Hastily leveling his field glass, he pronounced the strange figures, which were scarcely perceptible, to be neither more nor less than Indians. The officers brought into requisition their glasses, and were soon convinced of the correctness of Comstock's report. It was some time before the Indians perceived that they were discovered. Concealment then being no longer possible, they boldly rode to the crest and exposed themselves to full view. At first but twenty or thirty made their appearance; gradually their number became augmented, until about a hundred warriors could be seen.

It may readily be imagined that the appearance of so considerable a body of Indians produced no little excitement and speculation in the minds of the people with the train. The speculation was as to the intentions of the Indians, whether hostile or friendly. Upon this subject all doubts were soon dispelled. The Indians continued to receive accessions to their numbers, the reinforcements coming from beyond the crest of the hill on which their presence was first discovered. Finally, seeming confident in their superior numbers, the warriors, all of whom were mounted, advanced leisurely down the slope leading in the direction of the train and its escort. By the aid of field glasses, Comstock and the two officers were able to determine fully the character of the party now approaching them. The last doubt was thus removed. It was clearly to be seen that the Indians were arrayed in full war costume, their heads adorned by the brilliantly colored war bonnets, their faces, arms, and bodies painted in various colors, rendering their naturally repulsive appearance even more hideous. As they approached nearer they assumed a certain order in the manner of their advance. Some were to be seen carrying the long glistening lance with its pennant of bright colors; while upon the left arm hung the round shield, almost bulletproof, and ornamented with paint and feathers according to the taste of the wearer. Nearly all were armed with carbines and one or two revolvers, while many in addition to these weapons carried the bow and arrow.

When the entire band had defiled down the inclined slope, Comstock and the officers were able to estimate roughly the full strength of the party. They were astonished to perceive that between six and seven hundred warriors were bearing down upon them, and in a few minutes would undoubtedly commence the attack. Against such odds, and upon ground so favorable for the Indian mode of warfare, it seemed unreasonable to hope for a favorable result. Yet the entire escort, officers and men, entered upon their defense with the determination to sell their lives as dearly as possible.

As the coming engagement, so far as the cavalry was concerned, was to be a purely defensive one, Lieutenant Robbins at once set about preparing to receive his unwelcome visitors. Colonel Cook formed the train in two parallel columns, leaving ample space between for the horses of the cavalry. Lieutenant Robbins then dismounted his men and prepared to fight on foot. The led horses, under charge of the fourth trooper, were placed between the two columns of wagons, and were thus in a measure protected from the assaults which the officers had every reason to believe would be made for their capture. The dismounted cavalrymen were thus formed in a regular circle enclosing the train and horses. Colonel Cook took command of one flank, Lieutenant Robbins of the other, while Comstock, who as well as the two officers remained mounted, galloped from point to point wherever his presence was most valuable. These dispositions being perfected, the march was resumed in this order, and the attack of the savages calmly awaited.

The Indians, who were interested spectators of these preparations for their reception, continued to approach, but seemed willing to delay their attack until the plain became a little more favorable for their operations. Finally, the desired moment seemed to have arrived. The Indians had approached to within easy range, yet not a shot had been fired, the cavalrymen having been instructed by their officers to reserve their fire for close quarters. Suddenly, with a wild ringing war whoop, the entire band of warriors bore down upon the train and its little party of defenders.

On came the savages, filling the air with their terrible yells. Their first object, evidently, was to stampede the horses and draft animals of the train; then, in the excitement and consternation which would follow, to massacre the escort and drivers. The wagon master in immediate charge of the train had been ordered to keep his two columns of wagons constantly moving forward and well closed up. This last injunction was hardly necessary, as the frightened teamsters, glancing at the approaching warriors and hearing their savage shouts, were sufficiently anxious to keep well closed upon their leaders.

The first onslaught of the Indians was made on the flank which was superintended by Colonel Cook. They rode boldly forward as if to dash over the mere handful of cavalrymen, who stood in skirmishing order in a circle about the train. Not a soldier faltered as the enemy came thundering upon them, but waiting until the Indians were within short rifle range of the train, the cavalrymen dropped upon their knees, and taking deliberate aim poured a volley from their Spencer carbines into the ranks of the savages, which seemed to put a sudden check upon the ardor of their movements and forced them to wheel off to the right. Several of the warriors were seen to reel in their saddles, while the ponies of others were brought down or wounded by the effectual fire of the cavalrymen.

Those of the savages who were shot from their saddles were scarcely permitted to fall to the ground before a score or more of their comrades dashed to their rescue and bore their bodies beyond the possible reach of our men. This is in accordance with the Indian custom in battle. They will risk the lives of a dozen of their best warriors to prevent the body of any one of their number from falling into the white man's possession. The reason for this is the belief, which generally prevails among all the tribes, that if a warrior loses his scalp he forfeits his hope of ever reaching the happy hunting ground.

As the Indians were being driven back by the well-directed volley of the cavalrymen, the latter, overjoyed at their first success, became reassured, and sent up a cheer of exultation, while Comstock, who had not been idle in the fight, called out to the retreating Indians in their native tongue, taunting them with their unsuccessful assault.

The Indians withdrew to a point beyond the range of our carbines, and there seemed to engage in a parley. Comstock, who had closely watched every movement, remarked that "There's no sich good luck for us as to think them Injuns mean to give it up so. Six hundred red devils ain't agoin' to let fifty men stop them from gettin' at the coffee and sugar that is in these wagons. And they ain't agoin' to be satisfied until they get some of our scalps to pay for the bucks we popped out of their saddles a bit ago."

It was probable that the Indians were satisfied that they could not dash through the train and stampede the animals. Their recent attempt had convinced them that some other method of attack must be resorted to. Nothing but their greater superiority in numbers had induced them to risk so much in a charge.

The officers passed along the line of skirmishers—for this in reality was all their line consisted of—and cautioned the men against wasting their ammunition. It was yet early in the afternoon, and should the conflict be prolonged until night, there was great danger of exhausting the supply of ammunition. The Indians seemed to have thought of this, and the change in their method of attack encouraged such a result.

But little time was spent at the parley. Again the entire band of warriors, except those already disabled, prepared to renew the attack, and advanced as before—this time, however, with greater caution, evidently desiring to avoid a reception similar to the first. When sufficiently near to the troops the Indians developed their new plan of attack. It was not to advance *en masse,* as before, but fight as individuals, each warrior selecting his own time and method of attack. This is the habitual manner of fighting among all Indians of the Plains, and is termed "circling." First the chiefs led off, followed at regular intervals by the warriors, until the entire six or seven hundred were to be seen riding in single file as rapidly as their fleet-footed ponies could carry them. Preserving this order, and keeping up their savage chorus of yells, war whoops, and taunting epithets, this long line of mounted barbarians was guided in such manner as to envelop the train and escort, and make the latter appear like a small circle within a larger one.

The Indians gradually contracted their circle, although maintaining the full speed of their ponies, until sufficiently close to open fire upon the soldiers. At first the shots were scattering and wide of their mark; but, emboldened by the silence of their few but determined opponents, they rode nearer and fought with greater impetuosity. Forced now to defend themselves to the uttermost, the cavalrymen opened fire from their carbines, with most gratifying results. The Indians, however, moving at such a rapid gait and in single file, presented a most uncertain target. To add to this uncertainty, the savages availed themselves of their superior—almost marvelous—powers of horsemanship. Throwing themselves upon the sides of their well-trained ponies, they left no part of their persons exposed to the aim of the troopers except the head and one foot, and in this posture they were able to aim the weapons either over or under the necks of their ponies, thus using the bodies of the latter as an effective shield against the bullets of their adversaries.

At no time were the Indians able to force the train and its escort to come to a halt. The march was continued at an uninterrupted gait. This successful defense against the Indians was in a great measure due to the presence of the wagons, which, arranged in the order described, formed a complete barrier to the charges and assaults of the savages; and, as a last resort, the wagons could have been halted and used as a breastwork, behind which the cavalry, dismounted, would have been almost invincible against their more numerous enemies. There is nothing an Indian dislikes more in warfare than to attack a foe, however weak, behind

breastworks of any kind. Any contrivance which is an obstacle to his
pony is a most serious obstacle to the warrior.

The attack of the Indians, aggravated by their losses in warriors and
ponies, as many of the latter had been shot down, was continued without
cessation for three hours. The supply of ammunition of the cavalry was
running low. The "fourth troopers," who had remained in charge of
the led horses between the two columns of wagons, were now replaced
from the skirmishers, and the former were added to the list of active
combatants. If the Indians should maintain the fight much longer, there
was serious ground for apprehension regarding the limited supply of
ammunition.

If only night or reinforcements would come! was the prayerful hope
of those who contended so gallantly against such heavy odds. Night was
still too far off to promise much encouragement; while as to reinforcements, their coming would be purely accidental—at least so argued those
most interested in their arrival. Yet reinforcements were at that moment
striving to reach them. Comrades were in the saddle and spurring forward to their relief. The Indians, although apparently turning all their
attention to the little band inside, had omitted no precaution to guard
against interference from outside parties. In this instance, perhaps,
they were more than ordinarily watchful, and had posted some of their
keen-eyed warriors on the high line of bluffs which ran almost parallel
to the trail over which the combatants moved. From these bluffs not only
a good view of the fight could be obtained, but the country for miles in
either direction was spread out beneath them, and enabled the scouts
to discern the approach of any hostile party which might be advancing.
Fortunate for the savages that this precaution had not been neglected,
or the contest in which they were engaged might have become one of
more equal numbers. To the careless eye nothing could have been seen
to excite suspicion. But the warriors on the lookout were not long in
discovering something which occasioned them no little anxiety. Dis-
mounting from their ponies and concealing the latter in a ravine, they
prepared to investigate more fully the cause of their alarm.

That which they saw was as yet but a faint dark line on the surface
of the plain, almost against the horizon. So faint was it that no one but
an Indian or practiced frontiersman would have observed it. It was fully
ten miles from them and directly in their line of march. The ordinary
observer would have pronounced it a break or irregularity in the ground,
or perhaps the shadow of a cloud, and its apparent permanency of
location would have dispelled any fear as to its dangerous character.

But was it stationary? Apparently, yes. The Indians discovered otherwise. By close watching, the long faint line could be seen moving along, as if creeping stealthily upon an unconscious foe. Slowly it assumed a more definite shape, until what appeared to be a mere stationary dark line drawn upon the green surface of the plain developed itself to the searching eyes of the red man into a column of cavalry moving at a rapid gait toward the very point they were then occupying.

Convinced of this fact, one of the scouts leaped upon his pony and flew with almost the speed of the wind to impart this knowledge to the chiefs in command on the plain below. True, the approaching cavalry, being still several miles distant, could not arrive for nearly two hours; but the question to be considered by the Indians was, whether it would be prudent for them to continue their attack on the train—their ponies already becoming exhausted by the three hours' hard riding given them—until the arrival of the fresh detachment of the enemy, whose horses might be in condition favorable to a rapid pursuit, and thereby enable them to overtake those of the Indians whose ponies were exhausted. Unwilling to incur this new risk, and seeing no prospect of overcoming their present adversaries by a sudden or combined dash, the chiefs decided to withdraw from the attack, and make their escape while the advantage was yet in their favor.

The surprise of the cavalrymen may be imagined at seeing the Indians, after pouring a shower of bullets and arrows into the train, withdraw to the bluffs, and immediately after continue their retreat until lost to view.

This victory for the troopers, although so unexpected, was none the less welcome. The Indians contrived to carry away with them their killed and wounded. Five of their bravest warriors were known to have been sent to the happy hunting ground, while the list of their wounded was much larger.

After the Indians had withdrawn and left the cavalrymen masters of the field, our wounded, of whom there were comparatively few, received every possible care and attention. Those of the detachment who had escaped unharmed were busily engaged in exchanging congratulations and relating incidents of the fight.

In this manner nearly an hour had been whiled away, when far in the distance, in their immediate front, fresh cause for anxiety was discovered. At first the general opinion was that it was the Indians again, determined to contest their progress. Field glasses were again called into requisition, and revealed, not Indians, but the familiar blue blouses of the cavalry. Never was the sight more welcome. The next moment Colonel Cook, with Comstock and a few troopers, applied spurs to their horses and were soon dashing forward to meet their comrades.

The approaching party was none other than Colonel West's detachment, hastening to the relief of the train and its gallant little escort. A few words explained all, and told the heroes of the recent fight how it happened that reinforcements were sent to their assistance; and then was explained why the Indians had so suddenly concluded to abandon their attack and seek safety in quietly withdrawing from the field.

Rounding the Horn

by RICHARD HENRY DANA

The voyage which Dana here partly describes in his justly famous narrative, Two Years Before the Mast, *was a turning point in his career. Leaving Harvard because of difficulties with his eyesight, he shipped before the mast in an effort to regain his health, going to California via the tip of South America. He returned in 1836, healthy, energetic and with the raw materials for a classic about the sea.*

THERE BEGAN NOW TO BE A DECIDED CHANGE IN THE appearance of things. The days became shorter and shorter; the sun running lower in its course each day, and giving less and less heat, and the night so cold as to prevent our sleeping on deck; the Magellan Clouds in sight on a clear, moonless night; the skies looking cold and angry; and, at times, a long, heavy, ugly sea setting in from the southward, told us what we were coming to. Still, however, we had a fine strong breeze, and kept on our way under as much sail as our ship would bear.

Toward the middle of the week, the wind hauled to the southward, which brought us upon a taut bowline, made the ship meet, nearly head-on, the heavy swell which rolled from that quarter; and there was something not at all encouraging in the manner in which she met it. Being so deep and heavy, she wanted the buoyancy which should have carried her over the seas, and she dropped heavily into them, the water washing over the decks; and every now and then, when an unusually large sea met her fairly upon the bows, she struck it with a sound as dead and heavy as that with which a sledgehammer falls upon the pile, and took the whole of it upon the forecastle, and, rising, carried it aft in the scuppers, washing the rigging off the pins, and carrying along with it

167

everything which was loose on deck. She had been acting in this way all of our forenoon watch below; as we could tell by the washing of the water over our heads, and the heavy breaking of the seas against her bows, only the thickness of a plank from our heads, as we lay in our berths, which are directly against the bows.

At eight bells the watch was called, and we came on deck, one hand going aft to take the wheel, and another going to the galley to get the grub for dinner. I stood on the forecastle, looking at the seas, which were rolling high, as far as the eye could reach, their tops white with foam, and the body of them of a deep indigo blue, reflecting the bright rays of the sun. Our ship rose slowly over a few of the largest of them, until one immense fellow came rolling on, threatening to cover her, and which I was sailor enough to know, by the "feeling of her" under my feet, she would not rise over. I sprang upon the knightheads, and, seizing hold of the forestay, drew myself up upon it. My feet were just off the stanchion when the bow struck fairly into the middle of the sea, and it washed the ship fore and aft, burying her in the water. As soon as she rose out of it, I looked aft, and everything forward to the mainmast, except the longboat, which was gripped and double-lashed down to the ringbolts, was swept off clear. The galley, the pigsty, the hencoop, and a large sheeppen, which had been built upon the fore hatch, were all gone in the twinkling of an eye—leaving the deck as clean as a chin new reaped —and not a stick left to show where anything had stood. In the scuppers lay the galley, bottom up, and a few boards floating about—the wreck of the sheeppen—and half a dozen miserable sheep floating among them, wet through, and not a little frightened at the sudden change that had come upon them.

As soon as the sea had washed by, all hands sprang up out of the forecastle to see what had become of the ship; and in a few moments the cook and Old Bill crawled out from under the galley, where they had been lying in the water, nearly smothered, with the galley over them. Fortunately, it rested against the bulwarks, or it would have broken some of their bones. When the water ran off, we picked the sheep up, and put them in the longboat, got the galley back in its place, and set things a little to rights; but had not our ship uncommonly high bulwarks and rail, everything must have been washed overboard, not excepting Old Bill and the cook. Bill had been standing at the galley door, with the kid of beef in his hand for the forecastle mess, when away he went, kid, beef, and all. He held on to the kid to the last, like a good fellow, but the beef was gone, and when the water had run off we saw it lying high and dry, like a rock at low tide—nothing could hurt *that*. We took the loss of our beef very easily, consoling ourselves with the recollection that the cabin had more to lose than we; and chuckled not a little at seeing the remains of the chicken pie and pancakes floating in the scuppers.

"This will never do!" was what some said, and every one felt. Here we were, not yet within a thousand miles of the latitude of Cape Horn, and our decks swept by a sea not one-half so high as we must expect to find there. Some blamed the captain for loading his ship so deep when he knew what he must expect; while others said that the wind was always southwest off the Cape in the winter, and that, running before it, we should not mind the sea so much.

When we got down into the forecastle, Old Bill, who was somewhat of a croaker—having met with a great many accidents at sea—said that if that was the way she was going to act, we might as well make our wills, and balance the books at once, and put on a clean shirt.

" 'Vast there, you bloody old owl; you're always hanging out blue lights! You're frightened by the ducking you got in the scuppers, and can't take a joke! What's the use in being always on the lookout for Davy Jones?"

"Stand by!" says another, "and we'll get an afternoon watch below, by this scrape;" but in this they were disappointed; for at two bells all hands were called and set to work, getting lashings upon everything on deck; and the captain talked of sending down the long topgallant masts; but as the sea went down toward night, and the wind hauled abeam, we left them standing, and set the studding sails.

The next day all hands were turned to upon unbending the old sails, and getting up the new ones; for a ship, unlike people on shore, puts on her best suit in bad weather. The old sails were sent down, and three new topsails, and new fore and main courses, jib, and foretopmast staysail, which were made on the coast and never had been used, were bent, with a complete set of new earings, robands, and reef points; and reef tackles were rove to the courses, and spilling lines to the topsails. These, with new braces and clew lines fore and aft, gave us a good suit of running rigging.

The wind continued westerly, and the weather and sea less rough since the day on which we shipped the heavy sea, and we were making great progress under studding sails, with our light sails all set, keeping a little to the eastward of south; for the captain, depending upon westerly winds off the Cape, had kept so far to the westward that, though we were within about five miles of the latitude of Cape Horn, we were nearly

seventeen hundred miles to the westward of it. Through the rest of the
week we continued on with a fair wind, gradually, as we got more to
southward, keeping a more easterly course, and bringing the wind on
our larboard quarter, until—

Sunday, June 26th, when, having a fine, clear day, the captain got a
lunar observation, as well as his meridian altitude, which made us in lat.
47° 50′ S., lon. 113° 50′ W.; Cape Horn bearing, according to my calculation, E. S. E. ½ E., and distant eighteen hundred miles.

Monday, June 27th. During the first part of this day the wind continued fair, and, as we were going before it, it did not feel very cold, so
that we kept at work on deck in our common clothes and round jackets.
Our watch had an afternoon watch below for the first time since leaving
San Diego; and, having inquired of the third mate what the latitude was
at noon, and made our usual guesses as to the time she would need to
be up with the Horn, we turned in for a nap. We were sleeping away
"at the rate of knots," when three knocks on the scuttle and "All hands,
ahoy!" started us from our berths. What could be the matter? It did not
appear to be blowing hard, and, looking up through the scuttle, we could
see that it was a clear day overhead; yet the watch were taking in sail. We
thought there must be a sail in sight, and that we were about to heave to
and speak her; and were just congratulating ourselves upon it—for we
had seen neither sail nor land since we left port—when we heard the
mate's voice on deck (he turned in "all-standing," and was always on
deck the moment he was called) singing out to the men who were taking
in the studding sails, and asking where his watch was. We did not wait
for a second call, but tumbled up the ladder; and there, on the starboard
bow, was a bank of mist, covering sea and sky, and driving directly for
us. I had seen the same before in my passage round in the *Pilgrim,* and
knew what it meant, and that there was no time to be lost. We had nothing
on but thin clothes, yet there was not a moment to spare, and at it we
went.

The boys of the other watch were in the tops, taking in the topgallant
studding sails, and the lower and topmost studding sails were coming
down by the run. It was nothing but "haul down and clew up," until we
got all the studding sails in, and the royals, flying jib, and mizzen topgallant sail furled, and the ship kept off a little, to take the squall. The
fore and main top gallant sails were still on her, for the "old man" did
not mean to be frightened in broad daylight, and was determined to
carry sail till the last minute. We all stood waiting for its coming, when
the first blast showed us that it was not to be trifled with. Rain, sleet,

snow, and wind enough to take our breath from us, and make the toughest turn his back to windward! The ship lay nearly over upon her beam ends; the spars and rigging snapped and cracked; and her topgallant masts bent like whipsticks.

"Clew up the fore and main topgallant sails!" shouted the captain, and all hands sprang to the clewlines.

The decks were standing nearly at an angle of forty-five degrees, and the ship going like a mad steed through the water, the whole forward part of her in a smother of foam. The halyards were let go, and the yard clewed down, and the sheets started, and in a few minutes the sails smothered and kept in by clewlines and buntlines.

"Furl 'em, sir?" asked the mate.

"Let go the topsail halyards, fore and aft!" shouted the captain in answer, at the top of his voice.

Down came the topsail yards, the reef tackles were manned and hauled out, and we climbed up to windward, and sprang into the weather rigging. The violence of the wind, and the hail and sleet, driving nearly horizontally across the ocean, seemed actually to pin us down to the rigging. It was hard work making head against them. One after another we got out upon the yards. And here we had work to do; for our new sails had hardly been bent long enough to get the stiffness out of them, and the new earings and reef points, stiffened with the sleet, knotted like pieces of iron wire. Having only our round jackets and straw hats on, we were soon wet through, and it was every moment growing colder. Our hands were soon numbed, which, added to the stiffness of everything else, kept us a good while on the yard. After we had got the sail hauled upon the yard, we had to wait a long time for the weather earing to be passed; but there was no fault to be found, for French John was at the earing, and a better sailor never laid out on a yard; so we leaned over the yard and beat our hands upon the sail to keep them from freezing.

At length the word came, "Haul out to leeward," and we seized the reef points and hauled the band taut for the lee earing. "Taut band—knot away," and we got the first reef fast, and were just going to lay down, when—"Two reefs! two reefs!" shouted the mate, and we had a second reef to take in the same way. When this was fast, we went down on deck, manned the halyards to leeward, nearly up to our knees in water, set the topsail, and then laid aloft on the maintopsail yard, and reefed that sail in the same manner; for, as I have before stated, we were a good deal reduced in numbers, and, to make it worse, the carpenter, only two days before, had cut his leg with an ax, so that he could not go aloft.

This weakened us so that we could not well manage more than one top-sail at a time, in such weather as this, and, of course, each man's labor was doubled. From the maintopsail yard, we went upon the main yard, and took a reef in the mainsail. No sooner had we got on deck than— "Lay aloft there, and close-reef mizzen topsail!"

This called me; and, being nearest to the rigging, I got first aloft, and out to the weather earing. English Ben was up just after me, and took the lea earing, and the rest of our gang were soon on the yard, and began to fist the sail, when the mate considerately sent up the cook and steward to help us. I could now account for the long time it took to pass the other earings; for, to do my best with a strong hand to help me at the dog's ear, I could not get it passed until I heard them beginning to complain in the bunt. One reef after another we took in, until the sail was close reefed, when we went down and hoisted away at the halyards.

In the meantime, the jib had been furled and the staysail set, and the ship under her reduced sail had got more upright and was under management; but the two topgallant sails were still hanging in the bunt-lines, and slatting and jerking as though they would take the masts out of her. We gave a look aloft, and knew that our work was not done yet; and, sure enough, no sooner did the mate see that we were on deck again than—"Lay aloft there, four of you, and furl the topgallant sails!" This called me again, and two of us went aloft up the fore rig-ging, two more up the main, upon the topgallant yards. The shrouds were now iced over, the sleet having formed a crust round all the standing rigging, and on the weather side of the masts and yards. When we got upon the yard, my hands were so numb that I could not have cast off the knot of the gasket if it were to save my life. We both lay over the yard for a few seconds, beating our hands upon the sail, until we started the blood in our finger ends, and at the next moment our hands were in a burning heat. My companion on the yard was a lad (the boy, George Somerby) who came out in the ship a weak, puny boy, from one of the Boston schools—"no larger than a spritsail-sheet knot," nor "heavier than a paper of lampblack," and "not strong enough to haul a shad off a gridiron," but who was now "as long as a spare topmast, strong enough to knock down an ox, and hearty enough to eat him." We fisted the sail together, and, after six or eight minutes of hard hauling and pulling and beating down the sail, which was about as stiff as sheet iron, we managed to get it furled; and snugly furled it must be, for we knew the mate well enough to be certain that if it got adrift again we should be called up from our watch below, at any hour of the night, to furl it.

I had been on the lookout for a chance to jump below and clap on a thick jacket and southwester; but when we got on deck we found that eight bells had been struck, and the other watch gone below, so that there were two hours of dog watch for us, and a plenty of work to do. It had now set in for a steady gale from the southwest; but we were not yet far enough to the southward to make a fair wind of it, for we must give Tierra del Fuego a wide berth. The decks were covered with snow, and there was a constant driving of sleet. In fact, Cape Horn had set in with good earnest. In the midst of all this, and before it became dark, we had all the studding sails to make up and stow away, and then to lay aloft and rig in all the booms, fore and aft, and coil away the tacks, sheets, and halyards. This was pretty tough work for four or five hands, in the face of a gale which almost took us off the yards, and with ropes so stiff with ice that it was almost impossible to bend them. I was nearly half an hour out on the end of the fore yard, trying to coil away and stop down the topmast studding-sail tack and lower halyards. It was after dark when we got through, and we were not a little pleased to hear four bells struck, which sent us below for two hours, and gave us each a pot of hot tea with our cold beef and bread, and, what was better yet, a suit of thick, dry clothing, fitted for the weather, in place of our thin clothes, which were wet through, and now frozen stiff.

This sudden turn, for which we were so little prepared, was as unacceptable to me as to any of the rest; for I had been troubled for several days with a slight toothache, and this cold weather and wetting and freezing were not the best things in the world for it. I soon found that it was getting strong hold, and running over all parts of my face; and before the watch was out I went to the mate, who had charge of the medicine chest, to get something for it. But the chest showed like the end of a long voyage, for there was nothing that would answer but a few drops of laudanum, which must be saved for an emergency; so I had only to bear the pain as well as I could.

When we went on deck at eight bells, it had stopped snowing, and there were a few stars out, but the clouds were still black, and it was blowing a steady gale. Just before midnight, I went aloft and sent down the mizzen royal yard, and had the good luck to do it to the satisfaction of the mate, who said it was done "out of hand and shipshape." The next four hours below were but little relief to me, for I lay awake in my berth the whole time, from the pain in my face, and heard every bell strike, and, at four o'clock, turned out with the watch, feeling little spirit for the hard duties of the day. Bad weather and hard work at sea can be borne up against very well if one only has spirit and health; but there is nothing brings a man down at such a time like bodily pain and want of sleep.

There was, however, too much to do to allow time to think; for the gale of yesterday, and the heavy seas we met with a few days before, while we had yet ten degrees more southing to make, had convinced the captain that we had something before us which was not to be trifled with, and orders were given to send down the long topgallant masts. The topgallant and royal yards were accordingly struck, the flying jib boom rigged in, and the topgallant masts sent down on deck, and all lashed together by the side of the longboat. The rigging was then sent down and coiled away below, and everything made snug aloft. There was not a sailor in the ship who was not rejoiced to see these sticks come down; for, so long as the yards were aloft, on the least sign of a lull, the topgallant sails were loosed, and then we had to furl them again in a snow squall, and *shin* up and down single ropes caked with ice, and send royal yards down in the teeth of a gale coming right from the south pole.

It was an interesting sight, too, to see our noble ship dismantled of all her top hamper of long tapering masts and yards, and boom pointed with spear head, which ornamented her in port; and all that canvas which, a few days before, had covered her like a cloud, from the truck to the water's edge, spreading far out beyond her hull on either side, now gone; and she stripped like a wrestler for the fight. It corresponded, too, with the desolate character of her situation—alone, as she was, battling with storms, wind, and ice, at this extremity of the globe, and in almost constant night.

Friday, July 1st. We were now nearly up to the latitude of Cape Horn, and having over forty degrees of easting to make, we squared away the yards before a strong westerly gale, shook a reef out of the foretopsail, and stood on our way, east by south, with the prospect of being up with the Cape in a week or ten days. As for myself, I had had no sleep for forty-eight hours; and the want of rest, together with constant wet and cold, had increased the swelling, so that my face was nearly as large as two, and I found it impossible to get my mouth open wide enough to eat. In this state, the steward applied to the captain for some rice to boil for me, but he only got a "No! d—— you! Tell him to eat salt junk and hard bread, like the rest of them." This was, in truth, what I expected. However, I did not starve, for Mr. Brown, who was a man as well as a sailor, and had always been a good friend to me, smuggled a pan of rice into the galley, and told the cook to boil it for me, and not let the "old man" see it. Had it been fine weather, or in port, I should have gone below and laid by until my face got well; but in such weather as this, and shorthanded as we were, it was not for me to desert my post; so I kept on deck, and stood my watch and did my duty as well as I could.

Saturday, July 2nd. This day the sun rose fair, but it ran too low in the heavens to give any heat, or thaw out our sails and rigging; yet the sight of it was pleasant; and we had a steady "reef-topsail breeze" from the westward. The atmosphere, which had previously been clear and cold, for the last few hours grew damp, and had a disagreeable wet chilliness in it; and the man who came from the wheel said he heard the captain tell "the passenger" that the thermometer had fallen several degrees since morning, which he could not account for in any other way than by supposing that there must be ice near us; though such a thing was rarely heard of in this latitude at this season of the year. At twelve o'clock we went below, and had just got through dinner when the cook put his head down the scuttle and told us to come on deck and see the finest sight that we had ever seen.

"Where away, Doctor?"* asked the first man who was up.

"On the larboard bow."

And there lay, floating in the ocean, several miles off, an immense irregular mass, its top and points covered with snow, and its center of a deep indigo color. This was an iceberg, and of the largest size, as one of our men said who had been in the Northern Ocean. As far as the eye could reach, the sea in every direction was of a deep blue color, the waves running high and fresh, and sparkling in the light, and in the midst lay this immense mountain island, its cavities and valleys thrown into deep shade, and its points and pinnacles glittering in the sun. All hands were soon on deck, looking at it, and admiring in various ways its beauty and grandeur. But no description can give any idea of the strangeness, splendor, and, really, the sublimity, of the sight. Its great size—for it must have been from two to three miles in circumference, and several hundred feet in height—its slow motion, as its base rose and sank in the water, and its high points nodded against the clouds; the dashing of the waves upon it, which, breaking high with foam, lined its base with a white crust; and the thundering sound of the cracking

* The cook's title in all vessels.

of the mass, and the breaking and tumbling down of huge pieces; together with its nearness and approach, which added a slight element of fear—all combined to give to it the character of true sublimity.

The main body of the mass was, as I have said, of an indigo color, its base crusted with frozen foam; and as it grew thin and transparent toward the edges and top, its color shaded off from a deep blue to the whiteness of snow. It seemed to be drifting slowly toward the north, so that we kept away and avoided it. It was in sight all the afternoon; and when we got to leeward of it the wind died away, so that we lay to quite near it for a greater part of the night. Unfortunately, there was no moon, but it was a clear night, and we could plainly mark the long regular heaving of the stupendous mass, as its edges moved slowly against the stars, now revealing them, and now shutting them in. Several times in our watch loud cracks were heard, which sounded as though they must have run through the whole length of the iceberg, and several pieces fell down with a thundering crash, plunging heavily into the sea. Toward morning a strong breeze sprang up, and we filled away, and left it astern, and at daylight it was out of sight. The next day, which was—

Sunday, July 3rd, the breeze continued strong, the air exceedingly chilly, and the thermometer low. In the course of the day we saw several icebergs of different sizes, but none so near as the one which we saw the day before. Some of them, as well as we could judge at the distance at which we were, must have been as large as that, if not larger. At noon we were in latitude 55° 12′ S., and supposed longitude 89° 5′ W. Toward night the wind hauled to the southward, and headed us off our course a little, and blew a tremendous gale; but this we did not mind, as there was no rain nor snow, and we were already under close sail.

Monday, July 4th. This was "Independence Day" in Boston. What firing of guns, and ringing of bells, and rejoicing of all sorts, in every part of our country! The ladies (who have not gone down to Nahant for a breath of cool air and sight of the ocean) walking the streets with parasols over their heads, and the dandies in their white pantaloons and silk stockings! What quantities of ice cream have been eaten, and how many loads of ice brought into the city from a distance, and sold out by the lump and the pound! The smallest of the islands which we saw today would have made the fortune of poor Jack, if he had had it in Boston; and I dare say he would have had no objection to being there with it. This, to be sure, was no place to keep the Fourth of July. To keep ourselves warm, and the ship out of the ice, was as much as we

could do. Yet no one forgot the day; and many were the wishes and
conjectures and comparisons, both serious and ludicrous, which were
made among all hands.

The sun shone bright as long as it was up, only that a scud of black
clouds was ever and anon driving across it. At noon we were in
latitude 54° 27′ S., longitude 85° 5′ W., having made a good deal of
easting, but having lost in our latitude by the heading of the wind. Between daylight and dark—that is, between nine o'clock and three—we
saw thirty-four ice islands of various sizes; some no bigger than the
hull of our vessel, and others apparently nearly as large as the one that
we first saw; though, as we went on, the islands became smaller and more
numerous; and at sundown of this day a man at the masthead saw large
tracts of floating ice, called "field ice," at the southeast.

This kind of ice is much more dangerous than the large islands, for
those can be seen at a distance, and kept away from; but the ice field,
floating in great quantities, and covering the ocean for miles and miles,
in pieces of every size—large, flat, and broken cakes, with here and there
an island rising twenty and thirty feet, as large as the ship's hull—this
it is very difficult to steer clear of. A constant lookout was necessary;
for many of these pieces, coming with the heave of the sea, were large
enough to have knocked a hole in the ship, and that would have been
the end of us; for no boat (even if we could have got one out) could
have lived in such a sea; and no man could have lived in a boat in such
weather.

To make our condition still worse, the wind came out due east, just
after sundown, and it blew a gale dead ahead, with hail and sleet and a
thick fog, so that we could not see half the length of the ship. Our chief
reliance, the prevailing westerly gales, was thus cut off, and here we
were, nearly seven hundred miles to the westward of the Cape, with a
gale dead from the eastward, and the weather so thick that we could not
see the ice with which we were surrounded until it was directly under our
bows.

At four P.M. (it was quite dark) all hands were called, and sent aloft,
in a violent squall of hail and rain, to take in sail. We had now all got
on our "Cape Horn rig"—thick boots, southwesters coming down over
our neck and ears, thick trousers and jackets, and some with oilcloth
suits over all. Mittens, too, we wore on deck, but it would not do to go
aloft with them, as, being wet and stiff, they might let a man slip overboard, for all the hold he could get upon a rope: so we were obliged to
work with bare hands, which, as well as our faces, were often cut with

the hailstones, which fell thick and large. Our ship was now all cased with ice—hull, spars, and standing rigging; and the running rigging so stiff that we could hardly bend it so as to belay it, or, still less, take a knot with it; and the sails frozen. One at a time (for it was a long piece of work and required many hands) we furled the courses, mizzen topsail, and foretopmast staysail, and close-reefed the fore and main topsails, and hove the ship to under the fore, with the main hauled up by the clewlines and buntlines, and ready to be sheeted home, if we found it necessary to make sail to get to windward of an ice island. A regular lookout was then set, and kept by each watch in turn, until the morning.

It was a tedious and anxious night. It blew hard the whole time, and there was an almost constant driving of either rain, hail, or snow. In addition to this it was "as thick as muck," and the ice was all about us. The captain was on deck nearly the whole night, and kept the cook in the galley, with a roaring fire, to make coffee for him, which he took every few hours and once or twice gave a little to his officers; but not a drop of anything was there for the crew. The captain, who sleeps all the daytime, and comes and goes at night as he chooses, can have his brandy and water in the cabin, and his hot coffee at the galley; while Jack, who has to stand through everything, and work in wet and cold, can have nothing to wet his lips or warm his stomach.

This was a "temperance ship" by her articles, and, like too many such ships, the temperance was all in the forecastle. The sailor, who only takes his one glass as it is dealt out to him, is in danger of being drunk; while the captain, upon whose self-possession and cool judgment the lives of all depend, may be trusted with any amount, to drink at his will. Sailors will never be convinced that rum is a dangerous thing by taking it away from them and giving it to the officers; nor can they see a friend in that temperance which takes from them what they have always had, and gives them nothing in the place of it. By seeing it allowed to their officers, they will not be convinced that it is taken from them for their good; and by receiving nothing in its place, they will not believe that it is done in kindness. On the contrary, many of them look upon the change as a new instrument of tyranny. Not that they prefer rum. I never knew a sailor, who had been a month away from the grog shops, who would not prefer a pot of hot coffee or chocolate, in a cold night, to all the rum afloat. They all say that rum only warms them for a time; yet, if they can get nothing better, they will miss what they have lost. The momentary warmth and glow from drinking it; the break and change which it makes in a long dreary watch by the mere calling all hands aft and serving it out;

and the simply having some event to look forward to and to talk about
—all give it an importance and a use which no one can appreciate who
has not stood his watch before the mast.

On my passage out, the *Pilgrim* was not under temperance articles,
and grog was served out every middle and morning watch, and after
every reefing of topsails; and though I had never drunk rum before, nor
desire to again, I took my allowance then at the capstan, as the rest did,
merely for the momentary warmth it gave the system, and the change in
our feeling and aspect of duties on the watch. At the same time, as I have
said, there was not a man on board, who would not have pitched the
rum to the dogs (I have heard them say so a dozen times) for a pot of
coffee or chocolate; or even for our common beverage—"water bewitched
and tea begrudged," as it was.*

The temperance reform is the best thing that ever was undertaken
for the sailor; but when the grog is taken from him, he ought to have
something in its place. As it is now, in most vessels, it is a mere saving
to the owners; and this accounts for the sudden increase of temperance
ships, which surprised even the best friends of the cause. If every merchant, when he struck grog from the list of the expenses of his ship, had
been obliged to substitute as much coffee or chocolate as would give
each man a potful when he came off the topsail yard on a stormy night,
I fear Jack might have gone to ruin on the old road.†

But this is not doubling Cape Horn. Eight hours of the night our
watch was on deck, and during the whole of that time we kept a bright
lookout; one man on each bow, another in the bunt of the foreyard, the

---

* The proportions of the ingredients of the tea that was made for us (and ours,
as I have before stated, was a favorable specimen of American merchantmen)
were a pint of tea and a pint and a half of molasses to about three gallons of
water. These are all boiled down together in the "coppers," and, before serving it
out, the mess is stirred up with a stick, so as to give each man his fair share of
sweetening and tealeaves. The tea for the cabin is, of course, made in the usual
way, in a teapot, and drunk with sugar.

† I do not wish these remarks, so far as they relate to the saving of expense in
the outfit, to be applied to the owners of our ship, for she was supplied with an
abundance of stores of the best kind that are given to seamen; though the dis-
pensing of them is necessarily left to the captain. And I learned, on our return,
that the captain withheld many of the stores from us, from mere ugliness. He
brought several barrels of flour home, but would not give us the usual twice-a-
week duff, and so as to other stores. Indeed, so high was the reputation of "the
employ" among men and officers for the character and outfit of their vessels, and
for their liberality in conducting their voyages, that when it was known that they
had the *Alert* fitting out for a long voyage, and that hands were to be shipped at a
certain time—a half hour before the time, as one of the crew told me, sailors were
steering down the wharf, hopping over the barrels, like a drove of sheep.

third mate on the scuttle, one man on each quarter, and another always standing by the wheel. The chief mate was everywhere, and commanded the ship when the captain was below. When a large piece of ice was seen in our way, or drifting near us, the word was passed along, and the ship's head turned one way and another; and sometimes the yards squared or braced up. There was little else to do than to look out; and we had the sharpest eyes in the ship on the forecastle. The only variety was the monotonous voice of the lookout forward—"Another island!" "Ice ahead!" "Ice on the lee bow!" "Hard up the helm!" "Keep her off a little!" "Stead-y!"

In the meantime the wet and cold had brought my face into such a state that I could neither eat nor sleep; and though I stood it out all night, yet, when it became light, I was in such a state that all hands told me I must go below, and lie by for a day or two, or I should be laid up for a long time. When the watch was changed, I went into the steerage, and took off my hat and comforter, and showed my face to the mate, who told me to go below at once, and stay in my berth until the swelling went down, and gave the cook orders to make a poultice for me, and said he would speak to the captain.

I went below and turned in, covering myself over with blankets and jackets, and lay in my berth nearly twenty-four hours, half asleep and half awake, stupid from the dull pain. I heard the watch called, and the men going up and down, and sometimes a noise on deck, and a cry of "ice," but I gave little attention to anything. At the end of twenty-four hours the pain went down, and I had a long sleep, which brought me back to my proper state; yet my face was so swollen and tender that I was obliged to keep my berth for two or three days longer. During the two days I had been below, the weather was much the same that it had been —head winds, and snow and rain; or, if the wind came fair, too foggy, and the ice too thick, to run. At the end of the third day the ice was very thick; a complete fog bank covered the ship. It blew a tremendous gale from the eastward, with sleet and snow, and there was every promise of a dangerous and fatiguing night. At dark the captain called all hands aft, and told them that not a man was to leave the deck that night; that the ship was in the greatest danger, any cake of ice might knock a hole in her, or she might run on an island and go to pieces. No one could tell whether she would be a ship the next morning. The lookouts were then set, and every man was put in his station. When I heard what was the state of things, I began to put on my clothes to stand it out with the rest of them, when the mate came below, and looking at my face, ordered me back to my berth, saying that if we went down, we should all go down together, but if I went on deck I might lay myself up for life. This was the first word I had heard from aft; for the captain had done nothing, nor inquired how I was, since I went below.

In obedience to the mate's orders, I went back to my berth; but a more miserable night I never wish to spend. I never felt the curse of sickness so keenly in my life. If I could only have been on deck with the rest, where something was to be done and seen and heard, where there were fellow beings for companions in duty and danger; but to be cooped up alone in a black hole, in equal danger, but without the power to do, was the hardest trial. Several times, in the course of the night, I got up, determined to go on deck; but the silence which showed that there was nothing doing, and the knowledge that I might make myself seriously ill, for no purpose, kept me back. It was not easy to sleep, lying as I did with my head directly against the bows, which might be dashed in by an island of ice, brought down by the very next sea that struck her. This was the only time I had been ill since I left Boston, and it was the worst time it could have happened. I felt almost willing to bear the plagues of Egypt for the rest of the voyage, if I could but be well and strong for that one night.

Yet it was a dreadful night for those on deck. A watch of eighteen hours, with wet and cold and constant anxiety, nearly wore them out; and when they came below at nine o'clock for breakfast, they almost dropped asleep on their chests, and some of them were so stiff that they could with difficulty sit down. Not a drop of anything had been given them during the whole time (though the captain, as on the night that I was on deck, had his coffee every four hours), except that the mate stole a potful of coffee for two men to drink behind the galley, while he kept a lookout for the captain. Every man had his station, and was not allowed to leave it; and nothing happened to break the monotony of the night, except once setting the maintopsail, to run clear of a large island to leeward, which they were drifting fast upon. Some of the boys got so sleepy and stupefied that they actually fell asleep at their posts; and the young third mate, Mr. Hatch, whose post was the exposed one of standing on the forecastle, was so stiff, when he was relieved, that he could not bend his knees to get down. By a constant lookout, and a quick shifting of the helm, as the islands and pieces came in sight, the ship went clear of everything but a few small pieces, though daylight showed the ocean covered for miles.

At daybreak it fell a dead calm, and with the sun the fog cleared a little, and a breeze sprung up from the westward, which soon grew into a gale. We had now a fair wind, daylight, and comparatively clear weather; yet, to the surprise of every one, the ship continued hove to. "Why does not he run?" "What is the captain about?" was asked by everyone; and from questions it soon grew into complaints and murmuring. When the daylight was so short, it was too bad to lose it, and a fair wind, too, which every one had been praying for. As hour followed hour, and the captain showed no sign of making sail, the crew became impatient, and there was a good deal of talking and consultation together on the forecastle. They had been beaten out with the exposure and hardship, and impatient to get out of it, and this unaccountable delay was more than they could bear in quietness, in their excited and restless state.

Some said the captain was frightened—completely cowed by the dangers and difficulties that surrounded us, and was afraid to make sail; while others said that in his anxiety and suspense he had made a free use of brandy and opium, and was unfit for his duty. The carpenter, who was an intelligent man, and a thorough seaman, and had great influence with the crew, came down into the forecastle, and tried to induce them to go aft and ask the captain why he did not run, or request him, in the name of all hands, to make sail. This appeared to be a very reasonable request, and the crew agreed that if he did not make sail before noon they would go aft.

Noon came, and no sail was made. A consultation was held again, and it was proposed to take the ship from the captain, and give the command of her to the mate, who had been heard to say that if he could have his way the ship would have been half the distance to the Cape before night —ice or no ice. And so irritated and impatient had the crew become, that even this proposition, which was open mutiny, was entertained, and the carpenter went to his berth, leaving it tacitly understood that something serious would be done if things remained as they were many hours longer. When the carpenter left, we talked it all over, and I gave my advice strongly against it. Another of the men, too, who had known something of the kind attempted in another ship by a crew who were dissatisfied with their captain, and which was followed with serious consequences, was opposed to it. Stimson, who soon came down, joined us, and we determined to have nothing to do with it. By these means the crew were soon induced to give it up for the present, though they said they would not lie where they were much longer without knowing the reason.

The affair remained in this state until four o'clock, when an order came forward for all hands to come aft upon the quarterdeck. In about ten minutes they came forward again, and the whole affair had been blown. The carpenter, prematurely, and without any authority from the crew, had sounded the mate as to whether he would take command of the ship, and intimated an intention to displace the captain; and the mate, as in duty bound, had told the whole to the captain, who immediately sent for all hands aft. Instead of violent measures, or, at least, an outbreak of quarter-deck bravado, threats, and abuse, which they had every reason to expect, a sense of common danger and common suffering seemed to have tamed his spirit, and begotten in him something like a human fellow feeling; for he received the crew in a manner quiet, and even almost kind. He told them what he had heard, and said that he did not believe that they would try to do any such thing as was intimated; that they had always been good men—obedient, and knew their duty, and he had no fault to find with them, and asked them what they had to complain of; said that no one could say that he was slow to carry sail (which was true enough), and that, as soon as he thought it was safe and proper, he should make sail. He added a few words about their duty in their present situation, and sent them forward, saying that he should take no further notice of the matter; but, at the same time, told the carpenter to recollect whose power he was in, and that if he heard another word from him he would have cause to remember him to the day of his death.

This language of the captain had a very good effect upon the crew, and they returned quietly to their duty.

For two days more the wind blew from the southward and eastward, and in the short intervals when it was fair, the ice was too thick to run; yet the weather was not so dreadfully bad, and the crew had watch and watch. I still remained in my berth, fast recovering, yet not well enough to go safely on deck. And I should have been perfectly useless; for, from having eaten nothing for nearly a week, except a little rice which I forced into my mouth the last day or two, I was as weak as an infant. To be sick in a forecastle is miserable indeed. It is the worst part of a dog's life, especially in bad weather. The forecastle, shut up tight to keep out the water and cold air; the watch either on deck or asleep in their berths; no one to speak to; the pale light of the single lamp, swinging to and fro from the beam, so dim that one can scarcely see, much less read, by it; the water dropping from the beams and carlings, and running down the sides, and the forecastle so wet and dark and cheerless, and so lumbered up with chests and wet clothes, that sitting up is worse than lying in the berth. These are some of the evils. Fortunately,

I needed no help from any one, and no medicine; and if I had needed help, I don't know where I should have found it. Sailors are willing enough, but it is true, as is often said, no one ships for nurse on board a vessel. Our merchant ships are always undermanned, and if one man is lost by sickness, they cannot spare another to take care of him. A sailor is always presumed to be well, and if he's sick he's a poor dog. One has to stand his wheel, and another his lookout, and the sooner he gets on deck again the better.

Accordingly, as soon as I could possibly go back to my duty, I put on my thick clothes and boots and southwester, and made my appearance on deck. I had been but a few days below, yet everything looked strangely enough. The ship was cased in ice—decks, sides, masts, yards, and rigging. Two close-reefed topsails were all the sail she had on, and every sail and rope was frozen so stiff in its place that it seemed as though it would be impossible to start anything. Reduced, too, to her topmasts, she had altogether a most forlorn and crippled appearance. The sun had come up brightly; the snow was swept off the decks and ashes thrown upon them so that we could walk, for they had been as slippery as glass. It was, of course, too cold to carry on any ship's work, and we had only to walk the deck and keep ourselves warm. The wind was still ahead, and the whole ocean, to the eastward, covered with islands and field ice. At four bells the order was given to square away the yards, and the man who came from the helm said the captain had kept her off to N.N.E. What could this mean? The wildest rumors got adrift. Some said that he was going to put into Valparaiso, and winter; and others, that he was going to run out of the ice, and cross the Pacific, and go home round the Cape of Good Hope. Soon, however, it leaked out, and we found that we were running for the Straits of Magellan. The news soon spread through the ship, and all tongues were at work talking about it. No one on board had been through the straits, but I had in my chest an account of the passage of the ship *A. J. Donelson* of New York, through those straits a few years before. The account was given by the captain, and the representation was as favorable as possible. It was soon read by every one on board, and various opinions pronounced. The determination of our captain had at least this good effect, it gave us something to think and talk about, made a break in our life, and diverted our minds from the monotonous dreariness of the prospect before us. Having made a fair wind of it, we were going off at a good rate, and leaving the thickest of the ice behind us. This, at least, was something.

Having been long enough below to get my hands well warmed and softened, the first handling of the ropes was rather tough; but a few days hardened them, and as soon as I got my mouth open wide enough to take in a piece of salt beef and hard bread I was all right again.

Sunday, July 10th. Lat. 54° 10', lon. 79° 07'. This was our position at noon. The sun was out bright; and the ice was all left behind, and things had quite a cheering appearance. We brought our wet pea jackets and trousers on deck, and hung them up in the rigging, that the breeze and the few hours of sun might dry them a little; and, by leave of the cook, the galley was nearly filled with stockings and mittens, hung round to be dried. Boots, too, were brought up; and having got a little tar and slush from below, we gave them thick coats. After dinner all hands were turned to, to get the anchors over the bows, bend on the chains, etc. The fish tackle was got up, fish davits rigged out, and after two or three hours of hard and cold work both the anchors were ready for instant use, a couple of kedges got up, a hawser coiled away upon the fore hatch, and the deep-sea-lead line overhauled and made ready. Our spirits returned with having something to do; and when the tackle was manned to bowse the anchor home, notwithstanding the desolation of the scene, we struck up "Cheerly, men!" in full chorus. This pleased the mate, who rubbed his hands and cried out, "That's right, my boys; never say die! That sounds like the old crew!" and the captain came up, on hearing the song, and said to the passenger, within hearing of the man at the wheel, "That sounds like a lively crew. They'll have their song so long as there're enough left for a chorus!"

This preparation of the cable and anchors was for the passage of the straits; for, as they are very crooked, and with a variety of currents, it is necessary to come frequently to anchor. This was not by any means a pleasant prospect; for of all the work that a sailor is called upon to do in cold weather, there is none so bad as working the ground tackle. The heavy chain cables to be hauled and pulled about decks with bare hands; wet hawsers, slip ropes, and buoy ropes to be hauled aboard dripping in water, which is running up your sleeves and freezing; clearing hawse under the bows; getting under way and coming to at all hours of the night and day, and a constant lookout for rocks and sands and turns of tides—these are some of the disagreeables of such a navigation to a common sailor. Fair or foul, he wants to have nothing to do with the ground tackle between port and port. One of our hands, too, had unluckily fallen upon half of an old newspaper which contained an account of the passage, through the straits, of a Boston brig, called, I think, the

Peruvian, in which she lost every cable and anchor she had, got aground twice, and arrived at Valparaiso in distress. This was set off against the account of the *A. J. Donelson,* and led us to look forward with less confidence to the passage, especially as no one on board had ever been through, and we heard that the captain had no very satisfactory charts.

However, we were spared any further experience on the point; for the next day, when we must have been near the Cape of Pillars, which is the southwest point of the mouth of the straits, a gale set in from the eastward, with a heavy fog, so that we could not see half the ship's length ahead. This, of course, put an end to the project for the present; for a thick fog and a gale blowing dead ahead are not the most favorable circumstances for the passage of difficult and dangerous straits. This weather, too, seemed likely to last for some time, and we could not think of beating about the mouth of the straits for a week or two, waiting for a favorable opportunity; so we braced up on the larboard tack, put the ship's head due south, and stuck her off for Cape Horn again.

In our first attempt to double the Cape, when we came up to the latitude of it, we were nearly seventeen hundred miles to the westward, but in running for the Straits of Magellan we stood so far to the eastward that we made our second attempt at a distance of not more than four or five hundred miles; and we had great hopes, by this means, to run clear of the ice; thinking that the easterly gales, which had prevailed for a long time, would have driven it to the westward. With the wind about two points free, the yards braced in a little, and two close-reefed topsails and a reefed foresail on the ship, we made great way toward the southward; and almost every watch, when we came on deck, the air seemed to grow colder, and the sea to run higher. Still we saw no ice, and had great hopes of going clear of it altogether, when, one afternoon, about three o'clock, while we were taking a *siesta* during our watch below, "All hands!" was called in a loud and fearful voice. "Tumble up here, men! tumble up; don't stop for your clothes—before we're upon it!" We sprang out of our berths and hurried upon deck. The loud sharp voice of the captain was heard giving orders, as though for life or death, and we ran aft to the braces, not waiting to look ahead, for not a moment was to be lost. The helm was hard up, the after yards shaking, and the ship in the act of wearing. Slowly, with the stiff ropes and iced rigging, we swung the yards round, everything coming hard and with

a creaking and rending sound, like pulling up a plank which had been
frozen into the ice. The ship wore round fairly, the yards were steadied,
and we stood off on the other tack, leaving behind us, directly under
our larboard quarter, a large ice island, peering out of the mist, and
reaching high above our tops; while astern, and on either side of the
island, large tracts of field ice were dimly seen, heaving and rolling in
the sea. We were now safe, and standing to the northward; but, in a
few minutes more, had it not been for the sharp lookout of the watch,
we should have been fairly upon the ice, and left our ship's old bones
adrift in the Southern Ocean. After standing to the northward a few
hours, we wore ship, and the wind having hauled, we stood to the southward and eastward.

All night long a bright lookout was kept from every part of the deck;
and whenever ice was seen on the one bow or the other the helm was
shifted and the yards braced, and, by quick working of the ship, she was
kept clear. The accustomed cry of "Ice ahead!" "Ice on the lee bow!"
"Another island!" in the same tones, and with the same orders following
them, seemed to bring us directly back to our old position of the week
before. During our watch on deck, which was from twelve to four, the
wind came out ahead, with a pelting storm of hail and sleet, and we
lay hove-to, under a close-reefed foretopsail, the whole watch.

During the next watch it fell calm with a drenching rain until daybreak, when the wind came out to the westward, and the weather
cleared up, and showed us the whole ocean, in the course which we
should have steered, had it not been for the head wind and calm, completely blocked up with ice. Here, then, our progress was stopped, and
we wore ship, and once more stood to the northward and eastward; not
for the Straits of Magellan, but to make another attempt to double the
Cape, still farther to the eastward; for the captain was determined to get
round if perseverance could do it, and the third time, he said, never
failed.

With a fair wind we soon ran clear of the field ice, and by noon
had only the stray islands floating far and near upon the ocean. The
sun was out bright, the sea of a deep blue, fringed with the white foam
of the waves, which ran high before a strong southwester; our solitary
ship tore on through the open water as though glad to be out of her
confinement; and the ice islands lay scattered here and there, of various
sizes and shapes, reflecting the bright rays of the sun, and drifting
slowly northward before the gale. It was a contrast to much that we
had lately seen, and a spectacle not only of beauty, but of life; for it

required but little fancy to imagine these islands to be animate masses which had broken loose from the "thrilling regions of thick-ribbed ice," and were working their way, by wind and current, some alone, some in fleets, to milder climes. No pencil has ever yet given anything like the true effect of an iceberg. In a picture, they are huge, uncouth masses, stuck in the sea, while their chief beauty and grandeur—their slow, stately motion, the whirling of the snow about their summits, and the fearful groaning and cracking of their parts—the picture cannot give. This is the large iceberg, while the small and distant islands, floating on the smooth sea, in the light of a clear day, look like floating fairy isles of sapphire.

From a northeast course we gradually hauled to the eastward, and after sailing about two hundred miles, which brought us as near to the western coast of Tierra del Fuego as was safe, and having lost sight of the ice altogether, for the third time we put the ship's head to the southward, to try the passage of the Cape. The weather continued clear and cold, with a strong gale from the westward, and we were fast getting up with the latitude of the Cape, with a prospect of soon being round. One fine afternoon, a man, who had gone into the foretop to shift the rolling tackles, sung out at the top of his voice, and with evident glee, "Sail ho!" Neither land nor sail had we seen since leaving San Diego; and only those who have traversed the length of a whole ocean alone can imagine what an excitement such an announcement produced on board. "Sail ho!" shouted the cook, jumping out of his galley; "Sail ho!" shouted a man, throwing back the slide of the scuttle, to the watch below, who were soon out of their berths and on deck; and "Sail ho!" shouted the captain down the companionway to the passenger in the cabin.

Besides the pleasure of seeing a ship and human beings in so desolate a place, it was important for us to speak a vessel, to learn whether there was ice to the eastward, and to ascertain the longitude; for we had no chronometer, and had been drifting about so long that we had nearly lost our reckoning; and opportunities for lunar observations are not frequent or sure in such a place as Cape Horn. For these various reasons the excitement in our little community was running high, and conjectures were made, and everything thought of for which the captain would hail, when the man aloft sung out—"Another sail, large on the weather bow!" This was a little odd, but so much the better, and did not shake our faith in their being sails. At length the man in the top hailed, and said he believed it was land, after all. "Land in your eye!" said the mate, who was looking through the telescope; "they are ice islands, if I can see a hole through a ladder"; and a few moments showed the mate to be right; and all our expectations fled; and instead of what we most wished to see we had what we most dreaded, and what we hoped we had seen the last of. We soon, however, left these astern, having passed within two miles of them, and at sundown the horizon was clear in all directions.

Having a fine wind, we were soon up with and passed the latitude of the Cape, and, having stood far enough to the southward to give it a wide berth, we began to stand to the eastward with a good prospect of being round and steering to the northward, on the other side, in a very few days. But ill luck seemed to have lighted upon us. Not four hours had we been standing on in this course before it fell dead calm, and in half an hour it clouded up, a few straggling blasts, with spits of snow and sleet, came from the eastward, and in an hour more we lay hove to under a close-reefed maintopsail, drifting bodily off to leeward before the fiercest storm that we had yet felt, blowing dead ahead, from the eastward. It seemed as though the genius of the place had been roused at finding that we had nearly skipped through his fingers, and had come down upon us with tenfold fury. The sailors said that every blast, as it shook the shrouds, and whistled through the rigging, said to the old ship, "No, you don't!" "No, you don't!"

For eight days we lay drifting about in this manner. Sometimes—generally toward noon—it fell calm; once or twice a round copper ball showed itself for a few moments in the place where the sun ought to have been, and a puff or two came from the westward, giving some hope that a fair wind had come at last. During the first two days we made sail for these puffs, shaking the reefs out of the topsails and boarding the tacks of the courses; but finding that it only made work for us when the gale set in again, it was soon given up, and we lay to under our close reefs. We had less snow and hail than when we were farther to the westward, but we had an abundance of what is worse to a sailor in cold weather—drenching rain. Snow is blinding, and very bad when coming upon a coast, but, for genuine discomfort, give me rain with freezing weather. A snow storm is exciting, and it does not wet through the clothes (a fact important to a sailor); but a constant rain there is no escaping from. It wets to the skin, and makes all protection vain. We had long ago run through all our dry clothes, and as sailors have no other way of drying them than by the sun, we had nothing to do but to put on those which were the least wet. At the end of each watch, when we came below, we took off our clothes and wrung them out; two taking hold of a pair of trousers, one at each end—and jackets in the same way. Stockings, mittens, and all were wrung out also, and then hung up to drain and chafe dry against the bulkheads. Then, feeling all our clothes, we picked out those which were the least wet, and put them on, so as to be ready for a call, and turned in, covered ourselves up with blankets, and slept until three knocks on the scuttle, and the dismal sound of "All starbowlines ahoy! Eight bells, there below! Do you hear the news?" drawled out from on deck, and the sulky answer of "Aye, aye!" from below, sent us up again.

On deck all was dark, and either a dead calm, with the rain pouring steadily down, or, more generally, a violent gale dead ahead, with rain pelting horizontally, and occasional variations of hail and sleet; decks afloat with water swashing from side to side, and constantly wet feet, for boots could not be rung out like drawers, and no composition could stand the constant soaking. In fact, wet and cold feet are inevitable in such weather, and are not the last of those items which go to make up the grand total of the discomforts of a winter passage round Cape Horn. Few words were spoken between the watches as they shifted; the wheel was relieved, the mate took his place on the quarter-deck, and lookouts in the bows; and each man had his narrow space to walk fore and aft in, or rather to swing himself forward and back in, from one belaying pin to another, for the decks were too slippery with ice and water to allow of much walking.

To make a walk, which is absolutely necessary to pass away the time, one of us hit upon the expedient of sanding the decks; and afterward, whenever the rain was not so violent as to wash it off, the weather side of the quarter-deck and a part of the waist and forecastle were sprinkled with the sand which we had on board for holystoning, and thus we made a good promenade, where we walked fore and aft, two and two, hour after hour, in our long, dull, and comfortless watches. The bells seemed to be an hour or two apart, instead of half an hour, and an age to elapse before the welcome sound of eight bells. The sole object was to make the time pass on. Any change was sought for which would break the monotony of the time; and even the two hours' trick at the wheel, which came round to us in turn, once in every other watch, was looked upon as a relief. The never-failing resource of long yarns, which eke out many a watch, seemed to have failed us now; for we had been so long together that we had heard each other's stories told over and over again till we had them by heart; each one knew the whole history of each of the others, and we were fairly and literally talked out. Singing and joking we were in no humor for; and, in fact, any sound of mirth or laughter would have struck strangely upon our ears, and would not have been tolerated any more than whistling or a wind instrument. The last resort, that of speculating upon the future, seemed now to fail us, for our discouraging situation, and the danger we were really in (as we expected every day to find ourselves drifted back among the ice), "clapped a stopper" upon all that. From saying "*when* we get home," we began insensibly to alter it to "*if* we get home," and at last the subject was dropped by a tacit consent.

In this state of things, a new light was struck out, and a new field opened, by a change in the watch. One of our watch was laid up for two or three days by a bad hand (for in cold weather the least cut or bruise ripens into a sore), and his place was supplied by the carpenter. This was a windfall, and there was a contest who should have the carpenter to walk with him. As "Chips" was a man of some little education, and he and I had had a good deal of intercourse with each other, he fell in with me in my walk. He was a Finn, but spoke English well, and gave me long accounts of his country—the customs, the trade, the towns, what little he knew of the government (I found he was no friend of Russia), his voyages, his first arrival in America, his marriage and courtship; he had married a countrywoman of his, a dressmaker, whom he met with in Boston. I had very little to tell him of my quiet sedentary life at home; and in spite of our best efforts, which had protracted these yarns through five or six watches, we fairly talked each other out, and I turned him over to another man in the watch, and put myself upon my own resources.

I commenced a deliberate system of time killing, which united some profit with a cheering up of the heavy hours. As soon as I came on deck, and took my place and regular walk, I began with repeating over to myself in regular order a string of matters which I had in my memory —the multiplication table and the tables of weights and measures; the Kanaka numerals; then the States of the Union, with their capitals; the counties of England, with their shire towns; and the kings of England in their order, and other things. This carried me through my facts, and, being repeated deliberately, with long intervals, often eked out the first two bells. Then came the Ten Commandments, the thirty-ninth chapter of Job, and a few other passages from Scripture. The next in order, which I seldom varied from, came Cowper's *Cast away,* which was a great favorite with me; its solemn measure and gloomy character, as well as the incident it was founded upon, making it well suited to a lonely watch at sea. Then his lines to Mary, his address to the Jackdaw, and a short extract from "Table Talk" (I abounded in Cowper, for I happened to have a volume of his poems in my chest); "Ille et nefasto" from Horace, and Goethe's *Erlkönig*. After I had got through these, I allowed myself a more general range among everything that I could remember, both in prose and verse. In this way, with an occasional break by relieving the wheel, heaving the log, and going to the scuttlebutt for a drink of water, the longest watch was passed away; and I was so regular in my silent recitations that, if there was no interruption by ship's duty, I could tell very nearly the number of bells by my progress.

Our watches below were no more varied than the watch on deck. All washing, sewing, and reading were given up, and we did nothing but eat, sleep, and stand our watch, leading what might be called a Cape Horn life. The forecastle was too uncomfortable to sit up in; and whenever we were below we were in our berths. To prevent the rain and the sea water which broke over the bows from washing down, we were obliged to keep the scuttle closed, so that the forecastle was nearly airtight. In this little, wet, leaky hole we were all quartered, in an atmosphere so bad that our lamp, which swung in the middle from the beams, sometimes actually burned blue, with a large circle of foul air about it. Still, I was never in better health than after three weeks of this life. I gained a great deal of flesh, and we all ate like horses. At every watch when we came below, before turning in, the bread barge and beef kid were overhauled. Each man drank his quart of hot tea night and morning, and glad enough we were to get it; for no nectar and ambrosia were sweeter to the lazy immortals than was a pot of hot tea, a hard biscuit, and a slice of cold salt beef to us after a watch on deck. To be sure, we were mere animals, and had this life lasted a year instead of a month, we should have been little better than the ropes in the ship. Not a razor, nor a brush, nor a drop of water, except the rain and the spray, had come near us all the time; for we were on an allowance of fresh water; and who would strip and wash himself in salt water on deck, in the snow and ice, with the thermometer at zero?

After about eight days of constant easterly gales, the wind hauled occasionally a little to the southward, and blew hard, which, as we were well to the southward, allowed us to brace in a little, and stand on under all the sail we could carry. These turns lasted but a short while, and sooner or later it set in again from the old quarter; yet at each time we made something, and were gradually edging along to the eastward. One night, after one of these shifts of the wind, and when all hands had been up a great part of the time, our watch was left on deck, with the mainsail hanging in the buntlines, ready to be set if necessary. It came on to blow worse and worse, with hail and snow beating like so many furies upon the ship, it being as dark and thick as night could make it. The mainsail was blowing and slatting with a noise like thunder, when the captain came on deck and ordered it to be furled. The mate was about to call all hands, when the captain stopped him, and said that the men would be beaten out if they were called up so often; that, as our watch must stay on deck, it might as well be doing that as anything else.

Accordingly, we went upon the yard; and never shall I forget that piece of work. Our watch had been so reduced by sickness, and by some having been left in California, that, with one man at the wheel, we had only the third mate and three besides myself to go aloft; so that at most we could only attempt to furl one yardarm at a time. We manned the weather yardarm, and set to work to make a furl of it. Our lower masts being short, and our yards very square, the sail had a head of nearly fifty feet, and a short leech, made still shorter by the deep reef which was in it, which brought the clew away out on the quarters of the yard, and made a bunt nearly as square as the mizzen royal yard. Besides this difficulty, the yard over which we lay was cased with ice, the gaskets and rope of the foot and leech of the sail as stiff and hard as a piece of leather hose, and the sail about as pliable as though it had been made of sheets of sheathing copper. It blew a perfect hurricane, with alternate blasts of snow, hail and rain. We had to *fist* the sail with bare hands. No one could trust himself to mittens, for if he slipped he was a gone man. All the boats were hoisted in on deck, and there was nothing to be lowered for him. We had need of every finger God had given us. Several times we got the sail upon the yard, but it blew away again before we could secure it. It required men to lie over the yard to pass each turn of the gaskets, and when they were passed it was almost impossible to knot them so that they would hold. Frequently we were obliged to leave off altogether and take to beating our hands upon the sail to keep them from freezing.

After some time—which seemed for ever—we got the weather side stowed after a fashion, and went over to leeward for another trial. This was still worse, for the body of the sail had been blown over to leeward, and, as the yard was a-cockbill by the lying over of the vessel, we had to light it all up to windward. When the yardarms were furled, the bunt was all adrift again, which made more work for us. We got all secure at last, but we had been nearly an hour and a half upon the yard, and it seemed an age. It had just struck five bells when we went up, and eight were struck soon after we came down. This may seem slow work; but considering the state of everything, and that we had only five men to a sail with just half as many square yards of canvas in it as the mainsail of the *Independence* sixty-gun ship, which musters seven hundred men at her quarters, it is not wonderful that we were no quicker about it. We were glad enough to get on deck, and still more to go below. The oldest sailor in the watch said, as he went down, "I shall never forget that main-yard; it beats all my going a-fishing. Fun is fun, but furling one yardarm of a course at a time, off Cape Horn, is no better than man-killing."

During the greater part of the next two days the wind was pretty steady from the southward. We had evidently made great progress, and had good hope of being soon up with the Cape, if we were not there already. We could put but little confidence in our reckoning, as there had been no opportunities for an observation, and we had drifted too much to allow of our dead reckoning being anywhere near the mark. If it would clear off enough to give a chance for an observation, or if we could make land, we should know where we were; and upon these, and the chances of falling in with a sail from the eastward, we depended almost entirely.

Friday, July 22nd. This day we had a steady gale from the southward, and stood on under close sail, with the yards eased a little by the weather braces, the clouds lifting a little, and showing signs of breaking away. In the afternoon, I was below with Mr. Hatch, the third mate, and two others, filling the bread locker in the steerage from the casks, when a bright gleam of sunshine broke out and shone down the companionway and through the skylight, lighting up everything below, and sending a warm glow through the hearts of all. It was a sight we had not seen for weeks—an omen, a godsend. Even the roughest and hardest face acknowledged its influence. Just at that moment we heard a loud shout from all parts of the deck, and the mate called out down the companion-way to the captain, who was sitting in the cabin. What he said we could not distinguish, but the captain kicked over his chair, and was on deck at one jump. We could not tell what it was; and, anxious as we were to know, the discipline of the ship would not allow of our leaving our places. Yet, as we were not called, we knew there was no danger. We hurried to get through with our job, when seeing the steward's black face peering out of the pantry, Mr. Hatch hailed him to know what was the matter. "Lan'o, to be sure, sir! No you hear 'em sing out, 'Lan'o?' De cap'em say 'im Cape Horn!"

This gave us a new start, and we were soon through our work and on deck; and there lay the land, fair upon the larboard beam, and slowly edging away upon the quarter. All hands were busy looking at it—the captain and mates from the quarter-deck, the cook from his galley, and the sailors from the forecastle; and even Mr. Nuttall, the passenger, who had kept in his shell for nearly a month, and hardly been seen by anybody, and whom we had almost forgotten was on board, came out like a butterfly, and was hopping round just as bright as a bird.

The land was the island of Staten Land, just to the eastward of Cape Horn; and a more desolate-looking spot I never wish to set eyes upon— bare, broken, and girt with rocks and ice, with here and there, between the rocks and broken hillocks, a little stunted vegetation of shrubs. It was a place well suited to stand at the junction of the two oceans, beyond the reach of human cultivation, and encounter the blasts and snows of a perpetual winter. Yet, dismal as it was, it was a pleasant sight to us; not only as being the first land we had seen, but because it told us that we had passed the Cape—were in the Atlantic—and that, with twenty-four hours of this breeze, we might bid defiance to the Southern Ocean. It told us, too, our latitude and longitude better than any observation; and the captain now knew where we were, as well as if we were off the end of Long Wharf.

In the general joy, Mr. Nuttall said he should like to go ashore upon the island and examine a spot which probably no human being had ever set foot upon; but the captain intimated that he would see the island, specimens and all, in—another place, before he would get out a boat or delay the ship one moment for him.

We left the land gradually astern; and at sundown had the Atlantic Ocean clear before us.

Battle With a Whale

by WILLIAM M. DAVIES

Whoever has visited the whaling museum at Nantucket has probably paused for some minutes and dreamed of battles with Leviathan, while the tubs and anchors and South Sea souvenirs were momentarily forgotten. Melville's Moby-Dick *established the whale, one might almost say, as a new American animal, candidate for the head side of a coin. The virtue of "Battle With a Whale" is that it is, despite its quiet tone, authentic—the portrait of a brief, bloody and necessary battle.*

IT IS ABOUT THREE WEEKS SINCE WE TOOK OUR LAST WHALE, and we have had the greatest trial which attends the whalemen. The dullness and tedium of life on board ship at such quiet times is almost unendurable. The uninterrupted fine weather, the steady trade wind, the daily routine of make sail, man mastheads, scrub decks; breakfast, dinner, supper; shorten sail, boat's-crew watch, and "turn in" give not a line for a journal. The men become morose and quarrelsome; we hate each other, and numerous scores are run up, and appointments made to fight them out in the first port we make. The violin fails to move, the song to enliven, and the yarn to interest us. According to custom, and as a diversion, a red-flannel shirt has been offered as a prize to him who may *raise* the first whale captured, and a pair of duck trousers have been added. Pounds of tobacco are offered by the mate, but the days pass uninterestingly. A bright gold doubloon is nailed to the mainmast, well out of reach, but in sight of all, as another reward to good eyes. Now there is more life at the masthead. Not a whitecap can show, a porpoise jump, or finback spout, but that the alarm is given, in hope that it may lead to a capture, and so obtain for the discoverer the pretty piece of gold glittering on the white mast. In vain! All the whales seem to have gone to the bottom for a Rip Van Winkle nap. We all know they can do this, though it is contrary to the books, which tell us that they are warm-blooded mammals: even this is not the worst of the names the learned have given them. But whales are uneducated, don't take the papers, and without thought of irregularity stay down to suit their convenience an hour or a week. Like the original Kentuckian, Nimrod Wildfire, we were spoiling for a fight, when the captain ordered the sacrifice of a pig to propitiate our patron saints. The offering was accepted, for the protesting squeak of poor piggy was blended with the yell of "There she blows!" and "Sperm whale, sir." "Where away?" roared the officers. And in answer was heard Hinton's sweetest song, "Four points on lee bow." We squared in the yards and kept off, and away we ran merrily. At two miles' distance from what seemed a good whale the boats were lowered. The activity of the men, as they sprang barefooted into the boats and cast off the davit tackles; the readiness with which they handled the long, heavy oars, and dropped them silently into the well-thrummed thole mats, and the ease with which they fell into the stroke were wonderful. Four boats were down and heading to leeward, their course divergent, so that at two miles from the ship we peaked our oars with a space of about one third of a mile between the boats, thus commanding a reach of nearly two miles front.

As the boats thus ride the long, rolling swell of the sea lightly and gracefully as an albatross (and I know nothing more graceful than that), let us glance at the whaleboat and its fittings. It is the fruit of a century's experience, and the sharpened sense and ingenuity of an inventive people, urged by the peril of the chase and the value of the prize. For lightness and form; for carrying capacity, as compared with its weight and seagoing qualities; for speed and facility of movement at the word of command; for the placing of the men at the best advantage in the exercise of their power; by the nicest adaptation of the varying length of the oar to its position in the boat; and, lastly, for a simplicity of construction which renders repairs practicable on board the ship, the whaleboat is simply as perfect as the combined skill of the million men who have risked life and limb in service could make it. This paragon of a boat is twenty-eight feet long, sharp and clean-cut as a dolphin, bow and stern swelling amidships to six feet, with a bottom round and buoyant. The gunwale, amidships twenty-two inches above the keel, rises with an accelerated curve to thirty-seven inches at each end, and this rise of bow and stern, with the clipper-like upper form, gives it a ducklike capacity to top the oncoming waves, so that it will dryly ride when ordinary boats would fill. The gunwales and keel, of the best timber, are her heaviest parts, and give stiffness to the whole; the timbers, sprung to shape, are a half-inch or three quarters in depth, and the planking is half-inch white cedar. Her thwarts are inch pine, supported by knees of greater strength than the other timbers. The bow-oar thwart is pierced by a three-inch hole for the mast, and is double-kneed. Through the cuddy board projects a silk-hat-shaped loggerhead, for snubbing and managing the running line; the stem of the boat is deeply grooved on top, the bottom of the groove being bushed with a block of lead, or sometimes a bronze roller, and over this the line passes from the boat. Four feet of the length of the bow is covered in by a depressed box, in which the spare line, attached to harpoons, lies in carefully adjusted coils. Immediately back of the box is a thick pine plank, in which the "clumsy cleet," or knee brace, is cut. The gunwale is pierced at proper distances for tholepins, of wood, and all sounds of the working oars are muffled by well-thrummed mats, kept carefully greased, so that we can steal on our prey silent as the cavalry of the poor badgered Lear. The planking is carefully smoothed with sandpaper and painted. Here we have a boat which two men may lift, and which will make ten miles an hour in dead chase by the oars alone.

The equipment of the boat consists of a line tub, in which are coiled three hundred fathoms of hemp line, with every possible precaution against kinking in the outrun; a mast and spritsail; five oars; the harpoon and after oar, fourteen feet; the tub and bow oar, sixteen feet; and the midship, eighteen feet long; so placed that the two shortest and one longest pull against the two sixteen-feet oars, which arrangement preserves the balance in the encounter when the boat is worked by four oars, the harpoon oar being apeak. The boat is steered by an oar twenty-two feet long, which works through a grummet on the sternpost. The gear of the boat consists of two live harpoons, or those in use, i.e., harpoons secured to the side of the boat above the thwarts, and two or three lances, secured by cords in like position, the sharp heads of all these being guarded by well-fitted softwood sheaths. The harpoon is a barbed, triangular iron, very sharp on the edges, or it is a long, narrow piece of iron, sharpened only on one end, and affixed on the shank by a rivet, so placed that before use the cutting edge is on a line with the shank, but after penetrating the whale, and on being drawn back, the movable piece drops at right angles to the shank, and forms a square *toggle* about six inches across the narrow wound caused by its entrance. The porpoise

iron is preferred among the Arctic whalemen, as, owing to the softness
of the blubber, the fluked harpoon is apt to cut its way out. The upper
end of a shank thirty inches long terminates in a socket, into which a
heavy oak or hickory sapling pole six feet long is introduced. A short
piece of the whale line, with an eye splice at one end, is then wrapped
twice around the shank below the socket, and close spliced. This line is
stretched with great strain, and secured to the pole with a slight seizing
of rope yarn, intended to pay away and loose the pole in a long fight.
The tub line is secured to the eye of the short line after the boat is
lowered. The lance is simply an oval-headed instrument, with a cutting
edge, a shank five or six feet long, and a handle as long, with a light warp
to recover it. A hatchet and a sharp knife are placed in the bow box,
convenient for cutting the line, and a water keg, fire apparatus, candles,
lantern, compass, and bandages for wounds, with waif flags on poles, a
fluke spade, a boathook, and a "drug," or dragging float, complete the
equipment of a whaleboat. Among this crowd of dangerous lines and
threatening cutting gear are six pair of legs, belonging to six skilled
boatmen. Such a whaleboat is ours, as she floats two miles from the ship,
each man in the crew watching under the blade of his peaked oar for the
rising whale, and the captain and boat steerer standing on the highest
point, carefully sweeping the horizon with trained eye to catch the first
spout, and secure the chance of "getting on."

At this moment of rest, when on the point of entering a contest in
which the chances of mishap seem wonderfully provided for, I found that
a green hand is apt to run back over his life with something of regret
always, or forward, with a half vow that from then and there, for ever
and ever, he will be a better boy. The Frenchwoman found goodness
possible when she was well dressed. I found evil hateful when I was near
a sperm whale. But how one wakes up from such moralizing as the
captain lightly drops from his perch, runs out his steering oar, and lays
the boat around, with the words, "Take your oars, and spring; the
whale's half a mile off!" That means that we are just four minutes from
the whale, provided he is not running.

It would cheer a clubman's heart to watch the movements of the crew,
the splendid stroke and time, the perfect feather of the oars, their silent
dip on entering the foaming whirl of the lifted water, the ashen shaft
working silently in the oiled mat, the poise of the crew, as the five trained
athletes urge their perfect structure through the waves. Long and careful
training under danger breeds a unity in the men. The five work as a
single hand under the direction of him who is steering and throwing his

whole standing force in the push on the after oar. Every energy of my soul and body is centered in that bow oar, and I do not differ from four others who share in the excitement. An occasional glance at my springing ash, the leaping little waves, and the resolute face of the captain tells me to a fathom the position of the chase. His eyes are fixed on the rising and sinking whale; color has left his features; his pale lips are drawn tight, as he sways back and forth to the stroke of the oar. He, too, is straining on, and jerks out words of command, exhortation, and promise, to urge our energies to fiercer effort.

We are coming up at a killing pace. The captain, eloquent, unconscious of his words, yet with method in his frenzy, still urges us on. Now the puff of a spout joins the splash of the bow, and the old man's voice sinks to a fierce whisper as he promises all his tobacco, a share in his little farm at home, and his "lay" in the whale, as he adjures us to put him on. Human muscle cannot stand the strain much longer; the boat seems as lead; boiling foam curls and bubbles around the boat's head. The old man glances almost as low as the head of the boat; a puff is heard just under the bows; my oar blade dips in the eddying wake of the whale's last upward stroke, and right under its blade I see the broad half-moon of his flukes as we shoot across the corner of them. Now the odor of the whale, like a bank of seaweed, comes over us. "Stand up, Ben! Pull, pull for life! Good, good! Now again! Goody Lord, give it to him!" The backward start of the boat and the upward fling of the flukes tell the rest of that story. A stroke or two astern, and we pant for breath in safety.

But lest the reader might labor under the mistake that all our prizes are secured simply by the planting of the harpoon, I shall skip from the present whale, which gave us little trouble, to another.

Lat. 5° 40′ S., long. 107° 37′ W.—The watch was employed in breaking out, to make stowage for one hundred and fifteen barrels of oil now on deck, the fruit of two whales taken on the 11th and 14th inst. While the decks were all a "clutter," we raised a school of sperm whales. They were erratic in their movements, and it required several hours of maneuver to get the ship in a position for lowering the boats. But once we were down it was not long before the mate fastened to a large bull. This proved to be an ugly customer, cross-grained and bent on mischief. He ran swiftly a short distance under water, and took out considerable line; then, turning in his course, he rose to the surface and came down full speed, head far out of water, striking one boat partially with his jaw, staving in her broadside and rolling her over. Our boat hurried to the rescue, and as we pulled up the scene was stirring to our nerves, be assured. The crew of the overturned boat were swimming, and all six heads could be counted, which was a relief. The whale lay a short distance from the boat, thrashing the water madly with his flukes, and before we got on he again attacked the wreck and struck it with his jaw, cutting off about one third of her length. As we pulled past, two poor fellows who were clinging to the bottom begged for God's sake we would save them. The captain's quick eye saw that the swimming crew were well provided with means of support, and that the waist boat was fast coming up; so he told them to hold on, and that he would coax the whale away. The poor devils had a right to be *gallied* just then, for the mad beast was coming down on them, his ugly fifteen-foot jaw at right angles with his body, and ivory gleaming about it. Watching a chance, Ben made a long dart, and struck the bull before he reached the shattered boat. This seemed to astonish the creature, and with a grand flourish of flukes he put away to windward at a tremendous pace. Evidently we had a desperate fellow to deal with. What with this continued speed, and the promiscuous manner in which he tossed his tail, it was impossible to haul line and range alongside. Resort was had to the spade. We hauled line until the head of the boat was a little astern of the spiteful flukes, and, watching his chances, the captain pitched the broad-edged tool over the flukes into the small, with the hope of severing the tendons of the tail, which here came near the surface. If this piece of surgery had proved successful the whale must have heaved to on losing control of his propeller. But it was a difficult amputation to perform on a kicking, fighting whale. He ran with undiminished speed, often rolling as he went, so as to give his flukes a side-cutting power, with the amiable intent of smashing his little antagonist.

In this instance bow oar had been tugging at the line for an hour, but was utterly unable to get the boat in advance of the flukes. A little line might be gained for a short time, but it would soon be torn through the clinging hands, almost taking the flesh with it. This was certainly aggravating to the excited captain. Captain B—— was a religious man, and, under his own vine and fig tree, with none to rile or make afraid, I guess he would average well in patience line. But with our troubles on this day I believe he wished that there had been no sin in a ripping oath. He was a little hard on his bow oarsman, and rather more than hinted at somebody's cowardice. This was too much for my hot Welsh blood, and with the aid of two others I brought the boat right up to the iron, and coolly passed a bight around the thwart and made all fast. This suggested that there would be a thundering row in the boat directly if the whale was not killed.

The captain was delighted to be held so well up to his work, and he plied his lance, thrust after thrust; but the brute seemed to bear a charmed life. He would not spout blood, and the little jets of blood which spurt from a lance wound would not bleed a whale to death in a week. Our boat buried her nose in the waves, and the bloody spray leaped over her side as we swept right royally onward.

Now our majestic race horse grew impatient of our prodding. He milled short across our course, and we run plump against his head.

"Slack line!" roared the old man. "Starn all! Slack line and starn!"

He turned in his tracks to step aft of the bow oar, fearing the up-cut of the jaw, when he saw that the line was fast about the thwart. "For God's sake, clear that line!" he shouted, as he sprang forward for the hatchet to cut; but the loosened bight went over the side, as the whale came up under the forward part of the boat and carried the bow clear of the water as he rounded slowly forward.

At this moment the captain and old Ben occupied the stern of the boat, and in the perilous moment I was just mad enough to enjoy the expectant look with which the two old whalemen awaited the arrival of the oncoming flukes. Fortunately for us all, the blow was delayed a moment, and when the thundering concussion came it cleared our boat by a few feet.

The other boats were out of sight, and the ship's hull was dimly seen to leeward. Yet for two hours more the whale ran and fought with re-doubled energy. The captain got long darts with the lance, but to no good effect; the iron drew, and the victorious whale passed away from us. We were fagged and dead beat; almost worn to death, and we did not reach the ship until long after nightfall. The other boats picked up the mate's crew, no one having been hurt.

On the following day the captain did handsomely by his bow oar by remarking to me that an officer in the boat never meant half he said, and that such scolding was his habit. "But," he solemnly added, "never again, under any possible circumstances, make a line fast between the boat and a whale. Why, if that mad whale had gone down, the boat would have been a quarter of a mile under water in less than a minute, and half the crew might have been with it!" Bow oar suggested that it was better to be under water than live under a charge of cowardice. The old man overlooked this impudence, and turned on his heel. Thus I have shown that the harpoon is to fasten to the whale, the line to keep com-munication with it, and the lance is the instrument by which it is killed, a spade being sometimes used to check a running whale.

On the Bottom

by EDWARD ELLSBERG

The sunken submarine S-51 was 132 feet down in the open ocean off New England when Ellsberg, in charge of salvage, began the job which brought her up—lowering pontoons from the surface ship Falcon, *attaching them to the submarine, and then pumping them full of air. As this account shows, not even the most experienced divers can avoid the terrifying hazards of underwater operations.*

AT BOW AND STERN WE HAD BEEN ABLE TO PASS OUR REEVING lines under with no great difficulty, because there the keel, due to its rocker shape, rose clear of the bottom. However, for the other pontoons amidships, the case was far different.

Amidships the *S-51* was buried about six feet deep in a bed of hard blue clay, overlaid with a thin layer, a few inches thick, of hard packed gray sand. To get the reeving lines and the chains through here required that we provide a tunnel for their passage. There was only one way which appeared practicable for digging the tunnel. At that depth it was out of question for the divers to undertake the continued physical exertion of swinging pick and shovel in an excavation, disregarding the mechanical limitations of trying to do it in a diving rig. We all felt that the best solution lay in washing out a hole under the ship with a stream of water from a fire hose.

We coupled up two hundred and fifty feet of the *Falcon's* two and one-half inch fire hose, with a regular hose nozzle screwed to the end. Bailey was selected to go down and start the tunnel. I took him aboard the *S-50* and showed him the spot abreast frame forty-six, where he was to start. A torpedo davit projecting from the deck was the nearest visible mark. He was to spot this on the *S-51's* side, then measure off five feet forward of it, and start the tunnel there.

Bailey was small, but he was an excellent diver and a careful man. We could rely on him to hit the right spot and in case of any doubt, to ask questions rather than to guess.

Bailey was dressed, went down on the forward descending line, the fire hose dragging after him on a lanyard to his wrist. He found the torpedo davit, tied a small line to it, which he threw over the port side to mark the location, and then slid down the line to the bottom. He measured off the five feet against the side of the submarine, dragged the hose nozzle over, braced it between his heavy shoes against the sea bottom close to the ship's side, and sang out:

"On deck! Turn on the water!"

A sailor opened wide the valve to the *Falcon's* wrecking pump. The hose swelled out, and throbbing with each stroke of the pump as the water rushed through, disappeared over the rail.

Another call from Bailey:

"On deck! Turn off the water! I'm about fifty feet from the sub and I don't know where the hose is!"

We shut down the pump and the hose flattened out, hanging limply over our bulwarks.

It was easy to imagine what had happened. I remembered in my boyhood days the sight of four firemen clinging to a hose nozzle, trying to direct the stream against a burning building. Bailey, all alone, had tried the same thing except that his stream instead of meeting air, was discharged against solid water, making the reaction worse. The writhing hose had torn itself from his grasp and sent him flying backward through the water.

Bailey picked himself out of the sand, located the submarine, and after a search, found the hose again. He dragged the nozzle back, braced himself against the hull.

"On deck! Turn on the water again! Easy this time!"

Once more the wrecking pump started to throb. Gently we opened the valve from the firemain to the hose, watched the hose swell out slowly as we gradually raised the pressure. At forty pounds on our gauge, Bailey sang out from below:

"Hold it, that's enough!"

The engineer at the pump throttled it carefully to hold the pressure steady. We watched the stream pulsing through the hose, which was not very hard. A thumb could make a dent in the canvas covering.

Bailey worked his hour and came up.

"I could just hang on the second time, but I didn't get much done. That clay is awful hard, and the stream I had hardly made an impression. I don't think I made a hole a foot deep, and part of that was through the sand on top."

Other divers followed Bailey. We helped matters a little by tying a one hundred pound weight to the hose, just behind the nozzle, to assist the diver in holding the hose down. Still the low pressure prevented much progress, the stream had not force enough to cut the clay. We needed more pressure. To get it, we removed the last section of hose and replaced it with a one and one-half inch length and a nozzle to match. With the smaller nozzle, we were able to raise the pressure to sixty pounds before the divers complained. (The usual pressure on a two and one-half inch fire hose is one hundred and twenty pounds.) The sixty pound stream had force enough to do a little cutting, but of course the smaller hose greatly reduced the size of the jet.

Day after day, we worked on the tunnel at frame forty-six. It was slow work. We were never able to get more than six men in any one day down on the job, because of the loss of time in getting the old diver out and clear before his relief could get down, pick up the hose, and crawl in. Other complications arose. The clay turned out to be so heavy that when cut, it would not stay in suspension in the water, but after floating back a foot or so, would settle down in the tunnel around the diver. Consequently after cutting ahead for a few inches, the diver had to stop, and crawling out backward, turn his nozzle and wash the cuttings all the way out to the tunnel mouth before he could again advance.

As a final aggravation, after one or two days' work, a storm would drive us away. Coming back, we always found our tunnel filled in with hard packed sand, washed along the sea bottom by the currents, and this had to be removed regularly before we could again drive our bore ahead.

We worked along against constant difficulties. Hoses got fouled in the submarine's superstructure and tore in half when we tried to pull them free. Sometimes the divers could not find the tunnel, and wasted half their precious hour searching out the small entrance hole under the port bilge. Others, lying down in the tunnel, had their suits fill with water, and had to be dragged up, half frozen and nearly drowned.

We made progress, yes, but it had almost to be measured by the inch. As a result of two weeks' desperate work in May, the tunnel had advanced sixteen feet under the port side—about an average of one foot a day.

We were still two feet from the keel on the port side. Francis Smith was in the tunnel, burrowing his way along. Imagine his situation. In ice cold water, utter blackness, total solitude, he was buried one hundred and thirty-five feet below the surface of the sea. No sight, no sound, no sense of direction except the feel of the iron hull of the *S-51* against his back, as he lay stretched out flat in a narrow hole, scarcely larger than his body, not big enough for him to turn around in. Ahead in his outstretched arms he grasped the nozzle, burrowing his way deeper, while around him coursed backward a black stream of freezing water laden with mud and clay.

He had been working about twenty minutes, when on the *Falcon* the man at the telephone got a call from Smith. He could not understand and passed the telephone set to me.

"Hello, Smith!"

In an agonized voice came the reply:

"I'm in a very bad position, Mr. Ellsberg. Send someone to help!"

Joe Eiben was working aft on the other side of the submarine. I dropped Smith's phone, seized Eiben's, ordered Joe to stop whatever he was doing, climb over the boat to the tunnel and help Smith. Eiben acknowledged the message, started forward.

Meanwhile I tried to figure out what had happened. The fire hose leading over the rail was throbbing violently. Perhaps the nozzle had torn itself from Smith's grasp, was thrashing him to death.

I took Smith's phone again, called down:

"Shall I turn off the water?"

Almost a scream came the answer:

"No! For God's sake keep it going! The tunnel has caved in behind me!"

I felt faint. Hastily we coupled up another fire hose, slid it down the descending line for Eiben's use. But it had taken two weeks to drive the tunnel to where Smith lay! On deck we looked at each other helplessly. Over the telephone, I could hear Smith's labored breathing as he struggled in the darkness.

No further messages came. The sailors stood silently around the deck, waiting for Eiben to arrive at the tunnel, wondering what good he could do when he got there.

Eiben reached the descending line at the gun, cut loose the new hose, dragged it forward with him, and dropped over the port side to the bottom. Finally after what seemed an age, he reported himself at the tunnel mouth, said he was trying to enter.

I waited; then over Smith's telephone, I heard Smith say to Eiben:

"I'm all right now, Joe. Had a little accident. You go on back to your own job."

Though he could not turn round, Smith had managed to pass the nozzle back between his legs, and guiding it with his feet, he had washed his way out backward through the cave-in!

Eiben left. Smith sat down on the ocean floor a few minutes to rest, then picked up his hose, crawled back into the tunnel and for half an hour more continued to wash his way toward the keel.

No deed ever performed in the heat of battle with the enemy where thousands cheer you on, can compare with Francis Smith's bravery, when in the silent depths of the ocean beneath the hulk of the *S-51*, he washed his way out of what well might have been his grave, then deliberately turned round, went back into the black hole from which he had by the grace of God escaped, and worked his way deeper and deeper into it.

Other divers followed Smith; in a few more days we reached the keel on the port side. Then, marking the corresponding spot on the starboard side as carefully as possible, we started to drift another tunnel from that side to meet the port side hole. As the boat was heeled far over on her port side, the tunnel on the starboard side was not much over half as long as on the low side. While the divers worked on the starboard side hole, we sent one or two men a day into the port tunnel to keep it cleared out.

Only the most experienced of the divers managed to make any headway in the tunnels. Carr, Smith, Wilson, Eiben, Kelley, Eadie, Michels, and Bailey did practically all the work. We tried a few of the most promising of the newer divers on the job, but they never got anywhere at it. The reason was clear enough. Years of experience were necessary to develop the iron nerve and the forgetfulness of surroundings which were essential to allow the diver to concentrate on the job and ignore his situation.

The job proceeded, the divers coming up sometimes singly, sometimes in pairs. Eiben and Eadie, who had been working, one in the port tunnel, the other in the starboard one, met at the gun on the submarine's forecastle, climbed on the stage at the ninety-foot mark, and, according to ritual, began their setting-up exercises while decompressing.

Those two men were safely off the bottom. On the quarterdeck, we turned attention to the next diver, who, except for his helmet, was ready to go over. He was testing his telephone.

A voice came from the superstructure.

"Tom Eadie said something but I couldn't make it out. I can't get him now!"

Hartley tried, I tried, Gunner Tibbals tried. None of us could understand, though it did sound as if Eadie were shouting something. Eiben was on the stage down there with Eadie. I took Eiben's telephone.

"Hello, Joe! Ask Tom what he wants!"

A pause, then Eiben replied:

"Tom's not here! What did you pull him up for?"

Surprised, I looked at Eadie's tender. He had not pulled Eadie up.

"Where's Tom?" I asked him.

"He's still down there, sir. I'm trying to signal him. I've given him 'One' on his line, two or three times, but still he doesn't answer."

A shout over the telephone from Eiben.

"Eadie just fell back on the stage. His suit's nearly torn in half and he's full of water. Take him up quick!"

Half a dozen bears grabbed Eadie's lines and heaved hard. The weight was tremendous, evidently Eadie's suit was wholly waterlogged. Others grasped the lines wherever they could lay hands on them and we heaved rapidly. Over the side went another stage, two men on it, dropped into the water up to their waists. Hand over hand Eadie's lines came in, then at last Eadie's helmet. The men on the stage seized it, dragged his limp form on the stage; the winchman jerked the stage up, swung it in on deck.

Eadie's suit was nearly completely torn in two just below the breastplate, the leather straps over his shoulders were broken, his lead belt was hanging round his ankles. No need to take off his helmet. We cut loose his shoes, dragged him out of the suit through the hole around his breast.

Eadie was very pale, bleeding badly from the mouth and nose, but apparently still conscious. We did not wait to investigate. The tenders who pulled him out of the suit dragged him hurriedly to the recompression tank, thrust him in, together with Surgeon Flotte who hastily ran the pressure up to fifty pounds.

Hours later, after Eiben had come up, and Eadie was below, wrapped in blankets in his bunk, with Eiben resting in the next berth, I asked them what had happened. Eadie told me.

"Joe and I were on the stage at ninety feet, I was jumping up and down to decompress myself and I guess Joe was doing knee stoops.

"All of a sudden my exhaust valve jammed shut and my suit started to swell out. I tried to reach my control valve and turn off the air, but before I could swing my arm around, my suit stiffened out from the pressure inside, and it spread-eagled me. Both my sleeves shot out straight sideways and I couldn't bend my elbows to get my hand in on the control valve.

"By that time I was so light, I started to float up off the stage and I yelled in the telephone to the man on deck to turn the air off on my hose. I guess he didn't understand me."

I interrupted Eadie and turned to Eiben.

"Say, Joe, didn't you notice it when Eadie started up?"

Eiben looked at us sheepishly.

"Yes, I sort of saw him go, out of the corner of my faceplate, but I just thought he was taking an extra-high jump, and I went right on exercising. I wasn't thinking about Tom and I didn't look around again for him till you called me from the deck."

Eadie went on.

"As I started to float up, I thought fast. Of course I knew if I 'blew up' without any decompression I'd probably get 'the bends,' but that wasn't what worried me most. We were hanging from the *Falcon*, and if I came up from the bottom with all that buoyancy, I'd be going as if I'd been fired from a gun by the time I hit her hull. My copper helmet would flatten out like a pancake and that would be my finish right there.

"As I shot up, I saw the top of the steel bails from which the stage was hanging flash down past my faceplate. I couldn't do anything with my hands, but as I went by, I shoved out the toes of both my shoes, and I managed to hook the brass toe caps on my diving shoes into the triangle where the bails join. That stopped me with a jerk, and there I was, hanging onto the bails with my toes and just praying that the caps wouldn't tear off the shoes!

"I tried again to pull my hands in but I couldn't. My suit swelled out some more in a hurry, and burst the shoulder straps holding my belt up and my helmet down. The lead belt dropped around my feet, and my helmet flew up over my head. As it went by, the breastplate hit me a lick under the chin that nearly broke my jaw, and my suit then stretched out so the helmet was nearly two feet over my head. When the straps let go and the suit stretched that gave me still more buoyancy, and the pull on my toes was awful.

"I tried to yell in the telephone to you to have Joe climb up to me, shut off my air and open the petcock on my helmet so as to let some air out of my suit, but the telephone transmitter was up in the helmet and that was two feet over my head and I couldn't make you understand.

"Then the pressure increased with a rush and nearly broke my ears,* and I started to bleed from my mouth and nose. The strain on my toes was fierce, and I was wondering how much longer I could hang on, when all at once my suit tore apart under all that pressure, let out all the air, and I nearly burst as the extra pressure suddenly disappeared. My helmet sort of dropped back, my suit all filled up with water, and I fell down again on the stage.

"I felt you starting to pull me up. I tried to hold my breath, because there was no more air in the suit. Then I remembered that the lines you were hauling me with were only secured to my helmet, and I could feel that my suit was nearly torn in two just below the breastplate. I was down in the rest of the suit and I could feel my heavy shoes and that lead belt hanging round my ankles. I was afraid that what was left of the suit wouldn't stand the strain and it would tear all of the way across. Then you'd pull up the helmet and I'd just sink with those lead-soled shoes and the lead belt as anchors. I thought how surprised you'd be when my helmet came up empty. I tried to kick the belt free from round my feet. No use, I couldn't get it off, so I just held my breath and prayed that the suit wouldn't rip any more. I tried hard not to swallow any water, and the next thing I knew, they were dragging me onto the stage."

A terrible experience. In less than a minute's time, Eadie had seen death in four different horrible forms, successively staring him in the face—"the bends," concussion against the *Falcon*, sudden heavy pressure, and drowning had each in turn seemed about to kill him. He came through, saved by his quick thinking, weak and wounded, but with unshaken nerves. A wonderful diver, Tom Eadie. All the world learned what we already knew, when he later won the Medal of Honor on the *S-4*.

We examined Eadie's helmet to see what had jammed his automatic exhaust valve shut and stopped the air from escaping. We found out, but drew little comfort from the knowledge. While Eadie had been stretched out flat in the tunnel, washing, some mud had been carried into the exhaust valve of his helmet by the water that inevitably leaks in whenever a diver stoops over or lies down.

A few grains of sand had entered the sleeve in which the valve stem worked, jammed between the sleeve and the stem, and prevented the valve from sliding open. It was just as likely to happen to the next man

* With no escape for the air, the pressure in Eadie's suit went up till it balanced at the *Falcon's* compressor pressure of one hundred and thirty-five pounds, equal to diving to a depth of water of three hundred and four feet.

working in the tunnel, and added another danger to the multitude we had. We thereafter warned all divers working in the tunnel to leave the petcock on their helmets cracked open a trifle, while they were in the tunnel and later while coming up, so that if their exhaust valves jammed shut, they might have a brief period to shut off their air before the pressure could build up enough in their suits to spread-eagle them and prevent them from using their hands. The partly open petcock meant that a tiny stream of water would continually run into their suits while they lay down in the tunnel, but it had to be borne. If anyone ever spread-eagled and then had his suit burst inside the tunnel, he was sure to drown before aid could reach him.

There was a little delay on deck after Eadie was hauled up before Carr, the next diver ready, was finally dressed and on his way down, but in about thirty minutes all was quiet again on the *Falcon's* quarter-deck. The pulsating fire hose hanging over the rail and vanishing in the water showed that far below, Carr, prone in the tunnel, was carrying on. Eiben, hanging at the fifty foot stage, still had an hour to wait before he came aboard. The *Falcon* pitched easily as the waves rolled by; near at hand the *Vestal*, the *Iuka*, the *Sagamore*, and the *S-50* tugged at their anchors, and far off on the western horizon, a thin wisp of smoke indicated that the *Penobscot* was coming out with the mail. Altogether, the squadron presented a very peaceful scene, with no indication of the swift drama that had just been acted ninety feet below the gently heaving surface of the sea.

A few more days went by, and from the starboard side, the men reported that they could touch the box keel, which extended sixteen inches below the hull, with their hose nozzles. We knew we could do the same in the port tunnel.

To finish the job, Tug Wilson and Tom Eadie went down together, each one taking a fire hose, and each with a small manila line tied to one wrist. They entered the tunnels, Eadie on the port side, Wilson on the starboard side. When both had crawled in as far as they could go, they asked us for the water, and started from both sides to wash away the clay under the keel.

For communication, I wore Eadie's telephone receiver over one ear, Wilson's over the other one, with a transmitter in each hand.

The divers worked nearly an hour, digging steadily. Neither one made any report. On deck we waited anxiously for news, but did not wish to bother the men with needless conversation. Still it seemed as if they should have been able to wash away the barrier under the keel in that

time. As the minutes dragged by without a junction, I began to feel
that the two tunnels had not met, that one or the other had been drifted
at the wrong angle or perhaps a few feet too far forward to meet its mate.
Considering the difficulty of locating anything below, and the impossibility of checking up on the tunnel directions once they ran in under the
hull, such a failure of the tunnels to meet would be quite natural but
nevertheless it would be heartbreaking after all our struggles.

A call in my left ear. Wilson talking.

"On deck! Turn off my water. I think I can feel the water from Tom's
hose!"

We shut down on Tug's hose. It hung limply, while the other hose
throbbed vigorously.

"Tell Tom to point his hose aft." I gave Eadie the word. A few
minutes went by, then:

"Tell Tom to point his hose forward."

I passed that order also down to Eadie. Wilson, lying in the darkness
below, fumbled blindly around the keel, trying to locate the direction
of the current of water he could feel washing by him. He could find nothing definite.

"On deck, turn on my water again! I'll try to wash further aft along
the keel!"

The hour was up, but with the prospect of finishing the tunnel, it
looked best to leave them alone a little longer. Alternately, I shut off
Eadie's water, and then Wilson's, each one hoping to feel a stream coming under the keel from the other side. Nothing happened, both men
kept on digging.

A call in my right ear. Eadie talking.

"Turn off my water, Mr. Ellsberg!"

I ordered the water shut off. Eadie resumed:

"I got a hole under the keel. I'm going to shove my foot under. Tell
Tug to look out for it!" I turned off Wilson's water, told him to stand by.

Eadie crawled out of the tunnel, turned round, crawled in feet first,
lying on his face, till he touched the keel, and then shoved his right foot,
heel up, under the keel till his knee passed through, then bent his foot
upward as much as possible.

"On deck! I got my foot through! Tell Tug to look out for it!"

"Hello, Tug! Eadie says his foot is under! Feel around for it!"

Wilson fumbled in the blackness and the mud but encountered nothing.

Two hours had gone by, the men were long overtime. I could hear
Wilson cursing volubly as he fumbled in the water-filled tunnel.

"On deck! Tell Tom to wiggle his foot! I can't feel a damned thing!" I told Eadie. Burying his face deeper in the mud, Eadie struggled to push his leg through a few inches further, and wiggled his foot desperately.

A message in my right ear.

"Something is holding my foot!"

I seized Wilson's phone.

"That's Tom's foot you've got hold of, Tug! *Don't let go!*" and in Eadie's transmitter:

"Stop wiggling, Tom! Tug is going to tie his line on your foot!"

Then to Wilson, "Get a couple of good round turns and two half hitches with your line on that foot before you lose it!"

Carefully holding the foot with one hand to avoid losing it in the darkness, Wilson worked up a little slack in the line tied to his left wrist, wound it round Eadie's foot, then drew his knife, cut away the line from his wrist, and firmly secured the end to Eadie's ankle.

A far away growl came from Tug.

"All right, tell Tom he can have his foot now! I'm coming up!"

Wilson crawled out backward from the starboard hole. Eadie crawled headfirst out of the long port tunnel, dragging on his foot the first reeving line under the body of the ship. Outside the tunnel, he pulled through a little slack, cut the line off his foot, bent it to the line on his wrist, and we had a complete line around the ship.

Eadie and Wilson started up, cold and stiff. Their suits were filled with water nearly to their waists.

It was two hours and twenty-three minutes since they had gone down. It took nearly five hours to decompress them. They came aboard finally, utterly fagged out. They had won a point in our struggle against the sea, the first tunnel was at last completed, but on the *Falcon* we spent an anxious night till finally Surgeon Flotte assured us that neither pneumonia nor "the bends" would attack either Tom or Tug.

Another pair of divers took the reeving line, tied it securely to the rail on each side of the *S-51's* deck, cut off the excess lengths going to the surface, ready for running the larger lines through when a good day offered pontooning.

Lost in the Canadian Wilderness

by JOHN GRANT

The harrowing misadventure described below befell Grant while he was engaged on the Halifax and Quebec Railway Exploration Survey in the Tobique district in the year 1847. He spent five days and nights in the wilderness of New Brunswick without food and shelter and was rescued miraculously while close to death, having given up all hope. Many persons have experienced the calamity of being seriously lost. Grant's account is of particular interest because it indicates clearly the great unsuspected reserves which each of us has in store, and which become evident in crisis.

ON THE MORNING OF THE 5TH NOVEMBER WE WERE encamped on the line of survey in the Tobique district, about five miles from the Little Gulque. At eight o'clock the party, having struck tents and got their several loads in readiness, commenced their day's march along the line. When I left them, as I usually did for the purpose of examining the neighboring country, I took a course to the westward for about half a mile, toward a small mount, from the top of which I was led to believe I should obtain an excellent view of the surrounding country, observations from it of distant mountains having already been made by the surveying party during the summer's operations.

After making a few notes and sketches, I went to the top of the hill, where I remained for a short time similarly employed. I then descended with the intention of regaining the line of survey and joining the party. This, however, I found no such easy matter.

The country in this neighborhood has to an immense extent been laid waste by extensive fires, and the trees and even the soil in some places are so thoroughly burnt up that there is not a vestige of vegetation to be seen. In other places the naked trunks of the trees are left standing like grim ghosts of a stately forest race, charred by fire, or blanched by the storm; or they are tossed by the whirlwind into the most frightful heaps of confusion. These are termed "windfalls," and form some of the most formidable barriers to the progress of the traveler in the wilderness.

The surveyed line through this section of the country, owing to the facts above stated, was merely traced out with small stakes, placed at long intervals, and these, having become dark and discolored, could now scarcely be distinguished from the surrounding dead wood. I was not, therefore, in the least disconcerted at failing to find the line, but continued to advance in the direction which I knew it to take, stopping from time to time to take sketches and observations as before. As it was now getting late in the afternoon, and I felt confident I had gone quite as far as the party were likely to have advanced in their day's march, I again made an effort to discover them by traversing the country both to the right and left for a considerable distance, whooping and yelling as loud as I could. It was all in vain, however—I could neither hear nor see anything of them.

Very little more than half a mile from where I stood I recognized a rocky height from which I had, the year before, made some observations and I immediately proceeded thither in the hope of being able to discover from it the smoke of the camp.

On reaching the summit, there stood the post which I had placed for my instruments, exactly as I had left it a year ago. I carefully scanned the face of the country round in every direction, but the anxiously looked-for smoke was nowhere to be seen, and I was at last most reluctantly compelled to relinquish my hope of finding the party—for that night, at least. Not knowing whether the surveyed line lay to my right or left, I resolved on taking the direction in which I thought there was least personal risk, and therefore lost no time in getting on a line which had been run the year before by my directions, and along which I kept to the northward, as, in case I did not in the meantime cross either the other line or tracks of the party, I should at least have made some progress toward Campbell's, the nearest settlement on the Tobique.

I therefore continued to press forward, without, however, discovering the object of my search. I had reached the Beaver Brook, a branch of the Wapskihegan, when night overtook me, and it commenced to rain drearily. It was now quite certain that for one night I must forgo the comforts of food, fire, and shelter, having at the same time no doubt of my easily reaching Campbell's some time next day.

My situation at that time, although but the commencement of my disaster, was one of no ordinary suffering. I had already undergone twelve hours of the most harassing fatigue, without food or a moment's rest; and now, cold and wet, I stood alone amid wind and rain in a sterile and shelterless wilderness, and on a night so dark that the very skies seemed black. What was to be done? To follow a course and move forward in the dark I knew was impossible. There were thirteen long hours until daylight, yet I dared not lie down to rest for fear of perishing miserably. I at length resolved to endeavor to follow the course of the brook, in doing which I had difficulties to surmount which would, I have no doubt, appear to many almost like impossibilities, even by daylight. Such a night of falls, wounds, bruises, scratchings, and fatigue is, I confess, beyond my powers of description. On the morning of the 6th, I found I had got to within a short distance of the mouth of the brook, which I crossed, intending to follow down the Wapskihegan River until I came to a lumber road I had traveled the year before, leading by Shea's Mountain to the Campbell settlement, on the Tobique River.

The waters were now much swollen, so that I could only scramble along a very steep bank, thickly wooded with undergrowth and trees. I had gone some distance down, when, thinking that a little way back from the bank of the river I might probably find the traveling easier, I took that direction, and again found myself in a seemingly open country of burnt lands.

The surrounding highlands were distinctly seen on all sides in the distance, and among the most conspicuous was Shea's Mountain, which led me to the resolution of taking a direct course for it, not dreaming of the formidable difficulties I should have to encounter on the way. I toiled on with determined perseverance through a dreadful combination of windfalls, marshes, lakes, streams, etc., so that another day was nearly spent before I had reached the mountain. I at length found the lumber road, and now considered myself safe, and my journey nearly at an end, being only four miles from the settlement; but I reckoned without my host.

I followed the road for a short distance, until I came to an old lumber camp and road leading to the left, which I examined and unfortunately rejected, as it appeared to pass on a different side of the mountain to that which I knew was the proper road to take; from that moment I continued to go astray.

On traveling a little way farther, I came to a second old lumber camp, where the road again branched into two. A blinding snowstorm had commenced by this time, and night was once more fast approaching.

On going about a mile and a half down one of the roads, I did not like its appearance, and returning followed the other, which I found equally unsatisfactory, as it did not much resemble the road I had traveled during the summer of last year.

I, however, endeavored to console myself with the probability of the difference in its appearance being caused by its covering of snow. I continued to travel for some miles through a low, marshy ground, until I became quite convinced of my being in a strange part, when I returned with the intention if possible of regaining the old lumber camp before dark, and passing the night in it. Once more I was doomed to alarming and disheartening failure. The night came upon me so suddenly that I had only time to go a little way to the right, where the ground was higher and less swampy, and take up my quarters in the shelter of some low bushes, a few branches of which I threw on the ground before lying down. I need scarcely say I was wet, cold, hungry, and much fatigued, having now continued to walk without interruption for upwards of thirty-five hours.

On lying down I got into rather a distressing sort of slumber, from which I in a short time awoke, with much pain in my limbs and back, and quite stiff with cold. I got up and walked about, until once more overcome with fatigue, when I again lay down to endure a repetition of my sufferings. In this way I passed a dreadful night of about thirteen hours. On the morning of the 7th, as soon as it was sufficiently clear, I left my wretched couch, shivering with cold, and by no means refreshed after my fatigue. I was nevertheless in tolerable spirits, not considering myself lost, and feeling assured that within a few hours at least I should once more be in comfortable quarters.

The cravings of hunger were now becoming excessive, and not even a berry was to be seen with which I might allay them. The weather throughout had been, and still continued, appallingly dark, and the only compass then in my possession I had long considered as useless. I took off the glass, however, with the hope of repairing it, but my hands had become so benumbed with cold that the needle slipped from my fingers amongst the long grass, and I was unable, even after the most diligent search, to recover it. I now found that both roads leading from the lumber camp again united, and resolved to continue the one I had been following, under the impression that it must eventually bring me out somewhere on the Tobique. For a considerable distance it traversed a low, marshy district, where I found it very difficult to follow, being sometimes up to my knees in bitterly cold water. After a march of several hours I came to a timber brow on a river which appeared of doubtful size for the Tobique; but as, of course, my route lay down the stream, I, under a gradual mustering of doubts and fears, continued my journey in that direction. I leave you to imagine my feelings and sufferings.

I had felt, without at that moment comprehending them, very evident symptoms of approaching weakness. I frequently heard the sound of voices quite distinctly, and stopped to listen. I whooped loudly, but not a sound came in reply. The stream murmured on in its bed, the wind rustled mournfully amongst the leaves, or whistled shrilly through the long grass; and that was all. Everything else was as silent as the grave. In a short time after a most extraordinary illusion occurred. My attention was first attracted by distinctly hearing a tune whistled in the direction of the river, and on looking round, I saw through the trees an Indian with two squaws and a little boy. My joy at the sight may be readily conceived; their canoe, I thought, could not be far off, and I already fancied myself seated in it, and quietly gliding down the river. I halloed, but to my utter amazement not the slightest notice was taken or reply made. The Indian with folded arms leant against a tree, and still continued to whistle his tune with philosophic indifference. I approached, but they receded and appeared to shun me; I became annoyed and persisted, but in vain, in trying to attract their notice. The dreadful truth at length flashed upon my mind: it was really no more than an illusion, and that one of the most perfect description. Melancholy forebodings arose. I began to wonder fearfully if I were going mad.

I turned away, retraced my steps, and endeavored to think no more of it. I had turned my back upon the vision, but as I retreated, its accompaniment of ghostly music for some time continued to fall upon my unwilling ear like a far-off death knell. A sort of mirage next appeared to me to spread over the low grounds, and so completely real was it in its effect, that frequently, when expecting to step over my boots in water, I found that I was treading upon long, dry grass. And to be convinced of the truth of this, I frequently felt with my hands. My first vision was undoubtedly the result of delirium, brought on by exhaustion; but whether the latter arose from the same cause, or from real external phenomena, I cannot well determine. I continued my toilsome journey along the alternately flat and tangled or precipitous banks of the river, which, being now swollen, left me no beach to travel upon.

I presently crossed a large brook, which, owing to my mistaking it for the Clodell, led me to suppose myself but a very little way from the settlement, which, in reality, was upwards of twelve miles off. I had not advanced a great way farther, before I suddenly dropped down. Supposing I had merely tripped and fallen, I got up and endeavored to continue my march, but again staggered and fell. I got up a second time, and then, leaning against a tree in the hope of recovering from what I at first imagined to be temporary indisposition, I again made several fruitless attempts to walk, until at last the appalling fact forced itself upon me that I had really lost my strength; and that, moreover, as any further exertions of my own were now impossible, my case was indeed hopeless, unless I chanced to be discovered by some of the party, who, I had no doubt, were by this time in search of me. Or, what certainly did appear improbable, some persons going up the stream to lumber might come across me.

Under the circumstances I thought it best to endeavor to regain the banks of the river; but owing to my weak and disabled condition, I could scarcely do more than drag myself along on my hands and knees, and was consequently soon overtaken by the night and a sharp frost. I took shelter behind the roots of a fallen tree, and pulled off my boots, for the purpose of pouring out the water and rendering my feet as dry as I could make them to prevent their being frozen; after which, from my feet being much swollen, I found it quite impossible to get them on again.

I lay down excessively fatigued and weak, yet other sensations of suffering, both mental and physical, kept me through another dreary night of twelve or thirteen hours in a state which some may possibly conceive, but which I must confess my utter inability to describe. There was a sharp frost during the night, against which my flimsy jacket and trousers were but a poor "protection."

On the morning of the 8th, when it was sufficiently clear, I discovered that I was not more than a hundred yards from the bank of the river.

On endeavoring to get up, I was at first unable, and found both my feet and hands frozen; the former, as far as my ankles, felt as perfectly hard and dead as if composed of stone. I succeeded, however, with a good deal of painful exertion in gaining the bank of the river, where I sat as long as I was able with my feet in the water, for the purpose, if possible, of extracting the frost. The oiled canvas haversack in which I carried my sketching case I filled with water, of which I drank freely. The dreadful gnawings of hunger had by this time rather subsided, and I felt inclined to rest. Before leaving the bank of the river I laid hold of the tallest alder near, and drawing it down towards me fastened my handkerchief as a signal to the top, and let go. I also scrawled a few words on two slips of paper describing my situation, and, putting each into a piece of slit stick, threw them into the stream. I next moved back a little way amongst the long grass and alders, and striving to be as calm and collected as my sufferings and weakness would allow, I addressed myself to an all-seeing and merciful God, and endeavored to make my peace with Him, and place myself entirely at His disposal, feeling assured that, whatever the issue might be, whether for time or eternity, it would undoubtedly be for the best. I trust I was not presumptuous, but I felt perfectly calm and resigned to my fate.

I then lay down amongst the long, wet grass, having placed my papers under my head, and my haversack with some water near my side. My weakness seemed to favor the most extraordinary creations of the brain. I became surrounded, especially toward evening, with a distinct assemblage of grotesque and busy figures, with which could I have seen them under different circumstances I should have been highly amused; yet, even as it was, do I believe them to have been a great relief from the utter loneliness that must otherwise have surrounded me, as it really required an effort to establish the truth of my being alone. I passed another long and dreary night, and, from its being rather milder, had some little sleep, although of a distressing and disturbed nature, and not in the least refreshing. The morning of the 9th arrived, and I could then with difficulty support myself even on my knees. Still, after extraordinary exertions, I procured a fresh supply of water, and then lay down again— I thought, most likely, never to rise again. A violent, burning sensation in the stomach had now come on.

A few mouthfuls of water allayed this agony, but brought on violent spasms for five or ten minutes, after which I had, for a little while, comparative relief. In this state, gradually growing weaker and weaker, I continued until the morning of the 10th. During the night it rained in torrents, which, although in some respects inconvenient and disagreeable, had in a great measure drawn the frost from my feet and hands, which as well as my face had become terribly swollen.

In the course of the morning I suddenly heard, or thought I heard, the sound of voices.

I raised my head a little from the ground—all I could now accomplish —and looking through the alders, I saw a party of men and some horses on the opposite side of the river, and scarcely a hundred yards distant from where I lay. My surprise and joy were excessive; yet I had of late seen so many phantoms that I was quite at a loss to know for certain whether to consider it a reality or not. When at length convinced of the reality of help at hand, I discovered, alas! that both my strength and voice were so completely gone that I could neither make myself seen nor heard.

All my exertions were unavailing, and my horror and disappointment may be readily conceived at seeing the party depart again in the direction from which they had come. I had now given up all hope, and once more resigned myself to my apparently inevitable fate. Three more hours had passed, when I again thought I heard the sound of horses' feet on the bed of the river. On looking up I saw the men had returned to the same spot. My efforts to make myself heard were once more renewed, and I at last succeeded in producing a howl so inhuman, as to be mistaken by them for a wolf; but on looking up the stream they saw my handkerchief fluttering, which I had fastened to the alder, and knowing me to have been missing before they left the settlement, surmised the truth, and at once rushed to my assistance. I was taken into a cabin built at the stern of the towboat, in which there was a small stove. They there made a bed for me, and covered me with blankets and rugs. They made a sort of "pap" with bread and sugar, which they offered me, and also some potatoes. I declined their kind offering, but begged to have a little tea, which they gave me, and then I went to sleep. The towboat had to continue her voyage some distance up the river, with her freight, after which we returned and got to Campbell's late in the afternoon, where I met with every kindness and attention. The house of Mr. Campbell to which I was brought was but a very ordinary log house, yet with all its simple homeliness I felt quite comfortable, seeing I was surrounded with the most perfect cleanliness. Besides, the good dame was from long experience well skilled as to the case she had to deal with—at the same time saying mine was much the worst she had ever had under her care.

I have thus endeavored to give an imperfect (and certainly unvarnished) sketch of my wanderings during a period of more than five days and nights, without either food, fire, or shelter from the inclemency of the weather.

My recovery was rapid, although I at first suffered a great deal both from the returning circulation in my hands and feet, and after partaking of food. I was in a few days sufficiently well to be removed down to the mouth of the River Tobique, where I found my poor wife anxiously awaiting my arrival.

)

The Great Chicago Fire

by SAMUEL S. GREELEY

On October 8, 1871, a disastrous fire burned out an area in Chicago of more than 3 square miles, destroyed more than 17,000 buildings, left 100,000 people homeless, and cost 250 lives and $200,000,000 in property. According to legend, the fire was caused by a Mrs. O'Leary's cow, who is said to have kicked over a lantern in the barn. There seems to have been substance to the legend. There were a Mrs. O'Leary and her barn and cow, and numerous eyewitnesses claimed that the fire did indeed begin with her barn. Whatever the true story, conditions were ripe for a disaster. The summer had been very dry, the majority of the city's buildings were of wood, and a high wind was at hand to cause the flames to travel 2¼ miles in 6½ hours. In the following pages we have a first-hand account of the fire, which ranks with the London fire of 1666 as a city's ordeal by flames.

AT THE TIME OF THE GREAT FIRE I WAS LIVING AT THE NORTH-west corner of Erie and St. Clare Streets in the North Division of Chicago, in a new house which I had begun to occupy some ten weeks before. The whole region extending from the river north for half a mile to Chicago Avenue and east of St. Clare Street, and from St. Clare Street east 1,000 feet to the low, sandy shore of Lake Michigan was known as the "Sands," a waste tract without streets, largely covered with shanties and cottages, occupied by a motley population of laborers, teamsters, idlers and many persons without visible or avowable means of support. St. Clare Street was the boundary between two civilizations, and my house was on the frontier.

The members of my family then at home were my wife and myself, two of my sons, Frederick and Morris, aged respectively fifteen and eight years, and two babies, of two and a half years, and of four months. An extensive fire, or what we then thought was such, had on Friday night burned over two squares in the West Division, extending from Washington to Monroe Streets and from Canal Street to Clinton.

On Sunday afternoon we drove some friends to the railroad station to take a train for Boston and we stopped a moment in passing to wonder at the ravages of yesterday's fire. In the course of the evening, after our return home, we several times heard the peal of fire alarms and saw the glare of fire to the southwest, but we gave little heed, supposing that a strong wind had fanned a blaze in the ruins of the recent fire. Being somewhat fatigued, we retired early.

I think it must have been about eleven o'clock Sunday night that I awoke, as was my habit, and got up to see what the weather was and how the night was passing. To my astonishment the night was almost as light as the day: the sky to the southwest shone with a red, angry glare. Great masses of burning matter were sailing northeastward high up in the air, and a shower of sparks and cinders was falling on the sidewalks and roofs about us.

My house was the end one of a block of six new three-story brick houses, surrounded on the opposite sides of the two streets and in the rear by wooden houses and barns, and I saw at a glance that one of the myriad floating cinders might drift into the open window of a stable loft and set the neighborhood in a blaze in a moment. I felt rather than reasoned that the whole North Division was doomed and that we must leave the house while there was yet a way to flee from the wrath to come. My anxiety was the greater because, out of respect for my predatory neighbors, all my basement windows had been guarded by fixed iron bars; if the buildings opposite should ignite, the heat would make it impossible to get out by the front door; retreat by the rear might be equally cut off by the burning of my own stable, and we might be shut in and roasted alive.

I opened my chamber window; everything was quiet as usual, save the ominous roar and crackle of the then distant fire, and the slight rattle of falling cinders upon roofs and sidewalks. There were no lights in windows, and I heard neither voices nor bells. I awakened my wife, telling her that the whole city was afire, that the children must be dressed and everything got ready for a hasty flight.

Without a sign of surprise or emotion she got up, looked out for an instant on the fearful sight and then set to work to call the boys and servants and to dress the drowsy babies. I hurried to the roof with pails

of water to quench the blazing cinders that were falling thickly everywhere. Seeing no sign of alarm or consciousness among my neighbors,
I shouted "Fire, fire!" with all my force. Soon windows began to open
and lights to flash; some citizen more sleepy or more tipsy than the rest
gave forcible expression to his wrath and asked explosively—"What's
the matter with the fellow on the roof, yelling like a maniac in the
middle of the night?"

Meanwhile I had sent my son Frederick to sound the alarm in the
streets and to ring at the doors of friends and relatives living near. In a
very short time this quarter was alive with motion; men were harnessing
their teams or bringing furniture out of the houses, while those more
forward in preparation were starting in flight, some in family groups on
foot, carrying what they held most sacred or most useful in their hands or
on their backs, while others, more fortunate, were driving away in
buggies or wagons.

The scene was now indescribably grand and awful. In the half-hour
I had passed on my roof the fire had leaped forward with frightful speed
and was beginning to break out in detached spots in advance of the
general mass. The wind had risen and was now blowing almost a gale;
the masses of floating fire from roofs and warehouses were more numerous and more fiery and the roar of flames and of falling walls was more
appalling. Suddenly there came a crash like a broadside of artillery, and
a vast jet of smoke and sparks shot up to heaven. It almost seemed to me,
a mile away, that I felt the earth tremble. It was the fall of the roof and
of part of the walls of the new Court House and City Hall, the largest
building, except the grain warehouses, in the city.

The smoke was stifling, but through it the stars looked placidly down
from a clear, steel blue sky, and the full moon shed a cold white light, to
which the bloody glare of the fire made a ghastly contrast. All nature
seemed pitilessly indifferent to this fury and turmoil, wherein a city was
being shriveled and rolled together as a scroll. I was wholly possessed
and awed by this violent contrast between the supreme quiet and order
above and the fearful scene that was spread before me.

It was probably between one and two in the night that I saw flames
leaping up between me and the line of masts along the river, and then I
knew that the fire had crossed the only barrier in our front and was
devouring the North Side. Only a space of a third of a mile, crowded
with wooden buildings, was left to burn before our turn would come.

I heard my name called from the street and, looking down over the
cornice, I saw Matt Higgins, a faithful man, who had worked for me

several years about the house and at the office. He had moved his wife and some poor remnants of household stuff from his rooms near the river and had come to see what he could do for me. "What can I do to help you, Mr. Greeley?" he said.

"There's not much to be done, thank you, Matt," I shouted. "But wait, you might turn the horses out of the barn and give them a chance for their lives in the street. The barn has been on fire once and it might burn and roast them."

"Shure, and wont yez be wanting them yourself pretty soon to haul the family out of this?" asked Matt calmly.

Actually I had not thought of that. Blinded by the smoke and dazed by the general hurly-burly, I had only felt that we must fly, without thinking how or whither. Matt's way was clearly the best, and the horses were kept for future use. My barn took fire twice from falling cinders but the fire was put out by my son and some neighbors whose houses were in danger from it.

My wife came up to the roof once during this time to bring me a cup of coffee and to take one look at the "terror by night." Little was said. I held her as she braced herself against the gale for a moment, and then she went silently down to make her last preparations for the inevitable retreat.

Shortly after two o'clock flames began to shoot up in the hoop and stave yard of Lill's brewery on the lake shore at Chicago Avenue; the fire then had leaped over us and had broken out a quarter of a mile to the north. The city water works stood just north of the brewery with only the width of a street between. The great pumps disabled, the flow of liquid ammunition must stop, and then battle would give way to rout. The time for flight had come, and I went down into the house.

While I had been standing guard and quenching cinders on the house top I had not been unmindful of interests elsewhere. My office, which I shared with Messrs. Cleveland and French, landscape architects, was in the Shepherd Building, at the south east corner of Monroe and Dearborn Streets. In it were my surveying instruments and my field books and plats of surveys, the accumulation of eighteen years' work. They were my stock in trade and were of great value to me as guides in making surveys. But now in the destruction of the Court House and the Recorder's office, where were stored the official records of deeds and plats, and the probable loss of the records themselves, the plats and field notes of a surveyor would become of immense value to the public in restoring lines of ownership where all visible monuments were swept away. I did not dare to go to the South Side of the city to look after my property, fearing that the way back to my family might be cut off. I afterward learned that three of the young men attached to the offices went there early in the night and removed part of my papers, and of Messrs. Cleveland and French, to the office of a friend on Wabash Avenue, which they thought to be out of the range of the fire. On returning to the office after doing this, they found that the buildings to the windward of our block had fallen, leaving this unharmed. Apparently the danger was past; but even as they stood, rejoicing at this unlooked-for chance, a sudden eddy of flame seemed to sweep back upon the building as if determined to leave nothing standing. In a moment the interior was on fire, and the young men had barely time to reach the street from the third story. All witnesses concur, I think, as to the marvelous rapidity with which solid brick buildings seemed to melt and crumble at the touch of fire. This phenomenon is, I think, common to all great conflagrations. It is distinctly stated of the great London fire of 1666, by both Samuel Pepys and John Evelyn in their respective diaries; and we see it in the account of the great fire of San Francisco in 1851 and of Boston in 1873.

Finding their retreat cut off, the three young men ran to the windward side of the Post Office and Custom House on the diagonally opposite corner, where now stands the First National Bank. Here they were kept busy dancing on hot bricks for an hour, till the fire had so far swept by that they were able to escape by a circuitous route and by swift running. All the books, papers and instruments were burned in the place of deposit.

At the house, meanwhile, my wife and Annie Elm, our faithful servant —good friend as well—had dressed the two little children warmly, had chosen a few necessary articles of clothing for them—no more than could be stowed in two pillow cases and had spread a simple lunch of hot coffee and such cold provisions as were available, which we all ate together, standing round the table. All was now done, and had been done quietly and in good order, and good Annie said, "Now, Mrs. Greeley, if there is nothing more you would like to have me do, I will run over to my sister's and help her with the children."

We shook hands and bade good-by, and she hastened to her next field of duty. Annie afterward told me that she and her brood, finding all outlet to the west barred by fire, took refuge with hundreds more on the sands, at the lake shore, where they passed a hot and smoky night. By the dawn's light she saw our row of houses still unharmed; but while she

still gazed through the blinding smoke the fire whirled back, and in half
an hour all had fallen.

It was about two o'clock or a little after when the two horses, har-
nessed, one to the rockaway, the other to the buggy, stood at the door.
I placed my wife in the rockaway with Morris, the two little children
and their nurse, a young woman, whose helplessness and abject terror
make all further mention of her superfluous.

I arranged to drive the rockaway, leaving my son Frederick to follow
alone with the buggy containing the two pillowcases of children's
clothing, and the baby wagon.

We were just starting in this order when, to my great joy and relief,
my friend Mr. Richard Potts, an engineer in the department of public
works, appeared. He was living on the West Side, beyond the reach of
the fire, and had come to offer his services. He undertook to drive the
rockaway to the house of Mr. William H. Clarke, on Dearborn Avenue,
near Burton Place, while Frederick and I stayed behind to take one last
look through the house and to see if anything more could be done. We
passed through the parlor, glancing at the books and papers we had been
reading the evening before and which still lay on the table as we had
left them. We looked into the dining room, where the cloth was laid
for a breakfast never to be eaten. In the basement my eye was caught
by the iron safe and it suddenly occurred to me that the silverware might
be saved.

The gaslight had now failed, but by the light of a couple of matches
I unlocked the safe, swept its contents into the tablecloth, which I
dragged from the table, and threw the whole into the buggy. Just then
my brother-in-law came panting to the door with a huge bundle on his
back, which he threw onto my doorstep. It contained a heavy silver
service and tray valued at a thousand dollars, which had been forgotten
and left in his house when his carriage drove away with his family and
a few of their belongings. I placed it on top of my buggy load and we
started on our flight, noticing with a pang of regret that our poor canary
bird had been left, all unconscious of his doom, hanging in his cage at
an upper window.

Erie Street, on which my house fronted, was a mass of flames to the
west of us. We drove north on St. Clare Street, and saw that the next
street, Huron, too, was blocked. Superior Street looked less fiery, and
there I turned westward. At State Street the great Catholic Church of
the Holy Name was on fire, and its lofty spire was tottering to its ruin;

as we turned northward on Dearborn Avenue I glanced back and saw it swaying as if about to fall.

I think we must have been the last to escape from our neighborhood, for the late Mr. Edward I. Tinkham, banker, a near neighbor, afterward told me that he came to my house to ask my help in saving a trunk containing Government bonds and other securities, amounting to about a million dollars, belonging to his bank, and was told by a bystander that the Greeleys had just driven off. A teamster, who lived near my house, was harnessing his horses to a big truck wagon partly loaded with his household goods, and Mr. Tinkham offered him a thousand dollars for the use of his wagon and team for the night. "No," said the man, "that wagon is for my family; but there is a horse and buggy that you can have with a driver for as long as you want it." The bargain was struck and the trunk with its precious contents was placed in the buggy with the Negro driver.

The banker, finding all avenue of escape to the west and north closed by fire, betook himself with his family and treasure to the lake beach near by, and afterward to the North Pier of the river, whence they were removed the next afternoon by a passing tugboat, after some twelve hours of imprisonment.

As for my son Frederick and myself, we joined the innumerable throng in carriages and vehicles of all sorts, or on foot, all madly fleeing northward toward some unknown place of refuge. We soon reached Mr. Clarke's house, where we found the rest of my family, and with them a motley crowd of refugees, some friends or acquaintances of our host, and many entirely unknown to him. . . .

Bailing Out at Supersonic Speed

by ARTHUR RAY HAWKINS
as told to WESLEY PRICE

Within fifty years after man had made his first flight he had already banged his way through the sound barrier, a feat which only a decade ago was considered by some authorities as impossible. Now he regularly crosses the sound threshold and as regularly breaks speed and altitude records. The author of the following account, a much-decorated Navy pilot, tells what it is like to be fired out of a disabled plane at 40,000 feet while traveling faster than sound. He is the first man to live through the experience.

I AM A NAVY FIGHTER PILOT, AND THAT'S NOT JUST FOR NOW, a sometime thing. This is my settled profession, and so it will be, until the flight surgeon prescribes bifocals and a swivel chair. So far, I've logged almost 3000 hours of flying time, including combat off the carriers in World War II and in the Korean war. One thing about combat: you go looking for trouble, so you're not surprised to find it. It's the unexpected that really curls your hair. I've never been more scared or nearer to death than I was last summer on a routine flight from New York to Texas. I had this jet fighter at 40,000 feet, cruising level. It was so safe, so easy; and then, over Mississippi, the plane went crazily supersonic and tried to kill me.

I should explain that in peacetime I do a lot of acrobatic flying with the Navy's air-show team, the Blue Angels. I'm the leader. There are six of us, and we were all together, flying in line abreast, when my plane went out of control. It dived into an enormous outside loop—I was

vertical—then I was upside down, hanging by my safety belt, and beginning to red out as centrifugal force whirled blood into my brain at tremendous pressure.

That would put the fear of God into any man, especially when you
know that you're traveling faster than the speed of sound. If I was going
to bail out, I'd have to go now, before I lost consciousness—now or
never. But the slipstream outside my canopy was supersonic; plunging
into those granite-hard shock waves might conceivably smash the life
out of me. In all the history of aviation, no one had pierced the sonic
wall with his unarmored body—barehanded, so to speak. At least, no
one had survived to tell about it.

I remember thinking of all that; at the same time, I felt sorry that
my airplane was going to auger in and be destroyed. It was an F9F-6
Cougar, the last word in Grumman-built Navy fighters—wings swept
back, lots of fizz out the rear end, and a red-line speed above Mach 1.0.
["Mach" numbers indicate the ratio of a plane's speed to the speed of
sound at the temperature at which a plane is flying; the speed of sound
varies according to temperature.]

The F9F-6 Cougar was a new type, superseding the F9F-5 Panther.
As soon as dash-six production started, the Blue Angels wanted to trade
in their dash fives—all of a sudden the Panther was last year's airplane.
We had to wait, though, until a few active-duty squadrons got theirs.
Finally, after months of itching, we had the word: six Cougars were
waiting for our team at the Grumman factory in Bethpage, Long Island.

Our home base is the Naval Air Station at Corpus Christi, Texas;
we're all instructors there in the Advanced Training Command. We left
our old jets at Corpus and flew north in a Navy transport, arriving late
in the day. The next morning we swarmed out to the factory, six eager
guys. Texas, here we come!

But first we had to study the F9F-6 cockpit, noting how it differed
from the F9F-5 layout. There were important changes in the elevator
system. In the older Grumman, you had to take your hand off the throttle
to adjust elevator trim tabs. In this one there was a button on the control stick; you could trim nose up or nose down by flicking it with your
thumb. Electric motors did the rest. There was an emergency trim-tab
system, too, also electric.

Then, the Cougar had been given what we call a "flying" tail. The idea
behind it is fairly simple. You take a conventional tail, with its horizontal
surfaces—a movable elevator hinged to a rigid stabilizer. Now, unfreeze
the stabilizer, design it to tilt up and down like the elevator, and provide

a power drive. There's your flying tail. In effect, it gives a pilot a double-size elevator whenever he cuts it in.

So we had skull practice. After that we took the jets up for routine flight testing. The flying tail, we learned, was hardly needed at low altitude, where the air is thick enough to give standard elevators a good bite. But at high altitude, in thin air, it was invaluable. The tightest turn I could pull at 40,000 feet, with elevator alone, was a wide sweep, too wide for turning inside a MIG. When I cut in the flying tail, however, the Cougar really wrapped herself around.

We finished the hop well satisfied, bought the airplanes from Grumman and took off for home. On the way, we stopped at Sewart Air Force Base in Smyrna, Tennessee, for fuel and lunch. So far, so good. Leaving Smyrna, it took us about twenty minutes to get climbed out and formed in line abreast. We weren't pushing our engines, but another hour would see us in Corpus Christi.

Or so I thought. I had no premonition of danger. The controls felt a little sloppy, but that's natural at 40,000 feet. A normal stick movement isn't enough in skinny air. And then you move the stick big, and it's too much, and you get into a lope. But nothing to worry about.

I turned my head left, and right, to see the other jets. When I looked forward again, my nose had dropped a little below the horizon. That's no worry either. You ease back on the stick slightly, the nose rises, and there you are. But this time there was no response to stick movement. The nose stayed down. It went farther down.

I thought I could recover by adjusting the elevator trim tab. It was already set a little nose-up, just enough for level cruise at altitude. I thumbed the button on my stick, feeding more nose-up trim. Not too much.

The dive steepened. My air speed was getting very high. I fed in more trim tab. No response. More trim tab, and more, until I had all of it—fifteen degrees. Still no response; the airplane was getting away from me, diving steeper and steeper, building up speed every moment. I heard one of the boys call on the radio—it was Lieut. Bud Rich's voice—"There goes Hawk; he's in trouble!"

Centrifugal force was pulling me out of my seat, and I realized that I was in the first arc of an outside loop. What had gone wrong? I had only seconds left to figure this out.

Not the trim tab. Might be the flying tail, switched on accidentally. No, the switch is still at Off position. The engine, then a sudden flame-out

. . . but the gauge shows I'm pulling 90 per cent power . . . of course it might be stuck there——

To test instrument response, I shoved the throttle forward. The gauge went to 95 per cent; so power wasn't my trouble. The dive angle was now about thirty-five degrees, and my speed was approaching a dangerous level. Machmeter and air-speed needles were wheeling around together. I cut my power, dropped the dive brakes and went to my emergency trim-tab system, flicking the switch with my left hand. It had no effect.

Another glance at the instrument panel showed that I was already past the speed of sound—and the needles were still winding up. Dive angle fifty degrees——

Vertical! The loop's centrifugal force had me pinned up against the canopy, and a crimson haze began to cloud my vision. It was the first stage of a red-out. There was one last hope—keep pressure on the stick, full nose-up trim, and switch on the flying tail.

I flipped the switch. And with that, the airplane tucked under, and I was upside down, hanging in my harness. Vision was going; consciousness would go next. There was just time enough left to jettison the plastic canopy and fire the explosive charge that would cannon me into space, seat and all. I knew the bail-out drill by heart:

Depress this lever; it blows off the canopy and arms the explosive shell behind your seat. Draw your feet back into the stirrups. Reach overhead, grasp two handles and pull the protective curtain over your face. The last inch of pull will trigger a firing pin. Boom! Out you go.

But I couldn't get the sequence started. Hung up in the canopy as I was, my reach wasn't long enough to shove down the first lever. Stretching to the utmost, I could just graze it with a finger tip.

One last chance. Alongside my head was an emergency handle to be used only in desperate cases. It would arm the ejection seat. But it wouldn't blow off the canopy. To get out of this supersonic mantrap, I'd have to fire myself through thick plastic glass.

I pulled the handle.

How tough is my helmet? Duck down. Maybe the seat rails will punch a hole for you.

I pulled down the face curtain.

When the ejection charge fired, I was four or five inches off the seat. It came up and hit me like a pile driver. Too stunned to feel anything, I went through the canopy, a limp bundle traveling faster than sound. When the momentary blackout passed, I found myself clawing for my rip cord in a groggy attempt to open my parachute. Then I saw that I had missed the handle, and torn a pocket off my flight suit.

Then I thought, *How stupid! Wait until you slow down. A chute opened at this speed would be torn to shreds.*

The seat and I were tumbling over and over, but that soon stopped, and I was sitting upright in space, falling with a lot of forward motion, like an artillery shell. It was then I realized that I was bareheaded. The wind had torn away my face curtain, helmet and oxygen mask.

No oxygen, altitude still above 30,000 feet—I'd gasp my life out if I opened the parachute and dangled up here. I decided to fall free, two or three miles, to get into breathable air as soon as possible. So I fell, keeping one hand on the trip that would jettison my seat, and the other on the rip-cord handle. Two or three miles? Why, in about four seconds the lack of oxygen was graying me out. If I blacked out entirely, I knew that I might never wake up in time to pop the chute.

At an altitude later estimated as 29,000 feet, I opened my safety belt and pulled the rip cord. When the chute blossomed, it jerked the living fool out of me. The shock was so great that I thought the canopy had torn, but, looking up, I saw it was intact.

Next, I thought of my feet and legs. As far as I knew, I was the first Navy pilot to be fired through a canopy. But a lot of dummies had been shot through, in experiments, and I'd read the reports: most of them had feet torn off, legs shattered, heads bashed in. My head felt all right, and I saw that my feet were still attached to my legs.

The ground below was so far away that it didn't seem to be coming up at all. It was very quiet. The only sound was a soft whistling of air in my parachute. And then I couldn't see the ground, or the parachute, or anything. My vision faded away. I seemed to be suspended in gray fog. I needed oxygen.

After a while, I heard a jet go by. I was too grayed out to see it, but I knew it was one of the Blue Angels, following me down. I could think after a fashion, and hear, and feel—I remember feeling the intense cold. But I couldn't see. Then, finally, the blackout. I came back to gray; sank into blackness once more; again regained gray consciousness. The blackouts scared me. If I could only hang on until I got down where there was oxygen pressure!

The chute drifted down through a layer of rough air that swung me from side to side. I was violently sick at my stomach. Afterward, I felt better. My vision cleared, and in a space of mental clarity I remembered a lesson from Navy flight training, about "grunt breathing."

"If you lose your oxygen mask in a high-altitude bailout," we were told, "take deep breaths, close your mouth and grunt hard. That will put pressure on the air in your lungs, and force oxygen into your blood stream."

I tried it, inhaling, holding it and straining to put on pressure. Pressure is the thing; there's oxygen at high altitude, but it's at low pressure. A few seconds after each grunt, my vision would improve for a while. Now I could see the jet. He was flying figure eights to stay with me, but keeping a safe distance, so his jet blast wouldn't collapse my chute. I recognized the plane as an F9F-6. Where the four others were, I couldn't guess. It was explained to me later:

To begin, three jets were on my right, and two on my left, when my plane nosed over. Lieut. Bud Rich, the first to see me go, dived on my tail and had my plane in sight all the way to the ground. He didn't see me bail out. Nobody did—I was a mere speck in an enormous sky.

Lieut. Pat Murphy and Lieut. (j.g.) Frank Jones went screaming down right behind Rich. That left Lieut. (j.g.) Roland Aslund and Lieut. (j.g.) Dayl Crow to circle around, putting out "Mayday" distress calls, holding 40,000 feet to get maximum range on their transmitters. They hoped ground stations could take radio bearings on them, and thus pinpoint the crash location. It worked too.

The boys told me later that my plane completed only the first half of its outside loop. After it got on its back, it went down at a steep angle, augered in and exploded. Rich followed down—when he leveled out he was barely 500 feet off the ground—and saw the plane strike in a wooded area, doing no harm.

Murphy and Jones leveled off at 1000 feet, radioed news of the crash to the boys topside, and started climbing back. Topside flashed the word to Barksdale Air Force Base in Shreveport, and Corpus Christi had it on a hot line before Murphy and Jones got high enough to see something glinting in the sun—me and my parachute. For a minute, they mistook me for a high-altitude weather balloon. They still didn't know that I had bailed out.

We met at 22,000 feet. Murphy stayed up there, feeding radio reports to the nearest military air base, while Jones flew descending figure eights alongside me. It was a long, slow drop, and everybody was getting low on fuel. Aslund and Crow went into Barksdale, and reported to NAS Corpus Christi by phone. Murphy and Rich landed at NAS Memphis, and eventually Frank Jones went there too.

The entire accident, including the slow float down, took about half an hour. It seemed even longer, hanging in the chute. I wanted to give Jones a wave, to let him know I was alive, but being starved for oxygen, I lacked the strength to lift an arm. I thought, *Well, I'll save the energy and let him know later.*

Grunt breathing kept me alive all the way down to 10,000 feet, and there I could breathe normally. At 5,000 feet, I was able to raise my arms in a semaphore *R. R* for "Roger"—O.K. The ground was coming up fast—woods, cotton patches, highways. I was drifting toward a country road, and I could see a pickup truck moving to intercept me. People sitting in the back were looking up at me; I counted two men, a woman and three children.

I missed a barbwire fence and landed in a cotton patch. The chute quietly collapsed on the ground. People from the truck came running. I felt too weak to get up right away.

One of the men said, "Shall I help you up? I might fall down helping you. I'm scareder than you are."

I told him to let me sit awhile. Jones buzzed us in the Cougar. Since I didn't feel like getting up just yet, I asked one of the men—Mr. Arthur Edwards, a farmer and ex-deputy sheriff—to signal for me. "Wave to him on the next pass, so he'll know I'm all right."

Back came the jet, shrieking, and Mr. Edwards waved his hat. That didn't satisfy the pilot; he could see me sitting up, but I didn't look very lively. He came by again at 100 feet. I got on my feet, semaphoring "Roger" and a wave-off. He waggled his wings, and with drying tanks, went off on a beeline for NAS Memphis.

Mr. Edwards told me I was in Mississippi, near the small town of Pickens. About half an hour earlier, he said, he had heard three claps of thunder. Since the sky was clear, he was puzzled. He looked up; and he soon saw four jets diving toward him, one of them obviously out of control.

(Later, when accident investigators questioned local people, they found several who had heard three thunderclaps. There were "supersonic bangs," of course, and they originated as shock waves on my plane, about the time I bailed out. Three shock waves, three bangs; the effect is well known in high-speed test flying.)

Mr. Edwards drove me to the scene of the crash, about three miles away. I wanted to make sure the plane hadn't hurt anyone or destroyed property; and after that, I wanted the wreckage inspected for clues to the cause of my trouble. A rising column of smoke led us to a wooded area, where a crowd of farm people were standing around a deep crater.

Fire smoldered in the pit my plane had dug, and chunks of metal were scattered everywhere. I asked if anyone had seen the tail or parts of it.

"If there's enough left of it," I said, "the experts can tell what went wrong."

A man said, "I think it's back over there," and he showed me a good piece of the tail.

I asked him to see that no one picked up anything for a souvenir, and to phone the marshal for a guard. He said he would attend to it. Mr. Edwards then drove me into Pickens, to a drugstore, where I put in a long-distance call to my wife. Whenever I'm due in Corpus Christi, she always comes down to the flight line to meet me. She'd be waiting now, knowing I was overdue.

My wife is up on all the trouble we have with airplanes, and before I went north to get the F9F-6 she asked me if they had got all the bugs out of it. I told her entire squadrons had been flying F9F-6's, and anyway, I said, somebody has to make a start with every new plane. That satisfied her well enough. But now I had some explaining to do.

When she came on the phone, she was crying, and I told her if she didn't hush up, I couldn't tell her anything. It was awful, hearing her cry; she never cries. I assured her I was all right. She wasn't satisfied with that. She knew that I had bailed out; Aslund and Crow had phoned that much to the duty officer at Corpus, when they landed at Barksdale. Was I alive? They didn't know. About half an hour later, Bud Rich phoned my wife from Memphis: I'd been seen on the ground, waving. Whether I had broken bones or anything, he couldn't say.

No wonder she was crying. She kept asking, "Are you all right? Are you sure? Are you sure?"

I told her that one of my ribs was slightly out of kilter, but other than that, I was fine.

"Where are you calling from—a hospital?"

"A drugstore," I said; and I kidded her a little to let her be really sure everything was all right. She stopped crying.

I made my official call to the duty officer at Corpus. It was arranged that a Mississippi highway-patrol car would take me to a near-by airfield, where a Navy transport would be waiting to fly me to NAS Memphis. There was just time to see a local doctor. He taped up my rib and gave me a tetanus booster shot for scratches he found on my legs. My neck felt sore, my thighs ached from the two-and-a-half-ton spanking the ejection seat had given me, and altogether I felt as if I'd played an hour of football against a rough team. And I had butterflies in my stomach.

The highway-patrol officer who came for me, Jerry Wald, said he had the cure for my unsettled stomach. "We'll stop by my house, and my wife will give you a cold glass of buttermilk. It's an old Southern remedy."

Mr. and Mrs. Wald were wonderful, and I shall never forget their kindness, or Mr. Edwards' either. As for the buttermilk, it worked like magic.

It was after dark when I landed at the Naval Air Station in Memphis. Rich, Murphy and Jones were waiting for me, and there was an ambulance I didn't need. But I had to go to the Navy hospital, willy-nilly, where they looked me over—I had nothing worse than this one rib—and told me to return in the morning for X-rays. For a man who had been through a supersonic bailout, an unheard-of thing, I was in good shape. For instance, I might have frozen to death, floating so long in subzero temperatures at high altitude. Luckily, the slipstream hadn't torn off my shoes or gloves, and I was wearing my uniform under the flight suit. Only my ears were slightly frostbitten.

After X-rays the next day, I was flown back to Corpus Christi. I came stumbling off the transport plane, and there were all these people waiting—my wife with our small boys, Raymond and Michael, and a dozen of my best friends, Aslund and Crow, and my boss, Capt. H. J. Dyson, chief of staff of Naval Advanced Air Training—a very happy reunion. But my wife had tears in her eyes, and later on she said to me, "I'm never going to worry again. The Lord is saving you for something; you better start listening to find out what it is."

The doctors at Corpus re-examined me. This time there was much emphasis on eyes and lungs, and I remember a psychologist dropping in, sitting around and popping little questions at me to get my mental attitude. They couldn't find any reason to ground me. Yet it was six days before I could resume flying; I was swamped with paper work.

Regulations said I had to write a formal accident report at once. Also, I owed the Bureau of Medicine and Surgery in Washington a report on my physical condition, with long words in it like "metatarsal," which our flight surgeon stuck in for me. Then, the safety experts wanted a special report, written at great length. And I had a phone call from the Naval Air Material Center in Philadelphia. In tests of escape procedures, they'd been firing dummies through plastic-glass canopies, and most of them couldn't take it. Would I come east and talk over any ideas I might have?

I did visit NAMC, and, on seeing the dummies, suggested that they be made more flexible, so they'd squash down a little, as I had when the ejection seat walloped me, and go out with legs streamlining naturally after the torso. Perhaps I had the answer. But the big question was: Why had my F9F-6 gone out of control in the first place? Was this an isolated case? Or was there a basic defect in the Cougar design, some hidden fault that would cause many more accidents?

We had the verdict very quickly. Cougars in general were safe, but I'd been unlucky enough to get one with a malfunction in the flying tail. Power for the up or down tilting is supplied by hydraulic pressure. In my plane, a very slow leak in a valve permitted a gradual build-up of pressure on the nose-down side of the system. The mechanism, plucked from the wreckage, was found locked in full nose-down position.

The facts being known, a Navy order grounding all F9F-6's was lifted, on condition that they be flown with the stabilizer rigid, until Grumman could make a permanent fix. For a while, we had to pull a little harder on the stick, and we couldn't turn as tightly at high altitude. Grumman promptly began installing a manual control in all F9F-6's, so you can shut off all hydraulic pressure on the stabilizer in an emergency.

I ordered another F9F-6, before the fix was made, and the Blue Angels continued practice using the five others. We were doubtful of the swept wing, at first, because sweeping is apt to hurt the precise control you get with a straight wing. And you'd better be precise, doing barrel rolls in tight formation at low altitude. However, the wing gave us no trouble at all. It's a fine airplane; in a way, you might say it saved my life.

That emergency handle—the one that let me escape—existed at the time on only a few other aircraft. It was there because some of us wrote back from Korea and asked for it, suspecting that at least one of our friends died because he couldn't eject himself. Grumman pioneered the device in the F9F-6; and my experience has prompted the Bureau of Aeronautics to order it put in all previous F9F's in the field.

That's the story.

Death in the Afternoon

by ERNEST HEMINGWAY

It is difficult to bring to mind the name of any modern author who has had as much experience of "man against nature" as Ernest Hemingway, the colorful Byron of the twentieth century. Perhaps not since Tolstoy has any author lived the physical life as fully as he. His recent African safari, in which he escaped death twice in two air crashes, made headline news throughout the United States, a remarkable tribute to an American author. Hemingway has long been interested in the bullfight as a form of tragic ritual. His book Death in the Afternoon *is perhaps the most exciting narrative dealing with the bullfight as a spectacle and an institution ever written.*

THE BULLFIGHT IS NOT A SPORT IN THE ANGLO-SAXON SENSE of the word, that is, it is not an equal contest or an attempt at an equal contest between a bull and a man. Rather it is a tragedy; the death of the bull, which is played, more or less well, by the bull and the man involved and in which there is danger for the man but certain death for the animal. This danger to the man can be increased by the bullfighter at will in the measure in which he works close to the bull's horns. Keeping within the rules for bullfighting on foot in a closed ring formulated by years of experience, which, if known and followed, permit a man to perform certain actions with a bull without being caught by the bull's horns, the bullfighter may, by decreasing his distance from the bull's horns, depend more and more on his own reflexes and judgment of that distance to protect him from the points. This danger of goring, which the man creates voluntarily, can be changed to certainty of being caught and tossed by the bull if the man, through ignorance, slowness, torpidness, blind folly or momentary grogginess breaks any of these fundamental rules for the execution of the different suertes. Everything that is done by the man in the ring is called a "suerte." It is the easiest term to use as it is short. It means act, but the word act has, in English, a connotation of the theatre that makes its use confusing.

People seeing their first bullfight say, "But the bulls are so stupid. They always go for the cape and not for the man."

The bull only goes for the percale of the cape or for the scarlet serge of the muleta if the man makes him and so handles the cloth that the bull sees it rather than the man. Therefore to really start to see bullfights a spectator should go to the novilladas or apprentice fights. There the bulls do not always go for the cloth because the bullfighters are learning before your eyes the rules of bullfighting and they do not always remember or know the proper terrain to take and how to keep the bull after the lure and away from the man. It is one thing to know the rules in principle and another to remember them as they are needed when facing an animal that is seeking to kill you, and the spectator who wants to see men tossed and gored rather than judge the manner in which the bulls are dominated should go to a novillada before he sees a corrida de toros or complete bullfight. It should be a good thing for him to see a novillada first anyway if he wants to learn about technique, since the employment of knowledge that we call by that bastard name is always most visible in its imperfection. At a novillada the spectator may see the mistakes of the bullfighters, and the penalties that these mistakes carry. He will learn something too about the state of training or lack of training of the men and the effect this has on their courage.

One time in Madrid I remember we went to a novillada in the middle of the summer on a very hot Sunday when every one who could afford it had left the city for the beaches of the north or the mountains and the bullfight was not advertised to start until six o'clock in the evening, to see six Tovar bulls killed by three aspirant matadors who have all since failed in their profession. We sat in the first row behind the wooden barrier and when the first bull came out it was clear that Domingo Hernandorena, a short, thick-ankled, graceless Basque with a pale face who looked nervous and incompletely fed in a cheap rented suit, if he was to kill this bull would either make a fool of himself or be gored. Hernandorena could not control the nervousness of his feet. He wanted to stand quietly and play the bull with the cape with a slow movement of his arms, but when he tried to stand still as the bull charged his feet jumped away in short, nervous jerks. His feet were obviously not under his personal control and his effort to be statuesque while his feet jittered him away out of danger was very funny to the crowd. It was funny to them because many of them knew that was how their own feet would behave if they saw the horns coming toward them, and as always, they resented any one else being in there in the ring, making money, who had the same physical defects which barred them, the spectators, from that supposedly highly paid way of making a living. In their turn the other two matadors were very fancy with the cape and Hernandorena's nervous jerking was even worse after their performance. He had not been in the ring with a bull for over a year and he was altogether unable to control his nervousness. When the banderillas were in and it was time for him to go out with the red cloth and the sword to prepare the bull for killing and to kill, the crowd which had applauded ironically at every nervous move he had made knew something very funny would happen. Below us, as he took the muleta and the sword and rinsed his mouth out with water I could see the muscles of his cheeks twitching. The bull stood against the barrier watching him. Hernandorena could not trust his legs to carry him slowly toward the bull. He knew there was only one way he could stay in one place in the ring. He ran out toward the bull, and ten yards in front of him dropped to both knees on the sand. In that position he was safe from ridicule. He spread the red cloth with his sword and jerked himself forward on his knees toward the bull. The bull was watching the man and the triangle of red cloth, his ears pointed, his eyes fixed, and Hernandorena knee-ed himself a yard closer and shook the cloth. The bull's tail rose, his head lowered and he charged and, as he reached the man, Hernandorena rose solidly from his knees into the air, swung over like a bundle, his legs in all directions now, and then dropped to the ground. The bull looked for him, found a wide-spread moving cape held by another bullfighter instead, charged it, and Hernandorena stood up with sand on his white face and looked for his sword and the cloth. As he stood up I saw the heavy, soiled gray silk of his rented trousers open cleanly and deeply to show the thigh bone from the hip almost to the knee. He saw it too and looked very surprised and put his hand on it while people jumped over the barrier and ran toward him to carry him to the infirmary. The technical error that he had committed was in not keeping the red cloth of the muleta between himself and the bull until the charge; then at the moment of jurisdiction as it is called, when the bull's lowered head reaches the cloth, swaying back while he held the cloth, spread by the stick and the sword, far enough forward so that the bull following it would be clear of his body. It was a simple technical error.

That night at he café I heard no word of sympathy for him. He was ignorant, he was torpid, and he was out of training. Why did he insist on being a bullfighter? Why did he go down on both knees? Because he was a coward, they said. The knees are for cowards. If he was a coward why did he insist on being a bullfighter? There was no natural sympathy for uncontrollable nervousness because he was a paid public performer. It was preferable that he be gored rather than run from the bull. To be gored was honorable; they would have sympathized with him had he been caught in one of his nervous uncontrollable jerky retreats, which, although they mocked, they knew were from lack of training, rather than for him to have gone down on his knees. Because the hardest thing when frightened by the bull is to control the feet and let the bull come, and any attempt to control the feet was honorable even though they jeered at it because it looked ridiculous. But when he went on both knees, without the technique to fight from that position; the technique that Marcial Lalanda, the most scientific of living bullfighters, has, and which alone makes that position honorable; then Hernandorena admitted his nervousness. To show his nervousness was not shameful; only to admit it. When, lacking the technique and thereby admitting his inability to control his feet, the matador went down on both knees before the bull the crowd had no more sympathy with him than with a suicide.

For myself, not being a bullfighter, and being much interested in suicides, the problem was one of depiction and waking in the night I tried to remember what it was that seemed just out of my remembering and that was the thing that I had really seen and, finally, remembering all around it, I got it. When he stood up, his face white and dirty and the silk of his breeches opened from waist to knee, it was the dirtiness of the rented breeches, the dirtiness of his slit underwear and the clean, clean, unbearably clean whiteness of the thigh bone that I had seen, and it was that which was important.

At the novilladas, too, besides the study of technique, and the consequences of its lack you have a chance to learn about the manner of dealing with defective bulls since bulls which cannot be used in a formal bullfight because of some obvious defect are killed in the apprentice fights. Nearly all bulls develop defects in the course of any fight which must be corrected by the bullfighter, but in the novillada these defects, those of vision for instance, are many times obvious at the start and so the manner of their correcting, or the result of their not being corrected, is apparent.

The formal bullfight is a tragedy, not a sport, and the bull is certain to be killed. If the matador cannot kill him and, at the end of the allotted fifteen minutes for the preparation and killing, the bull is led and herded out of the ring alive by steers to dishonor the killer, he must, by law, be killed in the corrals. It is one hundred to one against the matador de toros or formally invested bullfighter being killed unless he is inexperienced, ignorant, out of training or too old and heavy on his feet. But the matador, if he knows his profession, can increase the amount of the danger of death that he runs exactly as much as he wishes. He should, however, increase this danger, *within the rules provided for his protection.* In other words it is to his credit if he does something that he knows how to do in a highly dangerous but still geometrically possible manner. It is to his discredit if he runs danger through ignorance, through disregard of the fundamental rules, through physical or mental slowness, or through blind folly.

The matador must dominate the bulls by knowledge and science. In the measure in which this domination is accomplished with grace will it be beautiful to watch. Strength is of little use to him except at the actual moment of killing. Once some one asked Rafael Gomez, "El Gallo," nearing fifty years old, a gypsy, brother of Jose Gomez, "Gallito," and the last living member of the great family of gypsy bullfighters of that name, what physical exercise he, Gallo, took to keep his strength up for bullfighting.

"Strength," Gallo said. "What do I want with strength, man? The bull weighs half a ton. Should I take exercises for strength to match him? Let the bull have the strength."

If the bulls were allowed to increase their knowledge as the bullfighter does and if those bulls which are not killed in the allotted fifteen minutes in the ring were not afterwards killed in the corrals but were allowed to be fought again they would kill all the bullfighters, if the bullfighters fought them according to the rules. Bullfighting is based on the fact that it is the first meeting between the wild animal and a dismounted man. This is the fundamental premise of modern bullfighting; that the bull has never been in the ring before. In the early days of bullfighting bulls were allowed to be fought which had been in the ring before and so many men were killed in the bull ring that on November 20, 1567, Pope Pius the Fifth issued a Papal edict excommunicating all Christian princes who should permit bullfights in their countries and denying Christian burial to any person killed in the bull ring. The Church only agreed to tolerate bullfighting, which continued steadily in Spain in spite of the edict, when it was agreed that the bulls should only appear once in the ring.

You would think then that it would make of bullfighting a true sport, rather than merely a tragic spectacle, if bulls that had been in the ring were allowed to reappear. I have seen such bulls fought, in violation of the law, in provincial towns in improvised arenas made by blocking the entrances to the public square with piled-up carts in the illegal capeas, or town-square bullfights with used bulls. The aspirant bullfighters, who have no financial backing, get their first experience in capeas. It is a sport, a very savage and primitive sport, and for the most part a truly amateur one. I am afraid however due to the danger of death it involves it would never have much success among the amateur sportsmen of America and England who play games. We, in games, are not fascinated by death, its nearness and its avoidance. We are fascinated by victory and we replace the avoidance of death by the avoidance of defeat. It is a very nice symbolism but it takes more cojones to be a sportsman when death is a closer party to the game. The bull in the capeas is rarely killed. This should appeal to sportsmen who are lovers of animals. The town is usually too poor to afford to pay for the killing of the bull and none of the aspirant bullfighters has enough money to buy a sword or he would not have chosen to serve his apprenticeship in the capeas. This would afford an opportunity for the man who is a wealthy sportsman, for he could afford to pay for the bull and buy himself a sword as well.

However, due to the mechanics of a bull's mental development the used bull does not make a brilliant spectacle. After his first charge or so he will stand quite still and will only charge if he is certain of getting the man or boy who is tempting him with a cape. When there is a crowd and the bull charges into it he will pick one man out and follow him, no matter how he may dodge, run and twist until he gets him and tosses him. If the tips of the bull's horns have been blunted this chasing and tossing is good fun to see for a little while. No one has to go in with the bull who does not want to, although of course many who want to very little go in to show their courage. It is very exciting for those who are down in the square, that is one test of a true amateur sport, whether it is more enjoyable to player than to spectator (as soon as it becomes enjoyable enough to the spectator for the charging of admission to be profitable the sport contains the germ of professionalism), and the smallest evidence of coolness or composure brings immediate applause. But when the bull's horns are sharp-pointed it is a disturbing spectacle. The men and boys try cape work with sacks, blouses and old capes on the bull just as they do when his horns have been blunted; the only difference is that when the bull catches them and tosses them they are liable to come off the horn with wounds no local surgeon can cope with. One bull which was a great favorite in the capeas of the province of Valencia killed sixteen men and boys and badly wounded over sixty in a career of five years. The people who go into these capeas do so sometimes as aspirant professionals to get free experience with bulls but most often as amateurs, purely for sport, for the immediate excitement, and it is very great excitement; and for the retrospective pleasure, of having shown their contempt for death on a hot day in their own town square. Many go in from pride, hoping that they will be brave. Many find they are not brave at all; but at least they went in. There is absolutely nothing for them to gain except the inner satisfaction of having been in the ring with a bull; itself a thing that any one who has done it will always remember. It is a strange feeling to have an animal come toward you consciously seeking to kill you, his eyes open looking at you, and see the oncoming of the lowered horn that he intends to kill you with. It gives enough of a sensation so that there are always men willing to go into the capeas for the pride of having experienced it and the pleasure of having tried some bullfighting maneuver with a real bull although the actual pleasure at the time may not be great. Sometimes the bull is killed if the town has the money to afford it, or if the populace gets out of control; every one swarming on him at once with knives, daggers, butcher knives and rocks; a man perhaps between his horns, being swung up and down, another flying through the air, surely several holding his tail, a swarm of choppers, thrusters and stabbers pushing into him, laying on him or cutting up at him until he sways and goes down. All amateur or group killing is a very barbarous, messy, though exciting business and is a long way from the ritual of the formal bullfight.

The bull which killed the sixteen and wounded the sixty was killed in a very odd way. One of those he had killed was a gypsy boy of about fourteen. Afterward the boy's brother and sister followed the bull around hoping perhaps to have a chance to assassinate him when he was loaded in his cage after a capea. That was difficult since, being a very highly valued performer, the bull was carefully taken care of. They followed him around for two years, not attempting anything, simply turning up wherever the bull was used. When the capeas were again abolished, they are always being abolished and re-abolished, by government order, the bull's owner decided to send him to the slaughterhouse in Valencia, for the bull was getting on in years anyway. The two gypsies were at the slaughter-house and the young man asked permission, since the bull had killed his brother, to kill the bull. This was granted and he started in by digging out both the bull's eyes while the bull was in his cage, and spitting carefully into the sockets, then after killing him by severing the spinal marrow between the neck vertebrae with a dagger, he experienced some difficulty in this, he asked permission to cut off the bull's testicles, which being granted, he and his sister built a small fire at the edge of the dusty street outside the slaughterhouse and roasted the two glands on sticks and when they were done, ate them. They then turned their backs on the slaughterhouse and went away along the road and out of town.

Bridging the Hellespont

by HERODOTUS

Man has challenged nature with bridges for centuries, bridges which have cost many lives to construct, and some of these bridges have become famous, such as London Bridge, Brooklyn Bridge and the Golden Gate Bridge. The latter are, of course, permanent structures, whereas the bridge described by Herodotus, the Greek historian and traveler, is a military bridge, constructed for a specific purpose and destined shortly to be dismantled.

XERXES, AFTER THIS, MADE PREPARATIONS TO ADVANCE TO Abydos, where the bridge across the Hellespont from Asia to Europe was lately finished. Midway between Sestos and Madytus in the Hellespontine Chersonese, and right over against Abydos, there is a rocky tongue of land which runs out for some distance into the sea. This is the place where no long time afterward the Greeks under Xanthippus, the son of Ariphron, took Artaÿctes the Persian, who was at that time governor of Sestos, and nailed him living to a plank. He was the Artaÿctes who brought women into the temple of Protesilaüs at Elæus, and there was guilty of most unholy deeds.

Toward this tongue of land then, the men to whom the business was assigned carried out a double bridge from Abydos; and while the Phœnicians constructed one line with cables of white flax, the Egyptians in the other used ropes made of papyrus. Now it is seven furlongs across from Abydos to the opposite coast. When, therefore, the channel had been bridged successfully, it happened that a great storm arising broke the whole work to pieces, and destroyed all that had been done.

So when Xerxes heard of it he was full of wrath, and straightway gave orders that the Hellespont should receive three hundred lashes, and

247

that a pair of fetters should be cast into it. Nay, I have even heard it said, that he bade the branders take their irons and therewith brand the Hellespont. It is certain that he commanded those who scourged the waters to utter, as they lashed them, these barbarian and wicked words: "Thou bitter water, thy lord lays on thee this punshment because thou has wronged him without a cause, having suffered no evil at his hands. Verily King Xerxes will cross thee, whether thou wilt or no. Well dost thou deserve that no man should honor thee with sacrifice; for thou art of a truth a treacherous and unsavory river." While the sea was thus punished by his orders, he likewise commanded that the overseers of the work should lose their heads.

Then they, whose business it was, executed the unpleasing task laid upon them; and other master builders were set over the work, who accomplished it in the way which I will now describe.

They joined together triremes* and penteconters,† 360 to support the bridge on the side of the Euxine Sea,‡ and 314 to sustain the other; and these they placed at right angles to the sea, and in the direction of the current of the Hellespont, relieving by these means the tension of the shore cables. Having joined the vessels, they moored them with anchors of unusual size, that the vessels of the bridge toward the Euxine might resist the winds which blow from within the straits, and that those of the more western bridge facing the Egean might withstand the winds which set in from the south and from the southeast. A gap was left in the penteconters in no fewer than three places, to afford a passage for such light craft as chose to enter or leave the Euxine. When all this was done, they made the cables taut from the shore by the help of wooden capstans. This time, moreover, instead of using the two materials separately, they assigned to each bridge six cables, two of which were of white flax, while four were of papyrus. Both cables were of the same size and quality; but the flaxen were the heavier, weighing not less than a talent the cubit. When the bridge across the channel was thus complete, trunks of trees were sawn into planks, which were cut to the width of the bridge, and these were laid side by side upon the tightened cables, and then fastened on the top. This done, brushwood was brought, and arranged upon the planks, after which earth was heaped upon the brushwood, and the whole trodden down into a solid mass. Lastly a bulwark was set up on either side of this causeway, of such a height as

* A galley having three banks of oars.
† A fifty-oared galley.
‡ Black Sea.

to prevent the sumpter-beasts and the horses from seeing over it and taking fright at the water.

And now when all was prepared—the bridges, and the works at Athos, the breakwaters about the mouths of the cutting, which were made to hinder the surf from blocking up the entrances, and the cutting itself; and when the news came to Xerxes that this last was completely finished—then at length the host, having first wintered at Sardis, began its march towards Abydos, fully equipped, on the first approach of spring. At the moment of departure, the sun suddenly quitted his seat in the heavens, and disappeared, though there were no clouds in sight, but the sky was clear and serene. Day was thus turned into night; whereupon Xerxes, who saw and remarked the prodigy, was seized with alarm, and sending at once for the Magians, inquired of them the meaning of the portent. They replied: "God is foreshowing to the Greeks the destruction of their cities; for the sun foretells for them, and the moon for us." So Xerxes, thus instructed, proceeded on his way with great gladness of heart.

The army had begun its march, when Pythius the Lydian, affrighted at the heavenly portent, and emboldened by his gifts, came to Xerxes and said: "Grant me. O my Lord! a favor which is to thee a light matter, but to me of vast account." Then Xerxes, who looked for nothing less than such a prayer as Pythius in fact preferred, engaged to grant him whatever he wished, and commanded him to tell his wish freely. So Pythius, full of boldness, went on to say:

"O my lord! thy servant has five sons; and it chances that all are called upon to join thee in this march against Greece. I beseech thee, have compassion upon my years; and let one of my sons, the eldest, remain behind, to be my prop and stay, and the guardian of my wealth. Take with thee the other four; and when thou hast done all that is in thy heart, mayest thou come back in safety."

But Xerxes was greatly angered, and replied to him: "Thou wretch! darest thou speak to me of thy son, when I am myself on the march against Greece, with sons, and brothers, and kinsfolk, and friends? Thou, who art my bond-slave, and art in duty bound to follow me with all thy household, not excepting thy wife! Know that man's spirit dwelleth in his ears, and when it hears good things, straightway it fills all his body with delight; but no sooner does it hear the contrary than it heaves and swells with passion. As when thou didst good deeds and madest good offers to me, thou wert not able to boast of having outdone the king in bountifulness, so now when thou art changed and grown impudent, thou shalt not receive all thy deserts, but less. For thyself and four of thy five sons, the entertainment which I had of thee shall gain protection; but as for him to whom thou clingest above the rest, the forfeit of his life shall be thy punishment." Having thus spoken, forthwith he commanded those to whom such tasks were assigned, to seek out the eldest of the sons of Pythius, and having cut his body asunder, to place the two halves, one on the right, the other on the left, of the great road, so that the army might march out between them.

Then the king's orders were obeyed, and the army marched out between the two halves of the carcass. First of all went the baggage-bearers, and the sumpter-beasts, and then a vast crowd of many nations mingled together without any intervals, amounting to more than one half of the army. After these troops an empty space was left, to separate between them and the king. In front of the king went first a thousand horsemen, picked men of the Persian nation—then, spearmen a thousand, likewise chosen troops, with their spearheads pointing toward the ground—next ten of the sacred horses called Nisæan, all daintily caparisoned. (Now these horses are called Nisæan, because they come from the Nisæan plain, a vast flat in Media, producing horses of unusual size) After the ten sacred horses came the holy chariot of Jupiter, drawn by eight milk-white steeds, with the charioteer on foot behind them holding the reins; for no mortal is ever allowed to mount into the car. Next to this came Xerxes himself, riding in a chariot drawn by Nisæan horses, with his charioteer, Patiramphes, the son of Otanes, a Persian, standing by his side.

Thus rode forth Xerxes from Sardis—but he was accustomed every now and then, when the fancy took him, to alight from his chariot and travel in a litter. Immediately behind the king there followed a body of a thousand spearmen, the noblest and bravest of the Persians, holding their lances in the usual manner—then came a thousand Persian horse, picked men—then ten thousand, picked also after the rest, and serving on foot. Of these last one thousand carried spears with golden pomegranates at their lower end instead of spikes; and these encircled the other nine thousand, who bore on their spears pomegranates of silver. The spearmen too who pointed their lances toward the ground had golden pomegranates; and the thousand Persians who followed close after Xerxes had golden apples. Behind the ten thousand footmen came a body of Persian cavalry, likewise ten thousand; after which there was again a void space for as much as two furlongs; and then the rest of the army followed in a confused crowd.

The march of the army, after leaving Lydia, was directed upon the river Caïcus and the land of Mysia. Beyond the Caïcus the road, leaving Mount Cana upon the left, passed through the Atarnean plain, to the city of Carina. Quitting this, the troops advanced across the plain of Thebé, passing Adramyttium, and Antandrus, the Pelasgic city; then, holding Mount Ida upon the left hand, it entered the Trojan territory. On this march the Persians suffered some loss; for as they bivouacked during the night at the foot of Ida, a storm of thunder and lightning burst upon them, and killed no small number.

TRANSLATED BY GEORGE RAWLINSON

Kon-Tiki

by THOR HEYERDAHL

Who has not dreamed of being wafted upon a gentle sea to Polynesia? The Norwegian ethnologist Thor Heyerdahl did not merely dream this but, as leader of an expedition to test a theory of his, actually lived it, and won worldwide fame by doing so. He believed that the prehistoric settlement of Polynesia had been made by pre-Inca Peruvians who had sailed about A.D. 500 to the South Pacific islands. The theory he proved is that it is possible to sail a balsa raft, with the aid of the Humboldt and South Equatorial currents, from Peru to Polynesia. Heyerdahl built the forty-five-foot raft Kon-Tiki in Peru and he and five male companions were set adrift on it at Callao, Peru, on April 28, 1947. They reached the Tuamotu Islands in the South Pacific on August 7, 101 days later, thus proving to the general public that the days of great adventure were not yet over, nor man's ability to return to nature, or to a state surprisingly similar to it.

USUALLY MEN WHO HAVE EMBARKED ON AN OCEAN RAFT IN modern times have been shipwrecked sailors whose sole desire was to escape the perils of the open sea and reach the nearest coast. But this was not the case in April of last year, when the tugboat "Guardian Rio" towed a clumsy raft away from the sheltered docks of the Peruvian port of Callao and left it adrift well outside the harbor entrance. The six of us that were left aboard the raft were filled with one single hope—that the wind and current would push our primitive craft far away from the South American mainland and right into the wide-open span of the vast Pacific Ocean.

Our purpose was not to flee the Republic of Peru. Leading officials of many nations had bidden us hearty farewell at the dock as the Peruvian Navy tugged us to our point of departure. Nor did we possess any desire to establish a world record in hazardous ocean drift. Yet the betting went high at the docks when we left.

Some claimed that we would be picked up off the coast in a few days or would never be seen again. The nine logs of porous balsa wood upon which we floated were too fragile and would break asunder in the heavy coastal swells, or they would at least be waterlogged and sink underneath us far short of the halfway mark to Polynesia, whose nearest islands lay some 4000 miles from Peru. With a foot and a half of free-board at the highest section of the bamboo deck, and with an open bamboo hut with thatched roof as our only shelter, we would be at the constant mercy of the waves and the weather and be lost in the first storm.

Others claimed that ropes were no good in the tropic sun and in the sea water and that the complete absence of nails, pegs, and wire in our raft would allow it to tear to pieces as soon as the constant movements of the logs started to chafe the hemp-rope lashings. And if a balsa-wood raft, against all the warnings of the experts, should prove to be sea-worthy, it would still not be navigable with its clumsy, square sail and primitive steering oar. How, then, could we possibly expect to hit one of the tiny, farflung islands? The distance ahead was twice the journey of Columbus and the clumsy raft not even comparable.

All these sinister but well-meant warnings were haunting my mind the first night after the last smoke of the tugboat had dissolved behind the horizon. When I was relieved from watch and tried to sleep, I realized how everything was in motion, not so much the pitching and rolling, as the restlessly undulating movement of the bamboo matting on which we lay on top of the great logs. Each time the stern was lifted by the seas, I saw dancing black hills of water, silhouetted against the stars as they chased along both sides of our raft, with whitecaps hissing at us as they passed. I listened to the squeaking and gnawing of a hundred ropes and the splashing and hammering of water everywhere. At regular intervals heavy seas thundered on board astern, but I noticed with comfort how the water, after whirling up to the waists of the two steersmen, instantly dwindled by falling between the open logs or over the sides of the raft. The seas fell in a pit before they could reach the unprotected bamboo hut lashed on deck a few feet from the stern. Therefore, we struggled to hold the stern to the weather and never let the seas in from the sides.

Gradually I felt happy and proud of our peculiar craft. But I could not quite get away from the complaining music of all the light and heavy ropes as everything aboard moved slowly up and down and even sideways as far as the ropes would permit.

What would the future bring us? How would the raft behave after a week, a month, or perhaps a year at sea?

I was not a sailor, and only one of my companions was experienced in handling an ordinary boat at sea. I had not been able, word by word, to answer the pessimistic warnings of naval authorities and other experts before we put out to sea. I was, nevertheless, firmly convinced that our raft could float across the ocean and bring us safely to some distant Polynesian shore. The secret of my stubborn confidence was that I felt certain that this same ocean route had been covered before by prehistoric men on the very same type of craft.

Already in 1937, after leaving the University of Oslo, I had made a zoological-ethnological survey on the lonely Marquesas Islands in the Southeast Pacific. What I found led me to suspect that an influence from early Central or South America had somehow preceded the present Polynesian culture in this area. It is well known that a number of striking similarities in the culture of South America and Polynesia have been noted. These include two of the important cultivated plants—the sweet potato and the bottle gourd—and many cultural features. The theory has therefore frequently been advanced—and again as frequently rejected—that there must have been a prehistoric contact between these two areas.

There can be no possibility of any land bridge having existed in human times, for a comparative study of the animal life of Polynesia proves its hoary isolation. The island people, when first discovered by Europeans, possessed good seagoing canoes, whereas the natives of Peru had only clumsy balsa rafts for their coastal navigation. Because of this, it has usually been assumed by the few who believe there was a cultural transfer that the South American cultures were influenced by the island people rather than vice versa. This view has never been fully accepted and is even doubted by competent scholars of the present day. It is too obvious that some of the Peruvian constructions, artifacts, and food plants in question date from an earlier period in America than A.D. 500, which is commonly accepted, through comparative genealogy, as the approximate date when the first Polynesians spread into the East Pacific.

Thus I had found myself inescapably drawn toward the alternative theory to explain the striking parallels between Peru and Polynesia—namely, that an offshoot from the amazing cultures of early Peru drifted, intentionally or otherwise, into the Pacific.

I was instantly met by one killing argument: How could the Peruvians have covered the thousands of miles of intermediate ocean when their only means of navigation in prehistoric times was an open balsa raft?

To me, there was only one satisfactory answer, and that was to build such a balsa raft and see if it could survive this journey.

I selected five dependable men who volunteered to join me on the experimental voyage. One of them, Herman Watzinger, was a technical engineer, and he directed the building of the balsa raft, guided by detailed accounts and sketches left in the earliest records after the conquest of Peru. First we had to get into the heart of the Ecuadorian jungle to find present-day balsa trees that would match the dimensions of the pre-historic rafts. We cut down nine giant trees, and floated on them down a jungle river to the Pacific coast. With the blessings of the President of Peru and his Naval Minister, the prehistoric type of craft was built in the main naval harbor of Callao under our own supervision.

The nine balsa logs were lashed together side by side with many separate pieces of hemp rope. The bow of the raft took an organ-pipe design, with the longest log in the middle measuring 45 feet and project-ing beyond the others both in the front and in the stern. In the stern it sup-ported a big chunk of balsa holding tholepins for the steering oar. Of the two-foot cross section of these logs, more than half was submerged in the water, but nine smaller crossbeams of light balsa covered with bamboo lifted the highest portion of the deck (including the floor of the open hut upon which we slept) eighteen inches above the sea. The little plaited bamboo hut with thatched roof; two hardwood masts side by side, with a square sail; five centerboards two feet wide and six feet deep, inserted at irregular intervals between the logs; and a long wooden steering oar astern completed our replica of the colorful prehistoric craft.

We named our raft "Kon-Tiki" in honor of the mythical sun king who the Incas claim built the enormous stone constructions near Lake Titicaca before he was defeated in war by local tribes. After the defeat, according to legend, he fled with his light-colored people down to the coast and then westward into the Pacific Ocean, never again to return to Peru. Throughout the Polynesian islands, Tiki is remembered as the mythical hero who was first in the line of aboriginal chiefs to settle the islands and to claim direct descent from the sun. The Peruvian prefix "Kon" means Sun.

The six of us went aboard on April 28 and were left at the mercy of the elements in the old Inca fishing grounds outside the port of Callao. Our ages ranged from twenty-five to thirty-two. Herman Watzinger, second in command, was in charge of testing and hydrographic and meteorologic measurements. Erik Hesselberg, an artist, was responsible for plotting our drift. Our radio operators were Knut Haugland and Torstein Raaby, both famous for their sabotage activities during the recent war (instrumental, respectively, in the important sabotage of the German Heavy-Water Plant and the battleship "Tirpitz"). Bengt Danielsson, lonely Swede on our Norwegian expedition, was an ethnologist from the University of Upsala who joined us in South America after an expedition in the jungles of Brazil.

Our voyage would carry us through a vast span of ocean that was very little known, since it was outside all the usual shipping lines. We had therefore been requested to make continuous observations and transfer them via the amateur radio network to the United States Weather Bureau. But unless we should use the radio for calling help, it would not alter the primitive conditions of our experiment in any way.

The first weeks at sea were hard. One man was seasick for several days and confined to the hut; consequently, with the ocean breaking over us, two of us at a time constantly had to battle with the clumsy steering oar, trying to hold our stern against the short, racing seas of the Humboldt Current. We were soon caught by the offshore trade winds and were then only able to sail before the wind. We now realized that we had cut all our bridges and that there was no road back to the coast.

We had been at sea only a couple of days when an airplane flew out to bring us a last farewell. We never saw the plane (our horizons were narrowly fenced in with watery hills on all sides), nor did they see us, but we spoke to them for several hours with our little radio.

After the first weeks we came into calmer seas with long, rolling swells. The great blue ocean was dotted with whitecaps, and trade-wind clouds drifted across the blue sky. We had soft days with swimming and rest, and we traveled along in comfort. Our drift turned from northwest to west as we left the green and cold Humboldt Current and entered the blue and increasingly warm South Equatorial Current. We made as much progress as 72 miles in one day, with a daily average of 42 miles for the entire voyage. The surface drift exceeded the current drift and occasionally blew us out of the main sweep of the central current.

We found little wearing on the ropes and learned the reason why. The balsa was too soft to chafe them. In case of friction, a rope would soon work itself into the waterlogged surface of the balsa logs and thus remain protected. It was more discomforting to observe that splinters cut from the surface of the logs had become waterlogged and sank when thrown overboard. It had been common opinion in Peru that the logs would be completely submerged before we sighted the islands.

Archaeologists no longer doubt that the prehistoric Peruvians used sails: Not only are there good historical descriptions of rafts equipped with sails, but centerboards of late pre-European date have been found. Our testings with centerboards clearly proved that they are useless on a raft if it is merely paddled or carried along by the current.

The first real excitement we ran into after entering the South Equatorial Current was the largest monster of the seas—the rare but famous whale shark. Accompanied by a shoal of pilot fish, this giant among all fishes slowly caught up with us from astern, and the water splashed around its enormous, white-speckled back as though on a small reef. The fish bumped into the steering oar and placed its huge, froglike head, with tiny eyes and a five-foot mouth, right up against the raft. The whale shark has been measured to a length of 45 feet and undoubtedly grows larger. We would never have dared such an estimate, but while the head appeared on one side of the raft, the tail simultaneously appeared on the other.

The whale shark kept us company for several hours, and the excitement on board was great, with everybody prepared with spears, hand harpoons, and motion picture camera. The peaceful visit ended when the excited navigator ran his harpoon with all his strength down between his legs and into the cartilaginous head of the monster. During the terrific commotion the whale shark dived, broke the harpoon, snapped the rope, and disappeared.

Only at one other time were we visited by what we suspected to be whale sharks. It was during a fairly calm night when three immensely large and phosphorescent bodies swam in circles under us. But occasionally we ran into schools of whales. The huge, snorting animals rolled right up beside us without the slightest fear. They could have splintered our raft with a single blow of their mighty tails, but after an exhibition of their swimming ability, they left us behind.

Some 600 miles southwest of the Galápagos we were twice visited by giant sea turtles. One was under constant attack by a dozen furious dolphins which tried to snap at the turtle's neck and fins. After sighting the raft, the turtle made its way right up to our side but swam away as soon as it saw us. Three of our men, equipped with rope, pursued the turtle in a tiny, inflatable rubber float, but our visitor escaped while the bewildered dolphins concentrated all their attention on the bouncing little float.

Weather permitting, we often got into our rubber float, two or three at a time, and took a "vacation" from our sturdy log raft to study our craft from a distance. We could imagine the sight that early Peruvian seafarers must have had when they sailed their flotillas of rafts side by side along the coast—or into the ocean like Inca Tupac Yupanqui, who according to legend discovered some East Pacific islands before the Spanish Conquest. Particularly at night, we experienced an unforgettable sight. Night-black seas, billowing on all sides, and twinkling stars formed our entire world.

The year 1947—A.D. *or* B.C.—what did it mean? We were at least alive. Time had little meaning; we were lost in the endless dark. Ahead of us "Kon-Tiki" rose and then sank between the seas. In moonlight there was an unbelievable atmosphere around the raft. The huge, wet logs fringed with seaweed, the square contour of the sail, the bushy jungle hut with a petrol lamp astern looked like something cut from a fairy tale rather than from reality. Now and then the raft would disappear entirely behind the black sea; then, with water pouring from the logs, it would rise high to be silhouetted against the stars.

Although we spent 101 days and nights drifting on our raft, we never sighted a ship or any floating debris left by mankind. If a ship had crossed our path during an average day at sea, it would have found us slowly dancing up and down over great rolling swells dotted with minor waves that were stirred up by the trade winds, which constantly blow from the New World into the island domain. A tanned and bearded man, devoid of clothing, would have been sighted at the stern of the raft, either desperately struggling with the ropes of a long steering oar or, if the wind were steady, sitting and dozing in the sun. Bengt would be found on his stomach in the doorway of the hut reading one of his 73 sociological books. Herman would be seen busily occupied anywhere, at the top of the mast, underneath the logs, or running around with instruments to measure wind and water. Knut and Torstein were always struggling with the weather-beaten radio sets, repairing damage and sending our reports at night to the amateur stations that could hear our signals.

Erik was always mending sail and splicing rope and sketching fishes and bearded men alike. And each noon he grabbed his sextant and gazed at the sun to determine how far we had moved since the day before. As to myself, I was writing logs, collecting plankton for food experimentation, and fishing or filming.

The day started with a glorious sunrise over the sea, the cook being relieved by the last night watchman to collect the flying fish that had flown on board during the night. These were fried on a small primus stove and devoured at the edge of the raft after a quick morning dip in the sea. Extra flying fish were used as bait for the great colorful dolphin fish that followed the raft day in and day out across the ocean. Dolphins that we did not eat were used as bait for the great sharks that calmly swam around us day and night. When the sea was high, we could see them sideways as though through a perpendicular glass wall raised high above the level of the raft. Then the raft tipped up and let the water and the slowly moving sharks pass beneath us. They never seemed treacherous except when we cleaned fish, and they scented blood. Then they would wake up in a fury. Yet we never quite trusted them, and in one day we pulled aboard nine six- to ten-foot sharks just to dispose of their intimate company.

When we slid the sharks up onto our shallow and slippery logs, the remoras, clinging to the sharks' skin by suction, would jump off and attach themselves to the side of the raft; and the pilot fish, having lost their king and master, would find a substitute in "Kon-Tiki," joining us in a nice formation before the bow or between the centerboards. If a big blue shark passed, they would occasionally follow him away, but more than 40 of them tailed us right across the ocean until our raft was shattered on the reef.

Although we carried our rations lashed to the logs beneath the bamboo deck, it was still of great importance to me to find out whether primitive man, accustomed to hardship as he was, would have been able to renew his supply of food and water on such a long-lasting drift. The answer was affirmative. After the fourth day at sea, there was not a single day throughout the journey when we were not accompanied by numbers of dolphin fish. They kept to the side of the raft or beneath us and could be fished, speared, or hooked whenever we desired. Edible barnacles and seaweeds grew all over the huge logs and could be picked like garden greens. And they often housed tiny, edible pelagic crabs or very small fishes. A dozen or more flying fish, often accompanied by baby squids, came aboard almost every night, sailing through the air in schools right above the surface if pursued by dolphins or sharks. Twice in mid-ocean on dark nights, a long snakelike fish with huge eyes and carnivorous jaws jumped right into our sleeping bags inside the bamboo hut and caused a great commotion. It was probably the *Gempylus*, which was seen this way by man for the first time, only a couple of skeletons having previously been found on South American shores. Soaked shark meat, delicious bonito, and yellow-fin tuna completed our seafood menu and made it clear enough that early, hardy raftsmen were not menaced by hunger.

We carried 200 coconuts and samples of the Peruvian sweet potato and gourd, which were important food plants that the aborigines of Peru shared with those of Polynesia. Those not eaten en route were successfully planted upon our arrival on the islands, to prove that they could be carried on a raft without loss of germinating power. These prehistoric food plants could never have drifted across the ocean without the aid and care of human hands, and the aboriginal name for sweet potato was *Kumara*—both in Peru and on the Polynesian islands.

The early raftsmen along the dry South American coast carried their water supply in gourds or pottery containers and in huge canes of bamboo with the joints pierced out. Left in the shade underneath the bamboo deck, where they were constantly washed by the seas, we found that our plain Peruvian spring water was preserved for more than two months before the first samples began to rot. At that time we had already entered a part of the ocean where drizzles were frequent and rains occasional, and we were able to collect sufficient rain water for our daily needs. We consumed a ton of water on the journey, along with more than ample rations, and the buoyancy of the balsa logs would have permitted us to double our water supply in easily stored bamboo canes under the deck. With the warm climate creating a demand for salt, we could mix up to 40 per cent of sea water with our drinking water without evil effects. Like our early predecessors and many sailors shipwrecked during the war, we found several simple methods of abstracting the thirst-quenching juice from raw fish, a supply that never ran short.

In this way, with the days full of testings and practical experiments, we found ourselves carried across the ocean bit by bit. By the forty-fifth day we had drifted from the seventy-eighth meridian to the one hundred-eighth and were exactly halfway to the first islands. During those days we were more than 2000 miles away from the nearest shore in any direction. When the ocean was smoothly rolling, we could leave our raft in the little float and row away into the blue space between eternal sea and sky. As we watched our grotesque craft growing smaller and smaller in the distance, an oppressive sense of loneliness came over us. It was as though we were suspended in space, like disembodied spirits. When we rowed back to our distant raft, we felt a strange feeling of relief and were happy to crawl on board our precious, weather-beaten logs and find shade from the glaring sun inside the bamboo hut. The now familiar scent of bamboo and thatched roof made us feel that we were back in our earthly home again, inside a jungle dwelling that was far away from the limitless sea.

We enjoyed our evening meals as the glorious sun sank into the sea before our bow, while sky and water became a dream of colors. Small, striped pilot fish would rush to the surface to snap at our crumbs, and they were occasionally followed by a lazy shark, like kittens by a bulldog.

As darkness came we would light our petrol lamp, and Erik would fetch his guitar. Then merry song and music from the raft spread with the dim light over the nearest waves of a trackless, endless ocean. We would soon roll up on the bamboo matting inside the hut, leaving the watchman alone with the stars and the steering oar.

We hit two storms when we approached the end of the journey. The first lasted one day and the second five. With sail down and ropes shrieking, "Kon-Tiki" rode the breaking ocean like a duck. A raft in high seas with wet and slippery logs and no railing requires careful stepping. The second storm had just begun when Herman went overboard. When visible again, he was seen struggling behind the stern. He struck for the blade of the steering oar, but a strong wind pushed us ahead, and he missed. We could not turn our raft around to go back a single inch. There was no possibility of even stopping our stubborn craft in its reckless trek to the west. The airy float would blow like a feather ahead of the raft if put to sea in such a wind. We threw out a life belt, once, twice, but it blew right back on board. We became desperate as Herman, our best swimmer, was left farther and farther behind. With a line in one hand Knut leaped into the sea, and slowly the two friends worked their way toward each other. Thirty yards behind the raft they joined hands, and the four of us on board pulled them in.

We had a green parrot as ship's pet. It was a perfect sailor and a joyous companion, until a big sea stole it on the sixtieth day.

At the end of the third month, we were constantly visited by Polynesian frigate birds and boobies in increasing numbers. Then we sighted a rising cumulo-nimbus cloud, revealing the existence of some hidden, sun-baked isle beneath the western horizon. We steered for the cloud as best we could, and as the golden sun rose from the sea on the ninety-third day, the blue haze of land was outlined against a reddish sky. We were passing the tiny atoll of Pukapuka, but wind and current would not permit us to turn around. We had covered 4000 miles of ocean heading west, and yet we could not force ourselves 4 miles to the east to reach the island. More than ever was this a plain and unmistakable lesson, stressing the fact that in this ocean a drifting craft and a natural migration would inevitably be pushed to the west. And it was with strange feelings that we sat quietly down on our raft and saw the little, solid speck of land— the first and only for twelve weeks—slide away on our port stern. For a moment the wind carried a mild whiff of verdant tropical foliage and smoky native household odors, and we filled our salty lungs before the fata morgana—the mirage of our hopes—sank into the sea.

On the ninety-seventh day another island grew up out of the ocean, straight ahead of us in line with the bow. As we approached, we saw from the top of the mast that a roaring reef was twisted like a submerged snake all around the island, blocking the approach to the palm-clad beaches behind. All day long we struggled in the current alongside the island to keep clear of the boiling reef and yet be close enough to attempt a landfall wherever an opening might be seen.

Late in the afternoon we sighted the first natives on a beach, and we hoisted all our flags in joy. A great commotion was seen on the beach, and shortly after, the first Polynesians in small outrigger canoes slid through a passage in the reef and swarmed aboard the "Kon-Tiki." A strong wind blew up, and our ocean raft struggled away from land as the sun went down in the sea. There was a desperate fight against the elements, in which we were assisted by all the friendly natives who were able to get out and join us in the open sea. As the dark night engulfed the island and the sea, a great campfire was lit on shore to show us the direction of the entrance through the reef. But the wind increased its grip and won another battle. When the glare of the great fire dwindled like a spark in the distance and the roar of the reef was no longer heard, our excited native friends jumped into their canoes to return to their homes on Angatau for fear of drifting with some crazy strangers into the open sea. And we drifted farther into the heart of the Tuamotu, or Dangerous Archipelago.

One night an unusual motion of the raft awakened me, and I suspected land ahead. Next morning, our one hundred-first at sea, we were alarmed by the watchman on the top of the mast, who had sighted an enormous reef that spanned the entire horizon ahead of us. It was the treacherous 20-mile reef of Raroia Atoll. With white spray shooting high into the air, the surf battered the endless reef in fury.

As we rode directly into this boiling inferno, we had three hours to prepare for all eventualities. We lowered the sail and threw out an improvised anchor on a long rope that kept sliding along the bottom. We carried valuable cargo into the hut and lashed it fast in watertight bags. We cut off all ropes holding the centerboards in position and pulled them up to get a shallow draft. With shoes on for the first time in 100 days, we concentrated on the last order: Hang on—hang onto the raft whatever happens!

The first walls of thundering water broke down upon us from above as soon as our logs ran against the solid coral reef. Tons of crashing water tore up the deck, flattened the hut, broke the hardwood mast like a match, and splintered the steering oar and stern crossbeam, while we were thrown in and dragged out, thrown in and dragged out, by the furious ocean. During these minutes, when we cramped every existing muscle to withhold the deadly grasp of the passing seas, we made up for all the leisure of the average ocean day. I felt the last of my strength giving away when a wave larger than the others lifted "Kon-Tiki" free of the water and tossed us high up on the reef. Other waves pushed us closer to shore, until we could jump off the raft and wade the shallow coral reef to a tiny, uninhabited coconut island. Never did any tiny piece of land embody paradise so perfectly to me as this verdant, palm-clad isle with its white and shiny beach facing a crystal-clear lagoon, calm as green glass.

A week later we were found by natives who had detected from another island six miles across the lagoon the drift wreckage and the light from our campfire. And about the same time "Kon-Tiki" was carried by high seas right across the solid reef and left becalmed inside the lagoon. The nine main logs that had carried us 4,300 miles across the ocean in 101 days were still intact, and after an unforgettable two-week Polynesian welcome party on lonely Raroia, our battered raft was towed to Tahiti by the French Government schooner "Tamara," which was sent expressly to pick us up.

We shall never forget the welcome on these Polynesian islands.

From Tahiti the "Kon-Tiki" was carried as deck cargo back to the Norwegian Museum of Navigation in Oslo.

To the Summit of Everest

by SIR EDMUND HILLARY

On May 29, 1953, Edmund Hillary, a New Zealander beekeeper, and Tenzing Norkey, a veteran Sherpa guide, together made the first complete ascent of Mt. Everest, earth's highest mountain. Both won immediate world fame, Hillary and the expedition chief, Colonel John Hunt, being knighted for the honor they had brought to Great Britain on the eve of the coronation of Elizabeth II. The final assault on the mountain was launched from an advance base at 21,000 feet. Thus fell the highest of all mountain pinnacles before man's desire to climb ever higher and to conquer—essentially for no other reason than that he liked to do so.

THE ASSAULT PARTY COMPOSED OF TENZING AND MYSELF arrived at Camp Seven, 24,000 feet high on the Lhotse face, after a three and one quarter hour trip up from Camp Four advanced base, 2,800 feet below. We found our support party, George Lowe and Alfred Gregory, already in residence together with the three Sherpa porters, Ang Nima, Ang Tembar and Pamber, who we were hoping would carry a camp for us high on the southeast ridge. We also had five other Sherpas who were to carry loads as far as South Col and then return to a lower camp.

After a restful night's sleep—the four of us used sleeping oxygen—we set off next morning in good heart for South Col. At 9:30, when we were nearly at the top of Lhotse glacier, we caught our first glimpse of tiny figures on the southeast ridge. It was Evans and Bourdillon, making their first assault on the mountain, and Col. Hunt, the leader of the expedition, and Da Namgyal, a Sherpa porter, carrying food and oxygen up the ridge for our future use. We were able to watch their progress almost continuously as we crossed the great traverse under Lhotse and moved up onto South Col.

At one P.M. we were greatly excited to see Evans and Bourdillon disappear over the south summit before they were blotted out by drifting clouds. By now Hunt and Da Namgyal were slowly descending to South Col camp and as they seemed in some distress we went up to meet and assist them. They were in an exhausted condition. Hunt, who had never spared himself throughout the trip, had made a magnificent effort and carried the loads some 150 feet above the old Swiss ridge camp to a height of approximately 27,350 feet. The two had then descended without oxygen in order to conserve supplies for the assault. At 3 P.M. Evans and Bourdillon appeared out of the mist on the southeast ridge and moved very slowly down the steep couloir leading to South Col. They were obviously very tired after their tremendous effort and we went up to meet them with hot drinks and escorted them back to camp. They confirmed they had successfully reached the south summit—28,720 feet—and so had been far higher than men had ever been before. They reported that the ridge along to the top looked like a very formidable proposition.

South Col can rarely be a cheerful spot but the night of May 26 was a particularly difficult one for the whole party. An extremely strong wind was blowing and it was very cold indeed. Few of us had much sleep. In the morning the wind was still blowing fiercely, and it was obvious that it would be impossible to venture on to the southeast ridge. Even movement between our tents, dressed in all our warm clothing, was a rigorous experience. During the morning the wind eased a little, although it was still very strong. Hunt, Evans and Bourdillon were all very weak after their previous day's efforts but prepared to descend to Camp Seven. Ang Tembar had become sick and was obviously incapable of carrying up any further so we decided to send him down too. Lowe and I assisted a very weary foursome to climb the slopes above the camp and then watched them start off on their slow and exhausting trip down to Camp Seven.

All day the wind blew furiously and it was in somewhat desperate spirit that we organized the loads for the establishment of the ridge camp on the following day. The violent wind gave us another uncomfortable night, but just before morning it eased considerably and a start became possible. However, another blow had fallen. Pamber had been violently ill all night and did not feel capable of going on. Only one Sherpa porter, Ang Nima, was left to carry for us out of our original band of three.

Our only alternatives were to carry the camp ourselves or abandon the attempt and this last was unthinkable. We repacked the loads, eliminating anything not vitally necessary and having no choice but to cut down our supplies of oxygen. At 8:45 Lowe, Gregory and Ang Nima departed, all carrying over 40 pounds each and breathing oxygen at four liters per minute.

Tenzing and I loaded all our personal clothing, sleeping bags and air mattresses and some food onto our oxygen frames and left at 10 A.M., carrying 50 pounds apiece. We followed slowly up the long slopes to the foot of the Great Couloir and then climbed the veritable staircase hewn by Lowe in the firm, steep snow. We reached the ridge at midday and joined the other party who were resting near the tattered ruins of the Swiss tent of the previous spring. It was a wonderful spot with remarkable views in every direction and we indulged in an orgy of photography. Then we heaved on our loads again and moved 150 feet up the ridge to the dump made by Hunt two days previously.

We were now at 27,350 feet but considered this was still far too low for an effective summit camp. We were all going extremely well so decided to add this extra gear to our already large loads. Gregory took some more oxygen and Lowe some food and fuel and I tied on the tent. Apart from Ang Nima, who was carrying just over 40 pounds, we all had loads of from 50 to 60 pounds. We continued on up the ridge at a somewhat reduced rate. The ridge here was quite steep, but the upward sloping strata of the rocks gave us good footholds. A little step-cutting was necessary in places, but generally the going was easy although loose snow over the steep rocks demanded care. By 2 P.M. we were starting to tire under our heavy burdens and commenced looking for a campsite. The ridge appeared to have no relief at all and continued upwards in one unbroken sweep. We plugged slowly on looking for a ledge without success and were getting a little desperate until Tenzing, remembering the ground from the previous year, suggested a traverse over steep slopes to the left which finally landed us on a relatively flat spot beneath a rocky bluff.

It was 2:30 and we decided to camp here. We estimated the height as 27,900. Our three "porters," Lowe, Gregory and Ang Nima, dropped their loads on the site with relief. They were tired but well satisfied with the height gained and to them must go a great deal of the credit for the successful climb of the following day. Wasting no time, they hurried off back to South Col. Tenzing and I removed our oxygen in order to conserve our supplies and set to work with our ice axes to clear a tiny platform. We scratched off all the snow to reveal a rocky slope at an angle of about 30°. The rocks were well frozen in, but by the end of a couple of hours of solid work we had managed to pry loose enough stones to level out two strips of ground, each a yard wide and six feet long but almost a foot different in levels. This was the best platform we could make. We pitched our tent on this double level and tied it down as best we could.

Then, while Tenzing started to heat up some soup, I made a tally of our limited oxygen supplies. They were much less than we had hoped. For the assault we had only one and two-thirds bottles each. It was obvious that if we were to have sufficient endurance we would be unable to use the four liters per minute we had originally planned, but I estimated that if we reduced our supply to three liters per minute we might still have a chance. I prepared the sets and made the necessary adjustments. One thing in our favor was that Evans and Bourdillon had left two bottles, each one-third full of oxygen, some hundreds of feet above our camp. We were relying on this oxygen to get us back to South Col.

In the evening the wind dropped almost completely except for an exceptionally strong gust every 10 minutes. We drank vast quantities of liquid and ate a satisfying meal out of our store of delicacies— sardines on biscuits, tinned apricots, dates, biscuits and jam and honey. Despite our great height our breathing was almost normal until a sudden exertion would cause us to pant a little.

Tenzing laid his air mattress on the lower shelf, half overhanging the steep slope below, and calmly settled down to sleep. I made myself as comfortable as possible, half sitting and half reclining on the upper shelf with my feet braced on the lower shelf. This position, while not particularly comfortable, had one decided advantage. When I received warning sounds of a gust of wind approaching, I could brace my feet and shoulders and assist our meager anchors to hold the tent steady while it temporarily shook and flapped in a most alarming manner.

We had sufficient spare oxygen for only four hours' sleeping on one liter per minute. We used this in two periods of two hours, from 9 to 11 P.M. and from one to 3 A.M. While wearing oxygen we dozed and were reasonably comfortable, but as soon as the supply ran out we started feeling cold and miserable. During the night the thermometer read 16° below zero, but fortunately the wind had dropped almost entirely.

At 4 A.M. the weather looked perfect and when I opened the tent door the view was indescribably beautiful, with all the icy peaks far below us glowing clearly in the early morning light as they towered above their still dark and sleeping valleys. Tenzing gleefully pointed out the monastery of Thyangboche, faintly visible on its dominant spur 16,000 feet below us. We started up our cooker and in a determined effort to prevent the weaknesses arising from dehydration, we drank large quantities of lemon juice and sugar and followed this with our last tin of sardines on biscuits.

I dragged our oxygen sets into the tent, cleaned the ice off them and then completely rechecked and tested them. Over our eiderdown clothing we donned our windproofs and on our hands we pulled three pairs of gloves—silk, woolen and windproof. Finally at 6:30 A.M. we crawled out of our tent into the snow, hoisted our 30 pounds of oxygen gear onto our backs, connected up our masks and turned on the valves to bring life-giving oxygen into our lungs. A few good deep breaths and we were ready to go.

Tenzing moved off and kicked a deep line of steps away from the rock bluff which protected our tent into the steep powder snow slope to the left of the main ridge. The ridge was now all bathed in sunlight and we could see our first objective—the south summit—far above us. Tenzing, moving purposefully, kicked steps in a long traverse back towards the ridge. We reached its crest just where it forms a great distinctive snow bump at about 28,000 feet.

From here the ridge narrowed to a knife edge and I took over the lead. We were moving slowly but steadily with plenty in reserve. Soft, unstable snow on the crest of the ridge made a route on it both uncomfortable and dangerous so I moved a little down on the steep left side where the wind had produced a thin crust. This sometimes held our weight but more often than not gave way with a sudden knock which had disturbing effects on our balance and morale. After several hundred feet of this the ridge suddenly eased and in a tiny hollow we came upon the two oxygen bottles left on the earlier attempt by Evans and Bourdillon. I scraped the ice off the gauges and was greatly relieved to find that they still contained several liters of oxygen—sufficient to get us down to the South Col if used sparingly.

I continued on up the ridge which soon steepened and broadened out into the very formidable snow face which formed the last 400 feet of the south summit. Snow conditions on this face were, we felt, distinctly dangerous, but as no alternative route seemed available we persisted in our strenuous and uncomfortable efforts to beat a trail up it. It was with some relief that we finally reached some firmer snow higher up and then chipped steps up the last steep slopes and cramponed onto the south summit. It was now 9 A.M.

We looked with some interest at the virgin ridge ahead of us. Both Bourdillon and Evans had been depressingly definite about its problems and difficulties and we realized it could form an almost insuperable barrier. At first glance it was certainly impressive and even rather frightening. On the right great contorted cornices, overhanging masses of ice and snow, thrust out like twisted fingers over the 12,000-foot drop of the Kangshung face. Any move into these cornices could only bring disaster. From the cornices the ridge dropped steeply to the left until the snow merged with the great rock face sweeping up from the Western Cwm. Only one encouraging feature was apparent. The steep snow slope between the cornices and the rock precipices seemed to be composed of firm hard snow. If we could cut a trail of steps along this slope we could make some progress at least.

Our first partly full bottles of oxygen were now exhausted so we disconnected them and threw them aside. We turned on our remaining full bottles—800 liters of oxygen which should give us four and a half hours' going at three liters per minute. Our apparatus was now much lighter, weighing only about 19 pounds, and as I cut steps down off the summit I felt a distinct sense of freedom and well being. As my ice ax bit into the first steep slope my highest hopes were realized. The snow was crystalline and firm. Two or three rhythmical blows of the ice ax produced a step large enough even for our oversized high altitude boots. And best of all, a firm thrust of the ice ax would sink it half-way up the shaft, giving a solid and comfortable belay.

We moved one at a time. I would cut a 40-foot line of steps, with Tenzing belaying me as I worked. Then in turn I would sink my ax, put a few loops of the rope around it and Tenzing—protected against a breaking step—would move up to me. Several of the cornices were particularly large and in order to escape them I cut a line of steps down to where the snow met the rocks. Half scrambling on the rocks and cutting handholds in the snow, we managed to shuffle past these difficult positions.

On one of these occasions I noted that Tenzing seemed to be breathing with difficulty and stopped to examine his oxygen set. I found that his exhaust tube, some two inches in diameter, was blocked with ice. I was able to clear it out and give him much needed relief. On checking my own set I found the same thing was occurring and from then on kept a much closer eye on this problem.

The weather for Everest was practically perfect. This did not mean that it would be an ideal day for the beach, but equipped as we were in all our eiderdown clothing and windproofs we suffered no discomfort from cold or wind. However, on the one occasion on which I removed my snow glasses in order to examine more closely a tricky section, I was very soon blinded by fine snow drawn by the cool wind. I hastily replaced my glasses.

After an hour's steady step-cutting we reached the foot of the most formidable-looking problem on the ridge, a 40-foot vertical rock step. We had seen this step through the binoculars from far away Thyangboche and realized that at this altitude it might well spell the difference between success and failure. The rock itself, smooth and almost holdless, might have been an interesting Sunday afternoon problem to a group of expert rock climbers in England's Lake District, but here it was a barrier far beyond our feeble strength to overcome.

But once again a possibility of tackling it remained. On its east side was another great cornice and running up the full 40 feet of the step was a narrow crack between the cornice and the rock. Leaving Tenzing to belay me as best he could, I moved into this crack. Then, kicking backwards with my crampons, I gained a purchase on the frozen snow behind me and levered myself off the ground. Taking advantage of every little rock hold and of all the friction of knee, shoulders and arms I could muster, I literally cramponed backwards up the crack, with the fervent prayer that the cornice would remain attached to the rock. My progress was slow but steady and as Tenzing paid out the rope I inched my way upwards until I could finally reach over the top of the rock and drag myself out of the crack onto a wide ledge. For a few moments I lay still, regaining my breath. For the first time I really felt the fierce determination that nothing now could stop our reaching the top.

When I had recovered I took a firm stance and commenced towing in the rope as Tenzing in his turn wiggled his way up the crack. He collapsed exhausted at the top like a giant fish that had just been hauled from the sea after a terrible struggle. I checked our remaining oxygen and roughly calculated our flow rates. Everything was going well. Tenzing had been moving rather slowly but was still climbing safely and well. His only comment when I enquired about his condition was to smile and wave along the ridge. The ridge continued as before—giant cornices on the right, steep slopes on the left. I went on cutting steps. We had no idea where the top was. The ridge curved away to the right and as

I cut around the back of one hump another higher one would swing into view. Time was passing and the ridge seemed never ending.

To save time I tried cramponing without cutting steps but quickly realized our margin of safety on these steep slopes at this altitude was too small so went on step cutting. I was starting to tire a little now. Tenzing was moving very slowly. As I chipped steps around still another corner, I wondered rather dully just how long we could keep it up. Then I realized that the ridge ahead, instead of still rising, now dropped sharply away and far below I could see the East Rongbuk Glacier! I looked upwards to see a narrow snow ridge running up to a sharp point. A few more whacks of the ice ax in the firm snow and we stood on the summit.

My initial feelings were of relief—relief that there were no more steps to cut, no more ridges to traverse and no more humps to tantalize us with hopes of success. Despite the knitted helmet, goggles and oxygen mask, all crusted with icicles, that concealed Tenzing's face, there was no disguising his infectious grin of pure delight as he looked all around him. We shook hands and then, casting those Anglo-Saxon formalities aside, Tenzing threw his arms around my shoulders and we thumped each other on the back until forced to stop from lack of breath.

I glanced at my watch: 11:30 A.M. The ridge had taken us two and a half hours, but it seemed more like five. I checked our oxygen again —yes, the slow rate seemed to be pretty constant. But if we intended to remain on three liters, we were going to have to waste no time on the return as we had only two hours' more endurance. In this time we had to return along the ridge and descend the dangerous slopes of the south summit to the two partly filled bottles waiting for us far below.

I turned off my oxygen and removed my set. I then produced my camera and set to work to photograph everything in sight. First of all some photographs of Tenzing waving a string of flags—Nepalese, British, United Nations and Indian. Then I endeavored to take photographs down all the ridges of Everest. I had little hope of the results being particularly successful, as I had a lot of difficulty in holding the camera steady in my clumsy gloves, but I felt they would at least serve as a record. After some 10 minutes of this I realized I was becoming rather clumsy-fingered and slow-moving. I quickly replaced my oxygen set and ex-perienced once more the stimulating effect of even a few liters of oxygen.

While I had been taking these photographs Tenzing had made a little hole in the snow and in it placed various articles of food, a bar of chocolate, a packet of biscuits and a handful of hard candy—small offerings indeed but at least a gift of some sort as a token offering to the gods that devout Buddhists believe have their home on this lofty summit.

After 15 minutes we turned to go. The whole world around us lay spread out like a giant relief map and I could take in with a glance country that we had spent months mapping and exploring on previous trips. Reaction was setting in and we must get off our mountain. Already, as the spur of ambition died under the glow of success, we felt weakness in our limbs and shortage of breath. I moved down off the summit. Wasting no time, we cramponed along our tracks, spurred by the urgency of diminishing oxygen.

Bump followed bump in rapid succession. In what seemed almost miraculous time we reached the top of the rock step. Now, with the almost casual indifference of familiarity, we kicked and jammed our way down it again. We were tired out but not too tired to be careful. We scrambled cautiously over the rock traverses, moved one at a time over shaky snow sections and finally cramponed on our steps and back onto the south summit. Only one hour back from the top! We were holding our own against time. A swig of sweetened lemonade refreshed us and we turned down again.

As I led the way down the great snow slope, I hacked each step with as much care as if our lives depended on it—as well they might. Every step down was a step nearer safety and, when we finally moved off the slope onto the ridge below, we both looked at each other and almost visibly shrugged off the sense of fear that had been with us all day.

We were now very tired but moved automatically down to the two oxygen cylinders cached on the ridge. We were only a short distance from camp, so we loaded the cylinders on to our frames, continued down our tracks and reached our tent on its crazy platform at 2 P.M. Already the moderate winds of the afternoon had wrenched the tent loose from some of its fastenings and it presented a forlorn sight.

We were very thirsty and still had to get down to the South Col. Tenzing lit the kerosene stove and started to make a lemonade drink heavily sweetened with sugar. I changed our oxygen sets onto the last partly filled bottles and cut down our flow rates to two liters a minute. Far below on the South Col we could see minute figures and knew that Lowe would be eagerly waiting for our descent.

We slowly packed up our sleeping bags and air mattresses and strapped them onto our frames. Then, with a last look at the camp that had served us so well, we turned downward with dragging feet and set ourselves to the task of safely descending the ridge. With our numbed faculties the time seemed to pass as in a dream, but finally we reached the site of the Swiss ridge camp and branched off down into the Great Couloir.

There an unpleasant surprise greeted us. The strong wind which was now blowing had completed wiped out all steps and only a steep, hard surface greeted our weary eyes. There was nothing to do but start cutting again. For 200 feet I chipped steps laboriously downward. Gusts of driving wind almost tore us from our steps. Tenzing took over the lead and cut down another 100 feet, then moved on to softer snow and kicked a track right down the couloir.

Two figures came toward us and met us a couple of hundred feet above camp. They were Lowe and Noyce, laden with hot soup and emergency oxygen. We were too tired to make any response to Lowe's enthusiastic acceptance of our news. We stumped down to the col and slowly ground our way up the short rise to the camp. Off came our oxygen and into the tent we crawled and with a sigh of pure delight collapsed into our sleeping bags while the tents flapped and shook under the perpetual South Col gale.

Yes, the South Col might be the worst spot in the world, but to us at the moment—with the Primus stove humming and our friends Lowe and Noyce fussing about us—it was home.

Man Against Bronco

by EMERSON HOUGH

Emerson Hough (1857-1923) was the author of several best-selling novels, among them The Covered Wagon, *which was made into a motion picture in the twenties. He was on intimate terms with many cowboys and with the various aspects of their life. A friend of Pat Garrett, the sheriff who killed Billy the Kid, he accompanied Garrett on a long horseback trip in New Mexico while gathering material for his* The Story of the Outlaw—*this not long before Garrett was shot and killed on a lonely road by a man he was riding in a wagon with. Hough's account of bronco busting is the best sustained and most exciting I have ever seen. Here, in very intimate terms, one watches man grappling with and finally subduing a seemingly untamable spirit.*

THE DIFFERENTIATION OF THE CATTLE TRADE HAS MADE horse breaking a trade of itself in much of the cow country, but at first the cowboys of each ranch usually did the breaking for the ranch, with such help as might come through the services of some neighboring rider of exceptional gifts at horse breaking. Such specially gifted men gradually became a class of themselves, known all over the range as "bronco busters," and they took to the hazardous trade of horse breaking as a steady business, usually working under contract, and "busting" horses at so much a head for all the big ranches having unbroken stock on hand. The name given this process of breaking is suggestive and not inaccurate. A horse was considered "busted" after he had been ridden two or three times under the hand of iron and the heel of steel. Out of such an ordeal the horse came with a temper perhaps ruined for life, and with a permanent grudge against all things human. It would really never be cured entirely of the habit of bucking, and was never absolutely safe unless ridden to the point of fatigue. Some of the best cow horses on a ranch will always buck when first mounted after a long rest, and some need a little preliminary training every time they are mounted. These animals probably had their first touch of the saddle at the gentle hands of the "buster," who got four or five dollars a head for proving ocularly that such and such a horse could actually be mounted and ridden without death to either horse or man. Sometimes the event was not thus for either the horse or the man. Horses were at times killed in the process of "busting," and very often the "buster" himself was the victim. The most successful of these men, who came of the hardiest and most daring of the range riders, rarely lasted more than a few years in the business. Sometimes their lungs were torn loose by the violent jolting of the stiff-legged bounds of the wild beasts they rode, and many busters would spit blood after a few months at their calling. Injury in the saddle at some stage of this wild riding was almost a certainty, and falls were a matter of course. A broken leg or arm was a light calamity, accepted philosophically with the feeling that it might have been much worse. The life of the soldier engaged in actual war is far safer than that of the bronco buster. There is no wilder or more exciting scene than the first riding of one of these wild range horses. It is a battle of man against brute, and of a quality to make the heart of a novice stand still in terror. Yet upon the range this is one of the necessities, and those who engage in this business go about it methodically and steadily, probably with no thought that they are doing anything extraordinary, because they have never done anything else.

Between the more modern methods, such as one may see practiced on Northern ranches today, and the methods of the earlier Southern ranches there is something of a distinction. On a Northern horse ranch, for instance, which sells sixty or eighty horses a year, the breaking is commonly done by a "contract buster." Perhaps thirty or forty horses are gathered in the big corral and are turned one by one into the small round corral, which has a snubbing post in the middle. Two or three men rope the horse by the forefeet and throw him, using the snubbing post if necessary. He is then quickly tied up and the "hackamore," which is provided with a blind already fastened to it, is put on his head. The blind is now slipped down over the horse's eyes, and he is allowed to stand up. The reins of the hackamore are led back, and the saddle is put on and cinched up. Sometimes the stirrups are tied together, but usually not, the buster perhaps being too proud to take advantage of this aid to easy riding, though it would perhaps save him some fatigue or danger. The blind is now lifted a little and the horse is led out, the blind then being slipped down again. Now the buster comes to the horse and mounts him, the beast usually standing quietly and cowering in its supposed helpless blindness. Two other men, sometimes known in these days of modern ranching as "hazers," now mount and ride up with their quirts in hand ready to drive on the horse that is to be broken. When all is ready the buster leans forward from his seat, lifts the blind, and sets whip and spur to the horse, the assistants meantime yelling, waving their hats, and pounding with their quirts. The horse so beset is apt to be "bad" for a time, but is likely to start away from sheer fright, and as soon as he leads off the assistants leave him, and the buster "rides it out," perhaps making a run of two or three miles, and then gradually getting back to the corral again. Here the horse is again blinded, and his saddle and hackamore are taken off. He is then turned into a separate corral, as a horse that has been "ridden." Another horse is then prepared for the buster. The latter may ride five or six horses in a day, all of these operations of course being repeated until each animal has been reduced to what seems near enough to the Western idea of docility.

In the early days of ranching in the Southwest the main ideas of horse breaking were much the same as above described, but the methods employed varied in some particulars. As those were the earliest days, they are perhaps the most interesting, and offer the best field for the examination of this essential phase of ranch work.

Some of the early Southern busters were Negroes, and very good breakers they made. Many were Mexicans, whose cruelty and roughness were practically certain to ruin the disposition of any horse, and who soon came into disrepute with American ranchers. Others were rough riders from the cowboy ranks, who had been riders from their youth and feared no horse that ever stood on earth. Many of them were graduated from the horse ranches where cow horses were bred and broken as a business. It is perhaps in such a school that a typical foreman, Jim, learned his splendid horsemanship, away back in the early days.

A horse ranch of average size would employ from six to ten men for the summer breaking season, and these would be busy from the middle of May till the end of summer. It took about a week to break a horse, and each breaker would usually handle two horses at the same time, riding them a part of the day each. After the first work was done, others might continue the handling of the horse through several weeks more, but about six days would usually fit a horse for the saddle so that a good rider could ride it; and none but good riders had any business about the cow country. For this sort of work the cowboys were usually paid about twenty to forty dollars a month, according to their value. Some Mexicans were employed, but they were not so much valued. Of course, there were always some of the young men about the ranch who were breaking their own saddle horses for themselves. Such horses were not run with the band, but usually kept up about the house. It was a notorious fact that one of the "pet horses" was sure to be about the worst case of the lot when it came to riding it, especially if it had been allowed to go late in life before it was ridden.

Any visitor to a cow ranch has seen the men at work among the horse herd, and has noticed how quickly a horse will stop as soon as it feels the rope touch it, even though it may perhaps not be caught by the noose at all. This submission to the magic of the rope is a cardinal principle in that horse's ideas of common sense. He bears deep within his mind the early lessons of his youth. The wildest bronco is very apt to cool down when he feels the iron grip of the rope. The first lesson of the rope he receives, as above mentioned, when a brawny cow puncher circles both his forelegs with a noose of this dreaded rope, throws him flat with a turn of the wrist, and hales him on his side through the dust away from his mother's side to the spot where the fiery iron is waiting. From that instant the colt hates man and all his doing. He hates the rope. He resolves that if ever he gets a fair chance he will break that rope into a thousand fragments. He is a couple of seasons older and bigger and stronger when he is at length driven into the round pen some fresh spring morning, so strong, he is sure, that he can rend any rope. He breaks into a run about the wall of the corral, but Jim, the lean and sinewy rider on the older cow horse, follows, about his head curling always that unpleasant snakelike thing the pony remembers and has hated from his babyhood. The rope comes at him with a wide curling sweep, and, in spite of his tossing and plunging, settles fair about his neck or forefeet. It tightens with a jerk. The old horse which Jim is riding stops in his stride and falls back, bracing his forelegs firmly. The young wild horse which was determined to break the rope finds himself upside down, the rope perhaps choking the life out of him. He has had lesson No. 2.

Jim, the cowpuncher and horse breaker, calmly waits till the young horse's eyes nearly start out of his head, and then signs to his assistants, who loosen the rope just in time to save the pony's life. The latter is furious at the indignity he has suffered, and as soon as he can breathe begins to plunge and kick and rear, throwing himself quite over in his struggles. Yet quietly he is pulled up, pulled down, pulled along, until he is ready for another lesson.

Upon the head of the horse now ready for breaking there is slipped a curious bitless bridle, or halter, of strands of rope, very strong and capable of being so arranged that too much pulling on it will close it fast upon a pony's nose and make the act of breathing difficult. This halter is called a "hackamore," and of course it was the invention of the Spaniard. The pony when put on the hackamore is staked out on the open ground on a long "stake rope." He is left alone for a while here, and soon learns his next lesson. Resolved again in his heart to break this hated rope, he runs full speed to the end of it, and there comes to a halt with his heels high in the air and his neck perhaps doubled under him. If his neck happens to be broken it makes no difference, for there are other ponies just as good, plenty of them. If his neck is not broken, he gets up and does it over again, and perhaps again. Then he shakes his head and thinks it over. His next act will be to get himself tied up thoroughly in the coils of the rope, tripping himself, throwing himself, and burning his heels terribly on the harsh fiber of the rope. In this he is allowed to follow his own sweet will, because he is not intended to be used on Broadway, and a little skin missing here or there constitutes no drawback for the purposes of the range. The pony cuts and bruises himself and falls down, and no doubt reviles and swears in Spanish, but it does no good, except that ever there grows in his mind a vast and vaster respect for this relentless thing, this rope which has him fast.

And then Jim comes along after a while, with a rope or blanket or something of the sort, and begins to whip it over the back of the pony, driving the latter half crazy with fright, for never has he had such a thing near him before. The pony cringes and plunges, but Jim lays a hard hand upon the hackamore and draws him into submission and into a personal contact resented with all the soul of the fiery little creature thus robbed of his loved liberty. A second man comes up on the other side of the pony and lays hands upon him. In a twinkling a red kerchief is slipped across his face and tied fast to the side strands of the hackamore. Smitten with blindness, the pony cowers and is motionless and dumb. The end of the world for him has come, for never in all his wild life did he ere this fail to see the light of day or the half light of night, which served him full as well. Surely, thinks the pony, all now is over, and the end has come. He shrinks and does not resist the hand laid upon his muzzle, the other hand laid upon his ear, the twist given to his head, the whipping of the blanket over and on his back, touching him where never any object has touched before. But with a jerk he may perhaps throw off the blinder of the handkerchief and begin instinctively the wild stiff-legged bucking of his breed. "He's shore bronc," says Jim. "You'll have to hold his head closter." Then the hackamore tightens again, and the hands lay hold of the ears and the trembling muzzle again, and—and then, before the frightened and frenzied pony has had time to dread or suspect anything further, there comes a rattle and a creak, and there falls with an awful thud and crash upon his back a vast thing the like of which he had never dreamed for himself, though he has seen it upon the tamed slaves which aided in his own undoing. The saddle has been thrown upon him. Unless closely blindfolded, he promptly bucks it off again, wildly kicking into the bargain, his head tossed high with terror and hatred, his legs straining back from the iron hands that hold him.

But the iron hands do not relax. They hold like the hands of fate. The saddle is bucked off time and again, a dozen times, but it comes back again with the thud and crash, and someway it does not actually kill, after all. The pony stops to think about it. Jim, who has been waiting for this moment of thought, cautiously reaches under the pony with a long crooked stick to the girth that hangs upon the farther side. Slowly and quietly he pulls this girth to him, talking to the pony the while. Slowly and quietly he puts the end of the girth through the iron ring or buckle. Then, quietly, slowly, Jim gets out to the end of the "cinch" as far as he can, because he knows what is going to happen. Commonly the girth of the breaking saddle has a big buckle with a tongue which will quickly engage in the holes punched through the girth. Taking the cinch strap firmly in his hands, Jim gives a sudden jerk backward and upward, and the pony feels an awful grip of something tightened about his body where never such a thing had been felt before. At once, wild and demonlike in his rage and terror at such indignities, he falls wildly to bucking again; but now Jim is close up at his side, pulling the harder at the cinch, which does not slip but holds its own. The men at the pony's head swing down and twist his head askew. The hackamore tightens, the saddle holds. Tighter and tighter the girth goes, and at length the trembling beast feels he must endure this also. Panting and red-eyed, courageous and full of fight still, he braces his feet apart and stands so, trembling with anger and shame. And Jim quietly pokes another stick under and gets hold of another girth, the hind cinch ("flank girth," it is called in the South), and soon the pony feels upon his stomach the grip of this hairy, hateful thing, which all his life he never ceases to resent, because it cuts off his lung room and makes him feel uncomfortable with its sinking into the soft part of a pony's anatomy, which ought to be respected even by a cow-puncher, but isn't. The pony rebels again and viciously at this flank girth, but it does no good. The great saddle stays with him.

And now Jim, with his eyes gleaming a little and his jaws set hard together, slips up to the side of the panting pony, who stands with his head down, his legs apart, his eyes bloodshot, flinging his head from side to side now and again in a wild effort to break away and win back that freedom for which his heart is sobbing. Jim puts a cautious foot against the stirrup. The pony whirls away and glares at him. He realizes now what is the purpose of these enemies. Jim speaks in low and soothing tones to him, but calls him perhaps by some such name as, "You d—d black devil, you hol' on a minute, kain't ye? Whoa, bronc!" Again and again Jim seeks a place with his left foot. He has now gathered up into a coil the long stake rope, and this he holds in his left hand or ties with a half turn at the saddle horn. He knows there may be a severance of the personal relations of himself and the pony, and if so the rope will be needed to re-establish them. At last Jim makes a swift run, a bound and a spring all in one. Before the pony knows how it has happened he feels upon his back a horrible crushing weight. He feels his side half crushed in by the grip of a long pair of human legs. He feels his head "turned loose." He hears a long keen yell from a dozen throats about him, answered by a similar shrill yell, not of fear but of confidence, above him from this creature which is crushing down his back, breaking in his sides. All the hate, the terror, the rage, the fear, the viciousness, the courage of this undaunted wild beast now become blended into a mad, unreasoning rage. He has fought the wolves, this pony, and is afraid of nothing. He will unseat this demon above him, he will kill him as he did the wolves; he will trample him into the dirt of the plains.

Down goes the pony's head and into the air he goes in a wild, serio-comic series of spectacular stiff-legged antics. His nose between his knees, he bounds from the ground with all four feet, and comes down again with all legs set and braced, only to go into the air again and again. He "pitches a-plungin' "—that is, jumping forward as he bucks, perhaps going six hundred yards before he stops for lack of wind. Or he may stand his ground and pitch. He may go up and down, fore and aft, in turn, or he may pitch first on one side and then the other, letting his shoulders alternately jerk up and droop down almost to the ground—

a very nasty sort of thing to sit through. He may spring clear up into the air and come down headed in the direction opposite to that he originally occupied, or he may "pitch fence cornered," or in a zigzag line as he goes on, bounding like a great ball from corner to corner of his rail-fence course of flight. The face of Jim may grow a little pale, his hand that pulls upon the hackamore may tremble a bit, and the arm that lashes the pony with the quirt may be a little weary, but still his legs hold their place, and his body, apparently loose and swaying easily from the waist up, keeps upright above the saddle. Jim knows this must be ridden out.

The pony soon exhausts himself with his rage. His breath comes short. He stops. The legs of the rider relax a trifle, but the eye does not. With a renewal of the wild screams or "bawling" with which he has punctuated his previous bucking performance the pony springs forward again at speed. He stops short with head down, expecting to throw the rider forward from the saddle. The rider remains seated, perhaps jarred and hurt, but still in the saddle. Then the pony rears up on his hind feet. The cowpuncher steps off with one foot, keenly watching to see whether the bronco is going over backward or going to "come down in front," and go on with his performance again. If he goes on, the rider is in the saddle as soon as the horse's feet are on the ground. If the pony throws himself over backward, as very likely he will, the rider does not get caught —at least, not always caught—but slips from the saddle, jerking up the pony's head sharply from the ground. He quickly puts his foot on the horn of the saddle, and there is the wild horse flat on the ground and absolutely helpless, trussed up by the bridle and held down by the foot at the saddle horn. If the horse could get his head to the ground he would have a leverage, and could break away and get up, but Jim is careful that he shall not get his head down. Meantime he "quirts him a-plenty." He does not talk soothingly now. He wants this pony to know that it is better to keep his feet on the ground than to acquire the habit of traveling on his back or on his hind feet. At last Jim lets the pony up, and, much to the surprise of the latter, the rider is someway again in the saddle.

Now the pony stands quiet, stubborn, with his head down, grunting at the stroke of the long roweled spurs which strike his sides. At once he bounds forward again wildly, repeating his former devices at accomplishing the undoing of the rider, whom he now begins to fear and dread as well as hate. The latter is immovable in purpose, relentless of hand and limb. All this time he is riding without a bridle bit, depending only on the hackamore, which allows the horse much more freedom to show his repertory of feats than does the savage Spanish bit. The pony in time grows weary, and determines to vary its campaign by a Fabian policy. Again he stops still, "sulling," his ears back, but his legs braced stiffly. Jim is talking soothingly to him now, for Jim is no cruel horse breaker, after all, and has no vindictiveness for his mount, whose breaking is purely an impersonal business matter to him.

The pony at length slowly turns his head around and bites with all his force straight into the leg that grips him. The heavy "chaps" protect the leg, and the spur strikes him upon the other side. He turns his head to that side also and bites that leg, but the same process occurs again. With a sullen fear eating at his heart, the pony tries yet another trick. Deliberately he drops to his knees and lies down quietly upon his side, perhaps holding the rider a willing prisoner fast by the leg which lies under his body. The rider need not be so caught unless he likes, but it is a superstition with Jim that the pony should never unseat the rider nor loosen the grip of the legs on his sides. Jim thinks that should he do this the matter of breaking would be longer and less effective, so he takes chances and holds his grip. Were the pony a big "States" horse, his maneuver would be effective, and the rider would be in a sad predicament; but this horse weighs scarcely more than six hundred pounds, and the big stirrup, perhaps tied to its fellow on the opposite side, is under him, protecting the foot of the rider, who is now stretched out at full length upon the ground beside the horse. Moreover, the grass is up a few inches in height perhaps, and all in all the leg is able to stand the weight of the horse without being crushed, there being no stone or stub to offer injury, and so long as that is true the cowpuncher does not worry about it.

He lies and talks to the pony kindly, and asks it how long it intends to stay there in that way, suggests that it is about time for him to go home for dinner, and that he has other work to do before the day is over. If the pony be very stubborn, he may lie so for several minutes, and Jim may take off his hat and put it under his own head to make the ground feel more comfortable. Both these wild creatures are watchful and determined. It is a battle of waiting. The pony is first to tire of it, for he does not clearly know how much damage he is doing the cowpuncher's leg, and would himself prefer to act rather than to wait. With a snort and a swift bound he is up on his feet and off, his spring jerking the rider's foot clear of the stirrup. At last he has won! He has unseated this clinging monster! He is free!

But almost as swift as the leap of the pony was that of the rider. He has tight in his hand the long stake rope, and with a flirt of the hand this unrolls. With a quick spring Jim gets to one side of the horse, for he knows that an "end pull" on the rope along the line of the horse's back will be hard to stop, whereas the matter is simpler if the rope makes an angle with the horse's course. His gloved hand grasps the rope and holds the end of it close against his right hip. His left hand runs out along the rope. His left leg is extended and braced firmly on the ground, and with all his weight he leans back on the rope until it is nearly taut. Then, just at the instant when the rope is about to tighten, he gives a swift rolling motion to it with his whole strength, sending a coiling wave along it as a boy does sometimes to a rope tied fast to a tree. This indescribable and effective motion is magical. The roll of the rope runs to the head of the pony just as the cowpuncher settles back firmly on his heels. The head of the horse comes down as though drawn by a band of iron. His heels go into the air, and over he comes, a very much surprised and chagrined cow pony. He awakes and arises to find the iron hand again at his head, the legs of steel again sitting him firmly. The pony has not known that, by this skilled handling of the stake rope at a time when a tenderfoot would be jerked clean from his feet, the cowpuncher can "bust wide open," as he calls it, the strongest pony on the range, the twist giving five times the power of a straight pull.

The heart of the pony fails at the shock of this sudden fall. His head droops. His ears relax from the side of his head where they have been tight tucked. Through his red, bloodshot eyes the landscape swims dully. He looks with a sob of regret at the wide sweep of the prairie lying out beyond, at the shade of the timber mottes on the horizon, at the companions of his kind, who look toward him now with heads uplifted. At last he begins to realize that he is a captive, that freedom is for him no more, that he has met his master in a creature stronger in will and in resource than himself. The cowpuncher urges him gently with his knee, talking to him softly. "Come, bronc," he says. "It's 'bout dinner time. Let's go back to the ranch." And the bronco, turning his head clear around at the pull on the hackamore—for he is not yet bridlewise—turns and goes back to the ranch, his head hanging down.

The next day the pony has regained something of his old wildness and self-confidence, but is not so bad as he was at first, and the result is the same. Meantime he has been learning yet more about the lesson of not "running against rope," and has cut his heels so much that he is beginning to be more careful how he plunges at the stake. The cowpuncher rides him at times in this way for four days or so on the hackamore, and then puts on a light bridle bit, riding him then a couple of days longer, gradually teaching the use of the bit and bridle. Then the hackamore is taken off, and the pony begins to learn that the best thing he can do is to turn at the touch of the rein on the neck and to stop at the instant the reins come up sharply. In two weeks the pony is quite a saddle horse, though it is well to watch him all the time, for he has a lightning estimation of the man about to ride him, will know if the latter is afraid, and will take advantage of his trepidation. All his life the pony will remember how to pitch a bit at times, perhaps just for fun, because he "feels good," perhaps for ugliness. All his life he will hate a hind cinch, but all his life he will remember the lesson about "going against rope," and will stop still when the rope touches him. Even if very late in life he resumes a bit of friskiness and evades the rope a little in the corral, the sight of another horse jerked end over end is apt to bring him to a sudden sense of what may happen, and he sobers down very quickly. The writer recalls a big black Spanish pony which was very bad on the stake, and had learned some way of getting up his picket pin and running off, contriving to loosen the pin by side pulls first on one side and then the other. One day he ran off in this way with rope and pin dangling, and started at full speed through a bit of timber. The jumping picket pin, whipped about at the end of the rope, caught about a tree with a sudden twist, and the horse got one of the worst falls it was ever the fortune of cow pony to experience, going into the air clear and coming down on his back with all four feet up. He was a dazed and repentant horse, and from that time on, in the words of the cowpunchers, he was "plum tender about rope."

The Tidal Wave

by LOUIS V. HOUSEL

Probably the greatest tidal wave of recorded history occurred immediately after the explosion in 1883 of Krakatoa, a volcanic island in the Sunda Strait, Netherlands Indies. An entire mountain was blown away, causing many tidal waves, the greatest of which was about 50 feet high. The effect was disastrous. More than 36,000 persons lost their lives and many villages and towns were utterly destroyed. Here we see at extremely close range some of the effects of a tidal wave, which is often one of the aftermaths of an earthquake occurring near the sea. Most sufferers from tidal waves are shore dwellers, either in port or in more exposed areas. The interest of the present account stems partly from the fact that it is viewed from the sea itself—at least in the beginning, for soon the unfortunate vessel is thrown upon shore.

SIX MONTHS AFTER RECEIVING OUR DIPLOMAS OF GRADUATION at Annapolis found us a disconsolate mess of six midshipmen attached to one of Uncle Sam's most unseaworthy "double-enders," fitting out at the Boston Navy Yard for the most disagreeable station in the world, the West Indies. We felt as if the Navy Department had put us on the black-list, and was determined to sit on us from the start in our active-service career. Our professional ardor was at a low ebb when the joyful news reached us that we were all to be detached from our double-bowed bugbear and ordered to the sloop of war ——, which shall be nameless in this narrative.

At length our ship was ready, and we bade adieu to Boston. We shaped our course southward, our destination being Cape Haytien, where we were ordered to report to Admiral Palmer, on his flagship *Susquehanna*. Here we learned from the American consul that the *Susquehanna* had left a week before for the United States, as yellow fever, the scourge of these fruitful islands, had appeared among her crew. We found orders for us to take an extended cruise among the islands, commencing with Santa Cruz, and returning to the same point by a certain date.

We carried out the instructions received from time to time from Admiral Palmer, to call among the various groups of islands, touching at all the principal ports, as well as Aspinwall and the ports on the Spanish Main, until, finally, the month of October found us lying in the harbor of Frederickstadt, Santa Cruz. We were there recuperating the health of our crew, having had eight cases of yellow fever aboard, one of which had proven fatal, the other patients having been sent ashore to the hospital. "It is an ill wind that blows nobody good"; for, had it not been for this sickness, our vessel, without doubt, would have anchored just outside Prince Rupert's Rocks, in the entrance to the harbor of St. Thomas, as had been our custom for several months, so as to meet the American mail, and would have been caught in that terrific hurricane of the 29th of October, 1867, which visited that island, wrecking in its harbor, in the space of two hours, sixty odd vessels of all sizes, from the magnificent iron steamer of the English mail lines to the small coasting schooner, and drowning over five hundred persons. But we were reserved for a different fate. Hearing of this catastrophe, our commanding officer immediately resolved to steam over and render all possible assistance. The first view of the scene impressed us with the terrible power that had been running riot among the shipping. The harbor was literally choked with wrecks; and, as if not content with that, some of the smaller craft were flung high upon the rocks. Vessels of all sizes became unmanageable, and were driven hither and thither about the harbor by the violence of the merciless gale, driving upon and sinking each other. One large collier, in ballast, the *British Empire* by name, broke from her moorings and charged three times across the harbor, maneuvered by the shifting wind, sinking steamers, ships, and schooners, until, shattered and stove, she finally sank upon the wrecks of two Danish brigs she had sent to the bottom before her.

After finishing our mission we returned to Santa Cruz, only to be ordered back in a couple of weeks. At this time the government was meditating the purchase of these Danish islands, and the commissioners who had been "viewing the landscape o'er" about St. Thomas were desirous of leaving that pestilential "hole in the wall" to survey the fairer one, of which they had many good reports. Consequently, we were detailed to carry them over to Frederickstadt, which was accomplished on the 17th of November. We anchored in the open roadstead which serves as a harbor to this town, about half a mile from the wharf. The weather was warm, but not remarkably so for the tropics, the thermometer ranging during the day in the eighties, touching the nineties in the middle of the day perhaps. The sky, we remembered by the light of after events, wore a coppery hue.

Nothing unusual attracted our attention until three o'clock in the afternoon of the 18th of November, when our vessel began to quiver and rock as if a mighty giant had laid hold of her and was trying to loosen every timber in her frame. Officers and men ran pell-mell on deck to ascertain the cause of such a phenomenon. The vibrations continued the space of perhaps a minute, accompanied by a buzzing noise somewhat like the draught of a smelting-furnace or the hum of innumerable swarms of bees. So certain were we that the cause was connected in some way with the ship that no one cast an eye on shore. Various suggestions were made by old and young.

"Blowing down the boilers!" said one. There being no fires under the boilers, such a solution was impossible.

"A drumfish fastened to the vessel's bottom," suggested another.

"It's an *earthquake,* sir; look ashore!" shouted from the bow an old bluejacket, who had felt the peculiar sensation before. I looked toward Frederickstadt and saw a dusty, hazy atmosphere over the town. I could see men, women and children running hither and thither and could catch faint cries of distress. Noticing that a part of the stone tower of the English church had fallen, I surmised great damage had been done the dwellings and was expecting to hear our boats called away to render assistance to the inhabitants. Full five minutes had elapsed since the shock, when I heard a peculiar, grating noise and, looking over the bow, I found the chain sawing on the cutwater and as taut as a harp string, full ten fathoms of it being out of water. On reporting the fact aft, the warp from the quarter, which was used to swing the ship broadside to the land breeze, was let go, when we found we were dragging anchor very rapidly, because of the powerful currents, the first effect of the shock. Orders were immediately given to "veer" chain; the executive officer ordered the "stoppers" to be cut. A sailor seized an axe and delivered but a stroke or two, when the tremendous strain broke them, and with the leap of a huge serpent the iron cable ran out the hawsepipe with continually increasing velocity, swaying and leaping in its mad career, defying the power of the men at the compressor with their powerful lever to stop it; on and on it dashed, making the vessel's bow rise and fall as it increased in momentum, marking its erratic course with a streak of fire, until, coming to the end, there was a perceptible rising of the deck, a tremendous jerk, and the heavy fourteen-inch bolt riveted in a solid oak beam was torn out, and the last links connecting the vessel to the anchor went flourishing and wriggling overboard with the rest. The last couple of fathoms swept the decks thoroughly under the top-gallant forecastle, upsetting and smashing the carpenter's bench and grindstone and whipping up the ladder, making it execute a back somersault in the air. We were now adrift, at the mercy of the currents.

An effort was made to man the starboard compressor so as to check the other anchor when let go; but the men had come on deck and were standing panic-stricken, gazing at the terrible appearance of the sea. A reef had risen off the northern point of the island where, but a few minutes before, were several fathoms of water. Our vessel advanced toward and receded from the shore with the waters until, as if some great power had raised up the bottom of the bay, the sea rapidly closed in on the town, filling the houses and covering the street running along the beach to the depth of twenty-four feet. Our ship, following the current, took a course toward the southern end of the town until, over the edge of the street, it swung her bow toward the north and was carried along, smashing a frame storehouse and breaking down a row of shade trees. During this maneuver an effort was made to hoist the jib, in the hope of catching a breeze to keep us off the town. The halliards were manned, when it was found that the cover (a strong piece of canvas) was holding it fast. Several men rushed out to remove the impediment, but their nervous fingers tugged in vain at the stubborn knots, when an officer ordered them to cut it loose; only one knife was convenient, and the man using it had ripped but a couple of feet of the cover when his trembling hand dropped it overboard. Men were then ordered aloft to loose the foretopsail. A dozen or more brave ones rushed up the rigging nearly to the top, when, catching a view of the angry and turbulent sea, they stopped, trembling in the presence of the mighty power that was abroad, and retreated to the deck. Again were the jib halliards manned, in the hope of tearing the sail from its cover. The men would tug at the rope with frantic efforts for a moment, then turn for a glimpse at the threatening sea, and the rope would drop from their hands. By this time the rush of waters was toward the ocean. We were carried out perhaps five hundred yards from the shore, when our vessel grounded, and, the water continuing its retreat, she careened over on her port beam's ends. The bottom of the roadstead was now visible, nearly bare, for a distance of half a

mile beyond us, and that immense body of water which had covered
the bay and part of the town was reforming, with the whole Atlantic
Ocean as an ally, for a tremendous charge upon us and the shore. This
was the supreme moment of the catastrophe. As far as the eye could
reach to the north and to the south was a high, threatening wall of green
water. It seemed to pause for a moment, as if marshaling its strength,
and then on it came in a majestic, unbroken column, more awe-inspiring
than an army with banners. The suspense was terrible. Our noble
vessel seemed as a tiny nutshell to withstand the shock of the mighty,
rushing Niagara that was advancing upon us. Many a hasty prayer was
muttered by lips unaccustomed to devotion. All expected to be engulfed,
and but few had any hope of surviving. We all seized hold of some
stationary object with the intent of preventing ourselves from being
washed overboard. "Hold fast!" was the cry, as the tidal wave struck the
ship with gigantic force, making every timber shiver. Yet, singular
enough, not a drop of water reached her decks. Being rather flat-
bottomed, the first effect of the blow was to send her over on her starboard beam's ends, which gave the water an opportunity of getting well
under her before righting, when she was buoyed to the crest of the wave
and carried broadside to the shore, finally landing on the edge of the
street in a cradle of rocks that seemed prepared for her reception.
Here she rested, with her decks inclined at an angle of fifteen degrees.
A small Spanish brig was carried bodily inland across the cane fields
and landed in the midst of the king's highway. The waters again retreated
and assumed such a threatening appearance that our commander, fearing
another tidal wave (which would have dashed us against the stone houses
or against the walls of a Danish fort just ahead of us), gave the order,
"Every man save himself!" In an instant ropes were thrown over the sides
and the crew began sliding down them like spiders and making for the
hills in the rear of the town. Seizing one of the fore-trysail vangs, I flung
it over the side, securing the part even with the deck to a cleat; after
the few men who still remained forward had descended on my rope and
I had cast a glance seaward to calculate the chances of getting clear of
the ship's bottom before the sea struck her again, I swung to it and
descended so rapidly that my hands paid a severe penalty, the rope cutting
the flesh nearly to the bone.

Upon striking the ground I immediately cut round the corner of the
street leading to the nearest hill. Like Lot, I looked not back but made
the best time possible, soon overtaking a squad of our men that had
preceded me. On arriving at the first cross street we were beset by a rush

of water that had been thrown far up in the town, seeking its way back to the sea. We were soon in water waist deep, contending with a strong current as best we could. The situation was not so critical, however, as to prevent us from noting some comical incidents. This water bore on its surface all manner of debris which it had gathered from the yards and houses in its course—chairs, cradles, bedsteads, broken fences and doors, together with flocks of ducks and geese quacking and gabbing, utterly bewildered by the sudden rise of their natural element.

We blundered and stumbled along, making all haste for fear the sea would overtake us. No injury resulting, we all arrived safely at the foot of the hill of refuge. Here was a scene never to be forgotten. Whites and blacks were collected in groups, praying, crying, and wringing their hands; some counting their beads and some on their knees reading aloud from their prayerbooks.

Many incidents of interest I might chronicle that occurred aboard our vessel during the interval between the shock and her final landing on the shore. When our apparently hopeless situation began to be realized by all of us it was curious to mark the manner in which it affected different individuals. Our chief boatswain's mate stood unmoved at his post, whistle in hand, never forgetting to pipe "haul away," or "belay," when appropriate, and, if I remember correctly, his whistle piped the men over the side when the order "every man save himself" was announced. Some were heard to remark, "We are all lost, but we must do the best we can," and worked with a will. One man ran about the decks exclaiming, in the face of the officers, "My God! we are all lost!" Two prisoners in double irons hobbled on deck from their prison below and begged, for God's sake, to have their iron removed, that they might have an equal chance for their lives with the rest of us. The master-at-arms was without his keys to unlock their shackles. He had given them to the ship's corporal, who was on shore. No time was to be lost, so I ordered their chains to be cut. One of the prisoners seized a hatchet and, seating himself on the deck, in one powerful stroke severed the chain confining his ankles. He then cut the chains of his fellow prisoner, who in turn cut those confining his wrists, leaving the bracelets still on wrists and ankles, but so as not to interfere with the free use of their limbs. When the commotion in the water first occurred, two men were sent in each of the boats to assist the keepers in getting them under the davits, the intention being to hoist them. But the time was too short and they drifted from the vessel. I watched the movements of one of these boats through a port as the wave approached. The three men in her manned their oars and pointed her bow toward the enemy, bending every effort to give her head-way in the shallow water, in the hope of topping the wave and riding it to shore. They did nobly. The boat's bow rose nearly to the crest of the wave, and I hoped for a moment they would be successful, but their oars were caught foul by the onrushing water, their boat thrown broadside to the wave, and crew and all were overwhelmed, two of them never to come up alive. The third one rose and, seizing hold of a sugar hogshead that had been washed from the wharf, after many immersions finally reached shore unhurt. The coxswain of the commodore's gig stood by his boat at the expense of his life. Keeping her under the quarter, when the final rush for the shore occurred, the vessel came down on boat and keeper. One poor fellow, who had just returned from liberty, lost his presence of mind and leaped overboard at a time when no effort could be made to save him. Another, in descending, lost his hold on the rope and fell to the ground, breaking both legs and sustaining other injuries. We carried him to a frame church on the hill, where the surgeons, after examination, announced to him it would be necessary to amputate both legs.

Leaving him in the hands of the surgeons, I collected what men I could and returned to the vessel. Many had remained on board, concluding that the threatening wave could not raise sufficient force for a second charge. When within hailing distance I was commanded by a superior officer to take a cutlass and clear the men out of a grogshop on the opposite side of the street from the ship. On entering I found twenty or thirty of our crew making away with all the liquor their stomachs could accommodate. They found themselves among a rare assortment of the vilest kind from which to select, and many of their faces already glowed with the liquid fire they had imbibed. Foremost among them I noticed our two prisoners with their chains still dangling to their limbs, far gone in intoxication. I ordered them all out and stood guard until relieved by the owner. His face elongated perceptibly when he surveyed the scene within. Billiard tables, chairs, counters, rum bottles and rubbish were piled together in a slimy heap at the farther end of the room.

On returning aboard ship for dry clothing I learned the full extent of damage sustained by our floating home. Her rudder was torn from its gimbals, forty feet of keel was gone, much copper was stripped off, two holes were in the bottom, and her frame was so racked that the engines were out of line, the shaft was bent near the propeller, and seams were gaping fore and aft.

Hearing that a widow lady and family who resided a half-mile from the

town were in great distress, three of us who were acquainted with them
proceeded to their assistance. We arrived at the house early in the evening
and found them huddled together in the yard almost paralyzed with terror,
without shelter, and their house so damaged that it would have to be
rebuilt. We removed what furniture and clothing was necessary for their
present comfort and, improvising a tent, we prepared for camping out for
the night. We built a large fire under the trees and made everyone as
comfortable as possible. But in vain did we woo sleep that night. Severe
shocks occurred at intervals of a half-hour during the entire night, which
had the effect of keeping us all on the *qui vive*. So there was nothing for
us to do but accept the situation and make the best of it. The night was
beautiful and clear, the heavens were filled with bright stars and, in spite
of the unfortunate condition in which we were all placed, there was a
charm in the situation, whether owing to the presence of the ladies or
the novelty of the surroundings I cannot say.

The Negroes from the plantations were terribly affected by the earthquakes; they saw water oozing from the sides of the hills, where no springs
were known, and the rumbling and shaking of the earth filled them with
superstitious terrors. Some of them died from fright, as I was informed
by a clergyman who ministered among them. Hundreds of them flocked
into town, and for the accommodation of them and others we constructed
a tent out of our mainsail. The scene in this palm grove was not unlike an
old-time camp meeting. If there was a cessation in their devotions at any
time, night or day, a shock was sure to revive them, and a long prayer
and one hymn, at least, would follow. But as days passed and the shocks
occurred with less frequency and violence, Sambo's natural gayety arose,
and as their repertoire of hymns had been exhausted, some of them
occasionally would venture to interject a popular ballad imported from
the States, and all would join in and render it with a full chorus. On one
occasion they were singing with great gusto,

I wish I were in Dixie

when whir-r-r-er came a tremendous vibration, which hushed every voice
in an instant and, as soon as recovered, fervent prayers took the place of
the worldly song, followed by the doubly appropriate hymn beginning,

On Jordan's stormy banks I stand

People outside of the tents conducted themselves during these trying
times in various manners. Some relied solely on their devotions, others

gave rum their exclusive attention, while still others there were who made, as they thought, a judicious admixture of the two.

At length, after fourteen days of anxiety, we were relieved by the appearance of the United States steamer *De Soto*, from St. Thomas (herself badly damaged by the tidal wave), with instructions to convey all but a few of us back to the United States. How glad we were to quit that island words cannot express. Ocean, with its uncertainties, its waves and tempests, even in a damaged vessel, was thrice welcome.

Our ark of refuge bore us safely to our native shores, and Uncle Sam, not forgetful of his own, had our noble vessel launched and repaired from keel to masthead, and today she sails the seas without a mark of her rough handling by the earthquake wave.

Hunting the African Buffalo

by J. A. HUNTER

Hunter, by the author of that name, is one of the most exciting and authentic books about hunting wild animals that I have read. In my mind it ranks second only to Jim Corbett's Man-Eaters of Kumaon *as the classic type of modern adventure book, modestly written, in brilliant detail, and with a large overall perspective. Captain A. T. A. Ritchie, Game Warden of Kenya from 1923 to 1949, has written of Hunter, "I can pay no greater tribute to his prowess than is provided by the fact that he is still alive." Hunter is one of the great white hunters of Africa of this century. Born in the south of Scotland with hunting in his blood as well as his name, he early emigrated to Africa to fulfill his ambition and establish his fame.*

WHEN HILDA AND I RETURNED FROM FUMVE, THERE WAS A note awaiting me from Captain Ritchie of the Kenya Game Department. I went to see him at once. The department was confronted by another control problem. In the vicinity of Thomson's Falls, a community some hundred miles north of Nairobi, a herd of buffalo had been doing great damage. The animals were destroying shambas and had killed several natives. Captain Ritchie had come to the conclusion that this herd must be dealt with.

In ordering these animals killed, Captain Ritchie was also interested in the general welfare of all the Kenya buffalo. This particular herd had become a nuisance and Captain Ritchie, ever out to assist the farming community, wanted their numbers kept in check.

Many hunters believe that the buffalo is Africa's most dangerous animal. When a buffalo attacks, he charges with admirable ferocity and will not flinch away from a bullet as do rhinos and even elephants. A buffalo usually continues to charge until he is killed or he has killed the hunter. They are most cunning. Frequently a wounded buffalo will double back and wait beside his trail, hoping to ambush the hunter. Then, too, a buffalo will often attack without any provocation at all, so he may well be regarded as a difficult and uncertain quarry.

I decided to use a heavy rifle on this trip, a .500 double Jeffery. I consider the heaviest weapon a man can conveniently carry is none too powerful for buffalo. Knowing that some of the wounded animals would escape into the bush and have to be driven out, I decided to use dogs. If this appears non-sporting, I can only say I was performing a task assigned to me by the department and I was not interested in personal glory.

The pound in Nairobi contained nothing but a small collection of worthless curs. Still, I was in no position to pick and choose, so I bought the lot. Later, I was able to add to this pack by buying a few larger and more alert dogs from settlers. I still badly needed a "head" dog, a leader of the pack, that would show his mates the way by his courage and determination. Dogs easily follow a leader and even one first-class dog can transform a group of curs into a reasonably respectable pack. No leader was forthcoming so I prepared to leave Nairobi with my mixed bunch of mongrels.

A few days before I left, I received a call from a prominent official asking me to get rid of his pet dog. This animal was considered to be incurably vicious. He had attacked and bitten several natives and was killing livestock near Nairobi. From the owner's description, I decided the dog was hopeless but at that moment anything was grist that came to my mill. I went over to collect him.

At first look, I liked the dog. He was big-boned, tawny in color, and about the size of an Alsatian. He had powerful jaws and clearly knew how to use them. He seemed to be a general crossbreed with a strong dash of bull terrier. I decided to call him Buff, an easy word for the tongue. He took to the name and I felt that we were going to get along well together. I believed him to be a keen, adventuresome animal, never intended by nature to be a house pet. He could not endure being confined in a city, and I knew that feeling well myself. If Buff had lost his temper and chewed up a few bad characters, well, I was not the man to hold that against him.

Buff soon established himself as leader of my pack. There were several that fought him, but they quickly learned discretion. Even the bitches showed preference by transferring their affections to him while the other dogs slunk about at a safe distance. Yet for all his ferocity, Buff was a true dog and would lie at my feet by the hour, looking up at me with his profound, wistful eyes, trying to read my thoughts. Even before we left Nairobi, I was more attached to Buff than I had ever been to any other dog. I could only hope he would prove himself in the buffalo hunts and learn to avoid the fierce animals' horns and sharp hooves.

Near Thomson's Falls, I began to realize why Buff's former owner had been so eager to part with him. I took the pack for a stroll one evening and on the way we passed a herd of sheep being driven by a native. The sight of the sheep was too much for Buff. He charged into the flock, cut out a fat-tailed ram, and in a matter of seconds the sheep was on its back with Buff's teeth buried deep in its throat. I tore him off and, removing my belt, gave the dog a beating that he never forgot. Buff took the punishment without a whimper, for which I liked him all the better. I paid the native for his sheep and we returned to camp, Buff cheerfully trotting by my heels all the way.

I had several Nderobo scouts attached to my control camp, a people one-quarter Masai and three-quarters bushman. They are a praiseworthy tribe, being reasonably good hunters, although they do some tilling. We had been at the village only a few hours when I heard a dreadful commotion outside my tent. Rushing out, I found that Buff had knocked down a native woman and was busy disrobing her. Her clothing was only a loincloth, but he had torn this off and fastened his teeth in her flank. I grabbed Buff by the tail and, exerting all my strength, managed to pull him off. The woman fled for the nearest hut, red and white marks showing on her plump black posterior. I expected a fearful protest from the natives, but the woman's husband was rolling on the ground shouting with laughter and the other natives were equally amused. Several of them came up and congratulated me on having such a fine animal. They considered Buff's aggressiveness a good omen for a buffalo dog.

I talked to the Nderobo concerning the buffalo and heard many stories of the animals' vindictiveness. I quote two of these stories to give the reader some idea of the determination with which a buffalo will follow his victims.

One of the Nderobo walked with a limp and I inquired the cause. The man showed me that his heel was gone—bitten clean off at the ankle. He told me that a buffalo had done it. I could hardly believe his statement, but when he had finished his story, I concluded that the man was telling the truth.

He had been walking through the bush on his way to his shamba, when he heard a snort from the underbrush. He turned and bolted; the thunder of hooves behind told him that his pursuer was a buffalo. The man had a fair start but the buffalo rapidly gained on him. The sound of the hooves grew steadily louder. At the last instant, the man made a desperate jump and managed to grab the limb of a tree just as the buffalo rushed under him. The animal turned and coming back stood below the man, pawing the ground and snorting with fury. The native had pulled his feet up under him but the strain of holding them there grew too much. His right leg became cramped and for a moment he had to extend it. Immediately the waiting buffalo rushed up and nipped off the man's heel with his teeth as though it were a twig. Then, seemingly appeased by the taste of blood, he went away, leaving the half-fainting man still clinging to the tree limb.

After thinking this story over, I saw nothing incredible in it. There is no reason why a buffalo should not use his teeth. A horse can give a vicious bite. Indeed, an angry stallion will fight with his teeth quite as much as with his hooves. Later, I was to discover that a buffalo will indeed use his teeth to tear his victims—and very deadly weapons they are.

The injuries produced by an infuriated buffalo are often extremely grisly. One afternoon a native came to my camp and asked me to employ him as a game scout. While I was talking to him, I noticed large, smooth scars on the insides of his thighs. I asked him the cause. As innocently as a child, he casually let fall his loincloth. To my horror, I saw the man had been completely castrated. At my astonished exclamation, the native said simply that he considered himself a very lucky man. If Mungu (God) had not been looking after him, he would now be dead.

I repeat his story as he told it to me. He had left his hut early one morning to visit his beehives. These hives are hollowed-out, wooden receptacles and natives hang them from the upper branches of trees throughout the bush. The boxes may become in succession the nesting site of birds, the home of snakes and the hive of a swarm of wild bees. If bees move in, the native collects the honey. Sugar of any kind is a rare commodity in the jungle and highly prized.

This native was walking through some high grass on his way to his beehives when he almost stepped on a resting buffalo bull. The bull leaped up and one of his great curved horns caught the man between the legs, tossing him into the air. The man fell straddle-legged over the withers of the maddened bull. In desperation he clutched the bull's ear with one hand and hung to his shoulder with the other. The grunting, infuriated beast broke into a heavy gallop, still ridden by the terrified native. The man did not dare to slip off, so he clung to the bull with all the power his life possessed. The buffalo carried him some sixty yards, and then, driven frantic by his burden, dashed under a heavy thorn bush, knocking the man to the ground.

The native was half stunned by the fall. Lying on his back, he saw the buffalo wheel and come back for him. The bull stopped a few feet away and then launched a terrific hook at the helpless man's belly. As the horn ripped into him, the man lost consciousness.

When he recovered his senses, the sun was sinking. His whole body was numb and seemed to be paralyzed. Forcing himself to think, he realized he was lying near a little stream. He managed to drag himself to the bank. One hand was broken, but with the other he was able to scoop up water and lift it to his mouth.

The man lay by the bank of that stream for two weeks. He kept alive by drinking water and eating what grass he could reach. He could do nothing for his wounds except to splash water on them. At night, he heard rhinos come down to drink and twice he heard the high-pitched screams of cow elephants near him. Often he heard hyenas wailing and laughing in the brush around him, but they never ventured close. Crocodiles would silently appear on the surface of the water and swim up to within a few feet of him. He was too weak to move and could only lie there watching them. After studying him for a few minutes, the reptiles would soundlessly submerge again.

The man was finally found by other honey seekers. He had long before been given up for dead by his village for after a man has been gone a few days in the bush, his relatives abandon all hope. His wounds had practically healed and he was soon as well as ever except for his terrible mutilation.

I asked the man why, after such an experience, he wanted to hunt buffalo. His eyes lighted up as he said, "Bwana, I will know that buffalo again by his horns. When I find him, I will cut off his makende (testicles) and eat them, just as surely as he galloped off with mine."

The buffalo herd I was after lived in the Marmanet Forest. The cover here is very dense, making hunting both difficult and dangerous. I do not consider a buffalo a formidable animal in the open, but in underbrush he can be very deadly indeed. I was glad I had my dogs with Buff at their head.

I let the pack rest a few days after their trip from Nairobi, then I started out early one morning with my pack and the game scouts. There were buffalo signs throughout the forest and the dogs showed little hesitation in following the tracks. My former pack in the Masai Reserve had been most reluctant to trail lion—the odor of the big cats seemed to daunt them—but apparently dogs are not fearful of buffalo scent. In a few minutes we could hear the buffaloes crashing through the bush with the dogs yelling on their heels. Followed by my native scouts, I kept as close to the pack as I could. Suddenly there came a shrill yelp and I saw one of the dogs go flying up above the bush as a buffalo tossed him. I could not see where he landed. Not wishing to lose dogs unnecessarily, I tried to call them back but in the hubbub of barking I could hardly hear my own voice.

When we came up with the pack, I found they were holding five buffalo bulls at bay. The bulls stood in a ring with their tails together and their horns pointing outward to keep off the dogs. Suddenly Buff rushed straight for the bunch and grabbed one of the bulls by the nose. The bull plunged forward and tried to dash the dog against the bole of a tree. Buff was not to be squashed so easily and slewed his hindquarters around at the last instant. A bullet from my gun put an end to the bull's struggles.

From then on, Buff always used the same tactics. After the pack had bayed a buffalo cow or bull, Buff would charge in and grab the animal by the nose. When attacked by dogs, buffaloes naturally hold their heads close to the ground to give their horns full play and this habit gave plucky Buff ample opportunity for his favorite hold. Apparently all cattle have tender noses. I remember how in Scotland farmers would put a ring through the nose of a dangerous bull, and as long as the man held the ring, the bull was comparatively helpless. Once Buff got his grip, the buffalo was seldom able to shake him off. Buff took a good stance with all four legs spread wide apart and a buffalo could not get sufficient purchase with his head held down to toss him.

A big buffalo bull is a grand creature, weighing up to 2,000 pounds, with great sweeping ink-black horns as thick as a man's leg at the boss and tapering to points as fine as daggers. When a bull charges with lowered head, he presents his thick skull to you, reinforced by the heavy boss. Under such conditions, only the heaviest-caliber rifle can bring him down. In hunting buffalo, I prefer to shoot for the chest, neck, shoulder or under the eye, but in case of a charge, you have little choice and must fire where you can.

The dogs were more effective in buffalo hunting than my other pack had been with lions. Dogs can keep out of a buffalo's way more easily

than they can avoid a lion's rush. As with my former pack, some of the
dogs had more courage than discretion. Instead of dodging an infuriated
buffalo's charge, they would stand their ground. A buffalo is so quick in
dealing a swipe with either horns or hooves that unless a dog takes good
care to leap clear, he will be instantly killed.

Several of the dogs were tossed on different occasions. As a dog went
up in the air, the buffalo would watch to see where he was coming down
and then make for the spot, hoping to catch the dog while he was still
dazed from the fall. The pack would rush in to help their friend, nipping
at the buffalo's hocks as I have seen dogs do with domestic cattle, and
try to turn him. If they could hold the beast even a moment I was
generally able to get in a shot.

The buffalo herds often grazed in the open along the edges of swamps,
frequently accompanied by egrets, which flutter about the big, dun-
colored beasts like bits of white paper. The egrets sometimes ride on the
buffaloes' backs and I believe they pick ticks off the animals. Occasionally
a hunter can locate buffalo in tall grass by the egrets flying above them.
It is a fine sight to come upon a herd of these magnificent beasts, proudly
bearing aloft their great ebony horns and walking through a pasture of
rich, green grass while the snowy white birds balance on their backs or
walk with stately strides beside them.

Even when we encountered a herd of buffalo in the open, I had great
trouble getting close enough to them for a shot. Their excellent eyesight
and hearing made it hard to approach them. Often I had to whistle on
the dogs. The pack would chase the buffalo into the cover and then out
again while I fired at the animals almost as though at target practice.

In cover, it was a different matter. A hunted buffalo is wise enough to
stand motionless in deep bush until the man is almost up to him before
starting his charge. Even shooting nearby will not make him move until
he is certain of getting his enemy. Here dogs are invaluable. The dogs
can often smell the waiting buffalo and give the alarm. If not, they are
fairly certain to come on him while they are trotting ahead of the hunter.
I have no hesitation in saying that the dogs saved my life a dozen times
during these hunts.

Buff was invaluable. He was that rare combination, seldom found
among either dogs or humans, of great courage mingled with intelligent
discretion. He knew enough to avoid a buffalo's rush and yet had absolutely no fear of the animal. Only when some unusual situation arose
was the gallant dog in any real danger.

On one occasion, the pack had taken off after a very large buffalo bull. To keep the dogs from closing with him, the bull had taken up his stand in the center of a stream. This is a common trick among hunted animals when pursued by dogs. The dogs lined up on the river bank, making a great din with their barking, but not caring to swim out to the bull. Not so Buff. When he came up, the plucky dog took a great leap into the water and sure enough, managed to grab the surprised bull by the nose. For a moment the old buffalo stood there astonished by such audacity but he quickly recovered from his surprise and countered by pushing Buff under water. Buff would have drowned in a few minutes had I not been able to end the unequal struggle with a bullet. When Buff swam back to shore, coughing and spitting up water, I discovered that he had taken such a fierce grip on the tough gristle of the bull's nose that the tips of his front teeth were broken off. This will give some idea of Buff's strength and determination.

Up to date, this was Buff's seventeenth kill, all the buffalo having been gripped and held until I dispatched them.

In the next scrap with a buffalo herd, Buff did not get off scotfree. The pack had surrounded a herd and were holding them together by barking and making quick, heel-nipping rushes. Buff tore in and grabbed a large buffalo cow by her nose. He was holding her but her half-grown calf came to her help and butted the dog in the side with its short, stubby horns. Buff gasped, but refused to release his grip. He would have been killed if my scouts had not shot the two buffalo.

After this misadventure, I retired Buff from hunting until his wounds healed. I had shot over two hundred buffalo and the task of wiping out the herds was almost completed. Buff moped in his enforced security, watching wistfully while the rest of the pack trotted out after me for the day's hunt. One of my scouts went daily to a nearby kraal to get milk for the pack, and I told him to take Buff along on these walks. I felt the exercise would keep Buff from getting stiff while he was recuperating and also give him something to do.

On one of these trips, a warthog crossed Buff's path. This was a familiarity he could not stand. In spite of the shouts of the scout, Buff started all out after him. The hog went down a hole, first turning around and backing in so he would have his tusks toward the entrance in true warthog style. Buff was about to go down the hole after him when the hog suddenly charged out. I firmly believe that if Buff had not broken off the points of his teeth, he would have succeeded in holding the animal. Instead, he lost his grip on the pig's sweaty hide. Instantly, the boar made a quick lunge with his tusks and caught Buff in the chest, ripping the brave dog open and killing him instantly. The scout shot the boar but the damage was done. When I returned from my day's hunt, there was the body of my noble Buff, killed at a time when I thought nothing could happen to him.

I have never owned another dog like Buff, before or since. The rest of the hunt was poisoned for me because of the loss of this great animal. I hoped some of Buff's puppies would take after him, but none of them were fit to run in the same pack with their father. You get too fond of a dog. Not until after his death do you realize how much he meant to you. I sometimes wonder if the pleasure in owning a dog is worth the misery caused by his death.

Because of their strength and ferocity, buffalo have always been a favorite quarry of mine. I have hunted them not only in Kenya, but also in Uganda and the Congo. Although I am far from underestimating the powers of this great animal, yet I think the dangers of buffalo hunting may have been somewhat overestimated. I have heard many a story of the danger of "buffalo stampedes." According to these accounts, a herd of buffalo will charge a man and trample him to death. Although I have shot over 350 buffalo, I never saw a herd charge as a group, unless they were in a ravine where they could not spread out, and even then the animals were trying to escape rather than making a proper charge. In my experience, a charge is always delivered by an individual animal, usually a beast that has been cut off from the rest of the herd. A solitary buffalo can be most aggressive, but as a member of a herd he is often no more savage than many breeds of domestic cattle.

Some years after this hunt, I was sent a second time to the Thomson's Falls area to control marauding buffalo. I had been in the district only a few days when a native named Abeya arrived at my camp to apply for a position as a game scout. He was of the Turkana tribe. The Turkanas are a very wild, primitive people, mainly distinguished by a sort of bracelet they wear made of a single curved knife, ground to razor sharpness. The Turkanas are very expert with the use of this bracelet and can cut a man's throat with one twist of the wrist. When I first met Abeya he was clothed in little more than his own skin. His hair was plastered with cow dung and seen from behind his head resembled a baked bun. Abeya had spent much of his life in prison for poaching game with his bow and poisoned arrows. Even though he was a savage-looking specimen I considered him a likable chap for he was unquestionably a keen hunter. Abeya was joining the game scouts because he had a passion to own a rifle. This in itself was a laudable ambition, but I knew that natives have a strong tendency to regard a rifle as a fetish that can do no wrong rather than as a useful tool. I agreed to take Abeya as a game scout but insisted that he first thoroughly understand the mechanism of a rifle before using the weapon on big game.

Abeya's poaching experience made him an expert scout. He quickly learned how to handle his rifle and became a more than passable shot. But nothing I said to the man could convince him that a rifle did not make him invulnerable. However, as he was one of my best men, I finally sent him out buffalo hunting with two other scouts.

A few days later, the two scouts returned to say that Abeya had refused to hunt with them. "We Turkanas always hunt alone," he told them proudly. This was a direct violation of my orders for I believe that no one man can hunt in safety. Two men are always necessary— one to follow the spoor and the other to watch in case of a charge. I determined to take Abeya very severely to task when he returned.

Abeya did not return. I was away up country on a five-day hunt and when I came back Abeya's wife was waiting for me. She was a recent purchase, clad mostly in layers of dirty white beads. She said that Abeya had not turned up and she feared the worst. I instantly organized a searching party and we started out to comb the vastness of the Marmanet Forest for the missing man.

Among the Marmanet's forested slopes are strips of open tableland. By a large tree on one of these open areas we found what was left of Abeya. The body had been eaten by hyenas and vultures but we were able to identify him by the skull. From all the signs, Abeya had been murdered by another native. Several of his ribs were broken, as though by blows from a club. There was also a long, oblique cut across two bones that resembled a spear thrust. His rifle and ammunition were gone. Certainly no animal would have carried off the man's equipment. I reported the circumstances to Inspector Jay of the local police.

At that time there were a number of bush outlaws in the district who had attacked and robbed several native communities. For a rifle and ammunition to fall into the hands of these "bad hats" was a very serious state of affairs. The inspector came up to inspect Abeya's body. The scout had dug out a little hollow under the tree where he could lie in wait for passing buffalo, but there were no signs of a struggle and no buffalo spoor around the spot. There seemed to be little doubt that Abeya had met with foul play.

Yet to make absolutely certain, Inspector Jay decided to examine the brush for miles around to see if there were any other explanation.

Police Askaris, the native constabulary, were brought up from Thomson's Falls and I joined the search with my scouts. Early one morning a large group of Askaris, scouts and local natives gathered under the tree where we had found poor Abeya's body. Dividing the crowd into small bands, we started out to comb the bush.

The search had been on for two hours or so when a native reported to me that he had found the body of a large buffalo. I accompanied the boy to his find. The ground around the carcass was completely covered with vicious safari ants, busily engaged in devouring it. The native had disturbed their trails when he found the buffalo, and the insects were on a rampage, ready to attack anything that approached within five yards of their meal.

I told the natives to cut a long pole and turn the body over. As they did so, I noticed a round hole in a rib bone. Making a dash through the biting ants, I pulled out the rib, and ran back again. I wanted to find out if an 8 mm. caliber bullet would fit the hole. That was the caliber of our scouts' rifles.

The bullet fitted perfectly. Knowing that a wounded buffalo will invariably run to a thicket and then turn around to face his assailant, I told the scouts to spread out and search in the direction the animal had been facing. A hundred yards away they came on a log covered with bloodstains. After examining the signs, I had no doubt that it was here the buffalo had caught and gored Abeya. A few feet from the log, I came on Abeya's missing rifle in the tall grass. There was an unfired cartridge partly in the chamber but not fully pressed home. A single empty cartridge case lay nearby.

Next I examined every foot of the ground between the log and the tree where we had found Abeya. Along the way, I picked up the balance of the scout's cartridges, scattered at intervals through the grass. I also found dried splotches of blood, mixed with the watery fluid that comes from a wounded animal shot through the stomach.

I pieced the scene together from the forest evidence. From his position under the tree, Abeya had fired at a passing buffalo, hitting him in the stomach. The wounded animal had run through the bush, leaving a blood trail. Abeya had followed him. The wounded bull, waiting in ambush, had suddenly charged while the scout's eyes were on the spoor. Abeya had fired but failed to stop the bull. Before he could get a second cartridge in the chamber, the buffalo was on him. He had dashed Abeya against the log, breaking his ribs, and then had died himself. Abeya, mortally injured, had managed to crawl back to his little hollow under the tree and there had died. On the way, the rest of his cartridges had trickled out of his pockets.

There only remained the spear thrust across his bones to be explained. I could tell by the nature of the injury that it had not been made by the bull's horns. On re-examining the log, I found a projecting knotted branch with a sharp point. This branch was covered with caked blood. The bull had thrown Abeya against the branch and it had gone through him as neatly as a short sword.

When I first came on the body, I would have been willing to swear that the scout had been murdered by other natives. Fortunately, due to the quiet common sense of Inspector Jay, the matter was carefully investigated and the mystery solved. Yet I still consider it one of the most remarkable combinations of circumstances I ever encountered in the bush.

I am far from underrating the buffalo as an antagonist, but I believe that deaths caused by this animal can generally be laid to two causes— either a man has become so intent on following the spoor of a wounded buffalo that he has forgotten to watch ahead or he has insisted on using a light-caliber gun that does not possess enough shocking power to stop a charge.

I have already mentioned my dislike of using light weapons against formidable game and the reader may think I am something of a fanatic on the subject. I can only say that the deepest personal loss I ever sustained in Africa came about because a sportsman insisted on using a light rifle to hunt big game. Two men lost their lives simply because this man did not want his shoulder bruised by the kick of a heavy gun.

This man was by rank a prince of royal blood; I do not care to identify him further. I was acting as his guide and with us was my dear friend and comrade Kirakangano. Ever since we first met on the Masai Reserve, I had often called him in to help me on hunting trips. There was also another native who acted as gunbearer for the prince. This gunbearer was a conceited chap who considered himself a great bushcraftsman although he actually knew little about the business.

We had completed a highly successful lion hunt and on the day we were to leave the district, the prince sighted several buffalo bulls grazing near the edge of some cover. Nothing would do but he must have one of these animals as a trophy. The prince was using a .416, excellent for lion but only capable of dropping a buffalo if the animal is hit in some vital part. Followed by Kirakangano and the prince's gunbearer, his highness and I stalked the herd. By keeping a small bush between us and the bulls, we were able to get to within eighty yards of them. The prince took careful aim at a good bull and fired. The animal dropped, but at the report of the gun another much finer bull dashed past us. The prince fired again, and from the noise of the impact I knew this second animal was hit in the stomach. The wounded bull plunged into the bush and vanished.

I prepared to follow him with Kirakangano and dispatch him. But the prince insisted on coming with us. He claimed that unless he was able to finish off the buffalo, the trophy would have no interest for him. Unfortunately, I yielded to his wishes and we started into the cover.

We had scarcely gone fifteen yards when Kirakangano pointed the animal out to me, standing in a little clump of bush. I tried to point him out to the prince but he could not see him. While we were whispering and gesticulating the buffalo realized he was spotted. He turned and ran farther into the cover.

The animal now knew he was being trailed and was sure to be on his guard. We went on into the thick bush, Kirakangano doing the spooring while I walked beside him with my rifle at the ready. The prince came next, followed by his gunbearer carrying an extra rifle. I had my Jeffrey .500 and Kirakangano, as usual, had nothing but his moran spear.

The cover was so thick that I could not see through the dense upper foliage. Several times we could smell the pungent, dairylike odor of the bull as he stopped to wait in ambush for us. Each time I lay down, hoping to catch a glimpse of his legs through the more open lower stalks, but he always saw me and dashed off again, uttering hoarse grunts of defeated anger.

This sort of hunting began to tell on the prince's nerves. Although at first he had been all eagerness to finish off the animal, he now suddenly announced, "I have a strange foreboding that something is going to happen. Take me out of here."

I wished his highness had had his foreboding before he shot a buffalo bull through the stomach with a .416. However, there was nothing to do but take the man out. I left Kirakangano and the gunbearer behind, warning them to wait there for me and to do no more spooring until I returned. I could see light through the bush on our right, showing that we were not far from the open plains. After taking the prince out of the cover, I left him there and started back to take up the hunt again.

I had scarcely gotten halfway to the two men when I heard a shot. For an instant there was silence. Then I heard the buffalo grunting. I knew what those quick, hard, savage grunts meant. They are the noises a buffalo makes when he is goring his victim. The bull was killing my natives. I tore through the tangle of wild briars and scrub like a lunatic. The vines wound themselves around me like lassos. I could hear the sodden thuds of the buffalo's horns as he pounded one of the men into the ground. I was now frantic, ripping up the clinging vines by the roots and plowing through the bushes by brute strength.

As I crashed through the last line of bush, I saw a terrible sight. The buffalo was down on his knees goring the motionless body of Kirakangano. The bull was so busy using his horns on the semiconscious man that he did not notice me until I was less than five yards away. Then he leaped up. As he rose, I fired for the point of his shoulder. The force of the heavy bullet knocked him backward onto Kirakangano. The buffalo fell dead on its knees, hind legs spread-eagled. Kirakangano was lying diagonally behind the dead buffalo's forelegs, the whole weight of the great body across him.

I tried to drag the flabby, sweating mass off my dying friend. I could hardly move it. I lay on my back and braced my feet against the carcass, shoving until I scraped the skin off my shoulders. It was no use. Then I grabbed a sapling in both hands and with my feet locked around the buffalo's neck, I tried to pull myself and the body toward the tree. I even grabbed the sapling in my teeth for more purchase. I still could not shift the carcass off Kirakangano. The man was conscious and I could tell he was suffering badly, but he did not complain or even moan.

I shouted for the prince to come and help me. After an interminable time, he finally gingerly entered the bush. By pulling together on the buffalo's tail, we were finally able to drag the carcass off Kirakangano. The Masai had been badly crushed by the buffalo's horns and forefeet. Two of his fingers were broken where he had tried to grab the animal by the mouth.

I promptly gave him an injection of a quarter grain of morphine to relieve his pain. Within a few minutes he appeared eased. His first question was "Is the gunbearer dead? If not, let me kill him while I still have the strength."

The gunbearer had been the direct cause of the tragedy. The Masai explained that after I left him, the gunbearer had sneaked on ahead, in spite of my orders and Kirakangano's protests. The man came on the buffalo lying down and had fired. The bull leaped up with a roar and charged. The terrified gunbearer had run back toward Kirakangano, apparently hoping that the bull would take off after the Masai. Just as the man reached Kirakangano, the bull caught up with him. He gave the man such a blow from behind that the gunbearer cannoned into Kirakangano, knocking him down. Kirakangano had not even had a chance to use his spear before the buffalo was on top of him.

I went to look for the gunbearer. Six yards to the right of Kirakangano, I found the man's body. He was lying on his back, his tongue protruding. I raised the limp body from the ground. The neck was supple, broken in two places from the force of the buffalo's blow. The buffalo had hit him with turned skull, both curves of the horns connecting at the same time. The man was still alive. He muttered "Maji," the native word for water. I took my bottle and tried to pour a little down his throat. The water trickled out of the sides of his mouth. While I held him, I could feel his breathing stop. His hunting days were over.

When I told Kirakangano that the man was dead, the faint flicker of a smile passed over his face. Later, I found the Masai's spear embedded in the buffalo's shoulder. I thought Kirakangano must have gotten in at least one thrust but he told me that the buffalo had actually speared himself in the shoulder while kneeling down to gore him.

I went back to camp and had our porters bring a motorcar to the edge of the bush. With their help, we carried Kirakangano and the dead gunbearer to the car. The nearest doctor was a hundred miles away over appallingly rutted roads. The prince drove while I sat beside Kirakangano. Rain commenced to fall, making the going skiddy and difficult. About halfway, the car got stuck in a deep ravine. The prince tried to force it up the muddy bank, but the car kept slipping back again. I remembered getting knocked and bumped by the gunbearer's dead body while I was trying to hold Kirakangano in my arms to spare him some of the jolts. Every jar shrieked through my nerves in sympathy with him.

At last we got out of the ravine and went on. The dying Masai pointed out a warthog we passed that had unusually fine tusks. Even though he was dying, he was still a hunter at heart. He talked to me about his wife, his children, and his cattle, quietly remarking that he would never see them again. I tried to cheer him by saying we would soon be hunting together. Kirakangano smiled. He knew he was dying.

My friend passed away that night. A brave man, a great bushcraftsman, a true African. My only small consolation is that Kirakangano died as many Masai dream of dying—killed during the hunt by a noble wild beast. I am glad that at the end his spear was bloody, even though it was only an accident. I don't think Kirakangano would have wished to die with a clean spear.

Masai Spearmen

by J. A. HUNTER

I SAW MY FIRST SPEAR HUNT WHEN I WAS STAYING IN A SMALL Masai community not far from Lake Magadi. The night before, a lion had jumped the twelve-foot boma that surrounded the village, seized a cow, and leaped back over the barrier with the cow in his mouth. I know this feat sounds incredible, as the lion weighed no more than four hundred pounds and the cow probably weighed nearly twice that. Yet a male lion can perform this exploit with no more trouble than a fox has in carrying off a chicken.

A lion shows a special knack in getting partly under the carcass and shifting the weight onto his back while still holding the cow's throat in his mouth. When jumping the barricade, the lion's tail becomes absolutely rigid and seems to act as a balance. The Masai have assured me that a lion without a tail could not possibly perform this feat.

I was prepared to start out on the lion's trail the next morning, but the moran in this community told me somewhat contemptuously that my help was not needed. They would handle the situation themselves. At that time, I found it hard to believe that a group of men could kill an adult lion with spears. I asked if I could go along and bring my gun. Permission was politely granted me. That night I loaded my .416 Rigby magazine rifle, never doubting that it would fall to my lot to kill any lions that we might find.

We started off at daybreak. I followed the spearmen. There were ten of them. Magnificent-looking men, slender but finely muscled, not one under six feet. To give their limbs free play, each man removed his one garment, the long piece of cloth they wear draped over their shoulders, and wrapped it around his left arm. They carried their brightly painted shields balanced on their shoulders. Their spears were

309

in their right hands. The warriors wore their ostrich-plume headdresses as though going into battle and bracelets of fur around their ankles. Otherwise, they were completely naked.

We picked up the spoor of the lion and the moran began to track. The lion had gorged on the cow during the night and was lying up in some dense cover. They threw stones into the bushes at random until the savage growls of the lion showed he had been hit. When the moran had spotted the cat by his angry grunts and snarls, they began to throw stones in good earnest; then the bushes began to shake. Suddenly the lion burst out a hundred yards from us and went bounding away across the plains, his gorged belly swinging from side to side as he ran.

Instantly the Masai were after him, giving their wild cries as they sped through the tall, yellow grass. The lion, still heavy with his great meal, did not run far. He stopped and turned at bay. The spearmen spread out to encircle him. The lion stood in the middle of the ring, looking this way and that, snarling in a way to make one's blood run cold as the spearmen slowly closed in.

The lion allowed the men to come within forty yards. Then I could tell that he was preparing to charge. His head was held low, just above his outstretched forepaws. His hindquarters were slightly arched so he could bring his rear legs well forward and get the maximum spring behind his rush. He began to dig his claws into the ground, much as a sprinter digs in with his spiked shoes to make sure he does not slip when he makes his first jump.

I concentrated on the sinister inverted curve of the lion's tail. Just before he charges, a lion always twitches the tasseled tip of his tail three times in rapid succession. On the third twitch he comes for you at amazing speed, going so fast he seems only a small part of his real size.

The spearmen knew as well as I did that the lion was preparing to attack. By what seemed to be a single impulse, all their spear arms moved back together for the cast. The men were so tense with excitement that their taut shoulder muscles twitched slightly, making ripples of sunlight play along the spear blades. You could have driven a nail into any one of them without his feeling it.

Suddenly the tip of the lion's tail began to twitch. One! Two! Three! Then he charged for the ring of spearmen. At once half a dozen spears leaped through the air toward him. I saw one plunge into his shoulder and the next instant the spear head broke through the hide on his other side. The lion never paused in his stride. In his path stood one of the moran, a youngster on his first hunt. The boy never flinched. He braced himself to meet the charge, holding his shield in front of him and swaying back slightly so as to put the whole weight of his body into his spear thrust. The lion sprang for the boy. With one blow he knocked the young moran's shield out of his hand as though it were cardboard. Then he reared up, trying to sweep the boy toward him with his outstretched paws.

The boy drove his spear a good two feet into the lion's chest. The mortally wounded beast sprang on him, fixing his hind claws in the boy's belly to insure his grip while at the same time he seized the boy's shoulder in his jaws.

The young warrior went down under the weight of the great cat. Instantly all the other moran were around the dying lion. It was too close quarters for spears. The men used their double-edged simis, heavy knives about two feet long. Shouldering each other out of the way, they hacked like madmen at the lion's head. In a matter of seconds, they had sliced the head to pieces, starting with the muzzle and shearing off an inch or so at a time. I saw one man deliver a terrible blow that split the lion's skull open, but whether the animal was still alive at the moment I can hardly say.

I had been quite unable to use my gun during this battle. A man with a gun is a positive menace at such times. Once the frenzied warriors begin to circle the lion, a rifleman cannot fire without running a grave chance of hitting them.

I examined the wounded boy. His wounds were truly frightful yet he seemed completely indifferent to them. I sewed him up with a needle and thread. He paid no more attention to the process than if I were patting him on the back.

The hide of the lion was so perforated with spear thrusts and simi-slashes that it was worthless as a trophy. It was simply a cut and bloody mass of dirty yellow hair. The dignity and majesty of the noble beast had completely departed, leaving only a sorry remnant.

When we returned to the Masai manyatta or village, the wounded boy was urged to eat great quantities of raw beef and then given cattle blood as a purgative so he could gorge himself again. Some of the other moran had been clawed by the lion but they made no attempt to guard against infection, except to wash their wounds with water. Later I saw some Masai communities soak the root of a bush called the "olkilorite" in water, which gives it a permanganate of potash color. It seems to act as an antiseptic and promotes healing.

I hope the lad recovered. He certainly held top honors for the day, and the young girls were looking at him with such admiration that, if he lived, he would have no trouble picking out a suitable sweetheart.

The Masai believe that the bravest act a man can perform is to grab a lion by the tail and hold the animal so the other warriors can close in with their spears and simis. Any man who performs this feat four times is given the title of "melombuki" and ranks as a captain. It is also an unwritten law among them that any man who gains this title must be willing to fight anything living. I doubt if more than two out of a thousand Masai ever become melombuki, although the competition among the moran to gain this honor is very keen.

I have seen several of these "tail pullings" during Masai lion hunts and it is a wonder to me that the men attempting the feat ever come out alive. I remember one hunt in which fifty or more spearmen were involved. They had put up two lions and a lioness. The animals tried to reach some heavy scrub but the warriors cut them off. The lions retreated into a small clump of bush near a dry, sandy watercourse. When possible, a pursued lion nearly always makes for one of these dry stream beds with its canopies of overhanging bush. In a matter of minutes, the moran had the thicket surrounded and began to move forward for the kill.

As the circle of yelling warriors closed in, the concealed lions began to growl. Then without any warning, the largest of the lions broke from the cover and made a rush for freedom. He was a fine sight as he dashed along the stream bottom, tail down and going all out at a gallop. He was headed straight for two moran, who raised their spears and prepared to meet his charge. But the big male had no desire to fight; he wished only to escape. He gave a mighty bound straight over the heads of the two spearmen, spinning one of them around sideways with a blow from his flank.

The other moran made tongue-clicking sounds of disapproval, partly because the two young men had allowed the lion to escape and partly because the lion had refused to fight. I have often noticed that the old lions with the finest manes are more reluctant to give battle than young males or females. The same is true of elephants. An old bull with fine ivory is shyer than a young bull or cow. I suppose they learn discretion with the years. It has also seemed to me that lions are able to tell young, inexperienced moran and will deliberately direct their attack at these youngsters. This may be nothing but my imagination yet the younger men are apt to be hesitant and uncertain in their actions and I believe the lions can detect it.

As the spearmen closed in around the thicket, they bunched together, jostling each other in their desire to be first to spill blood. The remaining two lions were clearly visible in the bush, standing shoulder to shoulder and both giving grating roars. When the moran were within ten yards of the lions, spears began to fly. One of the spears struck the lioness in the loin and she came out with a scream of rage and pain. For an instant she stood up on her hind legs, pawing the air like the crest on a coat of arms. Then she dropped to bite at the spear in her flank. At that moment, one of the moran threw down his spear and, rushing forward, grabbed her by the root of her tail. A moran never grabs a lion by the tasseled end of the tail. A lion can make his tail as stiff as a gun barrel, and a man would be swept aside by a single jerk.

At once the moran's comrades dashed in, slashing with their simis. At moments like this, the spearmen work themselves up to a pitch of blind frenzy. They seem to be mere automatic stabbers. Their faces are expressionless. There is no teamwork; each man is out to do the killing by himself. The lioness was digging her hind feet into the ground to get purchase forward and the tail puller was dragging her back. Suddenly the lioness went up on her hind legs, striking left and right with her paws at the men around her. Although I saw her blows go home, the men never flinched. They told me afterward that they never feel any pain at the time of a mauling—they are at too high a pitch of excitement. Apparently neither does the lion. Both sides continue to fight until one drops from loss of blood.

Slowly the lioness fell to the ground. Then all I could see were the flashing blades of the simis as the men hacked away in their blind fury. When it was over, the animal's head was cut into shreds. There must have been a dozen spears in the body. It looked like a bloody pincushion.

From the noise on the other side of the clump of bush, I knew another group of spearmen were busy with the second lion. I saw a warrior kneel and hold out his shield in a taunting fashion. The next instant the lion had leaped on it, knocking the man flat. The prone warrior tried vainly to get in a spear thrust while the lion mauled his exposed shoulder. I shouted to the other men to keep back and let me get in a shot, but nothing could be heard above the wild, falsetto yells of the warriors and the deep grunts of the lion as he lacerated the prostrate man. I saw two spears plunge into the lion's body and then the moran fell on the raging beast with their simis.

Before the lion was dead, he had seriously wounded one of the attacking moran besides ripping open the shoulder of the warrior lying under the shield. I did what I could for the injured men. They both had deep claw and fang incisions and were losing considerable blood. As I sewed up one man's injuries, he glanced down casually at the terrible cuts and made the same contemptuous clicking sound with his tongue that the moran had made when they saw the first lion escape. The warrior's attitude seemed to be "What a nuisance!" yet a white man in a similar situation would have been wild with pain.

Strangely enough, I have never heard of any bones being broken by the lion's teeth. The wounds are all flesh wounds. Apparently the lion's fang teeth are wide enough apart to close around the bones. Yet when a lion grabs a man by the shoulder, his fangs often meet in his victim's body. If you pour disinfectant into one wound, it will run out the other.

The spearmen have assured me that a lion's most dangerous weapon is neither his teeth nor his claws proper but what might be called his dewclaws. On the inside of each lion's forelegs is an extra claw about two inches long. These claws roughly correspond to a man's thumbs. They are curved and very sharp. The dewclaws are usually kept folded against the lion's legs and are difficult to see, but the lion can extend them at will so they stand out almost at right angles. These two claws are keen as brush hooks and very strong. A lion slashes with them and can disembowel a man with one blow of these terrible hooks.

The Masai spears are made by native smiths from bits of iron ore picked up in the streams. The smiths do not understand the art of tempering the metal so the spears are soft. A man can easily bend the blade over his knee. But the moran are able to throw their weapons with such skill that the spear will sometimes pass completely through an animal. If the spear strikes a bone, it will bend almost at right angles. The owner never straightens the blade until he returns to the village. The bent spear is proof positive that he was in at the kill, and so is highly prized.

While I was in the reserve, I also saw the Masai spear leopards. I consider this an even greater feat than killing lions. Although a leopard does not weigh more than two hundred pounds, he is far quicker and more aggressive than a lion. Leopards are cunning beasts and will lie quietly until you are almost on top of them. Then they will suddenly charge with the deadliest speed and determination. Also, leopards lie up in caves and other dark recesses, while lions prefer the open bush. A man crawling among boulders after a leopard is in an unenviable position.

I accompanied three spearmen who were after a leopard that had been killing their goats. Unlike the noble lions, a leopard will kill for the sheer lust of killing. This cat had left several dead goats behind him, never even bothering to eat their flesh. After considerable tracking, the moran finally marked the animal down in a narrow belt of high grass. If the cat had been a lion, a few stones would have brought him out charging or at least forced him to growl and show his hiding place. But a leopard is a wily brute and, although we threw a bushel of stones into the grass, he gave no sign. Unfortunately, I did not have my dogs with me so there was nothing for it but to drive the animal out.

With only three spearmen, I was able to use my gun without fear of hitting one of the men. I told the moran to spread out on either side of me and keep well back. I knew when the leopard came, he would come fast. I was sure that the men would not have time to use their spears, and I would have scarcely time for a quick snap shot at the cat as he sprang. I was underrating the moran, but I still did not realize their marvelous skill with their long, delicate blades.

We moved slowly through the waist-high grass, much as though beating for pheasants. The moran kept a few paces behind me, their shields held before them and their spears raised for the cast. We moved forward a foot at a time, stopping constantly to look around for the big cat. The strip of grass was not long, but this slow progress was nerve-racking, especially as we were all at a high point of tension.

Suddenly the leopard exploded out of the grass a yard or so in front of me and to my right. He made a great bound for me. Before I could get my rifle up, the moran on my right had transfixed the beast with his spear. The leopard had scarcely left the ground before the thin blade was through him. The spear hit the leopard between the neck and shoulders, pinning him to the ground. He lay there squirming and snarling, unable to free himself. Immediately the moran drew his simi and leaped forward to finish him off. I had great difficulty restraining him until I had time to put a bullet into the skewered animal and save a good skin from being slashed to ribbons.

When a moran is about to throw his spear, he takes up a position just like a shooting stance with his left foot slightly advanced for balance. When he throws, the whole weight of his body goes into the cast. The spear seems to shiver as its flies through the air. Most of the spears have a narrow ridge on either side of the blade and I believe this may cause the spear to rotate slightly in flight, somewhat like a rifle bullet. A moran is absolutely accurate with his spear up to twenty yards, even when throwing at a moving target.

At the end of three months, I started back to Nairobi with two oxcarts full of lion hides. In ninety days, I had shot eighty-eight lions and ten leopards—a record which I believe has never been approached and, I sincerely hope, will never be approached again. The natives had filled a hundred-weight drum with lion fat. I had a box full of lion "floating bones." These curved bones vary in size up to four inches and are found in the last shoulder muscle tissue. They are not attached to any other bones in the lion's body and apparently act as regulators, preventing shoulder rack when the lions make their great bounds. They are much in demand among the East Indians, who set them in gold and make ornaments out of them.

Only twenty of the lions I killed had really prime manes. The rest were either lionesses or had manes ruined by the thick brush. If I had been shooting only to get good trophies, I could have obtained more first-rate hides, but I was more interested in destroying cattle killers. Often these beasts had poor manes, for they were old or diseased, which may well be why they had turned to killing cows instead of their natural prey.

When the Masai heard I was leaving, they were greatly distressed. The elders of the tribe assembled and, after much jabbering, came to me with a proposition. They wanted to buy me from the Game Department. After due consideration, they had settled on five hundred cows as the price. As a good wife costs only three cows, I felt highly flattered.

We Jump into Fire

by STARR JENKINS

Forest fires are one of man's great natural enemies, consuming his woodland resources, his wildlife, taking human life and causing a state of soil erosion which in the long run is often more costly than the original fires. The government is always on the alert for such fires, striving to kill them in their infancy. One modern technique for controlling them uses smoke jumpers, trained air-borne firefighters who are also expert parachutists.

I'M UP IN THE HOT SUN CUTTING A TIN VALLEY DRAIN FOR THE new loft roof we're putting on when the call comes in. "Eight men on Yellowstone Park! One plane load. Cole, Jenkins, Samsel, Hall, Hellman, Bennett, Piper, Thol! Get your gear and let's go. Fire jump!"

It is 1:40 on a summer afternoon. The Forest Service Parachute Loft, at Missoula, Montana, is having a busy week. Fires are popping all over the region, and planes are shuttling men out to jump and back home to rest as long as daylight will let them. We're running out of jump rations and have to order truckloads of C rations from War Surplus, and the riggers are working overtime to get the chutes packed as those big white bundles of loose nylon come in. One fabulous Thursday within the last few weeks, sixty-four men jumped on fires scattered over the wild 25,000,000 acres that is the Forest Service's Region One. And a week later thirty-four men were dropped in twos and fours and sometimes dozens from the Gallatin Forest, down near Wyoming, to the Kaniksu, up in Washington State.

"All right, you guys, Shank will be spotting you, and you'll land at West Yellowstone to pick up the park man. He'll show you where the fires are. Four small ones they're supposed to be—little lightning strikes. He'll have maps for you and give you your best routes out. Now get that gear into the plane."

We've been loading a pickup with half a ton of equipment: Back-pack chutes in white canvas covers; chest-pack reserves, compact and olive drab with red rip rings; big bulky sacks that contain our canvas jump suits, helmets, letdown ropes and harnesses. Fire packs with rations, canteens, flashlights, fire tools—a shovel and a Pulaski, and a file for sharpening them—all wrapped tightly in new tarps and mounted on clack-board carriers for the hike out. Sleeping bags—big kapok ones this time instead of the tiny, efficient goose-down rolls we sometimes have along on fires. Five-gallon water cans—silvery square oblongs of steel that we know from experience smash as often as not on landing—tied in pairs to cargo chutes. Then lots of odds and ends, like a spotter's kit, map cases with compasses, climbing irons for retrieving chutes, extra signal streamers and a crosscut saw bolted between two boards, so that its sharp-set teeth won't be ruined on landing.

Outside, the plane is a sight to frighten the wits out of a modern air passenger. It is an ancient trimotor job, its engines uncowled, external control cables that slap its corrugated aluminum sides in the wind, truck tires on huge solid wheels, large square windows like a streetcar and the overall streamlining of a Model T. The wing is massive and fat, and the fuselage seems cut off square at the bottom to clear the turf of the airport. The wing-mounted engines have three dials each on the inboard side of one strut, so that the pilot, to check the engine's performance, must look through rain, darkness or fog and find those dials. This museum piece of an aircraft has been known variously as The Heap, The Tin Goose, The Flying Quonset Hut and Old Ironsides.

Yet we who are about to fly in her feel good inside, knowing that she is light for her size and can get in and out of canyons and postage-stamp airstrips. We know that the pudgy three-foot-thick wing gives her tremendous lift—she can glide and glide if the engines fail. We know that the high wing and big square windows give us visibility, and visibility is important in this business of jumping on fires. We know also that she, like her sister ships, has been kept up by her owner—Johnson Flying Service, contractor to the Forest Service in Region 1—to the best of man's ability.

Now the pickup roars out to where the plane is thundering in warm-up, and we transfer the load into her belly and climb in ourselves. Take-off time, two o'clock. We are scrambling around in the great jumble of equipment as the airport and the fairgrounds and Missoula drop away below. We swing past the big white M of Montana State University on the side of Sentinel Mountain and then settle on a southeast course bound for Yellowstone country.

Two hundred miles from Missoula to West Yellowstone. A two-hour flight in the slow-moving plane. We climb to clear the ridges that bristle up before us, and there always seem to be higher ones beyond. Getting cool as we climb. The door of the plane is off and back in Missoula, and a safety bar stretches across the middle of the doorway to keep guys from falling out.

Smitty, the chief rigger, is along for the ride and is telling us not to hit the ground in high country like Yellowstone or we'll break our ankles like he did on his last jump up there in '47.

"Hang up, whatever you do, because that ground at eight to ten thousand feet is just too hard to land on."

We think about it, the fact that air that high is a little thin for safe parachute jumping, and it sounds like good advice.

"Small reproduction, young trees—that's what you want to look for. Small reproduction for a soft landing. But hang up, whatever you do." Then Smitty goes up forward to gab with the pilot and fly the old Goose awhile, horsing it sloppily over the next pass till the pilot takes the controls away from him and adds a little throttle for good measure.

"Hey, that must be Georgetown Lake!"

"Yeah, there's Anaconda over there. See the big smelters?"

Eleven thousand feet to clear the highest range. It's cold up here in the air-conditioned plane. Seems funny; an hour ago I was sweating, out on that roof in Missoula's heat. Now I'm shaking with cold and pawing through the big white sacks to find mine and break out my high-collared canvas jump jacket.

Big stone mountains with jagged tops go by. I'd hate to jump into stuff like that. Don't worry, you won't have to. The Forest Service isn't out of its head.

The ranges are getting drier, less timbered, more and more just big humpy ridges of bareness separating the twisting river valleys with their bright-green irrigated fields. We're slanting down over Hebgen Reservoir, and my ears are popping in a glide. Must be close to West Yellowstone. We start suiting up—too early, but everybody starts, so I do too. Dumping our sacks out on the crowded floor of the plane, fighting our way into our girdles and jackets and jump pants with the big webbing crotch protection, and our quick-release harnesses.

"You can put on the chutes later, guys, after we pick up the park man."
So we don't fasten our legstraps, but sit comfortably half dressed for a jump, and I'm taking pictures with the 35-mm. camera that I take on all fires these days.

"Hey, there's West Yellowstone!"

We give the town a good buzz with two steeply banked circles to lose altitude, and West Yellowstone, with its railroad station and lodge and airstrip and stores, and two highways slicing away through the endless plateau of timber, is wheeling below us like a big, slow pinwheel. Then the pilot is down where he wants to be, and we skitter in over the clawing lodgepole to a landing on the dirt strip.

We taxi over for gas and to find the park man, and all pile out for a stretch. Hot again down here. Why did we suit up so soon? Smitty and Hank Shank are out hunting for the park man while we sprawl in the shade of the plane's protective wing. Soon they are back in a black Park Service car, and they pile out with two National Park rangers. These are dressed in snappy green-and-gray uniforms that we in the Forest Service think make them look just a little too much like tourist ushers. But forget the rivalry. We're working together this time. Besides, the Park Service pays for maintaining ten of our 150 jumpers at Missoula, so that the park people can call on the outfit for fire protection whenever Glacier or Yellowstone needs it.

"One of the fires has a ground crew on it already," Shank is saying. So Hellman and Bennett unsuit to stay here at West Yellowstone. Hellman fits his harness and reserve onto the ranger that's going to guide the remaining six of us to our three remote spot fires. Shank is reshuffling the jump list, and I want to jump last, so I can take pictures of the guys going out the door. But I don't say anything, and he puts me in the first pair—with Kermit Cole, of Missoula, a good boy.

Cole and I didn't find out till Saturday afternoon that the last four men of our eight-man load—Hellman, Bennett, Thol and Piper—all made dry runs on Yellowstone and went back to Missoula to jump on Friday and die in Helena National Forest. And I wanted to go last to take pictures!

We suit up again, this time chutes and all, and check one another out. Harnesses secure all around; safety catches of our quick-releases on; three little strings under the loop of each static line to secure the apex of the chute to its cover till our weight tears it loose. A dozen little details that have to be right. Our right legs look fat with a 100-foot coil of rope stuffed in the leg pocket. And my left leg is also bulging with a small strapped-on canvas sack of personal gear—soap, toothbrush, clean socks, underwear and dungarees. We'll be almost unrecognizable when we get our football helmets on with the wire-grill face masks buckled down. Six hundred dollars' worth of equipment. Seventy pounds of fabric and rope and metal per man, not counting the stuff that goes in by cargo chute.

The engines are thundering again, and the park man yells to the pilot, "Got plenty of gas? We've gotta fly fifty miles one direction, then seventy miles another, then forty miles back."

"Yeah, we've got plenty."

All aboard again except Hellman and Bennett—the last I ever see of them alive—and we're roaring down the runway in take-off. The park man has an armful of map scrolls, and he's having a tough time climbing forward over the jumble of men and equipment in the seatless tunnel-like plane. He's brought a feeble little water bag along to drop to one of his ground crews. A two-gallon job with about half a gallon in it—and that leaking out through the loose cap as the bag lies on its side by the door, jiggling with the plane vibration. Hate to be out on a mountain and have to depend on that. Our smashable square water cans don't look half bad alongside this park brand of water supply.

The ranger is a nice guy, and he's done this before. As soon as he knows that Cole and I are on the first stick, he gives me a little piece of a Yellowstone topographic map with some lakes and a couple of rivers on it and an inked-in X and some arrows running east and north from the X. The X is the fire, of course—as close as they can tell from the Mount Sheridan lookout, and incidentally about a half mile off, as we find out later—and the little river nearby is the headwaters of the Snake. The thick green line right below the X is the southern border of the park —less than three miles from the fire. So that'll put us 250 miles straight southeast of Missoula. The ranger is explaining that the arrows point the way out.

"Don't go back this way on the trail," he shouts above the roaring engines, "even though it looks closer, because that trail hasn't been maintained! Go north, the way it's marked, to the ranger station on Heart Lake!"

"Roger," I say, and put the map away and start taking pictures again. It's great being a second-year jumper and having a little experience to give you confidence. It's more fun knowing the little tricks that take your mind off yourself—enough to keep from sweating like Samsel, or Piper, there. Short Hall seems kinda quiet too. Oh, well, last year you sweated just as they're doing.

We're over the valley of the Snake, and the Grand Tetons rear their heads in jagged black majesty forty miles to the south. Hank Shank, our handsome spotter, is motioning me back to where Cole is sitting by the door, waiting. The ranger is up with Smitty and the pilot, looking for the smoke, and I take a last snapshot of Cole before tucking my camera inside my jacket and under my arm, where it hasn't smashed yet on a landing.

"There it is!" I say, poking Hank Shank and pointing to a smoke off the port quarter. The smoke isn't much, and Cole and I figure we really are going on a one-man fire, but two of us along for safety. Word is passed to the pilot, and we get down to business. Cole and I put on our gloves and helmets and snap our collars all the way up and get our static lines over our arms and into our right hands.

There's a wilderness of snags below us—miles and miles of dead-white tree skeletons marching over the hills as far as we can see individual trees. The old Heart Lake burn, the ranger said, in 1931, and still looking ugly after all those years.

Snags. One of the four dangerous horsemen facing the smoke jumper; the others being deep water, sheer rock and insecure tree hang-ups. Cole and Hank Shank and Smitty and I are all looking for a decent place to land in that tossing ocean of brittle dead bones; and we all simultaneously decide on the only spot available—a stand of thick young reproduction about a mile along the ridge from the smoke. I've got the map out again, getting oriented with the terrain, and 100 per cent of my attention is on the problem of getting to the ground safely. Ground altitude almost 8000 feet here. "Remember, hang up, whatever you do!" A little drift chute gives us the wind—something like twelve miles an hour—blowing east— and then comes the order to hook up.

Cole and I snap our static lines into the cable over the door and give ourselves a last fast check-out. Cole is going out first, so he kneels in the oval door and puts one foot out on the little step hanging there in space. I'm going out second, so I crouch behind him ready to follow him out as soon as the door is clear. Shank checks us over carefully again and briefs us once more on the spot we're to aim for and repeats what the ranger said about hiking out. Then we swing into the final pass, Shank jockeying the plane into position with hand signals to the pilot. The noisy engines die at last, and after one second of eerie silence, Cole gets the slap to go. He steps out easy and straight, wrapping his arms across the reserve on his chest, and the static line begins reeling the white silk off his back. I'm out with him a half second later, feeling the weird minutes-long moment of falling before the opening shock jolts me in the chest, and then that wonderful nylon flower is open above me with the sunlight streaming through.

No lines over—canopy functioning perfectly. Cole is far enough away. Okay, where is that spot? There it is, the lightest green of that patch of timber. Turn away from it and hold into the wind. I grab a guideline to spin myself west—for this is a steerable, slotted Forest Service chute I'm wearing—and haul down the front risers to gain forward speed.

I'm chinning myself on the risers to give myself eight or maybe ten miles an hour into the wind. The plane is circling around watching us closely and is completely out of my consciousness. Damned arms are getting tired, and I'm watching the ground through the V of my feet. I'm not going to make it; the wind's pushing me too far. And yet for some reason I'm not worried at all that I'm sailing beyond the thick safe stand of young trees toward the open, tree-dotted ridge.

Gettin' pretty close. Better stop planing and turn around. The slots start me around so I'll come in frontward, and I'm not quite around, and dumping both slots to kill forward speed, when the grassy ground with all the trees just out of reach rushes up into me with a thump. My feet are together from habit, and I flop into a loose sideways roll and come up tangled, unhurt and happy.

A soft landing, considering the 8000 feet. No harder than plenty of jumps I've made at 2000 or 3000. Well, that just shows what queer ducks parachutes are. The air must be perfect today.

Cole has also hit the ground 100 yards away from me and behind a couple of trees. We are both waving our signal streamers at the plane to show them we're all right, and then we're climbing out of our gear and sacking it up. The plane goes away to drop Samsel and Short on a smoke we can't see, beyond the Snake, and comes back ten minutes later to drop our cargo. We have piled our sacked-up gear in an orange-stream-ered cache on the ridge and watch our cargo come out of the plane a mile away through the forest of snags. The water-can chute hangs up in the top of a big snag right near the vague haze of smoke, and the silvery tin twirls and twinkles in the sun, making a perfect landmark for us to hike for.

Okay, Jenkins, the fun is over. Now begins the work you're getting paid for. The noise of the plane tapers away to nothing, and all of a sudden it's quiet on this mountain. Cole and I are two guys alone in the wilderness. Alone, many miles from the nearest road, in a sunny, dead forest.

"Damn Smitty for forgetting to drop the sleeping bags!"

"Oh, well," says Cole, full of good sense, as always, "that just means we'll work most of the night. And those kapoks are plenty big to pack out."

He's right, and I know it, and I don't mind working most of the night anyway to rake in a little overtime.

The fire is up on a knoll the way most lightning strikes and isn't going anywhere since the wind died down. It's really a tiny fire—at the size the Forest Service likes to catch them—not covering 100 square feet—in five or six little spots, where the lightning split off chunks of a snag and scattered them, burning, out on the grass. The stump of the snag is twenty feet high and burning all the way up and down inside, and dropping it will be our biggest single job in putting out this fire.

We're a little short on water because when we felled the snag that held our water can way up in the air, the can smashed to tinfoil and the water wetted up the ground good. Besides that, one of the canteens on the fire packs had a leak and is dry, so we have half a gallon from the other canteen to last us till we hike down to the Snake tomorrow sometime. Not that we'll need any more than that half gallon. But knowing that's all we've got is making us thirsty already.

It's been a big job falling a snag three feet through at the butt with a Pulaski just to get down the cargo chute—a Pulaski being a heavy-headed ax with an adz blade on the back. Cole and I have taken turns and are really warmed up by the time she sways and cracks and comes crashing down among the jumble of deadfalls around us.

We collect the gear and eat supper, hitting the liquid canned stuff first to save our water, and then settle down for a night of work. The tall butt of the burning snag comes down first and doubles the spread of the fire by taking an unexpected roll. We cool the burning logs by turning them warm side up and scraping the fire out of them with the adz blades of the Pulaskis. We break the big embers up into little ones and spread out the hot spots to cool and burn out. Then we trail each little spot of burn, scraping a shallow shovel-width trench around it down to fireproof mineral earth.

"Separate the fuel from the fire"—the old simplicity-itself fire-fighting method of the Forest Service. It doesn't take water or chemicals or bombs or pumps or hoses, though all those things may help if available. All it takes in essence is men, enough men with tools, and lots of sweat and backbending and shiny places on the insides of thumbs. And half-decent luck in regard to wind. But like any fire-fighting method, it works best at night, when everything cools down. . . .

It's midnight and cold, and the stars are so bright you can almost see by 'em, and the northern lights are a faint gray glow in the sky that looks like dawn coming up in the wrong place. Cole and I are sitting around patrolling our little line and taking turns going up to a muddy sump of a spring we found to fill two water bags with the stagnant stuff and pour it on what spots are still glowing red in the darkness. There's not much smoke drifting up through the cones of light from our head-lamp flashlights any more. The night is still and without wind. And the fire is just about dead.

So we decide to stretch out for a couple of hours, wrapping up in the tarps from the fire packs and the cargo chutes to keep warm. Not as cold as I'd expected it to be, and two hours of good shut-eye really pick me up. *Don't forget to put that on the time report, that we slept for two hours.*

Up again at two for a long cold morning of mop-up. We douse every square foot of the burn with undrinkable water and go over the charred ground with our gloves off, feeling for warm spots. It seems I'm spending half the night slogging back and forth to the shallow sump, filling the water bags tediously with a skillet, and climbing endlessly over the tangled maze of fallen snags back to the fire.

It's dawn and beautiful, and there's Mount Sheridan to the north and the valley of the Snake below us, and we're filthy and tired and unshaven, and the fire is dead. We eat breakfast, griping again because there's too much chocolate and ham in these jump rations, and the last of our canned fruit and juice goes, and all but a couple of swallows of water. Oh, well, there's a whole river of it right down there. We'll make out all right.

We know we'll have to watch the burn through at least two o'clock this afternoon to make sure that somewhere in that black wet mess of charcoal we haven't missed one spark, because the heat of the afternoon will show smoke if there's going to be any. So we figure we'll use this half day to start packing out. Chutes, suits, fire packs and tools will make a good muleload for each of us. And as we have time to burn, we might as well make two trips.

It's a mile back along the ridge to our jump gear, and then three miles down to the river trail—all through the maddening tangle of downed snags that blankets this country. About 80 per cent of the deadfalls lie with their tops to the east, telling us mutely that the winds roar through this saddle from the west most of the time. We pack down our jump gear— two big, heavy white sacks apiece lashed to a clackboard—and it's treacherous footing downhill over the never-ending snags. Five or six elk are moving down ahead of us, keeping a good half mile away and wondering what men are doing prowling around their domain. It's marshy grassland in the bottoms, with fresh elk wallows and lots of flies, and a flock of black-headed Canada geese takes off ahonking from the Snake as we trudge into sight.

A soft little rain starts to fall, and we know the fire is out for good—even though we'll check it again to make sure when we go back after the rations and fire tools. We get squared away with our map, discovering the half-mile error in the original fire location from the layout of the trail with the river; and it's good to have a full canteen again.

Six o'clock, Thursday evening. The sunlight is bright and warm, and I've just taken a bath in a creek because the mighty Snake here is too shallow to get under water in. Cole is busy eating supper—something I shall later regret not doing—and we've found, from horse tracks and shouting up and down the valley, what the dope is on the packer who is to lug this load the rest of the way out on packsaddles. The packer has been up here looking for us and has gone beyond where we have come out on the trail. So we quit looking for him, pile everything beside the trail, barber-pole a tree with streamers, so he can't miss, and start hiking for the ranger station up on Heart Lake.

Our map shows it to be six miles away. With all the twists and turns of the trail it turns out to be twelve. My boots are stretched and too big, and there's a place on my heel that makes a little squeaking sound with every step as it rubs on the inside of the boot.

Pretty soon it's dark and we wonder if we are on the right trail, and the moon comes up in time to help out Cole's waning flashlight. On a needlessly empty stomach and with one bad foot, I am a poor partner for a strong hiker like Cole, and he is constantly having to stop and wait for me. Another herd of elk is moving ahead of us in the darkness, crashing away intermittently when the tortured bawling of their scouts warns them of our persistent approach. The black peak of Mount Sheridan seems an eternity in creeping down to our left, and then at midnight we are finally marching along the shore of Heart Lake, feeling triumphantly near to rest. Suddenly we get a jolt, for there, a few hundred yards away, is a tall plume of smoke climbing into the moonlit sky. *Another fire.* But the fear quickly evaporates as a stink of sulphur drifts over us. *A hot spring. That isn't smoke; that's steam. You're still in Yellowstone, remember?*

The ranger station is nothing more than what the Forest Service calls a guard station—just a cabin that may or may not be manned during the summer, the fire season. This one is manned by the packer who is out looking for us, and is well stocked with provisions. It looks beautiful there in the moonlight on the sandy north shore of the lake, and we find the break-in window in the back with no strain. The lake is so clean and remote from people that a bucket dipped out of it is drinking water—a weird contrast to the highway cluttered with people and monoxide fumes just across the mountains.

A quick chow to stifle my gnawing, and the blankets close over us in sleep. . . .

"Hey, Kerm, did you shave back there in the cabin?" Cole is hiking ahead of me on the trail out from Heart Lake to the roadhead, and I can't see his face from where I'm walking.

"Hell, no! I wouldn't shave in cold water for all of Yellowstone National Park."

As if smarting under the insult, Yellowstone National Park produces, 100 yards farther up the trail, plenty of hot running water for all our needs. We squat on a steaming lime flat among countless bubbling hot springs for our first shave in three days. The water is too hot to be used for anything except dipping a washrag, but we make out. And we find the creek nearby has all degrees of mixtures from boiling to cold, as the surface water mixes with that from underground.

I get a scare a little later on when I slip shin-deep into some warm volcanic muck while crossing another open flat. It's not pleasant thinking of the people who have died of accidental scalding in Yellowstone's strange, naturally hot waters. But the mud goes to my boot tops and no farther, and I churn loose like a shying horse. The mud on my boots dries to white crust as we hike on out.

A truck meets us at the road five miles farther on, and after we make our fire report at the South Gate, the Park Service sends us on a personally conducted tour of the park, the first leg of our long ground trip home. We're stuck in Mammoth Village, on the north edge of the park, that evening because we can't get a train out of Livingston, Montana, till morning; and we kill time at a dance and a touristy wildlife lecture. Cole and I sit in the back row and grin when the ranger tells how nine forest fires are going in the park right now, and how they've called in extra crews and planes and even smoke jumpers.

All next day we ride the train back to Missoula and gripe because it's Saturday and we're traveling on our own time. But then, in the station at Missoula, we pick up a red-headlined paper that tells us twelve of our buddies were burned to death yesterday afternoon down in the Helena. It's hard to believe that Dave Navon, my best friend in this outfit, won't ever be back to get that laughing post card I sent him from Old Faithful. And Cole and I are shocked and hollow and hungry to know why, and we feel powerful lucky to have gone on our Yellowstone jump.

Rocket Shoot at White Sands

by JONATHAN NORTON LEONARD

Man, having released the atom's energy and flown much faster than the speed of sound, stands on the edge of his planet—the latter now seemingly small and confining—and peers into interplanetary space. In the last few years what had seemed only a wild dream has become a strategy and a determination, and now it is no longer dubious activity for scientists of august reputation to speak of space stations and flights to the moon as in the realm of probability. But before such visions can become actuality much must be known of the nature and habits of rockets, which the United States government is studying assiduously. Here Jonathan Leonard, on a visit to a great rocket installation, gives us a glimpse into this fabulous frontier activity.

A ROCKET SHOOT AT WHITE SANDS PROVING GROUND IS MORE than interesting, more than beautiful, more than exciting. It is inspiring in a way that is equaled by few sights on earth.

Behind the austere buildings of the military post rise the spectacular Organ Mountains of New Mexico, with a fringe of dark pine trees climbing to their highest ridges. An uninhabited wilderness presses from all sides upon this isolated outpost of technological man. Jack rabbits bounce among the cactus and yucca. Deer dance down from the mountains at night to browse on the post's garbage, and sometimes mountain lions follow to browse on the deer.

In front, for forty miles, sweeps the gray-green desert of the Tularosa Basin. Dust devils swirl across it like yellow tornadoes, and sometimes great sand storms blot out the sun. But much of the time the air is as clear as a vacuum, showing a rim of distant mountains around the flat desert floor. A person standing in the center beyond where the rockets fly can easily imagine himself in one of the Moon's great craters with the jagged rampart circling the horizon.

The works of man seen from a distance look small in this setting, but some of them are startling when seen from close by. On a steep mountain slope perches a massive concrete structure that has the soaring aloofness of a Tibetan monastery. This is a test-stand where the biggest rocket motors are put through their flaming paces. It really looks like an adjunct for a flight to the Moon.

Far out on the desert stands an even weirder structure—a peaked concrete igloo with walls and roof as solid as the stone of a pyramid. This "blockhouse" has narrow slits for windows with glass many inches thick. Its strength is a prudent precaution against the possibility that a rebellious rocket may turn on its creators and rend them to smoking shreds.

Near this modern donjon keep gather strange auxiliaries: tomblike underground storage places for violent chemical fuels; lacy steelwork towers; a forest of poles and a spiderweb of wires. The desert for miles around is dotted with grotesque instruments. Radars sweep the sky with their pulsed electronic beams. The wide glassy eyes of cameras and theodolites stare at the launching site. Far off on the mountain rim great telescopes with forty-inch mirrors wait to follow the rockets on their flights into space.

There are ghosts in this desert too. The hollows between the mesquite hummocks close to the launching site are sprinkled with fragments of brilliantly painted pottery. Long ago, when the Tularosa Basin was a fertile valley, it supported a dense population of Indians, whose burial grounds and building foundations can still be traced among the thorny scrub.

No one knows what happened to these ancient people. Perhaps the climate grew drier; perhaps some river changed its course or sank into the sand. At any rate they are gone. They lacked the knowledge and resource-fulness to deal with such changes of environment. They left their dead and their pottery shards and the flint fragments of their poor, weak weapons. Amateur archaeologists from the Proving Ground sometimes dig in the sand close by the launching site and find their crouched skeletons, each with a painted pot inverted over its skull.

II

Space enthusiasts who speak lightly about flights to the Moon or Mars should be privileged to see what happens at White Sands. It would give them a sobering glimpse of difficulties ahead. The rockets that roar into the sky above the New Mexico desert are primitive things compared with what real space vehicles must be. They rise only a few hundred miles at most, and their speed is hardly one-tenth of the speed that would be needed to blast them free of the earth. They carry no human crews, and they all crash to utter ruin.

But these crude "beasts" (some rocket-men call them "beasts"; others call them "birds") are the best that space-striving man has to offer at present. To White Sands come the highest products of technological achievement: strange metals with treated surfaces to resist the white-hot scour of racing gases; electronic brains packed with transistors or tiny vacuum tubes and finished as precisely as microscope lenses; pumps no bigger than coffee cups that can push corrosive fuels as fast as the massive flow of irrigation canals.

Marching into White Sands comes a continuous parade of new and incredible instruments—those thousands of specialized senses with which man must augment the senses built into his body. They take their stations in the central laboratories, in the blockhouse, or in solid little huts dotted over the desert. There they get busily to work flashing their impressions on fast-flowing strips of photographic film or scribbling with delicate pens on streams of paper like quick-fingered stenographers writing a strange shorthand.

The men who govern the instruments are as skilled as they. To White Sands come top experts on electronics, optics, solid state physics, chemistry, metallurgy, mathematics, and astronomy. Some of them stay for years; others stay only long enough to make specific contributions to this remote deposit of technical virtuosity.

What these experts do is mostly secret. White Sands, officially, is an Army Ordnance center for the development and testing of new weapons —intelligent and terrible weapons. Some of them are mechanical falcons that scream into the air at a human command and run down and destroy anything flying there. Others are avenging angels designed to fly over continents, steering by the stars, and strike down offending cities in the flash of a nuclear explosion.

The men of White Sands do not talk lightly about these fearful projects. They know that they are necessary and will always be necessary so long as mankind is committed to a course of mutual destruction. But when the quiet of night has crept over the desert and the brilliant, many-colored stars flash in the clear sky, the men of White Sands like to turn their thoughts, half apologetically, toward a more peaceful project—the conquest and occupation of the vacuum above their heads.

Even the enlisted men—some of them learned GIs who play hot chess in the crowded barracks and chat in the chow lines about quantum mechanics—realize that they are working at the closest place on earth to space. They appreciate both the accomplishments of man on his march toward space and the enormous difficulties that still lie in his path. They know, for instance, that rockets are as temperamental as the graceful, smooth-flanked dancers that they so strangely resemble.

In the early days when Americans were first learning to fly captured German V-2 rockets, one of these flaming monsters rose from the launching site with a mutinous plot in its gyroscopic brain. Instead of rising vertically, as a good rocket should, it veered toward the south. Its launchers—both Americans and Germans—stared after it helplessly. There was nothing that they could do.

Across the Rio Grande fifty miles away, the city of Juarez, Mexico, was having a fiesta. Its wide garish main street at the end of the bridge from El Paso was packed with a gay crowd. Bands were playing, and fireworks cracked overhead. Slanting down from the north at three thousand miles per hour came the rebellious V-2. It shot across the crowd and buried itself with a vast concussion in a hillside cemetery just outside the celebrating city.

The Mexicans rather enjoyed this super-firework; they are friends of death when it comes in heroic form. But the authorities at White Sands are still acutely conscious of what that V-2 might have done if its rebellious brain had chosen a slightly different course.

One result of this international incident, which almost produced a catastrophe, was an elaborate safety system. Another was the construction of the massive blockhouse. Not long after it was completed, a second V-2 rebelled, made a great loop in the air and screamed within six hundred feet of it, trailing its tail of flame.

The captured V-2s were tamed at last, but all rockets, especially the new ones, contain within them the seeds of possible disaster. To make sure that they will perform as expected, they are sometimes given static tests while held securely to the ground. Even this sort of test, intended to forestall disaster, may go wrong in spectacular ways.

Not long ago, one of the biggest rockets was being tested statically. It stood on its tail, screaming, while floods of flame and smoke shot out of its shackled motor. Then it began to struggle fiercely like a captive wild animal suddenly conscious of its bonds. The hold-downs broke. The rocket soared upward and hid behind the blue sky.

A panicky pulse of alarm swept across White Sands. The many-eyed net of instruments had not been watching, but the radars sprang to attention in seconds and swept the echoing sky. Telescopes groped for the fugitive rocket. Radio beams raced after it like lariats flung into space. No one knew where it had gone, and it had enough range at worst to fall as far north as Santa Fe or as far south as Chihuahua in Mexico.

The men of White Sands will give few details about the rocket that got away. They will not tell—or perhaps they do not know—whether their electronic lariats caught it and controlled it before it climbed out of the atmosphere. At any rate it fell in an uninhabited spot and did not dig its great crater in the plaza of Santa Fe.

There have been lesser disasters too, a multitude of them, and there will be more. White Sands is an outpost on the lawless frontier of technology. Each new rocket is acrawl with vindictive "bugs" that conspire to destroy it and its creators too. To eliminate these bugs every rocket part, even the tiniest of them, must be rigorously tested over and over.

The first of the testing is done in factories where the parts are made. They are strained and twisted, heated and cooled—even such inconsequential trifles as bolts and sealing rings. Then they are assembled into larger units and tested more elaborately. The rockets' electronic brains are put through intelligence tests. The aerodynamic performance of their fins and control surfaces is studied minutely in wind tunnels.

Most spectacular are the tests of the motors, which are done in desolate well-fenced places far from protesting neighbors. Even well away from the test-stands, these sites have an oppressive feeling of tense, pessimistic caution. Danger signs scream their warnings in loud colors. Visitors are searched for matches and cigarette lighters. Walls of buildings are apt to be many feet thick. If liquid oxygen is one of the chemicals used in the motors, it bubbles coldly and silently in gigantic Thermos bottles buried in concrete. Pipes carry upward the oxygen vapor, which drifts away from their tips in thin violet plumes.

The rocket motors themselves are surprisingly small. One type, which has power enough to drive several ocean liners, is a graceless pinch-waisted thing made of sheet metal and about as big as two bushel baskets. Massive steel work holds it to a frame, and a tangle of pipes and tubes leads into its bulbous head.

The men who run the test sit at a control panel behind many feet of concrete, and ranks of instruments stand at attention to record the motor's performance. Spectators, if any have been admitted, are kept at a good distance. If wise, they have wads of cotton stuffed into their ears.

Crouching close to the motor's tailpipe are television cameras which serve as expendable spectators, flashing their impressions to screens in the control room. If something goes wrong with the test, these non-human observers may die. Often they do. At one of the test sites the crumpled remains of the camera-casualties are buried in a special grave-yard where little white crosses commemorate their uncomplaining self-sacrifice.

To watch the test of a rocket motor is a shattering experience. Without the slightest warning, an enormous flame juts out of the tail pipe. The eyes cringe from its light, and a wave of heat beats against the skin. An indescribable bellowing sound pokes like an ice pick into cotton-stuffed ears. Even worse than the bellowing is a high-pitched waspish scream. This is the faintly audible edge of the motor's ultrasonic sound. It tears at the heart and groin and raises knife-edged vibrations echoing inside the skull.

But the screaming, bellowing flame is a beautiful thing. When certain fuels are used it is so bright that it sears the eyes through filters that shut out the sunlight. With other fuels the flame is a delicate, transparent violet with a line of diamond-shaped plates that look like gold leaf trembling in its center. These burnished "leaves" are caused by shock waves zigzagging through the flame. When the fuel is shut off, they chase one another into the motor like rabbits running down a hole.

The flame of one experimental fuel, a boron hydride, is brilliant green, and it fades into billows of purplish smoke. No Chinese dragon flying through the air was ever arrayed in colors as gay as these.

In some test setups the flame points horizontally; its gases scour the ground, leaving hot charred rocks where their tongue has licked. Some-times the flame is directed downward against a steel plate cooled from above and below by floods of cold water. If the plate were made of con-crete, as in some earlier tests, it would be destroyed by the flame, many inches of its substance clawed into gravel and dust.

The men who know about guided missiles will not say how many tests have been successful, certifying a rocket motor for future use in the sky. This is one of those dull statistics that have great military value. But they admit that in most cases the tests are still necessary, even at the risk of damaging a motor. The art of making rocket motors has not reached a point where all the pinch-waisted monsters can be expected to perform without practice.

Another kind of testing is done in quiet rooms. One of these simulated proving grounds is on Manhattan Island in a building which looks, except for the watchful guards outside its door, like a small factory making toys or dresses. Another is in the dry hills behind Pasadena, California. There are no screaming motors in these sheltered places and no other parts of a rocket. Instead, ranged around the walls, are panels of gleaming black plastic with row upon row of switches and dials and little winking red lights. These are the stolid impersonal faces of electronic computers whose brains of metal and glass can solve in fractions of a second problems that would employ for a lifetime a task force of mathematicians.

Only skilled mathematicians can get much of a thrill out of these flights-by-computer, but men with the necessary knowledge watch their outcome as tensely as if they were at White Sands. In preparation for the flight they have given the computer all the necessary data about the imaginary rocket that its brain contains. Dials are set to represent external factors such as gravitation and air resistance. When the machine is fully briefed, it knows what to expect from every part of the imaginary rocket, except a single crucial part that has not been tested yet.

The mathematicians know that this new part—perhaps a control surface—can have only a certain range of effects on the rocket's flight. They give the computer a formula that represents one extreme of this range. Then they set the machine to thinking. A blizzard of electronic impulses crisscrosses through its brain, and out come figures that tell how the simulated rocket has performed in its imaginary flight.

Sometimes the flight is a failure. Sometimes it is a disaster. The simulated rocket that exists only in the computer's electronic mind may shake itself to pieces or turn back in the air to crash upon a nonexistent desert.

Then comes another flight with the part to be tested set in a slightly different way. The success of this test, too, is written down in the books. At last after many mathematical flights, the behavior of the new component is as well understood as if twenty or thirty great rockets, each costing a quarter of a million dollars, had been flown into space to crash on the real wasteland of New Mexico.

III

On the day of a major shoot at White Sands the whole great apparatus spreading over the desert for hundreds of miles springs into tense activity. From the metal throats of invisible loud-speakers comes a slow throbbing sound. This is a half-second beat that binds all activities to the grid of time. Jeeps and trucks scurry across the desert, raising feathers of dust. The non-human eyes of the radars swing toward the launching site, where men swarm over the steel framework that surrounds the beautiful shape of the readied rocket.

Some of the rocket's attendants are muffled from head to foot, like Arabian women, in enveloping plastic garments to protect their skins from corrosive chemicals. Others wear earphones or carry walkie-talkie radios. They pump the rocket full of fuel, quiz its electronic brains, probe its valves and pumps with sensitive instruments. They are like midget masseurs grooming a tall and graceful ballerina for her first and last appearance on the stage of a great auditorium.

Inside the massive blockhouse, which feels part like a mine, part like a radio station, part like the bridge of a battleship going into action, is a hum of tense activity and purposeful running-around. Each man has a special duty, usually connected in some electronic way with the web of instruments spread over the desert. Squawking voices speak tersely with metallic tongues; vivid green lines zigzag across the faces of oscilloscopes.

On a long control panel under a slit window glows a line of little red lights. When one of them goes out, it means that some circuit is completed, some instrument far away has declared itself alert and ready. The half-second beat throbs on like a steady pulse.

Then a solemn, echoing voice comes over the loud-speaker. It says, "Zero minus thirty minutes."

This means that thirty minutes remain before the hour, the minute, and the second when the rocket will fly. The men in the blockhouse, climbing over the rocket or watching across the desert become a little more tense. Their blood runs a little faster. The moment is coming.

The little red lights on the control panel wink out one by one. Voices report trouble, then trouble overcome. "Zero minus twenty minutes," chants the loud-speaker.

Trucks and jeeps loaded with men dart away from the danger area. Gates are being closed; chains are being drawn taut across distant highways. The men on the framework around the rocket are administering to it a kind of extreme unction. They check its intricate instruments for the last time and close the flush-fitting doors that cover access ports. They climb down reluctantly, and the steel framework is wheeled away, revealing the graceful shape of the doomed rocket. At this moment of unveiling, it looks like the most beautiful thing that has ever been built by man.

"Zero minus ten minutes," chants the loud-speaker.

Now a solemn hush spreads across the desert. No men are in sight.

They have all fled away or gone inside the blockhouse like ants going underground ahead of an approaching shower. Only a few red lights still show on the control panel. Scientists who have worked for years on the rocket's burden of instruments are muttering over and over their profane technological prayers. Some of them finger incongruous rabbits' feet; some keep their fingers crossed like children in primary school.

"Zero minus one minute," chants the loud-speaker.

Now the impersonal voice at the unseen microphone shares the growing excitement. "Zero minus forty-five seconds," it chants in a higher key. Then, "Zero minus thirty seconds."

The last of the little red lights is gone from the control panel, leaving nothing between the rocket and its moment of glory. It stands naked and alone like a human sacrifice watched by a thousand priests. A plume of brilliant red smoke spurts from the ground beside it and drifts across the desert. This is a final visual warning to men, instruments, and airplanes with no electronic ears.

"Zero minus five seconds," chants the loud-speaker. Now its words come faster. "Four—three—two—one—ZERO!"

In the tense, hushed blockhouse, the firing officer throws a switch. A stab of yellow flame and a dense white cloud of smoke burst from the tail of the rocket, and a screaming roar rolls across the desert. The rocket rises slowly at first as if an invisible hoist were drawing it upward. It wobbles a little, standing on its tail of flame. Then it gains confidence, gathers speed, and shoots up toward space like a bellowing arrow. In a few seconds it is gone, leaving only a trail of smoke like a chalk mark against the blue sky.

For human eyes the flight is over, but instrument eyes are watching. The dish antennas of distant radars turn upward after the rocket. Cameras and theodolites crane upward their jointed necks. Down from the rocket, over a sheaf of radio channels, comes a flood of information for instruments below to gather and cherish.

The nose of the rocket is packed with delicate, specialized senses. They feel the air as it rushes past, measuring its temperature, its density, its motion. Spectrographs analyze the sunlight, which grows brighter as altitude increases. Geiger-tubes count the cosmic-ray particles striking fiercely out of space, and photon-counters feel for X-rays flooding out of the sun.

Some of their findings are recorded on photographic films that wind into steel cylinders that are strong enough to survive the final crash of the rocket. Other findings are radioed to earth, where skilled instrument-stenographers take them down on paper as swiftly waving lines.

Sometimes the information comes in the form of audible notes that sound for all the world like a small child playing a piano. The pitch of each note varies with the instruments' readings and can be analyzed by appropriate devices. This eerie music, which is to be inscribed on magnetic tape, tells the whole tale of the rocket's effort, of its triumph above the atmosphere, and of its ultimate death.

While the rocket is waiting on its launching platform, the singing instruments in its nose play a gentle, monotonous tune. Some of the tones are continuous, like the drones of a bagpipe. Others are "sampled" periodically so that they sound like piano notes. As the rocket rises, some of the tones remain steady; others vary in pitch in a strange modernistic way. The tinkling tune continues, but it becomes irregular, as if the child that is touching the keys were growing tired or frightened. As the rocket roars up toward space, it sends down groaning, quavering sounds. These record vibration, its struggle with the atmosphere. Long, low wails mean that the rocket is yawing or rolling. The tinkling music of the sampled tones plays on bravely above this background of discord, but the child at the piano sounds desperate now. The rocket is close to the peak of its speeds and struggling fiercely against the buffeting air.

As the rocket soars out of the atmosphere, the discords gradually die away. It is moving through space now, serene as an asteroid cruising around the sun, and the child at the piano plays his tinkling tune with confidence and skill.

His moment of peace in space does not last for long. The rocket reaches the top of its flight and then turns downward, tumbling over and over, toward the fringe of the atmosphere. When the air strikes it, the rocket straightens out, nose down, and points toward the spot on the desert where it will die. Vibration and yaw build up again, and discordant sounds obscure the tinkling tune. Louder and louder they grow as the rocket darts toward earth.

Radars and telescopes miles below slant downward gradually as the rocket falls. They are judging coldly just where its death will occur. The child at the piano continues his tinkling tune, now almost blotted out by warning screams from the instruments. The hard, unyielding earth rushes upward at three thousand miles per hour.

Then, without warning, the music stops. The rocket has come to its death on the desert, digging a great hole. Nothing is left but crumpled metal and a few photographic films inscribed with precious information. The child at the piano will never play another tune.

New York to Paris

by CHARLES A. LINDBERGH

In the early morning hours of May 20, 1927, Charles Augustus Lindbergh took off from Roosevelt Field, N. Y., on what was to become perhaps the most famous single flight of all time—and was certainly the outstanding flight up to that time. Flying alone via Newfoundland, Ireland and England, he landed his plane, The Spirit of St. Louis, at Paris the next day, having covered an estimated distance of 3,600 miles in 33½ hours. This leap into the void in a plane which by current standards is considered flimsy was man's challenge of the ocean, time and weather. Lindbergh had in his favor youth (he was born in 1902), courage and above all flying experience. Recently he has published a detailed account of his flight, but for sincerity, simplicity and candor the early account, written in 1927, which follows, is unsurpassed.

A T NEW YORK WE CHECKED OVER THE PLANE, ENGINE AND instruments, which required several short flights over the field.

When the plane was completely inspected and ready for the trans-Atlantic flight, there were dense fogs reported along the coast and over Nova Scotia and Newfoundland, in addition to a storm area over the North Atlantic.

On the morning of May 19th, a light rain was falling and the sky was overcast. Weather reports from land stations and ships along the great circle course were unfavorable and there was apparently no prospect of taking off for Paris for several days at least. In the morning I visited the Wright plant at Paterson, New Jersey, and had planned to attend a theatre performance in New York that evening. But at about six o'clock

338

I received a special report from the New York Weather Bureau. A high pressure area was over the entire North Atlantic and the low pressure over Nova Scotia and Newfoundland was receding. It was apparent that the prospects of the fog clearing up were as good as I might expect for some time to come. The North Atlantic should be clear with only local storms on the coast of Europe. The moon had just passed full and the percentage of days with fog over Newfoundland and the Grand Banks was increasing so that there seemed to be no advantage in waiting longer.

We went to Curtiss Field as quickly as possible and made arrangements for the barograph to be sealed and installed, and for the plane to be serviced and checked.

We decided partially to fill the fuel tanks in the hangar before towing the ship on a truck to Roosevelt Field, which adjoins Curtiss on the east, where the servicing would be completed.

I left the responsibility for conditioning the plane in the hands of the men on the field while I went into the hotel for about two and one-half hours of rest; but at the hotel there were several more details which had to be completed and I was unable to get any sleep that night.

I returned to the field before daybreak on the morning of the twentieth. A light rain was falling which continued until almost dawn; consequently we did not move the ship to Roosevelt Field until much later than we had planned, and the take-off was delayed from daybreak until nearly eight o'clock.

At dawn the shower had passed, although the sky was overcast, and occasionally there would be some slight precipitation. The tail of the plane was lashed to a truck and escorted by a number of motorcycle police. The slow trip from Curtiss to Roosevelt was begun.

The ship was placed at the extreme west end of the field heading along the east and west runway, and the final fueling commenced.

About 7:40 A.M. the motor was started and at 7:52 I took off on the flight for Paris.

The field was a little soft due to the rain during the night and the heavily loaded plane gathered speed very slowly. After passing the halfway mark, however, it was apparent that I would be able to clear the obstructions at the end. I passed over a tractor by about fifteen feet and a telephone line by about twenty, with a fair reserve of flying speed. I believe that the ship would have taken off from a hard field with at least five hundred pounds more weight.

I turned slightly to the right to avoid some high trees on a hill directly ahead, but by the time I had gone a few hundred yards I had sufficient altitude to clear all obstructions and throttled the engine down to 1750 R.P.M. I took up a compass course at once and soon reached Long Island Sound where the Curtiss Oriole with its photographer, which had been escorting me, turned back.

The haze soon cleared and from Cape Cod through the southern half of Nova Scotia the weather and visibility were excellent. I was flying very low, sometimes as close as ten feet from the trees and water.

On the three hundred mile stretch of water between Cape Cod and Novia Scotia I passed within view of numerous fishing vessels.

The northern part of Nova Scotia contained a number of storm areas and several times I flew through cloudbursts.

As I neared the northern coast, snow appeared in patches on the ground and far to the eastward the coastline was covered with fog.

For many miles between Nova Scotia and Newfoundland the ocean was covered with caked ice but as I approached the coast the ice disappeared entirely and I saw several ships in this area.

I had taken up a course for St. Johns, which is south of the great Circle from New York to Paris, so that there would be no question of the fact that I had passed Newfoundland in case I was forced down in the North Atlantic.

I passed over numerous icebergs after leaving St. Johns, but saw no ships except near the coast.

Darkness set in about 8:15 and a thin, low fog formed over the sea through which the white bergs showed up with surprising clearness. This fog became thicker and increased in height until within two hours I was just skimming the top of storm clouds at about ten thousand feet. Even at this altitude there was a thick haze through which only the stars directly overhead could be seen.

There was no moon and it was very dark. The tops of some of the storm clouds were several thousand feet above me and at one time, when I attempted to fly through one of the larger clouds, sleet started to collect on the plane and I was forced to turn around and get back into clear air immediately and then fly around any clouds which I could not get over.

The moon appeared on the horizon after about two hours of darkness; then the flying was much less complicated.

Dawn came at about 1 A.M. New York time and the temperature had risen until there was practically no remaining danger of sleet.

Shortly after sunrise the clouds became more broken although some of them were far above me and it was often necessary to fly through them, navigating by instruments only.

As the sun became higher, holes appeared in the fog. Through one the open water was visible, and I dropped down until less than a hundred feet above the waves. There was a strong wind blowing from the northwest and the ocean was covered with white caps.

After a few miles of fairly clear weather the ceiling lowered to zero and for nearly two hours I flew entirely blind through the fog at an altitude of about 1500 feet. Then the fog raised and the water was visible again.

On several more occasions it was necessary to fly by instrument for short periods; then the fog broke up into patches. These patches took on forms of every description. Numerous shorelines appeared, with trees perfectly outlined against the horizon. In fact, the mirages were so natural that, had I not been in mid-Atlantic and known that no land existed along my route, I would have taken them to be actual islands.

As the fog cleared I dropped down closer to the water, sometimes flying within ten feet of the waves and seldom higher than two hundred.

There is a cushion of air close to the ground or water through which a plane flies with less effort than when at a higher altitude, and for hours at a time I took advantage of this factor.

Also, it was less difficult to determine the wind drift near the water. During the entire flight the wind was strong enough to produce white caps on the waves. When one of these formed, the foam would be blown off, showing the wind's direction and approximate velocity. This foam remained on the water long enough for me to obtain a general idea of my drift.

During the day I saw a number of porpoises and a few birds but no ships, although I understand that two different boats reported me passing over.

The first indication of my approach to the European Coast was a small fishing boat which I first noticed a few miles ahead and slightly to the south of my course. There were several of these fishing boats grouped within a few miles of each other.

I flew over the first boat without seeing any signs of life. As I circled over the second, however, a man's face appeared, looking out of the cabin window.

I have carried on short conversations with people on the ground by flying low with throttled engine, shouting a question, and receiving the answer by some signal. When I saw this fisherman I decided to try to get him to point towards land. I had no sooner made the decision than the futility of the effort became apparent. In all likelihood he could not speak English, and even if he could he would undoubtedly be far too astounded to answer. However, I circled again and closing the throttle as the plane passed within a few feet of the boat I shouted, "Which way is Ireland?" Of course the attempt was useless, and I continued on my course.

Less than an hour later a rugged and semi-mountainous coastline appeared to the northeast. I was flying less than two hundred feet from the water when I sighted it. The shore was fairly distinct and not over ten or fifteen miles away. A light haze coupled with numerous local storm areas had prevented my seeing it from a long distance.

The coastline came down from the north, curved over towards the east. I had very little doubt that it was the southwestern end of Ireland but in order to make sure I changed my course towards the nearest point of land.

I located Cape Valentia and Dingle Bay, then resumed my compass course towards Paris.

After leaving Ireland I passed a number of steamers and was seldom out of sight of a ship.

In a little over two hours the coast of England appeared. My course passed over Southern England and a little south of Plymouth; then across the English Channel, striking France over Cherbourg.

The English farms were very impressive from the air in contrast to ours in America. They appeared extremely small and unusually neat and tidy with their stone and hedge fences.

I was flying at about a fifteen hundred foot altitude over England and as I crossed the Channel and passed over Cherbourg, France, I had probably seen more of that part of Europe than many native Europeans. The visibility was good and the country could be seen for miles around.

People who have taken their first flight often remark that no one knows what the locality he lives in is like until he has seen it from above. Countries take on different characteristics from the air.

The sun went down shortly after passing Cherbourg and soon the beacons along the Paris-London airway became visible.

I first saw the lights of Paris a little before ten P.M., or five P.M. New York time, and a few minutes later I was circling the Eiffel Tower at an altitude of about four thousand feet.

The lights of Le Bourget were plainly visible, but appeared to be very close to Paris. I had understood that the field was farther from the city, so continued out to the northeast into the country for four or five miles to make sure that there was not another field farther out which might be Le Bourget. Then I returned and spiralled down closer to the lights. Presently I could make out long lines of hangars, and the roads appeared to be jammed with cars.

I flew low over the field once, then circled around into the wind and landed.

After the plane stopped rolling I turned it around and started to taxi back to the lights. The entire field ahead, however, was covered with thousands of people all running towards my ship. When the first few arrived, I attempted to get them to hold the rest of the crowd back, away from the plane, but apparently no one could understand, or would have been able to conform to my request if he had.

I cut the switch to keep the propeller from killing some one, and attempted to organize an impromptu guard for the plane. The impossibility of any immediate organization became apparent, and when parts of the ship began to crack from the pressure of the multitude I decided to climb out of the cockpit in order to draw the crowd away.

Speaking was impossible; no words could be heard in the uproar and nobody apparently cared to hear any. I started to climb out of the cockpit, but as soon as one foot appeared through the door I was dragged the rest of the way without assistance on my part.

For nearly half an hour I was unable to touch the ground, during which time I was ardently carried around in what seemed to be a very small area, and in every position it is possible to be in. Every one had the best of intentions but no one seemed to know just what they were.

The French military flyers very resourcefully took the situation in hand. A number of them mingled with the crowd; then, at a given signal, they placed my helmet on an American correspondent and cried: "Here is Lindbergh." That helmet on an American was sufficient evidence. The correspondent immediately became the center of attraction, and while he was being taken protestingly to the Reception Committee via a rather devious route, I managed to get inside one of the hangars.

Meanwhile a second group of soldiers and police had surrounded the plane and soon placed it out of danger in another hangar.

The French ability to handle an unusual situation with speed and capability was remarkably demonstrated that night at Le Bourget.

Attempts on the Eigerwand

by C. F. MEADE

It sometimes seems that the greater man's technological triumphs, the greater also is his desire to continue the tradition of conquest by hand and foot, as if to offset the dehumanizing effects of an ever-expanding technology. In the following pages we are witnesses of a tragedy in the Swiss Alps, in which several young climbers, using a so-called "mechanical" method, stubbornly attempted to force their way to the summit of one of the most difficult of mountains—the Eigerwand— all to meet with death despite courageous efforts to save them. They were young and foolhardy—that, at any rate, seemed to be the verdict of the many eyewitnesses and would-be rescuers—and they threw their lives away. Perhaps so. This feature too—foolhardiness—is an aspect of man's duel with nature.

THE SENSATIONAL EXPLOITS OF A NEW SCHOOL OF ALPINE climber have scandalized the mountaineering world, and with good cause. Nevertheless, there may be some excuse for the extravagances of the innovators. The fact is that the young desperadoes belonging to what is known as the "mechanical" school of climbing have begun to take alarm. These virtuosos who delight in forcing their way up a mountain by hammering pegs into overhanging rocks or vertical ice-falls —"conquering" the mountain they would call it—have realized that since the classical era of exploration has come to an end, there will now be no more laurels left for them to win.

However, this state of affairs that they describe as "the exhaustion of the Alps" is not yet quite complete, for at least one great climb survived untried until recently.

At Grindelwald, in 1935, the appalling northern precipice of the Eiger that overshadows the valley, and forms the sensational feature of the view from the village, still remained unclimbed, and its forbidding appearance had deterred everyone from meddling with it. It is true that a daring party in 1932 had skirted the brink of the huge cliff by following a difficult route that led along its eastern margin over very steep snow and ice to the summit; nevertheless the direct and dangerous route up the very center of the colossal wall had never been attempted.

It is not surprising that such a climb should never have been seriously thought of before 1935, for this amazing north wall of the Eiger, the Eigerwand as it is called, is one of the biggest cliffs in the Alps. Throughout its five thousand feet of rock its steepness is such that, in spite of the altitude, permanent snow cannot rest anywhere. From top to bottom, too, the whole of the vast rock-face is shattered by constant bombardments of ice fragments and boulders. Besides these there are smaller missiles in the shape of flying stones, and most of these projectiles, big and little, travel at a speed that renders them invisible, as they whistle and scream past the cowering climber clinging precariously to the precipice.

It seems as if the present phase in the evolution of mountaineering has evoked a new type of climber adapted to an environment that has become more and more exacting in consequence of the so-called exhaustion of the Alps. This new type of climber, proud of his skill in the use of hammers, pegs, rope rings, balustrades, stirrups, slings and pulleys, finds a new source of joy in a mystical worship of danger as an end in itself, so that he considers even the most foolish feat praiseworthy, as long as courage, skill and endurance are displayed in performing it. In the sinister shadow of the Eigerwand the votaries of this strange cult have sought their Valhalla. It may be profitable to learn from the story of their adventures the consequences of the doctrine that they profess. At any rate the self-sacrificing heroism of the guides who staked their lives repeatedly in desperate attempts at rescue deserves to be remembered.

In August of 1935 two young men from Munich reached Grindelwald. They spent some time reconnoitering the lower cliffs of the Eigerwand, and one of them devoted a whole day to ascending the Eiger by the ordinary way in order to leave a depot of provisions on the summit. Meanwhile at the foot of the mighty wall the two men prepared a tent and sleeping bags as their base camp where they could remain with their stores of rope and tools. They then waited in hopes of an improvement in the weather, which, in fact, was so bad that they were several times sorely tempted to abandon their enterprise and go home.

At last, on Wednesday the 21st, the weather improved, and they began their attack upon the precipice. By the evening they could be well observed from the Eigerwand station of the Jungfraujoch Railway, through the window cut in the solid flank of the Eiger where the passengers pause on their way up inside the mountain in order to enjoy the panorama of northern Switzerland, and gaze down at the chalets of Grindelwald nestling in the green depths far below.

Everything seems to have gone well, for the climbers were now on a level with the station, and succeeded in accomplishing about one-third of their immense journey up the cliff.

On Thursday, however, the rate was not maintained. Moreover, as a critic has expressed it, the first half of the wall is only about a quarter as difficult as the whole; and still there were two-thirds of the formidable task to be achieved, for during the whole of this day, hampered as they were by the steepness of the ice, the climbers could only by their utmost efforts accomplish a paltry increase of some three hundred feet.

Already the prospects were disquieting enough, and again on Friday they had only ascended another three hundred feet. Obviously there was no longer any chance of victory, and the difficulties they were contending with were evident, for observers with telescopes could see the climbers hauling up their rucksacks after them by means of the rope. Later that evening a terrible storm suddenly concealed them from view.

On Saturday the whole mountain was ominously swathed in cloud, so that the men were still invisible. There was much fresh snow higher up the mountain, and avalanches, big as well as small, were pouring down the rocks.

On Sunday the anxiety of the watchers was reaching a climax, yet in such weather rescue operations were out of the question. The doomed men were again momentarily visible. They had made little progress, and were making their fifth bivouac, at about two-thirds of the way up the wall. Doubtless they spent the night in the customary manner of these devotees, crouching against the cliff without sleeping bags or blankets, and with the climbing rope that united them fastened for the sake of security by means of a steel clasp to a ringed metal peg driven into any available crevice in the rock. The clasp, it may be mentioned, is an important feature of the mechanical mountaineer's equipment, and is a contrivance resembling the clasp on some brobdingnagian watch chain.

Meanwhile it had begun to rain all over the Oberland, and although snow was falling only at great heights, the danger from waterfalls, stone-falls and the increasing exhaustion of the climbers was growing constantly. At Grindelwald a rescue party had been formed, but the weather remained prohibitive. An airplane had been warned to stand by, and on Tuesday, the first clear day, a pilot from Thun in a military plane flew for a full hour to and fro across the Eigerwand, scanning the cliffs. There were masses of fresh snow everywhere, and no living being was in sight. Several days later, when fine weather had definitely returned, another pilot, accompanied by an Alpine guide, actually flew to within twenty yards of the precipice, and caught sight of one of the two men standing upright, frozen to death, up to his knees in the snow, as if gazing down into the valley. The other man, they thought, must have been already buried in a drift. Probably both men had died where they had last been seen, on the fifth day of their attempt.

In 1936 another summer had come round, the tragedy of the Eiger was fresh in men's minds, but a party was gathered once more at the foot of the same forbidding precipice with the same desperate ambition that had led the two youths to destruction in the previous year. Eight young men had been dreaming the same dream of the Eigerwand, and were mustering their resources for the assault. They had collected quantities of rope and the usual paraphernalia employed by climbers of their way of thinking. Yet already death had taken its toll among the aspirants, for two of them who had been doing a practice climb on the Guggi route up the north face of the Jungfrau had fallen, and one of them had been killed. Of the others now waiting to make an attempt, Kurz, the youngest, had qualified as a guide in the Eastern Alps. With his friend, Hinter-stoisser, who was to accompany him, he had already accomplished formidable ascents such as the storming of the vertical north wall of the Grosse Zinne. Two other young men of the party, Rainer and Angerer, were from Innsbruck. All these four showed equal determination. "The Eigerwand is ours or we shall leave our bones on it," they declared.

Yet the weather was even worse than in 1935; it rained constantly, and the Eiger was hidden in cloud. Only brief glimpses through the cloud-curtain revealed the wall frowning down at them and loaded with masses of fresh snow. Avalanches thundered, and the crackling reverberations caused by stonefall were almost continuous. Doubt began to spread among the party, and no wonder. They must have known that before committing themselves to a five days' struggle on such a precipice a preliminary spell of settled weather was essential, in order to stabilize the conditions, and that only a prolonged spell of equable weather is likely to give more than a day's warning before it breaks up. With several days' warning it might be possible to retreat in time to escape before conditions prohibitive to life have supervened. In seasons that are variable the onset of dangerous conditions can occur with terrible abruptness. No wonder, then, that four of the less infatuated members of the group abandoned the adventure. However, the Bavarians, Kurz and Hinterstoisser, remained, and so did the Austrians, Rainer and Angerer. These four now decided to join forces.

In the meantime there were many visitors to the tents at the foot of the Eigerwand, and many sought to reason with the party, but the camp resounded with youthful laughter, and the four protested that they had no wish to die, although they admitted that luck was necessary for the undertaking. Down at Grindelwald they had even been told that the local authorities would take no responsibility for rescue operations, but they were confident that none would be required. All that was necessary was one more preliminary reconnaissance, and, with this object in view, the four set out together. They soon reached a suitable bivouac place under a huge overhanging cliff known as the Rothe Fluh. They had once passed the night there during a previous exploratory climb. Unfortunately, when they had got thus far, instead of staying where they were for the night, in order to reconnoiter further next day, they decided to return to their base, and at this juncture the Eigerwand gave its first warning. Hinterstoisser was beginning to descend, and was about fifty feet above Kurz's head. He trusted his weight to a peg that Angerer and Rainer had hammered into the rock some days previously. The peg suddenly gave way, and Hinterstoisser was hurled down for a hundred and twenty feet through the air past his horrified companion. The latter could do nothing to check the fall, for it happened with the rapidity of lightning, so that there was not even time to make a futile attempt to belay the rope. By a miracle the falling man not only hunched himself into a ball, but dropped into a patch of deep soft snow, where he saved himself from a further fall by acrobatic dexterity. Strange to say, the only damage was a wounded knee, and, although when they got back to camp the rain had begun again, the four men never wavered in their determination to pursue their adventure to its end.

On Friday the 17th of July the weather looked better, and all were satisfied that up to 10,000 feet the precipice had been sufficiently reconnoitered. Rucksacks were packed, and there was much amusement when Kurz made a comic story for the pressmen out of Hinterstoisser's hundred-and-twenty-foot fall. Hinterstoisser meanwhile was packing some photographs away in a sack that was to be left behind. "If anything happens to us," he remarked to the reporters, "you will know where to find our photographs."

It was regrettable that more food could not be carried. Sixty hand-forged pegs with rings attached were a heavy burden. Twenty of them, about a foot long, were for use on ice walls, and forty of a shorter kind were intended for hammering into crevices in the rock-face in places where otherwise handholds would be lacking. Besides this weight of metal they had to carry hammers, a few steel clasps, two hundred and forty feet of spare rope, some string and the spirit cooker. Consequently, without overloading their rucksacks, the only provisions they could take were two pounds of bacon, five pounds of black bread, six tins of sardines, tea, sugar and solidified spirit. It was not nearly enough, but greater loads could not be managed.

Finally, at two o'clock in the morning of Saturday the 18th of July, the four set out from the Kleine Scheidegg. The news spread through Switzerland, and the ethics of the enterprise began to be discussed once more. A telegram from the commanding officer of the Bergsjaeger regiment forbidding Hinterstoisser and Kurz from taking part in the expedition came too late, for the young men had already started and were out of reach. By half-past nine that morning the whole party had gathered at the reconnoiterers' sleeping place under the Rothe Fluh. Everything seemed favorable, and progress had been rapid, but from now on difficulties began, and observers at the Kleine Scheidegg and Grindelwald thronged the telescopes. It could be seen that from the sleeping place a difficult traverse had to be made over some very smooth cliffs. Hinterstoisser succeeded in crossing at a point where Rainer and Angerer had already failed. A narrow belt of snow and a difficult descending traverse then enabled the party to join the route of 1935 at the lower of two small snow fields. To the distant watchers at the telescopes progress seemed agonizingly slow, yet the men wasted no time, for they were expert at their work, hammering and chiseling the rock whenever one of the precious pegs could be spared, and there was a chance of forcing it into a suitable crevice. The rocks indeed were so steep and difficult that it was a long time before the party reached the second bivouac used by the two Bavarians in 1935, and situated between the lower and the upper snow fields.

By five-thirty in the afternoon the last man had reached the foot of the cliff below the upper snow field, night was approaching, and a site for a bivouac had to be found. The formidable overhang of the Rothe

Fluh was now behind them, and they settled down to pass the night, partly sheltered by another overhanging cliff. They were now on a level with the third and last bivouac of the Munich pair where the latter were supposed to have perished. Here the four men remained all night without sleeping bag or blanket, while the stones that thundered down the mountain continuously were deflected by the overhang above the sleepers' heads.

On the following day, Sunday, dawn broke threatening with thunder clouds, and only occasionally were patches of blue sky visible. At Zurich it was already raining, and although a north wind was driving the clouds upward, the party in their bivouac, condemned to inaction by the cloud bank surrounding them, could hardly have realized that there were signs of a momentary improvement in the weather. By six-forty-five that morning, however, they had started, and Hinterstoisser was leading, cutting steps up the steep *névé* of the upper snow field, in order to rejoin the route taken by the party of the previous year. An hour later they were suddenly hidden by a curtain of cloud, and nothing more was to be seen of the Eiger that day.

It was not until eight o'clock on Monday morning that they were again observed to be on the move. Their second bivouac must have been at a height of about 11,800 feet, a little above the highest point reached in 1935, but soon they began to retreat and were back at the second bivouac once more. One climber was seen to be so long immobile that it was concluded he was injured, and it was believed that Angerer had been wounded by a stone, as he appeared to be wearing a bandage on his head. As late as five o'clock that evening they were still to be seen descending the upper snow field, above the overhanging precipice called the Rothe Fluh. Two of the party seemed to be helping a third, presumably Angerer, but the prevalence of clouds made it difficult to see what was happening. The situation had now become extremely serious, for the food supply had only been calculated to last over the third night, and the third night was now beginning, while the climbers were still far up on the mountain. The supply of pegs, too, was being used up, the weather was not improving, and avalanches of stones and snow continued to fall.

Tuesday's weather, unfortunately, was much worse, with pouring rain and quantities of fresh snow everywhere covering the rocks. The roar of avalanches became almost continuous. Cries could be heard. At nine in the morning three of the party were seen descending. Could the fourth have dropped out? However, two hours later all four were seen still descending the upper snow field. Below them was a vertical and overhanging cliff that they had avoided on the way up. In order to avoid it again they must ascend the smooth and difficult rock traverse down which Hinterstoisser had led them on their way up the mountain, three days before. It was at this point that they met with a fatal reverse. The passage had taken them only two hours on the outward journey, but now, facing the traverse in its ascending direction, foodless and frozen as they were, short of iron pegs, too, and with a rope frozen so stiff that it was unmanageable, they failed repeatedly to force their way up the smooth ice-glazed slabs. At length they must have realized that retreat was now cut off, and that the one remaining hope was to face the appalling precipice below them and make a desperate attempt at a direct descent of it. After two hours had been wasted in fruitless struggles to ascend the traverse, the conclusion became inevitable, although the ghastly prospect of attempting to lower themselves by ropes into the abyss below them may well have seemed hopeless. Clouds, too, were seething round them, and the artillery of the Eigerwand was incessantly in action.

Meanwhile, from a point only six hundred feet below the four men, through an opening cut to serve as a rubbish-shoot for the tunnel of the Jungfraujoch Railway a workman, peering out from inside the mountain, had been for several hours anxiously watching the maneuvers of the climbers, and was now exchanging shouts with them. At first they still hoped, and they shouted down courageously that all was well. Later, when the whole party became involved in lowering themselves down the three hundred feet of precipice, cries for help could be heard, and the anxious spectator hurried down to give the alarm at the Eigergletscher station. The assailants of the Eigerwand had all been warned before starting that they could expect no guides to risk their lives in futile attempts at rescue, but it so happened that at that moment three of the best guides in Switzerland were working for a cinema company at the Eigergletscher station, and the railway company at once supplied a train to take them to the workman's observation post at the hole in the tunnel. The three guides then climbed out through the hole, and in only three quarters of an hour, at an astonishing speed, traversed the face of the deadly Eigerwand in a horizontal direction, and reached the foot of the precipice that the four men had been trying to descend. As they toiled across the face, pebbles, invisible like bullets, hummed past them, and a flying boulder burst like a shell, close to the leader. From the first it had been evident that it would be impossible to effect a rescue that night, and now it appeared that Kurz alone of all the climbers was alive. He was suspended in a sling from the overhanging cliff, and was exposed to stone-falls as

well as torrents of snow and water. "Can you hold out till morning?" he
was asked, and "No, no, no!" came the heart-rending reply. But it was
already night, and the guides had no choice but to retreat and disregard
his cries. The return journey in storm and darkness must have been an
unforgettable nightmare.

During the night another guide of the same caliber joined the original
three, and by daybreak of Wednesday all four, Adolf Rubi, Christian
Rubi, Hans Schlunegger and Arnold Glatthard, climbed through the
rubbish-shoot once more and again raced across the terrible wall. Kurz
was still calling for help, and was even capable of telling something of
his dreadful experiences. "Are none of your friends alive?" he was asked.
"No, I am alone, they all died yesterday; one is frozen above me, one
has fallen, and one lies hanging on the rope below."

It seems that the four men had fixed a rope to the cliff, and had begun
to rope themselves down into space over the overhang. As there had not
been enough rope for them all, Hinterstoisser had been obliged to untie
himself. In doing so he fell, perhaps having been knocked over by falling
stones, and was dashed to destruction at the bottom of the precipice.
Angerer is said to have been strangled in the coils of falling rope, and
Rainer was flung against one of the iron pegs with such violence that
he died. Pegs and rope rings had all been expended, and Kurz was helpless, third on the rope that linked him to his dead comrades, and crippled
by having an arm and hand useless owing to frostbite. The guides, too,
were in a desperate position, secured by their rope to a peg driven into
an ice-slope of sixty degrees, and under fire from the relentless mountain.
Glatthard, indeed, had narrowly escaped destruction. Moreover, they were
still at a distance of a hundred and fifty feet below Kurz, and the interval
that separated them consisted of smooth, vertical and overhanging rock,
veneered with ice.

Since it was impossible to climb up to Kurz he was asked: "Try and
cut the dead man loose from you." In order to do this he had to climb
down forty feet—handicapped as he was by his crippled arm—and then
with his ice-axe laboriously saw through the rope close to the loop round
his friend's body. Afterward he had to climb up again to where he was
before in order to fix the severed rope to the peg to which he had been
suspended. By a miracle of resolution and endurance, after hours of toil,
he succeeded in carrying out these exhausting maneuvers. At first the
corpse could not be detached, for it was frozen to the cliff; then, when
it suddenly plunged into space, it narrowly missed sweeping the guides
with it, as it hurtled past them in its three thousand foot fall. Then, after

Kurz, working with one hand and often with his teeth, had climbed back to his former position, he had to lower the severed rope to the guides, who attached to it some pegs and rope rings. These were then drawn up to Kurz, who hammered in a peg, and passed the rope through the ring in the head of the peg. The guides were so placed that it was impossible for them to help Kurz, by lowering him in pulley fashion, and the whole series of Kurz's heroic efforts seemed endless. Four hours were consumed in the terrible work before the unfortunate man could begin the descent. As he did so, it was noticed that he carefully removed any loose stones which might otherwise have been dislodged and have fallen on to the guides below him. As he slowly descended, an avalanche swept over the whole party, concealing Kurz from view for some moments.

And now, at the end of this heroically prolonged struggle, Kurz's consciousness was beginning to fail. Yet he was almost down. "Another step and you'll be saved," cried the guides, and then with a supreme effort, one guide climbing on the shoulders of another, while a third held him in position, it became just possible to touch the ice-coated climbing irons of Kurz with the tip of an ice-axe, but he was still just out of reach. At this moment occurred the final disaster; the knot that joined the ropes together caught fast in the ring fifty feet above the victim's head, and would allow him to descend no further. This was the end. Suddenly, throwing his axe to the guides, he let go his hold, and, swinging slowly out into space, he died. The devoted efforts of the heroic rescuers had been in vain, and death had come to Kurz at a moment when the reward of his unparalleled endurance and courage seemed to be close at hand. The guides, overcome by the spectacle of such unavailing fortitude, returned by the way they had come.

Note.—The north wall of the Eiger was eventually ascended by an Austro-German party in July, 1938. In spite of bad weather they succeeded in reaching the summit alive, and encountered the rescue party during the descent by the ordinary route.

The Buffalo Chase

by FRANCIS PARKMAN

Inasmuch as I have included tiger hunting in India and lion hunting in Africa, it seems only fair to recall, through this selection, that the United States was once a wilderness where man could easily pit himself against great animals. The exploits of many come to mind, among them Davy Crockett and Kit Carson, but I have drawn on Parkman's classic, The Oregon Trail, *because of the richness of its authentic detail and the high quality of his style. His was a broad and sympathetic mind. Afflicted by nervous ailments and ill health, he managed to live for seventy years despite the rigors of the American wilderness, to which he sometimes exposed himself. These qualities are evident in "The Buffalo Chase."*

THE NEXT DAY WAS ONE OF ACTIVITY AND EXCITEMENT, FOR about ten o'clock the man in advance shouted the gladening cry of "Buffalo! Buffalo!" and in the hollow of the prairie just below us, a band of bulls were grazing. The temptation was irresistible and Shaw and I rode down upon them. We were badly mounted on our traveling horses, but by hard lashing we overtook them, and Shaw, running alongside a bull, shot into him both balls of his double-barreled gun. Looking round as I galloped by, I saw the bull in his mortal fury rushing again and again upon his antagonist, whose horse constantly leaped aside and avoided the onset. My chase was more protracted, but at length I ran close to the bull and killed him with my pistols. Cutting off the tails of our victims by way of trophy, we rejoined the party in about a quarter of an hour after we had left it. Again and again that morning rang out the same welcome cry of "Buffalo! Buffalo!" Every few moments, in the broad meadows along the river, we saw bands of bulls, who, raising their shaggy heads, would gaze in stupid amazement at the approaching horsemen, and then, breaking into a clumsy gallop, file off in a long line across the trail in front, toward the rising prairie on the left. At noon the plain before us was alive with thousands of buffalo, bulls, cows, and calves, all moving rapidly as we drew near; and far off beyond the river the swelling prairie was darkened with them to the very horizon. The party was in gayer spirits than ever. We stopped for a nooning near a grove of trees by the river.

"Tongues and hump ribs tomorrow," said Shaw, looking with contempt at the venison steaks which Deslauriers placed before us. Our meal finished, we lay down to sleep. A shout from Henry Chatillon aroused us, and we saw him standing on the cart wheel, stretching his tall figure to its full height while he looked toward the prairie beyond the river. Following the direction of his eyes, we could clearly distinguish a large dark object, like the black shadow of a cloud, passing rapidly over swell after swell of the distant plain; behind it followed another of similar appearance though smaller, moving more rapidly, and drawing closer and closer to the first. It was the hunters of the Arapahoe camp chasing a band of buffalo. Shaw and I caught and saddled our best horses and went plunging through sand and water to the farther bank. We were too late. The hunters had already mingled with the herd, and the work of slaughter was nearly over. When we reached the ground we found it strewn far and near with numberless carcasses, while the remnants of the herd, scattered in all directions, were flying away in terror, and the Indians still rushing in pursuit. Many of the hunters, however, remained upon the spot, and among the rest was our yesterday's acquaintance, the chief of the village. He had alighted by the side of a cow, into which he had shot five or six arrows, and his squaw, who had followed him on horseback to the hunt, was giving him a draught of water from a canteen purchased or plundered from some volunteer soldier. Recrossing the river, we overtook the party, who were already on their way.

We had gone scarcely a mile when we saw an imposing spectacle. From the river bank on the right, away over the swelling prairie on the left, and in front as far as the eye could reach, was one vast host of buffalo. The outskirts of the herd were within a quarter of a mile. In many parts they were crowded so densely together that in the distance their rounded backs presented a surface of uniform blackness; but elsewhere they were more scattered, and from amid the multitude rose little columns of dust where some of them were rolling on the ground. Here and there a battle was going forward among the bulls. We could distinctly see them rushing against each other, and hear the clattering of their horns and their hoarse bellowing. Shaw was riding at some distance in advance, with Henry Chatillon; I saw him stop and draw the leather covering from his gun. With such a sight before us, but one thing could be thought of. That morning I had used pistols in the chase. I had now a mind to try the virtue of a gun. Deslauriers had one, and I rode up to the side of the cart; there he sat under the white covering, biting his pipe between his teeth and grinning with excitement.

"Lend me your gun, Deslauriers."

"Oui, Monsieur, oui," said Deslauriers, tugging with might and main to stop the mule, which seemed obstinately bent on going forward. Then everything but his moccasins disappeared as he crawled into the cart and pulled at the gun to extricate it.

"Is it loaded?" I asked.

"Oui, bien chargé; you'll kill, mon bourgeois; yes, you'll kill—c'est un bon fusil."

I handed him my rifle and rode forward to Shaw.

"Are you ready?" he asked.

"Come on," said I.

"Keep down that hollow," said Henry, "and then they won't see you till you get close to them."

The hollow was a kind of wide ravine; it ran obliquely toward the buffalo, and we rode at a canter along the bottom until it became too shallow; then we bent close to our horses' necks, and, at last, finding that it could no longer conceal us, came out of it and rode directly toward the herd. It was within gunshot; before its outskirts numerous grizzly old bulls were scattered, holding guard over their females. They glared at us in anger and astonishment, walked toward us a few yards, and then, turning slowly round, retreated at a trot which afterward broke into a clumsy gallop. In an instant the main body caught the alarm. The buffalo began to crowd away from the point toward which we were approaching, and a gap was opened in the side of the herd. We entered it, still restraining our excited horses. Every instant the tumult was thickening. The buffalo, pressing together in large bodies, crowded away from us on every hand. In front and on either side we could see dark columns and masses, half hidden by clouds of dust, rushing along in terror and confusion, and hear the tramp and clattering of ten thousand hoofs. That countless multitude of powerful brutes, ignorant of their own strength, were flying in a panic from the approach of two feeble horsemen. To remain quiet longer was impossible.

"Take that band on the left," said Shaw. "I'll take these in front."

He sprang off and I saw no more of him. A heavy Indian whip, or
"quirt," was fastened by a band to my wrist; I swung it into the air and
lashed my horse's flank with all the strength of my arm. Away she
darted, stretching close to the ground. I could see nothing but a cloud of
dust before me but I knew that it concealed a band of many hundreds
of buffalo. In a moment I was in the midst of the cloud, half suffocated
by the dust and stunned by the trampling of the flying herd; but I was
drunk with the chase and cared for nothing but the buffalo. Very soon
a long dark mass became visible, looming through the dust; then I could
distinguish each bulky carcass, the hoofs flying out beneath, the short
tails held rigidly erect. In a moment I was so close that I could have
touched them with my gun.

Suddenly, to my amazement, the hoofs were jerked upward, the tails
flourished in the air, and amid a cloud of dust the buffalo seemed to sink
into the earth before me. One vivid impression of that instant remains
upon my mind. I remember looking down upon the backs of several
buffalo dimly visible through the dust. We had run unawares upon a
ravine. At that moment I was not the most accurate judge of depth and
width, but when I passed it on my return, I found it about twelve feet
deep and not quite twice as wide at the bottom. It was impossible to
stop; I would have done so gladly if I could; so, half sliding, half plunging,
down went the little mare. She came down on her knees in the loose
sand at the bottom; I was pitched forward against her neck and nearly
thrown over her head among the buffalo, who amid dust and confusion
came tumbling in all around. The mare was on her feet in an instant
and scrambling like a cat up the opposite side. I thought for a moment
that she would have fallen back and crushed me, but with a violent effort
she clambered out and gained the hard prairie above.

Glancing back I saw the huge head of a bull clinging as it were by the
forefeet at the edge of the dusty gulf. At length I was fairly among the
buffalo. They were less densely crowded than before, and I could see
nothing but bulls, who always run at the rear of herd to protect their
females. As I passed among them they would lower their heads, and
turning as they ran, try to gore my horse; but as they were already at
full speed there was no force in their onset, and as Pauline ran faster
than they, they were always thrown behind her in the effort.

I soon began to distinguish cows amid the throng. One just in front of
me seemed to my liking, and I pushed close to her side. Dropping the
reins I fired, holding the muzzle of the gun within a foot of her shoulder.
Quick as lightning she sprang at Pauline; the little mare dodged the

attack, and I lost sight of the wounded animal amid the tumult. Immediately after, I selected another, and urging forward Pauline, shot into her both pistols in succession. For a while I kept her in view, but in attempting to load my gun lost sight of her also in the confusion. Believing her to be mortally wounded and unable to keep up with the herd, I checked my horse.

The crowd rushed onward. The dust and tumult passed away, and on the prairie, far behind the rest, I saw a solitary buffalo galloping heavily. In a moment I and my victim were running side by side. My firearms were all empty, and I had in my pouch nothing but rifle bullets, too large for the pistols and too small for the gun. I loaded the gun, however, but as often as I leveled it to fire, the bullets would roll out of the muzzle and the gun returned only a report like a squib as the powder harmlessly exploded. I rode in front of the buffalo and tried to turn her back; but her eyes glared, her mane bristled and, lowering her head, she rushed at me with the utmost fierceness and activity. Again and again I rode before her and again and again she repeated her furious charge. But little Pauline was in her element. She dodged her enemy at every rush, until at length the buffalo stood still, exhausted with her own efforts, her tongue lolling from her jaws.

Riding to a little distance, I dismounted, thinking to gather a handful of dry grass to serve the purpose of wadding, and load the gun at my leisure. No sooner were my feet on the ground than the buffalo came bounding in such a rage toward me that I jumped back again into the saddle with all possible despatch. After waiting a few minutes more, I made an attempt to ride up and stab her with my knife; but Pauline was near being gored in the attempt. At length, bethinking me of the fringes at the seams of my buckskin trousers, I jerked off a few of them and, reloading the gun, forced them down the barrel to keep the bullet in its place; then approaching, I shot the wounded buffalo through the heart. Sinking to her knees, she rolled over lifeless on the prairie. To my astonishment, I found that, instead of a cow, I had been slaughtering a stout young bull. No longer wondering at his fierceness, I opened his throat and, cutting out his tongue, tied it at the back of my saddle. My mistake was one which a more experienced eye than mine might easily make in the dust and confusion of such a chase.

Then for the first time I had leisure to look at the scene around me. The prairie in front was darkened with the retreating multitude, and on either hand the buffalo came filing up in endless columns from the low plains upon the river. The Arkansas was three or four miles distant. I turned and moved slowly toward it. A long time passed before, far in the distance, I distinguished the white covering of the cart and the litttle black specks of horsemen before and behind it. Drawing near, I recognized Shaw's elegant tunic, the red flannel shirt, conspicuous far off. I overtook the party and asked him what success he had had. He had assailed a fat cow, shot her with two bullets, and mortally wounded her. But neither of us was prepared for the chase that afternoon, and Shaw, like myself, had no spare bullets in his pouch; so he abandoned the disabled animal to Henry Chatillon, who followed, dispatched her with his rifle, and loaded his horse with the meat.

We encamped close to the river. The night was dark, and as we lay down we could hear, mingled with the howlings of wolves, the hoarse bellowing of the buffalo, like the ocean beating upon a distant coast.

The North Pole Conquered

by ROBERT E. PEARY

Peary (1856-1920), sometimes called the man who refused to fail, attained his life's ambition when he reached the North Pole on April 6, 1909. He was then fifty-three. That he was still very vigorous is attested to by the fact that he survived the series of treks which finally brought him, Matt Henson and four Eskimos to the Pole. He had visited arctic regions as early as 1886. Shortly thereafter he determined to be the Pole's conqueror. After privations and failure, hinted at in the following pages, he experienced the exultation of a man whose vision and fortitude have finally been rewarded. Here we observe him and his small party reaching the Pole and share with him his feelings in that white wasteland.

WITH EVERY PASSING DAY EVEN THE ESKIMOS WERE BECOMing more eager and interested, notwithstanding the fatigue of the long marches. As we stopped to make camp, they would climb to some pinnacle of ice and strain their eyes to the north, wondering if the Pole was in sight, for they were now certain that we should get there this time.

We slept only a few hours the next night, hitting the trail again a little before midnight between the 3d and 4th of April. The weather and the going were even better than the day before. The surface of the ice, except as interrupted by infrequent pressure ridges, was as level as the glacial fringe from Hecla to Cape Columbia, and harder. I rejoiced at the thought that if the weather held good I should be able to get in my five marches before noon of the 6th.

Again we traveled for ten hours straight ahead, the dogs often on the trot and occasionally on the run, and in those ten hours we reeled off at least twenty-five miles. I had a slight accident that day, a sledge runner having passed over the side of my right foot as I stumbled while running beside a team; but the hurt was not severe enough to keep me from traveling.

Near the end of the day we crossed a lead about one hundred yards wide, on young ice so thin that, as I ran ahead to guide the dogs, I was obliged to slide my feet and travel wide, bear style, in order to distribute my weight, while the men let the sledges and dogs come over by themselves, gliding across where they could. The last two men came over on all fours.

I watched them from the other side with my heart in my mouth—watched the ice bending under the weight of the sledges and the men. As one of the sledges neared the north side, a runner cut clear through the ice, and I expected every moment that the whole thing, dogs and all, would go through the ice and down to the bottom. But it did not.

This dash reminded me of that day, nearly three years before, when in order to save our lives we had taken desperate chances in recrossing the "Big Lead" on ice similar to this—ice that buckled under us and through which my toe cut several times as I slid my long snowshoes over it. A man who should wait for the ice to be really safe would stand small chance of getting far in these latitudes. Traveling on the polar ice, one takes all kinds of chances. Often a man has the choice between the possibility of drowning by going on or starving to death by standing still, and challenges fate with the briefer and less painful chance.

That night we were all pretty tired, but satisfied with our progress so far. We were almost inside of the 89th parallel, and I wrote in my diary: "Give me three more days of this weather!" The temperature at the beginning of the march had been minus 40°. That night I put all the poorest dogs in one team and began to eliminate and feed them to the others, as it became necessary.

We stopped for only a short sleep, and early in the evening of the same day, the 4th, we struck on again. The temperature was then minus 35°, the going was the same, but the sledges always haul more easily when the temperature rises, and the dogs were on the trot much of the time. Toward the end of the march we came upon a lead running north and south, and as the young ice was thick enough to support the teams, we traveled on it for two hours, the dogs galloping along and reeling off the miles in a way that delighted my heart. The light air which had blown from the south during the first few hours of the march veered to the east and grew keener as the hours wore on.

I had not dared to hope for such progress as we were making. Still the biting cold would have been impossible to face by anyone not fortified by an inflexible purpose. The bitter wind burned our faces so that they cracked, and long after we got into camp each day they pained us so that we could hardly go to sleep. The Eskimos complained much, and at every camp fixed their fur clothing about their faces, waists, knees, and wrists. They also complained of their noses, which I had never known them to do before. The air was as keen and bitter as frozen steel.

At the next camp I had another of the dogs killed. It was now exactly six weeks since we left the *Roosevelt*, and I felt as if the goal were in sight. I intended the next day, weather and ice permitting, to make a long march, "boil the kettle" midway, and then go on again without sleep, trying to make up the five miles which we had lost on the 3d of April.

During the daily march my mind and body were too busy with the problem of covering as many miles of distance as possible to permit me to enjoy the beauty of the frozen wilderness through which we tramped. But at the end of the day's march, while the igloos were being built, I usually had a few minutes in which to look about me and to realize the picturesqueness of our situation—we, the only living things in a trackless, colorless, inhospitable desert of ice. Nothing but the hostile ice, and far more hostile icy water, lay between our remote place on the world's map and the utmost tips of the lands of Mother Earth.

I knew of course that there was always a *possibility* that we might still end our lives up there, and that our conquest of the unknown spaces and silences of the polar void might remain forever unknown to the world which we had left behind. But it was hard to realize this. That hope which is said to spring eternal in the human breast always buoyed me up with the belief that, as a matter of course, we should be able to return along the white road by which we had come.

Sometimes I would climb to the top of a pinnacle of ice to the north of our camp and strain my eyes into the whiteness which lay beyond, trying to imagine myself already at the Pole. We had come so far, and the capricious ice had placed so few obstructions in our path, that now I dared to loose my fancy, to entertain the image which my will had heretofore forbidden to my imagination—the image of ourselves at the goal.

We had been very fortunate with the leads so far, but I was in constant and increasing dread lest we should encounter an impassable one toward the very end. With every successive march, my fear of such impassable leads had increased. At every pressure ridge I found myself hurrying breathlessly forward, fearing there might be a lead just beyond it, and when I arrived at the summit I would catch my breath with relief—only to find myself hurrying on in the same way at the next ridge.

At our camp on the 5th of April I gave the party a little more sleep than at the previous ones, as we were all pretty well played out and in need of rest. I took a latitude sight, and this indicated our position to be 89° 25', or thirty-five miles from the Pole; but I determined to make the next camp in time for a noon observation, if the sun should be visible.

Before midnight on the 5th we were again on the trail. The weather was overcast, and there was the same gray and shadowless light as on the march after Marvin had turned back. The sky was a colorless pall gradually deepening to almost black at the horizon, and the ice was a ghastly and chalky white, like that of the Greenland icecap—just the colors which an imaginative artist would paint as a polar ice-scape. How different it seemed from the glittering fields, canopied with blue and lit by the sun and full moon, over which we had been traveling for the last four days.

The going was even better than before. There was hardly any snow on the hard granular surface of the old floes, and the sapphire blue lakes were larger than ever. The temperature had risen to minus 15°, which, reducing the friction of the sledges, gave the dogs the appearance of having caught the high spirits of the party. Some of them even tossed their heads and barked and yelped as they traveled.

Notwithstanding the grayness of the day and the melancholy aspect of the surrounding world, by some strange shift of feeling the fear of the leads had fallen from me completely. I now felt that success was certain and, notwithstanding the physical exhaustion of the forced marches on the last five days, I went tirelessly on and on, the Eskimos following almost automatically, though I knew that they must feel the weariness which my excited brain made me incapable of feeling.

When we had covered, as I estimated, a good fifteen miles, we halted, made tea, ate lunch, and rested the dogs. Then we went on for another estimated fifteen miles. In twelve hours' actual traveling time we made thirty miles. Many laymen have wondered why we were able to travel faster after the sending back of each of the supporting parties, especially after the last one. To any man experienced in the handling of troops this will need no explanation. The larger the party and the greater the number of sledges, the greater is the chance of breakages or delay for one reason or another. A large party cannot be forced as rapidly as a small party.

Take a regiment, for instance. The regiment could not make as good an average daily march for a number of forced marches as could a picked company of that regiment. The picked company could not make as good an average march for a number of forced marches as could a picked file of men from that particular company; and this file could not make the same average for a certain number of forced marches that the fastest traveler in the whole regiment could make.

So that, with my party reduced to five picked men, every man, dog, and sledge under my individual eye, myself in the lead, and all recognizing that the moment had now come to let ourselves out for all there was in us, we naturally bettered our previous speed.

When Bartlett left us the sledges had been practically rebuilt, all the best dogs were in our pack, and we all understood that we must attain our object and get back as quickly as we possibly could. The weather was in our favor. The average march for the whole journey from the land to the Pole was over fifteen miles. We had repeatedly made marches of twenty miles. Our average for five marches from the point where the last supporting party turned back was about twenty-six miles.

The last march northward ended at ten o'clock on the forenoon of April 6. I had now made the five marches planned from the point at which Bartlett turned back, and my reckoning showed that we were in the immediate neighborhood of the goal of all our striving. After the usual arrangements for going into camp, at approximate local noon, of the Columbia meridian, I made the first observation at our polar camp. It indicated our position as 89° 57'.

We were now at the end of the last long march of the upward journey. Yet with the Pole actually in sight I was too weary to take the last few steps. The accumulated weariness of all those days and nights of forced marches and insufficient sleep, constant peril and anxiety, seemed to roll across me all at once. I was actually too exhausted to realize at the moment that my life's purpose had been achieved. As soon as our igloos had been completed and we had eaten our dinner and double-rationed the dogs, I turned in for a few hours of absolutely necessary sleep, Henson and the Eskimos having unloaded the sledges and got them in readiness for such repairs as were necessary. But, weary though I was, I could not sleep long. It was, therefore, only a few hours later when I woke. The first thing I did after awaking was to write these words in my diary: "The Pole at last. The prize of three centuries. My dream and goal for twenty years. Mine at last! I cannot bring myself to realize it. It seems all so simple and commonplace."

Everything was in readiness for an observation at 6 P.M., Columbia meridian time, in case the sky should be clear, but at that hour it was, unfortunately, still overcast. But as there were indications that it would clear before long, two of the Eskimos and myself made ready a light sledge carrying only the instruments, a tin of pemmican, and one or two skins; and drawn by a double team of dogs, we pushed on an estimated distance of ten miles. While we traveled, the sky cleared, and at the end of the journey, I was able to get a satisfactory series of observations at Columbia meridian midnight. These observations indicated that our position was then beyond the Pole.

Nearly everything in the circumstances which then surrounded us seemed too strange to be thoroughly realized; but one of the strangest of those circumstances seemed to me to be the fact that, in a march of only a few hours, I had passed from the western to the eastern hemisphere and had verified my position at the summit of the world. It was hard to realize that, in the first miles of this brief march, we had been traveling due north, while on the last few miles of the same march, we had been traveling south, although we had all the time been traveling precisely in the same direction. It would be difficult to imagine a better illustration of the fact that most things are relative. Again, please consider the uncommon circumstance that, in order to return to our camp, it now became necessary to turn and go north again for a few miles and then to go directly south, all the time traveling in the same direction.

As we passed back along that trail which none had ever seen before or would ever see again, certain reflections intruded themselves which, I think, may fairly be called unique. East, west, and north had disappeared for us. Only one direction remained and that was south. Every breeze which could possibly blow upon us, no matter from what point of the horizon, must be a south wind. Where we were, one day and one night constituted a year, a hundred such days and nights constituted a century. Had we stood in that spot during the six months of the arctic winter night, we should have seen every star of the northern hemisphere circling the sky at the same distance from the horizon, with Polaris (the North Star) practically in the zenith. . . .

If it were possible for a man to arrive at 90° north lattitude without being utterly exhausted, body and brain, he would doubtless enjoy a series of unique sensations and reflections. But the attainment of the Pole was the culmination of days and weeks of forced marches, physical discomfort, insufficient sleep, and racking anxiety. It is a wise provision of nature that the human consciousness can grasp only such degree of intense feeling as the brain can endure, and the grim guardians of earth's remotest spot will accept no man as guest until he has been tried and tested by the severest ordeal.

Perhaps it ought not to have been so, but when I knew for a certainty that we had reached the goal, there was not a thing in the world I wanted but sleep. But after I had a few hours of it, there succeeded a condition of mental exaltation which made further rest impossible. For more than a score of years that point on the earth's surface had been the object of my every effort. To its attainment my whole being, physical, mental, and moral, had been dedicated. Many times my own life and the lives of those with me had been risked. My own material and forces and those of my friends had been devoted to this object. This journey was my eighth into the arctic wilderness. In that wilderness I had spent nearly twelve years out of the twenty-three between my thirtieth and my fifty-third year, and the intervening time spent in civilized communities during that period had been mainly occupied with preparations for returning to the wilderness. The determination to reach the Pole had become so much a part of my being that, strange as it may seem, I long ago ceased to think of myself save as an instrument for the attainment of that end. To the layman this may seem strange, but an inventor can understand it, or an artist, or anyone who has devoted himself for years upon years to the service of an idea.

But though my mind was busy at intervals during those thirty hours spent at the Pole with the exhilarating thought that my dream had come true, there was one recollection of other times that, now and then, intruded itself with startling distinctness. It was the recollection of a day three years before, April 21, 1906, when after making a fight with ice, open water, and storms, the expedition which I commanded had been forced to turn back from 87° 6' north latitude because our supply of food would carry us no further. And the contrast between the terrible depression of that day and the exaltation of the present moment was not the least pleasant feature of our brief stay at the Pole. During the dark moments of that return journey in 1906, I had told myself that I was only one in a long list of arctic explorers, dating back through the centuries, all the way from Henry Hudson to the Duke of the Abruzzi, and including Franklin, Kane, and Melville—a long list of valiant men who had striven and failed. I told myself that I had only succeeded, at the price of the best years of my life, in adding a few links to the chain that led from the parallels of civilization toward the polar center, but that, after all, at the end the only word I had to write was failure.

But now, while quartering the ice in various directions from our camp, I tried to realize that, after twenty-three years of struggles and discouragement, I had at last succeeded in placing the flag of my country at the goal of the world's desire. It is not easy to write about such a thing, but I knew that we were going back to civilization with the last of the great adventure stories—a story the world had been waiting to hear for nearly four hundred years, a story which was to be told at last under the folds of the Stars and Stripes, the flag that during a lonely and isolated life had come to be for me the symbol of home and everything I loved—and might never see again.

The thirty hours at the Pole, what with my marchings and countermarchings, together with the observations and records, were pretty well crowded. I found time, however, to write to Mrs. Peary on a United States postal card which I had found on the ship during the winter. It had been my custom at various important stages of the journey northward to write such a note in order that, if anything serious happened to me, these brief communications might ultimately reach her at the hands of survivors. This was the card, which later reached Mrs. Peary at Sydney:—

90 NORTH LATITUDE, April 7th.

My dear Jo,

I have won out at last. Have been here a day. I start for home and you in an hour. Love to the "kidsies."

BERT

In the afternoon of the 7th, after flying our flags and taking our photographs, we went into our igloos and tried to sleep a little, before starting south again.

I could not sleep and my two Eskimos, Seegloo and Egingwah, who occupied the igloo with me, seemed equally restless. They turned from side to side, and when they were quiet I could tell from their uneven breathing that they were not asleep. Though they had not been specially excited the day before when I told them that we had reached the goal, yet they also seemed to be under the same exhilarating influence which made sleep impossible for me.

Finally I rose, and telling my men and the three men in the other igloo, who were equally wakeful, that we would try to make our last camp, some thirty miles to the south, before we slept, I gave orders to hitch up the dogs and be off. It seemed unwise to waste such perfect traveling weather in tossing about on the sleeping platforms of our igloos.

Neither Henson nor the Eskimos required any urging to take to the trail again. They were naturally anxious to get back to the land as soon as possible—now that our work was done. And about four o'clock on the afternoon of the 7th of April we turned our backs upon the camp at the North Pole.

Though intensely conscious of what I was leaving, I did not wait for any lingering farewell of my life's goal. The event of human beings standing at the hitherto inaccessible summit of the earth was accomplished, and my work now lay to the south, where four hundred and thirteen nautical miles of ice floes and possibly open leads still lay between us and the north coast of Grant Land. One backward glance I gave—then turned my face toward the south and toward the future.

The Eruption of Vesuvius

by PLINY THE YOUNGER

Pliny the Younger was in his eighteenth year when he witnessed the historic eruption of Vesuvius, A. D. 79, which destroyed Pompeii and incidentally killed his uncle, Pliny the Elder. Through the latter's will he became the elder Pliny's adopted son. We probably owe the famous descriptions of the eruption to the Roman historian, Tacitus, who apparently elicited them. Pliny's Letters are not noted for simple effusion or unguarded candor. On the contrary, they are extremely polished and mannered. For this reason I have chosen an eighteenth-century translation, which mirrors the original. These two letters stir in one's memory images of excavated Pompeii, with its evidence of sudden death, licentiousness and incredible "modernity."

To Tacitus

YOUR REQUEST THAT I WOULD SEND YOU AN ACCOUNT OF MY uncle's end, so that you may transmit a more exact relation of it to posterity, deserves my acknowledgments; for if his death shall be celebrated by your pen, the glory of it, I am aware, will be rendered forever deathless. For notwithstanding he perished, as did whole peoples and cities, in the destruction of a most beautiful region, and by a misfortune memorable enough to promise him a kind of immortality; notwithstanding he has himself composed many and lasting works; yet I am persuaded, the mentioning of him in your immortal writings, will greatly contribute to eternize his name.

He was at that time with the fleet under his command at Misenum. On the 24th of August, about one in the afternoon, my mother desired him to observe a cloud of very unusual size and appearance. He had sunned himself, then taken a cold bath, and after a leisurely luncheon was

369

engaged in study. He immediately called for his shoes and went up an eminence from whence he might best view this very uncommon appearance. It was not at that distance discernible from what mountain this cloud issued, but it was found afterward to be Vesuvius. I cannot give you a more exact description of its figure, than by resembling it to that of a pine tree, for it shot up a great height in the form of a trunk, which extended itself at the top into several branches; because I imagine, a momentary gust of air blew it aloft, and then failing, forsook it; thus causing the cloud to expand laterally as it dissolved, or possibly the downward pressure of its own weight produced this effect. It was at one moment white, at another dark and spotted, as if it had carried up earth or cinders.

My uncle, true savant that he was, deemed the phenomenon important and worth a nearer view. He ordered a light vessel to be got ready, and gave me the liberty, if I thought proper, to attend him. I replied I would rather study; and, as it happened, he had himself given me a theme for composition. As he was coming out of the house he received a note from Rectina, the wife of Bassus, who was in the utmost alarm at the imminent danger (his villa stood just below us, and there was no way to escape but by sea); she earnestly entreated him to save her from such deadly peril. He changed his first design and what he began with a philosophical, he pursued with an heroical turn of mind. He ordered large galleys to be launched, and went himself on board one, with the intention of assisting not only Rectina, but many others; for the villas stand extremely thick upon that beautiful coast. Hastening to the place from whence others were flying, he steered his direct course to the point of danger, and with such freedom from fear, as to be able to make and dictate his observations upon the successive motions and figures of that terrific object.

And now cinders, which grew thicker and hotter the nearer he approached, fell into the ships, then pumice stones too, with stones blackened, scorched, and cracked by fire, then the sea ebbed suddenly from under them, while the shore was blocked up by landslips from the mountains. After considering a moment whether he should retreat, he said to the captain who was urging that course, "Fortune befriends the brave; carry me to Pomponianus." Pomponianus was then at Stabiae, distant by half the width of the bay (for, as you know, the shore, insensibly curving in its sweep, forms here a receptacle for the sea). He had already embarked his baggage; for though at Stabiae the danger was not yet near, it was full in view, and certain to be extremely near, as soon as it spread; and he resolved to fly as soon as the contrary wind should cease. It was full favorable, however, for carrying my uncle to Pomponianus. He embraced, comforted, and encouraged his alarmed friend, and in order to soothe the other's fears by his own unconcern, desired to be conducted to a bathroom; and after having bathed, he sat down to supper with great cheerfulness, or at least (what is equally heroic) with all the appearance of it.

In the meanwhile Mount Vesuvius was blazing in several places with spreading and towering flames, whose refulgent brightness the darkness of the night set in high relief. But my uncle, in order to soothe apprehensions, kept saying that some fires had been left alight by the terrified country people, and what they saw were only deserted villas on fire in the abandoned district. After this he retired to rest, and it is most certain that his rest was a most genuine slumber; for his breathing, which, as he was pretty fat, was somewhat heavy and sonorous, was heard by those who attended at his chamber door. But the court which led to his apartment now lay so deep under a mixture of pumice stones and ashes, that if he had continued longer in his bedroom, egress would have been impossible. On being aroused, he came out, and returned to Pomponianus and the others, who had sat up all night. They consulted together as to whether they should hold out in the house, or wander about in the open. For the house now tottered under repeated and violent concussions, and seemed to rock to and fro as if torn from its foundations. In the open air, on the other hand, they dreaded the falling pumice stones, light and porous though they were; yet this, by comparison, seemed the lesser danger of the two; a conclusion which my uncle arrived at by balancing reasons, and the others by balancing fears. They tied pillows upon their heads with napkins; and this was their whole defense against the showers that fell round them.

It was now day everywhere else, but there a deeper darkness prevailed than in the most obscure night; relieved, however, by many torches and divers illuminations. They thought proper to go down upon the shore to observe from close at hand if they could possibly put out to sea, but they found the waves still run extremely high and contrary. There my uncle having thrown himself down upon a disused sail, repeatedly called for, and drank, a draught of cold water; soon after, flames, and a strong smell of sulphur, which was the forerunner of them, dispersed the rest of the company in flight; him they only aroused. He raised himself up with the assistance of two of his slaves, but instantly fell; some unusually gross vapor, as I conjecture, having obstructed his breathing and blocked his windpipe, which was not only naturally weak and constricted, but chronically inflamed. When day dawned again (the third from that he last beheld) his body was found entire and uninjured, and still fully clothed as in life; its posture was that of a sleeping, rather than a dead man.

Meanwhile my mother and I were at Misenum. But this has no connection with history, and your inquiry went no farther than concerning my uncle's death. I will therefore put an end to my letter. Suffer me only to add, that I have faithfully related to you what I was either an eyewitness of myself, or heard at the time, when report speaks most truly. You will select what is most suitable to your purpose; for there is a great difference between a letter, and an history; between writing to a friend, and writing for the public. Farewell.

To Cornelius Tacitus

The letter which, in compliance with your request, I wrote to you concerning the death of my uncle, has raised, you say, your curiosity to know not only what terrors, but what calamities I endured when left behind at Misenum (for there I broke off my narrative).

"Though my shock'd soul recoils, my tongue shall tell."

My uncle having set out, I gave the rest of the day to study—the object which had kept me at home. After which I bathed, dined, and retired to short and broken slumbers. There had been for several days before some shocks of earthquake, which the less alarmed us as they are frequent in Campania; but that night they became so violent that one might think that the world was not being merely shaken, but turned topsy-turvy. My mother flew to my chamber; I was just rising, meaning on my part to awaken her, if she was asleep. We sat down in the forecourt of the house, which separated it by a short space from the sea. I know not whether I should call it courage or inexperience—I was not quite eighteen—but I called for a volume of Livy, and began to read, and even went on with the extracts I was making from it, as if nothing were the matter. Lo and behold, a friend of my uncle's who was just come to him from Spain, appeared on the scene; observing my mother and me seated, and that I had actually a book in my hand, he sharply censured her patience and my indifference; nevertheless I still went on intently with my author.

It was now six o'clock in the morning, the light still ambiguous and faint. The buildings around us already tottered, and though we stood upon open ground, yet as the place was narrow and confined, there was certain and formidable danger from their collapsing. It was not till then we resolved to quit the town. The common people followed us in the utmost consternation, preferring the judgement of others to their own (wherein the extreme of fear resembles prudence), and impelled us onward by pressing in a crowd upon our rear. Being got outside the houses, we halted in the midst of a most strange and dreadful scene. The coaches which we had ordered out, though upon the most level ground, were sliding to and fro, and could not be kept steady even when stones were put against the wheels. Then we beheld the sea sucked back, and as it were repulsed by the convulsive motion of the earth; it is certain at least the shore was considerably enlarged, and now held many sea animals captive on the dry sand. On the other side, a black and dreadful cloud bursting out in gusts of igneous serpentine vapor now and again yawned open to reveal long fantastic flames, resembling flashes of lightning but much larger.

Our Spanish friend already mentioned now spoke with more warmth and instancy: "If your brother—if your uncle," said he, "is yet alive, he wishes you both may be saved; if he has perished, it was his desire that you might survive him. Why therefore do you delay your escape?" We could never think of our own safety, we said, while we were uncertain of his. Without more ado our friend hurried off, and took himself out of danger at the top of his speed.

Soon afterward, the cloud I have described began to descend upon the earth, and cover the sea. It had already begirt the hidden Capreae, and blotted from sight the promontory of Misenum. My mother now began to beseech, exhort, and command me to escape as best I might; a young man could do it; she, burdened with age and corpulency, would die easy if only she had not caused my death. I replied, I would not be saved without her, and taking her by the hand, I hurried her on. She complied reluctantly and not without reproaching herself for retarding me. Ashes now fell upon us, though as yet in no great quantity. I looked behind me; gross darkness passed upon our rear, and came rolling over the land after us like a torrent. I proposed while we yet could see, to turn aside, lest we should be knocked down in the road by the crowd that followed us and trampled to death in the dark. We had scarce sat down, when darkness overspread us, not like that of a moonless or cloudy night, but of a room when it is shut up, and the lamp put out. You could hear the shrieks of women, the crying of children, and the shouts of men; some were seeking their children, others their parents, others their wives or husbands, and only distinguishing them by their voices; one lamenting his own fate, another that of his family; some praying to die, from the very fear of dying; many lifting their hands to the gods; but the greater part imagining that there were no gods left anywhere, and that the last and eternal night was come upon the world.

There were even some who augmented the real perils by imaginary terrors. Newcomers reported that such or such a building at Misenum had collapsed or taken fire—falsely, but they were credited. By degrees it grew lighter; which we imagined to be rather the warning of approaching fire (as in truth it was) than the return of day: however, the fire stayed at a distance from us: then again came darkness, and a heavy shower of ashes; we were obliged every now and then to rise and shake them off, otherwise we should have been buried and even crushed under their weight. I might have boasted that amidst dangers so appalling, not a sigh or expression of fear escaped from me, had not my support been founded in that miserable, though strong consolation, that all mankind were involved in the same calamity, and that I was perishing with the world itself.

At last this dreadful darkness was attenuated by degrees to a kind of cloud or smoke, and passed away; presently the real day returned, and even the sun appeared, though lurid as when an eclipse is in progress. Every object that presented itself to our yet affrighted gaze was changed, covered over with a drift of ashes, as with snow. We returned to Misenum, where we refreshed ourselves as well as we could, and passed an anxious night between hope and fear; though indeed with a much larger share of the latter, for the earthquake still continued, and several enthusiastic people were giving a grotesque turn to their own and their neighbors' calamities by terrible predictions. Even then, however, my mother and I, notwithstanding the danger we had passed, and that which still threatened us, had no thoughts of leaving the place, till we should receive some tidings of my uncle.

And now, you will read this narrative, so far beneath the dignity of a history, without any view of transferring it to your own; and indeed you must impute it to your own request, if it shall appear scarce worthy of a letter. Farewell.

TRANSLATED BY WILLIAM MELMOTH
TRANSLATION REVISED BY W. M. L. HUTCHINSON

On the Edge of the Primeval Forest

by ALBERT SCHWEITZER

Few men are as revered in their lifetime as Albert Schweitzer. He is considered by many to be the outstanding authority on Johann Sebastian Bach. He is also a fine organist, a theologian, philosopher and a physician. When he was thirty and famous as a musician, Schweitzer decided to become a doctor in order to help the natives of French Equatorial Africa. Born in Alsatia in 1875, in 1913 Schweitzer left for Lambaréné, Gabon, and has since established extensive medical facilities there with the financial aid of various groups and persons from the outside world. In the following selection he describes some early struggles at Lambaréné.

THE NUMBER OF PEOPLE WITH HEART COMPLAINTS astonishes me more and more. They, on the other hand, are astonished that I know all about their trouble as soon as I have examined them with the stethoscope. "Now I believe we've got a real doctor!" said an old woman to Joseph not long ago. "He knows that I can often hardly breathe at night, and that I often have swollen feet, yet I've never told him a word about it and he has never even looked at my feet." I cannot help saying to myself that there is something really glorious in the means which modern medicine has for treating the heart. I give digitalis according to the new French method (daily doses of a tenth of a milligram of digitalin continued for weeks and months) and am more than pleased with the results obtained. It must be said that it is easier to treat heart disease here than it is in Europe, for when patients are told that they must rest and keep quiet for weeks, they are never obliged to object that they will lose their wages and perhaps their work. They simply live at home and "recruit," and their family, in the widest sense of that word, supports them.

Mental complaints are relatively rarer here than in Europe, though I have already seen some half-dozen such. They are a great worry as I do not know how to dispose of them. If they are allowed to remain on the station they disturb us with their cries all the night through, and I have to get up again and again to quieten them with a subcutaneous injection. I can look back on several terrible nights which resulted in my feeling tired for many a day afterwards. The difficulty can be surmounted in the dry season, for then I can make the mental patients and their friends camp out on a sandbank about 600 yards away, although getting across to see them twice a day consumes a great deal both of time and of energy.

The condition of these poor creatures out here is dreadful. The natives do not know how to protect themselves from them. Confinement is impossible, as they can at any time break out of a bamboo hut. They are therefore bound with cords of bast, but that only makes their condition worse, and the final result almost always is that they are somehow or other got rid of. One of the Samkita missionaries told me once that a couple of years before, while sitting one Sunday in his house, he had heard loud cries in a neighbouring village. He got up and started off to see what was the matter, but met a native who told him it was only that some children were having the sand flies cut out from their feet; he need not worry, but might go home again. He did so, but learnt the next day that one of the villagers, who had become insane, had been bound hand and foot and thrown into the water.

My first contact with a mentally-diseased native happened at night. I was knocked up and taken to palm tree to which an elderly woman was bound. Around a fire in front of her sat the whole of her family, and behind them was the black forest wall. It was a glorious African night and the shimmering glow of the starry sky lighted up the scene. I ordered them to set her free, which they did, but with timidity and hesitation. The woman was no sooner free than she sprang at me in order to seize my lamp and throw it away. The natives fled with shrieks in every direction and would not come any nearer, even when the woman, whose hand I had seized, sank quietly to the ground as I told her, and offered me her arm for an injection of morphia and scopolamin. A few moments later she followed me to a hut, where, in a short time, she went to sleep. The case was one of an attack of recurrent maniacal disturbance, and in a fortnight she was well again, at least for a time. In consequence of this the report spread that the doctor was a great magician and could cure all mental diseases.

Unfortunately, I was soon to learn that there are forms of maniacal disturbance here with which our drugs can do little or nothing. The second case was an old man, and he, too, was brought with hands and feet bound. The ropes had cut deeply into his flesh, and hands and feet alike were covered with blood and sores. I was amazed at the small effect produced by the strongest doses of morphia, scopolamin, chloral hydrate, and bromide of potassium. On the second day Joseph said to me: "Doctor, believe me, the man is out of his mind because he has been poisoned. You will make nothing of him; he will get weaker and wilder, and at last he will die." And Joseph was right; in a fortnight the man was dead. From one of the Catholic fathers I learnt that he had robbed some women, and, therefore, had been followed up and poisoned by their relatives.

A similar case I was able to study from the beginning. One Sunday evening there arrived in a canoe a woman who was writhing with cramp. I thought at first that it was simple hysteria, but the next day maniacal disturbance supervened, and during the night she began to rave and shriek. On her, too, the narcotics had hardly any effect, and her strength rapidly diminished. The natives surmised that she had been poisoned, and whether they were right or not I am not in a position to decide.

From all I hear it must be true that poison is much used in these parts, and further south that is still oftener the case: the tribes between the Ogowe and the Congo are notorious in this respect. At the same time there are, among the natives, many inexplicable cases of sudden death which are quite unjustifiably regarded as the result of poison.

Anyhow, there must be many plants the juices of which have a peculiarly stimulating effect on the system. I have been assured by trustworthy persons that there are certain leaves and roots which enable men to row for a whole day without experiencing either hunger, thirst, or fatigue, and to display at the same time an increasingly boisterous merriment. I hope in time to learn something more definite about these "medicines," but it is always difficult to do so, because the knowledge about them is kept a strict secret. Anyone who is suspected of betraying anything about them, and, above all, if it is to a white man, may count with certainty on being poisoned.

That the medicine men employ poison to maintain their authority I learnt in a peculiar way through Joseph. About the middle of the dry season his village went off to a sandbank about three hours upstream from here, on a fishing expedition. These fishing days are not unlike the Old Testament harvest festivals, when the people "rejoiced before Yahweh." Old and young live together for a fortnight in "booths" made with branches of trees and eat at every meal fresh fish, broiled, baked, or stewed. Whatever is not consumed is dried and smoked, and if all goes well, a village may take home with it as many as ten thousand fish. As Joseph's eyes nearly start from their sockets whenever the conversation turns on fish, I proposed to allow him to go out with his village for the first afternoon, and asked him to take a small tub in which to bring back a few fishes for the doctor. He showed, however, no enthusiasm at the prospect, and a few questions put me in possession of the reason. On the first day there is no fishing done, but the place is blessed. The "elders" pour rum and throw tobacco leaves into the water to put the evil spirits into a good humour, so that they may let the fish be caught in the nets and may injure no one. These ceremonies were once omitted several years ago, but the following year an old woman wrapped herself up in a net and let herself be drowned. "But—why? Most of you are Christians!" I exclaimed; "you don't believe in these things!" "Certainly not," he replied, "but anyone who spoke against them or even allowed himself to smile while the rum and tobacco were being offered, would assuredly be poisoned sooner or later. The medicine men never forgive, and they live among us without any one knowing who they are." So he stayed at home the first day, but I allowed him to go some days later.

Besides the fear of poison there is also their dread of the supernatural power for evil which one man can exert over another, for the natives here believe that there are means of acquiring such powers. Whoever has the right fetish can do anything; he will always be successful when hunting, and he can bring bad luck, sickness, and death on anyone whom he wishes to injure. Europeans will never be able to understand how terrible is the life of the poor creatures who pass their days in continual fear of the fetishes which can be used against them. Only those who have seen this misery at close quarters will understand that it is a simple human duty to bring to these primitive peoples a new view of the world which can free them from these torturing superstitions. In this matter the greatest sceptic, did he find himself out here, would prove a real helper of mission work.

What is fetishism? It is something born of the fears of primitive man. Primitive man wants to possess some charm to protect him from the evil spirits in nature and from those of the dead, as well as from the power for evil of his fellow men, and this protecting power he attributes to certain objects which he carries about with him. He does not worship his fetish, but regards it as a little bit of property which cannot but be of service to him through its supernatural powers.

What makes a fetish? That which is unknown is supposed to have magical power. A fetish is composed of a number of little objects which fill a small bag, a buffalo horn, or a box; the things most commonly used are red feathers, small parcels of red earth, leopard's claws and teeth, and . . . bells from Europe! Bells of an old-fashioned shape which date from the barter transactions of the eighteenth century! Opposite the mission station a Negro has laid out a small cocoa plantation, and the fetish which is expected to protect it hangs on a tree in a corked bottle. Nowadays valuable fetishes are enclosed in tin boxes, so that they may not be damaged by termites, from whose ravages a wooden box gives no permanent protection.

There are big fetishes and little ones. A big one usually includes a piece of human skull, but it must be from the skull of someone who was killed expressly to provide the fetish. Last summer at a short distance below the station an elderly man was killed in a canoe. The murderer was discovered, and it is considered to have been proved that he committed the crime in order to secure a fetish by means of which he hoped to ensure the fullfillment of their contracts by people who owed him goods and money!

A few weeks later my wife and I took a walk one Sunday through the forest to Lake Degele, which is about two hours distant. In the village in which we took a midday rest the people had nothing to eat because for several days the women had been afraid to go out to the banana field. It had become known that several men were prowling about the neighborhood who wanted to kill someone in order to obtain a fetish. The women of Lambaréné asserted that these men had also been seen near one of our wells, and the whole district was in a state of excitement for several weeks.

I am myself the possessor of a fetish. The most important objects in it are two fragments of a human skull, of a longish oval shape and dyed with some sort of red coloring matter; they seem to me to be from the parietal bones. The owner was ill for many months, and his wife also, both suffering tortures from sleeplessness. Several times, however, the man heard in a dream a voice which revealed to him that they could only get well if they took the family fetish he had inherited to Mr. Haug,

the missionary in N'Gômô, and followed Mr. Haug's orders. Mr. Haug
referred him to me, and made me a present of the fetish. The man and his
wife stayed with me several weeks for treatment, and were discharged
with their health very much improved.

The belief that magical power dwells in human skulls which have
been obtained expressly for this purpose, must be a quite primitive one.
I saw not long ago in a medical periodical the assertion that the supposed cases of trephining which have often been recognized during the
excavation and examination of prehistoric graves were by no means
attempts at treatment of tumors on the brain or similar growths, as had
been assumed, but were simply operations for the securing of fetish
objects. The author of the article is probably right.

In the first nine months of my work here I have had close on two
thousand patients to examine, and I can affirm that most European
diseases are represented here; I even had a child with whooping cough.
Cancer, however, and appendicitis I have never seen. Apparently they
have not yet reached the Negroes of Equatorial Africa. On the other
hand, chills play a great part here. At the beginning of the dry season
there is as much sneezing and coughing in the church at Lambaréné as
there is in England at a midnight service on New Year's Eve. Many
children die of unrecognized pleurisy.

In the dry season the nights are fresher and colder than at other
times, and as the Negroes have no bedclothes they get so cold in their
huts that they cannot sleep, even though according to European standards
the temperature is still fairly high. On cold nights the thermometer shows
at least 68 degrees F., but the damp of the atmosphere, which makes
people sweat continually by day, makes them thereby so sensitive that
they shiver and freeze by night. White people, too, suffer continually
from chills and colds in the head, and there is much truth in a sentence
I came across in a book on tropical medicine, though it seemed at the
time rather paradoxical: "Where the sun is hot, one must be more careful
than elsewhere to avoid chills." Especially fatal to the natives is the
camp life on the sandbanks when they are out on their summer fishing
expeditions. Most of the old folk die of pneumonia which they have
caught on these occasions.

Rheumatism is commoner here than in Europe, and I not infrequently
come across cases of gout, though the sufferers cannot be said to bring
it on by an epicurean diet. That they eat too much flesh food cannot

possibly be alleged, as except for the fish days in summer they live almost exclusively on bananas and manioc.

That I should have to treat chronic nicotine poisoning out here I should never have believed. At first I could not tell what to think of acute constipation which was accompanied by nervous disturbances and only made worse by aperients, but while treating a black Government official who was suffering severely I came to see clearly, through observation and questioning, that the misuse of tobacco lay at the root of it. The man soon got well and the case was much talked of, as he had been a sufferer for years and had become almost incapable of work. From that time, whenever a case of severe constipation came to me, I asked at once: "How many pipes a day do you smoke?" and I recognized in a few weeks what mischief nicotine produces here. It was among the women that cases of nicotine poisoning are most frequent. Joseph explained to me that the natives suffer much from insomnia, and then smoke all through the night in order to stupefy themselves.

Tobacco comes here from America in the form of leaves, seven of which form a head (*tête de tobac*). It is a plant which is frightfully common and also frightfully strong (much stronger than that which is smoked by white people), and it largely takes the place of small coins: e.g., one leaf, worth about a halfpenny, will buy two pineapples, and almost all temporary services are paid for by means of it. If you have to travel, you take for the purchase of food for the crew, not money, for that has no value in the forest, but a box of tobacco leaves, and to prevent the men from helping themselves to its valuable contents you make it your seat. A pipe goes from mouth to mouth during the journey; and anybody who wants to travel fast and will promise his crew an extra two leaves each, is sure to arrive an hour or two sooner than he otherwise would. . . .

Abdominal tumors are very common here with the women.

My hope that I should not need to perform any major operation before the medical ward was ready for use was disappointed. On August 15th I had to operate on a case of strangulated hernia which had been brought in the evening before. The man, whose name was Aïnda, begged me to operate, for, like all natives, he knew well enough the dangers of his condition. There was, in fact, no time to lose, and the instruments were brought together as quickly as possible. Mr. Christol allowed me to use his boys' bedroom as an operating theater; my wife undertook to give the anesthetic, and a missionary acted as assistant. Everything went off better than we could have expected, but I was almost staggered by the quiet confidence with which the man placed himself in position on the operating table.

A military doctor from the interior, who is going to Europe on leave, tells me that he envies me the excellent assistance I had for my first operation on hernia! He himself, he said, had performed his with one native prisoner handing him the instruments and another administering the chloroform by guesswork, while each time they moved the fetters on their legs rattled; but his regular assistant was ill and there was no one who could take his place.

The aseptic precautions were, naturally, far from perfect, but the patient recovered. . . .

At the end of January and the beginning of February my wife and I were in Talagouga busy looking after Mr. Hermann, a missionary, who was suffering from a bad attack of boils with high fever, and at the same time I treated the sick of the neighborhood. Among the latter was a small boy who, with every sign of extreme terror, refused to enter the room, and had to be carried in by force. It transpired later that he quite thought the doctor meant to kill and eat him! The poor little fellow had got his knowledge of cannibalism, not from nursery tales, but from the terrible reality, for even today it has not been quite extirpated among the Pahouins. About the area over which it still prevails it is hard to say anything definite, as fear of the heavy penalties attached to it makes the natives keep every case as secret as possible. A short time ago, however, a man went from the neighborhood of Lambaréné into some outlying villages to collect arrears of debt, and did not come back. A laborer disappeared in the same way from near Samkita. People who know the country say that "missing" is often to be interpreted as "eaten."

The hut for the sleeping sickness victims is now in course of erection on the opposite bank, and costs me much money and time. When I am not myself superintending the laborers whom we have secured for grubbing up the vegetation and building the hut, nothing is done. For whole afternoons I have to neglect the sick to play the part of foreman there.

Sleeping sickness prevails more widely here than I suspected at first. The chief focus of infection is in the N'Gounje district, the N'Gounje being a tributary of the Ogowe about ninety miles from here, but there are isolated centers round Lambaréné and on the lakes behind N'Gômô.

What is the sleeping sickness? How is it spread? It seems to have existed in Equatorial Africa from time immemorial, but it was confined to particular centers, since there was little or no traveling. The native method of trade with the sea coast was for each tribe to convey the goods to the boundary of its territory, and there to hand them over to the traders of the adjoining one. From my window I can see the place where the N'Gounje enters the Ogowe, and so far only might the Galoas living round Lambaréné travel. Anyone who went beyond this point, further into the interior, was eaten.

When the Europeans came, the natives who served them as boats' crews, or as carriers in their caravans, moved with them from one district to another, and if any of them had the sleeping sickness they took it to fresh places. In the early days it was unknown to the Ogowe, and it was introduced about thirty years ago by carriers from Loango. Whenever it gets into a new district it is terribly destructive, and may carry off a third of the population. In Uganda, for example, it reduced the number of inhabitants in six years from 300,000 to 100,000. An officer told me that he once visited a village on the Upper Ogowe which had two thousand inhabitants. On passing it again two years later he could only count five hundred; the rest had died meanwhile of sleeping sickness. After some time the disease loses its virulence, for reasons that we cannot as yet explain, though it continues to carry off a regular, if small, number of victims, and then it may begin to rage again as destructively as before.

The first symptom consists of irregular attacks of fever, sometimes light, sometimes severe, and these may come and go for months without the sufferer feeling himself really ill. There are victims who enter the sleep stage straight from this condition of apparent health, but usually severe headaches come during the fever stage. Many a patient have I had come to me crying out: "Oh, doctor! my head, my head! I can't stand it any longer; let me die!" Again, the sleep stage is sometimes preceded by torturing sleeplessness, and there are patients who at this stage get mentally deranged; some become melancholy, others delirious. One of my first patients was a young man who was brought because he wanted to commit suicide.

As a rule, rheumatism sets in with the fever. A white man came to me once from the N'Gômô lake district suffering from sciatica. On careful examination, I saw it was the beginning of the sleeping sickness, and I sent him at once to the Pasteur Institute at Paris, where French sufferers are treated. Often, again, an annoying loss of memory is experienced, and this is not infrequently the first symptom which is noticed by those around them. Sooner or later, however, though it may be two or three years after the first attacks of fever, the sleep sets in. At first it is only an urgent need of sleep; the sufferer falls asleep whenever he sits down and is quiet, or just after meals.

A short time ago a white non-commissioned officer from Mouila, which is six days' journey from here, visited me because, while cleaning his revolver, he had put a bullet through his hand. He stayed at the Catholic mission station, and his black boy accompanied him whenever he came to have his hand dressed, and waited outside. When the N.C.O. was ready to go, there was almost always much shouting and searching for his attendant, till at last, with sleepy looks, the latter emerged from some corner. His master complained that he had already lost him several times because, wherever he happened to be, he was always taking a long nap. I examined his blood and discovered that he had the sleeping sickness.

Toward the finish the sleep becomes sounder and passes at last into coma. Then the sick man lies without either feeling or perception; his natural motions take place without his being conscious of them, and he gets continually thinner. Meanwhile his back and sides get covered with bed-sores; his knees are gradually drawn up to his neck, and he is altogether a horrible sight. Release by death has, however, often to be awaited for a long time, and sometimes there is even a lengthy spell of improved health. Last December I was treating a case which had reached this final stage, and at the end of four weeks the relatives hurried home with him that, at least, he might die in his own village. I myself expected the end to come almost at once, but a few days ago I got the news that he had recovered so far as to eat and speak and sit up, and had only died in April. The immediate cause of death is usually pneumonia.

Knowledge of the real nature of sleeping sickness is one of the latest victories of medicine, and is connected with the names of Ford, Castellani, Bruce, Dutton, Koch, Martin, and Leboeuf. The first description of it was given in 1803 from cases observed among the natives of Sierra Leone, and it was afterwards studied also in Negroes who had been taken from Africa to the Antilles and to Martinique. It was only in the 'sixties that extensive observations were begun in Africa itself, and these first led to a closer description of the last phase of the disease, no one even suspecting a preceding stage or that there was any connection between the disease and the long period of feverishness. This was only made possible by the discovery that both these forms of sickness had the same producing cause.

Then in 1901 the English doctors, Ford and Dutton, found, on examining with the microscope the blood of fever patients in Gambia, not the malaria parasites they expected, but small, active creatures which on account of their form they compared to gimlets, and named Trypanosomata, i.e., boring-bodies. Two years later the leaders of the English expedition for the investigation of sleeping sickness in the Uganda district found in the blood of a whole series of patients similar little active creatures. Being acquainted with what Ford and Dutton had published on the subject, they asked whether these were not identical with those found in the fever patients from the Gambia region, and at the same time, on examination of their own fever patients, they found the fever to be due to the same cause as produced the sleeping sickness. Thus it was proved that the "Gambia fever" was only an early stage of sleeping sickness.

The sleeping sickness is most commonly conveyed by the *Glossina palpalis*, a species of tsetse fly which flies only by day. If this fly has once bitten anyone with sleeping sickness, it can carry the disease to others for a long time, perhaps for the rest of its life, for the trypanosomes which entered it in the blood it sucked live and increase and pass in its saliva into the blood of anyone it bites.

Still closer study of sleeping sickness revealed the fact that it can be also conveyed by mosquitoes, if these insects take their fill of blood from a healthy person immediately after they have bitten anyone with sleeping sickness, as they will then have trypanosomes in their saliva. Thus the mosquito army continues by night the work which the *glossina* is carrying on all day. Poor Africa!*

In its essential nature sleeping sickness is a chronic inflammation of the meninges and the brain, one, however, which always ends in death, and this ensues because the trypanosomes pass from the blood into the cerebro-spinal fluid. To fight the disease successfully it is necessary to kill them before they have passed from the blood, since it is only in the blood that atoxyl, one weapon that we at present possess, produces effects which can to any extent be relied on; in the cerebro-spinal marrow the trypanosomes are comparatively safe from it. A doctor must, therefore, learn to recognise the disease in the early stage, when it first produces fever. If he can do that, there is a prospect of recovery.

In a district, therefore, where sleeping sickness has to be treated, its

---

* I must, however, in justice add that the mosquito does not harbor the trypanosomes permanently, and that its saliva is poisonous only for a short time after it has been polluted by the blood of a sleeping sickness victim.

diagnosis is a terribly complicated business because the significance of every attack of fever, of every persistent headache, of every prolonged attack of sleeplessness, and of all rheumatic pains must be gauged with the help of the microscope. Moreover, this examination of the blood is, unfortunately, by no means simple, but takes a great deal of time, for it is only very very seldom that these pale, thin parasites, about one eighteen-thousandth of a millimeter long, are to be found in any considerable number in the blood. So far I have only examined one case in which three or four were to be seen together. Even when the disease is certainly present one can, as a rule, examine several drops of blood, one after another, before discovering a single trypanosome, and to scrutinise each drop properly needs at least ten minutes. I may, therefore, spend an hour over the blood of a suspected victim, examining four or five drops without finding anything, and even then have no right to say there is no disease; there is still a long and tedious testing process which must be applied. This consists in taking ten cubic centimeters of blood from a vein in one of the sufferer's arms, and keeping it revolving centrifugally for an hour according to certain prescribed rules, at the same time pouring off at intervals the outer rings of blood. The trypanosomes are expected to have collected into the last few drops, and these are put under the microscope; but even if there is again a negative result, it is not safe to say that the disease is not present. If there are no trypanosomes to-day, I may find them ten days hence, and if I have discovered some to-day, there may be none in three days' time and for a considerable period after that. A white official, whose blood I had proved to contain trypanosomes, was subsequently kept under observation for weeks, in Libreville, without any being discovered, and it was only in the Sleeping Sickness Institute at Brazzaville that they were a second time proved to be there.

If, then, I wish to treat such patients conscientiously, a couple of them together can tie me for a whole morning to the microscope while outside there are sitting a score of sick people who want to be seen before dinner-time! There are also surgical patients whose dressings must be renewed; water must be distilled, and medicines prepared; sores must be cleansed, and there are teeth to be drawn! With this continual drive, and the impatience of the waiting sick, I often get so worried and nervous that I hardly know where I am or what I am doing.

Atoxyl is a frightfully dangerous drug. If the solution is left for some time in the light it decomposes, just like salvarsan, and works as a poison but even if it is prepared faultlessly and is in perfect condition, it may cause blindness by injuring the nerves of sight. Nor does this depend on the size of the dose; small ones are often more dangerous than large ones, and they are never of any use. If one begins with too small a dose, in order to see whether the patient can take the drug, the trypanosomes get inured to it; they become "atoxylproof," as it is called, and then can defy the strongest doses. Every five days my sleeping sick come to me for an injection, and before I begin I always ask in trepidation whether any of them have noticed that their sight is not as good as usual. Happily, I have so far only one case of blinding to record, and that was a man in whom the disease had already reached a very advanced stage. Sleeping sickness now prevails from the east coast of Africa right to the west, and from the Niger in the northwest to the Zambesi in the southeast. Shall we now conquer it? A systematic campaign against it over this wide district would need many doctors and the cost would be enormous. . . . Yet, where death already stalks about as conqueror, the European States provide in most niggardly fashion the means of stopping it, and merely undertake stupid defensive measures which only give it a chance of reaping a fresh harvest in Europe itself. . . .

As to operations, one undertakes, naturally, in the forest only such as are urgent and which promise a successful result. The one I have had to perform oftenest is that for hernia, a thing which afflicts the Negroes of Central Africa much more than it does white people, though why this should be so we do not know. They also suffer much oftener than white people from strangulated hernia, in which the intestine becomes constricted and blocked, so that it can no longer empty itself. It then becomes enormously inflated by the gases which form, and this causes terrible pain. Then after several days of torture death takes place, unless the intestine can be got back through the rupture into the abdomen. Our ancestors were well acquainted with this terrible method of dying, but we no longer see it in Europe because every case is operated upon as soon as ever it is recognised. "Let not the sun go down upon your— strangulated hernia," is the maxim continually impressed upon medical students. But in Africa this terrible death is quite common. There are few Negroes who have not as boys seen some man rolling in the sand of his hut and howling with agony till death came to release him. So now, the moment a man feels that his rupture is a strangulated one—rupture is far rarer among women—he begs his friends to put him in a canoe and bring him to me.

How can I describe my feelings when a poor fellow is brought me in this condition? I am the only person within hundreds of miles who can help him. Because I am here and am supplied by my friends with the necessary means, he can be saved, like those who came before him in the same condition and those who will come after him, while otherwise he would have fallen a victim to the torture. This does not mean merely that I can save his life. We must all die. But that I can save him from days of torture, that is what I feel as my great and ever new privilege. Pain is a more terrible lord of mankind than even death himself.

So, when the poor, moaning creature comes, I lay my hand on his forehead and say to him: "Don't be afraid! In an hour's time you shall be put to sleep, and when you wake you won't feel any more pain." Very soon he is given an injection of omnipon; the doctor's wife is called to the hospital, and, with Joseph's help, makes everything ready for the operation. When that is to begin she administers the anesthetic, and Joseph, in a long pair of rubber gloves, acts as assistant.

The operation is finished, and in the hardly-lighted dormitory I watch for the sick man's awaking. Scarcely has he recovered consciousness when he stares about him and ejaculates again and again: "I've no more pain! I've no more pain!" . . . His hand feels for mine and will not let it go. Then I begin to tell him and the others who are in the room that it is the Lord Jesus who has told the doctor and his wife to come to the Ogowe, and that white people in Europe give them the money to live here and cure the sick Negroes. Then I have to answer questions as to who these white people are, where they live, and how they know that the natives suffer so much from sickness. The African sun is shining through the coffee bushes into the dark shed, but we, black and white, sit side by side and feel that we know by experience the meaning of the words: "And all ye are brethren" (Matt. xxiii, 8). Would that my generous friends in Europe could come out here and live through one such hour!

TRANSLATED BY C. T. CAMPION

The Last March

by ROBERT FALCON SCOTT

No modern compilation of man's defiance of nature can be complete without Scott's classic account. This document, in a great British tradition of fortitude sotto voce, *is one of the noblest and most moving ever written. One of its finest aspects is its tragic "rightness"— that Scott should have outlived his companions in catastrophe and that he should have been able to write his journal until very close to the end. Scott and his four companions reached the South Pole on January 18, 1912, only to find the tent that Amundsen had left there some three weeks before. It was a great disappointment to them. Their return journey to their base was beset by illness, hunger and storms. Evans and Oates died first. The rest perished on or about March 27, 1912, when further advance was made impossible by constant blizzards. On November 12, 1912, a search party from the main base discovered Scott's tent, containing the bodies of Scott, Wilson and Bowers, as well as Scott's records and journals.*

SUNDAY, FEBRUARY 18.—R. 32. TEMP. −5.5°. AT SHAMBLES Camp. We gave ourselves 5 hours' sleep at the lower glacier depot after the horrible night, and came on at about 3 today to this camp, coming fairly easily over the divide. Here with plenty of horsemeat we have had a fine supper, to be followed by others such, and so continue a more plentiful era if we can keep good marches up. New life seems to come with greater food almost immediately, but I am anxious about the Barrier surfaces.

Monday, February 19.—Lunch T. −16°. It was late (past noon) before we got away today, as I gave nearly 8 hours sleep, and much camp work was done shifting sledges and fitting up new one with mast, &c., packing horsemeat and personal effects. The surface was every bit as bad as I expected, the sun shining brightly on it and its covering of soft loose sandy snow. We have come out about 2′ on the old tracks. Perhaps lucky to have a fine day for this and our camp work, but we shall want wind or change of sliding conditions to do anything on such a surface as we have got. I fear there will not be much change for the next 3 or 4 days.

R. 33. Temp. −17°. We have struggled out 4.6 miles in a short day over a really terrible surface—it has been like pulling over desert sand, not the least glide in the world. If this goes on we shall have a bad time, but I sincerely trust it is only the result of this windless area close to the coast and that, as we are making steadily outward, we shall shortly escape it. It is perhaps premature to be anxious about covering distance. In all other respects things are improving. We have our sleeping bags spread on the sledge and they are drying, but, above all, we have our full measure of food again. Tonight we had a sort of stew fry of pemmican and horseflesh, and voted it the best hoosh we had ever had on a sledge journey. The absence of poor Evans is a help to the commissariat, but if he had been here in a fit state we might have got along faster. I wonder what is in store for us, with some little alarm at the lateness of the season.

Monday, February 20.—R. 34. Lunch Temp. −13°; Supper Temp. −15°. Same terrible surface; four hours' hard plodding in morning brought us to our Desolation Camp, where we had the four-day blizzard. We looked for more pony meat, but found none. After lunch we took to ski with some improvement of comfort. Total mileage for day 7—the ski tracks pretty plain and easily followed this afternoon. We have left another cairn behind. Terribly slow progress, but we hope for better things as we clear the land. There is a tendency to cloud over in the SE tonight, which may turn to our advantage. At present our sledge and ski leave deeply ploughed tracks which can be seen winding for miles behind. It is distressing, but as usual trials are forgotten when we camp, and good food is our lot. Pray God we get better traveling as we are not so fit as we were, and the season is advancing apace.

Tuesday, February 21.—R. 35. Lunch Temp. −9½°; Supper Temp. −11°. Gloomy and overcast when we started; a good deal warmer. The marching almost as bad as yesterday. Heavy toiling all day, inspiring gloomiest thoughts at times. Rays of comfort when we picked up tracks and cairns. At lunch we seemed to have missed the way, but an hour or two after we passed the last pony walls, and since, we struck a tent ring, ending the march actually on our old pony tracks. There is a critical spot here with a long stretch between cairns. If we can tide that over we get on the regular cairn route, and with luck should stick to it; but everything depends on the weather. We never won a march of 8½ miles with greater difficulty, but we can't go on like this. We are drawing away from the land and perhaps may get better things in a day or two. I devoutly hope so.

Wednesday, February 22.—R. 36. Supper Temp. −2°. There is little doubt we are in for a rotten critical time going home, and the lateness of the season may make it really serious. Shortly after starting today the wind grew very fresh from the SE with strong surface drift. We lost the faint track immediately, though covering ground fairly rapidly. Lunch came without sight of the cairn we had hoped to pass. In the afternoon, Bowers being sure we were too far to the west, steered out. Result, we have passed another pony camp without seeing it. Looking at the map tonight there is no doubt we are too far to the east. With clear weather we ought to be able to correct the mistake, but will the weather get clear? It's a gloomy position, more especially as one sees the same difficulty returning even when we have corrected this error. The wind is dying down tonight and the sky clearing in the south, which is hopeful. Meanwhile it is satisfactory to note that such untoward events fail to damp the spirit of the party. Tonight we had a pony hoosh so excellent and filling that one feels really strong and vigorous again.

Thursday, February 23.—R. 37. Lunch Temp. −9.8°; Supper Temp. −12°. Started in sunshine, wind almost dropped. Luckily Bowers took a round of angles and with help of the chart we fogged out that we must be inside rather than outside tracks. The data were so meager that it seemed a great responsibility to march out and we were none of us happy about it. But just as we decided to lunch, Bowers' wonderful sharp eyes detected an old double lunch cairn, the theodolite telescope confirmed it, and our spirits rose accordingly. This afternoon we marched on and picked up another cairn; then on and camped only 2½ miles from the depot. We cannot see it, but given fine weather, we cannot miss it. We are, therefore, extraordinarily relieved. Covered 8.2 miles in 7 hours, showing we can do 10 to 12 on this surface. Things are again looking up, as we are on the regular line of cairns, with no gaps right home, I hope.

Friday, February 24.—Lunch. Beautiful day—too beautiful—an hour after starting loose ice crystals spoiling surface. Saw depot and reached it middle forenoon. Found store in order except shortage oil—shall have to be *very* saving with fuel—otherwise have ten full days' provision from tonight and shall have less than 70 miles to go. Note from Meares who passed through December 15, saying surface bad; from Atkinson, after fine marching (2¼ days from pony depot), reporting Keohane better after sickness. Short note from Evans, not very cheerful, saying surface bad, temperature high. Think he must have been a little anxious. It is an immense relief to have picked up this depot and, for the time, anxieties are thrust aside. There is no doubt we have been rising steadily since leaving the Shambles Camp. The coastal Barrier descends except where glaciers press out. Undulation still, but flattening out. Surface soft on top, curiously hard below. Great difference now between night and day temperatures. Quite warm as I write in tent. We are on tracks with half-march cairn ahead; have covered 4½ miles. Poor Wilson has a fearful attack snow blindness consequent on yesterday's efforts. Wish we had more fuel.

Night camp R. 38. Temp. −17°. A little despondent again. We had a really terrible surface this afternoon and only covered 4 miles. We are on the track just beyond a lunch cairn. It really will be a bad business if we are to have this pulling all through. I don't know what to think, but the rapid closing of the season is ominous. It is great luck having the horsemeat to add to our ration. Tonight we have had a real fine hoosh. It is a race between the season and hard conditions and our fitness and good food.

Saturday, February 25.—Lunch Temp. −12°. Managed just 6 miles this morning. Started somewhat despondent; not relieved when pulling seemed to show no improvement. Bit by bit surface grew better, less sastrugi, more glide, slight following wind for a time. Then we began to travel a little faster. But the pulling is still *very* hard; undulations disappearing but inequalities remain.

Twenty-six Camp walls about 2 miles ahead, all tracks in sight—Evans' track very conspicuous. This is something in favor, but the pulling is tiring us, though we are getting into better ski drawing again. Bowers hasn't quite the trick and is a little hurt at my criticisms, but I never doubted his heart. Very much easier—write diary at lunch—excellent meal—now one pannikin very strong tea—four biscuits and butter.

Hope for better things this afternoon, but no improvement apparent. Oh! for a little wind—E. Evans evidently had plenty.

R. 39. Temp. −20°. Better march in afternoon. Day yields 11.4 miles—the first double figure of steady dragging for a long time, but it meant and will mean hard work if we can't get a wind to help us.

Evans evidently had a strong wind here, SE I should think. The temperature goes very low at night now when the sky is clear as at present. As a matter of fact this is wonderfully fair weather—the only drawback the spoiling of the surface and absence of wind. We see all tracks very plain, but the pony walls have evidently been badly drifted up. Some kind people had substituted a cairn at last camp 27. The old cairns do not seem to have suffered much.

Sunday, February 26.—Lunch Temp. −17°. Sky overcast at start, but able see tracks and cairn distinct at long distance. Did a little better, 6½ miles to date. Bowers and Wilson now in front. Find great relief pulling behind with no necessity to keep attention on track. Very cold nights now and cold feet starting march, as day footgear doesn't dry at all. We are doing well on our food, but we ought to have yet more. I hope the next depot, now only 50 miles, will find us with enough surplus to open out. The fuel shortage still an anxiety.

R. 40. Temp. −21°. Nine hours' solid marching has given us 11½ miles. Only 43 miles from the next depot. Wonderfully fine weather but cold, very cold. Nothing dries and we get our feet cold too often. We want more food yet and especially more fat. Fuel is woefully short. We can scarcely hope to get a better surface at this season, but I wish we could have some help from the wind, though it might shake us up badly if the temp. didn't rise.

Monday, February 27.—Desperately cold last night: −33° when we got up, with −37° minimum. Some suffering from cold feet, but all got good rest. We *must* open out on food soon. But we have done 7 miles this morning and hope for some 5 this afternoon. Overcast sky and good surface till now, when sun shows again. It is good to be marching the cairns up, but there is still much to be anxious about. We talk of little but food, except after meals. Land disappearing in satisfactory manner. Pray God we have no further setbacks. We are naturally always discussing possibility of meeting dogs, where and when, &c. It is a critical position. We may find ourselves in safety at next depot, but there is a horrid element of doubt.

Camp R. 41. Temp. −32°. Still fine clear weather but very cold—absolutely calm tonight. We have got off an excellent march for these days (12.2) and are much earlier than usual in our bags. 31 miles to depot, 3 days' fuel at a pinch, and 6 days' food. Things began to look a little better; we can open out a little on food from tomorrow night, I think.

Very curious surface—soft recent sastrugi which sink underfoot, and between, a sort of flaky crust with large crystals beneath.

Tuesday, February 28.—Lunch. Thermometer went below −40° last night; it was desperately cold for us, but we had a fair night. I decided to slightly increase food; the effect is undoubtedly good. Started marching in −32° with a slight northwesterly breeze—blighting. Many cold feet this morning; long time over footgear, but we are earlier. Shall camp earlier and get the chance of a good night, if not the reality. Things must be critical till we reach the depot, and the more I think of matters, the more I anticipate their remaining so after that event. Only 24½ miles from the depot. The sun shines brightly, but there is little warmth in it. There is no doubt the middle of the Barrier is a pretty awful locality.

Camp 42. Splendid pony hoosh sent us to bed and sleep happily after a horrid day, wind continuing; did 11½ miles. Temp. not quite so low, but expect we are in for cold night (Temp. −27°).

Wednesday, February 29.—Lunch. Cold night. Minimum Temp. −37.5°; −30° with northwest wind, force 4, when we got up. Frightfully cold starting; luckily Bowers and Oates in their last new finnesko; keeping my old ones for present. Expected awful march and for first hour got it. Then things improved and we camped after 5½ hours marching close to lunch camp—22½. Next camp is our depot and it is exactly 13 miles. It ought not to take more than 1½ days; we pray for another fine one. The oil will just about spin out in that event, and we arrive 3 clear days' food in hand. The increase of ration has had an enormously beneficial result. Mountains now looking small. Wind still very light from west—cannot understand this wind.

Thursday, March 1.—Lunch. Very cold last night—minimum −41.5°. Cold start to march, too, as usual now. Got away at 8 and have marched within sight of depot; flag something under 3 miles away. We did 11½ yesterday and marched 6 this morning. Heavy dragging yesterday and *very* heavy this morning. Apart from sledging considerations the weather is wonderful. Cloudless days and nights and the wind trifling. Worse luck, the light airs come from the north and keep us horribly cold. For this lunch hour the exception has come. There is a bright and comparatively warm sun. All our gear is out drying.

Friday, March 2.—Lunch. Misfortunes rarely come singly. We marched to the depot fairly easily yesterday afternoon, and since that have suffered three distinct blows which have placed us in a bad position. First we found a shortage of oil; with most rigid economy it can scarce carry us to the next depot on this surface. Second, Titus Oates disclosed his feet, the toes showing very bad indeed, evidently bitten by the late temperatures. The third blow came in the night, when the wind, which we had hailed with some joy, brought dark overcast weather. It fell below −40° in the night, and this morning it took 1½ hours to get our footgear on, but we got away before night. We lost cairn and tracks together and made as steady as we could N by W, but have seen nothing. Worse was to come—the surface is simply awful. In spite of strong wind and full sail we have only done 5½ miles. We are in a very queer street since there is no doubt we cannot do the extra marches and feel the cold horribly.

Saturday, March 3.—Lunch. We picked up the track again yesterday, finding ourselves to the eastward. Did close on 10 miles and things looked a trifle better; but this morning the outlook is blacker than ever. Started well and with good breeze; for an hour made good headway; then the surface grew awful beyond words. The wind drew forward; every circumstance was against us. After 4½ hours things so bad that we camped, having covered 4½ miles. One cannot consider this a fault of our own—certainly we were pulling hard this morning—it was more than three parts surface which held us back—the wind at strongest, powerless to move the sledge. When the light is good it is easy to see the reason. The surface, lately a very good hard one, is coated with a thin layer of woolly crystals, formed by radiation no doubt. These are too firmly fixed to be removed by the wind and cause impossible friction on the runners. God help us, we can't keep up this pulling, that is certain. Amongst ourselves we are unendingly cheerful, but what each man feels in his heart I can only guess. Pulling on footgear in the morning is getting slower and slower, therefore every day more dangerous.

Sunday, March 4.—Lunch. Things looking *very* black indeed. As usual we forgot our trouble last night, got into our bags, slept splendidly on good hoosh, woke and had another, and started marching. Sun shining brightly, tracks clear, but surface covered with sandy frost rime. All the morning we had to pull with all our strength, and in 4½ hours we covered 3½ miles. Last night it was overcast and thick, surface bad; this morning sun shining and surface as bad as ever. One has little to hope for except perhaps strong dry wind—an unlikely contingency at this time of year. Under the immediate surface crystals is a hard sastrugi surface, which must have been excellent for pulling a week or two ago. We are about 42 miles from the next depot and have a week's food, but only about 3 to 4 days' fuel—we are as economical of the latter as one can possibly be, and we cannot afford to save food and pull as we are pulling. We are in a very tight place indeed, but none of us despondent *yet*, or at least we preserve every semblance of good cheer, but one's heart sinks as the sledge stops dead at some sastrugi behind which the surface sand lies thickly heaped. For the moment the temperature is on the −20°—an improvement which makes us much more comfortable, but a colder snap is bound to come again soon. I fear that Oates at least will weather such an event very poorly. Providence to our aid! We can expect little from man now except the possibility of extra food at the next depot. It will be real bad if we get there and find the same shortage of oil. Shall we get there? Such a short distance it would have appeared to us on the summit! I don't know what I should do if Wilson and Bowers weren't so determinedly cheerful over things.

Monday, March 5.—Lunch. Regret to say going from bad to worse. We got a slant of wind yesterday afternoon, and going on 5 hours we converted our wretched morning run of 3½ miles into something over 9. We went to bed on a cup of cocoa and pemmican solid with the chill off. (R. 47.) The result is telling on all, but mainly on Oates, whose feet are in a wretched condition. One swelled up tremendously last night and he is very lame this morning. We started march on tea and pemmican as last night—we pretend to prefer the pemmican this way. Marched for 5 hours this morning over a slightly better surface covered with high moundy sastrugi. Sledge capsized twice; we pulled on foot, covering about 5½ miles. We are two pony marches and 4 miles about from our depot. Our fuel dreadfully low and the poor Soldier nearly done. It is pathetic enough because we can do nothing for him; more hot food might do a little, but only a little, I fear. We none of us expected these terribly low temperatures, and of the rest of us Wilson is feeling them most; mainly, I fear, from his self-sacrificing devotion in doctoring Oates' feet. We cannot help each other, each has enough to do to take care of himself. We get cold on the march when the trudging is heavy, and the wind pierces our warm garments. The others, all of them, are unendingly cheerful when in the tent. We mean to see the game through with a proper spirit, but it's tough work to be pulling harder than we ever pulled in our lives for long hours, and to feel that the progress is so slow. One can only say "God help us!" and plod on our weary way, cold and very miserable, though outwardly cheerful. We talk of all sorts of subjects in the tent, not much of food now, since we decided to take the risk of running a full ration. We simply couldn't go hungry at this time.

Tuesday, March 6.—Lunch. We did a little better with help of wind yesterday afternoon, finishing 9½ miles for the day, and 27 miles from depot. (R. 48.) But this morning things have been awful. It was warm in the night and for the first time during the journey I overslept myself by more than an hour; then we were slow with footgear; then, pulling with all our might (for our lives) we could scarcely advance at rate of a mile an hour; then it grew thick and three times we had to get out of harness to search for tracks. The result is something less than 3½ miles for the forenoon. The sun is shining now and the wind gone. Poor Oates is unable to pull, sits on the sledge when we are track-searching—he is wonderfully plucky, as his feet must be giving him great pain. He makes no complaint, but his spirits only come up in spurts now, and he grows more silent in the tent. We are making a spirit lamp to try and replace the primus when our oil is exhausted. It will be a very poor substitute and we've not got much spirit. If we could have kept up our 9-mile days we might have got within reasonable distance of the depot before running out, but nothing but a strong wind and good surface can help us now, and though we had quite a good breeze this morning, the sledge came as heavy as lead. If we were all fit I should have hopes of getting through, but the poor Soldier has become a terrible hindrance, though he does his utmost and suffers much I fear.

Wednesday, March 7.—A little worse I fear. One of Oates' feet *very* bad this morning; he is wonderfully brave. We still talk of what we will do together at home.

We only made 6½ miles yesterday. (R. 49.) This morning in 4½ hours we did just over 4 miles. We are 16 from our depot. If we only find the correct proportion of food there and this surface continues, we may get to the next depot but not to One Ton Camp. We hope against hope that the dogs have been to Mt. Hooper; then we might pull through. If there is a shortage of oil again we can have little hope. One feels that for poor Oates the crisis is near, but none of us are improving, though we are wonderfully fit considering the really excessive work we are doing. We are only kept going by good food. No wind this morning till a chill northerly air came ahead. Sun bright and cairns showing up well. I should like to keep the track to the end.

Thursday, March 8.—Lunch. Worse and worse in morning; poor Oates' left foot can never last out, and time over footgear something awful. Have to wait in night footgear for nearly an hour before I start changing, and then am generally first to be ready. Wilson's feet giving trouble now, but this mainly because he gives so much help to others. We did 4½ miles this morning and are now 8½ miles from the depot— a ridiculously small distance to feel in difficulties, yet on this surface we

know we cannot equal half our old marches, and that for that effort we
expend nearly double the energy. The great question is, What shall we
find at the depot? If the dogs have visited it we may get along a good
distance, but if there is another short allowance of fuel, God help us
indeed. We are in a very bad way, I fear, in any case.

Saturday, March 10.—Things steadily downhill. Oates' foot worse.
He has rare pluck and must know that he can never get through. He
asked Wilson if he had a chance this morning, and of course Bill had
to say he didn't know. In point of fact he has none. Apart from him,
if he went under now, I doubt whether we could get through. With great
care we might have a dog's chance, but no more. The weather conditions
are awful, and our gear gets steadily more icy and difficult to manage.
At the same time of course poor Titus is the greatest handicap. He keeps
us waiting in the morning until we have partly lost the warming effect of
our good breakfast, when the only wise policy is to be up and away at
once; again at lunch. Poor chap! it is too pathetic to watch him; one
cannot but try to cheer him up.

Yesterday we marched up the depot, Mt. Hooper. Cold comfort.
Shortage on our allowance all round. I don't know that anyone is to
blame. The dogs which would have been our salvation have evidently
failed. Meares had a bad trip home I suppose.

This morning it was calm when we breakfasted, but the wind came
from the WNW as we broke camp. It rapidly grew in strength. After
traveling for half an hour I saw that none of us could go on facing such
conditions. We were forced to camp and are spending the rest of the day
in a comfortless blizzard camp, wind quite foul. (R. 52.)

Sunday, March 11.—Titus Oates is very near the end, one feels. What
we or he will do, God only knows. We discussed the matter after breakfast; he is a brave fine fellow and understands the situation, but he
practically asked for advice. Nothing could be said but to urge him to
march as long as he could. One satisfactory result to the discussion; I
practically ordered Wilson to hand over the means of ending our troubles
to us, so that any one of us may know how to do so. Wilson had no
choice between doing so and our ransacking the medicine case. We have
30 opium tabloids apiece and he is left with a tube of morphine. So far
the tragical side of our story. (R. 53.)

The sky completely overcast when we started this morning. We could
see nothing, lost the tracks, and doubtless have been swaying a good
deal since—3.1 miles for the forenoon—terribly heavy dragging—expected it. Know that 6 miles is about the limit of our endurance now, if

we get no help from wind or surfaces. We have 7 days' food and should be about 55 miles from One Ton Camp tonight, $6 \times 7 = 42$, leaving us 13 miles short of our distance, even if things get no worse. Meanwhile the season rapidly advances.

Monday, March 12.—We did 6.9 miles yesterday, under our necessary average. Things are left much the same, Oates not pulling much, and now with hands as well as feet pretty well useless. We did 4 miles this morning in 4 hours 20 min.—we may hope for 3 this afternoon, $7 \times 6 =$ 42. We shall be 47 miles from the depot. I doubt if we can possibly do it. The surface remains awful, the cold intense, and our physical condition running down. God help us! Not a breath of favorable wind for more than a week, and apparently liable to head winds at any moment.

Wednesday, March 14.—No doubt about the going downhill, but everything going wrong for us. Yesterday we woke to a strong northerly wind with temp. $-37°$. Couldn't face it, so remained in camp (R. 54.) till 2, then did 5¼ miles. Wanted to march later, but party feeling the cold badly as the breeze (N) never took off entirely, and as the sun sank the temp. fell. Long time getting supper in dark. (R. 55.)

This morning started with southerly breeze, set sail and passed another cairn at good speed; halfway, however, the wind shifted to W by S or WSW, blew through our wind clothes and into our mits. Poor Wilson horribly cold, could not get off ski for some time. Bowers and I practically made camp, and when we got into the tent at last we were all deadly cold. Then temp. now midday down $-43°$ and the wind strong. We *must* go on, but now the making of every camp must be more difficult and dangerous. It must be near the end, but a pretty merciful end. Poor Oates got it again in the foot. I shudder to think what it will be like tomorrow. It is only with greatest pains rest of us keep off frostbites. No idea there could be temperatures like this at this time of year with such winds. Truly awful outside the tent. Must fight it out to the last biscuit, but can't reduce rations.

Friday, March 16 or Saturday 17.—Lost track of dates, but think the last correct. Tragedy all along the line. At lunch, the day before yesterday, poor Titus Oates said he couldn't go on; he proposed we should leave him in his sleeping bag. That we could not do, and we induced him to come on, on the afternoon march. In spite of its awful nature for him he struggled on and we made a few miles. At night he was worse and we knew the end had come.

Should this be found I want these facts recorded. Oates' last thoughts were of his mother, but immediately before he took pride in thinking that his regiment would be pleased with the bold way in which he met his death. We can testify to his bravery. He has borne intense suffering for weeks without complaint, and to the very last was able and willing to discuss outside subjects. He did not—would not—give up hope till the very end. He was a brave soul. This was the end. He slept through the night before last, hoping not to wake; but he woke in the morning—yesterday. It was blowing a blizzard. He said, "I am just going outside and may be some time." He went out into the blizzard and we have not seen him since.

I take this opportunity of saying that we have stuck to our sick companions to the last. In case of Edgar Evans, when absolutely out of food and he lay insensible, the safety of the remainder seemed to demand his abandonment, but Providence mercifully removed him at this critical moment. He died a natural death, and we did not leave him till two hours after his death. We knew that poor Oates was walking to his death, but though we tried to dissuade him, we knew it was the act of a brave man and an English gentleman. We all hope to meet the end with a similar spirit, and assuredly the end is not far.

I can only write at lunch and then only occasionally. The cold is intense, −40° at midday. My companions are unendingly cheerful, but we are all on the verge of serious frostbites, and though we constantly talk of fetching through I don't think any one of us believes it in his heart.

We are cold on the march now, and at all times except meals. Yesterday we had to lay up for a blizzard and today we move dreadfully slowly. We are at No. 14 pony camp, only two pony marches from One Ton Depot. We leave here our theodolite, a camera, and Oates' sleeping bags. Diaries, &c., and geological specimens carried at Wilson's special request, will be found with us or on our sledge.

Sunday, March 18.—Today, lunch, we are 21 miles from the depot. Ill fortune presses, but better may come. We have had more wind and drift from ahead yesterday; had to stop marching; wind NW, force 4, temp. −35°. No human being could face it, and we are worn out *nearly*.

My right foot has gone, nearly all the toes—two days ago I was proud possessor of best feet. These are the steps of my downfall. Like an ass I mixed a small spoonful of curry powder with my melted pemmican—it gave me violent indigestion. I lay awake and in pain all night; woke and felt done on the march; foot went and I didn't know it. A very small measure of neglect and have a foot which is not pleasant to contemplate. Bowers takes first place in condition, but there is not much to choose after all. The others are still confident of getting through—or pretend to

be—I don't know! We have the last *half* fill of oil in our primus and a
very small quantity of spirit—this alone between us and thirst. The wind
is fair for the moment, and that is perhaps a fact to help. The mileage
would have seemed ridiculously small on our outward journey.

Monday, March 19.—Lunch. We camped with difficulty last night,
and were dreadfully cold till after our supper of cold pemmican and
biscuit and a half a pannikin of cocoa cooked over the spirit. Then,
contrary to expectation, we got warm and all slept well. Today we
started in the usual dragging manner. Sledge dreadfully heavy. We are
15½ miles from the depot and ought to get there in three days. What
progress! We have two days' food but barely a day's fuel. All our feet
are getting bad—Wilson's best, my right foot worst, left all right. There
is no chance to nurse one's feet till we can get hot food into us. Amputation is the least I can hope for now, but will the trouble spread? That is
the serious question. The weather doesn't give us a chance—the wind
from N to NW and $-40°$ temp. today.

Wednesday, March 21.—Got within 11 miles of depot Monday night;
had to lay up all yesterday in severe blizzard. Today forlorn hope,
Wilson and Bowers going to depot for fuel.

Thursday, March 22 and 23.—Blizzard bad as ever—Wilson and
Bowers unable to start—tomorrow last chance—no fuel and only one or
two of food left—must be near the end. Have decided it shall be natural
—we shall march for the depot with or without our effects and die in
our tracks.

Thursday, March 29.—Since the 21st we have had a continuous gale
from WSW and SW. We had fuel to make two cups of tea apiece and
bare food for two days on the 20th. Every day we have been ready to
start for our depot *11 miles* away, but outside the door of the tent it
remains a scene of whirling drift. I do not think we can hope for any
better things now. We shall stick it out to the end, but we are getting
weaker, of course, and the end cannot be far.

It seems a pity, but I do not think I can write more.

R. SCOTT.

Last entry.

For God's sake look after our people.

NOTE: The curious repetition of Monday on page 390, apparently a lapse on
Scott's part, appears in the London and New York editions of *Scott's Last Expedition,* 1913, vol. I.

The Open Boat

by SIR ERNEST SHACKLETON

"After the conquest of the South Pole by Amundsen . . . there remained but one great main object of Antarctic journeyings—the crossing of the South Polar continent from sea to sea." Thus wrote Sir Ernest Shackleton in the preface to his volume, South, from which the story below has been drawn. Shackleton, one of the great modern explorers, tried and failed to cross that continent, but, as with Scott, the failure was in some respects a glorious one—a triumph of the human spirit over great adversities. Shackleton set sail for Antarctica in 1914. His ship Endurance was eventually trapped in the ice and crushed, and he and his men drifted northward for months, icebound castaways. They landed finally at Elephant Island, and there Shackleton and a few men set out in an open boat to seek help, crossing 800 miles of Antarctic water to the Norwegian whaling station in South Georgia and thus making it possible to effect the rescue of the rest of his stranded crew. His is one of the most celebrated open-boat voyages ever made.

THE INCREASING SEA MADE IT NECESSARY FOR US TO DRAG the boats farther up the beach. This was a task for all hands, and after much labor we got the boats into safe positions among the rocks and made fast the painters to big boulders. Then I discussed with Wild and Worsley the chances of reaching South Georgia before the winter locked the seas against us. Some effort had to be made to secure relief. Privation and exposure had left their mark on the party, and the health and mental condition of several men were causing me serious anxiety. Blackborrow's feet, which had been frostbitten during the boat journey, were in a bad way, and the two doctors feared that an operation would be necessary. They told me that the toes would have to be amputated unless animation could be restored within a short period. Then the food supply was a vital consideration. We had left ten cases of provisions in the crevice of the rocks at our first camping place on the island. An examination of our stores showed that we had full rations for the whole party for a period of five weeks. The rations could be spread over three months on a reduced allowance and probably would be supplemented by seals and sea elephants to some extent. I did not dare to count with full confidence on supplies of meat and blubber, for the animals seemed to have deserted the beach and the winter was near. Our stocks included three seals and two and a half skins (with blubber attached). We were mainly dependent on the blubber for fuel, and, after making a preliminary survey of the situation, I decided that the party must be limited to one hot meal a day.

A boat journey in search of relief was necessary and must not be delayed. That conclusion was forced upon me. The nearest port where assistance could certainly be secured was Port Stanley, in the Falkland Islands, 540 miles away, but we could scarcely hope to beat up against the prevailing northwesterly wind in a frail and weakened boat with a small sail area. South Georgia was over 800 miles away, but lay in the area of the west winds, and I could count upon finding whalers at any of the whaling stations on the east coast. A boat party might make the voyage and be back with relief within a month, provided that the sea was clear of ice and the boat survive the great seas. It was not difficult to decide that South Georgia must be the objective, and I proceeded to plan ways and means. The hazards of a boat journey across 800 miles of stormy subantarctic ocean were obvious, but I calculated that at worst the venture would add nothing to the risks of the men left on the island. There would be fewer mouths to feed during the winter and the boat would not require to take more than one month's provisions for six men, for if we did not make South Georgia in that time we were sure to go under. A consideration that had weight with me was that there was no chance at all of any search being made for us on Elephant Island.

The case required to be argued in some detail, since all hands knew that the perils of the proposed journey were extreme. The risk was justified solely by our urgent need of assistance. The ocean south of Cape Horn in the middle of May is known to be the most tempestuous storm-swept area of water in the world. The weather then is unsettled, the skies are dull and overcast, and the gales are almost unceasing. We had to face these conditions in a small and weather-beaten boat, already strained by the work of the months that had passed. Worsley and Wild realized that the attempt must be made, and they both asked to be allowed to accompany me on the voyage. I told Wild at once that he would have to stay behind. I relied upon him to hold the party together while I was away and to make the best of his way to Deception Island with the men in the spring in the event of our failure to bring help. Worsley I would take with me, for I had a very high opinion of his accuracy and quickness as a navigator, and especially in the mapping and working out of positions in difficult circumstances—an opinion that was only enhanced during the actual journey. Four other men would be required, and I decided to call for volunteers, although, as a matter of fact, I pretty well knew which of the people I would select. Crean I proposed to leave on the island as a right-hand man for Wild, but he begged so hard to be allowed to come in the boat that, after consultation with Wild, I promised to take him. I called the men together, explained my plan, and asked for volunteers. Many came forward at once. Some were not fit enough for the work that would have to be done, and others would not have been much use in the boat since they were not seasoned sailors, though the experiences of recent months entitled them to some consideration as seafaring men. McIlroy and Macklin were both anxious to go but realized that their duty lay on the island with the sick men. They suggested that I should take Blackborrow in order that he might have shelter and warmth as quickly as possible, but I had to veto this idea. It would be hard enough to fit men to live in the boat. Indeed, I did not see how a sick man, lying helpless in the bottom of the boat, could possibly survive in the heavy weather we were sure to encounter. I finally selected McNeish, McCarthy, and Vincent in addition to Worsley and Crean. The crew seemed a strong one, and as I looked at the men I felt confidence increasing.

The decision made, I walked through the blizzard with Worsley and Wild to examine the *James Caird*. The 20-ft. boat had never looked big; she appeared to have shrunk in some mysterious way when I viewed her in the light of our new undertaking. She was an ordinary ship's whaler, fairly strong, but showing signs of the strains she had endured since the crushing of the *Endurance*. Where she was holed in leaving the pack was, fortunately, about the water line and easily patched. Standing beside her, we glanced at the fringe of the storm-swept, tumultuous sea that formed our path. Clearly, our voyage would be a big adventure. I called the carpenter and asked him if he could do anything to make the boat more seaworthy. He first inquired if he was to go with me, and seemed quite pleased when I said "Yes." He was over fifty years of age and not altogether fit, but he had a good knowledge of sailing boats and was very quick. McCarthy said that he could contrive some sort of covering for the *James Caird* if he might use the lids of the cases and the four sledge runners that we had lashed inside the boat for use in the event of a landing on Graham Land at Wilhelmina Bay. This bay, at one time the goal of our desire, had been left behind in the course of our drift, but we had retained the runners. The carpenter proposed to complete the covering with some of our canvas, and he set about making his plans at once.

Noon had passed and the gale was more severe than ever. We could not proceed with our preparations that day. The tents were suffering in the wind and the sea was rising. We made our way to the snow slope at the shoreward end of the spit, with the intention of digging a hole in the snow large enough to provide shelter for the party. I had an idea that Wild and his men might camp there during my absence, since it seemed impossible that the tents could hold together for many more days against the attacks of the wind; but an examination of the spot indicated that any hole we could dig probably would be filled quickly by the drift. At dark, about 5 P.M., we all turned in, after a supper consisting of a pannikin of hot milk, one of our precious biscuits, and a cold penguin leg each.

The gale was stronger than ever on the following morning (April 20). No work could be done. Blizzard and snow, snow and blizzard, sudden lulls and fierce returns. During the lulls we could see on the far horizon to the northeast bergs of all shapes and sizes driving along before the gale, and the sinister appearance of the swift-moving masses made us thankful indeed that, instead of battling with the storm amid the ice, we were required only to face the drift from the glaciers and the inland heights. The gusts might throw us off our feet, but at least we fell on solid ground and not on the rocking floes. Two seals came up on the beach that day, one of them within ten yards of my tent. So urgent was our need of food and blubber that I called all hands and organized a line of beaters instead of simply walking up to the seal and hitting it on the nose. We were prepared to fall upon this seal *en masse* if it attempted to escape. The kill was made with a pick handle, and in a few minutes five days' food and six days' fuel were stowed in a place of safety among the boulders above high-water mark. During this day the cook, who had worked well on the floe and throughout the boat journey, suddenly collapsed. I happened to be at the galley at the moment and saw him fall.

I pulled him down the slope to his tent and pushed him into its shelter with orders to his tent mates to keep him in his sleeping bag until I allowed him to come out or the doctors said he was fit enough. Then I took out to replace the cook one of the men who had expressed a desire to lie down and die. The task of keeping the galley fire alight was both difficult and strenuous, and it took his thoughts away from the chances of immediate dissolution. In fact, I found him a little later gravely concerned over the drying of a naturally not overclean pair of socks which were hung up in close proximity to our evening milk. Occupation had brought his thoughts back to the ordinary cares of life.

There was a lull in the bad weather on April 21, and the carpenter started to collect material for the decking of the *James Caird*. He fitted the mast of the *Stancomb Wills* fore and aft inside the *James Caird* as a hogback and thus strengthened the keel with the object of preventing our boat "hogging"—that is, buckling in heavy seas. He had not sufficient wood to provide a deck, but by using the sledge runners and box lids he made a framework extending from the forecastle aft to a well. It was a patched-up affair, but it provided a base for a canvas covering. We had a bolt of canvas frozen stiff, and this material had to be cut and then thawed out over the blubber stove, foot by foot, in order that it might be sewn into the form of a cover. When it had been nailed and screwed into position it certainly gave an appearance of safety to the boat, though I had an uneasy feeling that it bore a strong likeness to stage scenery, which may look like a granite wall and is in fact nothing better than canvas and lath. As events proved, the covering served its purpose well. We certainly could not have lived through the voyage without it.

Another fierce gale was blowing on April 22, interfering with our preparations for the voyage. The cooker from No. 5 tent came adrift in a gust, and, although it was chased to the water's edge, it disappeared for good. Blackborrow's feet were giving him much pain, and McIlroy and Macklin thought it would be necessary for them to operate soon. They were under the impression then that they had no chloroform, but they found some subsequently in the medicine chest after we had left. Some cases of stores left on a rock off the spit on the day of our arrival were retrieved during this day. We were setting aside stores for the boat journey and choosing the essential equipment from the scanty stock at our disposal. Two ten-gallon casks had to be filled with water melted down from ice collected at the foot of the glacier. This was a rather slow business. The blubber stove was kept going all night, and the watchmen emptied the water into the casks from the pot in which the ice was melted. A working party started to dig a hole in the snow slope about forty feet above sea level with the object of providing a site for a camp. They made fairly good progress at first, but the snow drifted down unceasingly from the inland ice, and in the end the party had to give up the project.

The weather was fine on April 23, and we hurried forward our preparations. It was on this day I decided finally that the crew for the *James Caird* should consist of Worsley, Crean, McNeish, McCarthy, Vincent, and myself. A storm came on about noon, with driving snow and heavy squalls. Occasionally the air would clear for a few minutes, and we could see a line of pack ice, five miles out, driving across from west to east. This sight increased my anxiety to get away quickly. Winter was advancing, and soon the pack might close completely round the island and stay our departure for days or even for weeks. I did not think that ice would remain around Elephant Island continuously during the winter, since the strong winds and fast currents would keep it in motion. We had noticed ice and bergs going past at the rate of four or five knots. A certain amount of ice was held up about the end of our spit, but the sea was clear where the boat would have to be launched.

Worsley, Wild, and I climbed to the summit of the seaward rocks and examined the ice from a better vantage point than the beach offered. The belt of pack outside appeared to be sufficiently broken for our purposes, and I decided that, unless the conditions forbade it, we would make a start in the *James Caird* on the following morning. Obviously the pack might close at any time. This decision made, I spent the rest of the day looking over the boat, gear, and stores, and discussing plans with Worsley and Wild.

Our last night on the solid ground of Elephant Island was cold and uncomfortable. We turned out at dawn and had breakfast. Then we launched the *Stancomb Wills* and loaded her with stores, gear, and ballast, which would be transferred to the *James Caird* when the heavier boat had been launched. The ballast consisted of bags made from blankets and filled with sand, making a total weight of about 1000 lb. In addition we had gathered a number of round boulders and about 250 lb. of ice, which would supplement our two casks of water.

The stores taken in the *James Caird*, which would last six men for one month, were as follows:

> 30 boxes of matches.
> 6½ gallons paraffin.
> 1 tin methylated spirit.

10 boxes of flamers.
1 box of blue lights.
2 Primus stoves with spare parts and prickers.
1 Nansen aluminum cooker.
6 sleeping bags.
A few spare socks.
A few candles and some blubber oil in an oil bag.

Food:
3 cases sledging rations = 300 rations.
2 cases nut food   = 200   „
2 cases biscuits   = 600 biscuits.
1 case lump sugar.
30 packets of Trumilk.
1 tin of Bovril cubes.
1 tin of Cerebos salt.
36 gallons of water.
112 lb. of ice.

Instruments:

Sextant.	Sea anchor.
Binoculars.	Charts.
Prismatic compass.	Aneroid.

The swell was slight when the *Stancomb Wills* was launched and the boat got under way without any difficulty; but half an hour later, when we were pulling down the *James Caird*, the swell increased suddenly. Apparently the movement of the ice outside had made an opening and allowed the sea to run in without being blanketed by the line of pack. The swell made things difficult. Many of us got wet to the waist while dragging the boat out—a serious matter in that climate. When the *James Caird* was afloat in the surf she nearly capsized among the rocks before we could get her clear, and Vincent and the carpenter, who were on the deck, were thrown into the water. This was really bad luck, for the two men would have small chance of drying their clothes after we had got under way. Hurley, who had the eye of the professional photographer for "incidents," secured a picture of the upset, and I firmly believe that he would have liked the two unfortunate men to remain in the water until he could get a "snap" at close quarters; but we hauled them out immediately, regardless of his feelings.

The *James Caird* was soon clear of the breakers. We used all the available ropes as a long painter to prevent her drifting away to the northeast, and then the *Stancomb Wills* came alongside, transferred her load, and went back to the shore for more. As she was being beached this time the sea took her stern and half filled her with water. She had to be turned over and emptied before the return journey could be made. Every member of the crew of the *Stancomb Wills* was wet to the skin. The water casks were towed behind the *Stancomb Wills* on this second journey, and the swell, which was increasing rapidly, drove the boat on to the rocks, where one of the casks was slightly stove in. This accident proved later to be a serious one, since some sea water had entered the cask and the contents were now brackish.

By midday the *James Caird* was ready for the voyage. Vincent and the carpenter had secured some dry clothes by exchange with members of the shore party (I heard afterward that it was a full fortnight before the soaked garments were finally dried), and the boat's crew was standing by waiting for the order to cast off. A moderate westerly breeze was blowing. I went ashore in the *Stancomb Wills* and had a last word with Wild, who was remaining in full command, with directions as to his course of action in the event of our failure to bring relief, but I practically left the whole situation and scope of action and decision to his own judgment, secure in the knowledge that he would act wisely. I told him that I trusted the party to him and said good-by to the men. Then we pushed off for the last time, and within a few minutes I was aboard the *James Caird*. The crew of the *Stancomb Wills* shook hands with us as the boats bumped together and offered us the last good wishes. Then, setting our jib, we cut the painter and moved away to the northeast. The men who were staying behind made a pathetic little group on the beach, with the grim heights of the island behind them and the sea seething at their feet, but they waved to us and gave three hearty cheers. There was hope in their hearts and they trusted us to bring the help that they needed.

I had all sails set, and the *James Caird* quickly dipped the beach and its line of dark figures. The westerly wind took us rapidly to the line of pack, and as we entered it I stood up with my arm around the mast, directing the steering, so as to avoid the great lumps of ice that were flung about in the heave of the sea. The pack thickened and we were forced to turn almost due east, running before the wind toward a gap I had seen in the morning from the high ground. I could not see the gap now, but we had come out on its bearing and I was prepared to find that it had been influenced by the easterly drift. At four o'clock in the afternoon we found the channel, much narrower than it had seemed in the morning but still navigable. Dropping sail, we rowed through

without touching the ice anywhere, and by 5:30 P.M. we were clear of
the pack with open water before us. We passed one more piece of ice in
the darkness an hour later, but the pack lay behind, and with a fair
wind swelling the sails we steered our little craft through the night, our
hopes centered on our distant goal. The swell was very heavy now, and
when the time came for our first evening meal we found great difficulty
in keeping the Primus lamp alight and preventing the hoosh splashing out
of the pot. Three men were needed to attend to the cooking, one man
holding the lamp and two men guarding the aluminum cooking pot,
which had to be lifted clear of the Primus whenever the movement of
the boat threatened to cause a disaster. Then the lamp had to be
protected from water, for sprays were coming over the bows and our
flimsy decking was by no means watertight. All these operations were
conducted in the confined space under the decking, where the men lay
or knelt and adjusted themselves as best they could to the angles of our
cases and ballast. It was uncomfortable, but we found consolation in
the reflection that without the decking we could not have used the cooker
at all.

The tale of the next sixteen days is one of supreme strife amid heaving
waters. The subantarctic Ocean lived up to its evil winter reputation. I
decided to run north for at least two days while the wind held and so get
into warmer weather before turning to the east and laying a course for
South Georgia. We took two-hourly spells at the tiller. The men who
were not on watch crawled into the sodden sleeping bags and tried to
forget their troubles for a period; but there was no comfort in the boat.
The bags and cases seemed to be alive in the unfailing knack of pre-
senting their most uncomfortable angles to our rest-seeking bodies. A
man might imagine for a moment that he had found a position of ease,
but always discovered quickly that some unyielding point was impinging
on muscle or bone. The first night aboard the boat was one of acute
discomfort for us all, and we were heartily glad when the dawn came
and we could set about the preparation of a hot breakfast.

This record of the voyage to South Georgia is based upon scanty notes
made day by day. The notes dealt usually with the bare facts of distances,
positions, and weather, but our memories retained the incidents of the passing days in a period never to be forgotten. By running north for the first
two days I hoped to get warmer weather and also to avoid lines of pack
that might be extending beyond the main body. We needed all the advantage that we could obtain from the higher latitude for sailing on the
great circle, but we had to be cautious regarding possible ice streams.

Cramped in our narrow quarters and continually wet by the spray, we suffered severely from cold throughout the journey. We fought the seas and the winds and at the same time had a daily struggle to keep ourselves alive. At times we were in dire peril. Generally we were upheld by the knowledge that we were making progress toward the land where we would be, but there were days and nights when we lay hove to, drifting across the storm-whitened seas and watching, with eyes interested rather than apprehensive, the uprearing masses of water, flung to and fro by Nature in the pride of her strength. Deep seemed the valleys when we lay between the reeling seas. High were the hills when we perched momentarily on the tops of giant combers. Nearly always there were gales. So small was our boat and so great were the seas that often our sail flapped idly in the calm between the crests of two waves. Then we would climb the next slope and catch the full fury of the gale where the woollike whiteness of the breaking water surged around us. We had our moments of laughter—rare, it is true, but hearty enough. Even when cracked lips and swollen mouths checked the outward and visible signs of amusement we could see a joke of the primitive kind. Man's sense of humor is always most easily stirred by the petty misfortunes of his neighbors, and I shall never forget Worsley's efforts on one occasion to place the hot aluminum stand on top of the Primus stove after it had fallen off in an extra heavy roll. With his frostbitten fingers he picked it up, dropped it, picked it up again, and toyed with it gingerly as though it were some fragile article of lady's wear. We laughed, or rather gurgled with laughter.

The wind came up strong and worked into a gale from the northwest on the third day out. We stood away to the east. The increasing seas discovered the weaknesses of our decking. The continuous blows shifted to box lids and sledge runners so that the canvas sagged down and accumulated water. Then icy trickles, distinct from the driving sprays, poured fore and aft into the boat. The nails that the carpenter had extracted from cases at Elephant Island and used to fasten down the battens were too short to make firm the decking. We did what we could to secure it, but our means were very limited, and the water continued to enter the boat at a dozen points. Much baling was necessary, and nothing that we could do prevented our gear from becoming sodden. The searching runnels from the canvas were really more unpleasant than the sudden definite douches of the sprays. Lying under the thwarts during watches below, we tried vainly to avoid them. There were no dry places in the boat, and at last we simply covered our heads with our Burberrys

and endured the all-pervading water. The baling was work for the watch.
Real rest we had none. The perpetual motion of the boat made repose
impossible; we were cold, sore, and anxious. We moved on hands and
knees in the semi-darkness of the day under the decking. The darkness
was complete by 6 P.M., and not until 7 A.M. of the following day could
we see one another under the thwarts. We had a few scraps of candle,
and they were preserved carefully in order that we might have light at
mealtimes. There was one fairly dry spot in the boat, under the solid
original decking at the bows, and we managed to protect some of our
biscuit from the salt water; but I do not think any of us got the taste of
salt out of our mouths during the voyage.

The difficulty of movement in the boat would have had its humorous
side if it had not involved us in so many aches and pains. We had to
crawl under the thwarts in order to move along the boat, and our knees
suffered considerably. When a watch turned out it was necessary for me
to direct each man by name when and where to move, since if all hands
had crawled about at the same time the result would have been dire
confusion and many bruises. Then there was the trim of the boat to be
considered. The order of the watch was four hours on and four hours
off, three men to the watch. One man had the tiller ropes, the second
man attended to the sail, and the third baled for all he was worth. Sometimes when the water in the boat had been reduced to reasonable proportions, our pump could be used. This pump, which Hurley had made
from the Flinders bar case of our ship's standard compass, was quite
effective, though its capacity was not large. The man who was attending
the sail could pump into the big outer cooker, which was lifted and
emptied overboard when filled. We had a device by which the water
could go direct from the pump into the sea through a hole in the gunwale, but this hole had to be blocked at an early stage of the voyage, since
we found that it admitted water when the boat rolled.

While a new watch was shivering in the wind and spray, the men who
had been relieved groped hurriedly among the soaked sleeping bags and
tried to steal a little of the warmth created by the last occupants; but it
was not always possible for us to find even this comfort when we went
off watch. The boulders that we had taken aboard for ballast had to be
shifted continually in order to trim the boat and give access of the pump,
which became choked with hairs from the moulting sleeping bags and
finneskoe. The four reindeer-skin sleeping bags shed their hair freely
owing to the continuous wetting, and soon became quite bald in appearance. The moving of the boulders was weary and painful work. We

came to know every one of the stones by sight and touch, and I have vivid memories of their angular peculiarities even today. They might have been of considerable interest as geological specimens to a scientific man under happier conditions. As ballast they were useful. As weights to be moved about in cramped quarters they were simply appalling. They spared no portion of our poor bodies. Another of our troubles, worth mention here, was the chafing of our legs by our wet clothes, which had not been changed now for seven months. The insides of our thighs were rubbed raw, and the one tube of Hazeline cream in our medicine chest did not go far in alleviating our pain, which was increased by the bite of the salt water. We thought at the time that we never slept. The fact was that we would doze off uncomfortably, to be aroused quickly by some new ache or another call to effort. My own share of the general unpleasantness was accentuated by a finely developed bout of sciatica. I had become possessor of this originally on the floe several months earlier.

Our meals were regular in spite of the gales. Attention to this point was essential, since the conditions of the voyage made increasing calls upon our vitality. Breakfast, at 8 A.M., consisted of a pannikin of hot hoosh made from Bovril sledging ration, two biscuits, and some lumps of sugar. Lunch came at 1 P.M., and comprised Bovril sledging ration, eaten raw, and a pannikin of hot milk for each man. Tea, at 5 P.M., had the same menu. Then during the night we had a hot drink, generally of milk. The meals were the bright beacons in those cold and stormy days. The glow of warmth and comfort produced by the food and drink made optimists of us all. We had two tins of Virol, which we were keeping for an emergency; but, finding ourselves in need of an oil lamp to eke out our supply of candles, we emptied one of the tins in the manner that most appealed to us, and fitted it with a wick made by shredding a bit of canvas. When this lamp was filled with oil it gave a certain amount of light, though it was easily blown out, and was of great assistance to us at night. We were fairly well off as regarded fuel, since we had 6½ gallons of petroleum.

A severe southwesterly gale on the fourth day out forced us to heave to. I would have liked to have run before the wind, but the sea was very high and the *James Caird* was in danger of broaching to and swamping. The delay was vexatious, since up to that time we had been making sixty or seventy miles a day; good going with our limited sail area. We hove to under double-reefed mainsail and our little jigger, and waited for the gale to blow itself out. During that afternoon we saw bits of wreckage, the remains probably of some unfortunate vessel that had failed to weather the strong gales south of Cape Horn. The weather conditions did not improve, and on the fifth day out the gale was so fierce that we were compelled to take in the double-reefed mainsail and hoist our small jib instead. We put out a sea anchor to keep the *James Caird's* head up to the sea. This anchor consisted of a triangular canvas bag fastened to the end of the painter and allowed to stream out from the bows. The boat was high enough to catch the wind, and, as she drifted to leeward, the drag of the anchor kept her head to windward. Thus our boat took most of the seas more or less end on. Even then the crests of the waves often would curl right over us and we shipped a great deal of water, which necessitated unceasing baling and pumping. Looking out abeam, we would see a hollow like a tunnel formed as the crest of a big wave toppled over on to the swelling body of water. A thousand times it appeared as though the *James Caird* must be engulfed; but the boat lived. The southwesterly gale had its birthplace above the Antarctic Continent, and its freezing breath lowered the temperature far toward zero. The sprays froze upon the boat and gave bows, sides, and decking a heavy coat of mail. This accumulation of ice reduced the buoyancy of the boat, and to that extent was an added peril; but it possessed a notable advantage from one point of view. The water ceased to drop and trickle from the canvas, and the spray came in solely at the well in the after part of the boat. We could not allow the load of ice to grow beyond a certain point, and in turns we crawled about the decking forward, chipping and picking at it with the available tools.

When daylight came on the morning of the sixth day out we saw and felt that the *James Caird* had lost her resiliency. She was not rising to the oncoming seas. The weight of the ice that had formed in her and upon her during the night was having its effect, and she was becoming more like a log than a boat. The situation called for immediate action. We first broke away the spare oars, which were encased in ice and frozen to the sides of the boat, and threw them overboard. We retained two oars for use when we got inshore. Two of the fur sleeping bags went over the side; they were thoroughly wet, weighing probably 40 lb. each, and they had frozen stiff during the night. Three men constituted the watch below, and when a man went down it was better to turn into the wet bag just vacated by another man than to thaw out a frozen bag with the heat of his unfortunate body. We now had four bags, three in use and one for emergency use in case a member of the party should break down permanently. The reduction of weight relieved the boat to some extent, and vigorous chipping and scraping did more. We had to be very careful not to put axe or knife through the frozen canvas of the decking as we crawled over it, but gradually we got rid of a lot of ice. The *James Caird* lifted to the endless waves as though she lived again.

About 11 A.M. the boat suddenly fell off into the trough of the sea. The painter had parted and the sea anchor had gone. This was serious. The *James Caird* went away to leeward, and we had no chance at all of recovering the anchor and our valuable rope, which had been our only means of keeping the boat's head up to the seas without the risk of hoisting sail in a gale. Now we had to set the sail and trust to its holding. While the *James Caird* rolled heavily in the trough, we beat the frozen canvas until the bulk of the ice had cracked off it and then hoisted it. The frozen gear worked protestingly, but after a struggle our little craft came up to the wind again, and we breathed more freely. Skin frostbites were troubling us, and we had developed large blisters on our fingers and hands. I shall always carry the scar of one of these frostbites on my left hand, which became badly inflamed after the skin had burst and the cold had bitten deeply.

We held the boat up to the gale during that day, enduring as best we could discomforts that amounted to pain. The boat tossed interminably on the big waves under gray, threatening skies. Our thoughts did not embrace much more than the necessities of the hour. Every surge of the sea was an enemy to be watched and circumvented. We ate our scanty meals, treated our frostbites, and hoped for the improved conditions that the morrow might bring. Night fell early, and in the lagging hours of darkness we were cheered by a change for the better in the weather. The wind dropped, the snow squalls became less frequent, and the sea moderated. When the morning of the seventh day dawned there was not much wind. We shook the reef out of the sail and laid our course once more for South Georgia. The sun came out bright and clear, and presently Worsley got a snap for longitude. We hoped that the sky would remain clear until noon, so that we could get the latitude. We had been six days out without an observation, and our dead reckoning naturally was uncertain. The boat must have presented a strange appearance that morning. All hands basked in the sun. We hung our sleeping bags to the mast and spread our socks and other gear all over the deck. Some of the ice had melted off the *James Caird* in the early morning after the gale began to slacken, and dry patches were appearing in the decking. Porpoises came blowing round the boat, and Cape pigeons wheeled and swooped within a few feet of us. These little black-and-white birds have an air of friendliness that is not possessed by the great circling albatross.

They had looked gray against the swaying sea during the storm as they darted about over our heads and uttered their plaintive cries. The albatrosses, of the black or sooty variety, had watched with hard, bright eyes, and seemed to have a quite impersonal interest in our struggle to keep afloat amid the battering seas. In addition to the Cape pigeons an occasional stormy petrel flashed overhead. Then there was a small bird, unknown to me, that appeared always to be in a fussy, bustling state, quite out of keeping with the surroundings. It irritated me. It had practically no tail, and it flitted about vaguely as though in search of the lost member. I used to find myself wishing it would find its tail and have done with the silly fluttering.

We reveled in the warmth of the sun that day. Life was not so bad, after all. We felt we were well on our way. Our gear was drying, and we could have a hot meal in comparative comfort. The swell was still heavy, but it was not breaking and the boat rode easily. At noon Worsley balanced himself on the gunwale and clung with one hand to the stay of the mainmast while he got a snap of the sun. The result was more than encouraging. We had done over 380 miles and were getting on for half-way to South Georgia. It looked as though we were going to get through.

The wind freshened to a good stiff breeze during the afternoon, and the *James Caird* made satisfactory progress. I had not realized until the sunlight came how small our boat really was. There was some influence in the light and warmth, some hint of happier days, that made us revive memories of other voyages, when we had stout decks beneath our feet, unlimited food at our command, and pleasant cabins for our ease. Now we clung to a battered little boat, "alone, alone, all, all alone, alone on a wide, wide sea." So low in the water were we that each succeeding swell cut off our view of the sky line. We were a tiny speck in the vast vista of the sea—the ocean that is open to all and merciful to none, that threatens even when it seems to yield, and that is pitiless always to weakness. For a moment the consciousness of the forces arrayed against us would be almost overwhelming. Then hope and confidence would rise again as our boat rose to a wave and tossed aside the crest in a sparkling shower like the play of prismatic colors at the foot of a waterfall. My double-barreled gun and some cartridges had been stowed aboard the boat as an emergency precaution against a shortage of food, but we were not disposed to destroy our little neighbors, the Cape pigeons, even for the sake of fresh meat. We might have shot an albatross, but the wandering king of the ocean aroused in us something of the feeling that inspired, too late, the Ancient Mariner. So the gun remained among the stores and sleeping-bags in the narrow quarters beneath our leaking deck, and the birds followed us unmolested.

The eighth, ninth, and tenth days of the voyage had few features worthy of special note. The wind blew hard during those days, and the strain of navigating the boat was unceasing, but always we made some advance toward our goal. No bergs showed on our horizon, and we knew that we were clear of the ice fields. Each day brought its little round of troubles, but also compensation in the form of food and growing hope. We felt that we were going to succeed. The odds against us had been great, but we were winning through. We still suffered severely from the cold, for, though the temperature was rising, our vitality was declining owing to shortage of food, exposure, and the necessity of maintaining our cramped positions day and night. I found that it was now absolutely necessary to prepare hot milk for all hands during the night, in order to sustain life till dawn. This meant lighting the Primus lamp in the darkness and involved an increased drain on our small store of matches. It was the rule that one match must serve when the Primus was being lit. We had no lamp for the compass and during the early days of the voyage we would strike a match when the steersman wanted to see the course at night; but later the necessity for strict economy impressed itself upon us, and the practice of striking matches at night was stopped. We had one watertight tin of matches. I had stowed away in a pocket, in readiness for a sunny day, a lens from one of the telescopes, but this was of no use during the voyage. The sun seldom shone upon us. The glass of the compass got broken one night, and we contrived to mend it with adhesive tape from the medicine chest. One of the memories that comes to me from those days is of Crean singing at the tiller. He always sang while he was steering, and nobody ever discovered what the song was. It was devoid of tune and as monotonous as the chanting of a Buddhist monk at his prayers; yet somehow it was cheerful. In moments of inspiration Crean would attempt "The Wearing of the Green."

On the tenth night Worsley could not straighten his body after his spell at the tiller. He was thoroughly cramped, and we had to drag him beneath the decking and massage him before he could unbend himself and get into a sleeping bag. A hard northwesterly gale came up on the eleventh day (May 5) and shifted to the southwest in the late afternoon. The sky was overcast and occasional snow squalls added to the discomfort produced by a tremendous cross sea—the worst, I thought, that we had experienced. At midnight I was at the tiller and suddenly noticed a line of clear sky between the south and southwest. I called to the other men that the sky was clearing, and then a moment later I realized that what I had seen was not a rift in the clouds but the white crest of an enormous wave. During twenty-six years' experience of the ocean in all its moods I had not encountered a wave so gigantic. It was a mighty upheaval of the ocean, a thing quite apart from the big white-capped seas that had been our tireless enemies for many days. I shouted, "For God's sake, hold on! It's got us!" Then came a moment of suspense that seemed drawn out into hours. White surged the foam of the breaking sea around us. We felt our boat lifted and flung forward like a cork in breaking surf. We were in a seething chaos of tortured water; but somehow the boat lived through it, half full of water, sagging to the dead weight and shuddering under the blow. We baled with the energy of men fighting for life, flinging the water over the sides with every receptacle that came to our hands, and after ten minutes of uncertainty we felt the boat renew her life beneath us. She floated again and ceased to lurch drunkenly as though dazed by the attack of the sea. Earnestly we hoped that never again would we encounter such a wave.

The conditions in the boat, uncomfortable before, had been made worse by the deluge of water. All our gear was thoroughly wet again. Our cooking stove had been floating about in the bottom of the boat, and portions of our last hoosh seemed to have permeated everything. Not until 3 A.M., when we were all chilled almost to the limit of endurance, did we manage to get the stove alight and make ourselves hot drinks. The carpenter was suffering particularly, but he showed grit and spirit. Vincent had for the past week ceased to be an active member of the crew, and I could not easily account for his collapse. Physically he was one of the strongest men in the boat. He was a young man, he had served on North Sea trawlers, and he should have been able to bear hardships better than McCarthy, who, not so strong, was always happy.

The weather was better on the following day (May 6), and we got a glimpse of the sun. Worsley's observation showed that we were not more than a hundred miles from the northwest corner of South Georgia. Two more days with a favorable wind and we would sight the promised land. I hoped that there would be no delay, for our supply of water was running very low. The hot drink at night was essential, but I decided that the daily allowance of water must be cut down to half a pint per man. The lumps of ice we had taken aboard had gone long ago. We were dependent upon the water we had brought from Elephant Island, and our thirst was increased by the fact that we were now using the brackish water in the breaker that had been slightly stove in in the surf when the boat was being loaded. Some sea water had entered at that time.

Thirst took possession of us. I dared not permit the allowance of water to be increased since an unfavorable wind might drive us away from the island and lengthen our voyage by many days. Lack of water is always the most severe privation that men can be condemned to endure, and we found, as during our earlier boat voyage, that the salt water in our clothing and the salt spray that lashed our faces made our thirst grow quickly to a burning pain. I had to be very firm in refusing to allow anyone to anticipate the morrow's allowance, which I was sometimes begged to do. We did the necessary work dully and hoped for the land. I had altered the course to the east so as to make sure of our striking the island, which would have been impossible to regain if we had run past the northern end. The course was laid on our scrap of chart for a point some thirty miles down the coast. That day and the following day passed for us in a sort of nightmare. Our mouths were dry and our tongues were swollen. The wind was still strong and the heavy sea forced us to navigate carefully, but any thought of our peril from the waves was buried beneath the consciousness of our raging thirst. The bright moments were those when we each received our one mug of hot milk during the long, bitter watches of the night. Things were bad for us in those days, but the end was coming. The morning of May 8 broke thick and stormy, with squalls from the northwest. We searched the waters ahead for a sign of land, and though we could see nothing more than had met our eyes for many days, we were cheered by a sense that the goal was near at hand. About ten o'clock that morning we passed a little bit of kelp, a glad signal of the proximity of land. An hour later we saw two shags sitting on a big mass of kelp, and knew then that we must be within ten or fifteen miles of the shore. These birds are as sure an indication of the proximity of land as a lighthouse is, for they never venture far to sea. We gazed ahead with increasing eagerness, and at 12:30 P.M., through a rift in the clouds, McCarthy caught a glimpse of the black cliffs of South Georgia, just fourteen days after our departure from Elephant Island. It was a glad moment. Thirst-ridden, chilled, and weak as we were, happiness irradiated us. The job was nearly done.

We stood in toward the shore to look for a landing place, and presently we could see the green tussock grass on the ledges above the surf-beaten rocks. Ahead of us and to the south, blind rollers showed the presence of uncharted reefs along the coast. Here and there the hungry rocks were close to the surface, and over them the great waves broke, swirling viciously and spouting thirty and forty feet into the air. The rocky coast appeared to descend sheer to the sea. Our need of water and rest was well-nigh desperate, but to have attempted a landing at that time would have been suicidal. Night was drawing near, and the weather indications were not favorable. There was nothing for it but to haul off till the following morning, so we stood away on the starboard tack until we had made what appeared to be a safe offing. Then we hove to in the high westerly swell. The hours passed slowly as we awaited the dawn, which would herald, we fondly hoped, the last stage of our journey. Our thirst was a torment and we could scarcely touch our food; the cold seemed to strike right through our weakened bodies. At 5 A.M. the wind shifted to the northwest and quickly increased to one of the worst hurricanes any of us had ever experienced. A great cross sea was running, and the wind simply shrieked as it tore the tops off the waves and converted the whole seascape into a haze of driving spray. Down into valleys, up to tossing heights, straining until her seams opened, swung our little boat, brave still but laboring heavily. We knew that the wind and set of the sea was driving us ashore, but we could do nothing. The dawn showed us a storm-torn ocean, and the morning passed without bringing us a sight of the land; but at 1 P.M., through a rift in the flying mists, we got a glimpse of the huge crags of the island and realized that our position had become desperate. We were on a dead lee shore, and we could gauge our approach to the unseen cliffs by the roar of the breakers against the sheer walls of rock. I ordered the double-reefed mainsail to be set in the hope that we might claw off, and this attempt increased the strain upon the boat. The *James Caird* was bumping heavily, and the water was pouring in everywhere. Our thirst was forgotten in the realization of our imminent danger, as we baled unceasingly, and adjusted our weights from time to time; occasional glimpses showed that the shore was nearer. I knew that Annewkow Island lay to the south of us, but our small and badly marked chart showed uncertain reefs in the passage between the island and the mainland, and I dared not trust it, though as a last resort we could try to lie under the lee of the island. The afternoon wore away as we edged down the coast, with the thunder of the breakers in our ears. The approach of evening found us still some distance from Annewkow Island, and, dimly in the twilight, we could see a snow-capped mountain looming above us. The chance of surviving the night, with the driving gale and the implacable sea forcing us on to the lee shore, seemed small. I think most of us had a feeling that the end was very near. Just after 6 P.M., in the dark, as the boat was in the yeasty backwash from the seas flung from this iron-bound coast, then, just when things looked their worst, they changed for the best. I have marveled often at the thin line that divides success from failure and the sudden turn that leads from apparently certain disaster to comparative safety. The wind suddenly shifted, and we were free once more to make an offing. Almost as soon as the gale eased, the pin that locked the mast to the thwart fell out. It must have been on the point of doing this throughout the hurricane, and if it had gone nothing could have saved us; the mast would have snapped like a carrot. Our backstays had carried away once before when iced up and were not too strongly fastened now. We were thankful indeed for the mercy that had held that pin in its place throughout the hurricane.

We stood off shore again, tired almost to the point of apathy. Our water had long been finished. The last was about a pint of hairy liquid, which we strained through a bit of gauze from the medicine chest. The pangs of thirst attacked us with redoubled intensity, and I felt that we must make a landing on the following day at almost any hazard. The night wore on. We were very tired. We longed for day. When at last the dawn came on the morning of May 10 there was practically no wind, but a high cross sea was running. We made slow progress toward the shore. About 8 A.M. the wind backed to the northwest and threatened another blow. We had sighted in the meantime a big indentation which I thought must be King Haakon Bay, and I decided that we must land there. We set the bows of the boat toward the bay and ran before the freshening gale. Soon we had angry reefs on either side. Great glaciers came down to the sea and offered no landing place. The sea spouted on the reefs and thundered against the shore. About noon we sighted a line of jagged reef, like blackened teeth, that seemed to bar the entrance to the bay. Inside, comparatively smooth water stretched eight or nine miles to the head of the bay. A gap in the reef appeared, and we made for it. But the fates had another rebuff for us. The wind shifted and blew from the east right out of the bay. We could see the way through the reef, but we could not approach it directly. That afternoon we bore up, tacking five times in the strong wind. The last tack enabled us to get through, and at last we were in the wide mouth of the bay. Dusk was approaching. A small cove, with a boulder-strewn beach guarded by a reef, made a break in the cliffs on the south side of the bay, and we turned in that direction. I stood in the bows directing the steering as we ran through the kelp and made the passage of the reef. The entrance was so narrow that we had to take in the oars, and the swell was piling itself right over the reef into the cove; but in a minute or two we were inside, and in the gathering darkness the *James Caird* ran in on a swell and touched the beach. I sprang ashore with the short painter and held on when the boat went out with the backward surge. When the *James Caird* came in again three of the men got ashore, and they held the painter while I climbed some rocks with another line. A slip on the wet rocks twenty feet up nearly closed my part of the story just at the moment when we were achieving safety. A jagged piece of rock held me and at the same time bruised me sorely. However, I made fast the line, and in a few minutes we were all safe on the beach, with the boat floating in the surging water just off the shore. We heard a gurgling sound that was sweet music in our ears, and, peering around, found a stream of fresh water almost at our feet. A moment later we were down on our knees drinking the pure, ice-cold water in long draughts that put new life into us. It was a splendid moment.

Craters of Fire

by HAROUN TAZIEFF

Tazieff, a geologist by training, was born in Warsaw in 1914, was educated in Belgium, and fought with both regular and Resistance soldiers in World War II. A scientist, photographer and adventurer, he has helped explore the world's deepest cave, and numerous volcanoes on land as well as undersea. One senses with him the ferocity of the power locked inside our planet, made manifest now and then by earthquakes, explosions and great lava flows and eruptions.

The Crater of Kituro

Standing on the summit of the growling cone, even before I got my breath back after the stiff climb, I peered down into the crater.

I was astonished. Two days previously the red lava had been boiling up to the level of the gigantic lip; now the funnel seemed to be empty. All that incandescent magma had disappeared, drawn back into the depths by the reflux of some mysterious ebb and flow, a sort of breathing. But there, about fifty feet below where I was standing, was the glow and the almost animate fury of the great throat which volcanologists call the conduit or chimney. It was quite a while before I could tear my eyes away from that lurid fiery center, that weird palpitation of the abyss. At intervals of about a minute, heralded each time by a dry clacking, bursts of projectiles were flung up, running away up into the air, spreading out fanwise, all aglare, and then falling back, whistling, on the outer sides of the cone. I was rather tense, ready to leap aside at any moment, as I watched these showers, with their menacing trajectories.

Each outburst of rage was followed by a short lull. Then heavy rolls of brown and bluish fumes came puffing out, while a muffled grumbling,

423

rather like that of some monstrous watchdog, set the whole bulk of the volcano quivering. There was not much chance for one's nerves to relax, so swiftly did each follow on the other—the sudden tremor, the burst, the momentary intensification of the incandescence, and the outbreak of a fresh salvo. The bombs went roaring up, the cone of fire opening out overhead, while I hung in suspense. Then came the hissing and sizzling, increasing in speed and intensity, each 'whoosh' ending up in a muffled thud as the bomb fell. On their black bed of scoriae, the clots of molten magma lay with the fire slowly dying out of them, one after the other growing dark and cold.

Some minutes of observation were all I needed. I noted that today, apart from three narrow zones to the west, north, and northeast, the edges of the crater had scarcely been damaged at all by the barrage from underground. The southern point where I stood was a mound rising some twelve of fifteen feet above the general level of the rim, that narrow, crumbling lip of scoriae nearer to the fire, where I had never risked setting foot. I looked at this rather alarming ledge all round the crater, and gradually felt an increasing desire to do something about it. . . . It became irresistible. After all, as the level of the column of lava had dropped to such an exceptional degree, was this not the moment to try what I was so tempted to do and go right round the crater?

Still, I hesitated. This great maw, these jaws sending out heat that was like the heavy breathing of some living creature, thoroughly frightened me. Leaning forward over that hideous glow, I was no longer a geologist in search of information, but a terrified savage.

"If I lose my grip," I said aloud, "I shall simply run for it."

The sound of my own voice restored me to normal awareness of myself. I got back my critical sense and began to think about what I could reasonably risk trying. "De l'audace, encore de l'audace. . . ." That was all very well, of course, but one must also be careful. Past experience whispered a warning not to rush into anything blindly. Getting the upper hand of both anxiety and impatience, I spent several minutes considering, with the greatest of care, the monster's manner of behaving. Solitude has got me into the habit of talking to myself, and so it was more or less aloud that I gave myself permission to go ahead.

"Right, then. It can be done."

I turned up my collar and buttoned my canvas jacket tight at the throat—I didn't want a sly cinder down the back of my neck! Then I tucked what was left of my hair under an old felt hat that did service for a helmet. And now for it!

Very cautiously indeed, I approach the few yards of pretty steep slope separating the peak from the rim I am going to explore. I cross, in a gingerly manner, a first incandescent crevasse. It is intense orange in color and quivering with heat, as though opening straight into a mass of glowing embers. The fraction of a second it takes me to cross it is just long enough for it to scorch the thick cord of my breeches. I get a strong whiff of burned wool.

A promising start, I must say!

Here comes a second break in the ground. Damn it, a wide one, too! I can't just stride across this one: I'll have to jump it. The incline makes me thoughtful. Standing there, I consider the unstable slope of scoriae that will have to serve me for a landing ground. If I don't manage to pull up . . . if I go rolling along down this funnel with the flames lurking at the bottom of it . . . My little expedition all at once strikes me as thoroughly rash, and I stay where I am, hesitating. But the heat under my feet is becoming unbearable. I can't endure it except by shifting around. It only needs ten seconds of standing still on this enemy territory, with the burning gases slowly and steadily seeping through it, and the soles of my feet are already baking hot. From second to second the alternative becomes increasingly urgent: I must jump for it or retreat.

Here I am! I have landed some way down the fissure. The ashes slide underfoot, but I stop without too much trouble. As so often happens, the anxiety caused by the obstacle made me overestimate its importance.

Step by step, I set out on my way along the wide wall of slaglike debris that forms a sort of fortification all round the precipice. The explosions are still going on at regular intervals of between sixty and eighty seconds. So far no projectile has come down on this side, and this cheers me up considerably. With marked satisfaction I note that it is pretty rare for two bombs of the same salvo to fall less than three yards apart: the average distance between them seems to be one of several paces. This is encouraging. One of the great advantages of this sort of bombardment, compared with one by artillery, lies in the relative slowness with which the projectiles fall, the eye being able to follow them quite easily. Furthermore, these shells don't burst. But what an uproar, what an enormous, prolonged bellowing accompanies their being hurled out of the bowels of the earth!

I make use of a brief respite in order to get quickly across the ticklish northeastern sector. Then I stop for a few seconds, just long enough to see yet another burst gush up and come showering down a little ahead of me, after which I start out for the conquest of the northern sector.

Here the crest narrows down so much that it becomes a mere ridge, where walking is so difficult and balancing so precarious that I find myself forced to go on along the outer slope, very slightly lower down. Little by little, as I advance through all this tumult, a feeling of enthusiasm is overtaking me. The immediate imperative necessity for action has driven panic far into the background. And under the hot, dry skin of my face, taut on forehead and cheekbones, I can feel my compressed lips parting, of their own accord, in a smile of sheer delight. But look out!

A sudden intensification of the light warns me that I am approaching a point right in the prolongation of the fiery chimney. In fact, the chimney is not vertical, but slightly inclined in a northwesterly direction, and from here one can look straight down into it. These tellurian entrails, brilliantly yellow, seem to be surging with heat. The sight is so utterly amazing that I stand there, transfixed.

Suddenly, before I can make any move, the dazzling yellow changes to white, and in the same instant I feel a muffled tremor all through my body and there is a thunderous uproar in my ears. The burst of incandescent blocks is already in full swing. My throat tightens as, motionless, I follow with my gaze the clusters of red lumps rising in slow, perfect curves. There is an instant of uncertainty. And then down comes the hail of fire.

This time the warning was too short: I am right in the middle of it all. With my shoulders hunched up, head drawn back, chin in air, buttocks as much tucked in as possible, I peer up into the vault of sinister whining and whizzing there above me. All around bombs are crashing down, still pasty and soft, making a succession of muffled *plops*. One dark mass seems to have singled me out and is making straight for my face. Instinctively I take a leap to one side, and *feel* the great lump flatten itself out a few inches from my left foot. I should like to have a look, but this is not the moment! Here comes another projectile. I take another leap to dodge it. It lands close beside me. Then suddenly the humming in the air begins to thin out. There are a few more whizzing sounds, and then the downpour is over.

Have you ever tried to imagine a snail's state of mind as it creeps out of its shell again, the danger past? That was the way my head, which had been drawn back between hunched-up shoulders, gradually began to rise up again on my neck, and my arched back began to straighten, my arms to loosen, my hands to unclench. Right, then—it's better not to hang about in this sector! So I set out again. By this time I have got round three-quarters of the crater, and am in the gap between the northern and western zones, which are those that get the worst pounding. From here I can get back on the ridge proper.

I am now almost directly over the roaring chasm, and my gaze goes straight down into it like a stone dropping into the pit. After all, it's nothing but a tunnel. That's all. It's a vertical tunnel, ten or fifteen yards across, its walls heated to such a degree that they stretch and 'rise' like dough, and up from its depths every now and then enormous drops of liquid fire spurt forth, a great splashing sweat that falls and vanishes, golden flash upon flash, back into the dazzling gulf. Even the brownish vapors emanating from the pit cannot quite veil its splendor. It is nothing but a tunnel running down into viscous copper-colored draperies; yet it opens into the very substance of another world. The sight is so extraordinary that I forget the insecurity of my position and the hellish burning under the soles of my feet. Quite mechanically, I go on lifting first the left foot, then the right. It is as though my mind were held fast in a trap by the sight of this burning well from which a terrifying snore continually rises, interrupted by sharp explosions and the rolling of thunder.

Suddenly I hurl myself backward. The flight of projectiles has whizzed past my face. Hunched up again, instinctively trying to make as small a target of myself as I can, I once more go through the horrors that I am beginning to know. I am in the thick of this hair's-breadth game of anticipation and dodging.

And now it's all over; I take a last glance into the marvelous and terrible abyss, and am just getting ready to start off on the last stage of this burning circumnavigation, all two hundred yards of it, when I get a sudden sharp blow in the back. A delayed-action bomb! With all the breath knocked out of me, I stand rigid.

A moment passes. I wonder why I am not dead. But nothing seems to have happened to me—no pain, no change of any sort. Slowly I risk turning my head, and at my feet I see a sort of huge red loaf with the glow dying out of it.

I stretch my arms and wriggle my back. Nothing hurts. Everything seems to be in its proper place. Later on, examining my jacket, I discovered a brownish scorchmark with slightly charred edges, about the size of my hand, and I drew from it a conclusion of immense value to me in future explorations: so long as one is not straight in the line of fire, volcanic bombs, which fall in a still pasty state, but already covered with a kind of very thin elastic skin, graze one without having time to cause a deep burn.

I set off at a run, as lightly as my 165 pounds allow, for I must be as quick as I can in crossing this part of the crater edge, which is one of the most heavily bombarded. But I am assailed by an unexpected blast of suffocating fumes. My eyes close, full of smarting tears. I am caught in a cloud of gas forced down by the wind. I fight for breath. It feels as if I were swallowing lumps of dry, corrosive cotton wool. My head swims, but I urge myself at all costs to get the upper hand. The main thing is not to breathe this poisoned air. Groping, I fumble in a pocket. Damn, not this one. How about this other one, then? No. At last I get a handkerchief out and, still with my eyes shut, cover my mouth with it. Then, stumbling along, I try to get through the loathsome cloud. I no longer even bother to pay any attention to the series of bursts from the volcano, being too anxious to get out of this hell before I lose grip entirely. I am getting pretty exhausted, staggering . . . The air filtered through the handkerchief just about keeps me going, but it is still too poisonous, and there is too little of it for the effort involved in making this agonizing journey across rough and dangerous terrain. The gases are too concentrated, and the great maw that is belching them forth is too near.

A few steps ahead of me I catch a glimpse of the steep wall of the peak, or promontory, from the other side of which I started about a century ago, it seems to me now. The noxious mists are licking round the peak, which is almost vertical and twice the height of a man. It's so near! But I realize at once that I shall never have the strength to clamber up it.

In less than a second, the few possible solutions to this life-and-death problem race through my mind. Shall I turn my back to the crater and rush away down the outer slope, which is bombarded by the thickest barrages? No. About face and back along the ledge? Whatever I do, I must turn back. And then make my escape. By sliding down the northern slope? That is also under too heavy bombardment. And the worst of it would be that in making a descent of that sort there would be no time to keep a watch for blocks of lava coming down on me.

Only one possibility is left: to make my way back all along the circular ridge, more than a hundred yards of it, till I reach the eastern rim, where neither gas nor projectiles are so concentrated as to be necessarily fatal.

I swing round. I stumble and collapse on all fours, uncovering my mouth for an instant. The gulp of gas that I swallow hurts my lungs, and leaves me gasping. Red-hot scoriae are embedded in the palms of my hands. I shall never get out of this!

The first fifteen or twenty steps of this journey back through the acrid
fumes of sulphur and chlorine are a slow nightmare; no step means any
progress and no breath brings any oxygen into the lungs. The threat of
bombs no longer counts. Only these gases exist now. Air! Air!

I came to myself again on the eastern rim, gasping down the clean
air borne by the wind, washing out my lungs with deep fresh gulps of it,
as though I could never get enough. How wide and comfortable this
ledge is! What a paradise compared with the suffocating, torrid hell
from which I have at last escaped! And yet this is where I was so anxious
and so tense less than a quarter of an hour ago.

Several draughts of the prevailing breeze have relieved my agony. All
at once, life is again worth living! I no longer feel that desire to escape
from here as swiftly as possible. On the contrary, I feel a new upsurge
of explorer's curiosity. Once more my gaze turns toward the mouth, out
of which sporadic bursts of grapeshot are still spurting forth. Now and
then there are bigger explosions and I have to keep a lookout for what
may come down on my head, which momentarily interrupts the dance I
keep up from one foot to the other, that *tresca* of which Dante speaks—
the dance of the damned, harried by fire. True, I have come to the
conclusion that the impact of these bombs is not necessarily fatal, but
I am in no hurry to verify the observation.

The inner walls of the crater do not all incline at the same angle. To
the north, west and south, they are practically vertical, not to say overhanging, but here on the east the slope drops away at an angle of no
more than fifty degrees. So long as one moved along in a gingerly way,
this might be an incline one could negotiate. It would mean going down
into the very heart of the volcano. For an instant I am astounded by my
own foolhardiness. Still, it's really too tempting . . .

Cautiously, I take a step forward . . . then another . . . and another . . .
seems all right . . . it *is* all right. I begin the climb down, digging my heels
as deep as I can into the red-hot scoriae. Gradually below me, the oval
of the enormous maw comes nearer, growing bigger, and the terrifying
uproar becomes more deafening. My eyes, open as wide as they will go,
are drunken with its monstrous glory. Here are those ponderous draperies
of molten gold and copper, so near—so near that I feel as if I, human
being that I am, had entered right into their fabulous world. The air is
stifling hot. I am right in the fiery furnace.

I linger before this fascinating spectacle. But then, by sheer effort, I
tear myself away. It's time to get back to being 'scientific' and measure
the temperatures, of the ground, and of the atmosphere. I plunge the

long spike of the thermometer into the shifting scoriae, and the steel of it glitters among these brownish and gray screes with their dull shimmer. At a depth of six inches the temperature is two hundred and twenty degrees centigrade. It's amusing to think that when I used to dream it was always about polar exploration!

Suddenly, the monster vomits out another burst; so close that the noise deafens me. I bury my face in my arms. Fortunately almost every one of the projectiles comes down outside the crater. And now all at once I realize that it is I who am here—*alive* in this crater, surrounded by scorching walls, face to face with the very mouth of the fire. Why have I got myself in this trap, alone and without the slightest chance of help? Nobody in the world has any suspicion of the strange adventure on which I have embarked, and nobody, for that matter, could now do the slightest thing about it. Better not think about it . . .

Without a break the grim, steady growling continues to rise from the depths of that throat, only outroared at intervals by the bellowing and belching of lava. It's too much; I can feel myself giving up. I turn my back on it, and try, on all fours, to scramble up the slope, which has now become incredibly steep and crumbles and gives way under my weight, which is dragging me down, down . . . "Steady, now," I say to myself. "Keep calm for a moment. Let's work it out. Let's work it out properly. Or else, my boy, this is the end of *you*."

Little by little, by immense exertions, I regain control of my movements, as well as the mental steadiness I need. I persuade myself to climb *calmly* up this short slope, which keeps crumbling away under my feet. When I reach the top, I stand upright for just a moment. Then, crossing the two glowing fissures that still intersect my course, I reach the part of the rim from where there is a way down to the world of ordinary peaceful things.

Night on la Sciara

About the end of the afternoon, accompanied by one of our porters, a slim, shaggy youth with very dark eyes, we set off again, taking it easily, up the path that zigzags between the agaves and the wild fig trees in the northwestern corner of the island, slowly climbing toward the volcano. We crossed a zone where the vegetation had been ravaged by a fire the previous day. The wonderful hillside ablaze with scented broom was no longer anything but a charred slope bristling with hard stubble, the remains of the tall grasses that had been burned. It was a startling experience to sniff again the acrid smell of bush fires. . . .

We climbed the mountain slowly. Below, almost a straight drop, the blue of the sea grew ever more and more immense. High above, great brownish coils of fumeroles were boiling up out of the craters and blowing away over the summit in the wind.

It was nine o'clock. The sun was low on the horizon. It was reflected on the endless glassy surface of the sea.

"I think this is it—isn't it?"

"Yes. We'll have to go round the side to the big shaft, and then cut across toward that rock."

Coming down the day before we had spent a long time looking at the dizzy slopes of la Sciara, trying to make out a possible track that would enable us to get to the edge of the river of lava. Would we still be able to find our landmarks—the light rocks, white flecks of alkaline salts, sulphur deposits—when darkness fell?

The beginning was easier than we had expected. In the long twilight, following an almost horizontal line, we passed under the summit and along the upper edge of some extensive sulphur deposits, and reached the lip of the big conduit. We could hear the lava splashing in that vast hole, and that muffled sound of churning activity made us hurry on. We reached the very end of the ledge and began the climb down. Night had almost fallen. In the dark blue dusk the streams of fire were monstrous red serpents far away.

Step by step, one foot after the other, we went down the rough slope in the darkness. By now the last trace of daylight was gone, and the only glimmer we had was from the red glare of the lava on the low smoke screen being blown this way and that in the wind.

A rocky drop in the ground, the depth of which we could not guess, worried us. With my face close to the stone, my fingers clawing at it, I explored this unknown quantity with my foot. It took us a quarter of an hour to descend ten feet. Then again there was the slope of rubble, scoriae and coarse sand. On and off these unstable screes would crumble and slide away from under our feet, dragging us away, pulling us down with them, with the same fine-drawn hissing sound that snow makes in the same circumstances. With an effort we would manage to stop ourselves, holding fast to the alpenstock or the axe. With pebbles and sand trickling and rustling all round our ankles, we would listen tensely. Supposing we suddenly started an avalanche? Then the sliding mass would gradually slow down and stop. And so we would continue on our way.

After covering some fair distance, we made a swing away over to the left, aiming for the center of la Sciara. Now that we had the glow from the incandescent torrents, reflected on the vapor, straight ahead of us, it was more of a nuisance than a help to us and we stumbled miserably among the indescribable chaos of smashed boulders.

Suddenly, in the coolness of the night, I felt puffs of air on my face that were hot—too hot. Among the blocks I was stumbling along over there was lava, still live, burning like a somber furnace.

"Hi, Pit! Tell Peppino to stay where he is!"

The two of us went on together. Ahead of us the jagged ridge stood out against the diffuse crimson glimmer that betrayed the presence of the molten river. But there was also this furnace under our feet, with its burning breath! A glance uphill, to the left, quickly increased our desire to beat a retreat: glowing blocks, like *séracs* of fire, formed the front of an outflow that was just solidifying up there. Every moment or so one of them would break loose and go vaulting down toward the invisible sea, lighting up the black hillside with its leaps and bounds and scarlet showers of sparks.

Peppino had been calmly waiting where we had left him. Together we continued our exhausting progress over the unstable mountainside. We could not help feeling a little forlorn, here in this darkness full of red glare and hot breath, fumbling over this uncertain ground where no human being had ever ventured before. All around us we could feel the power of an extraordinary world on a scale that was not our own, and absolutely indifferent to our existence. It gave us a queer heartache, feeling the overwhelming grandeur of it.

"Damnation!" Tripping, I had smashed the lamp that I was carrying fixed to my rucksack, which was to have lighted us on our return journey. It had turned out to be more trouble than it was worth coming down and we had soon decided it was best to switch it off. We were going to miss it badly in a very short time.

We had been going downhill for hours. Still we had got no chance of moving up to the rivers of lava: what was in our way was sometimes these sinister furnaces hidden under an all too thin layer of blackish coke, sometimes rocky inclines that we could not get over, sometimes corridors of avalanches—either incandescent avalanches or avalanches of dark and gloomy boulders. Weariness lay heavy on my shoulders and I felt myself being slowed up as a result of breathing this air, which was full of toxic vapors. Thirst, too, was making itself more and more urgently felt—that chlorine-tasting thirst one gets on active volcanoes.

I was beginning to feel like giving up—like turning back uphill again as soon as possible, although the very idea of the return climb horrified me. The further down we went, the harder and more hazardous the return would be. . . .

Pit must also be dreading the upward climb. I heard him ask Peppino, in Italian:

"Do you think if we go right down to the sea some fisherman might see us from his boat and come and take us off?"

"*No. Non credo.*"

Pity . . . I too would have preferred, on the whole, to go all the way down la Sciara del Fuoco to the seashore.

Twice, three times, we had had to turn back from an attempt to cut across the slope to the left. Suddenly, coming out on the top of a last ridge, I found myself right in the red blaze of the incandescent river and saw it running along, swift and silent, only five yards ahead of me. I went nearer still. The heat struck into my face. My eyes were dazzled. What a vision it was!

Picciotto caught up with me. Another step . . . And another . . . But then the burning glow of it made it impossible to go any closer. Peppino had stopped just behind us. Speechless, spellbound, we gazed on something resembling the birth of our planet itself.

How many times had I already beheld such a spectacle? But the wonder of it is new to me every time. This river flowed along in a silence that was not silence. There was a steady hissing that was both thin and powerful, a sound that seemed as though in its inexorability it must be everlasting. It brought to my mind those armies of tropical ants advancing on their irresistible march, always with that pitiless rustling murmur. . . .

I don't know how long we stayed there, staring in rapture at this indescribable splendor, and then taking measurements, photographing, filming . . . Pit burned the bridge of his nose by trying to get some inches nearer. Our hands holding the instruments were half toasted. The sweat poured off us. Our thirst was frightful . . . agonizing . . .

After the dazzling red and yellow of the molten magma the pitch darkness of the night into which we turned back seemed like a solid wall. We climbed uphill at random, blindly, twisting our ankles, skinning our knees, sometimes upright, more often on all fours. Scarps of rock drove us to the left; slabs of slippery smoothness sent us to the right. . . . It was impossible, absolutely impossible, to find any point of reference. Sometimes we crossed ravines, sometimes we clambered up steep hillocks formed by heaps of breccia. To the right was the sheer drop into the great crater, with incandescent boulders breaking loose, like ice blocks breaking loose from some glacier of fire and pitching headlong down the steep incline, tracing huge, bright festoons of light in the darkness.

But a rumbling sound above us made us stop short. It immediately became louder, punctuated by sharp crashes. The avalanche! We could not see anything, but the din filled our ears—even, it seemed, our bodies —so suddenly did it increase in volume. It seemed to last an age. Straining our eyes in the darkness, we were all suspense. How long it lasted! An eternity, it seemed.

Then there was a roar, and a huge, pale rock, the size of one of the houses in the village, crashed to the bottom of the corridor only five paces away from us, and then, with a colossal leap, bounced onward downhill.

"Pietra molto grossa," Peppino remarked.

We could not find the way we had come. Cliffs that we had not noticed on the way down now drove us back. We were utterly lost. Fatigue made our legs heavy, lay heavy on our shoulders.

Here was a bastion of light-colored rock. While Pit was doing his best to get up it, I went along the base of it to the right, plunging up to the ankles in sand I could not see, glad to be able to keep one hand against the solid rock. Each of us hoped he had chosen the right way on and would not have to come back. Peppino, standing at the foot of the rock, awaited the result of our reconnoitering.

At first we kept in touch by shouting to each other. Each of us was doing his utmost, alone with his own problem. I was still making progress upward, on all fours. Quick! I glanced swiftly upward. Yes, it looked almost as though there were a way through there. . . . Oh, heavens! Here came a pack of pallid wolves swarming down on me, sulphurous vapors making a slanting attack on me in mid-climb. Should I go on? Should I get back as fast as I could? No—damn it all, I wasn't going to have climbed all this way up for nothing! So I pushed on upward, the suffocating fog catching up with me. With a handkerchief over my mouth, I climbed doggedly on. Oof! the dreadful cloud had passed.

Just at that moment, eighty or ninety feet above me, a great red cone of fire burst into the air! There was the uproar of the explosion, then the slow ascent of the incandescent clots, and finally, more and more violent, more and more concentrated, the whistling of the bombs and the crash of heavy lumps of lava falling to the ground.

No, they didn't get me that time. But I cleared out! At the bottom I found Pit, who had been driven back by insurmountable overhangs, and Peppino, composed as ever. There was nothing else to be done but to go round the bastion to the left, continuing on our endless way. For a long, long time we dragged thirstily on through that darkness, up those infernal slopes, with the ground shifting underfoot, until at last we reached the earthenware wine jar that stood in a corner of our tent, full of the beautiful cold water that had been waiting there for us all the time.

The sun got us out of our sleeping bags.

Lighting the solidified alcohol under the spirit cooker, Pit made tea with what was left of the water since the night before. Squatting on the ground, we sipped the drink gratefully. How good it seemed!

There in front of us clouds of smoke were ceaselessly unfurling over the summit and the rocky ridge that rises over it to the north, from where the track went down to San Vincenzo.

We were more or less in bliss. After the difficulties, the fears, the fiery torrents, the infernal thirst, and all the fatigues of the night, now to be here drinking this hot tea, in this magnificent early morning sunshine, gave us a feeling of intense well-being.

"Look! Mules!"

There were really mules looming up out of the smoky mist that enveloped the peak. They came at a trot, with their drivers pulling at the bridle and encouraging them with shouts. Certainly that was no place to hang about, in all those clouds of sulphur and chlorine! It was at a run that they came down the last few yards that still lay between them and our gully, and at that moment one more mule came over the top, but at a walk, and rather unsteadily. There was nobody leading it. It carried a rider. Slowly they drew nearer. Frowning in the brightness of the light, we watched this very odd rider with increasing astonishment. Then something about the man's attitude made us think there was something wrong. . . . In the same moment we all got up and ran to meet him.

He literally fell into our arms. It was the film director's right-hand man, General Muratori. Livid, he just managed to gasp out: "Fumes— air!"

There was a rattle in his throat. The muleteers gathered around us, explaining that the Commendatore had wanted to come and see for himself the place we had told him about a few days previously. But he had got caught in the blanket of gas. They had run with handkerchiefs over their mouths, but he must have taken deep breaths and got the gas right into his lungs.

It is a terrible thing to feel oneself powerless to help a human being. We tried laying him flat, sitting him up, giving him a drink of tea. . . . It didn't help. The minutes passed, and he got no better. On the contrary, he seemed to be suffocating more and more. There was nothing for it, we must get him down. And as fast as possible.

Six of us carried him. We set off at top speed. Our heels dug into the black sand. We started along the path down to the village.

The sky was absolutely pure blue and as though tightly stretched. The immense sea sparkled, even more intensely blue. The world was miraculously wide and clean.

Two hundred yards further down General Muratori, having been slowly asphyxiated, died in my arms.

TRANSLATED BY EITHNE WILKINS

The Johnstown Flood

by PETER J. TONER

The city of Johnstown, Pennsylvania, lies more than 1,000 feet above the sea, along the Conemaugh River at the mouth of Stony Creek. Precipitous hills nearly surround it. On May 31, 1889, as the result of a series of unprecedented rains, a dam twelve miles above the city gave way, and Johnstown was engulfed in a major catastrophe, whose details are vividly given below.

FRIDAY MORNING, MAY 31, DAWNED DARK AND DREARY—A dismal setting for the disaster that was to come. At 8:30 A.M. both rivers overflowed their banks. It was not long before the area below Market Street was covered with water, and within a few hours the greater part of the city was inundated, the water ranging from two to ten feet in depth. Mills and stores had closed early in the morning. Members of families were at home busily engaged in moving their furniture to upper floors. This was especially true of the residents of the lower areas, where the water ascended nearly to the first-floor ceilings. Some families deserted their homes and moved to safer ground.

Before noon the Poplar Street Bridge and the Cambria City Bridge had been carried away. Swiftly it was noised about that the South Fork Dam would be unable to withstand the pressure against its breast. Scant attention was paid to such reports, as similar rumors had proved false in the past. The Johnstown *Tribune,* however, cocked a ready ear to a report received at the central telephone office at three in the afternoon that the dam was in danger of breaking.

"It is idle to speculate," the *Tribune* observed, "what would be the result if this tremendous body of water—three miles long, a mile wide in places, and 60 feet deep at the breast at its normal state—should be thrown into the already submerged valley of the Conemaugh."

The dam broke at about 3:10 in the afternoon. Those who saw it go said it seemed at first as though the dam itself were moving rapidly down the valley. Due to the disruption of telegraph and telephone service the people could be given no warning after the break had occurred. But even had Johnstown received the alarm, nine-tenths of its inhabitants could not have escaped. The already flooded streets precluded the possibility of mass flight to the hills.

The tales told of the Daniel Peytons, John Parkes, and others, who on "foam-flecked steeds" rode through town warning the people to flee to safety are utterly fantastic. Even Pegasus, equipped with water wings, would have had difficulty in negotiating the canal-like streets of Johnstown. The myths owe their origins to McLauren's story of young John Baker who, mounted on horseback, witnessed the break while some distance away from the dam. Riding furiously toward South Fork, he warned several households along the route, as well as a few families in South Fork, of the coming avalanche.

There were loosed 4,500,000,000 gallons of water. Rushing down the mountain gorge, the black wall swept away nearly everything in its path. Trees, rocks, houses, lumber, and locomotives were engulfed and carried along like straw in a brook. Nothing could withstand the onslaught; the conglomerate mass of wreckage moved relentlessly toward Johnstown.

Witnesses along the path of death afterward declared that the movement of the water was frequently retarded at places where the valley narrowed. The wreckage and debris would form a temporary dam, but these checks were only momentary, and the flood swept on. Sections of houses, logs, trees, and other objects were tossed continually above the surface by the grinding movement of the rolling mass. In front of the gigantic wave rushed a powerful wind that pushed houses from their foundations before the water reached them. This invisible buffer was caused by the water and debris whipping the still air into motion and shoving it relentlessly onward. Only when the water reached Woodvale, where the valley widened, did the wreckage mix with the water. The flood swept through Woodvale, about one mile northeast of the center of the city, at approximately 24 miles an hour. It struck the central part of Johnstown with terrific force.

After the largest wave had passed through Conemaugh Borough it was deflected on Clinton Street, sweeping down Main and Locust Streets. This wave, the central one of three, pounded futilely at the rear wall of the Methodist Church. Passing through Central Park, it encircled Vine Street, destroying on the way the public buildings on Market Street. Nearly 200 persons found refuge in the Union Street schoolhouse, which stood against the flood. The three titanic waves united at the Point.

The hill on the west side of the Stonycreek River was an insurmountable barrier. It caused the water to surge toward the Stone Bridge, which withstood the shock without a visible tremor. The low arches of the bridge—which still constitute a distinct hazard to the city during high water—quickly piled up the debris. This obstacle impeded the flood, which receded as far as the Eighth Ward (then known as Grubtown, about one mile south of the city) before it seemed to gain fresh impetus. Retracing its path of destruction, the wave of death swept back as though to destroy completely and forever what little remained of Johnstown.

While many deaths were directly attributed to the immovability of the Stone Bridge, no one will deny that it was also the cause of saving many lives. Had it been swept from its supports when the first wave struck it, Cambria City and Morrellville—not excluding the Cambria Iron Works —would have been utterly destroyed. The span and the debris jammed against it enabled thousands of persons to escape death in the deluge. And, as the flood backed up from the bridge, there was afforded opportunities for many rescues.

The first huge wave derailed several railroad cars containing crude petroleum, which saturated driftwood and houses. When the wreckage piled against the Stone Bridge an overturned stove set fire to one of the houses. Despite the water which raged around it, the whole mass of debris soon became a roaring, crackling conflagration, forming a flaming breastwork for a dam of destruction and death. Death by fire in the midst of a flood! To dislodge the blazing wreckage by dynamite was impossible, not because the bridge itself was indestructible, but because it was inaccessible for the placing of explosives. As the flames roared upward, the sickening odor of burned human flesh assailed the nostrils of those who watched helplessly on the river banks. Within a few hours nearly 300 persons were burned to death. The town lay under water from 15 to 20 feet deep.

That night there was no moon, no stars. The pall of darkness elsewhere was made more apparent by the glare from the funeral pyre at the Stone Bridge. A scream, the crash of a building, the splash of cold rain, were the only sounds to break the silence.

Saturday morning dawned clear and bright. Streams still swollen separated different parts of the town. How many bodies lay strewn among animal carcasses and the wreckage could only be conjectured. Those watching on the hillsides beheld one of the most devastating scenes in the annals of American disasters. The few buildings that still occupied their original sites were damaged almost irreparably.

There were no thoroughfares. From Clinton Street to Jackson Street not a house was left standing, with the exception of a wing of the chapel of St. John's Convent. In that part of the chapel which contained the altar, the Sisters of Charity of Greensburg had knelt and recited their prayers till the fury of the flood had spent itself. Every nun survived to work untiringly to allay the sufferings of the afflicted.

While searchers clambered over debris, rafts were hastily constructed to carry the more venturesome across the well-nigh impassable streams to perform works of helpfulness—to clothe the naked, to feed the hungry, to give drink to the thirsty, to comfort the afflicted, to bury the dead.

In the days that followed appalling sights bore witness to the misery of the city's people. So ghastly had been the experiences of many survivors that they prayed for death as a surcease. Nearly everyone who survived had lost some relative or close friend in the flood. One unidentified woman had been killed while giving birth to a child.

The heroism displayed by those who had risked their lives to save others found its counterpart in the calm fortitude with which many met their deaths. One witness relates that he saw a large raft bearing an entire family singing "Nearer, My God, to Thee." While the hymn was yet half sung the raft crashed against a tree. All of its occupants perished.

A five-months-old baby—who were its parents no one ever knew— was rescued uninjured at Pittsburgh Saturday morning, after floating the entire distance on the floor of a house. Stories of rescue, adventure, and escape were myriad, but it was no time for story telling. Bodies had to be recovered, identified if possible, and buried. It was necessary to guard against pestilence. A city had to be rebuilt.

To recover the bodies was not easy. So woven into the wreckage were the corpses that many weeks elapsed before an approximately accurate death toll could be made. To learn definitely the extent of the casualties was impossible, although it was estimated that approximately 2,200 persons had perished.

James J. Flannery, Pittsburgh undertaker, organized a relief corps of undertakers. Embalming supplies were hurried to Johnstown. It was not until Monday evening, however, that the full corps of 55 undertakers began their work of washing, embalming, and preparing the bodies for burial. To add to the danger of disease after disaster was the large number of animal carcasses.

A room in Alma Hall was set aside for the reception of articles that might lead to the identification of the dead and the missing. Scenes of indescribable grief took place in this room. A glimpse at some of the entries in the records:

> Three rings on female, weight 185 lbs., 5 ft. 8 in.
> $25 found in black silk stocking with foot of female, high button shoe.
> $7.04 found on male, light hair, weight about 150 lbs.
> Ring with initials "F. M.—L. H."—woman about 55, hair partly gray, dress black.
> Foot of child burned at the bridge, slightly charred.
> Girl, about 6 months old, dark hair, white dress, brown bib.
> Child, 6 years old, no means of identification.

Upon such meager information thousands of survivors visited the morgues searching for missing relatives and friends. One of every three victims buried was unidentified. Frequently the dead were labeled for the living.

Many of the cemeteries were inaccessible because of the debris-littered streets and the lack of bridges. A plot of land back of Prospect, a hill suburb one-half mile north of the central part of the city, was therefore used for shallow graves. The bodies temporarily interred here were removed months later to Grandview Cemetery, where 779 unidentified dead now rest high in the hills.

Alarmed by the drunkenness, disorder, and depredations so prevalent on Saturday afternoon, a citizens' committee was organized to bring about order. There were many cases of robbery, mutilation, and pillage. Telegraph communication with the outside world was broken, and rumor took the place of fact in many newspapers.

When the committee found itself powerless to subdue the lawless element, a public meeting was held on Wednesday. J. B. Scott, of Pittsburgh, was unanimously chosen director, with the virtual powers of a dictator. Some semblance of order was restored during his brief administration, which lasted until the coming of the militia.

On Sunday night Sheriff Burgess asked the governor for troops. The following day the Fourteenth Regiment, Pennsylvania National Guard, under command of Col. E. C. Perchment, started for Johnstown. It was not until June 9, as a result of a conference between Governor James A. Beaver, Adj. Gen. D. H. Hastings, and Mr. Scott and his staff, that the

State took charge. The town was virtually, if not officially, placed under martial law, with General Hastings in command. The Fourteenth continued on duty until July 13, with one company remaining through the summer. The largest number of troops in Johnstown at one time was 550.

More than 6,000 laborers, under the direction of William Flinn of Pittsburgh, were engaged to clear the wreckage. Most of this force was withdrawn on June 12, the worst part of the job having been completed.

Hunger became a factor on Saturday, the day after the flood. A few grocers whose places of business had escaped at first demanded extortionate prices. They were quickly made to realize that profiteering constituted what might be considered a criminal act. The first carload of supplies was sent from Somerset, arriving in Johnstown early Sunday morning. Pittsburgh, Philadelphia, and Altoona soon followed suit, and it was not long before the survivors were assured that famine would not overtake them. At the various commissaries, during the first two weeks following the catastrophe, 30,000 persons were fed daily.

Five days after the flood Miss Clara Barton, President of the Red Cross Society, arrived in Johnstown. She and her assistants immediately began to give aid to the sick and injured, and later undertook the distribution of food and clothing to the survivors. From her headquarters on Walnut Street, Miss Barton directed the work of hospitalization and housing until she left the city late in the fall.

Sanitary conditions in the town were alarming, with sewers stopped up, streams polluted, and wreckage saturated with filth. As many as 50 cases of typhoid fever were reported in a single day, and illness of a malarial type became almost epidemic. Meanwhile the State Board of Health struggled to provide some measure of security. Disinfectants were used freely; nuisances were abated; sewers were opened; and the river channel was cleared to permit the escape of sewage. Normal sanitary facilities were not restored until October.

Relief money poured into the city from all parts of the world. From presidents and kings, to children with their pennies, the golden stream flowed in, giving life, courage, and hope. More than $3,000,000 was contributed to the sufferers of Johnstown. Governor Beaver appointed a commission to distribute the money according to the needs and losses of the survivors.

Soon the work of rehabilitation was begun. From its ruins a new and greater Johnstown arose, attesting the indomitable courage and will of the stricken people. The city grew and prospered—but it never could forget those who had perished.

Ten Thousand Miles in the Saddle

by A. F. TSCHIFFELY

*By birth Swiss-Argentine, Tschiffely was educated in England,
where he became a schoolmaster. He emigrated to Argentina and there
spent much time on horseback in the pampas and on several expeditions
into the northern wilds of that country. The present story was delivered
by him as a broadcast for the British Broadcasting Corporation in 1932.
It was part of a series of broadcasts, each being given by a man who
had, either in peace or in war, "hazarded his life in some notable adventure or important work." Undoubtedly many men have spent more
time in the saddle than Tschiffely—one thinks of working cowboys and
gauchos—but none more hazardously or on so sustained a ride. The
courage, hardihood and ingenuity which he required in order to survive
his self-imposed ordeal with nature may be surmised from his story.*

IT WASN'T JUST MADNESS OR A DESIRE FOR PUBLICITY THAT
induced me to ride two horses from the extreme south of
South America to the United States when comfortable ships would have
taken me from point to point in three weeks or less.

The two horses I took with me were descendants of the stock which
was shipped to South America by the Spanish Conquistadores about
four hundred years ago. Many of them were turned loose by the Spaniards
and others managed to escape during hostile attacks by the Indians.
But—owing to various circumstances—this wild breed of horses was
becoming nearly extinct, and the object of my ride was to prove to the
Government that it was hardy and useful and worth saving from ex-
tinction.

My journey took me two and a half years and was probably the
longest expedition ever made on horseback.

I traveled over vast plains, through deserts, jungles, swamps and over lofty mountains. In one place in the Andes we were close on 18,000 feet above sea level, and then again we found ourselves in steaming tropical swamps and jungles where it was often necessary to use a bush knife to open a trail through the dense vegetation. I say "we" although I was traveling without human companionship, for—after all—my two faithful horses did most of the hard work, and if it hadn't been for their instincts and thinking I should have come to grief on more than one occasion.

I had to go down to the far south of the Argentine Republic to find them, for I wanted a couple of animals which would be able to stand so long and arduous an expedition. There I bought thirty horses from a Tehuelche Indian Chief named "Liempichun," which means "I have feathers," and when they had been driven I chose two which looked good and tough to me.

Although they were sixteen and eighteen years old respectively, neither of these horses had ever been ridden, and you can imagine what kind of a war dance they led me when I first jumped on to their backs. Rodeo horses may be showy goat jumpers but for real unadulterated buck jumping I recommend the hurricane deck of a wild horse. However, after a great deal of patience and kindness on my part, and one or two nasty falls, the horses became more friendly and I was ready to start.

I had spent something like two years studying the road I proposed to follow and had gathered as much information about the different countries as I could. This, incidentally, was very little and vague, as I found out later.

Although I tried to avoid publicity the press soon heard about my proposed journey and the comments were many and varied. Most of the papers thought the trip was impossible and one or two said frankly that I ought to consult a doctor. Others were of the opinion that the expedition involved cruelty to animals. If these worthy gentlemen of the press had only thought a little they might have realized that if a man sets out into the wilds with two horses, his life will depend on them to a great extent and he will make it his first duty to attend to their welfare.

Usually I rode on one horse while the other carried the pack, and I changed from one to the other whenever I thought the change would do them good. When the trail was steep or the going difficult I divided the pack between them and went on foot, for the horses made faster progress in this way and there was less danger of a nasty fall. Although

I had to sleep out in the open very often I could not carry a tent, for even the lightest would have meant extra weight for the pack horse. I often had to sleep in huts, but I much preferred to curl up somewhere in the open where there were fewer insects than are to be found in most of the habitations of Indians and half-breeds.

I rarely bothered about wild beasts, for most of them are afraid of man and are only too glad to keep out of his way. Crushed garlic, rubbed on a rope made of horsehair, will usually keep snakes away from a sleeping man if he places this rope in a circle around him before he lies down to sleep on the ground. The only beast of prey which might attack a man in South or Central America is the jaguar, but since it isn't found in many places, one is fairly safe.

I have read in books and heard travelers tell how they made fires all night to keep pumas away. The puma is the American lion; in North America they often call him "cougar." This animal is very cowardly but rather curious and, after all, if the nervous traveler wishes to make fires all night one can hardly blame the poor puma for that. No; the real dangers I had to face were lack of water and food; and dangerous trails in the mountains. Then there were burning deserts and steaming tropical swamps and the possibility of fever and sickness.

I once had to stay for four days in a filthy settlement where over 150 natives were down with bubonic plague, and during my stay in the place twenty-four died of this horrible disease.

The swimming of torrential mountain rivers also presents many hazards, and in some of the tropical waters one has to look out for alligators and crocodiles. Even worse than these are the small cannibal fish, called caribes or piranhas. They attack in thousands and will tear to pieces in a few seconds any human being or animal which happens to have a cut or scratch, for they are attracted by the smell of blood.

Another unpleasant customer which lurks in some of the muddy waters is an ugly flat fish; the poisonous stinging ray. The tremblador or electric eel—one of nature's most extraordinary freaks—is another very dangerous denizen of some tropical streams and rivers. The discharge of one of these living electric batteries is powerful enough to paralyze a horse and cause him to sink like lead. They are from three to five feet long and about as thick as a man's arm. As well as poisonous fish, all sorts of different poisonous herbs and weeds grow in some parts of South America, and they will kill a horse if he eats them. I came across several varieties of these herbs and had to take great care that my animals did not get them.

From Buenos Aires we set out in a northwesterly direction toward the distant Bolivian border. There are few roads in that mountainous country, so I had carefully planned to arrive in Bolivia during the dry season; for I knew that the only means of communication would be the dry river beds. I had plenty of time, so I took things easy. But I had no end of trouble with the horses for the first few days, for they were none too tame and shied at such things as houses and traffic, which they had never seen in their desolate native regions in the far south. As soon as we were out in the open pampas things became more pleasant, and Mancha and Gato—as I had called the horses—gradually became more friendly. Mancha means "Spot," and Gato "Cat."

I had two .45 caliber six-shooters strapped to my hips, and the pack horse also carried a .44 rifle and a 16-bore repeating shotgun, for I knew I would have to rely a good deal on firearms for food. The type of saddle I used was a light framework of wood covered with leather. I piled sheepskins on this and was able to use it as a comfortable bed as well as for riding.

We jogged along for days over the vast flatness, which suggested eternity. There was little wild life to be seen except prairie owls and other birds. Herds of cattle were grazing and occasionally a *gaucho*, or Argentine cattle boy, passed us.

It got warmer as we continued north, and when we entered the huge alkali flats the sun rays seemed to penetrate to the very bones. The water is so scarce and bad there and the place is so barren, excepting for a few cactus plants and other shrubs, that I had been told that I should never get my horses across. But we managed all right and, when we came out safe and sound on the other side, I was well satisfied with my animals, for they had given the first real proof of their toughness.

At length we entered the mighty Andes, and traveled for days through vast valleys, using the dry river beds as roads and guessing our direction with more luck than judgment.

As we approached the Bolivian border we occasionally met Indians who were on their way down to distant villages or towns. Once a year— during the dry season—the hardy mountaineers make their long journeys. Their woven goods and beautifully made pottery are packed on llamas, the pretty and elegant South American beasts of burden, which they drive before them. When they have sold or exchanged their goods they return home before the rains set in and the wild rivers thunder down the deep ravines and canyons, on their way to the distant Atlantic.

The further we penetrated into this vast and imposing labyrinth of mountains the rougher and less hospitable the country became. Icy blasts swept down from the high peaks, and there was nothing green to be seen. For days we stumbled over rocks and boulders in river beds, and sometimes we threaded our way along giddy precipices where the horses had to pick their way with the greatest care.

It was bitterly cold in the high passes, and mountain sickness—caused by the low air pressure—sometimes made my nose bleed profusely and caused a feeling of giddiness. This mountain sickness—called *sorroche* or *puna* in the Andes—often affects animals as well and, unless the traveler takes care never to overexert his mount, it may collapse and even die.

The natives in some of these regions have a very rough but quite effective cure for it. If one of their animals falls they quickly cut a gash in the roof of its mouth to bleed it and then blow a little pure alcohol up its nostrils. I never hurried my horses where the trails were steep, and gave them a rest whenever they asked for it—and I assure you that once a horse gets used to a man he learns how to ask for many things.

In many parts of Bolivia it is advisable not to drink water. It looks clear enough but it is often bad and even dangerous. The natives make themselves a strong alcoholic beverage with corn. This abounds wherever Indians live, and its preparation is original, though not very appetizing. First of all, a quantity of corn is boiled for some hours, and in the meantime more corn is chewed by the Indians. When it has been masticated into a soft paste and well mixed with saliva, they spit it into a wooden bowl. The resulting paste is called *moco*, and acts rather as yeast does in the making of bread. When the boiled corn is ready, the chewed *moco* is added to it and soon the concoction begins to fizz and bubble, and after a day or so the native beer, or *chicha*, is ready. Owing to the scarcity of good water, I had to drink quite a lot of *chicha*—and what the eye has seen the heart can grieve over.

After weeks of traveling we reached La Paz, the capital of Bolivia, and shortly afterward a bloody uprising broke out in the Indian territory which we had just left, and many whites lost their lives. In most cases my sympathy goes to the poor and oppressed Indians, who have suffered untold injustices and misery ever since the Spaniards, under Pizarro, invaded their land.

We continued north from La Paz, skirted Lake Titicaca, and finally reached Curco, the ancient capital of the Inca Empire. This lake is some 14,000 feet above sea level and, although it does not look very big on the map, it took me a week to ride along its full length, from south to north. In this neighborhood we passed several most interesting ruins, which date back to Incaic and pre-Incaic times, and, although I am a keen student of archæology, I could not stay in these regions as long as I would like to have done. From there we swung due west and entered another terrific network of mountains—frightfully rough country where nature works on so gigantic a scale that it often made me gasp.

When we were on the mountaintops it was bitterly cold, and when we had stumbled down over neck-breaking trails into steaming tropical valleys, swarms of mosquitoes attacked us, whilst flocks of parrots screeched as if protesting against our invasion. Sometimes we had to cross Indian hanging bridges across deep chasms. When we came to the first of these hammocklike structures, which sagged dangerously in the middle, I thought my horses would never get across it, but the animals picked their way with great care, and when the bridge swayed too much they stopped until it was safe to proceed. Some of these bridges were only about three feet wide, and I always unsaddled the horses and took them across singly, for I did not think these wobbly and giddy pieces of primitive engineering would have stood the weight of two horses. I sometimes feared that one animal would be too much for these frail but daring constructions.

Once, while we were following a narrow trail, one of the horses lost his foothold and shot down a steep incline to what looked like certain death. Luckily, however, his descent was stopped by a solitary tree on the very edge of a deep precipice. It was not at all an easy job to rescue him, but he seemed to realize the danger for he never moved until ropes and lassos had been tied to him and he had been pulled back to safety with the assistance of friendly Indians.

Eventually we reached Lima, the capital of Peru, and from there we continued north along the coast.

We had to travel through sandy deserts where the heat was terrific. It never rains in these coastal regions and water can only be found where rivers come down from the Andes. One desert which we had to cross was ninety-six miles from river to river; a dangerous journey which took us twenty hours to accomplish. We did most of the traveling at night but, since we could only do this when there was a moon to help us, we often had to forge ahead during the daytime, when the tropical sun baked the sand to such a degree that I could feel it burn through my heavy riding boots.

Often I rode for miles over the wet sands along the beach where thousands of sea birds circled above us. The monotony of the scenery and the regular breaking of the waves often made me feel very sleepy and I found it very difficult to keep awake. When we came nearer to the equator I again changed the route and took to the mountains once more. It was cooler there, though the broken country made progress very slow. But I had had enough of deserts, heat and quicksands along the Peruvian coast, and had no desire to attempt crossing the low swamp land along the coast of Ecuador.

Up and down wound our trail, sometimes through dense vegetation in hot, tropical valleys, where the horses had to wade through deep mud, and where we had to be on the lookout for mud holes. These and quicksands are very dangerous traps; they are extremely difficult to distinguish from the rest of the ground, and should the traveler happen to blunder on to one of them he will be sucked down and perish unless help is at hand.

Once the horse I was riding refused to go a step further, and the more I tried to urge him on the fussier he became. When I finally used my spurs he reared up and snorted, but still refused to go forward. Luckily an Indian who spoke Spanish appeared on the scene and told me that I was on the very edge of a dangerous mud hole. How my horse sensed the danger is really mysterious, for there were none of these mud holes in his native regions. He probably saved my life, anyway, for I remember how a mounted guide, who once worked for me, trod on one of these places. His pony at once sank in, and if I had not carried lassos and ropes it would never have got free. As it was, we had a very difficult and exciting time pulling the poor beast out.

I was very proud and pleased when we crossed the equator not far from Quito, the capital of Ecuador. Strange as it may seem, it was very cool there, for we were high above sea level, and near us towered several beautiful snow-capped peaks and volcanoes, their snows glittering in the dark blue sky.

The Indians in every region through which we passed varied a lot in dress and general appearance, and many were the languages they spoke. If they did not understand any Spanish I had to make myself understood by signs, and this was often none too easy and required a great deal of patience.

Colombia was not an easy nut to crack but we finally reached the shores of the Caribbean Sea at the extreme north of South America. We had been on the road just about one year. The rainy season had now set in, and in many places we had to do almost as much swimming as walking—at least so it seemed to me at the time. Once, during a severe thunderstorm, I was knocked off my mount and stunned by a flash of lightning, but luckily I was not much hurt.

The overland trip from the north of Colombia to Panama is impossible because of swamps and impenetrable jungles and so I was obliged to embark the horses as far as Cristobal, near the Panama Canal. We stayed hereabouts for nearly a month and a half—about the longest stay I made anywhere—until the rains subsided and the jungles had dried up. Then I saddled up and set out again toward the forests and dense jungles which lie between Panama and Costa Rica. For several weeks we fought our way through dense vegetation and dark forests. We had to cross an 11,000-foot mountain range from which I could see both the Pacific and Atlantic Oceans, and the jungles below us looked like another angry sea of green.

In some parts it was very difficult to find food and I often fed off parrots, wild turkeys, wood pigeons and similar birds, and occasionally a wild pig provided me with meat. But I was once so hard up for food that I had to shoot and eat monkeys, though it made me feel like a common murderer, and the meat was extremely tough. My menu was often a strange one, and among other rare dishes I have had to eat large lizards, or iguanas as they are called in Latin America; crocodile, horse meat, ostrich eggs, armadillo; and even a snake once figured on my bill of fare. The latter tasted rather like a mixture of chicken and fish, and in some parts it is considered a delicacy by the native gourmets.

The horses had their share of strange fodder, too, for grass does not grow everywhere. They also provided unwilling food for others, for in the jungles ticks, vampire bats and many other pests made life unpleasant for them. Some of the South American vampire bats are much bigger than the useful European bats and, though they never bothered me, I had no end of trouble when they attacked my horses. The big ones can suck as much as half pint of blood, and if a few of these repulsive creatures get at a horse they weaken him terribly. But I soon found a way of protecting my two pets against vampires and ticks, and managed to keep them healthy and strong.

What with jungles and revolutions, I had plenty of excitement in Central America, and later, when I thought the rest of the journey would be just plain sailing, I ran into more revolutions in Mexico, where I had a very lively time of it. Fighting and banditry obliged me to make a big detour over the mountains and, in spite of the delay caused by this, we slowly approached our goal. I soon found out that a pleasant smile will take a man further than all the guns will, and somehow I managed to wriggle through without worse consequences than a black eye and a bullet through my saddle sheepskin.

When things became too hot the Mexican Government provided me with military escorts who accompanied me through the most dangerous parts. Long before I had reached that country the authorities and people knew about my ride, and since Mexicans are keen horsemen and lovers of the open, our long journey appealed to them, and they saw to it that nothing should happen to us on our way through their beautiful but turbulent country. After we had crossed the Rio Grande into Texas things were easy, but the further we went the heavier the traffic became. Finally I unsaddled in New York, and we took a ship back to the Argentine.

Thanks to delays caused by an official reception, I missed sailing on the ill-fated *Vestris,* which sank with over a hundred lives lost. We left the United States in the next boat, and you may be sure that I did not leave my two horses behind but took them back home with me on a comfortable passenger liner.

Thus they lived again to see their beloved pampas, where they were turned loose to roam from horizon to horizon and enjoy the life that is natural to them. They had done their duty!

Buzzing Death

by TURSA

In general, man's war with insects is impersonal—for example, they attack our crops and we spray the crops with insecticides—but occasionally it comes down to a bitterly intimate conflict, as was the experience of J. W. Beagle-Atkins of Great Britain, who writes under the pseudonym of Tursa. Beagle-Atkins fortunately survived his experience. Many others have succumbed to the bites and stings of poisonous insects. (Spiders and scorpions, technically known as arachnids, are by general usage considered insects.) And of course thousands of people have died from bacterial infections caused by the bites of such insects as the mosquito.

OF THE MANY VICIOUS PESTS OF NORTHEASTERN INDIA, THE tree bee, half cousin of the Indian hornet, tops the list. These bees go about in immense swarms, making their hives in the highest trees. Unlike the hornet, which will sting only when thoroughly annoyed, the tree bee has the habit of swooping down in attacking thousands, for no apparent reason, and chasing one for his life.

One sunny morning, riding along a dusty cart track, I found myself, without the least warning, the center of such an assault. The sky above me suddenly became thick with bees. With an icy shiver down my spine, I put my pony, Souvenir, to a gallop. Flight seemed the only hope of safety, but Souvenir's speed availed us nothing; the bees were after us in earnest. Souvenir jumped, bucked, reared and lashed out in all directions to rid himself of the bees, while I, attempting to protect my face and limbs, had the greatest difficulty in retaining my saddle. In a few moments, an angry buck while turning a corner at full gallop threw me into the dust.

With less than a mile to safety, I began to leg it with far greater determination than I had ever done in my life. But I was covered from head to foot with bees; they crawled in thousands all over me, stinging with excruciating pain. The under-rim of my topee became an angry hive, bees clustered inches deep. My forehead, ears and neck were blanketed in a buzzing, stinging swab of agony. Bees crawled inside my open-necked shirt and up my unprotecting shorts; they were everywhere. I tore them away in handfuls, but only to make room for others about me in clouds.

As I staggered on I yelled frantically to distant workers; but seeing the swarms about me, they bolted in every direction but mine. Gasping for breath, each time I opened my swollen mouth, more bees entered, until my tongue was stung to twice its normal size, and I was crunching them with my teeth. My nostrils had swollen into uselessness; my eyes, stung and running with water, were rapidly closing.

Stumbling weakly into the factory compound, I groped my way toward a building that was being erected. As soon as the men working there saw the droning battle array accompanying me, they made for cover at top speed. With the certainty of being half killed themselves, there was no alternative for them.

I was now a pitiful specimen, blind and deaf, and only able to breathe with extreme difficulty. Scrambling about with unseeing eyes ended by my falling unexpectedly into a huge heap of something soft and powdery, which I sensed must be a mound of red brick dust, used for building purposes. Into this I burrowed madly until my head and shoulders were covered. I quickly found myself in a worse quandary, brick dust choking out what little life I had remaining, and the angry swarm concentrating a renewed attack on my lower regions. Withdrawing from the brick dust, I used my remaining strength in a search for the water tank I knew was near. Staggering about in circles, I tore bees from my face and crushed them in handfuls, until I went down in a state of coma, powerless to defend myself. The bees had won.

After what seemed a lifetime, an unpleasant sensation of great heat crept over me. Presently I faintly felt the touch of human hands as rescuers hurried me away to safety. The reaction proved too strong, and I passed out.

My timely rescue was effected by two quick-witted Ghurkas, who had raced to a thatch stack and, bringing bundles of dry grass, had quickly surrounded me with a dense wall of fire and smoke, until the bees were beaten off. Later, as I lay unconscious, while the district was being scoured for a doctor, these same two staunch men insisted upon remaining and extracting stings from my inflated carcass. It took two days to free my body of the discarded stings. When, eventually, I recovered consciousness I was beamingly informed that I had had at least two thousand punctures, probably a record.

I lay in torment for several days, unable to move. My body, blown up like an oversized sausage, was black, blue and purple, and as hard as frozen meat. For several days I could see and speak only with the greatest difficulty, and it took many applications of antiswelling lotions before what had once been my nose and ears again emerged from the general mess.

My convalescence was a lengthy business of some six months in the hospital and several weeks in the cool hills of Darjeeling. When I returned to my old haunts I could never refrain from ducking and looking for the nearest cover whenever a droning swarm passed overhead.

Annapurna

by JAMES RAMSEY ULLMAN

James Ramsey Ullman, mountain climber and author, here recounts the exploits of a French expedition, led by Maurice Herzog, to climb Annapurna in the Himalayas and win fame as the first conquerors of a mountain 8,000 meters high. It was a long way from France to Annapurna, but longer still the way from the mountain's base to its peak. Why does man spend much and hazard all to climb a mountain? Perhaps the best answer is a shrug, or the same answer to the question why he wants fame or love. The joys of climbing many understand, but even the non-climber can know the thrill of the mountaintop: the heady air, the sense of freedom, the great perspective. These, together with great pain, are reflected in Ullman's pages.

TWO ALMOST EXHAUSTED MEN CREPT UP A STEEP, WIND-scoured slope of snow and reached a small level space. There they saw that there was nowhere higher to go. They were standing on the summit of the highest mountain yet climbed by man.

The mountain was Annapurna, 26,496 feet high. The climbers, Maurice Herzog and Louis Lachenal, were members of the French Expedition of 1950 to the Himalayas. And before they so much as laid eyes on the great peak they, and the men behind them, had had to win formidable struggles against both physical and political obstacles.

Men have gone higher than Annapurna on other, loftier mountains. In 1924 and again in 1933 climbers got to within 1,000 feet of Everest's 29,141. But until June 3, 1950 the highest peak yet climbed to the top was 25,710-foot Nanda Devi, in the Garhwal Himalayas, ascended by the Englishmen Tilman and Odell in 1936. During the war years, of course, there was no high mountaineering at all; and since war's end Asia has been in such turmoil that expeditions have been few in number and limited in scope. The Roof of the World—comprising some 14 known peaks of the Himalayas more than 8,000 meters (26,247 feet) in height—remained as inviolate as it had been through the ages since it rose out of the prehistoric sea.

An "8,000-er"—the first "8,000-er"—has been the goal of mountaineers the world over. And that was what the French wanted: the first *huit mille*. But in the mid-20th Century mere access to the highest mountains is almost as difficult a matter as their ascent. The road to Everest lies through Tibet, and since the war Tibet has denied admission to all large expeditions. India and Pakistan have been in ferment, Kashmir virtually in a state of civil war.

Then came the great chance—and from the unlikeliest of sources. The tiny Kingdom of Nepal, on India's northern border, had long been the most implacably closed of all Asiatic states. But the French envoy to Katmandu had become a close friend of the maharajah. And when the request for permission was, none too hopefully, submitted, years of tradition were swept away by the nod of a jeweled turban.

This was in the fall of 1949. Back in France, as soon as the word arrived, the machinery was put in motion for launching a major expedition. The French government itself supplied a third of the necessary funds, and the rest was raised by the French Alpine Club and other mountaineering organizations, which together formed a central committee to launch the venture. Supplies and equipment were drawn from the French army, from scores of manufacturers and merchants, from specialists in every conceivable field which might contribute to the success of the enterprise.

Most important of all, of course, was the selection of the climbers, and out of hundreds of aspirants a team of nine was finally selected by the committee of climbing clubs. As leader there was 31-year-old Maurice Herzog, by profession an engineer, by avocation a widely experienced Alpinist. The others chosen primarily as climbers were five men still in their 20s—Louis Lachenal, Lionel Terray, Gaston Rebuffat, Jean Couzy and Marcel Schatz—all outstanding among the postwar crop of French mountaineers. Rounding out the party were three men for specialized jobs: Dr. Jacques Oudot as physician, Marcel Ichac as photographer and Francis de Noyelle as transport officer. It was to prove a strong, well-balanced team. If it had not been so, all nine would not be alive today.

On March 30 a DC-4 carried them off from Paris' Le Bourget Airport, and some two weeks later a mountain train set them down at a railhead on the frontier of Nepal. Ahead of them lay the highest mountains on earth and, guarding the mountains, a wilderness in which no white man had ever set foot.

No one has seen the Himalayas without being awe-struck. Explorer Hermann Keyserling wrote in 1914, "Never have I found myself in the presence of such immense power. . . . One would say that the frozen moon had transfixed itself onto the green earth, so supernatural is their impact, so out of proportion their grandeur to the usual aspects of this planet. They are a pyramid of formation upon formation, flora upon flora, fauna upon fauna. A tropical world transforms itself, little by little, into an arctic world; the kingdom of the elephant gives way to the kingdom of the bear, and that in turn to the kingdom of the snow leopard. It is not until one has reached the top of this world that the Himalaya proper begins."

For days the long caravan of the expedition crept through the jungle and up onto the higher open land beyond. Porters and pack animals carried their four tons of supplies. Back in France it had been decided that there would be two alternative objectives: first, Dhaulagiri, the huge 26,795-foot citadel of central Nepal; second, if that proved impossible, the neighboring and slightly lower snow peak of Annapurna. Now, as the great wall of the Himalayas rose up before them, the summits of the two "8,000-ers" appeared and disappeared in the distant mists.

But seeing the remote crests was one thing, finding a way to their bases quite another. The few available maps were worse than useless. The valley-dwelling Nepalese knew virtually nothing about the uplands beyond, which they believed to be the home of gods and demons. The expedition climbed up, climbed down, zigzagged and backtracked through a wilderness of ridges, gorges, choked valleys and swollen torrents, searching out the route to their goal.

Speed was important, for the only time of year when the great peaks can even be attempted is the brief period between the melting of the winter snows and the coming of the summer monsoon. This year meteorologists predicted the monsoon for early June. And it was now the end of April.

Dhaulagiri was investigated thoroughly before the verdict was reached. An immense tapering pyramid, shaped like the Matterhorn but almost twice as high, it was, if not impossible, so formidable that there would be no margin of safety at all. Now it was Annapurna or nothing.

"The Goddess of the Harvests" the Nepalese call her, watching high in the sky above the fertile plateau of Pokhara. But there was nothing womanlike about the grim world of rock and ice through which the climbers struggled in their circuit around her. The southern side was impossible. East and west were impossible. All presented either unclimbable rock faces or cliffs of ice that daily crumbled down in gigantic avalanches. The only hope was on the northwest flank. Here, at last, a way was found. And no less important, there appeared to be a way still farther, still higher.

So climbers, porters and equipment were all assembled at the foot of Annapurna's northwestern glacier. Above them still loomed two vertical miles of snow and ice, wind and cold, ridge and precipice. It was now mid-May, and the inevitable monsoon was a scant three weeks off.

Finally on the mountain itself, they began the backbreaking work of establishing the chain of higher camps. The expedition's food supply consisted largely of French army field rations, and enough of this had to be packed up not only to maintain them if all went well, but also to see them through if they should be pinned down in their bivouacs by storms. Day after day, therefore, the climbers and high-altitude porters moved up and down the mountainside in relays, under 40-pound loads, carrying their food, their tents, their sleeping bags, their extra clothing and spirit stoves and can openers and all the other impedimenta that was needed—not to conquer the heights, but simply to live on them.

Camp 1 was set up on the lower glacier, some 2,000 feet above the base, No. 2 near the head of the glacier, another 2,500 feet up. Then, while the others moved back and forth with their burdens, Herzog, alone, reached the snowfield above the glacier and picked the site for Camp 3, at a height of more than 21,000 feet.

The weather held good. No serious climbing difficulties were encountered. The principal danger was from the avalanches that were forever rumbling and crashing down the mountainside; but the climbers chose their routes and camp sites carefully, and while there were several near misses, they succeeded in keeping out of the path of the great snowfalls.

Excerpts from Terray's report:

"Camp 1 to 2: Cross the level surface of the glacier. A few crevasses, but an hour of absolute calm during which one feels safe from snow-slides and falling *séracs* (ice towers). A snow-covered spur rises up ahead, and we tackle it by skirting two overhanging walls of ice.

"Camp 2 to 3: The slope suddenly becomes very steep again. The route winds between walls of *séracs* and across two sharp iceridges, onto which we fix static ropes.

"At Camp 3: My two porters and I spent a terrible night, for I couldn't find the second tent that was supposed to have been left there in a bag. Even worse, avalanches were crashing down all night to the left and right of our single tent, in which we were huddled one on top of another."

Before the next camp could be established the weather took a turn for the worse. Fog sifted in over the mountainside and late each day it snowed. Even the indefatigable and optimistic Herzog admitted, "All our efforts will be wasted if the snow doesn't stop falling at least for two days."

Then providentially it did stop snowing. The wind fell, the sun blazed out and once again on the dazzling ice walls men moved up and down like columns of ants. At 22,700 feet, on a huge, curving arch of cliffs that supported the snow dome of the summit, they succeeded, on June 1, in establishing Camp 4. Meanwhile, on the radio in base camp far below, word came through from New Delhi that the monsoon, moving up from the Indian Ocean, had already reached Calcutta.

Throughout the ascent the climbers had for the most part worked in teams of two. Now, as the moment for the final thrust approached, Herzog and Lachenal moved up ahead as Team No. 1. On June 2 they were on their way again, to set up a final camp as near the summit as possible.

A great band of cliffs blocked direct access to the top; so they struck off to the left and, hour after hour, threaded their way upward. But the weather held, and toward midafternoon they set up Camp 5, at 24,300 feet. Here a single rib of rock lay like a dark wrinkle across the slope; here their hope was to find a flat ledge for their tent. But there was no flatness anywhere. They dug themselves in as best they could against a curve of the rock, and when the inevitable evening storm broke, the wind threatened to lift the tiny tent bodily from the mountainside.

The night dragged past—a night in which they thought only of the morning. The summit slope above them appeared of itself easy, a mere 2,200 feet of gently rising snow. The two great imponderables were the weather and how they would react to the now tremendous altitude. They dozed. At first light they crept from their sleeping bags, pulled on their frost-stiffened boots and set off for the top. Simultaneously, below them, the two supporting teams moved upward, according to plan: Couzy and Schatz from Camp 3 to 4, Terray and Rebuffat from 4 to 5. For better or worse, the day to which all their months of preparation and struggle had been directed had come at last.

The day was sunny, but clouds of snow whipped into their faces. Step by step, hour after hour, Herzog and Lachenal plodded on, as if up the tilt of a blazing white roof. The tilt was not steep and they climbed unroped, but at every step their feet broke through the thin crust into deep, powdery snow, and soon their hearts were pounding and their lungs burning from the exertion. Every 50 paces they alternated leadership, so as to share equally the strain of opening up the track.

They felt themselves all but drowned in the glaring light of the tropical sun. Their heads seemed on fire, yet at the same time the cold stiffened their clothing and pinched their fingers beneath their gloves. Half suffocated, they stopped again and again to suck the raw, thin air into their lungs, but it gave them only a fraction of the oxygen they needed. Minutes blurred into hours, and hours into eternity. Then at last a black patch danced before their eyes—a final band of rock directly beneath the summit dome. Was there a way up the rock? As they approached it, they saw a cleft splitting its center. . . . One foot forward, then the other. One foot. The other. . . . A blast of wind struck them. It came from the *other* side of the mountain, and even in their dazed and exhausted condition they knew what it meant. Another few gasping steps, and they stopped—for the last time. Maurice Herzog reached out and touched a delicate icy crest that changed shape before his eyes as the wind swirled over it. Annapurna was theirs: the first "8,000-er" ever climbed.

The day may come when men will climb a mountain and be lifted gently from its summit by a helicopter. But that day is not yet, and, until it arrives, getting down a mountain will remain almost as difficult—and invariably more dangerous—than getting up it. Herzog and Lachenal had won a great victory. Now they were to pay the great price.

Even while they stood on the summit, the sun receded and gray veils of mist streamed in on an icy wind. The world beneath them was blotted from sight. But there was one traditional act that had to be performed: removing his gloves, Herzog opened his pack and took out his camera and a small French flag. Handing the camera to Lachenal, he fastened the flag to his ice ax and then held the ax above his head while his companion snapped the shutter. In a few minutes the two men were inching down the snow slopes, bent almost double against the still rising wind. By now both their bodies and brains were sluggish from fatigue and lack of oxygen, so it was not until long afterward that Lachenal suddenly shouted, "Maurice! Maurice!" When Herzog turned, Lachenal pointed.

Herzog looked down in dull surprise and saw that his hands were bare. He had lost his gloves.

This was the first in a long chain of mishaps that was now to plunge the expedition into near tragedy and almost into total disaster. Herzog, now all too aware of his already numb hands, rushed on to Camp 5 ahead of his companion. Terray and Rebuffat were waiting there, according to plan, and had just begun to minister to Herzog when there was a sudden cry from outside the tent.

Within a few steps of the camp Lachenal had slipped and fallen, and now he lay among an outcropping of ice hummocks 300 feet below. Terray made his way to him and found that, while miraculously he had broken no bones, he was suffering from shock and scarcely knew where he was or what had happened. With the utmost difficulty Terray got him back up to the tent, and for the rest of that day and all night he and Rebuffat tended the two battered men. Not only Herzog's hands, but his and Lachenal's feet, were badly frozen, and for a time the two others almost despaired of restoring their circulation. In the end, however, they were successful; and during the night, happily, Lachenal's mind cleared. He and Herzog told of the day's great victory. Congratulations were passed around. The worst seemed over.

But the worst had not even begun. For no sooner had the four started their descent the next morning than the storm, which had threatened all the previous afternoon, burst in full fury. In clear weather the down trip from Camp 5 to 4 would have taken no more than three hours; but now all landmarks were effaced in a caldron of boiling snow, and for hours they groped and stumbled through white nothingness—numbed, blinded and lost. Once, they discovered later, they passed within 300 yards of Camp 4, but neither could they see it nor could Couzy and Schatz, who were awaiting them there, hear their desperate, snow-muffled shouts.

All day they wandered, and as darkness approached they knew that they would have to face that most dreadful, and usually lethal, Himalayan ordeal: spending a night in the open. While they were burrowing into the snow, Lachenal, standing a little apart from the others, vanished before their eyes. For a moment it seemed certain that tragedy had been added to catastrophe, but then they heard Lachenal's voice, telling them that the crevasse into which he had fallen was only a few yards deep. Investigation proved that its floor was solid and that its walls gave good protection from the wind; and, climbing down, the others settled themselves as best they could. What had seemed disaster was turned for a while into a stroke of luck.

But only for a very short while; for no sooner did they stop moving than the cold, even in their windless cavern, began gnawing through to their very bones. Taking off their boots (since keeping them on in such conditions would have meant certain frostbite), they put their feet into a bag and lay practically one on top of another to generate such warmth as they could. So the night passed, without sleep, without surcease from the cold. And shortly before dawn came the worst blow of all. A mass of snow, near the lip of the crevasse above, worked loose and plunged down, burying them in a white shroud.

Stifled and stunned, they struggled and managed to fight free. But everything they had had with them—their packs, climbing equipment and, above all, their boots—remained buried under the white tons of snow. For more than an hour, in stockinged feet, the exhausted, half-frozen men dug and groped with the last frantic desperation of the will to live. And at last they uncovered the four pairs of boots. Almost simultaneously day broke above them—a day bright with sunlight, for the storm had passed.

It was nearly too late, however. Both Herzog and Lachenal had again lost all feeling in their feet, and Herzog's hands were as cold and hard as blocks of ice. By now Terray and Rebuffat too had begun to suffer from frostbite; and all four were partly snowblind from the effect of invisible ultraviolet rays when they had removed their goggles the previous day to find their way through the blizzard.

They were lost. Their legs could scarcely support their weight. They could not open their eyes against the white stab of daylight. Creeping to the rim of the crevasse, Lachenal and Rebuffat stood up where they might be seen and shouted for help. Ironically, they were seen and heard by Ichac, the photographer, almost 4,000 feet down the mountainside at Camp 2, but from Camp 4, only a few hundred yards away, both their figures and voices were blocked off by an intervening ice cliff. Herzog and Terray struggled up from the crevasse beside them. They all shouted. No answer. Half limping and half crawling, they began working their way down the snow slopes. If they were going to die, they were going to die trying.

Then at last, after all their bad fortune, came the one great stroke of good. At 8 o'clock that morning Marcel Schatz began to climb upward from Camp 4. Having seen no sign of the higher men the previous evening, he assumed that they had decided not to make the descent during the storm, but would be coming down that day; and now he was making a track to guide them on the last stage of their journey. Not more than a few minutes above camp he stopped and stared at the four apparitions who stood swaying, blind and crippled, on the white slope above him. Then he went up to them and led them down.

That was the end of the ordeal of climbing, but not of that of the climbers. Led by Schatz and Couzy, with Sherpa porters assisting, the descent from Camp 4 to 2 was made all in that same day. Just above Camp 3 the mountain struck its final blow at them, hurling down an alavanche that almost swept Herzog, Rebuffat and two Sherpas to destruction. Rebuffat, however, managed at the last moment to leap from its path, and Herzog, though swept from his feet, was providentially wedged against the side of a small crevasse, from which point he was able to hold the porters on the rope. They were still alive—though not much more—and toward evening the whole straggling, exhausted caravan limped into Camp 2.

Ichac and Oudot had gone part way up to meet them. "The first to come toward us," reported Ichac, "was Maurice [Herzog]. He walked straight, his legs stiff, his face worn with fatigue and covered with bruises, his hands wrapped in rags. With difficulty he recognized me. 'It was terrible, old man,' he said. 'My feet and hands are frozen. I can't see properly. But we've scored a fine victory for you. We did Annapurna day before yesterday, Lachenal and I!. . .' "

Now the climbers had had their day, and it was the doctor, Oudot, who became the key man of the expedition. Of the four men who had spent the night out, Terray was all right, and Rebuffat, though suffering from frostbite and the pain in his eyes, would recover. But with Herzog and Lachenal it was another matter. The toes of both had turned blue-black, and on Herzog's feet the leaden color extended to the middle of the soles. His hands, from which shreds of rotted skin were hanging, were numb as far as the wrists. In a cramped, dimly lit tent, Oudot worked through the night and all the next day over the two men, administering novocaine to relieve their suffering and injecting them repeatedly with acetylcholine to stimulate the circulation of their blood.

One day, however, was all that could be spared at Camp 2, for the monsoon was now due, and at any moment torrential rains would begin turning the mountainside into a death trap of melting snow. Sledges were improvised out of skis and stretched canvas, and the crippled men were roped onto them for the descent. Inching down the white slopes, their eyes blindfolded, their arms and legs swathed in bandages, they seemed less living men than mummies.

Almost miraculously, the operation was accomplished without mishap, and a few days later, on June 10, the whole party was assembled at the base camp, at the foot of the mountain. A single bottle of champagne had been brought from France to celebrate victory—when and if; and now Herzog, lying in his tent, called everyone in to drink it. When his own turn came, his companions had to hold the bottle to his lips.

The next morning they awoke to the unfamiliar sound of beating rain. The monsoon had come, and above them the white walls of Annapurna had started to peel off in roaring avalanches.

Later that same day they broke camp and set off—the mountain behind them, a month's nightmare ahead. Herzog and Lachenal had to be carried every step of the way; over steep ridges, swollen rivers, and finally through the underbrush of the lowland jungles. Instead of bitter cold there was now cloying, sweltering heat. The two crippled men stank of putrefying flesh, and their pain became so great that Oudot kept them almost constantly under morphine. Herzog, with septicemia, was often delirious; one day his fever reached 105.6° and it was touch and go whether he would live or die. Massive doses of penicillin pulled him through, however, and the weary caravan struggled on.

Rain beat down incessantly. The wet earth smoked. And almost every day, amid swarms of flies and crowds of curious villagers, Oudot did the grim work that had to be done on Herzog and Lachenal. For by now it had become obvious that the toes of both men—and Herzog's fingers as well—would have to go; and one by one the doctor amputated them, before the deathly infection could spread further into their bodies. By the time the journey was over Lachenal had lost all his toes and Herzog all his toes and fingers.

In the second week of July they reached railhead and civilization. But, characteristically, Herzog refused to leave Nepal until he had paid a long-arranged visit to the maharajah, who had made the whole venture possible by granting his permission. So there followed still another journey, through mountains and valleys, to Katmandu, the capital, where, amid oriental pomp, he was carried on a chair into the Durbar Palace to discharge his last duties as expedition leader. Then Maurice Herzog and his companions flew back home: to their rewards—and their memories.

The two conquerors of Annapurna are still convalescing. On the day I visited Herzog in Chamonix, in the French Alps, there were other guests in his room. Presently, of course, someone asked the inevitable question: "Was it worth it?"

Herzog's only answer was a smile. It was a needless question. To him and to his companions of course it was worth it. This is the story of brave men. Some may think it also a story of foolhardy men. But if nothing else, it demonstrates that there are still among us those who are willing to struggle greatly and suffer greatly for wholly ideal ends; for whom security is not the be-all and end-all of living; for whom there are conquests to be won in the world other than over their fellow men.

A Waterspout in the Pacific

by JAMES J. WAIT

Often it is not so much a matter of man against nature as of nature against man. When one senses the enormous power which nature can display even in one of her minor moods, such as this waterspout, one is likely to reflect on man's puniness and to marvel at his incredible effrontery in daring to challenge her at all.

A waterspout is essentially a whirling column of cloud or air extending between the surface of a body of water and low-hanging clouds. As in a tornado, its suction and its destructive powers are tremendous when reckoned by the standards of man. The following account brilliantly describes what it is like to be near and inside one.

WE HAD JUST LEFT THE PHILIPPINE ISLANDS—THE CLIPPER *Wasatch*, bound for New York, with some fifteen hundred tons of sugar—and were then bowling easily across the Celebes Sea toward the Straits of Macassar, with the last of the southwest monsoon. Very little wind seemed left in the bag, for as the ship lifted on the remnants of the long Pacific rollers the sails lost their snowy fullness and slapped shudderingly against the spars and rigging; the reef points rattled like hail, the masts creaked in their fittings and the yards jerked uneasily at the braces. The whole ship had a rattling, unsteady, loose-jointed motion, until she rolled ponderously to windward again and tautened everything with a quick jerk that seemed powerful enough to carry away the lighter spars.

The monsoon was about breaking up; and although the sky was now as serene as possible, unsettled weather, with violent squalls, was to be expected.

It was with such surroundings that I left the ship when I went below at eight bells, turned into my bunk, and soon fell asleep.

I was roused by the boatswain thrusting his head hurriedly in at the door and saying, "All hands shorten sail, Mr. Wait. A water-spout to windward, sir!" Bounding up, I soon jumped into the few clothes necessary in that latitude and ran on deck.

What a sight! To leeward the sky, air and water were, as before, hot, breathless and glittering; but to windward was a vault of billowy black nimbus cloud, rent by incessant lightning and acting as an immense reverberator for the thunder which rolled along over the water, crash after crash, shaking the ship like a leaf, until it was almost deafening. The lower surfaces of the clouds were torn into white and ragged fragments, and these were spun and blown about by the resistless currents of the whirlwind, while in the center of the mass, like a sturdy column supporting the vast dome, writhed an enormous waterspout. Within a radius of many rods about its twirling base the sea was lashed into boiling fury, and rose and fell in irregular tumultuous waves, whose crests were whipped off by the wind and blown hither and thither like smoke.

The spout was dead to windward and bearing down upon us with fearful speed. Already its roaring was in our ears. All hands were working for their very lives to get sail off the vessel, pulling and hauling like steam engines, every one of them, and jumping aloft like monkeys to roll up the slatting canvas. For once Captain Mason lost his habitual coolness and seemed almost beside himself with excitement and apprehension. When I came on deck the ship was beginning to heel over from the effect of the outside currents of the whirlwind upon her bare spars and half-furled canvas. Our signal howitzer had been unlashed by the cabin boy and the captain shouted, "Mr. Wait, will you serve that gun." I sighted the piece and pulled the lock string with such a trembling hand that the ball missed its mark, and called forth a cry of disappointment from those aloft, who had watched its ricochet course with the eagerness of men intent on a forlorn hope. "Load again!—quick, for God's sake!— load again!" This time the ball went crashing through the watery column, but with no more effect than if my piece had been a popgun. There was no time for another shot. The ship was now staggering under the violence of the wind. The men aloft, knowing the insecurity of the spars, came sliding down the backstays in their haste to reach the deck. Every second the force of the wind was stronger, bearing the good ship down upon her beam-ends as a skilful wrestler forces an antagonist to his knees. Slowly the cloud began to swing around, and we backed our bare main yards to deaden any headway the ship might now have, until we could get some little patch of sail up forward to pay her off from the wind and thus escape the spout, which in its altered course we hoped would pass ahead of us. Suddenly the half-furled missen-topsail blew from the gaskets, and, filling out like a balloon, sent the ship spinning around toward the wind and tearing through the water as though she had all sail set. "Up helm, there—run up the fore-topmast staysail—keep her away!" shouted the captain, wildly, through his hands. One of the ordinary seamen was at the wheel, and I saw him jamming down the spokes in his vain endeavors to move the helm. Calling to one of my watch to follow, I sprang to the wheel, and with our united strength had the helm hard up, when the fore-topmast staysail they were trying to set forward blew clear from the bolt-roping at the first slap, and it became a certainty that all our endeavors were fruitless and the waterspout must strike us. The ponderous fabric of the vessel, quivering like a whale at the stroke of the harpoon, was tossed like a cork on the seething base of the column. Her masts bent like coach whips before they snapped. Great patches of canvas were torn from the yards and, spreading out, sped off like frightened ghosts, their long arms of tatters waving wildly as they vanished in the misty air. Each man almost involuntarily secured himself as best he might, and in an instant more the waterspout was upon us— with a roaring and bellowing as of a thousand demons, the cannonlike crash of breaking spars, the snapping of cordage, and the rending of timber. Then an irresistible rush of water poured down upon the deck, seemingly with the concussions of Niagara; it bore me back against the wheel casing and held me as in a vise, tore off my shirt and shoes and pressed with such a weight upon my chest that my eyeballs almost started from their sockets and I thought I had been caught under a falling spar.

A moment of deathlike stillness succeeded this awful pandemonium and then the rain fell, not in drops but in solid masses that beat us down upon the deck, filled our eyes, mouths and nostrils, and nearly drowned us. The decks were afloat even with the tops of the demolished bulwarks; and ropes and half-alive but struggling men were washing back and forth as the ship's bare hulk rolled about in the trough of the sea.

When I recovered from the shock of being half drowned and half crushed, and had succeeded in getting my breath and dashing the water from my eyes, I saw—instead of the gallant clipper of an hour before, whose graceful build and lofty spars excited the admiration of every seaman and made the *Wasatch* the "smartest" ship in port, wherever she went—instead of this, a dismantled wreck shorn of every semblance of her former beauty. Our fore and mizzen masts were gone close to the deck and the mainmast had been taken out bodily from the stepping, tearing up the deck from rail to rail as it went. Of the forward house and forecastle not a vestige remained. The bowsprit was twisted off close to the stem and both bulwarks were gone from the bows clear aft to the quarter-deck. The cabin was partly unroofed and the body of the captain's son was visible, jammed into a corner of the companionway, broken and crushed into an almost unrecognizable mass. As soon as they were able, the remnant of the crew crawled aft to the quarter-deck. Instead of our complement of twenty-five, we only mustered eleven. The captain and mate were gone; the cook and steward had vanished with their galley. There were six of the men, one with a broken arm, the boatswain with a wound in his head deluging his face with blood, the carpenter, two of the boys, and myself left in command. Getting out the medicine chest, I at once began to dress the hurts of the wounded men and gave the order to clear away the wreck. It was considerable of a surprise when the men returned saying there was no wreckage to clear away. Such had been the force of the whirlwind that all our heavy top-hamper had been entirely torn away. Not a spar or a timber, except a few odds and ends, was hanging by the ship, but pieces of both could be seen heaving about in the swell for a mile or so to leeward.

Where the mainmast had been torn out, the gaping decks revealed the hold half full of water, swashing around among the sugar bags, while at every roll of the shattered hulk tons of it burst in over the stumps of the demolished bulwarks. The pumps were nearly destroyed in the general upheaval of the decks in their vicinity. The carpenter immediately went to work upon them, while the rest of us broke out old sails from the locker to nail over the openings in the decks, and stretched life lines along fore and aft.

To the stump of the mizzen-mast we lashed a studding-sail boom and on it spread an old trysail. This kept the ship nearly head to wind, decreasing the rolling motion and preventing the deluge of water upon the decks, so that we could work with greater safety and expedition. The afternoon was now well advanced and we were sadly in need of food. The galley in which our dinner had been preparing was completely gone, and on further investigation we found that the mainmast in its fall had torn out the forward end of the storeroom under the half deck, emptying overboard nearly all our provisions. What little of perishable goods remained were about spoiled by salt water. Hastily conveying this remnant of our former supply into the after-cabin, I detailed as steward a man who had served in that capacity on a former voyage and told him to save all he could and try to improvise a galley out of the cabin heater.

Returning to the deck, I found that the sun was out again. The sky, air and water were as placid and innocent looking as they had been before the squall. The heavy sea had nearly subsided and the wind, but a few hours ago a tornado, had now failed utterly. The ship rolled slowly but heavily in the trough of the sea, the water in her hold rushing back and forth through the cargo with a force that made the hulk tremble in every timber. Its rumbling and gurgling sounded as if we were over a volcano. By this time the men had covered all the breaks in the deck and sides, as far as possible, with plank and canvas, and water was no longer taken in in large quantities, although there must have been enormous leakage both there and through the vessel's seams, which had been opened by the awful strain to which she had been subjected. There was fully eight feet of water in the hold, bringing our decks amidships nearly even with the surface of the sea. After working all hands at the pumps for about half an hour, we lowered it not quite a foot. It was very fatiguing work. Our pumps were of the old-fashioned pattern, with brakes and plungers like a hand fire engine, but they were large and would raise about five gallons at a stroke. The falling mainmast had so thoroughly bent and twisted them that it was with the greatest difficulty they were made to work at all, and then with so much friction that we could not give more than twenty strokes without a rest.

I now had leisure to question the survivors of the port watch about the waterspout and ask how it happened that the ship was caught so unprepared. They said they were all seated on deck as I had left them when I went below, making mats, the mate and boatswain both among them giving directions, leaving, for the time, no one actually on the lookout except one of the boys at the wheel. He was somewhat green at steering and consequently must have kept his eyes fast on the compass card. Our high bulwarks forward shut out the horizon from the men on the main deck and the sky was so bright overhead that no one thought of the squall, which came up with exceptional rapidity, even for those latitudes, until they were called into action by a clap of thunder and the "old man" suddenly appearing on the poop and singing out, "Clew up the royals!" The squall had promised to be one of only ordinary severity, until the boys who had gone aloft to furl were down again and standing by the top-gallant gear with the rest, when, as if by magic, the waterspout was formed. All hands were then called and set to work in earnest to take in the kites. After dinner I tossed up with the boatswain for the watch, and as it fell to his lot I left him to do what he could toward rigging jury masts, and went below. On the captain's desk I found the half-worked *Sumner's* sight of the morning, which I finished, and, allowing for our drift, found that we were in latitude 3° 15' north, longitude 163° 41' east, or almost the center of the Celebes Sea. Plotting down this position on the chart, it appeared that Cape Rivers, on the island of Celebes, was the nearest land, bearing south by east one hundred and twenty-five miles. This was so nearly to windward that we could hardly hope to reach it under jury masts.

The nearest islands of the Sooloo Archipelago bore about northwest by west, nearly two hundred miles away. There was every reason for trying to reach Celebes. The Bughis were semi-civilized and friendly to Caucasians, and their propensity for trading with the neighboring islands and passing ships would give us a good chance to reach some frequented port.

I called a council of the more intelligent of the men and put before them my ideas concerning the best course to steer, etc. It was decided that working to windward was not to be thought of, and as the monsoon was late in changing we would have to take our chances and run for the Sooloo Islands. It would take us three or four days at least to rig any sort of sail that would give the ship a speed of two knots in a good breeze; so that we could not hope to reach land in less than ten days at the quickest, and it was a question if we could endure the labor of pumping for that length of time. Our stores, too, were scanty and could not last us longer than three weeks by the strictest economy above short allowance. During all our consultations and work the steady clank of the pumps had continued, broken only by the occasional "Spell, oh!"

On the seventh day my observation showed that we had made barely ninety miles in all in the direction of the Sooloos. That day we all knew, by the actions of the barometer and the unmistakable appearance of the sky, that the scourge of the China seas, a typhoon, would be upon us in less than twenty hours. We were several degrees south of the probable path of its vortex, but still far enough within its influence to make it extremely probable that our shaky hulk would founder in its first stages; or if we did manage to keep afloat, we could hardly hope to escape being driven upon some of the reefs or iron-bound coasts surrounding the Sooloo Sea.

The remainder of the day we spent in securing with extra stays and lashings our pitiful jury masts, putting new battens around the hatches and breaks in the deck, and endeavoring with but poor success to put the bilge pumps in order. That night the wind increased to a gale, with blinding lightning and scourging squalls of rain and electric hail that stung like whip lashes. The ship was too water-logged to attempt successfully the seaman's usual maneuver in a heavy blow and lay her to. She only fell off again into the trough of the sea, which swept her decks completely and drove us from the pumps. It soon became apparent that the hulk must in some way be kept head to sea. With the greatest difficulty we succeeded in overhauling enough of the chain cable, outside the vessel and in over the bows, to reach our jury foremast, and there lashed it. Securing to the chain all the spars, lumber and old sails we could find, we let go the anchors easily and, cutting away the steppings of the foremast, managed to slide the whole mass overboard with a heavy lurch of the ship, immediately paying out through the hawse pipes fifteen or twenty fathoms more of chain.

The tangle of spars, chain and rigging floated a hundred yards or so ahead and, being almost under water, drifted much more slowly than the ship, so that by their action as a drag, together with the little rag of a mizzen hauled flat aft, the only sail remaining set, the hulk was kept almost head to sea.

The sails ahead, spreading out in the water, served to break the force of the waves, making the ship ride more comfortably, although each heavy sea broke over the bows like a deluge and, running aft waist-deep clear to the taffrail, poured out in great spouts through the shattered bulwarks.

The straining ship, wallowing like a mad buffalo in the sea, sent up the most lifelike groans and screams of pain from her tortured timbers as, buffeted back and forth from sea to sea, she rolled and pitched till our brains began to reel. As I recall the resounding blows of the waves upon the vessel's sides and deck, the bellowing of the wind, the swash and crash of the tons of water in the hold, the cargo adrift, and sugar bags tumbling around as pebbles roll up and down a beach, each one a hundred-pound battering-ram upon the white-pine ceiling of the hold, the wild convulsions of the laboring hulk, the seams opening and closing and planks sawing back and forth against each other as if the wreck were breaking up, the pumps clogged with half-dissolved sugar and pieces of bamboo bags, while the water swept the decks so as to drive us into the scanty rigging of our jury mizzenmast, where we lashed ourselves to keep from being blown away, expecting that each heavy plunge of the quivering bows would be the last—as I recall all this, I wonder that our reason held, and can hardly understand how we calculated so logically as we did our chances of survival, discussed so coolly such projects as lashing a leaky oil barrel alongside the bowsprit to becalm the sea ahead, and even joked about the ship's being like Paddy's boot—a hole in her forefoot to let the water in, and a hole in her heel to let it out—or, like the *Mary Dunn* of Dover, with three decks and no bottom.

The morning of the ninth day dawned, or rather glimmered, upon a cheerless, cold, gray sky streaked with flying scud, and the air full of rain and spume flakes that stung our faces and hands like the pricking of needles and almost blinded us if we attempted to look to windward. Toward the close of the forenoon one of the men above me in the rigging scrambled down and, placing his face close to mine, shouted excitedly from the hollow of his hand, "Sail on the port quarter, sir!" On drawing ourselves higher up the rigging we saw, through the flying spume drift, a large vessel lying-to under storm canvas and apparently weathering the gale handsomely. With much difficulty and considerable danger of being washed overboard, we brought an ensign from the locker and secured it, union down, to the rigging above us, where it blew out straight and stiff as a board. Our hulk was by this time low enough in the water not to be visible at any great distance, and the entire absence of top-hamper made it extremely doubtful that we could be seen by the watch of the ship, who were in all probability crouched behind their weather cloth for protection from the gale. As the vessel drew nearer and her outline became more distinct we made out that she was on the port tack and forereaching enough to carry her across our bows. Thus we were on her lee beam and had a much better chance of being seen than if we had been to windward.

As she was slowly forging by us not a quarter of a mile away our hearts were gladdened by the sight of the American flag, and below it an answering pennant flying out from her monkey gaff. In another instant her watch below tumbled out of the forecastle and we could see them all busy upgriping their lee boat and running a line forward outside of all to the bows. Then we began to feel that we had done wrong in flying our signal of distress, for no boat, we thought, could live a moment in such an awful sea, and any attempt to take us off would only result in the drowning of the brave fellows who were coming to our relief, without bettering our condition a whit. They soon showed us that we were discounting Yankee skill and bravery at sea. We almost held our breath as we saw their whaleboat half lowered, the crew in place with oars apeak, and then saw it dropped on the crest of a huge rolling sea when the ship lurched heavily leeward. The boat's crew slewed her quickly round head to wind as she was swept away from the ship, and let her drive down toward us with the gale, keeping her "bows on" with the oars, and checking her sternway to meet each combing breaker. They caught the line we hove them and rode astern clear of the swash of the wallowing wreck.

The wounded men, who had been up to this time lashed securely in the rigging, were slung by a rope's end from the tip of the spanker boom and, watching for a comparatively smooth spell, the boat was hauled up and we lowered them into it. Then we tied bowlines around our waists and, jumping one at a time from the taffrail, struck out for the boat and were hauled in over its stern. Meanwhile the ship, after working slowly across our bows, had worn short round and, squaring her yards, sped by us like an arrow, and now lay rolling about, hove-to again to leeward, waiting for us to drift down to her.

The boat was what I had never seen before on board a merchant ship —an iron self-baling lifeboat, of the whaleboat model; and most gallantly she behaved, overloaded as she was, in that awful sea, which no ordinary ship's boat could have weathered for five minutes. You may imagine what a difficult matter it was to get aboard the ship and hoist in the boat. After about half an hour of hard work we were on the deck of the good ship *Iceberg*, Captain Blaney, who received us with a hearty welcome, declining with a gruff good nature our protestations of gratitude and our admiration for the skilful seamanship that had carried his vessel and whaleboat safely through such dangerous maneuvers. As I turned to go below, a cry from the men caused me to look to windward, and I saw the *Wasatch* throw up her stern and go down headforemost, like a sounding whale. Our rescuers gave us what we then most wanted, a substantial meal, and generously supplied us with clothing until we reached Java Head, where, at our request, we were put ashore.

Success at Kitty Hawk

by ORVILLE WRIGHT

Here Orville Wright describes his brother's epoch-making flight, the first powered flight of a heavier-than-air machine of any duration in the world's history. The flight was made on December 17, 1903, at Kitty Hawk, N. C., in a plane with a four-cylinder engine of twelve horsepower. The duration of flight was 59 seconds, the speed about 30 miles per hour. Machine and pilot weighed about 750 pounds. After the flight—the longest of several that day—the Wrights, Orville and Wilbur, were not particularly impressed: they had expected their success, having worked hard and intelligently step by step in its direction. Icarus, of Greek mythology, had fallen into the sea because he had flown too high, so that the heat of the sun had melted the wax which held his wings together. Leonardo da Vinci had dreamed of devices which would permit man to fly. But the Wrights had taken the first long step in translating such dreams into reality. Within fifty years man was flying across the oceans, over the poles, at speeds more than double the speed of sound, and was seriously preparing for a venture into interplanetary space.

I TOOK A POSITION AT ONE OF THE WINGS, INTENDING TO HELP balance the machine as it ran down the track. But when the restraining wire was slipped, the machine started off so quickly I could stay with it only a few feet. After a 35- to 40-foot run, it lifted from the rail.

But it was allowed to turn up too much. It climbed a few feet, stalled, and then settled to the ground near the foot of the hill, 105 feet below. My stop watch showed that it had been in the air just 3½ seconds. In landing, the left wing touched first. The machine swung around, dug the skids into the sand and broke one of them. Several other parts were also broken, but the damage to the machine was not serious. While the tests had shown nothing as to whether the power of the motor was sufficient to keep the machine up, since the landing was made many feet below the starting point, the experiment had demonstrated that the method adopted for launching the machine was a safe and practical one. On the whole, we were much pleased.

Two days were consumed in making repairs, and the machine was not ready again till late in the afternoon of the 16th. While we had it out on the track in front of the building, making the final adjustments, a stranger came along. After looking at the machine a few seconds he inquired what it was. When we told him it was a flying machine he asked whether we intended to fly it. We said we did, as soon as we had a suitable wind. He looked at it several minutes longer and then, wishing to be courteous, remarked that it looked as if it would fly, if it had a "suitable wind." We were much amused, for, no doubt, he had in mind the recent 75-mile gale when he repeated our words, "a suitable wind"!

During the night of December 16th a strong cold wind blew from the north. When we arose on the morning of the 17th, the puddles of water, which had been standing about the camp since the recent rains, were covered with ice. The wind had a velocity of 10 to 12 meters per second (22 to 27 miles an hour). We thought it would die down before long, and so remained indoors the early part of the morning. But when ten o'clock arrived, and the wind was as brisk as ever, we decided that we had better get the machine out and attempt a flight. We hung out the signal for the men of the Life Saving Station. We thought that by facing the flyer into a strong wind, there ought to be no trouble in launching it from the level ground about camp. We realized the difficulties of flying in so high a wind, but estimated that the added dangers in flight would be partly compensated for by the slower speed in landing.

We laid the track on a smooth stretch of ground about one hundred feet west of the new building. The biting cold wind made work difficult, and we had to warm up frequently in our living room, where we had a good fire in an improvised stove made of a large carbide can. By the time all was ready, J. T. Daniels, W. S. Dough and A. D. Etheridge, members of the Kill Devil Life-Saving Station; W. C. Brinkley of Manteo; and Johnny Moore, a boy from Nag's Head, had arrived.

We had a "Richard" hand anemometer with which we measured the velocity of the wind. Measurements made just before starting the first flight showed velocities of 11 to 12 meters per second, or 24 to 27 miles per hour. Measurements made just before the last flight gave between 9 and 10 meters per second. One made just afterward showed a little over 8 meters. The records of the Government Weather Bureau at Kitty Hawk gave the velocity of the wind between the hours of 10:30 and 12 o'clock, the time during which the four flights were made, as averaging 27 miles at the time of the first flight and 24 miles at the time of the last.

With all the knowledge and skill acquired in thousands of flights in the last ten years, I would hardly think today of making my first flight on a strange machine in a twenty-seven-mile wind, even if I knew that the machine had already been flown and was safe. After these years of experience, I look with amazement upon our audacity in attempting flights with a new and untried machine under such circumstances. Yet faith in our calculations and the design of the first machine, based upon our tables of air pressures, obtained by months of careful laboratory work, and confidence in our system of control developed by three years of actual experiences in balancing gliders in the air, had convinced us that the machine was capable of lifting and maintaining itself in the air, and that, with a little practice, it could be safely flown.

Wilbur having used his turn in the unsuccessful attempt on the 14th, the right to the first trial now belonged to me. After running the motor a few minutes to heat it up, I released the wire that held the machine to the track, and the machine started forward into the wind. Wilbur ran at the side of the machine, holding the wing to balance it on the track. Unlike the start on the 14th, made in a calm, the machine, facing a 27-mile wind, started very slowly. Wilbur was able to stay with it till it lifted from the track after a forty-foot run. One of the Life Saving men snapped the camera for us, taking a picture just as the machine had reached the end of the track and had risen to a height of about two feet. The slow forward speed of the machine over the ground is clearly shown in the picture by Wilbur's attitude. He stayed along beside the machine without any effort.

The course of the flight up and down was exceedingly erratic, partly due to the irregularity of the air and partly to lack of experience in handling this machine. The control of the front rudder was difficult on account of its being balanced too near the center. This gave it a tendency to turn itself when started, so that it turned too far on one side and then too far on the other. As a result, the machine would rise suddenly to about ten feet, and then as suddenly dart for the ground. A sudden dart when a little over a hundred feet from the end of the track, or a little over 120 feet from the point at which it rose into the air, ended the flight. As the velocity of the wind was over 35 feet per second and the speed of the machine over the ground against this wind ten feet per second, the speed of the machine relative to the air was over 45 feet per second, and the length of the flight was equivalent to a flight of 540 feet made in calm air.

This flight lasted only 12 seconds, but it was nevertheless the first in the history of the world in which a machine carrying a man had raised itself by its own power into the air in full flight, had sailed forward without reduction of speed, and had finally landed at a point as high as that from which it started.

With the assistance of our visitors we carried the machine back to the track and prepared for another flight. The wind, however, had chilled us all through, so that before attempting a second flight, we all went to the building again to warm up. Johnny Moore, seeing under the table a box filled with eggs, asked one of the Station men where we got so many of them. The people of the neighborhood eke out a bare existence by catching fish during the short fishing season, and their supplies of other articles of food are limited. He probably never had seen so many eggs at one time in his whole life.

The one addressed jokingly asked him whether he hadn't noticed the small hen running about the outside of the building. "That chicken lays eight to ten eggs a day!" Moore, having just seen a piece of machinery lift itself from the ground and fly, a thing at that time considered as impossible as perpetual motion, was ready to believe nearly anything. But after going out and having a good look at the wonderful fowl, he returned with the remark, "It's only a common-looking chicken!"

At twenty minutes after eleven Wilbur started on the second flight. The course of this flight was much like that of the first, very much up and down. The speed over the ground was somewhat faster than that of the first flight, due to the lesser wind. The duration of the flight was less than a second longer than the first, but the distance covered was about seventy-five feet greater.

Twenty minutes later, the third flight started. This one was steadier than the first one an hour before. I was proceeding along pretty well when a sudden gust from the right lifted the machine up twelve to fifteen feet and turned it up sidewise in an alarming manner. It began a lively sidling off to the left. I warped the wings to try to recover the lateral balance and at the same time pointed the machine down to reach the ground as quickly as possible. The lateral control was more effective than I had imagined and before I reached the ground the right wing was lower than the left and struck first. The time of this flight was fifteen seconds and the distance over the ground a little over 200 feet.

Wilbur started the fourth and last flight at just 12 o'clock. The first few hundred feet were up and down, as before, but by the time three hundred feet had been covered, the machine was under much better control. The course for the next four or five hundred feet had but little undulation. However, when out about eight hundred feet the machine began pitching again, and, in one of its darts downward, struck the ground. The distance over the ground was measured and found to be 852 feet; the time of the flight 59 seconds. The frame supporting the front rudder was badly broken, but the main part of the machine was not injured at all. We estimated that the machine could be put in condition for flight again in a day or two.

While we were standing about discussing this last flight, a sudden strong gust of wind struck the machine and began to turn it over. Everybody made a rush for it. Wilbur, who was at one end, seized it in front. Mr. Daniels and I, who were behind, tried to stop it by holding to the rear uprights.

All our efforts were in vain. The machine rolled over and over. Daniels, who had retained his grip, was carried along with it, and was thrown about, head over heels, inside of the machine. Fortunately he was not seriously injured, though badly bruised in falling about against the motor, chain guides, etc. The ribs in the surfaces of the machine were broken, the motor injured and the chain guides badly bent, so that all possibility of further flights with it for that year were at an end.

Sources and Acknowledgments

I owe thanks to William Beebe, to the Explorers Club, and to Edward Weyer, Jr., president of the Explorers Club, for courtesies extended to me; to the United States Navy Department for a submarine cruise, and specifically to Lt. Commander Philip Jones of the submarine base at Groton, Conn., and to Lt. Commander Jack Hudson, skipper of *U.S.S. Spikefish*, for personal and professional courtesies; to Evan Thomas and Genevieve Young of Harper & Brothers for useful suggestions and aids, and particularly to John Appleton of Harper & Brothers for many valuable detailed editorial consultations; and to my wife, Joan Merrick, who lent a sympathetic ear even while engrossed in her own studies.

Grateful acknowledgment is made to the following authors and publishers for the material included in this volume:

"Adventure—The Unending Challenge." By Maurice Herzog, author of *Annapurna. The New York Times Magazine,* October 4, 1953, pp. 14-15.

"Earthquake at San Francisco." *A History of the Earthquake and Fire in San Francisco,* by Frank W. Aitken and Edward Hilton (San Francisco, The E. Hilton Co., 1906), pp. 13-30.

"The Strange Death of Louis Slotin." *Saturday Evening Post,* March 6, 1954, pp. 25ff.

"Voyage to the South Pole." *The South Pole,* by Roald Amundsen (London, J. Murray; New York, L. Keedick, 1913), vol. 2, pp. 107-34.

"The Just Vengeance of Heaven." *The Just Vengeance of Heaven Exemplified* . . . (Philadelphia, William Bradford, 1748).

"Forty-five Seconds Inside a Tornado." *Saturday Evening Post,* July 11, 1953, pp. 17ff.

"Descent Into Perpetual Night." *Half Mile Down,* by William Beebe (New York, Duell, Sloan & Pearce, Inc., 1951), pp. 197-225.

"The Plague." *The Decameron,* by Giovanni Boccaccio, "The First Day."

"Head Hunters of New Guinea." *Kachalola,* by Sidney Spencer Broomfield (London, Peter Davies, Ltd.; New York, William Morrow & Co., Inc., 1930), pp. 234-40.

"Alone." *Alone,* by Richard E. Byrd (New York, G. P. Putnam's Sons, 1938), pp. 146-56.

"Lost in the Sahara." *A Saharan Venture,* by Donald R. G. Cameron (London, Edward Arnold, Ltd.; New York, Longmans, Green & Co., 1928), pp. 140-73.

"The Great Lisbon Earthquake." *Library of Universal Adventure by Sea and Land,* edited by William Dean Howells and Thomas S. Perry (New York, Harper & Brothers, 1888), pp. 482-94.

"The Champawat Man-Eater." *Man-Eaters of Kumaon,* by Jim Corbett (New York, Oxford University Press, 1946), pp. 3-32.

"The Silent World." *The Silent World,* by J. Y. Cousteau, with Frédéric Dumas (New York, Harper & Brothers, 1953), pp. 69-83.

"Indians!" *My Life on the Plains,* by George A. Custer (New York, Sheldon & Co., 1874), pp. 63-68.

"Rounding the Horn." *Two Years Before the Mast,* by Richard Henry Dana (New York, Harper & Brothers, 1840), chaps. 31 and 32.

"Battle With a Whale." *Nimrod of the Seas,* by William M. Davies, reprinted in *Library of Universal Adventure by Sea and Land,* edited by William Dean Howells and Thomas S. Perry (New York, Harper & Brothers, 1888), pp. 912-17.

"On the Bottom." *On the Bottom,* by Edward Ellsberg (New York, Dodd, Mead & Co., 1929), pp. 171-87.

"Lost in the Canadian Wilderness." *Wide World Magazine,* October, 1898, pp. 19-25.

"The Great Chicago Fire." *Memories of the Great Chicago Fire of October 1871,* by Samuel S. Greeley (Chicago, the author, 1904), pp. 1-7.

"Bailing Out at Supersonic Speed" (original title "I Had to Bail Out at Supersonic Speed"), *Saturday Evening Post,* March 13, 1954, pp. 32ff.

"Death in the Afternoon." *Death in the Afternoon,* by Ernest Hemingway (New York, Charles Scribner's Sons, 1932), pp. 16-25.

"Bridging the Hellespont." *History,* by Herodotus, Book VIII.

"Kon-Tiki." *Natural History Magazine,* June, 1948, pp. 256ff.

"To the Summit of Everest." *Life,* July 13, 1953, pp. 124ff., and *The Times* (London).

"Man Against Bronco." *The Story of the Cowboy,* by Emerson Hough (New York, D. Appleton & Co., 1897), pp. 88-103.

"The Tidal Wave." *The Century Magazine,* reprinted in *Library of Universal Adventure by Sea and Land,* edited by William Dean Howells and Thomas S. Perry (New York, Harper & Brothers, 1888), pp. 988-97.

"Hunting the African Buffalo." *Hunter,* by J. A. Hunter (New York, Harper & Brothers, 1952), pp. 134-51.

"Masai Spearmen." *Hunter,* by J. A. Hunter (New York, Harper & Brothers, 1952), pp. 101-10.

"We Jump Into Fire." *Saturday Evening Post*, April 28, 1951, pp. 26ff.

"Rocket Shoot at White Sands" (original title, "Sacrifice at White Sands"). *Flight Into Space*, by Jonathan Norton Leonard (New York, Random House, 1953), pp. 9-17.

"New York to Paris." *We*, by Charles A. Lindbergh (New York, G. P. Putnam's Sons, 1927), pp. 213-26.

"Attempts on the Eigerwand." *Approach to the Hills*, by C. F. Meade (London, John Murray, Ltd.; New York, E. P. Dutton & Co., 1940), pp. 63-74.

"The Buffalo Chase." *The Oregon Trail*, by Francis Parkman (Boston, Little, Brown & Co., 1892), pp. 356-66.

"The North Pole Conquered." *The North Pole*, by Robert E. Peary (Philadelphia, J. B. Lippincott Co., 1910), pp. 280-90, 297-301.

"The Eruption of Vesuvius." *Letters*, by Pliny the Younger, Book VI, xvi and xx.

"On the Edge of the Primeval Forest." *On the Edge of the Primeval Forest*, by Albert Schweitzer (London, A. & C. Black, Ltd.; New York, The Macmillan Company, 1922), pp. 45-56, 69, 78-86, 91-93.

"The Last March." *Scott's Last Expedition* (New York, Dodd, Mead & Co., 1913), vol. 1, pp. 396-410.

"The Open Boat." *South*, by Sir Ernest Shackleton (London, William Heinemann, 1919), pp. 156-80.

"Craters of Fire." *Craters of Fire*, by Haroun Tazieff (New York, Harper & Brothers, 1952), pp. 11-21; 183-90.

"The Johnstown Flood." *The Floods of Johnstown*, by Peter J. Toner (Johnstown, Pa., The Mayors' Committee, 1939), pp. 8-15, 18-19.

"Ten Thousand Miles in the Saddle." *Tales of Hazard*, ed. by H. C. Armstrong (John Lane, The Bodley Head, Ltd., 1932), pp. 231-38.

"Buzzing Death" (reprinted by permission of J. W. Beagle-Atkins). *Blackwood's Magazine*, May, 1937; *Reader's Digest*, August, 1937, pp. 63-64.

"Annapurna" (reprinted by permission of Harold Matson). *Life*, July 9, 1951, pp. 84-95.

"A Waterspout in the Pacific." *The Century Magazine*, reprinted in *Library of Universal Adventure by Sea and Land*, edited by William Dean Howells and Thomas S. Perry (New York, Harper & Brothers, 1888), pp. 997-1006.

"Success at Kitty Hawk." *The Wright Brothers*, by Fred C. Kelly (New York, Farrar, Straus & Young, Inc., 1950), pp. 96-102.

Set in Linotype Times Roman
Format by Katharine Sitterly
Manufactured by The Haddon Craftsmen, Inc.
Published by HARPER & BROTHERS, *New York*